Fodor's 2000

Cape Cod, Martha's Vineyard, Nantucket

The complete guide, thoroughly up-to-date

Packed with details that will make your trip

The must-see sights, off and on the beaten path

What to see, what to skip

Mix-and-match vacation itineraries

City strolls, countryside adventures

Smart lodging and dining options

Essential local do's and taboos

Transportation tips, distances, and directions

Key contacts, savvy travel tips

When to go, what to pack

Clear, accurate, easy-to-use maps

Books to read, background essays

Fodor's Travel Publications • New York, Toronto, London, Sydney, Auckland
www.fodors.com/capecod

Fodor's Cape Cod, Martha's Vineyard, Nantucket 2000

EDITOR: Linda Cabasin

Editorial Contributors: Carolyn Heller, Ellen LeBow, Karl Luntta, Seth Rolbein, Laura V. Scheel
Editorial Production: Rebecca Zeiler
Maps: David Lindroth, *cartographer*; Rebecca Baer and Bob Blake, *map editors*
Design: Fabrizio La Rocca, *creative director*; Guido Caroti, *art director*; Jolie Novak, *photo editor*
Cover Design: Pentagram
Production/Manufacturing: Mike Costa
Cover Photo: Jake Rajs/Tony Stone Images

Copyright

ISBN 0–679–00394–0

ISSN 1093–7986

Special Sales

Fodor's Travel Publications are available at special discounts for bulk purchases for sales promotions or premiums. Special editions, including personalized covers, excerpts of existing guides, and corporate imprints, can be created in large quantities for special needs. For more information, contact your local bookseller or write to Special Markets, Fodor's Travel Publications, 201 East 50th Street, New York, NY 10022. Inquiries from Canada should be directed to your local Canadian bookseller or sent to Random House of Canada, Ltd., Marketing Department, 2775 Matheson Boulevard East, Mississauga, Ontario L4W 4P7. Inquiries from the United Kingdom should be sent to Fodor's Travel Publications, 20 Vauxhall Bridge Road, London SW1V 2SA, England.

PRINTED IN THE UNITED STATES OF AMERICA

10 9 8 7 6 5 4 3 2 1

Important Tip

Although all prices, opening times, and other details in this book are based on information supplied to us at press time, changes occur all the time in the travel world, and Fodor's cannot accept responsibility for facts that become outdated or for inadvertent errors or omissions. So **always confirm information when it matters,** especially if you're making a detour to visit a specific place.

CONTENTS

Maps

ON THE ROAD WITH FODOR'S

EVERY Y2K TRIP is a significant trip. So if there was ever a time you needed excellent travel information, it's now. Acutely aware of that fact, we've pulled out all stops in preparing Fodor's *Cape Cod, Martha's Vineyard, Nantucket 2000.* To guide you in putting together your Cape and islands experience, we've created multiday itineraries and neighborhood walks. And to direct you to the places that are truly worth your time and money in this important year, we've rallied the team of endearingly picky know-it-alls we're pleased to call our writers. Having seen all corners of the Cape, the Vineyard, and Nantucket, they're real experts. If you knew them, you'd poll them for tips yourself.

One of **Carolyn Heller**'s early memories is of digging in the tide pools along Cape Cod Bay—now she's introducing her own daughters to the Cape beaches. A Cambridge-based travel writer, she tracks the area's dining and arts scenes as the Boston bureau chief of the on-line business travel site *ontheroad.com.* Her recent travel articles have appeared in the *Boston Globe,* the *Los Angeles Times,* the *Philadelphia Inquirer,* the *Miami Herald,* and *Family Fun* magazine. For this edition, she covered the Upper and Mid Cape sections of Cape Cod and updated Smart Travel Tips A to Z; she has also contributed to several other Fodor's guidebooks, including *Boston.*

Ellen LeBow is a writer and well-known artist who has lived and worked on Cape Cod for more than 20 years. This year she worked with Seth Rolbein to update the guide's dining reviews—look for plenty of new reviews, particularly in the Cape section.

Karl Luntta has lived on Cape Cod for more than 10 years and is a frequent visitor to Martha's Vineyard, where he took his children while updating this year's chapter. Despite the fact that on the return ferry trip his seven-year-old asked, "Daddy, are we going back to America now?" he assures all that Martha's Vineyard is indeed a wonderful part of the republic. Karl has covered the Cape and islands for publications such as *Cape Cod Travel Guide, Cape Cod Life,* and the *Cape Cod*

Times. In addition to his published travel guides to Jamaica, St. Lucia, the Virgin Islands, and the Caribbean region, he is a frequent contributor to Fodor's *Caribbean.*

We're pleased to have as one of our dining critics writer and documentary filmmaker **Seth Rolbein,** who has lived on the Cape for most of the past 20 years. He is the editor-in-chief of the Community Newspaper Company's four Cape Cod newspapers. He has also been published by many regional and national publications, including the *Boston Globe Sunday* magazine and *Yankee* magazine.

Yet another Cape Cod transplant, **Laura V. Scheel** was attracted to both the area's natural splendor and the unique way of life. As a freelance writer and editor living in Wellfleet, she works on projects including travel pieces, profiles of the arts, and textbooks. Her articles have appeared in *Cape Cod Life, Cape Cod Travel Guide, The Cape Codder, The Provincetown Banner,* and *On the Water.* She is also the editor of *A-Plus,* a local monthly arts and antiques publication.

New York–based Fodor's editor **Linda Cabasin** has spent many happy hours on the Cape Cod Rail Trail and on Nauset Light Beach during vacations with her husband and son.

The authors and editor wish to thank Cape Air for help with transportation.

Don't Forget to Write

Keeping a travel guide fresh and up-to-date is a big job. So we love your feedback—positive and negative—and follow up on all suggestions. Contact the Cape Cod, Martha's Vineyard, Nantucket editor at editors@fodors.com or c/o Fodor's, 201 East 50th Street, New York, New York 10022. And have a wonderful trip!

Karen Cure
Editorial Director

Cape Cod, Martha's Vineyard, and Nantucket

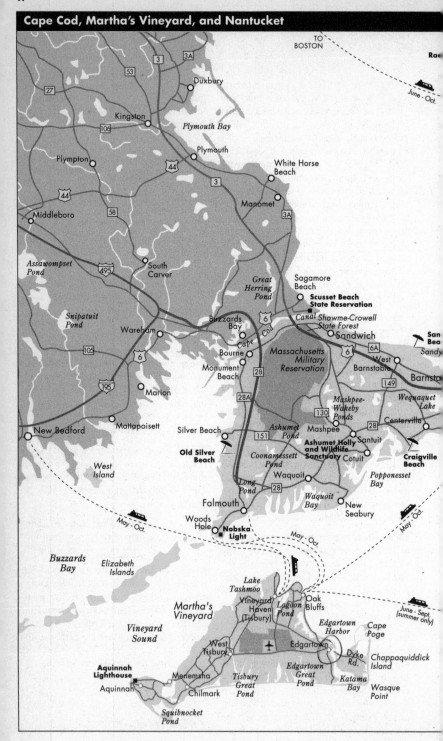

TO
BOSTON

Rac

June - Oct.

Duxbury

3 3A

53

27

Kingston

106

Plymouth Bay

Plymouth

Plympton

US 44

White Horse
Beach

3

44

Manomet

3A

Middleboro

58

*Assawompset
Pond*

495

South
Carver

*Great
Herring
Pond*

Sagamore
Beach

Scusset Beach
State Reservation

*Snipatuit
Pond*

Wareham

Buzzards
Bay

6

Cape Cod Canal

Shawme-Crowell
State Forest

Sandwich

San
Bea

105

US 6

Bourne

Cape Cod Canal

Massachusetts
Military
Reservation

6

6A

West
Barnstable

Sandy

Barnsta

Monument
Beach

28

195

Marion

Mattapoisett

28A

Silver Beach

151

*Mashpee-
Wakeby
Ponds*

130

Mashpee

149

*Wequaquet
Lake*

Centerville

28

Santuit

Barnsto

New Bedford

*West
Island*

Old Silver
Beach

*Ashumet
Pond*

*Coonamessett
Pond*

Ashumet Holly
and Wildlife
Sanctuary

Cotuit

Craigville
Beach

Waquoit

28

*Long
Pond*

*Popponesset
Bay*

Falmouth

Woods
Hole

Nobska
Light

*Waquoit
Bay*

New
Seabury

May - Oct.

May - Oct.

May - Oct.

*Buzzards
Bay*

*Elizabeth
Islands*

*Lake
Tashmoo*

Vineyard
Haven
(Tisbury)

*Lagoon
Pond*

Oak
Bluffs

June - Sept.
(summer only)

Martha's
Vineyard

*Vineyard
Sound*

West
Tisbury

*Edgartown
Harbor*

Edgartown

*Cape
Poge*

Dyke
Rd.

Chappaquiddick
Island

Aquinnah
Lighthouse

Aquinnah

Menemsha

Chilmark

*Tisbury
Great
Pond*

*Edgartown
Great
Pond*

*Katama
Bay*

Wasque
Point

*Squibnocket
Pond*

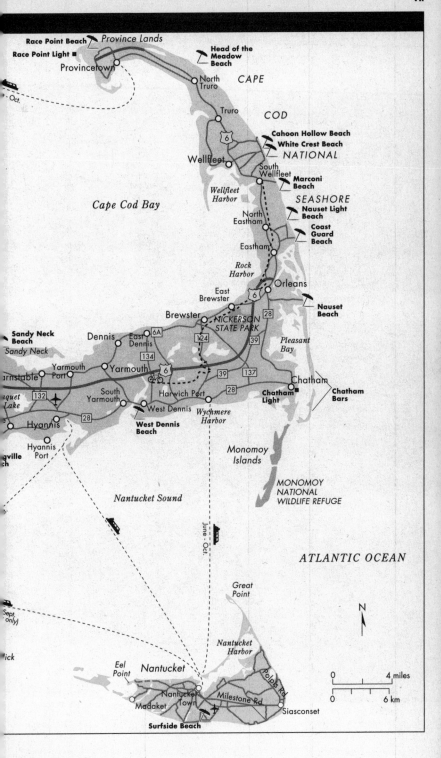

Race Point Beach
Race Point Light ■
Province Lands
Provincetown
- Oct.

Head of the Meadow Beach

North Truro

CAPE

Truro

COD

U.S. 6
Cahoon Hollow Beach
White Crest Beach
NATIONAL

Wellfleet

South Wellfleet
Marconi Beach

Cape Cod Bay

Wellfleet Harbor

SEASHORE

North Eastham
Nauset Light Beach

Coast Guard Beach

Eastham

Rock Harbor

Orleans

East Brewster
U.S. 6
Brewster
NICKERSON STATE PARK
6A
124
28
Nauset Beach

Sandy Neck Beach
Sandy Neck

Dennis
East Dennis

134
Yarmouth
U.S. 6

Pleasant Bay

rnstable
Yarmouth Port

39
137
Chatham

132
aquet Lake

South Yarmouth
39
28
Chatham Light
Chatham Bars

Hyannis
28
Harwich Port

West Dennis
West Dennis Beach
Wychmere Harbor

qville ch

Hyannis Port

Monomoy Islands

Nantucket Sound

June - Oct.

MONOMOY NATIONAL WILDLIFE REFUGE

ATLANTIC OCEAN

Sept. only)

ick

Great Point

N

Nantucket Harbor

Eel Point
Nantucket

0   4 miles
0   6 km

Madaket
Nantucket Town
Milestone Rd

Siasconset

Surfside Beach

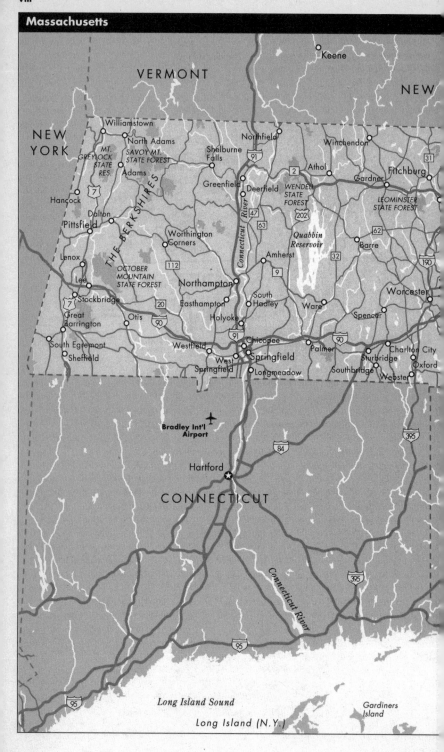

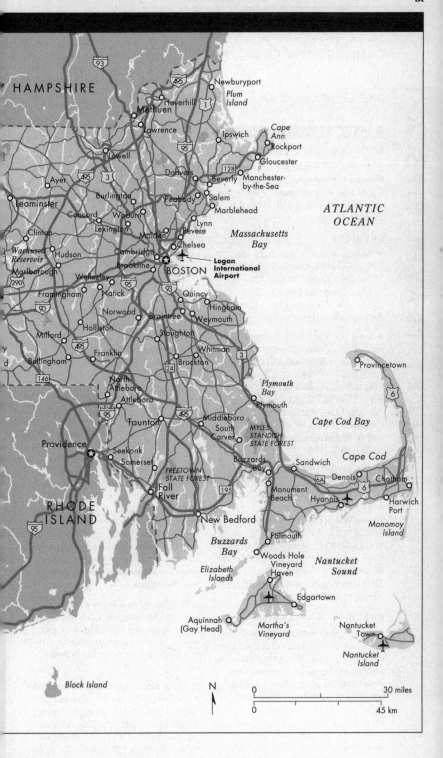

New HAMPSHIRE

93

495

Newburyport
Plum Island

Methuen
Haverhill
1
Lawrence
95
Ipswich

Cape Ann
Rockport

Lowell
Danvers
128
Beverly
Gloucester

Ayer
Burlington
Peabody
Manchester-by-the-Sea

Leominster
Concord
Woburn
Salem
Marblehead

Clinton
Lexington
ATLANTIC OCEAN

Wachusett Reservoir
Hudson
Cambridge
Lynn
Revere

Marlborough
Brookline
Chelsea
Massachusetts Bay

290
Wellesley
95
BOSTON
Logan International Airport

Framingham
Natick
93

90
Norwood
Quincy
Hingham

Milford
Hollistøn
Braintree
Weymouth

Bellingham
Franklin
Stoughton

146
24
Whitman
3

North Attleboro
Brockton

Attleboro
Plymouth Bay
Plymouth

Provincetown
6

Providence
Taunton
495
Middleboro
South Carver
MYLES STANDISH STATE FOREST
Cape Cod Bay

Seekonk
Somerset
FREETOWN STATE FOREST
Buzzards Bay
Sandwich
Cape Cod

95
195
6A
Dennis
Chatham

RHODE ISLAND
Fall River
Monument Beach
6
Hyannis
Harwich Port

95
New Bedford
Buzzards Bay
Falmouth
Monomoy Island

Woods Hole
Vineyard Haven
Nantucket Sound

Elizabeth Islands
Edgartown

Aquinnah (Gay Head)
Martha's Vineyard
Nantucket Town

Nantucket Island

Block Island

N

0   30 miles
0   45 km

SMART TRAVEL TIPS A TO Z

Basic Information on Traveling on Cape Cod and the Islands, Savvy Tips to Make Your Trip a Breeze, and Companies and Organizations to Contact

AIR TRAVEL

BOOKING YOUR FLIGHT

When you book **look for nonstop flights** and **remember that "direct" flights stop at least once.** Try to avoid connecting flights, which require a change of plane.

CARRIERS

➤ MAJOR AIRLINES: **American** (☎ 800/433–7300). **Continental** (☎ 800/525–0280). **Delta** (☎ 800/221–1212). **Northwest** (☎ 800/225–2525). **TWA** (☎ 800/221–2000). **US Airways** (☎ 800/428–4322).

➤ SMALLER AIRLINES: **Business Express/Delta Connection** (☎ 800/345–3400). **Cape Air/Nantucket Airlines** (☎ 508/771–6944, 508/228–6252, 508/228–6234, 800/352–0714, or 800/635–8787 in MA). **Colgan Air** (☎ 508/325–5100 or 800/272–5488). **Continental Express** (☎ 800/525–0280). **Island Airlines** (☎ 508/228–7575 or 800/248–7779).

➤ CHARTERS: **Air New England** (☎ 508/693–8899), serving Martha's Vineyard. **Direct Flight** (☎ 508/693–6688), serving Martha's Vineyard. **Ocean Wings** (☎ 508/693–4646, 508/228–3350, 800/262–7858, or 800/253–5039), serving Martha's Vineyard and Nantucket. **Westchester Air** (☎ 914/761–3000 or 800/759–2929), serving Cape Cod, Martha's Vineyard, and Nantucket.

CHECK-IN & BOARDING

Assuming that not everyone with a ticket will show up, airlines routinely overbook planes. When that happens, airlines ask for volunteers to give up their seats. In return these volunteers usually get a certificate for a free flight and are rebooked on the next flight out. If there are not enough volunteers, the airline must choose who will be denied boarding. The first to get bumped are passengers who checked in late and those flying on discounted tickets, so **get to the gate and check in as early as possible,** especially during peak periods.

Always **bring a government-issued photo I.D. to the airport.** You may be asked to show it before you are allowed to check in.

CUTTING COSTS

The least-expensive airfares to Cape Cod must usually be purchased in advance and are non-refundable. It's smart to **call a number of airlines, and when you are quoted a good price, book it on the spot**—the same fare may not be available the next day. Always **check different routings** and look into using different airports. Travel agents, especially low-fare specialists (☞ Discounts & Deals, *below*), are helpful.

Consolidators are another good source. They buy tickets for scheduled international flights at reduced rates from the airlines, then sell them at prices that beat the best fare available directly from the airlines, usually without restrictions. Sometimes you can even get your money back if you need to return the ticket. Carefully read the fine print detailing penalties for changes and cancellations, and **confirm your consolidator reservation with the airline.**

When you **fly as a courier** you trade your checked-luggage space for a ticket deeply subsidized by a courier service. There are restrictions on when you can book and how long you can stay.

➤ CONSOLIDATORS: **Cheap Tickets** (☎ 800/377–1000). **Up & Away Travel** (☎ 212/889–2345). **Discount Airline Ticket Service** (☎ 800/576–1600). **Unitravel** (☎ 800/325–2222). **World Travel Network** (☎ 800/409–6753).

ENJOYING THE FLIGHT

For more legroom **request an emergency-aisle seat.** Don't sit in the row in front of the emergency aisle or in front of a bulkhead, where seats may not recline. If you have dietary concerns, **ask for special meals when booking.** These can be vegetarian, low-cholesterol, or kosher, for example. On long flights, try to maintain a normal routine, to help fight jet lag. At night **get some sleep.** By day **eat light meals, drink water** (not alcohol), and **move around the cabin** to stretch your legs.

FLYING TIMES

Flying time is one hour from New York, 2½ hours from Chicago, 6 hours from Los Angeles, and 3½ hours from Dallas.

HOW TO COMPLAIN

If your baggage goes astray or your flight goes awry, complain right away. Most carriers require that you **file a claim immediately.**

➤ AIRLINE COMPLAINTS: U.S. Department of Transportation **Aviation Consumer Protection Division** (✉ C-75, Room 4107, Washington, DC 20590, ☎ 202/366–2220). **Federal Aviation Administration Consumer hot line** (☎ 800/322–7873).

AIRPORTS

The major gateway to Cape Cod is Boston's Logan International Airport. Smaller airports include Barnstable Municipal Airport in Hyannis, Martha's Vineyard Airport, and Nantucket Memorial Airport. For further information, *see* Arriving and Departing *in* the A to Z section at the end of Chapters 2, 3, and 4.

➤ AIRPORT INFORMATION: Boston: **Logan International Airport** (☎ 617/561–1806 or 800/235–6426). Hyannis: **Barnstable Municipal Airport** (☎ 508/775–2020). Martha's Vineyard: **Martha's Vineyard Airport** (☎ 508/693–7022). Nantucket: **Nantucket Memorial Airport** (☎ 508/325–5300). Provincetown: **Provincetown Municipal Airport** (☎ 508/487–0241).

BIKE TRAVEL

Biking is very popular on Cape Cod and the islands; some popular trails can be as busy as the roads in summer. Note that Massachusetts law requires children under 13 to wear protective helmets when they are operating a bike or riding as a passenger. For information on trails, maps, and rentals, *see* Getting Around *in* the A to Z sections at the end of Chapters 2 and 4; rental shops and bike trails are listed with the various towns, too.

BIKES IN FLIGHT

Most airlines accommodate bikes as luggage, provided they are dismantled and boxed. For bike boxes, often free at bike shops, you'll pay about $5 (at least $100 for bike bags) from airlines. International travelers can sometimes substitute a bike for a piece of checked luggage at no charge; otherwise, the cost is about $100. Domestic and Canadian airlines charge $25–$50.

BOAT & FERRY TRAVEL

Ferries to Provincetown leave from Boston and Plymouth in season.

Ferries leave for Martha's Vineyard from Woods Hole year-round and from Falmouth, Hyannis, and New Bedford in season.

Hyannis ferries serve Nantucket year-round. In season, a passenger ferry connects the islands, and a cruise out of Hyannis makes a one-day round-trip with stops at both islands.

See the A to Z sections *in* Chapters 2, 3, and 4 for fares, schedules and contact numbers of ferry companies.

BUS TRAVEL

Bus service is available to Cape Cod, with stops at many Cape towns and some connecting service to the islands by ferry. Greyhound serves Boston from all over the country; from there you can connect to a local carrier, such as Bonanza Bus Lines, which offers direct service to Falmouth/Woods Hole from Boston and New York City. Plymouth & Brockton Street Railway travels to Provincetown from Boston and Logan Airport, with stops en route.

➤ BUS INFORMATION: **Bonanza Bus Lines** (☎ 508/548–7588 or 800/556–3815, www.bonanzabus.com). **Greyhound** (☎ 800/231–2222, www.greyhound.com). **Plymouth & Brockton Street Railway** (☎ 508/746–0378, www.p-b.com).

BUS TRAVEL WITHIN CAPE COD AND THE ISLANDS

See Getting Around *in* the A to Z section of Chapters 2, 3, and 4 for local bus travel information.

BUSINESS HOURS

MUSEUMS & SIGHTS

Hours for sights on the Cape and islands vary widely from place to place and from season to season. Some places are staffed by volunteers and have limited hours (a few hours several days a week) even in summer, although major museums and attractions will be open daily in summer. Always check the hours of a place you plan to visit, and call ahead to confirm if you'll be traveling some distance.

SHOPS

Shop hours are generally 9 or 10 to 5, though in high season many tourist-oriented stores stay open until 10 PM or later. Except in the main tourist areas, shops are often closed on Sundays.

CAMERAS & PHOTOGRAPHY

➤ PHOTO HELP: **Kodak Information Center** (☎ 800/242–2424). *Kodak Guide to Shooting Great Travel Pictures,* available in bookstores or from Fodor's Travel Publications (☎ 800/533–6478; $16.50 plus $4 shipping).

EQUIPMENT PRECAUTIONS

Always **keep your film and tape out of the sun.** Carry an extra supply of batteries, and **be prepared to turn on your camera or camcorder** to prove to security personnel that the device is real. Always **ask for hand inspection of film,** which becomes clouded after successive exposures to airport X-ray machines, and **keep videotapes away from metal detectors.**

CAR RENTAL

Rates in Boston begin at $48 a day and $179 a week for an economy car with air-conditioning, an automatic transmission, and unlimited mileage. Rates in Hyannis range from $33 to $45 a day (with most $40–$45) and

from $180 to $235 a week (with most about $225). These rates do not include tax on car rentals, which is 5%.

➤ MAJOR AGENCIES: **Alamo** (☎ 800/327–9633; 020/8759–6200 in the U.K.). **Avis** (☎ 800/331–1212; 800/879–2847 in Canada; 02/9353–9000 in Australia; 09/525–1982 in New Zealand). **Budget** (☎ 800/527–0700; 0144/227–6266 in the U.K.). **Dollar** (☎ 800/800–4000; 020/8897–0811 in the U.K., where it is known as Eurodollar; 02/9223–1444 in Australia). **Hertz** (☎ 800/654–3131; 800/263–0600 in Canada; 0990/90–60–90 in the U.K.; 02/9669–2444 in Australia; 03/358–6777 in New Zealand). **National InterRent** (☎ 800/227–7368; 0345/222525 in the U.K., where it is known as Europcar InterRent).

CUTTING COSTS

To get the best deal **book through a travel agent, who will shop around.** Also **price local car-rental companies,** although the service and maintenance may not be as good as those of a major player. Remember to ask about required deposits, cancellation penalties, and drop-off charges if you're planning to pick up the car in one city and leave it in another. If you're traveling during a holiday period, also make sure that a confirmed reservation guarantees you a car.

Do **look into wholesalers,** companies that do not own fleets but rent in bulk from those that do and often offer better rates than traditional car-rental operations.

➤ LOCAL AGENCIES: Nantucket: **Nantucket Windmill** (☎ 508/228–1227 or 800/228–1227). Martha's Vineyard: **Adventure Rentals** (☎ 508/693–1959). **Vineyard Classic and Specialty Cars** (☎ 508/693–5551). Also *see* Contacts and Resources *in* the A to Z sections in Chapters 2, 3, and 4.

INSURANCE

When driving a rented car you are generally responsible for any damage to or loss of the vehicle as well as for any property damage or personal injury that you may cause. Before you rent see what coverage your personal auto-insurance policy and credit cards already provide.

For about $15 to $20 per day, rental companies sell protection, known as a collision- or loss-damage waiver (CDW or LDW), that eliminates your liability for damage to the car. In Massachusetts the car-rental company must pay for damage to third parties up to a preset legal limit, beyond which your own liability insurance kicks in. However, **make sure you have enough coverage to pay for the car.** If you do not have auto insurance or an umbrella policy that covers damage to third parties, purchasing liability insurance and a CDW or LDW is highly recommended.

REQUIREMENTS & RESTRICTIONS

In Massachusetts you must be 21 to rent a car, and rates may be higher if you're under 25. You'll pay extra for child seats (about $3 per day), which are compulsory for children under five, and for additional drivers (about $2 per day). Non-U.S. residents will need a reservation voucher, a passport, a driver's license, and a travel policy that covers each driver, in order to pick up a car.

SURCHARGES

Before you pick up a car in one city and leave it in another **ask about drop-off charges or one-way service fees,** which can be substantial. Note, too, that some rental agencies charge extra if you return the car before the time specified in your contract. To avoid a hefty refueling fee **fill the tank just before you turn in the car,** but be aware that gas stations near the rental outlet may overcharge.

CAR TRAVEL

Driving on the Cape and islands has a number of unique and sometimes frustrating aspects addressed in individual chapters (☞ Cape Cod A to Z *in* Chapter 2 for information on Cape roads).

To get to Martha's Vineyard with your car, you'll have to take a ferry from Woods Hole, and to reach Nantucket, take the ferry from Hyannis (☞ Martha's Vineyard A to Z *in* Chapter 3 and Nantucket A to Z *in* Chapter 4).

AUTO CLUBS

➤ IN AUSTRALIA: **Australian Automobile Association** (☎ 02/6247–7311).

➤ IN CANADA: **Canadian Automobile Association** (CAA, ☎ 613/247–0117).

➤ IN NEW ZEALAND: **New Zealand Automobile Association** (☎ 09/377–4660).

➤ IN THE U.K.: **Automobile Association** (AA, ☎ 0990/500600). **Royal Automobile Club** (RAC; ☎ 0990/722722 for membership; 0345/121345 for insurance).

➤ IN THE U.S.: **American Automobile Association** (☎ 800/564–6222).

ROAD CONDITIONS

For information *see* Getting Around *in* the A to Z section at the end of Chapters 2, 3, and 4.

RULES OF THE ROAD

Right turns on red after a full stop are permitted in Massachusetts unless otherwise indicated.

In Massachusetts highway speed limits are 55 mph near urban areas, 65 mph elsewhere. Speed limits on U.S. 6 on the Cape vary as it changes from four lanes to two lanes.

CHILDREN IN CAPE COD

Cape Cod is very family oriented and provides every imaginable diversion for kids, including lodgings and restaurants that cater to them and that are affordable for families on a budget. Cottages and condominiums are popular with families, offering privacy, room, kitchens, and sometimes laundry facilities. Often cottage or condo communities have play yards and pools, sometimes even full children's programs.

You should consult the Children's Activities heading in the A to Z sections of the Cape Cod and Martha's Vineyard chapters. For other kid-friendly events, check the Festivals and Seasonal Events guide in Chapter 1 as well as Summertime: Week-at-a-Glance Close-Up feature box in Chapter 2.

SMART TRAVEL TIPS A TO Z

If you are renting a car don't forget to **arrange for a car seat** when you reserve.

➤ LOCAL INFORMATION: The **Bristol County Convention & Visitors Bureau** (✉ Box 976, New Bedford, MA 02741, ☎ 508/997–1250 or 800/288–6263) has a calendar of family-oriented events along south-coastal New England in its "Southern Coastal New England Americana Trail Guide."

FLYING

If your children are two or older **ask about children's airfares.** As a general rule, infants under two not occupying a seat fly at greatly reduced fares or even for free.

Experts agree that it's a good idea to use safety seats aloft for children weighing less than 40 pounds. Airlines set their own policies: U.S. carriers usually require that the child be ticketed, even if he or she is young enough to ride free, since the seats must be strapped into regular seats. Do **check your airline's policy about using safety seats during takeoff and landing.** And since safety seats are not allowed just everywhere in the plane, get your seat assignments early.

When reserving, **request children's meals or a freestanding bassinet** if you need them. But note that bulkhead seats, where you must sit to use the bassinet, may lack an overhead bin or storage space on the floor.

LODGING

Most hotels on Cape Cod allow children under a certain age to stay in their parents' room at no extra charge, but others charge for them as extra adults; be sure to **find out the cutoff age for children's discounts.**

If you're planning to stay at a bed-and-breakfast, be sure to **check in advance with the owners** to be sure that the B&B welcomes children. Some establishments are filled with fragile antiques, and owners may not accept families with children of a certain age.

SIGHTS & ATTRACTIONS

Child-friendly historical, cultural, and natural sights are indicated by a rubber duckie icon (🐥) in the margin.

CONSUMER PROTECTION

Whenever shopping or buying travel services on Cape Cod, **pay with a major credit card** so you can cancel payment or get reimbursed if there's a problem. If you're doing business with a particular company for the first time, **contact your local Better Business Bureau and the attorney general's offices** in your state and the company's home state, as well. Have any complaints been filed? Finally, if you're buying a package or tour, always **consider travel insurance** that includes default coverage (☞ Insurance, *below*).

➤ LOCAL BBBs: **Council of Better Business Bureaus** (✉ 4200 Wilson Blvd., Suite 800, Arlington, VA 22203, ☎ 703/276–0100, FAX 703/525–8277).

CUSTOMS & DUTIES

When shopping, **keep receipts** for all purchases. Upon reentering the country, **be ready to show customs officials what you've bought.** If you feel a duty is incorrect or object to the way your clearance was handled, note the inspector's badge number and ask to see a supervisor. If the problem isn't resolved, write to the appropriate authorities, beginning with the port director at your point of entry.

IN AUSTRALIA

Australian residents who are 18 or older may bring home $A400 worth of souvenirs and gifts (including jewelry), 250 cigarettes or 250 grams of tobacco, and 1,125 ml of alcohol (including wine, beer, and spirits). Residents under 18 may bring back $A200 worth of goods. Prohibited items include meat products. Seeds, plants, and fruits need to be declared upon arrival.

➤ INFORMATION: **Australian Customs Service** (Regional Director, ✉ Box 8, Sydney, NSW 2001, ☎ 02/9213–2000, FAX 02/9213–4000).

IN CANADA

Canadian residents who have been out of Canada for at least 7 days may bring home C$500 worth of goods duty-free. If you've been away less than 7 days but more than 48 hours, the duty-free allowance drops to

C$200; if your trip lasts 24–48 hours, the allowance is C$50. You may not pool allowances with family members. Goods claimed under the C$500 exemption may follow you by mail; those claimed under the lesser exemptions must accompany you. Alcohol and tobacco products may be included in the 7-day and 48-hour exemptions but not in the 24-hour exemption. If you meet the age requirements of the province or territory through which you reenter Canada, you may bring in, duty-free, 1.14 liters (40 imperial ounces) of wine or liquor *or* 24 12-ounce cans or bottles of beer or ale. If you are 16 or older you may bring in, duty-free, 200 cigarettes and 50 cigars. Check ahead of time with Revenue Canada or the Department of Agriculture for policies regarding meat products, seeds, plants, and fruits.

You may send an unlimited number of gifts worth up to C$60 each duty-free to Canada. Label the package UNSOLICITED GIFT—VALUE UNDER $60. Alcohol and tobacco are excluded.

➤ INFORMATION: **Revenue Canada** (⊠ 2265 St. Laurent Blvd. S, Ottawa, Ontario K1G 4K3, ☎ 613/993–0534; 800/461–9999 in Canada).

IN NEW ZEALAND

Homeward-bound residents 17 or older may bring back $700 worth of souvenirs and gifts. Your duty-free allowance also includes 4.5 liters of wine or beer; one 1,125-ml bottle of spirits; and either 200 cigarettes, 250 grams of tobacco, 50 cigars, or a combination of the three up to 250 grams. Prohibited items include meat products, seeds, plants, and fruits.

➤ INFORMATION: **New Zealand Customs** (Custom House, ⊠ 50 Anzac Ave., Box 29, Auckland, New Zealand, ☎ 09/359–6655, FAX 09/ 359–6732).

IN THE U.K.

From countries outside the EU, including the U.S., you may bring home, duty-free, 200 cigarettes or 50 cigars; 1 liter of spirits or 2 liters of fortified or sparkling wine or liqueurs; 2 liters of still table wine; 60 ml of perfume; 250 ml of toilet water; plus £136 worth of other goods, including gifts

and souvenirs. If you are returning from outside the EU, prohibited items include meat products, seeds, plants, and fruits.

➤ INFORMATION: **HM Customs and Excise** (⊠ Dorset House, Stamford St., Bromley Kent BR1 1XX, ☎ 020/ 7202–4227).

IN THE U.S.

Non-U.S. residents ages 21 and older may import into the United States 200 cigarettes or 50 cigars or 2 kilograms of tobacco, 1 liter of alcohol, and gifts worth $100. Meat products, seeds, plants, and fruits are prohibited.

➤ INFORMATION: **U.S. Customs Service** (inquiries, ⊠ 1300 Pennsylvania Ave. NW, Washington, DC 20229, ☎ 202/927–6724; complaints, ⊠ Office of Regulations and Rulings, 1300 Pennsylvania Ave. NW, Washington, DC 20229; registration of equipment, ⊠ Registration Information, 1300 Pennsylvania Ave. NW, Washington, DC 20229, ☎ 202/927–0540).

DINING

The restaurants we list are the cream of the crop in each price category. Properties indicated by an ✕⊡ are lodging establishments whose restaurant warrants a special trip.

Category	Cape Cod and Martha's Vineyard*	Nantucket*
$$$$	over $40	over $45
$$$	$25–$40	$35–$45
$$	$15–$25	$25–$35
$	under $15	under $25

per person for a three-course meal, excluding drinks, service, and 5% sales tax

RESERVATIONS & DRESS

Reservations are always a good idea: we mention them only when they're essential or are not accepted. Book as far ahead as you can, and reconfirm as soon as you arrive. We mention dress only when men are required to wear a jacket or a jacket and tie.

DISABILITIES & ACCESSIBILITY

➤ LOCAL RESOURCES: **Cape Organization for Rights of the Disabled** (CORD; ☎ 508/775–8300; 800/541– 0282 in MA) will supply information on accessibility of restaurants, hotels, beaches, and other tourist facilities on Cape Cod and the islands. **Sight Loss Services** (☎ 508/394–3904; 800/427–6842 in MA) provides accessibility and other information and referrals for people with vision impairments. The **Cape Cod National Seashore** (✉ South Wellfleet 02663, ☎ 508/349–3785) has facilities, services, and programs accessible to visitors with disabilities. Write for information on what is available. You can ask at the **Cape Cod National Seashore visitor centers** (☎ 508/255–3421 in Eastham; 508/487–1256 in Provincetown; ☞ Web Sites, *below* for site). For information about accessibility in Massachusetts state parks and beaches, contact the **Massachusetts Department of Environmental Management** (☞ Visitor Information, *below*).

LODGING

When discussing accessibility with an operator or reservations agent **ask hard questions.** Are there any stairs, inside *or* out? Are there grab bars next to the toilet *and* in the shower/tub? How wide is the doorway to the room? To the bathroom? For the most extensive facilities meeting the latest legal specifications **opt for newer accommodations.**

➤ COMPLAINTS: **Disability Rights Section** (✉ U.S. Department of Justice, Civil Rights Division, Box 66738, Washington, DC 20035-6738, ☎ 202/514–0301; 800/514–0301; 202/514–0301 TTY; 800/514–0301 TTY, FAX 202/307–1198) for general complaints. **Aviation Consumer Protection Division** (☞ Air Travel, *above*) for airline-related problems. **Civil Rights Office** (✉ U.S. Department of Transportation, Departmental Office of Civil Rights, S-30, 400 7th St. SW, Room 10215, Washington, DC 20590, ☎ 202/366–4648, FAX 202/366–9371) for problems with surface transportation.

TRAVEL AGENCIES

In the United States, although the Americans with Disabilities Act requires that travel firms serve the needs of all travelers, some agencies specialize in working with people with disabilities.

➤ TRAVELERS WITH MOBILITY PROBLEMS: **Access Adventures** (✉ 206 Chestnut Ridge Rd., Rochester, NY 14624, ☎ 716/889–9096), run by a former physical-rehabilitation counselor. **CareVacations** (✉ 5-5110 50th Ave., Leduc, Alberta, Canada T9E 6V4, ☎ 780/986–6404 or 877/478–7827, FAX 780/986–8332) has group tours and is especially helpful with cruise vacations. **Flying Wheels Travel** (✉ 143 W. Bridge St., Box 382, Owatonna, MN 55060, ☎ 507/451–5005 or 800/535–6790, FAX 507/451–1685). **Hinsdale Travel Service** (✉ 201 E. Ogden Ave., Suite 100, Hinsdale, IL 60521, ☎ 630/325–1335, FAX 630/325–1342).

➤ TRAVELERS WITH DEVELOPMENTAL DISABILITIES: **Sprout** (✉ 893 Amsterdam Ave., New York, NY 10025, ☎ 212/222–9575 or 888/222–9575, FAX 212/222–9768).

DISCOUNTS & DEALS

Be a smart shopper and **compare all your options** before making decisions. A plane ticket bought with a promotional coupon from travel clubs, coupon books, and direct-mail offers may not be cheaper than the least expensive fare from a discount ticket agency. And always keep in mind that what you get is just as important as what you save.

DISCOUNT RESERVATIONS

To save money **look into discount-reservations services** with toll-free numbers, which use their buying power to get a better price on hotels, airline tickets, even car rentals. When booking a room, always **call the hotel's local toll-free number** (if one is available) rather than the central reservations number—you'll often get a better price. Always ask about special packages or corporate rates.

➤ AIRLINE TICKETS: ☎ **800/FLY–4–LESS.** ☎ **800/FLY–ASAP.**

➤ HOTEL ROOMS: **RMC Travel** (☎ 800/245–5738).

PACKAGE DEALS

Don't confuse packages and guided tours. When you buy a package, you travel on your own, just as though you had planned the trip yourself. Fly-drive packages, which combine airfare and car rental, are often a good deal.

GAY & LESBIAN TRAVEL

Provincetown, at the tip of the Cape, is one of the East Coast's leading lesbian and gay seaside destinations and also has a large year-round lesbian and gay community. Dozens of P-town establishments, from B&Bs to bars, cater specifically to lesbian and gay visitors, and most of the town's restaurants are gay-friendly; several are gay-owned and -operated. Hyannis has the one gay bar on the Cape that's not in P-town (☞ Nightlife in Hyannis *in* Chapter 2).

➤ BOOKS: *Fodor's Gay Guide to the USA,* available in bookstores or from Fodor's Travel Publications (☎ 800/533–6478; $19.50 plus $4 shipping), has a chapter on Provincetown.

➤ GAY- AND LESBIAN-FRIENDLY TOUR OPERATORS: **New England Vacation Tours** (✉ Box 560, West Dover, VT 05356, ☎ 802/464–2076 or 800/742–7669, ℻ 802/464–2629) offers vacation packages to Cape Cod and the islands.

➤ GAY- AND LESBIAN-FRIENDLY TRAVEL AGENCIES: **Different Roads Travel** (✉ 8383 Wilshire Blvd., Suite 902, Beverly Hills, CA 90211, ☎ 323/651–5557 or 800/429–8747, ℻ 323/651–3678). **Kennedy Travel** (✉ 314 Jericho Turnpike, Floral Park, NY 11001, ☎ 516/352–4888 or 800/237–7433, ℻ 516/354–8849). **Now Voyager** (✉ 4406 18th St., San Francisco, CA 94114, ☎ 415/626–1169 or 800/255–6951, ℻ 415/626–8626). **Skylink Travel and Tour** (✉ 1006 Mendocino Ave., Santa Rosa, CA 95401, ☎ 707/546–9888 or 800/225–5759, ℻ 707/546–9891), serving lesbian travelers.

HEALTH

A common problem on the East Coast is Lyme disease (named after Lyme, Connecticut, where it was first diagnosed). This bacterial infection is transmitted by deer ticks and can be very serious, leading to chronic arthritis and worse if left untreated. Pregnant women are advised to **avoid areas of possible deer tick infestation**; if contracted during early pregnancy, Lyme disease can harm a fetus.

Deer ticks are most prevalent April–October but can be found year-round. They are about the size of a pinhead. Wear light-color clothing, which makes it easier to spot any ticks that might have attached themselves to you. Anyone planning to explore wooded areas or places with tall grasses (including dunes) should **wear long pants, socks drawn up over pant cuffs, and a long-sleeve shirt with a close-fitting collar**; boots are also recommended. The National Centers for Disease Control recommends that DEET repellent be applied to skin (not face!) and that permethrin be applied to clothing directly before entering infested areas; **use repellents very carefully** and conservatively with small children. Ticks also attach themselves to pets.

Recent research suggests that if ticks are removed within 12 hours of attachment to the body, the infectious bacteria is not likely to enter the bloodstream. That makes evenings a good opportunity to check yourself for ticks—look at the warm spots and hairlines on the body that attract ticks.

To remove a tick, apply tweezers to where it is attached to the skin and pull on the mouth parts. Try not to squeeze the body of the tick, which can send the body fluids containing the bacteria into the bloodstream. (Heating the tip of the tweezers before grasping the tick will cause the bug to release its bite, allowing for removal of the entire tick, including the sometimes-embedded head.) Disinfect the bite with alcohol and save the tick in a closed jar in case symptoms of the disease develop.

The first symptom of Lyme disease may be a ringlike rash or flulike symptoms, such as general feelings of malaise, fever, chills, and joint or facial pains. If diagnosed early, it can be treated with antibiotics. If you suspect your symptoms may be due to a tick bite, inform your doctor and ask to be tested.

Also **ask your physician about Lymerix, the new Lyme disease vaccine**; it takes three shots and 12 months to be 80% effective but is worth considering. Brochures on the disease are available at many tourist information areas.

Poison ivy is a pervasive vinelike plant, recognizable by its leaf pattern: three shiny green leaves together. In spring, new poison ivy leaves are red; likewise, they can take on a reddish tint as fall approaches. The oil from these leaves produces an itchy skin rash that spreads with scratching. If you think you may have touched some leaves, **wash as soon as you can** with soap and cool water.

➤ LYME DISEASE INFO: **Centers for Disease Control** (☎ 404/332–4555) or the **Massachusetts Department of Public Health** (✉ Southeast Office, 109 Rhode Island Rd., Lakeville, MA 02347, ☎ 508/947–1231).

HOLIDAYS

Major national holidays include New Year's Day (Jan. 1); Martin Luther King, Jr., Day (3rd Mon. in Jan.); President's Day (3rd Mon. in Feb.); Memorial Day (last Mon. in May); Independence Day (July 4); Labor Day (1st Mon. in Sept.); Thanksgiving Day (4th Thurs. in Nov.); Christmas Eve and Christmas Day (Dec. 24 and 25); and New Year's Eve (Dec. 31). Patriot's Day (3rd Mon. in Apr.) is a Massachusetts state holiday.

INSURANCE

The most useful travel insurance plan is a comprehensive policy that includes coverage for trip cancellation and interruption, default, trip delay, and medical expenses (with a waiver for preexisting conditions).

Without insurance you will lose all or most of your money if you cancel your trip, regardless of the reason. Default insurance covers you if your tour operator, airline, or cruise line goes out of business. Trip-delay covers expenses that arise because of bad weather or mechanical delays. Study the fine print when comparing policies.

British and Australian citizens need extra medical coverage when traveling overseas.

Always **buy travel policies directly from the insurance company**; if you buy it from a cruise line, airline, or tour operator that goes out of business you probably will not be covered for the agency or operator's default, a major risk. Before you make any purchase **review your existing health and home-owner's policies** to find what they cover away from home.

➤ TRAVEL INSURERS: In the U.S. **Access America** (✉ 6600 W. Broad St., Richmond, VA 23230, ☎ 804/285–3300 or 800/284–8300), **Travel Guard International** (✉ 1145 Clark St., Stevens Point, WI 54481, ☎ 715/345–0505 or 800/826–1300). In Canada **Voyager Insurance** (✉ 44 Peel Center Dr., Brampton, Ontario L6T 4M8, ☎ 905/791–8700; 800/668–4342 in Canada).

➤ INSURANCE INFORMATION: In the U.K. the **Association of British Insurers** (✉ 51–55 Gresham St., London EC2V 7HQ, ☎ 020/7600–3333, FAX 020/7696–8999). In Australia the **Insurance Council of Australia** (☎ 03/9614–1077, FAX 03/9614–7924).

LODGING

The Cape and islands have a wide range of lodging options, from campsites to B&Bs to luxurious self-contained resorts offering all kinds of sporting facilities, restaurants, entertainment, services (including business services and children's programs), and all the assistance you'll ever need in making vacation arrangements.

Single-night lodgings for those just passing through can be found at countless tacky but cheap and conveniently located little roadside motels, as well as at others that are spotless and cheery yet still inexpensive, or at chain hotels at all price levels; these places often have a pool, TVs, or other amenities to keep children entertained in the evening.

Families may want to **consider condominiums, cottages, and efficiencies,** which offer more space, living areas, kitchens, and sometimes laundry facilities, children's play areas, or children's programs.

The lodgings we list are the cream of the crop in each price category. We always list the facilities that are available—but we don't specify whether they cost extra: when pricing accommodations, always ask what's included and what costs extra. Properties indicated by an ✕🏨 are lodging establishments whose restaurant warrants a special trip.

Category	Cost*
$$$$	over $200
$$$	$150–$200
$$	$100–$150
$	under $100

All prices are for a standard double room in high season and do not include tax or gratuities. Some inns add a 15% service charge. The state tax on lodging is 5.7%; Nantucket and Martha's Vineyard (Down-Island only) impose an additional 4% tax.

Assume that hotels operate on the European Plan (EP, with no meals) unless we specify that they use the Continental Plan (CP, with a Continental breakfast daily), Breakfast Plan (BP, with a full breakfast daily), Modified American Plan (MAP, with breakfast and dinner daily), or the Full American Plan (FAP, with all meals).

APARTMENT, HOUSE & VILLA RENTALS

If you want a home base that's roomy enough for a family and comes with cooking facilities, **consider a furnished rental.** In fact, many visitors to the Cape and the islands rent a house for a week or longer rather than stay at a B&B or hotel. These can save you money; however, some rentals are luxury properties, economical only when your party is large. Many local Cape and islands agencies specialize in rentals. If you do decide to rent, be sure to book a property well in advance of your trip, as many properties are rented out to the same families or groups year after year. See the A to Z sections at the ends of Chapters 2, 3, and 4 for information on renting houses on the Cape and islands and for the names of agencies. Also see Close-Up: Home, Sweet Rental Home in Chapter 2 for tips on arranging a rental.

Home-exchange directories (☞ Home Exchanges, below) list rentals (often second homes owned by prospective house swappers), and some services search for a house or apartment for you (even a castle if that's your fancy) and handle the paperwork. Some send an illustrated catalog; others send photographs only of specific properties, sometimes at a charge. Up-front registration fees may apply.

➤ INTERNATIONAL AGENTS: **Rent-a-Home International** (✉ 7200 34th Ave. NW, Seattle, WA 98117, ☎ 206/789–9377 or 800/964–1891, FAX 206/789–9379). **Hideaways International** (✉ 767 Islington St., Portsmouth, NH 03801, ☎ 603/430–4433 or 800/843–4433, FAX 603/430–4444; membership $99).

B&BS

Bed-and-breakfasts are very popular on Cape Cod, Martha's Vineyard, and Nantucket. Many are housed in interesting old sea captains' homes and other 17th-, 18th-, and 19th-century buildings; others are in newer homes in which a few rooms and bathrooms have been set aside for rent. In many cases, B&Bs are not appropriate for families; be sure to ask. Noise travels easily, rooms are often small, and the furnishings are often fragile. Usually a B&B will not offer a phone or TV in guest rooms; also, more and more B&Bs do not allow smoking. You should also ask if the rooms are air-conditioned.

Numerous B&B reservation agencies serve the Cape and the islands; for some leading agencies, see Contacts and Resources in the A to Z sections of Chapters 2, 3, and 4. For additional information, get a free B&B guide from the Massachusetts Office of Travel & Tourism (☞ Visitor Information, below). The Cape Cod Chamber of Commerce (☞ Visitor Information, below) also publishes a free B&B guide.

CAMPING

Camping is not allowed on Nantucket, but there are many private and state-park camping areas on Cape Cod and a few on Martha's Vineyard. Write to the Massachusetts Office of Travel & Tourism and the Cape Cod Chamber of Commerce (☞ Visitor Information, below). For additional camping information, look for the ⚠ icon in Dining and Lodging sections in individual chapters and consult the Contacts and Resources section of Cape Cod A to Z in Chapter 2.

HOME EXCHANGES

If you would like to exchange your home for someone else's **join a home-exchange organization,** which will send you its updated listings of available exchanges for a year and will include your own listing in at least one of them. It's up to you to make specific arrangements.

➤ EXCHANGE CLUBS: **HomeLink International** (✉ Box 650, Key West, FL 33041, ☎ 305/294–7766 or 800/638–3841, FAX 305/294–1448; $93 per year). **Intervac U.S.** (✉ Box 590504, San Francisco, CA 94159, ☎ 800/756–4663, FAX 415/435–7440; $83 for catalogs.

HOSTELS

No matter what your age you can **save on lodging costs by staying at hostels.** In some 5,000 locations in more than 70 countries around the world, Hostelling International (HI), the umbrella group for a number of national youth-hostel associations, offers single-sex, dorm-style beds and, at many hostels, couples rooms and family accommodations. Membership in any HI national hostel association, open to travelers of all ages, allows you to stay in HI-affiliated hostels at member rates (one-year membership is about $25 for adults; hostels run about $10–$25 per night). Members also have priority if the hostel is full; they're eligible for discounts around the world, even on rail and bus travel in some countries. Membership in the U.S. is $25, in Canada C$26.75, in the U.K. £9.30, in Australia $44, in New Zealand $24.

There are very good hostels on the Cape and islands. In season, when all other rates are jacked up beyond belief, hostels are often the only budget accommodation option, but you must plan ahead to reserve space. You may luck out on last-minute cancellations, but it would be unwise to rely on them. *See* the lodging listings *in* Chapters 2, 3, and 4 for specific information.

➤ ORGANIZATIONS: **Australian Youth Hostel Association** (✉ 10 Mallett St., Camperdown, NSW 2050, ☎ 02/9565–1699, FAX 02/9565–1325). **Hostelling International—American Youth Hostels** (✉ 733 15th St. NW,

Suite 840, Washington, DC 20005, ☎ 202/783–6161, FAX 202/783–6171). **Hostelling International—Canada** (✉ 400–205 Catherine St., Ottawa, Ontario K2P 1C3, ☎ 613/237–7884, FAX 613/237–7868). **Youth Hostel Association of England and Wales** (✉ Trevelyan House, 8 St. Stephen's Hill, St. Albans, Hertfordshire AL1 2DY, ☎ 01727/855215 or 01727/845047, FAX 01727/844126). **Youth Hostels Association of New Zealand** (✉ Box 436, Christchurch, New Zealand, ☎ 03/379–9970, FAX 03/365–4476).

HOTELS

All hotels listed have private bath unless otherwise noted.

MEDIA

Glossy magazines on the area include *Cape Cod Life, Provincetown Arts, P'Town Women, Martha's Vineyard Magazine,* and *Nantucket Journal.*

On the Cape, the *Cape Cod Times* is a daily newspaper. *A-Plus,* available free in galleries and as several newspaper supplements, has arts listings. In Provincetown, look for the *Advocate,* the *Banner,* and *Provincetown Magazine,* all weeklies, for art and entertainment listings.

On the Vineyard, both island newspapers, the *Martha's Vineyard Times* and the *Vineyard Gazette,* publish weekly calendars of events. Also scan the *Best Read Guide,* free at many shops and hotels.

On Nantucket, see the free seasonal weekly *Nantucket Map & Legend,* the ferry companion paper *Yesterday's Island,* and the island newspaper, the *Inquirer and Mirror.*

MONEY MATTERS

Prices throughout this guide are given for adults. Substantially reduced fees are almost always available for children, students, and senior citizens. For information on taxes, *see* Taxes, *below.*

ATMS

Cape Cod has an abundance of ATM machines in its many towns, but they are a bit more sparse on the islands.

➤ ATM LOCATIONS: **Cirrus** (☎ 800/424–7787). **Plus** (☎ 800/843–7587)

for locations in the U.S. and Canada, or visit your local bank.

➤ ON MARTHA'S VINEYARD: ATMs are at the following locations: by the **Compass Bank** (✉ Opposite steamship offices in Vineyard Haven and Oak Bluffs; ✉ 19 Lower Main St., Edgartown; ✉ Up-Island Cronig's Market, State Rd., West Tisbury; ☎ 508/693–9400); **Edgartown National Bank** (✉ 2 S. Water St. and 251 Upper Main St., ☎ 508/627–1140); **Martha's Vineyard Cooperative Bank** (✉ S. Main St., Vineyard Haven, ☎ 508/693–0161); and **Park Avenue Mall** (✉ Oak Bluffs, ☎ 508/627–1167).

➤ ON NANTUCKET: ATMs are at the following locations: **Finast** (✉ Lower Pleasant St.); **Nantucket Bank** (✉ 2 Orange St. or 104 Pleasant St.); **Nantucket Memorial Airport** (☎ 508/325–5300); **Pacific National Bank** (✉ 61 Main St.); and **A&P** (✉ Straight Wharf).

CREDIT CARDS

Throughout this guide, the following abbreviations are used: **AE,** American Express; **D,** Discover; **DC,** Diners Club; **MC,** Master Card; and **V,** Visa.

➤ REPORTING LOST CARDS: To report lost or stolen credit cards, call the following toll-free numbers: **American Express** (☎ 800/327–2177); **Discover Card** (☎ 800/347–2683); **Diners Club** (☎ 800/234–6377); **Master-Card** (☎ 800/307–7309); and Visa (☎ 800/847–2911).

NATIONAL PARKS

Look into discount passes to **save money on park entrance fees.** The Golden Eagle Pass ($50) gets you and your companions free admission to all parks for one year. (Camping and parking are extra.) Both the Golden Age Passport ($10), for those 62 and older, and the Golden Access Passport (free), for travelers with disabilities, entitle holders to free entry to all national parks, plus 50% off fees for the use of many park facilities and services. You must show proof of age and of U.S. citizenship or permanent residency (such as a U.S. passport, driver's license, or birth certificate) and, if requesting Golden Access, proof of disability. All three passes are available at all national park entrances where entrance fees are charged. Golden Eagle and Golden Access passes are also available by mail.

➤ PASSES BY MAIL: **National Park Service** (National Capitol Area Office, ✉ 1100 Ohio Dr. SW, Washington, DC 20242).

OUTDOORS & SPORTS

Cape Cod and the islands are popular for their beaches and for opportunities to do everything from bike to sail. For specific information, *see* the specific towns in Chapters 2, 3, and 4 *and* the Contacts and Resources sections *in* the A to Z sections of these chapters.

PACKING

Only a few restaurants on Cape Cod, Martha's Vineyard, and Nantucket require formal dress, as do some dinner cruises. The area prides itself on informality. Do **pack a sweater or jacket, even in summer,** for nights can be cool. For suggested clothing regarding deer ticks and Lyme disease *see* Health, *above.*

In your carry-on luggage **bring an extra pair of eyeglasses or contact lenses** and **enough of any medication you take** to last the entire trip. You may also want your doctor to write a spare prescription using the drug's generic name, since brand names may vary from country to country. In luggage to be checked, **never pack prescription drugs or valuables.** To avoid customs delays, carry medications in their original packaging. And don't forget to copy down and carry addresses of offices that handle refunds of lost traveler's checks.

Perhaps most important of all, **don't forget a swimsuit** (or two).

CHECKING LUGGAGE

How many carry-on bags you can bring with you is up to the airline. Most allow two, but not always, so make sure that everything you carry aboard will fit under your seat, and get to the gate early. Note that if you have a seat at the back of the plane, you'll probably board first, while the overhead bins are still empty.

If you are flying internationally, note that baggage allowances may be determined not by piece but by weight—generally 88 pounds (40 kilograms) in first class, 66 pounds (30 kilograms) in business class, and 44 pounds (20 kilograms) in economy.

Airline liability for baggage is limited to $1,250 per person on flights within the United States. On international flights it amounts to $9.07 per pound or $20 per kilogram for checked baggage (roughly $640 per 70-pound bag) and $400 per passenger for unchecked baggage. You can buy additional coverage at check-in for about $10 per $1,000 of coverage, but it excludes a rather extensive list of items, shown on your airline ticket.

Before departure **itemize your bags' contents** and their worth, and label the bags with your name, address, and phone number. (If you use your home address, cover it so that potential thieves can't see it readily.) Inside each bag **pack a copy of your itinerary.** At check-in **make sure that each bag is correctly tagged** with the destination airport's three-letter code. If your bags arrive damaged or fail to arrive at all, file a written report with the airline before leaving the airport.

PASSPORTS & VISAS

➤ U.K. CITIZENS: **U.S. Embassy Visa Information Line** (☎ 01891/200290; calls cost 49p per minute, 39p per minute cheap rate) for U.S. visa information. **U.S. Embassy Visa Branch** (✉ 5 Upper Grosvenor Sq., London W1A 1AE) for U.S. visa information; send a self-addressed, stamped envelope. Write the **U.S. Consulate General** (✉ Queen's House, Queen St., Belfast BTI 6EO) if you live in Northern Ireland. Write the **Office of Australia Affairs** (✉ 59th fl., MLC Centre, 19-29 Martin Pl., Sydney NSW 2000) if you live in Australia. Write the **Office of New Zealand Affairs** (✉ 29 Fitzherbert Terr., Thorndon, Wellington) if you live in New Zealand.

PASSPORT OFFICES

The best time to apply for a passport or to renew is during the fall and winter. Before any trip, check your

passport's expiration date, and, if necessary, renew it as soon as possible.

➤ AUSTRALIAN CITIZENS: **Australian Passport Office** (☎ 131–232).

➤ NEW ZEALAND CITIZENS: **New Zealand Passport Office** (☎ 04/494–0700 for information on how to apply; 04/474–8000 or 0800/225050 in New Zealand for information on applications already submitted).

➤ U.K. CITIZENS: **London Passport Office** (☎ 0990/210410) for fees and documentation requirements and to request an emergency passport.

SENIOR-CITIZEN TRAVEL

To qualify for age-related discounts **mention your senior-citizen status up front** when booking hotel reservations (not when checking out) and before you're seated in restaurants (not when paying the bill). When renting a car ask about promotional car-rental discounts, which can be cheaper than senior-citizen rates.

➤ EDUCATIONAL PROGRAMS: **Elderhostel** (✉ 75 Federal St., 3rd floor, Boston, MA 02110, ☎ 877/426–8056, FAX 877/426–2166).

SHOPPING

For a general overview of some of the local specialties, *see* Pleasures and Pastimes *in* Chapter 1. On the islands the majority of shops close down in winter. Because of the Cape's large year-round population, its shops tend to remain open, though most Provincetown and Wellfleet shops and galleries do close.

On the Cape, Provincetown and Wellfleet are the main centers for art, and their gallery associations have pamphlets about local galleries. For a directory of area antiques dealers and auctions, contact the Cape Cod Antique Dealers Association. For a listing of crafts shops on the Cape, write to the Artisans' Guild of Cape Cod, Cape Cod Potters, or the Society of Cape Cod Craftsmen.

Throughout the Cape and islands, shop owners respond to the flow of tourists as well as to their own inclinations. Especially off-season, it's best to **phone a shop before going out of your way to visit it.**

➤ LOCAL RESOURCES: **Cape Cod Antique Dealers Association** (send business-size SASE to ✉ Box 191, Yarmouth Port 02675). **Provincetown Gallery Guild** (✉ Box 242, Provincetown 02657). **Wellfleet Art Galleries Association** (✉ Box 916, Wellfleet 02667).

Artisans' Guild of Cape Cod (send business-size SASE to ✉ 46 Debs Hill Rd., Yarmouth 02675). **Cape Cod Potters** (✉ Box 76, Chatham 02633). **Society of Cape Cod Craftsmen** (✉ Box 1709, Wellfleet 02667-1709).

STUDENTS IN CAPE COD

➤ STUDENT IDs & SERVICES: **Council on International Educational Exchange** (CIEE, ✉ 205 E. 42nd St., 14th fl., New York, NY 10017, ☎ 212/822–2600 or 888/268–6245, FAX 212/822–2699) for mail orders only, in the U.S. **Travel Cuts** (✉ 187 College St., Toronto, Ontario M5T 1P7, ☎ 416/979–2406 or 800/667–2887) in Canada.

TAXES

SALES TAX

Massachusetts state sales tax is 5%.

TIME

Cape Cod and the islands are in the Eastern time zone.

TIPPING

At restaurants, a 15% tip is standard for waiters; up to 20% may be expected at more expensive establishments. The same goes for taxi drivers, bartenders, and hairdressers. Coat-check operators usually expect $1; bellhops and porters should get 50¢ to $1 per bag; hotel maids in upscale hotels should get about $1.50 per day of your stay. On package tours, conductors and drivers usually get $10 per day from the group as a whole; check whether this has already been figured into your cost. For local sightseeing tours, you may individually tip the driver-guide $1–$5, depending on the length of the tour and the number of people in your party, if he or she has been helpful or informative. Ushers in theaters do not expect tips.

TOURS & PACKAGES

On a prepackaged tour or independent vacation everything is prearranged so you'll spend less time planning—and often get it all at a good price.

BOOKING WITH AN AGENT

Travel agents are excellent resources. But it's a good idea to collect brochures from several agencies because some agents' suggestions may be influenced by relationships with tour and package firms that reward them for volume sales. If you have a special interest **find an agent with expertise in that area**; ASTA (☞ Travel Agencies, *below*) has a database of specialists worldwide.

Make sure your travel agent knows the accommodations and other services of the place he or she is recommending. Ask about the hotel's location, room size, beds, and the availability of a pool, room service, or programs for children, if you care about these. Has your agent been there in person or sent others whom you can contact?

Do some homework on your own, too: local tourism boards can provide information about lesser-known and small-niche operators, some of which may sell only direct.

BUYER BEWARE

Each year consumers are stranded or lose their money when tour operators—even large ones with excellent reputations—go out of business. So **check out the operator.** Ask several travel agents about its reputation, and try to **book with a company that has a consumer-protection program.** (Look for information in the company's brochure.) In the United States, members of the National Tour Association and United States Tour Operators Association are required to set aside funds to cover your payments and travel arrangements in case the company defaults. It's also a good idea to choose a company that participates in the American Society of Travel Agent's Tour Operator Program (TOP); ASTA will act as mediator in any disputes between you and your tour operator.

Remember that the more your package or tour includes the better you can predict the ultimate cost of your vacation. Make sure you know exactly what is covered, and **beware of hidden costs.** Are taxes, tips, and transfers included? Entertainment and excursions? These can add up.

➤ TOUR-OPERATOR RECOMMENDATIONS: **American Society of Travel Agents** (☞ Travel Agencies, *below*). **National Tour Association** (NTA, ✉ 546 E. Main St., Lexington, KY 40508, ☎ 606/226–4444 or 800/682–8886). **United States Tour Operators Association** (USTOA, ✉ 342 Madison Ave., Suite 1522, New York, NY 10173, ☎ 212/599–6599 or 800/468–7862, FAX 212/599–6744).

TRAIN TRAVEL

Because of continuing financial difficulties, Amtrak service to the Cape was suspended in 1998; it is not currently scheduled to resume in 2000, but call for an update.

➤ TRAIN INFORMATION: **Amtrak** (☎ 800/872–7245).

TRANSPORTATION AROUND CAPE COD

For information about getting around Cape Cod and the islands, *see* Getting Around *in* the A to Z sections at the end of Chapters 2, 3, and 4.

TRAVEL AGENCIES

A good travel agent puts your needs first. Look for an agency that has been in business at least five years, emphasizes customer service, and has someone on staff who specializes in your destination. In addition **make sure the agency belongs to a professional trade organization.** The American Society of Travel Agents (ASTA), with 27,000 agents in some 170 countries, is the largest and most influential in the field. Operating under the motto "Integrity in Travel," it maintains and enforces a strict code of ethics and will step in to help mediate any agent-client disputes if necessary. ASTA also maintains a Web site that includes a directory of agents. If a travel agency is also acting as your tour operator, *see* Buyer Beware *in* Tours & Packages, *above.*

➤ LOCAL AGENT REFERRALS: **American Society of Travel Agents** (ASTA, ☎ 800/965–2782 24-hr hot line, FAX 703/684–8319, www.astanet.com). **Association of British Travel Agents** (✉ 68–271 Newman St., London W1P 4AH, ☎ 020/7637–2444, FAX 020/7637–0713). **Association of Canadian Travel Agents** (✉ 1729 Bank St., Suite 201, Ottawa, Ontario K1V 7Z5, ☎ 613/521–0474, FAX 613/521–0805). **Australian Federation of Travel Agents** (✉ Level 3, 309 Pitt St., Sydney 2000, ☎ 02/9264–3299, FAX 02/9264–1085). **Travel Agents' Association of New Zealand** (✉ Box 1888, Wellington 10033, ☎ 04/499–0104, FAX 04/499–0786).

VISITOR INFORMATION

Before you go, contact the state's office of tourism and the area's chambers of commerce for general information, seasonal events, and brochures. For specific information on Cape Cod's state forests and parks, the area's farmers' markets and fairs, or wildlife, contact the special-interest government offices below. You can also check Web sites on the Internet (☞ Web Sites, *below*). When you arrive, you can pay a visit to the chambers of commerce for additional information.

➤ CHAMBERS OF COMMERCE: **Cape Cod Chamber of Commerce** (✉ Junction of Rtes. 6 and 132, Hyannis 02601, ☎ 508/862–0700 or 888/332–2732, FAX 508/862–0727). **Martha's Vineyard Chamber of Commerce** (✉ Box 1698, Beach Rd., Vineyard Haven 02568, ☎ 508/693–0085, FAX 508/693–7589). **Nantucket Chamber of Commerce** (✉ 48 Main St., Nantucket 02554, ☎ 508/228–1700, FAX 508/325–4925). For a list of local Cape Cod chambers of commerce that can also provide information, *see* Cape Cod A to Z *in* Chapter 2.

➤ STATE: **Massachusetts Office of Travel & Tourism** (✉ 10 Park Plaza, Suite 4510, Boston 02116, ☎ 800/227–6277; 800/447–6277 for brochures; FAX 617/973–8525).

➤ SPECIAL INTERESTS: The **Department of Environmental Management** (✉ Division of Forests and Parks, 100 Cambridge St., Room 1905, Boston

02202, ☎ 617/727–3180, FAX 617/727–9402). The **Department of Food and Agriculture** (✉ 100 Cambridge St., Suite 2103, Boston 02202, ☎ 617/727–3000, FAX 617/727–7235). The **Division of Fisheries and Wildlife** (✉ Field Headquarters, North Drive, Westborough 01581, ☎ 508/792–7270, FAX 508/792–7275).

WEB SITES

Do check out the World Wide Web when you're planning. You'll find everything from the latest weather forecast to wedding planners to fishing tips. Fodor's Web site, www.fodors.com, is a great place to start your on-line travels. The various chamber-of-commerce sites are also quite helpful.

➤ WEB SITES: **Cape Cod Chamber of Commerce** (www.capecodchamber.org). **Cape Cod National Seashore** (www.nps.gov/caco). **Martha's Vineyard Chamber of Commerce** (www.mvy.com). **Nantucket Chamber of Commerce** (www.nantucketchamber.org). Other general sites include the **Cape Cod Information Center** (www.allcapecod.com/); **Cape Cod Online** (www.capecodonline.com/), which has links to the *Cape Cod Times* and other local publications; **Martha's Vineyard Online** (www.mvol.com); **Nantucket.net** (www.nantucket.net); **Massachusetts Office of Travel & Tourism** (www.massvacation.com)

Cape Cod Commission (www.gocapecod.org) for updates on the Cape Cod Rail Trail. **Massachusetts Bicycle Coalition** (www.massbike.org) for information for bicyclists. **Rails-to-Trails Conservancy** (www.railtrail.org) for Cape Cod Rail Trail riders.

Martha's Vineyard Times (www.mvtimes.com/) has news and listings for community events. The **Nantucket Nectar** site (www.juiceguys.com/), though associated with the juice company, has lots of interesting trivia.

For Cape Cod bus and trolley schedules, **Cape Cod Regional Transit Authority** (www.allcapecod.net/ccrta). The transportation information site of the **Cape Cod Commission** (www.gocapecod) has links to transportation providers, updates on transportation-related construction projects, and information on bicycling and walking.

Island ferry information and schedules are available online from the **Steamship Authority** (www.islandferry.com) and from **Hy-Line** (www.hy-linecruises.com).

Directory of Accessible Facilities in Massachusetts (www.state.ma.us/dem/access.htm). **Cape Cod Disability Access Directory** (www.capecod.net/ccdad/).

WHEN TO GO

Memorial Day through Labor Day (in some cases, Columbus Day) is high season on Cape Cod, Martha's Vineyard, and Nantucket. This is summer with a capital *S,* a time for barbecues, beach bumming, water sports, and swimming. During summer everything is open for business on the Cape, but you can also expect high-season evils: high prices, crowds, and traffic.

The Cape and the islands, however, are increasingly a year-round destination. *See* "The Cape's Six Seasons" *in* Chapter 5 for some highlights of the off-season.

CLIMATE

Although there are plenty of idyllic beach days to go around on the Cape, rain or fog is not an uncommon part of even an August vacation here. Visitors who do not learn to appreciate the beauty of the land and sea in mist and rain may find themselves mighty cranky.

Temperatures in winter and summer are milder on the Cape and islands than on the mainland, due in part to the warming influence of the Gulf Stream and the moderating ocean breezes. As a rule (and there have been dramatically anomalous years— 1994 and 1999 in particular), the Cape and islands get much less snow than the mainland, and what falls generally does not last. Still, winter can bring bone-chilling dampness, especially on the windswept islands.

The following are average daily maximum and minimum temperatures for Hyannis; it's likely to be two or three degrees cooler on the coast and on the islands.

SMART TRAVEL TIPS A TO Z

➤ FORECASTS: For local Cape weather, coastal marine forecasts, and today's tides, call the weather line of **WQRC** in Hyannis (☎ 508/771–5522). **Weather Channel Connection**(☎ 900/932–8437), 95¢ per minute from a Touch-Tone phone.

Climate

Jan.	40F	+4C	May	62F	17C	Sept.	70F	21C
	25	−4		48	+9		56	13
Feb.	41F	+5C	June	71F	22C	Oct.	59F	15C
	26	−3		56	13		47	8
Mar.	42F	+6C	July	78F	26C	Nov.	49F	9C
	28	−2		63	17		37	3
Apr.	53F	12C	Aug.	76F	24C	Dec.	40F	4C
	40	+4		61	16		26	−3

1 DESTINATION: CAPE COD, MARTHA'S VINEYARD, NANTUCKET

THE SEASONS OF AMERICA PAST AND PRESENT

THE WORLD TO-DAY is sick to its thin blood for lack of elemental things," wrote Henry Beston in his 1928 Cape Cod classic, *The Outermost House,* "for fire before the hands, for water welling from the earth, for air, for the dear earth itself underfoot." It is this that the Cape and its neighboring islands most have to offer an increasingly complex and artificial world: the chance to reconnect with elemental things. Walking along the shore poking at the washed-up sea life or watching birds fish in the surf, listening to the rhythm of the waves, experiencing the tranquillity of night on the beach or the power of a storm on water—all this is somehow life-affirming and satisfyingly real.

Cape Cod—the craggy arm of peninsula 60 mi southeast of Boston—and the islands of Martha's Vineyard and Nantucket share their geologic origins as debris deposited by a retreating glacier in the last ice age. They also share a moderate coastal climate and a diversity of terrain that foster an equally diverse assortment of plant and animal life, some of which exist nowhere else in northern climes.

Barrier beaches (sandbars that protect an inner harbor from the battering of the ocean), such as Monomoy on the Cape and Coatue on Nantucket, are breeding and resting grounds for a stunning variety of shore and seabirds, and the marshes and ponds are rich in waterfowl. Stellwagen Bank, just north of Provincetown, is a prime feeding ground for whales and dolphins, and shallow sandbars are favorite playgrounds for harbor and gray seals.

Among the flotsam and jetsam along the shores, beachcombers find horseshoe crabs, starfish, sea urchins, sponges, jellyfish, and a plethora of shells: white quahogs; elegant scallops; blue mussels; long, straight razor clams; spiraling periwinkles; pointy turret shells; smooth, round moon snails; conical whelks; rough-ridged oysters.

Much of the land, including a third of Nantucket's acreage and a quarter of the Vineyard's, is protected from development.

Nature preserves encompassing pine forests, marshes, swamps, cranberry bogs, and many other varieties of terrain are laced with well-marked walking and bicycling trails. On Nantucket, acres of moorland are spread with a rough tapestry of gnarled scrub oaks, low-lying blueberry bushes, fragrant bayberry, bearberry, and heather (the last originally brought to Nantucket from Scotland by accident in a shipment of pine trees).

Thanks to the establishment of the Cape Cod National Seashore in 1961, you can walk for almost 30 mi along the Atlantic beach and rarely see a trace of human habitation, other than a few old shacks in the dunes of Provincetown or the lighthouses that stand watch over the Cape's dangerous shoals. Across dunes anchored by poverty grass sprawl beach plums, pink salt-spray roses, and purple beach peas.

Through the creation of many National Historic Districts, in which change is kept to a minimum to preserve the historical integrity of the area, similar protection has been extended to the Cape and islands' oldest and loveliest man-made landscapes. One of the most important, as well as most visually harmonious, is along the Old King's Highway (Route 6A) on the north shore of the Cape, where some of the Cape's first towns were incorporated in the mid-1600s. Lining this tree-shaded country road are simple saltboxes from the earliest days, fancier houses built later by prosperous sea captains, and the traditional Cape cottages, shingles weathered to a silvery gray, with soft pink roses spilling across them. Here, too, are the Cape's windmills, as well as the white-steepled churches, taverns, and village greens that savor of old New England.

Nearly the entire island of Nantucket is part of its historic district. A rigid enforcement of district guidelines has created a town architecturally almost frozen in time, and one of the world's great treasures. Among the neat clapboard and weathered-shingle houses that line its cobblestone streets and narrow lanes are former warehouses, factories, and mansions that date from the golden age of whaling. Provincetown, too, has been designated an historic district, preserving for posterity its cheerful mix of tiny waterfront shops (former fish shacks) and captains' mansions, with everything from a 1746 Cape house to a mansarded French Second Empire building.

The Cape and islands also preserve their past in a wealth of small museums—nearly every town has one—that document local history, often back to the days when Native Americans were the sole inhabitants. (In 1620, when the Pilgrims first anchored at Provincetown, exploring the Cape before heading on to Plymouth, an estimated 30,000 Wampanoags lived on Cape Cod.) Often set in houses that are themselves historic, these museums provide a visual history of the lives of the English settlers and their descendants, including their economic pursuits: from farming to harvesting salt, salt hay, and cranberries (still an important local crop) to fishing and whaling to tourism, which began as far back as the late 19th century.

The importance of whaling to the area—Nantucket was the world's premier whaling port in the early to mid-19th century—is reflected in the historical museums. The travels of the area's whaling and packet-schooner seamen and captains are illustrated with such items as antique nautical equipment, harpoons, charts, maps, journals, scrimshaw created during the often years-long whaling voyages, and gifts brought back from exotic ports for wives who had waited so patiently (those who had waited, that is; some women chose to go along with their husbands for the ride).

Remote Nantucket has just one town, with a few outlying villages, one of them full of rose-covered cottages that once housed an actors' colony. Large tracts of undeveloped moorland and nature preserves give the island an open, breezy feel. It has long been a summer bastion of the wealthy, who are likely to be seen dressed down to the hilt and tooling around on beat-up bicycles.

Martha's Vineyard, on the other hand, is known as the celebrity island for its famous summer (and year-round) residents in the arts and entertainment, many of whom participate in the annual Possible Dreams Auction and other high-visibility charitable events. More than twice the size of Nantucket, the Vineyard offers more variety than its smaller neighbor 19

mi to the east: its six towns range from a young and rowdy seaside hamlet of Victorian cottages to a rural New England village to an elegant, well-manicured town of sea captains' homes and flower gardens. The landscape, too, is more varied, including a 5,146-acre pine forest, rolling farmland enclosed by drystone walls, and dramatic clay cliffs.

Both islands are ringed with beautiful sandy beaches, some backed with high or low dunes, others bordering moorland or marshes. You can visit them on a day trip from a Cape Cod base, but three days is a practical minimum for getting a real sense of island life.

ALL THREE AREAS are noted for their shopping (for crafts, art, and antiques especially); for theater, both small community groups and professional summer stock companies; and for plenty of recreational offerings that take advantage of the marine environment, including water sports, fishing charters, and even Jeep safaris to isolated beaches for surf casting. (Piping plovers nest on beaches, and access to beaches is sometimes severely limited, so check about restrictions before renting that Jeep.) All three are also family oriented—especially the Cape, which has endless amusements to offer children beyond the ever-beckoning beach. There are also such typical New England entertainments as chowder suppers and clambakes.

The "season" used to be strictly from Memorial Day to Labor Day, but the boundaries have blurred; many places now open in April or earlier and close as late as November, and a core remain open year-round. Unfortunately, most of the historic sites and museums, staffed largely by volunteers, still adhere to the traditional dates and so are inaccessible in the off-season.

In fact, all seasons invite a different kind of visit. In summer, you have your choice of plunking down somewhere near a beach and never moving, filling your schedule with museums and activities, or combining the two in whatever mix suits you. In fall, the water may be warm enough for swimming as late as October, crowds are gone, and prices are lower. Turning foliage, though nothing like the dramatic displays found elsewhere in New England, is still an enjoyable addition to a fall visit; it usually reaches its peak around the end of October. The peak can be as much as a few weeks earlier or later than this, though, depending on the weather in the preceding months. Moors turn purple and gold and rust; burning bush along roadsides flames a brilliant red. Cranberries ripen to a bright burgundy color and are harvested by a method fascinating to watch. Trees around freshwater marshes, ponds, and swamps tend to color earlier and brighter; the red maple swamps, Beech Forest in Provincetown, and Route 6A from Sandwich to Orleans are particularly colorful spots.

Fall and winter are oyster and scallop season, and restaurants that remain open serve a wide selection of dishes made with these freshly harvested delicacies. Winter is a quiet time, when many tourist-oriented activities and facilities shut down, but prices are low and you can walk the beaches in often total solitude. For a quiet or romantic weekend getaway, country inns offer cozy rooms with canopy beds, where you can curl up before the fireplace after returning from a leisurely dinner by candlelight.

As for spring, it gets a wee bit wet, and on Nantucket expect a good dose of fog. Still, when daffodils come bursting up from roadsides, especially on Nantucket, everything begins to turn green. By April, seasonal shops and restaurants begin to open, and locals prepare for yet another summer.

NEW AND NOTEWORTHY

Cape Cod

The **Waquoit Bay National Estuarine Research Reserve** in Waquoit opened a new exhibit center in 1999, with displays about the bay's plants and animals, the Cape Cod watershed, and Wampanoag culture. An interactive exhibit allows you to trace the path of a raindrop.

In Dennis, the **Cape Museum of Fine Arts** was embarking on a major expansion in late 1999; new gallery space is scheduled to open in summer 2000. The new facilities will include a gallery for special exhibitions and added space to display works from the museum's permanent collections.

Provincetown celebrated its third annual **Portuguese Week** in summer 1999. The festival has evolved into quite an event, with bands playing in the streets, ethnic foods and crafts, dances, a children's fishing derby, and a parade with people in traditional Portuguese dress. The festival honors the history of the Portuguese in Provincetown and their role in the fishing industry; it winds up on Sunday with a procession from St. Peter's Church to MacMillan Wharf, where the bishop blesses the fishing vessels.

The year 1999 marked the **100-year anniversary** of Provincetown's existence as an art colony. In 1899, Charles W. Hawthorne opened the Cape Cod School of Art, attracting students and fellow artists to the town in droves. By 1916, five additional art schools had been established, and more than 300 artists lived and worked in Provincetown. The prominence of artists and art schools has continued through the century; today the Cape Cod School of Art, the Hawthorne School of Art, the Provincetown Art Association and Museum School, and the Provincetown Fine Arts Work Center serve hundreds of students.

The Cape Cod Chamber of Commerce has expanded its transportation "Smart Map" into a more detailed **"Smart Guide,"** which lists the Cape's transportation options, including trolley, bus, ferry, and flight services. It also includes information about traveling by train, bicycling, and walking, as well as sources of traffic condition reports. The guide is designed to encourage tourists to take advantage of local transportation, thus easing the severe summer traffic congestion. The guides are available at all Chamber offices, and at many shops and attractions.

In 1999, the **Cape Cod Central Railroad** began offering two-hour, 42-mi scenic rail tours from Hyannis to the Cape Cod Canal and back. Dinner train service was also expected to be in full swing by the year 2000.

Martha's Vineyard

The Vineyard has become one of the nation's leading **summer hot spots** for the elite from the worlds of entertainment, media, and politics. Sharon Stone, Spike Lee, Walter Cronkite, Ted Danson and Mary Steenburgen, Beverly Sills, Billy Joel, Art Buchwald, Patricia Neal, and Diane Sawyer and Mike Nichols spend their summers here, rubbing creative elbows with such year-round residents as Carly Simon and James Taylor. President Clinton, First Lady Hillary Rodham Clinton, and daughter Chelsea have visited the island several times since Clinton took office.

The **art scene** on the Vineyard has really blossomed, with more than 35 galleries displaying the work of internationally recognized artists and photographers. Weekly openings are eagerly awaited social events, where guests can nibble, sip, and meet-and-greet the men and women behind the works. The Granary Gallery in Chilmark still carries the late photographer Alfred Eisenstaedt's work. And don't miss the breathtaking photography of Peter Simon (Carly's brother) that can be found at his gallery at the Feast of Chilmark restaurant.

The Trustees of Reservations report an **increased rate of erosion** on south-facing beaches—up to 75 ft in some spots. Although 60 to 75 acres of beach were created at Wasque over the past 20 years, the current cycle of erosion reclaims an average of 17 ft annually. In Oak Bluffs, the town, the state, and the Army Corps of Engineers are continuing the battle to save Beach Road, a narrow, view-rich strip between the ocean and Sengekontacket Pond.

Martha's Flavor Fest, an independent black film and script competition based in Oak Bluffs, showcases work by undiscovered black actors, directors, and script writers. The first Flavor Fest in summer 1998 included screenings at the Island Theater, an evening script reading at the Tabernacle with such notables as Gil Harper and Ruby Dee, and a women's forum at Lola's discussing the issues of black women in the film industry. The festival expanded with workshops and panel discussions in 1999.

Nantucket

The annual **Nantucket Film Festival,** a weeklong series of screenings, readings, panel discussions, and Q&A sessions, has gained a secure footing. From 10 AM until midnight, an array of films, from 20-minute shorts to full-length features, is shown at two venues in town.

A full restoration of the **African School and Church** in Nantucket Town was completed in 1999, returning the structure to its authentic 1880s appearance, both inside and out. New space for lectures, concerts, and readings will be dedicated to the education of the public about the experiences of the black and Cape Verdean communities on Nantucket. A guided walk on the Black Heritage Trail takes you to nine significant historic spots.

The new **Polpis bike path,** an 8-mi stretch between Nantucket Town and the Life Saving Museum, and on to a winding path along Polpis Road to Siasconset, was completed in time for the 1999 season.

The third annual **Nantucket Wine Festival,** held in May 1999, has continued its success, welcoming several vineyards from around the world, including France, Australia, Chile, Italy, and California's Napa Valley, to participate. The vineyards team up with Nantucket's best restaurants and host tastings and dinners in some of Nantucket's historic old homes.

WHAT'S WHERE

Cape Cod

Continually shaped by ocean currents, this windswept land of sandy beaches and dunes has an amazing natural beauty. Everyone comes for the seaside, yet crimson cranberry bogs, forests of birch and beech, and grassy meadows and marshlands gracing the interior are equally splendid. Local history is fascinating; whale-watching provides an exhilarating experience of the natural world; cycling trails lace the landscape; shops purvey everything from antiques to useful items to pure kitsch; and you can dine on simple, as-fresh-as-it-comes seafood, delicious, thoughtfully prepared cuisine, or most anything in between.

Martha's Vineyard

With all of the star appeal that's come to it in recent years, you might think that the Vineyard has changed. Yes, more and more visitors come to the island every year, but Vineyarders have risen to the occasion. As a result, some restaurants have acquired a pleasant, easygoing sophistication, while others hold on to their local traditions. The bustle and crush of Vineyard Haven, Oak Bluffs, and Edgartown's summertime crowds continue to belie the quieter feeling that off-season visitors have come to love. In season, you can always step back into rural time Up-Island—at the fantastic West Tisbury Farmers' Market or on a conservation area's delightful walking trails. And the fresh fish loaded onto the docks in Menemsha is as delicious as it's ever been.

Nantucket

Herman Melville may never have set foot on Nantucket, but he was right about its exuberance—in summer, the place brims over with activity. To the eye, Nantucket Town's museum-quality houses and the outlying beaches and rolling moors make the island an aesthetic world unto itself. So hop a ferry to the "Gray Lady of the Sea" to measure your gait on its historic cobblestone streets, stand knee-deep in surf casting for stripers, pick up some old whaling lore, or set yourself up on the sand as the sun arcs its way across the sky.

PLEASURES AND PASTIMES

Beaches

Cape Cod, Martha's Vineyard, and Nantucket are known for long, dune-backed sand beaches, with both surf and calm water, depending on the body of water. Swimming season is approximately mid-June–September (sometimes into October). The Cape Cod National Seashore on the ocean side of the Lower and Outer Cape has the Cape's best beaches, with high dunes, wide strands of sand, and no development on the shore.

Beaches on the Vineyard and Nantucket are no less spectacular. The botanically curious will find plants that do not appear on the Cape, and it's even more possible on the islands to feel the delight of having an isolated beach all to yourself. There may, in fact, be something about island beaches that heightens their appeal—knowing that you must cross the water in front of you in order to return to your other life gives them a more precious quality.

Conservation Areas

With all of the bustle that can seem unavoidable on a Cape Cod, Martha's Vineyard, or Nantucket vacation, a sure bet for escape is any one of the numerous Audubon, Land Bank, Sherrif's Meadow, Nature Conservancy, or Trustees of the Reservations refuges. There you can delight in seeing an osprey nest or the slow-motion stalking of a great blue heron, the head of a river otter coursing through the water, great shorebird colonies, a meadow in late summer, or that stray, berry-studded blueberry bush. This is simply the best way to experience the vitality and diversity of the region.

Flora and fauna of local interest to look out for are beach-plum bushes, which bloom in late May and bear fruit in the fall; spring-blooming, white-flowered shadbush and its red-purple June berries; shade- and moisture-loving cinnamon ferns; June-blooming pasture rose and the lovely rosa rugosa, which bloom throughout the summer; the brilliant orange butterfly weed, so named for the affinity that monarch butterflies have for the nectar of its summer flowers; the fragrant midsummer blooms of the sweet pepper bush; blueberry and huckleberry bushes; the low-slung, waxy-leaved, dark green teaberry with its early fall red berries; fall-flowering yellow seaside goldenrod and purple sea lavender; caribou moss, also near the sea; the plentiful beach grass (which you should avoid treading upon in order to keep it plentiful); oval-leaf bayberry bushes, whose scent is a wintertime household delight; and tupelo, sassafras, pygmy beech, cottonwood, Norway spruce, red cedar, pitch pine, tamarack, and numerous other trees. Unfortunately, you need to watch out for poison ivy, that invasive spoiler of human comfort (its berries are a great boon to birds, however).

As for wildlife, there are hawks and harriers, ospreys, pheasants, quail, numerous ducks and geese, terns, bobwhites, meadowlarks, catbirds, towhees, swallows, orioles, goldfinches, yellowthroats, a great variety of warblers, and more spring and fall migrants than can be mentioned; a kingdom of mollusks and sea creatures—horseshoe, hermit, fiddler, and blue crabs, oysters, scallops, quahogs, and so on; and rabbits, raccoons, otter, muskrats, mice, and deer. From beach to marsh to meadow to salt-sprayed sand plains, the variety of habitats is tremendous.

Note: Along with the poison ivy alert, check yourself for deer ticks after a day's walk or hike in the outdoors (☞ Health *in* Smart Travel Tips A to Z).

Restaurants

What's new in Cape and island cuisine? Influenced by arrivals from Boston and New York, a generation of young chefs—many of whom own their restaurants—is serving eclectic, inventive, cosmopolitan menus, with prices to match. First-rate, sophisticated dining is now available in most towns, but particularly in Provincetown and on the islands. The latest trend among these smart young chefs is to offer menus that range from reasonable burgers to expensive full dinners, blurring the line between hot and haute spots, allowing families and younger diners to enjoy a more upscale ambience.

Although the fish that gave the Cape its name is much harder to find now than in Pilgrim days, seafood remains the area's major culinary attraction. Flounder and hake are more often available than haddock and cod, but for freshness and preparation, no one does it better than local chefs. Bass has made a good comeback; locals much prefer it to salmon or even swordfish steaks. At one time certain restaurants boasted that they used "underutilized species" such as hake and monkfish. Now there is no such thing as underutilized—everything is being used and all the fish are more expensive.

The very best New England clam chowder—made from large native clams called quahogs (pronounced "*ko*-hawgs"), potatoes, and cream—doesn't hide the taste with a flour thickener. Roadside stands still serve tasty fried clams or fish-and-chips, either of which, eaten at a picnic table overlooking the bay or the ocean, may be more memorable than the fanciest meal in town.

For generations, Cotuit and Wellfleet have vied to produce the world's best-tasting oyster. That neither has emerged victorious over the other is to everyone's benefit; try a half dozen of both and judge for yourself. Other specialties include scallops (at their very best at the end of the summer season), mussels, and of course the nation's favorite crustacean, the large-clawed North Atlantic lobster.

Shopping

Art galleries and crafts shops abound on Cape Cod, Martha's Vineyard, and Nantucket, a reflection of the long attraction the area has held for artists and craftspeople. The region is also a popular antiquing spot—which means both the genuine article and kitschy wanna-bes. Coastal environments and a seafaring past account for the proliferation of sea-related crafts (as well as marine-antiques dealers) on the Cape and the islands. A craft form that originated on the years-long voyages to whaling grounds is scrimshaw, the etching of finely detailed designs of sailing ships and sea creatures onto a hard surface. In the beginning, the bones or teeth of whales were used; today's ecologically minded (and legally constrained) scrimshanders use a synthetic substitute like Corian, a DuPont countertop material.

Another whalers' pastime was the sailor's valentine: a glass-enclosed wood box, often in an octagonal shape (derived from the shape of the compass boxes that were originally used), containing an intricate mosaic of tiny seashells. The shells were collected on stopovers in the West Indies and elsewhere; sorted by color, size, and shape; and then glued into elaborate patterns during the long hours aboard ship. Exquisite examples can be found in Nantucket museums.

The Nantucket lightship basket was developed in the mid-19th century on a lightship off the island's coast. In good weather there was little to do, and so (the story goes) crew members began weaving intricately patterned baskets of cane, a trade some continued onshore and passed on. Later a woven lid and decoration were added, and the utilitarian baskets were on their way to becoming the handbags that today cost hundreds of dollars. Although Nantucket is still the locus of the craft, antique and new baskets can be found on the Cape and the Vineyard as well (☞ Close-Up: Nantucket Lightship Baskets *in* Chapter 4).

Cranberry glass, a light ruby glass made by fusing gold with glass or crystal, is sold in gift shops all over the Cape. It was once made by the Sandwich Glass company (among others) but now retains only the association with Cape Cod, as it is made elsewhere in the United States and in Europe.

For some great vacation reading, there are also a number of highly browsable new- and used-book stores on the Cape and islands. Many have strong sections of books on topics of local interest that you won't find in bookstores at home.

Sports and the Outdoors

The Cape and the islands are top spots for swimming, surfing, windsurfing, sailing, and enjoying virtually all other water sports. Shipwrecks make for interesting dive sites, but don't expect a tropical underwater landscape. Golfers have a number of excellent courses to choose from, including championship layouts, and most courses remain open nearly year-round. Bicycling is a joy on the mostly level roads, along paved and scenic bike paths, and through the many nature preserves. Birdwatchers have a wide variety of habitats to choose from, often in a single nature preserve. Fishing, especially for bluefish and striped bass, brings many people to the area year after year, and there are some major derbies around. Remember, adults will need a license (available at most tackle shops for a nominal fee) for freshwater fishing.

Spectators can choose from a plethora of bike and running races, golf competitions, horse shows, sailboat races, and the well-attended Cape Cod Baseball League games, breeding ground of champions (☞ Close-Up: The Cape Cod Baseball League *in* Chapter 2).

Theater

In 1916 a young aspiring writer arrived in Provincetown to try his hand at writing plays. In July of that same year, Eugene O'Neill's first play, *Bound East for Cardiff*, made its debut in a waterfront fish house to tremendous success. More than 80 years later, theater continues to thrive on the Cape. The country's most renowned summer theater, the Cape Playhouse in Dennis—where Bette Davis got her start first as an usher, then as an actress (in 1928, in *Mr. Pim Passes By*)—tops the list for the best and brightest stage fare. The Wellfleet Harbor Actors Theater has staged many important New England and world premieres. The Cape Cod Theatre Project, in Falmouth and Woods Hole, presents staged readings of new works by leading

playwrights, followed by an audience discussion with the author.

Then there's the newest kid on the creative block: Provincetown Repertory Theatre. Founded in 1995 by Ken Hoyt, PRT brought legendary director Jose Quintero out of retirement in the summer of 1996 to direct two one-act O'Neill plays. In 1997 three-time Pulitzer Prize–winning playwright Edward Albee appeared at a benefit reading to help raise money for PRT's new theater on the grounds of the Pilgrim Monument and Provincetown Museum. Community theater abounds as well, most notably at the Academy Playhouse in Orleans, the Cape Cod Repertory Theatre Co. in Brewster, and the Harwich Junior Theatre.

FODOR'S CHOICE

No two people will agree on what makes a perfect vacation, but it's fun and helpful to know what others think. We hope you'll have a chance to experience some of Fodor's Choices yourself while visiting Cape Cod and the islands. For detailed information about each, refer to the appropriate chapters this guidebook.

Old New England

★ The town of **Sandwich,** with its abundance of old houses, its cemetery, museums, salt marsh, and its lovely setting on Shawme Pond, is unsurpassed for regional charm.

★ **Bright crimson cranberries** floating on flooded bogs just before the fall harvest on Cape Cod and Nantucket are a perfect reminder of the handwork that was one of the joys of the seasonal roundup.

★ At **Hallet's century-old drugstore** in Yarmouth Port, life can be sweet, especially when you're sipping an ice cream soda while swiveling on a stool at a marble bar.

★ The **Wednesday-night community sing-along** (in July and August only) at the Tabernacle in the Oak Bluffs Camp Ground on Martha's Vineyard is great old-time fun, as much for the melody as for the sense of community you can't help but feel.

★ The brick **Aquinnah Lighthouse** overlooking the dramatic cliffs at Aquinnah on Martha's Vineyard quietly speaks, like a time-tested sentinel, of the elemental forces of wind and sea.

★ More than the past works of any other town in America, **Nantucket's cobblestone streets and historic architecture** continue to glow with the dignity and charm of early American life.

Natural Phenomena

★ If you crave a little rejuvenation, or just want to commune with nature, spend an afternoon observing life on the salt marsh at **Bass Hole Boardwalk** in Yarmouth Port or taking a walk onto the tidal flats when the water is out.

★ From Chatham Light, looking out at the **Chatham Break** in the sandbar is a reminder of the power of the sea and a fascinating display of the process of geological change.

★ **Seeing harbor seals off Race Point** in Provincetown in winter is one of the pleasures of the seaside Cape at a time when you feel like you have the place to yourself.

★ **Sunset over Cape Cod Bay** on any bay beach from Eastham to Provincetown is an unforgettable delight at any time of year.

★ **Whales breaching** alongside your whale-watch boat will fill you with a sense of wonder unlike any you've ever felt—the creatures are simply marvelous. It's also quite a treat to see dolphins jumping in and out of the boat's bow waves or in its wake.

★ The **moors of Nantucket** in fall, next to cranberry bogs, turn colors that you can almost hear, if you listen closely enough.

★ **Stargazing from Nantucket's Loines Observatory** is so astonishing because the island's isolation from mainland lights makes the sky virtually blaze with starlight.

Beaches and Conservation Areas

★ **Monomoy National Wildlife Refuge,** two islands off Chatham, is a bird and birders' haven, particularly during spring and fall migrations.

★ **Massachusetts Audubon Wellfleet Bay Wildlife Sanctuary** in South Wellfleet, with its numerous adult and kids' programs and its beautiful salt-marsh setting, is a favorite migration stop for Cape vacationers year-round.

★ **Nauset Light, Coast Guard, Marconi, and Race Point beaches** stretch majestically along the length of the Cape Cod National Seashore. Backed by dunes, they are the truly classic Cape beaches.

★ **Felix Neck Wildlife Sanctuary** on Martha's Vineyard is another Massachusetts Audubon Society jewel, its ponds, marshes, fields, and woods teeming with plant and animal life.

★ **Lucy Vincent Beach** in Chilmark on Martha's Vineyard is quite simply the best beach on the island. It is restricted to resident use in summer, at which point you may want to venture out to Aquinnah to take in the sights on the beach under the phenomenal cliffs and lighthouse.

★ At the **Coatue–Coskata–Great Point reserves** in Nantucket, you may see a marsh hawk or an oystercatcher floating in the air or coming and going from stands of cedar and oak, or you might just land a striped bass or bluefish if you brought along a surf-casting pole. Or you could just put your feet in the sand and walk out to the Great Point Light.

★ **Eel Point,** at the western end of Nantucket, blossoms at various times of year with wild roses, bayberry, heather, and goldenrod. It is a great beach and surf-casting and birding area, with small, sandbar islands close to shore serving as perches for shorebirds.

Shopping

★ **Sandwich Auction House** has been holding weekly auctions for more than two decades, with periodic theme sales of toys, silver, paperweights, and collectibles.

★ The **weekly flea market** (Wednesday, Thursday, and weekends in summer; weekends before and after) at the Wellfleet Drive-In Theater is one big browse, whether or not you take anything home with you.

★ **Herridge Books** in Wellfleet reflects the town's longtime appeal to vacationing writers, with an outstanding collection of interesting reading. A book lover could easily take a day or more to do justice to what's on the shelves in this store.

★ The seasonal **West Tisbury Farmers' Market** on Martha's Vineyard is the largest in Massachusetts, with about 50 vendors of local produce and homemade jam and preserves.

★ **Bunch of Grapes** in Vineyard Haven on the Vineyard contains an amazing array of books, books, and more books, including island-related titles. Don't be surprised to find yourself browsing through the shelves next to the Hollywood celebs and assorted literati who shop here.

★ **Rafael Osona auction house** in Nantucket Town is for buyers and spectators alike. Whether or not you buy any of the fine antiques, the auction can be great entertainment.

★ **Lightship baskets and scrimshaw** on Nantucket continue a crafts tradition unique to the area.

★ **Farm stands** throughout the Cape and islands provide one of the best ways to get close to the land and the rhythm of rural life.

Flavors

★ **Front Street, Provincetown, Cape Cod.** In a town that consistently continues to raise the level of the Cape's cuisine, this small, unassuming venue serves nothing short of superb, original food, offered by a marvelous staff. You couldn't ask for much more at Cape's end. $$$

★ **Inaho, Yarmouth Port, Cape Cod.** To recommend a Japanese restaurant on Cape Cod is only superficially surprising. Inaho uses the great Cape fresh seafood to maximum effect, and the setting and presentation, from lighting to service, perfectly celebrate a remarkably conscious kitchen. $$–$$$

★ **Sagamore Inn, Sagamore, Cape Cod.** Rustic, roomy, family run, not pretentious or expensive—this is the kind of place you might stop in for lunch on a rainy day, and then dinner the following night. $$

★ **Mojo's, Provincetown, Cape Cod.** If every hole-in-the-wall were as inventive as this one, and cared as much about its menu, the world would be a cheaper, better place. You'll find everything from fried clams and steak subs to veggie burgers and salads here. $

★ **L'étoile, Edgartown, Martha's Vineyard.** Set in the incomparable Charlotte Inn, this longtime contemporary French favorite is one of the finest restaurants outside of major cities on the east coast. $$$$

★ **Savoir Fare, Edgartown, Martha's Vineyard.** Its short rise to the top on the Vineyard has been driven by the constantly inventive and delicious menu devised by the uncle-nephew team here. $$$$

★ **Sweet Life Café, Oak Bluffs, Martha's Vineyard.** Relaxed, gracious, young but not trendy, intimate but not cloying, the Sweet Life serves terrific new American food. $$$–$$$$

★ **Larsen's, Menemsha, Martha's Vineyard.** There is precious little seating here, but you may find that raw oysters, steamers, lobster, crab cakes, and chowder have never tasted better than they do on the dock outside Larsen's market. $

★ **American Seasons, Nantucket Town, Nantucket.** Creative fare from all four corners of the country and wine from the best of the American vineyards are served in a romantic, artistic setting. $$$–$$$$

Comforts

★ **Brass Key, Provincetown, Cape Cod.** This elegant complex encompasses several fully restored structures that unite Victorian splendor and modern luxury.$$$$

★ **Captain's House Inn, Chatham, Cape Cod.** Friendly and professional service, colonial atmosphere, and wonderful old buildings make this one of the Cape's most pleasant B&Bs. $$–$$$$

★ **Augustus Snow House, Harwich Port, Cape Cod.** This elegant Victorian inn takes you back to another era, with a tearoom where you can savor afternoon tea on weekends. $$$

★ **Heaven on High, West Barnstable, Cape Cod.** Perfectly named, perfectly decorated, and perfectly comfortable, Heaven on High is such a blessed hilltop haven you might never want to leave to explore the town's nearby sights and sounds. $$–$$$

★ **Charlotte Inn, Edgartown, Martha's Vineyard.** In this Edwardian period piece, friendliness and relaxed elegance speak volumes. Go ahead and treat yourself. $$$$

★ **Inn at Blueberry Hill, Chilmark, Martha's Vineyard.** Rural, Up-Island escapes are a favorite reason to go to the Vineyard, and this laid-back yet stylish retreat puts you smack in the middle of a nature preserve threaded with walking trails. $$$–$$$$

★ **Wauwinet, in Wauwinet, Nantucket.** Very likely Nantucket's best-kept and best-equipped inn, with a great lawn and immediate proximity to ocean and harbor beaches, the historic Wauwinet is the all-out option on the island. *$$$$*

⭐ **Centerboard Guest House, Nantucket Town, Nantucket.** This polished property radiates calm with puffy white comforters on the beds and murals of the sky on the walls. *$$$–$$$$*

Children's Activities

⭐ Sandwich has the **Thornton W. Burgess Museum,** namesake of the creator of Peter Rabbit and great for children; **Heritage Plantation,** with superb old cars, a working 1912 carousel, and grounds to run around; and the **Green Briar Nature Center and Jam Kitchen,** with walking trails, "Smiling Pool" pond, natural-history exhibits, and Peter Rabbit's great-great-grandchildren.

⭐ The **Cape Cod Museum of Natural History** in Brewster offers a great variety of bay, marsh, and estuary cruises with naturalists who haul up traps so kids can ob-serve aquatic creatures up close. There are also field walks, exhibits, and a pond- and sea-life room with live specimens.

⭐ **Pirate's Cove** in South Yarmouth far outdoes the average miniature golf course, architecturally speaking. Give in and pick up a putter at least once—you may have a good time even if your kids aren't along-side you.

⭐ **Whale watches** out of Provincetown can be a tremendous thrill—genuinely ex-citing and pleasantly educational.

⭐ **Flying Horses Carousel** in Oak Bluffs on Martha's Vineyard isn't just for kids, you know. But we wouldn't recommend it for anyone who's too old to feel like a kid. Across the street, the Game Room has the authentic seaside arcade game, Skee-ball.

⭐ **Vineyard Playhouse and the Actors Theatre of Nantucket,** in Vineyard Haven on Martha's Vineyard and Nantucket Town, respectively, have entertaining children's events in July and August.

FESTIVALS AND SEASONAL EVENTS

The Massachusetts Office of Travel & Tourism (☞ Visitor Information *in* Smart Travel Tips A to Z) offers events listings and a whale-watch guide for the entire state. Also see the events calendar in *Cape-Week,* an arts and entertainment supplement published every Friday in the *Cape Cod Times.*

➤ EARLY DEC.: Many Cape and island towns do up the Christmas season in grand style. The best-known celebration is the Nantucket **Christmas Stroll** (☎ 508/228–1700), which takes place the first Saturday of the month. Carolers and musicians entertain strollers as they walk the festive cobblestone streets and sample shops' wares and seasonal refreshments. Activities include theatrical performances, art exhibitions, crafts sales, and a tour of historic homes. To avoid the throngs, visit on one of the surrounding weekends (festivities begin the day after Thanksgiving and last through New Year's Eve).

Various Cape towns also have **holiday strolls**; call the Cape Cod Chamber of Commerce for a free brochure (☎ 508/862–0700).

On Martha's Vineyard, **Christmas in Edgartown** (☎ 508/693–0085), the second weekend of December, includes tours of historic homes, teas, carriage rides, a parade, caroling, and other entertainment. Vineyard Haven packs a chowder contest, church bazaars, tours, plays, and concerts into its **Come Home for the Holidays** festival (☎ 508/693–2725).

Falmouth's **Christmas by the Sea** (☎ 508/548–8500 or 800/526–8532), the first full weekend of December, includes lighting ceremonies at the Village Green, caroling at Nobska Light in Woods Hole, a house tour, church fairs, and a parade.

➤ DEC. 1–3, 8–9: Ashumet Holly and Wildlife Sanctuary, in East Falmouth, holds its annual **Holly Days** (☎ 508/563–6390), where you can pick up cut holly, wreaths, and greens.

➤ DEC.: Chatham's **Main Street Open House** (☎ 508/945–0342) includes hayrides, caroling, a book-and-author tea, and more, culminating in a dinner dance at the grand Chatham Bars Inn. The open house is part of a monthlong celebration beginning just after Thanksgiving and ending with a lavish First Night celebration, including fireworks over Oyster Pond, on New Year's Eve.

➤ LATE APR.: Nantucket's four-day **Daffodil Festival** (☎ 508/228–1700) celebrates spring with a flower show, shop-window displays, and a procession of antique cars adorned with daffodils that ends in tailgate picnics at Siasconset. For about five weeks from mid-April to mid-May, millions of daffodils bloom along Nantucket roadsides and in private gardens.

The weekend-long **Brewster in Bloom** (☎ 508/896–3500) greets the spring season with a daffodil fest each year. Geared to promote small-town life, the festival includes arts-and-crafts shows, a parade, tours of historic homes and inns, a golf tournament, and a giant flea market.

➤ MAY 13: As this year's spring production, **Opera New England of Cape Cod** (☎ 508/775–3974) performs Donizetti's *Lucia Di Lammermoor* at the Tilden Art Center at the Cape Cod Community College in Hyannis (✉ Rte. 132).

➤ MID-MAY: In Hyannis, **Cape Cod Maritime Week** (☎ 508/362–3828) celebrates Cape Cod's maritime history.

The Green Briar Nature Center and Jam Kitchen in Sandwich holds its annual **Green Briar Herb Festival** (☎ 508/888–6870), where you can pick up perennials, wildflowers dug out of their garden, plus dozens of herb varieties.

➤ MAY 21–23: During the **Nantucket Wine Festival,** viticulturists from around the world host tastings and dinners in the island's top restaurants and some historic homes.

SUMMER

➤ JUNE–AUG.: The Cape and islands are all busy with **summer theater, town band concerts,** and **arts-and-crafts fairs.**

➤ EARLY JUNE: **Cape Cod Antique Dealers Association Annual Antiques Show** at Sandwich's Heritage Plantation (☎ 508/888–3300) is attended by 50 dealers in fine 18th- and 19th-century English and American furniture, folk art, Sandwich glass, jewelry, paintings, and quilts.

➤ MID- TO LATE JUNE: **Cape Heritage '00** (☎ 508/362–3225) is a weeklong celebration of the Cape's history and culture hosted by museums, historical societies, theater groups, libraries, and the Cape Cod National Seashore.

In Edgartown's **A Taste of the Vineyard** (☎ 508/627–4440), ticket holders sample treats provided by local restaurants, caterers, and wine merchants.

The **Nantucket Film Festival** (☎ 508/228–1700) draws actors, screenwriters, directors, and film enthusiasts to the island for a weeklong series of screenings, readings, and panel discussions.

The **Blessing of the Fleet** (☎ 508/487–3424) in Provincetown is the culmination of a weekend of festivities, including a banquet and dance. On the last Sunday of the month, a parade ends at the wharf, where fishermen and their families

pile onto their boats and form a procession. The bishop stands on the dock and blesses the boats with holy water as they pass by.

The **Portuguese Festival** coincides with the Blessing of the Fleet (☞ above), with traditional foods, dances, games, fireworks, and events honoring the Portuguese heritage in Provincetown.

➤ JUNE 17–30: Falmouth welcomes the **Soundfest Chamber Music Festival** (☎ 508/548–2290), including the Colorado Quartet and guest artists. During the weeklong festival, daily events, including student performances, concerts, master classes, and lectures, are held at the String Quartet Institute.

➤ JULY 4 WEEKEND: The **Mashpee Powwow** (☎ 508/477–0208) brings together Wampanoags from North and South America for three days of dance contests, drumming, a fireball game, and a clambake, plus the crowning of the Mashpee Wampanoag Indian princess on the final night.

Fireworks displays are a part of July 4 celebrations in several Cape towns and on Nantucket.

➤ EARLY JULY–MID-AUG.: **Martha's Vineyard Chamber Music Society** (☎ 508/696–8055) performs a dozen concerts over six weeks, Mondays in Edgartown and Tuesdays in Chilmark.

➤ MID-JULY: **Edgartown Regatta** (☎ 508/627–4361), started in 1923, is three days of yacht racing around Martha's Vineyard.

In East Sandwich, the **Cape Cod Antiquarian Book Fair** (☎ 508/888–2331) welcomes more than 70 dealers in old and rare books. The night before the book fair, the Greenbriar Nature Center hosts an auction that deals with books related to Thornton W. Burgess.

➤ LATE JULY: The Cape Symphony Orchestra sets up at the Mashpee Commons for the first of two annual **Sounds of Summer Pops Concert** (☎ 508/362–1111).

The **Barnstable County Fair** (☎ 508/563–3200) in East Falmouth, begun in 1844, is Cape Cod's biggest event. The nine-day affair features livestock and food judging; horse, pony, and oxen pulls and shows; arts-and-crafts demonstrations; carnival rides; lots of food; and appearances by the formerly famous, bent on comebacks.

Billed as a gala event that the Great Gatsby and his counterparts would never have missed, the annual **Lawn Cotillion** (☎ 508/896–9000), held on the grounds of Brewster's grand Ocean Edge resort, is indeed quite the affair. Participants are encouraged to dress in the whites of the 1920s era for the Celebrity Croquet Tournament. Other activities include a fashion show and fine art auction.

➤ AUG.: The **Cape & Islands Chamber Music Festival** (☎ 508/945–8060) is three weeks of top-caliber performances, including a jazz night, at various locations in August.

On Nantucket, an **Annual House Tour** is held by the

garden club, and a **Sand-castle Contest** at Jetties Beach results in some amazing sculptures (☎ 508/228–1700 for both events).

On Martha's Vineyard, **fireworks** (☎ 508/693–0085) explode over the ocean while the town watches from the Oak Bluffs village green and the town band plays on the gazebo.

➤ EARLY AUG.: At the **Possible Dreams Auction** (☎ 508/693–7900), held the first Monday of August in Edgartown as a benefit for Martha's Vineyard Community Services, a guest auctioneer (Art Buchwald in the past) sells off such starry prizes as a sail with Walter Cronkite and lunch with Carly Simon.

The Boston Pops Esplanade Orchestra wows the crowds with its annual **Pops by the Sea** concert (☎ 508/362–0066), held at the Hyannis Village Green at 5 PM. Each year, a guest conductor strikes up the band.

The Otis Air Base near Falmouth generally holds a free two-day **open house and air show** (☎ 508/968–4090) with exhibitions that may include precision flying by teams of the Air Force's Thunderbirds or the Navy's Blue Angels; call to confirm.

➤ MID-AUG.: The **Falmouth Road Race** (✉ Box 732, Falmouth 02541, ☎ 508/540–7000) is a world-class race covering the coast from Woods Hole to Falmouth Heights; apply by mail the previous fall or winter.

Sails Around Cape Cod (☎ 508/430–1165) is a two-day, 140-nautical-mi race that circumnavigates the Cape, starting at the west end of the Cape Cod canal and ending at the east end.

Martha's Flavor Fest (☎ 508/693–4486 or 212/726–2179) on Martha's Vineyard celebrates the work of black actors, directors, and scriptwriters in independent films.

➤ MID–LATE AUG.: **Martha's Vineyard Agricultural Fair** (☎ 508/693–4343) is pure Americana, with livestock and food judging, animal shows, a carnival, plus evening musical entertainment.

➤ AUG. 22: The Cape Symphony Orchestra comes to Eldridge Field Park in Orleans for its **Sounds of Summer Pops Concert** (☎ 508/362–1111).

➤ LATE AUG.: The annual **New England Jazz Festival** (☎ 508/477–2580), produced by the Boch Center for the Performing Arts, takes place at Mashpee Commons.

The Osterville Historical Society holds its annual **antiques show** (☎ 508/428–5861).

AUTUMN

➤ SEPT.: The 30th **Annual Bourne Scallop Fest** (☎ 508/759–6000), the weekend after Labor Day, attracts thousands of people to Buzzards Bay for three days of fried scallops.

The **Harwich Cranberry Festival** (☎ 508/430–2811) features a country-western jamboree, an arts-and-crafts show, fireworks, pancake breakfasts, an antique-car show, and much more.

➤ MID-SEPT.: **Tivoli Day** (☎ 508/696–7643), an end-of-summer celebration in Oak Bluffs on Martha's Vineyard, has a street fair with live entertainment and crafts.

➤ MID-SEPT.–MID-OCT.: Locals go crazy over the monthlong **Martha's Vineyard Striped Bass and Bluefish Derby** (✉ Box 2101, Edgartown 02539, ☎ 508/627–8510), one of the East Coast's premier fishing contests, with more than $100,000 in prizes for albacore, bluefish, striped bass, and bonito catches. It raises money for the island's conservation projects and scholarships for Vineyard students pursuing marine sciences.

➤ LATE SEPT.: **Bird Carvers' Exhibit and Auction** (☎ 508/896–3867) at the Cape Cod Museum of Natural History in Brewster showcases local and regional bird carvers' art over three days.

➤ MID-OCT.: **Nantucket Cranberry Harvest Festival** (☎ 508/228–1700) is a three-day celebration, including bog tours, a cookery contest, and a crafts exhibition.

Seafest, an annual tribute to the maritime industry, marks one of the few times that Chatham Light (☎ 508/945–0719) is open to the public.

➤ OCT. 29: For its annual fall production, **Opera**

New England of Cape Cod (☎ 508/775–3974) performs Verdi's *Il Trovatore* at the Tilden Art Center at Cape Cod Community College in Hyannis.

➤ THANKSGIVING EVE: **Provincetown Festival of Lights** (☎ 508/487–3424), commemorating the Pilgrims' landing, begins with the lighting of 5,000 white and gold bulbs draped over the Pilgrim Monument. The lights are lit nightly until Little Christmas (January 6). A performance of Handel's "Hallelujah Chorus" accompanies the lighting, and the monument museum offers an open house and tours. Other events include a reenactment of the first landing of the Pilgrims on Provincetown shores, dramatic readings of the Mayflower Compact (which was signed in Provincetown harbor), fireworks, and an abundance of Thanksgiving dinner celebrations.

2 CAPE COD

Continually shaped by ocean currents, this windswept land of sandy beaches and dunes has an amazing natural beauty. Everyone comes for the seaside, yet crimson cranberry bogs, forests of birch and beech, and grassy meadows and marshlands gracing the interior are equally splendid. Local history is fascinating, whale-watching provides an exhilarating experience, cycling trails lace the landscape, and shops purvey everything from antiques to kitsch. You can dine on simple, as-fresh-as-it-comes seafood or creative, thoughtfully prepared cuisine— or most anything in between.

Updated by
Carolyn Heller
and Laura V.
Scheel

Dining
updated by
Seth Rolbein
and Ellen
LeBow

A PATTI PAGE SONG FROM THE 1950S PROMISES that "If you're fond of sand dunes and salty air, quaint little villages here and there, you're sure to fall in love with old Cape Cod." The tourism boom since the '50s has certainly proved her right. So popular has the Cape become that today parts of it have lost the charm that brought everyone here in the first place. Although traditional associations of weathered-shingle cottages, long dune-backed beaches, and fog-enshrouded lighthouses still hold, the serenity of the landscape has in many places been crowded out by suburbanization—the housing developments, condominium complexes, and strip malls built to serve an expanding year-round population. In summer, large crowds make you work for the tranquillity once met at every turn.

Still, much of the Cape remains compellingly beautiful and unspoiled. Even at the height of the season, there won't be crowds at the less-traveled nature preserves and historic old villages. Off-season, many beaches are dream material for solitary walkers, and life returns to a small-town hum.

In 1961 the Cape Cod National Seashore was established to preserve virtually all of the eastern shoreline in its natural state for all time, and in 1990 the Cape Cod Commission was created to put a stop to the unchecked development of years past. For the sake of its economy, largely based on the area's continued appeal to tourists, and for the sake of preserving a landscape just as dear to most of the people who live here, Cape Cod has moved toward responsible management of its principal resources.

Separated from the Massachusetts mainland by the 17½-mi Cape Cod Canal—at 480 ft, the world's widest sea-level canal—and linked to it by two heavily trafficked bridges, the Cape is always likened in shape to an outstretched human arm bent at the elbow, its Provincetown fist turned back toward the mainland. (The Cape "winds around to face itself," is how the writer Philip Hamburger has put it.) Cape Cod Bay rests within the arm's embrace. The open Atlantic lies to the east, and Nantucket Sound washes the southern shore.

Being surrounded by all this water has its cost: tides regularly eat away at the land, sometimes at an alarming rate. In *Cape Cod,* Henry David Thoreau described the Atlantic-side beach, which he walked from end to end on several trips in the mid-19th century, as "the edge of a continent wasting before the assaults of the ocean." Through the years, many lighthouses—some built hundreds of feet from water's edge—have fallen into the sea, and others are now in danger of being lost. Both Highland Light in Truro and Eastham's Nauset Light were moved to safety from their precarious perches in 1996. Billingsgate Island off Wellfleet, which once held a number of cottages and a lighthouse, today is a bare sandbar occupied only by resting birds. And the once continuous Chatham bar was breached by storms in the winter of 1987. Sand eroded from one shore often ends up on another; Provincetown and Monomoy Island, for instance, continue to grow. Nevertheless, the U.S. Geological Survey estimates that "at some distant time—not for many generations, however—Cape Cod will be nothing more than a few low sandy islands surrounded by shoals."

The Cape's Atlantic coast is notorious for its shoals, shifting sandbanks that wrecked more than 3,000 ships in 300 years of recorded history. Nicknamed "the graveyard of ships," the area once had 13 lifesaving stations from Monomoy to Provincetown. They were manned by a crew of surf men who drilled in lifesaving techniques during the day and took turns walking the beach at night in all kinds of weather, watching for ships in distress. Their motto: "You have to go out, but you don't have to come back." In the service's 43-year history, hundreds of victims were rescued, but only twice were surf men's lives lost. Thoreau's stories of shipwrecks and those in Henry Beston's *The Outermost House* fascinate with their revelations of the awesome power of the sea, the tragedy of lives lost in icy waters, and the bravery of the men of the U.S. Life Saving Service. When the tide is low on the Cape, you can sometimes see the skeletons of wrecked ships emerge briefly, still caught in the treacherous sands where they lie buried.

Cape Cod is only about 70 mi from end to end, and you can make a cursory circuit of it in about two days. But it is really a place for relaxing—for swimming and sunning, for fishing, boating, and playing golf or tennis, for attending the theater, hunting for antiques, and making the rounds of art galleries, for buying lobster and fish fresh from the boat, or for taking leisurely walks, bike rides, or drives along pretty country roads that continue to hold out against modernity.

Pleasures and Pastimes

Beaches

Cape Cod has more than 150 ocean and freshwater beaches, with something for just about every taste. Bay-side beaches generally have more temperate waters and gentle waves. South-side beaches, on Nantucket Sound, have rolling surf and are warmed by the Gulf Stream. Ocean beaches on the Cape Cod National Seashore have cold water, serious surf, and are by and large superior—wide, long, sandy, and dune-backed, with great views. They're also contiguous: you can walk from Eastham to Provincetown practically without leaving sand. This almost always ensures privacy, if you stroll far enough away from crowds. From late July through August, Outer Cape beaches are sometimes troubled with red algae in the water, which, while harmless, can be annoying; check with the Cape Cod National Seashore about conditions. To mitigate the crowd factor, arrive either early in the morning or later in the afternoon—those long-light hours when the water is warmest. Parking lots tend to fill up by 10 AM in summer.

In season, you will have to pay for parking at public beaches; parking at restricted beaches is open to residents and visitors with permits. Walkers and bicyclists can enter these restricted beaches without permits, however. The latest official take on seasonal boundaries: between the last June weekend before July 1 and Labor Day. Plan accordingly.

Biking

Biking on the Cape will satisfy avid and occasional cyclists alike. There are plenty of flat back roads, as well as a number of well-developed bike trails. The Cape's top bike path, the Cape Cod Rail Trail, offers a scenic ride through the area. Following the paved right-of-way of the old Penn Central Railroad, it is about 25 mi long, stretching from South Dennis to South Wellfleet (☞ Close-Up: Riding the Rail Trail *in* West Dennis, *below*). The Cape Cod National Seashore maintains three bicycle trails. Head of the Meadow Trail is 2 mi of easy cycling between dunes and salt marshes from High Head Road, off Route 6A in North Truro, to the Head of the Meadow Beach parking lot. Province Lands Trail is a 5¼-mi loop off the Beech Forest parking lot on Race Point Road in Provincetown, with spurs to Herring Cove and Race Point beaches and to Bennett Pond. The paths wind up and down hills amid dunes, marshes, woods, and ponds and offer spectacular views—on an exceptionally clear day, you can see the Boston skyline. There's a picnic grove at Pilgrim Spring. Nickerson State Park in Brewster has 8 mi of trails through forest (trail map available).

Dining

Cape Cod received its name from the thickness of the schools of cod that early explorers found around its shores. These days, the ominous local joke is that the peninsula should be renamed, except that there is no alternative species certain to be around for the next few generations. But don't give up hope and expect to eat steaks. Plenty of great seafood can still be had, and here's one encouraging little secret: largely because of strict federal regulations, codfish have been making a quiet but remarkable comeback in the past few years. You'll see more and more cod on the menus, and it will be fresh.

The other interesting new development is that many Cape fisherfolk took a look at the offshore problems and decided to become less hunter and more farmer. Many have moved into aquaculture, staking grants along the tidal flats of Cape Cod Bay and planting quahogs or oysters. These shellfish are not fed any artificial food, and they aren't laced with any chemicals. They are simply planted in one area, protected from predators, and harvested when they reach market size. As a result, fresh shellfish is a great bet at restaurants and markets. If you buy some littlenecks or quahogs, turn the shell over and see if there are little rays or lines of lighter color radiating from the base of the shell. If so, you've gotten a cultured clam, known by scientists as a "notata." They're as sweet to eat as their wild cousins.

Traditionally, Cape restaurants have not favored fancy sauces or sophisticated cooking techniques. Now there is a new, younger generation of Cape Cod chefs who aren't afraid to bring more ingredients and international influence to the table, who know that if they keep everything else on the plate as fresh as the fish, the results can be truly memorable. This new approach has tended to drive the price of dinner ever higher. Prices have not reached chic New York levels by a long shot, but good Cape restaurants are charging as much as good Boston restaurants—and delivering equally impressive quality. The emerging cuisine speaks to a new confidence among chefs; they are willing to mix and match, to grab something from Italy and something from Thailand and marry ingredients and techniques to the fish from Cape Cod Bay. That confidence is matched by a shift in their audience, who have come to appreciate the culinarily adventurous and experimental.

The other emerging trend at many Cape restaurants is toward a menu that runs up and down the price ladder. Except for at the fanciest spots, it is common to find both expensive full dinners and fancy burgers and eclectic pizzas side by side. This can help hold down the price of an evening out.

That said, there's a—you name it—Lobster Pot/Trap/Claw/Bowl/Net in every town. These restaurants are still authentic and the best place to go with a family, although there is no place left where good seafood could be called inexpensive. You don't need to be a stodgy traditionalist to agree that the fry-o-lators in many home-style seafood restaurants and clam shacks impart the real lusciousness to classic Cape Cod cooking. For a quintessential summertime Cape experience, nothing beats simple standbys. The standard summer lunch is a lobster roll—very light lobster salad with practically no mayonnaise on a plain white frankfurter roll. One of the best meals you may ever have on the Cape might just consist of nothing more than a "Catch of the Day" dinner and a drive to a sunset beach: a plate of local steamers or mussels, a six-pack of Sam Adams, and a special someone.

Cape Cod *(Boxes Refer to Detail Maps)*

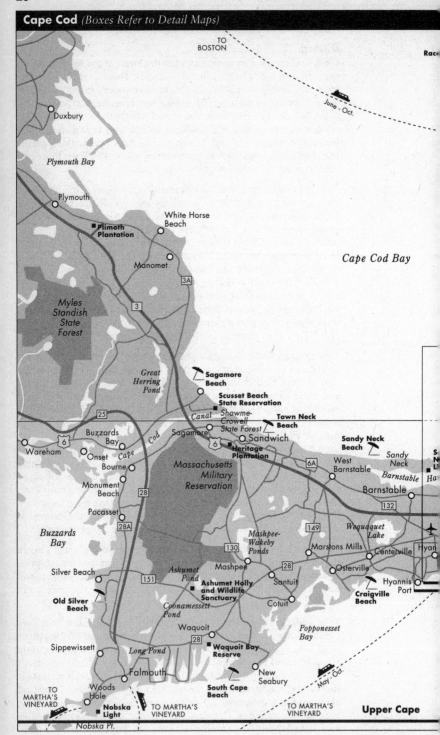

TO BOSTON

Race

June - Oct.

Duxbury

Plymouth Bay

Plymouth

■ Plimoth Plantation

White Horse Beach

Manomet

3A

3

Cape Cod Bay

Myles Standish State Forest

Great Herring Pond

Sagamore Beach

Scusset Beach State Reservation

Canal

Shawme-Crowell State Forest

Town Neck Beach

25

Buzzards Bay

Cod

Sagamore

6

Sandwich

Sandy Neck Beach

Sandy Neck

6 Wareham

Onset

Cape

Heritage Plantation

6A

West Barnstable

Barnstable

Bourne

Monument Beach

Massachusetts Military Reservation

28

132

Pocasset

28A

149

Weguaquet Lake

Buzzards Bay

Mashpee-Wakeby Ponds

130

Marstons Mills

Centerville

Hyan

Silver Beach

Ashumet Pond

151

Mashpee

28

Osterville

Old Silver Beach

Coonamessett Pond

Ashumet Holly and Wildlife Sanctuary

Santuit

Cotuit

Craigville Beach

Hyannis Port

Sippewissett

Long Pond

28

Waquoit

Waquoit Bay Reserve

Popponesset Bay

Falmouth

New Seabury

May - Oct.

Woods Hole

TO MARTHA'S VINEYARD

Nobska Light

TO MARTHA'S VINEYARD

South Cape Beach

TO MARTHA'S VINEYARD

Upper Cape

Nobska Pt.

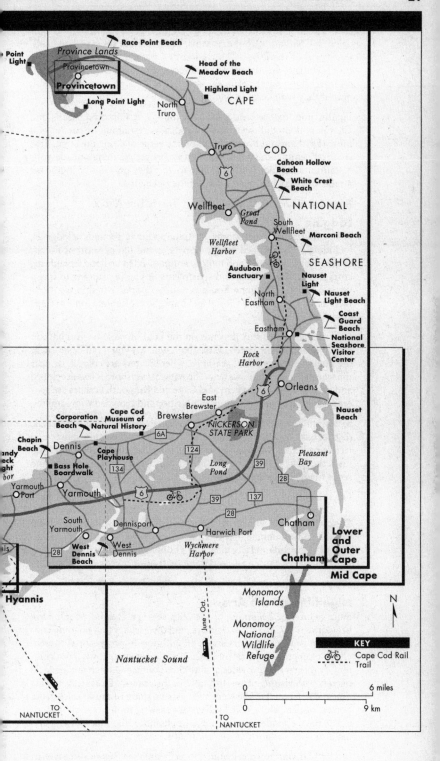

Point
Light

Province Lands

Provincetown

Provincetown

Long Point Light

Race Point Beach

Head of the
Meadow Beach

Highland Light

North
Truro

CAPE

Truro

6

COD

Cahoon Hollow
Beach

White Crest
Beach

Wellfleet

Great
Pond

South
Wellfleet

NATIONAL

Marconi Beach

Wellfleet
Harbor

Audubon
Sanctuary

SEASHORE

Nauset
Light

Nauset
Light Beach

North
Eastham

Coast
Guard
Beach

Eastham

National
Seashore
Visitor
Center

Rock
Harbor

Orleans

6

East
Brewster

Brewster

NICKERSON
STATE PARK

Nauset
Beach

Corporation
Beach

Cape Cod
Museum of
Natural History

6A

Chapin
Beach

Dennis

Cape
Playhouse

124

Long
Pond

Pleasant
Bay

39

28

andy
eck
ght
bor

Bass Hole
Boardwalk

134

Yarmouth
Port

6

Yarmouth

39

137

South
Yarmouth

Dennisport

28

Chatham

**Lower
and
Outer
Cape**

is

West
Dennis
Beach

28

West
Dennis

Harwich Port

Wychmere
Harbor

Chatham

Mid Cape

Hyannis

Monomoy
Islands

N

June - Oct.

Monomoy
National
Wildlife
Refuge

TO
NANTUCKET

Nantucket Sound

0   6 miles

0   9 km

TO
NANTUCKET

At dinnertime, dress is largely casual. One older Cape Codder takes this edict so seriously that he chops off any ties he sees and adorns his cabin in Chatham with the remains. But in certain rooms—like Chillingsworth or the Dan'l Webster Inn or Chatham Bars Inn—a sports coat is virtually mandatory. Another recent and important development: an increasing number of restaurants are remaining open year-round, even if they scale back in winter.

Finally, note that several towns on the Cape, notably Orleans and Chatham, do not allow smoking inside any restaurant or bar. Several more (Eastham and Brewster) are on the verge of doing the same. This is strictly enforced, so if you see some people standing outside your restaurant of choice in one of these towns, they may not be in line for a table but may be taking a puff in the open air.

For price ranges *see* Dining *in* Smart Travel Tips A to Z.

Lodging

With a tourism-based economy, the Cape naturally abounds in lodgings, including self-contained luxury resorts, grand old oceanfront hotels, chain hotels, mom-and-pop motels, antiques-filled bed-and-breakfasts, cottages, condominiums, and apartments. If you're planning to stay a week or longer, renting a house is another popular option (☞ Contacts and Resources *and* Close-Up: Home, Sweet Rental Home *in* Cape Cod A to Z, *below*).

Choosing where to stay depends on the kind of vacation you have in mind. If you love the beach, think about whether you'd rather stay near the dune-backed national seashore, where waters are coldest, or near the warmer south-shore waters. The national seashore is less developed and great for walking, where Mid Cape and Falmouth beaches are generally, but not always, more circumscribed and crowded with families.

Sandwich and other towns along the north-shore Route 6A historic district have quiet, traditional villages with old-Cape atmosphere and charming B&Bs. If you want more action head for the Mid Cape. Hyannis is the center of it all, with a busy Main Street, active nightlife, and some fine warm-water beaches.

For the austere Cape of dunes and sea, try the beach cottages of the sparsely developed Lower Cape between Wellfleet and Provincetown. "P-town" itself is something completely different, in summer a frantic wall-to-wall jumble of shops and houses bursting with a large contingent of lesbians and gay men, and a hopping nighttime scene. Staying in town makes getting to everything by foot or bike possible.

For price ranges *see* Lodging *in* Smart Travel Tips A to Z.

Nightlife and the Arts

Since before the beginning of the 20th century, creative people have been drawn to Cape Cod summers, and their legacy and ongoing contribution is a thriving arts scene. In addition to professional theater, which offers top-name talent in season, almost every town has a community theater that provides quality entertainment—often mixing local players with visiting pros—throughout the year (☞ Pleasures and Pastimes *in* Chapter 1). The Cape also gets its share of music stars, from pop to classical, along with local groups ranging from barbershop quartets to Bach chorales to early music or chamber ensembles, often playing at school auditoriums or town halls.

In 1999 Provincetown celebrated its centennial as America's oldest art colony, a tradition that still thrives today. Its many galleries exhibit Cape and non-Cape artists, and the Fine Arts Work Center has launched the careers of many well-known award-winning authors. Wellfleet and Orleans have emerged as vibrant art centers. Both towns have attracted craftspeople who sell through a number of unique and sophisticated shops.

Nighttime on Cape Cod can be very special in many ways. In less developed areas, the stars are amazingly bright and make beach walks even more wondrous. Lighthouse beacons cutting shafts through the night sky have a fascination impossible to resist. If you're up *really* late, or really early, head for Chatham Light or a national seashore beach to catch a terrific sunrise.

Another Cape twist on nightlife is that many daytime activities, such as fishing, take on a completely different aspect at night. Scuba enthusiasts might consider night diving: colors are more vivid by flashlight, much sea life is phosphorescent or bioluminescent, and nocturnal species come out to play. It's important to know the tides and safe locations—check with a dive shop.

Outdoor Activities and Sports

On the water, canoeing and sea kayaking are great around the bay's marshy inlets. Fishing on the Cape is both a profession and a pastime. Hundreds of freshwater ponds are good for perch, pickerel, and trout; surf casting off beaches and deep-sea fishing for blues, bass, and flounder is also popular. You'll need a license for freshwater fishing, available for a nominal fee at most tackle and bait shops. Bird-watchers have a variety of habitats to choose from, and the Cape is a great place to come for spring and fall migrants. The Cape is one of the world's finest whale-watching spots; a whale breaching alongside your boat is truly an impressive sight (☞ Outdoor Activities and Sports *in* Provincetown, *below*).

The Cape Cod National Seashore has nine walking trails through varied terrain. In winter, ponds and shallow flooded cranberry bogs sometimes freeze hard enough for skating. Check conditions with the local fire department before venturing onto unfamiliar territory.

Shopping

Like it or not, shopping is an important part of a Cape Cod vacation. On rainy days, enclosed malls and factory outlets are mobbed. Even on a beautiful day, you may find yourself antiquing, bookstore browsing, or gallery hopping. Throughout the Cape you'll find weavers, candle makers, glassblowers, papermakers, and potters, as well as an inordinate number of shops specializing in country crafts from straw dolls to handmade Christmas-tree ornaments. And you'll run across plenty of junk that will make you wish conspicuous consumption would go the way of the break in the Chatham bar.

You'll find an auction going on somewhere on the Cape all year long from country-barn types to the internationally known Eldred's auctions. Though the high-end auctions deal in very fine antiques, they also include some lower-priced merchandise and often yield interesting Cape pieces, such as old sea chests, at good prices.

Town Band Concerts

Traditional New England town band concerts are held weekly each summer in many Cape towns—take along chairs, blankets, sweaters, and a picnic supper if you like, and go early to get a good spot.

Exploring Cape Cod

There are essentially two ways to visit the Cape: either station yourself in one town and take excursions from there, or stay in a string of towns as you make your way from one end to the other. Neither is right or wrong; it all depends on your idea of a good trip.

Cape Geography, Highways, and Byways

The Cape consists of 15 towns, each broken up into villages, which is where things can get complicated. The town of Barnstable, for example, consists of Barnstable, West Barnstable, Cotuit, Marstons Mills, Osterville, Centerville, and Hyannis. Likewise the terms Upper Cape and Lower Cape may be confusing. They derive from sailing days and latitudes increasing as one sails south. **Upper Cape**—think upper arm, as in the shape of the Cape—refers to the towns of Bourne, Falmouth, Mashpee, and Sandwich. **Mid Cape** includes Barnstable, Yarmouth, and Dennis. **Lower Cape** covers Brewster, Harwich, Chatham, Orleans, Eastham, Wellfleet, Truro, and Provincetown. **Outer Cape,** as in outer reaches, is essentially synonymous with Lower Cape. Technically it includes only Wellfleet, Truro, and Provincetown.

There are three major roads on the Cape. U.S. 6 is the fastest way to get from the mainland to Orleans. Route 6A winds along the north shore through scenic towns, while Route 28 dips south through some of the overdeveloped parts of the Cape. Generally speaking, if you want to avoid malls, heavy traffic, and tacky motels, avoid Route 28 from Falmouth to Chatham. Past Orleans on the way out to Provincetown, the roadside clutter of much of U.S. 6 belies the beauty of what surrounds it.

Numbers in the text correspond to numbers in the margin and on the Upper Cape, Mid Cape, Hyannis, Lower and Outer Cape, Chatham, and Provincetown maps.

Great Itineraries

The itineraries below are divided geographically to present the best of the Upper, Mid, Lower, and Outer Cape section by section. If you have three days, decide on one area to explore and divide your days into museum or historical outings and outdoor activities. With beaches and lakes all around you'll probably want to spend half of each day in the fresh air. In five days, it would be reasonable to see two parts of the Cape or the length of it if you don't get the car crazies. You could otherwise take all of your time—two weeks, two months—relaxing and getting to know one area. There isn't a better place than the Cape to just unwind—period.

THE UPPER CAPE

It's astonishing that so close to the mainland the lovely old town of **Sandwich** ① is one of the best examples of the Cape of yesteryear. Visit the Hoxie House, the Sandwich Glass Museum, or **Heritage Plantation**'s ② beautiful grounds and old car collection; have a picnic lunch on the banks of Shawme Pond; or spend the afternoon at the old-timey Green Briar Nature Center and Jam Kitchen walking the nature trails and picking out homemade jam to take with you. Here and all along the bay shore, you can explore salt marshes full of sea and bird life. If history's your thing, take a step back and start your Upper Cape trip at **Plimoth Plantation,** about 22 mi northwest of the Sagamore Bridge on Route 3A. The reconstructed settlement, where actors dress in period clothing and carry out the activities typical of earlier days, relates a very tangible sense of the Cape's history.

To reach the Upper Cape's south shore, take Route 28A south through some lovely little towns with detours to beautiful white-sand beaches. This is the way to Falmouth and to **Woods Hole** ⑥, the center for international marine research and the year-round ferry port for Martha's Vineyard. A small aquarium in town has regional sea-life exhibits, and there are several shops and museums. On the way out of town, the view from Nobska Light is breathtaking. In **Falmouth** ④, stroll around the village green, look into some of the historic houses, and stop at the Waquoit Bay National Estuarine Research Reserve for a walk along the estuary and barrier beach. Inland, on the eastern extent of the Upper Cape, the Wampanoag Indian township of **Mashpee** ⑧ is one of the best places to learn about the Cape's Native American heritage.

THE MID CAPE

The crowded belly of the Cape is a center of activity unlike any other here, except perhaps Provincetown at the height of its summer crush. **Hyannis** ⑬–⑯ is the hub of Cape Cod, with plenty to do and see. Take a cruise around the harbor, or go on a deep-sea fishing trip. There are shops and restaurants along Main Street, and plenty of amusements for the kids. Kennedy fans will want to spend time at the JFK Museum. End the day with a concert at the Cape Cod Melody Tent. **Barnstable** ⑨, the county seat, has plenty of its own history and the wonderful Sandy Neck Beach to keep you occupied. Scenic Route 6A passes through **Yarmouth Port** ⑰ and **Dennis** ㉓. There are beaches and salt marshes, museums, walking trails, and old graveyards all along this route if you feel like stopping. Yarmouth Port's **Bass Hole Boardwalk** ⑲ makes for a particularly beautiful stroll. In Dennis there are historic houses to tour, the Cape Museum of Fine Arts will introduce you to the work of Cape-associated artists, and the Cape Cod Rail Trail provides a premier path for bicyclists. Toward the end of the day, head for Scargo Hill and climb 30-ft **Scargo Tower** ㉔ to watch the sun set. At night you could catch a film at the Cape Cinema, on the grounds of the **Cape Playhouse** ㉕. The south shore has plenty of activities for kids, from **Centerville** ⑫ to **Dennisport** ㉗.

THE LOWER CAPE

The Lower Cape stretches from Brewster and Harwich out to Provincetown. **Brewster** ㉘ has something for everyone—antiques shops, museums, an old gristmill open to the public, Bassett's Wild Animal Farm for kids, freshwater ponds for swimming or fishing, the beach and tidal flats to explore when the water is low, and miles of biking and hiking trails through **Nickerson State Park** ㉛. Don't miss the **Cape Cod Museum of Natural History** ㉚, which will take a couple of hours to explore. Main Street in the handsome town of **Chatham** ㉝–㊳ is perfect for strolling, shopping, and dining. A trip to the Monomoy Islands is a must for bird-watchers. Back in town, you can watch glassblowing in process at the Chatham Glass Company, visit the Old Atwood House and Railroad Museums, and drive over to take in the view from Chatham Light.

On the way north from Chatham, take the less commercial end of Route 28 to **Orleans** ㊴, driving alongside sailboat-speckled views of Pleasant Bay. You might want to allow time for a good long bike ride on the Cape Cod Rail Trail, or for an afternoon relaxing at Nauset Beach. **Eastham** ㊵ is the next stop on the way up the arm, where the **Ft. Hill Area** ㊶ has the historic Penniman House Museum and some wonderful walks along the adjacent trails. Stop at the national seashore's **Salt Pond Visitor Center** ㊷ for some interesting information about the area; then take the bike trails to Coast Guard Beach and Nauset Light, with a view of the Three Sisters Lighthouses, now settled in a small park area.

THE OUTER CAPE

The Outer Cape refers to the wrist and fist of Cape Cod, the towns that rooted and grew amid dunes and marshland—Wellfleet, Truro, and Provincetown. **Wellfleet** ㊸, with pleasant shops and galleries along Main Street, is also rich in dune-backed ocean beaches and marshes great for canoeing and kayaking. Historic **Marconi Station** ㊺ was the landing point for the transatlantic telegraph early this century, and its White Cedar Swamp trail is quite beautiful. In Wellfleet, visit art galleries, browse through great bookstores, take a dip in the bay or the ocean, rent a canoe or kayak and tour the marshes, and have dinner at one of the fine area restaurants. Don't leave without visiting the **Massachusetts Audubon Wellfleet Bay Sanctuary** ㊹, especially if you are a bird-watcher. It's a fantastic place to catch a sunset over the bay. **Truro** ㊻ solidly represents the quietude of this end of the Cape, at least until you reach the seasonally bustling **Provincetown** ㊾–㊿ out at the tip. Catch a whale-watch boat from P-town—the Cape ranks fourth in the world for sighting whales. Take a trolley tour in town or bike through the national seashore on its miles of trails. Climb the Pilgrim Monument for a spectacular view of the area—on an exceptionally clear day you can see the Boston skyline. Visit the museums and shops and art galleries, or spend the afternoon swimming and sunning on one of the beaches. To escape the crowds, walk across the breakwater to Long Point. Rent a sailboat, or relax in the sand, taking in the splendid views of the bay. Then choose from an abundance of restaurants and the Cape's wildest nightlife.

When to Tour Cape Cod

Summer is by far the most popular season on Cape Cod—from mid-June through the end of August, everything is open and happening and busy. These are the months for maritime history celebrations, Fourth of July fireworks, county fairs, and all manner of summer-only activities, like summer theater and town band concerts. Fall has come into its own on the Cape in recent years and extends the "season" with Halloween and Thanksgiving events and all sorts of harvest celebrations. Winter has its own charm, and Christmas Strolls and First Nights also make for good getaways. In spring, everything is in bloom, and there are open houses and garden tours. If you're planning to travel outside of summer, however, be sure to check for reduced hours or seasonal closings at sights, restaurants, and lodgings.

THE UPPER CAPE

Especially considering the difference between towns on its north and south shores, the Upper Cape contains enough diversity to make generalizations about its character close to impossible. It just happens to be the closest part of the Cape to the mainland. There are four major towns. On the north shore, **Sandwich,** gracious and lovely, is the Cape's oldest town. Centered inland, **Mashpee** is a long-standing Native American township whose native-owned land is governed by local Wampanoags. **Falmouth,** the Cape's second most-populous town, is still green and historic, if seemingly overrun with strip malls. **Woods Hole,** one port from which to ferry over to Martha's Vineyard, is an international center of marine and biological scientific research. Along the west coast you'll find wooded areas ending in secluded coves and, on the south coast, long-established seaside resort communities.

The towns are listed as you would approach them, first from the Sagamore Bridge along Route 6A to Sandwich, then from the Bourne Bridge down Route 28 to Falmouth and Woods Hole.

Sagamore

60 mi southeast of Boston, 30 mi northeast of New Bedford.

The village of Sagamore straddles both sides of the Cape Cod Canal and is perhaps best known to visitors for the canal-spanning bridge,

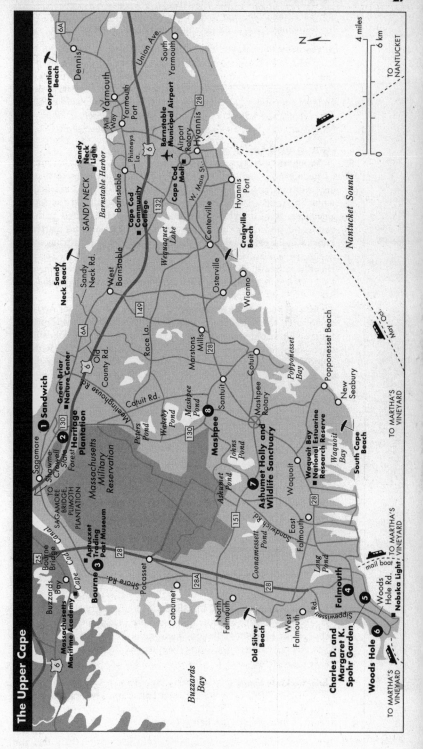

The Upper Cape

6A

Corporation Beach

Dennis

Union Ave

South Yarmouth

Mill Way

Yarmouth Port

Yarmouth

SANDY NECK

Sandy Neck Light

Phinneys La.

6

28

Barnstable Municipal Airport

Airport Rotary

Hyannis

Barnstable Harbor

Cape Cod Mall

W. Main St.

Hyannis Port

Sandy Neck Beach

Barnstable

Cape Cod Community College

132

Hyannis Port

West Barnstable

Sandy Neck Rd.

Wequaquet Lake

Centerville

Craigville Beach

6A

149

Osterville

Wianno

Nantucket Sound

Old County Rd.

Race La.

Marstons Mills

28

Cotuit

Poppanesset Beach

Meetinghouse Rd.

6

Cotuit Rd.

Mashpee Pond

Santuit

Mashpee Rotary

Poppanesset Bay

1 Sandwich

2 Green Briar Nature Center

Heritage Plantation

130

Forest Crowell Store

Shawme-

Sagamore

TO SAGAMORE BRIDGE, PILMOTH PLANTATION

25

Bourne Bridge

Buzzards Bay

Cape Cod Canal

Aptucxet Trading Post Museum

3 Bourne

28

Massachusetts Military Reservation

Peters Pond

Wakeby Pond

8 Mashpee

130

Johns Pond

7 Ashumet Holly and Wildlife Sanctuary

New Seabury

Waquoit Bay National Estuarine Research Reserve

Waquoit Bay

South Cape Beach

TO MARTHA'S VINEYARD

Ashumet Pond

151

Coonamessett Pond

Sandwich Rd.

Waquoit

East Falmouth

28

TO MARTHA'S VINEYARD

Shore Rd.

Pocasset

28A

North Falmouth

Long Pond

Falmouth

4

mail boat

TO MARTHA'S VINEYARD

Massachusetts Maritime Academy

6

Cataumet

West Falmouth

Old Silver Beach

28

Woods Hole Rd.

5 Nobska Light

Sippewissett Rd.

Charles D. and Margaret K. Spohr Garden

6 Woods Hole

TO MARTHA'S VINEYARD

Buzzards Bay

N

4 miles

6 km

0

TO NANTUCKET

completed in 1935, that bears its name. The town has several stores for those interested in bargain hunting or gift shopping.

At **Pairpoint Crystal,** you can watch richly colored lead crystal being hand-blown in the factory as it has been since 1837. The shop sells candlesticks, vases, stemware, sun catchers, ornamental cup plates (used to hold the cup in the days when tea was poured into saucers to drink), and reproductions of original Boston and Sandwich glass pieces. ⊠ 851 *Rte. 6A,* ☏ *508/888–2344 or 800/899–0953.* ▣ *Free.* ☉ *Showroom Mon.–Sat. 9–6, Sun. 10–6; demonstrations weekdays 9–4:30.*

Dining and Lodging

$$ ✕ **Sagamore Inn.** This local favorite—owned by the Pagliarani fam-
★ ily since 1963—keeps old Cape Cod traditions alive. Pressed-tin walls and ceilings, fans, old wooden booths and tables, lace curtains, and white linen add up to a dining room so casual you almost overlook its elegance. All the food here is homemade (except the stuffed quahogs), very good, and traditional at the same time. The seafood platter is a knockout, the chicken potpie substantial, and the prime rib huge. Luncheon specials attract regulars from all over town, and the service is friendly as family. A cozy, handsome old bar is under the same roof. ⊠ *1131 Rte. 6A,* ☏ *508/888–9707. Reservations not accepted. AE, MC, V. Closed Tues. and Dec.–Mar.*

$ ⚠ **Scusset Beach State Reservation.** This park (☞ Outdoor Activities and Sports, *below*), which encompasses 490 acres near the Cape Cod Canal with a cold-water beach on the bay, has tent and RV camping on its sites; some are wooded. One site is accessible to people with disabilities. There are cold showers on the beach and hot showers in the campground. ⊠ *140 Scusset Beach Rd., off Rte. 3 at the Sagamore Bridge rotary, 02532,* ☏ *877/422–6762 for campsite reservations; 508/888–0859 for general information. 103 sites. Beach. MC, V.*

Outdoor Activities and Sports

The **Scusset Beach State Reservation** is a pleasant place for a swim, walk, or a bike ride near the mainland side of the Sagamore Bridge. The beach sweeps along Cape Cod Bay, although the view inland is marred by the nearby power plant. Its pier is a popular fishing spot; other activities include hiking, picnicking, and camping (☞ Lodging, *above*). ⊠ *140 Scusset Beach Rd., off Rte. 3 at the Sagamore Bridge rotary,* ☏ *508/888–0859.* ▣ *Parking $2.* ☉ *Daily 8–8.*

Shopping

Cape Cod Factory Outlet Mall (⊠ Factory Outlet Rd., Exit 1 off U.S. 6, ☏ 508/888–8417) has more than 20 outlets, including Corning/Revere, Carter's, Bass, Bugle Boy, Van Heusen, Izod, London Fog, and Champion/Hanes.

Chocolate House Fudge and Gift Shop (⊠ 11 Cranberry Hwy. [Rte. 6A], ☏ 508/888–7065), just over the Sagamore Bridge on the Cape side, sells creamy fudge in 12 flavors, hand-dipped chocolates and truffles, saltwater taffy, and penny candy. The gift shop has cranberry glass and other Cape items.

Christmas Tree Shops (⊠ Cranberry Hwy. [Rte. 6A], Exit 1 off U.S. 6, ☏ 508/888–7010; other locations at Falmouth, Hyannis, Yarmouth Port, West Yarmouth, West Dennis, and Orleans) sell everything from furniture to clothes to kitchen goods.

En Route   Before crossing the Sagamore Bridge on your way to the Cape, you can journey back to the Pilgrims' time with a visit to Plymouth. **Plymouth** is the settlement site the Pilgrims chose in December 1620 after scouting locations from their base at Provincetown. In addition to a number of historical museums, you can view **Plymouth Rock** (reputed first footfall) and tour *Mayflower II,* a replica of the *Mayflower* built in 1957. (After hundreds of years of wear and tear, Plymouth Rock is not much more than a boulder; it's protected by a pillared structure.)

Plimoth Plantation is a painstaking reconstruction of the original Pilgrim settlement, from the thatched roofs, cramped quarters, and open fireplaces to the long-horned livestock. At the plantation, actors in period costume speak Jacobean English as they walk the grounds and carry on the daily life of the 17th century. Feel free to engage them in conversation about their life, and expect curious looks if you ask them about anything beyond 1627. A crafts center features demonstrations of early techniques of making pottery, baskets, furniture, and woven goods. Self-guided tours start with a 12-minute film. ⊠ *Warren Ave., Rte. 3A, about 22 mi northwest of the Sagamore Bridge via Rte. 3 or the coastal Rte. 3A,* ☎ *508/746–1622.* ☞ *$16 Plantation only; $6.50 Mayflower II only; $19 combination Plantation/Mayflower II.* ☉ *Apr.–Nov., daily 9–5.*

Sandwich

★ ❶ *3 mi east of the Sagamore Bridge, 11 mi west of Barnstable.*

The oldest town on Cape Cod, Sandwich was established in 1637 by some of the Plymouth Pilgrims and incorporated on March 6, 1638. Today it is a well-preserved, quintessential New England village that wears its history proudly. Driving through town past the white-columned town hall, the gristmill on Shawme Pond, the spindlelike spire of the First Church of Christ, and the 18th- and 19th-century homes that line the streets is like driving back in time—you'll feel as if you should be holding a horse's reins rather than the steering wheel of a car. When you reach Main Street, park the car and get out for a stroll. Look at old houses on Main Street, stop at a museum or two, and work your way to the delightful Shawme Pond. While you walk, look for etched Sandwich glass from the old factory on front doors—there probably aren't two identical glass panels in town.

Unlike other Cape towns, whose deepwater ports opened the doors to prosperity in the whaling days, Sandwich was an industrial town for much of the 19th century. The main industry was the production of vividly colored glass, called Sandwich glass, which is now sought by collectors. The glass was made in the Boston and Sandwich Glass Company's factory here from 1825 until 1888, when competition with glassmakers in the Midwest—and finally a union strike—closed it. The **Sandwich Glass Museum** holds information about the history of the company, including a diorama showing how the factory looked in its heyday, and an outstanding collection of blown and pressed glass in many shapes and shimmering hues. Large glass lamps, vases, and pitchers are impressive, but so are the hundreds of small cup plates on display. Glassmaking demonstrations are held in the summer. A few galleries contain relics of the town's early history. The gift shop sells some handsome reproductions, including some made by local artisans. ⊠ *129 Main St.,* ☎ *508/888–0251.* ☞ *$3.50.* ☉ *Apr.–Dec., daily 9:30–5; Feb.–Mar., Wed.–Sun. 9:30–4.*

Ⓒ The impressive roster of dolls in the **Yesteryears Doll Museum** includes everything from a toy Henry VIII and his wives, elegantly clothed in velvets and brocades, to samurai warriors and Balinese shadow puppets. There are also antique German, French, and Chinese dolls in bisque, china, wax, and other media as well as some wonderful miniature sets, such as a toy millinery shop with display cases, hatboxes, even ladies trying on hats; period German kitchens; and an elaborately detailed four-story late-Victorian dollhouse with a wedding feast going on. The gift shop sells antique dolls, books, and toys, as well as doll costumes and the patterns with which to make them. The museum is housed in the 1833 First Parish Meetinghouse. ⊠ *143 Main St.,* ☎ *508/888–1711.* ⊡ *$3.* ⊙ *Mid-May–Sept., Tues.–Sat. 10–4.*

A lovely place for a stroll or a picnic is the park around **Shawme Pond** (⊠ Water and Grove Sts.), a favorite fishing spot for kids. The ducks and swans love to be fed, though posted signs warn you not to indulge them. Across the way—it's a perfect backdrop for this setting—is the spired, white 1848 First Church of Christ, inspired by a design by British architect Christopher Wren.

Where Shawme Pond drains over its dam, a little wooden bridge leads over a watercourse to the waterwheel-powered **Dexter Gristmill,** built in 1654. In season, the miller demonstrates and talks about the mill's operation and sells the ground corn. ⊠ *Water and Grove Sts.,* ☎ *508/ 888–4910.* ⊡ *$1.50; combination ticket with Hoxie House (☞ below), $2.50.* ⊙ *Late May, Sat. 10–4:45, Sun. 1–4:45; June–Labor Day, Mon.–Sat. 10–4:45, Sun. 1–4:45; Labor Day–mid-Oct., Tues.–Sat. 10–4:45.*

NEED A BREAK?

Stop in at the delightful **Dunbar Tea Shop** (⊠ 1 Water St. [Rte. 130], ☎ 508/833–2485), a former billiards room–carriage house now converted into a country cottage with paneled walls, a beamed ceiling, and assorted antiques and kitschy doodads. Breakfast is available from 8 to 11, and lunch—everything from a smoked fish platter with salad to quiche or a salmon tart—English cream tea, and tasty sweets are served from 11 to 6 daily, July through October (till 4:30 the rest of the year). A gift shop sells British tea, specialty foods, and home decorating items.

The **Thornton W. Burgess Museum** is dedicated to the Sandwich native whose tales of Peter Rabbit, Reddy Fox, and a host of other creatures of the Old Briar Patch have been part of children's bedtimes for decades. Thornton Burgess (1874–1965), an avid conservationist, made his characters behave true to their species to educate children as he entertained them. A storytelling session, featuring the live animal that the Burgess story is about, is held regularly in July and August. The many displays crowded into the small old house include some of Burgess's 170 books (although kids are welcome, the exhibits are of the don't-touch variety). The small gift shop carries puppets, Burgess books, and Pairpoint Crystal cup plates decorated with Burgess characters. ⊠ *4 Water St. [Rte. 130],* ☎ *508/888–4668.* ⊡ *$2 suggested donation.* ⊙ *Apr.–Oct., Mon.–Sat. 10–4, Sun. 1–4; 1st 2 wks in Dec., Sat. 10–4, Sun. 1–4.*

Overlooking Shawme Pond is the **Hoxie House,** a remarkable old saltbox that has been virtually unaltered since it was built in 1675. Even though people lived in it until the 1950s, the house was never modernized with electricity or plumbing. It has been furnished to reflect daily life in the colonial period, with some pieces on loan from the Museum of Fine Arts in Boston. Highlights are diamond-shape leaded-glass windows and a collection of antique textile machines. ⊠ *18 Water St. [Rte. 130],* ☎ *508/888–1173.* ⊡ *$1.50; combination ticket with Dexter Gristmill (☞ above) $2.50.* ⊙ *Mid-June–mid-Oct., Mon.–Sat. 10– 5, Sun. 1–5.*

The **Old Town Cemetery** (⊠ Grove St.), on the opposite side of Shawme Pond (☞ *above*) from Hoxie House, is a classic, undulating, New England graveyard. Stop in for a peaceful moment and trace the genealogy of old Sandwich.

 On 76 beautifully landscaped acres overlooking the upper end of Shawme Pond is the **Heritage Plantation,** an impressive complex of museum buildings and gardens and a café. In 1967 pharmaceuticals magnate Josiah K. Lilly III purchased the estate and turned it into a nonprofit museum. The Shaker Round Barn showcases classic and historic cars—including a 1930 yellow-and-green Duesenberg built for Gary Cooper, a 1919 Pierce-Arrow, and a 1911 Stanley Steamer—as well as art exhibitions. The Military Museum houses antique firearms, a collection of 2,000 hand-painted miniature soldiers, military uniforms, and Native American arts. The Art Museum has an extensive Currier & Ives collection, Americana (including a mechanical-bank collection), antique toys such as a 1920 Hubley Royal Circus, and a working 1912 Coney Island–style carousel.

The grounds are crisscrossed by paths and planted with daylily, hosta, heather, herb, fruit-tree, and other gardens. Rhododendron enthusiasts will recognize the name of onetime estate owner and hybridizer Charles O. Dexter; the rhododendrons are in full glory from mid-May through mid-June. Daylilies reach their peak from mid-July through early August. Families visiting with children should ask at the ticket office for the "family funpacks" with kids' activities or the "clue tours," scavenger-hunt games for exploring the grounds. In summer, concerts are held in the gardens, often on Saturday evenings and Sunday afternoons. The center of the complex is about ¾ mi on foot from the in-town end of Shawme Pond. ⊠ *Grove and Pine Sts.,* ☎ *508/888–3300.* ☞ *$9.* ☉ *Mid-May–late Oct., daily 10–5.*

For a view of the bay, you can walk to Town Neck Beach on the **Sandwich Boardwalk,** built over a salt marsh, creek, and low dunes. In 1991 Hurricane Bob and an October nor'easter destroyed the previous boardwalk. Individuals and businesses donated planks to rebuild it, which volunteers then installed. The donors' names, jokes (GET OFF OUR BOARD), thoughts (SIMPLIFY/THOREAU), and memorials to lovers, grandparents, and boats are inscribed on the planks. The long sweep of Cape Cod Bay stretches out around the beach at the end of the walk, where a platform provides fine views, especially at sunset. Stone jetties, dunes and waving grasses, and the entrance to the canal are in the foreground, and you can look out toward Sandy Neck, Wellfleet, and Provincetown or toward the white cliffs beyond Sagamore. The sandy strip on this mostly rocky beach is near the rugosa rose–patched dunes; the flowers have a delicious fragrance, and it's a good place for birding. If you have a canoe, the creeks running through the salt marsh make for great paddling. From the town center, it's about a mile to the boardwalk; cross Route 6A on Jarves Street, and at its end turn left, then right, and continue to the boardwalk parking lot.

At the **Sandwich Fish Hatchery,** you'll see more than 200,000 brook, brown, and rainbow trout at various stages of development, being raised to stock the state's ponds. The mesh over the raceways is to keep kingfishers and herons from a free lunch. You can buy feed for 25¢ and watch the fish jump for it. There's a modest interpretive center. ⊠ *164 Rte. 6A,* ☎ *508/888–0008.* ☞ *Free.* ☉ *Daily 9–3.*

OFF THE BEATEN PATH

GREEN BRIAR NATURE CENTER AND JAM KITCHEN – Is it the soothing pond-side setting or its simple earthiness—who's to say? The Green Briar Nature Center and Jam Kitchen, owned and operated by the Thornton Burgess Society, is as solid a symbol of the old Cape as you could find. You'll pass a wildflower garden on your way in, and the

Smiling Pool sparkles out back. Birds flit about the grounds, and great smells waft from vintage stoves in the Jam Kitchen, where you can watch as jams and pickles are made according to Ida Putnam's recipes, used here since 1903. (Sun-cooked fruit preserves are especially superb.) Come weekdays mid-April through mid-December to see jam being made in the Jam Kitchen; you can even take a jam-making class some evenings or Saturdays. The nature center has classes for adults and children, as well as walks, lectures, and a May herb festival, where you can take home herbs, wildflowers, and perennials. The Briar Patch Conservation Area behind the building has nature trails to explore—take a walk and visit with Peter Rabbit, Grandfather Frog, and other creatures that inspired the beloved Thornton Burgess characters. ⊠ *6 Discovery Hill Rd., off Rte. 6A east of Sandwich Center,* ☎ *508/888–6870.* ⊟ *$1 suggested donation.* ☉ *Apr.–Dec., Mon.–Sat. 10–4, Sun. 1–4; Jan.–Mar., Tues.–Sat. 10–4.*

Dining and Lodging

$ ✕ **Marshland Restaurant and Bakery.** This tiny coffee shop tucked onto a parking lot is Sandwich's version of down-home, the sure antidote to the overspending you're susceptible to if you eat all your meals out while you're on the Cape. For breakfast try an Italian omelet, a rich mix of Italian sausage, fresh vegetables, and cheese. The lunch specials—grilled chicken club sandwich, lobster salad, turkey Reuben, a daily quiche, and the like—are the best choices midday, and for dinner the prime rib does not quit. ⊠ *109 Rte. 6A,* ☎ *508/888–9824. No credit cards. No lunch or dinner Sun., no dinner Mon.*

$ ✕ **Seafood Sam's.** Across from the Coast Guard station, in the shadow of the canal power plant and a stone's throw from the Cape Cod Canal, Sam's is all about fried seafood. You order from the counter, get a number, and sit in an airy dining room where the sound of lobsters cracking open is accompanied by the munch of fried clams. It's casual enough that a sign near the entrance reminds you that shirt and shoes are required. Sam has gotten around, with branches in Harwich, Falmouth, and South Yarmouth. ⊠ *6 Coast Guard Rd.,* ☎ *508/888–4629. MC, V. Closed Nov.–Mar.*

$$$–$$$$ ✕🏠 **Dan'l Webster Inn.** Built in 1971 on the site of a 17th-century inn, the Dan'l Webster is essentially a contemporary hotel with old New England friendliness and hospitality. In the more formal restaurant, the menu and wine list are interesting and up-to-date; some hydroponic vegetables and fish come from the local, family-run D. W. Aquafarm. Standout dishes include striped bass crusted with cashews and macadamia nuts, accompanied by mango sauce. (If you don't feel like a starched-napkin meal, there's also a casual tavern.) Guest rooms, in the main inn and wings or in two nearby historic houses with four suites each, have floral fabrics and fine reproduction mahogany and cherry furnishings, including some canopy beds. The eight rooms on the second floor of the Jarves Wing, which were added in 1999, are particularly spacious and have fireplaces and whirlpool tubs, as do some of the suites; one suite even has a baby grand piano. Guests have access to nearby golf courses and a local health club. ⊠ *149 Main St., 02563,* ☎ *508/888–3622 or 800/444–3566,* FAX *508/888–5156. 54 rooms, 9 suites. 2 restaurants, bar, air-conditioning, no-smoking rooms, room service, pool. AE, D, DC, MC, V. MAP available.*

$$$–$$$$ 🏠 **Bay Beach.** Oceanfront accommodations are few in this part of the Cape, but if you want to wake to broad vistas of the bay, this B&B in two adjacent contemporary houses is a fine choice. The seven rooms are appointed like a well-turned-out suburban home, with lots of wicker, floral comforters, CD players, refrigerators, and, best of all, picture windows facing the water or the adjacent marshes. Four rooms

have whirlpool tubs, three have gas fireplaces, and several have private decks. Breakfast is served buffet-style in the casual dining room, with floor-to-ceiling windows for still more bay views, and a boardwalk leads to a private beach. ⊠ *1–3 Bay Beach La., 02563,* ☎ *508/888–8813 or 800/475–6398,* FAX *508/888–5416. 7 rooms. Air-conditioning, exercise room, beach. MC, V. Closed Nov.–Apr. CP.*

$$–$$$ 🖫 **Belfry Inne & Bistro.** In an 1882 Victorian manor house, a former church rectory in the center of town, owner Christopher Wilson has created a comfortably stylish inn. The nine rooms are decorated with a whimsical blend of iron, spool, or sleigh beds; Laura Ashley prints; and pastel-painted furnishings for a look that's fresh but traditional. If you need to relax, sink into one of the armchairs in the bar or climb up to the widow's walk, where the cozy sitting room is painted as a tiny Alice-in-Wonderland fantasy. The bistro serves contemporary fare: swordfish with mango salsa, filet mignon with pesto mashed potatoes, or duck breast in a corn-chili sauce. At press time, the inn was expanding into the former church next door, creating six guest rooms (several with the original stained-glass windows intact) and a new space for the bistro and lounge. ⊠ *8 Jarves St., 02563,* ☎ *508/888–8550,* FAX *508/888–3922. 9 rooms. Restaurant, bar. AE, D, DC, MC, V. BP.*

$$–$$$ 🖫 **Sandwich Lodge & Resort.** Set amid 10 rolling acres, this glorified motel—emphasis on glorified—offers a variety of rooms, all nicely decorated in soft mauve and navy. Suites (the deluxe are the newest), like efficiencies, are equipped with gleaming kitchens with refrigerators and two-burner stoves or microwave ovens; two even have two-person whirlpool tubs. The grounds include private volleyball and shuffleboard courts, game rooms, hot tub, and two of the cleanest pools on the Cape. The on-site restaurant serves lunch and dinner (ample portions, great prices) in a homey atmosphere. Pets are allowed, with advance notice, for a $15 fee. ⊠ *54 Rte. 6A, Box 1038, 02563,* ☎ *508/888–2275 or 800/282–5353,* FAX *508/888–8102. 24 rooms, 36 suites, 4 efficiencies. Restaurant, bar, no-smoking rooms, indoor-outdoor pool, hot tub. AE, D, MC, V. CP.*

$$ 🖫 **Captain Ezra Nye House.** Elaine and Harry Dickson's 1829 house in the heart of town belonged to one of the old local families. The cozy, country-style rooms aren't crammed with state-of-the-period pieces or overly precious from a museumlike restoration, but the house is brimming with the Dicksons' hospitality—they cook full breakfasts and offer suggestions for activities by day or night—for which there is no substitute. ⊠ *152 Main St., 02563,* ☎ *508/888–6142 or 800/388–2278,* FAX *508/833–2897. 5 rooms, 1 suite. No smoking. AE, D, MC, V. BP.*

$$ 🖫 **Dunbar House.** Stepping into the Dunbar House is like stepping through time. Built in 1741 by descendants of Sandwich founder John Dillingham, the modernized inn is still filled with history. The rooms—each named for an English lake—have views of Shawme Pond (☞ *above*). Buttermere, on the first floor, has a king-size bed and antique furnishings. Upstairs, Ennerdale edges out the slightly smaller Loweswater; it has a fine selection of antiques, a four-poster queen-size bed, and a bathtub as well as a shower. In summer, guests eat breakfast at the Dunbar Tea Shop (☞ *above*) next door, where the selections include Wiltshire crumpets and a traditional British breakfast of fried egg, English bacon, banger, grilled tomato, and beans. You'll also receive a voucher good for a complimentary tea. ⊠ *1 Water St. (Rte. 130), 02563,* ☎ *508/833–2485,* FAX *508/833–4713. 3 rooms. No smoking. D, MC, V. BP.*

$$ 🖫 **Wingscorton Farm.** This is, perhaps, the Upper Cape's best-kept se-
★ cret: an enchanting working farm with ducks, chickens (you can help gather eggs), sheep, a donkey, and a pair of llamas. Built in 1763, the main house, once a stop on the Underground Railroad, has a dining room with one of the largest fireplaces in New England—the hearth

alone is 9 ft long. Oriental rugs, wing chairs, and a TV are in the paneled library-den. The main house has two second-floor suites, each with a fireplace, Oriental rugs topping wide-plank floors, wainscoting, and, adjoining the main guest room, a smaller bedroom, once the house's "birthing rooms." (Today, they hold twin beds.) The property also includes a detached cottage. A stone carriage house offers a fully equipped kitchen, a living room with a pull-out queen-size sofa and a wood-burning stove; a spiral staircase leads to a loft (with a queen-size bed) and an oversize sundeck. Traditional clambakes are prepared year-round (for large groups) by visiting members of Martha's Vineyard's Wampanoag tribe, and a private bay beach is a five-minute walk away. ✉ *11 Wing Blvd., off Rte. 6A, about 4½ mi east of Sandwich Center, East Sandwich 02537,* ☎ *508/888–0534,* FAX *508/888–0545. 2 suites, 1 carriage house, 1 two-bedroom cottage. Library, beach. AE, MC, V. BP.*

$–$$ 🏨 **Earl of Sandwich Motor Manor.** Single-story Tudor-style buildings are arranged in a U around a duck pond and wooded lawn set with lawn chairs. Rooms in the main building (1966) and the newer buildings (1981–83) have rather somber decor, with dark exposed beams on white ceilings, dark paneled walls, quarry-tile floors with Oriental throw rugs, and chenille bedspreads, but they are of good size and have large windows and small-tiled baths. Pets are permitted with advance notice. ✉ *378 Rte. 6A, East Sandwich 02537,* ☎ *508/888–1415 or 800/442–3275,* FAX *508/833–1039. 24 rooms. Air-conditioning, no-smoking rooms. AE, D, DC, MC, V. CP.*

$–$$ 🏨 **Inn at Sandwich Center.** This house directly across from the Sandwich Glass Museum is listed on the National Register of Historic Places. All rooms have Laura Ashley comforters and bedding, and hooked rugs; three have fireplaces. At night you can slip into a terry robe and indulge in the handmade chocolates left on your pillow. Each room is named after its signature color (white, green, yellow, beige, and blue). Particularly lovely is the Blue Room, which has a two-poster bed, comfortable rockers, a chintz chaise, and a library of travel books crammed in the room's original nooks and crannies and built-in cabinets—great material to peruse on the private deck overlooking the lush gardens. Owner Eliane Thomas's breakfast specialties include rhubarb muffins and crepes with raspberry sauce, served by candlelight in the antiques-furnished "Keeping Room," which has a fireplace and the original 1750 beehive oven. ✉ *118 Tupper Rd., 02563,* ☎ *508/888–6958 or 800/249–6949,* FAX *508/ 888–6958. 5 rooms. No smoking. AE, D, MC, V. CP.*

$ 🏕 **Shawme-Crowell State Forest.** Less than a mile from the Cape Cod Canal, this 742-acre state forest is a good base for local biking and hiking, and campers get free day use of Scusset Beach. Open-air campfires are allowed at the wooded tent and RV (no hookups) campsites. There are also heated bathroom and shower facilities—a blessing on chilly mornings. ✉ *Rte. 130, 02563,* ☎ *508/888–0351; 877/422– 6762 for reservations. 285 sites. MC, V.*

Nightlife and the Arts

THE ARTS

Heritage Plantation (☞ *above*) sponsors summer jazz and other concerts in its gardens from June to mid-September; bring chairs or blankets. Most concerts are free with admission to the complex.

Opera New England of Cape Cod (☎ 508/775–3974 for schedules, locations, and reservations) has two performances a year, in spring and fall, by the National Lyric Opera Company.

Town band concerts (✉ Bandstand, Henry T. Wing Elementary School, Rte. 130 and Beale Ave., ☎ 508/888–5144) are held Thursday evenings from July through late August starting at 7:30.

Bobby Byrne's Pub (✉ 65 Rte. 6A, ☎ 508/888–6088) offers a comfortable pub atmosphere, a jukebox, and good light and full menus.

Rof-Mar Diplomat Club (✉ Popple Bottom Rd., South Sandwich, ☎ 508/428–8111), a function room, has ballroom dinner dances and dancing year-round. There's a large dance floor and seating on outdoor porches overlooking Lawrence Pond; you'll need a reservation.

Shopping

Brown Jug (✉ 155 Main St., at Jarves St., ☎ 508/833–1088) specializes in antique glass, such as Sandwich glass and Tiffany iridescent glassware, as well as Staffordshire china.

The **Giving Tree** (✉ 550 Rte. 6A, East Sandwich, ☎ 508/888–5446), an art gallery and sculpture garden, shows contemporary crafts, jewelry, ceramics, and prints. It has walking paths through a peaceful bamboo grove, along the marsh, and over a narrow wooden suspension bridge. A café serves coffee and pastries.

Horsefeathers (✉ 454 Rte. 6A, East Sandwich, ☎ 508/888–5298) sells antique linens, lace, vintage baby and children's clothing, and Victoriana such as valentines.

H. Richard Strand (✉ Town Hall Sq., ☎ 508/888–3230), in an 1800 home opposite the Sandwich Glass Museum, displays very fine pre-1840 and Victorian antique furniture, paintings, and American glass.

Sandwich Auction House (✉ 15 Tupper Rd., ☎ 508/888–1926) is a great place to spend part of a Wednesday night (Saturday in the off-season); come after 2 to preview the items for sale. It's a local institution, with weekly sales; in addition, there are specialty sales every four to six weeks that present the cream of the crop of antiques received in that period. Specialty sales are also held for collections of modern rugs, silver, or toys.

Titcomb's Bookshop (✉ 432 Rte. 6A, East Sandwich, ☎ 508/888–2331) has used, rare, and new books, including a large collection of Cape and nautical titles and Americana, as well as an extensive selection of new children's books.

En Route   **Route 6A** heads east from Sandwich, passing through the oldest settlements on the Cape. It is part of the Old King's Highway historic district and is therefore protected from development. Classic inns and enticing antiques shops alternate with traditional gray-shingled homes on this tree-lined route, and the woods periodically give way to broad vistas across the marshes. In autumn the foliage along the road is bright; maples with their feet wet in ponds and marshes put on a good display. Along Route 6A just east of Sandwich center, you can stop to watch cranberries being harvested in flooded bogs. If you're heading to Orleans and you're not in a hurry, this is a lovely route to take.

Bourne

❸ *6 mi southwest of Sandwich.*

The town of Bourne includes nine villages—Bourne Village, Bournedale, Buzzards Bay, Cataumet, Gray Gables, Monument Beach, Pocasset, Sagamore (☞ *above*), and Sagamore Beach—along Buzzards Bay and both sides of the Cape Cod Canal. The villages range from honky-tonk commercial districts to bucolic waterfront suburbs. The Bourne area includes places for learning about the region's marine life and early commercial history, as well as several attractive spots for biking and hiking along the canal.

SUMMERTIME:
A WEEK-AT-A-GLANCE

EVERY SUMMER the Cape's social and cultural calendar fills up with regularly scheduled weekly events. Before setting out, phone in advance, as even long-standing events change.

Monday West Yarmouth's summertime **town band concerts** (☎ 508/778–1008) take place at 7 at Mattacheese Middle School.

Tuesday Tales of Cape Cod (☎ 508/362–8927), Barnstable's historical society, sponsors **slide-illustrated lectures.** In Woods Hole, **free guided village walking tours** begin at 4 at the Woods Hole Historical Museum (☎ 508/548–7270). The 2,500-acre **Waquoit Bay National Estuarine Research Reserve** (☎ 508/457–0495) in Waquoit holds evening talks on environmental, historical, and artistic subjects; you can bring a picnic dinner. **Town band concerts** in Harwich take place at 7:30 in Brooks Park (☎ 508/432–1600). The Nau-Sets (☎ 508/255–5079 or 508/385–9841) hold **weekly square dances** (year-round) in Dennis.

Wednesday Hyannis's Cape Cod Melody Tent (☎ 508/775–9100) hosts a morning **children's theater** series at 11 AM for ages 3–11. Also in Hyannis, **town band concerts** (☎ 508/362–5230) are held at 7:30 on the Village Green. The bidding begins at 6 each week at the **Sandwich Auction House** (☎ 508/888–1926).

Thursday In Bourne, **town band concerts** begin at 7 in Buzzards Bay Park (☎ 508/759–6000). Sandwich's **town band concerts** get under way at 7:30 at the bandstand at the Henry T. Wing Elementary School (☎ 508/888–5144). Falmouth's **town band concerts** start at 8 in Marina Park (☎ 508/548–8500).

Also in Falmouth, the **Nimrod Inn** (☎ 508/540–4132) offers the Big Band and jazz sounds of Stage Door Canteen (September–June); in July and August, the band plays at the **Dome** in Woods Hole. At Provincetown's Old Harbor Station (✉ Race Point Beach, ☎ no phone), you can see **reenactments of an old-fashioned lifesaving procedure.**

Friday Look for **Molly Benjamin's fishing column** in the *Cape Cod Times*. The Cape Playhouse in Dennis (☎ 508/385–3911) puts on morning **children's theater** shows. Chatham's **town band concerts** (☎ 508/945–5199) begin at 8. You may see 500 fox-trotting on the roped-off dance floor; there are special dances for children and sing-alongs for all. It's **Rock Night** at the Charles Moore Arena (☎ 508/255–2971) in Orleans. From 8 to 10 PM, kids 9–14 ice-skate to DJ-spun rock.

Saturday During Wellfleet's **Gallery Crawl,** walk from gallery to gallery meeting artists and checking out the works in their just-opened shows. Do a turn around the Cape's largest dance floor at **Betsy's Ballroom** (☎ 508/362–9538) in South Yarmouth.

Sunday Between 4:30 and 7:30, tours are given of the relocated and relit **Nauset Light** (☎ 508/240–2612) in Eastham. At 8 PM you can hear a **concert** at Wellfleet's Congregational Church, with its 1873 organ. The Ashumet Holly and Wildlife Sanctuary sponsors all-day **tours to Cuttyhunk Island** (☎ 508/563–6390), which leave Falmouth Harbor at 9 AM and return at 5.

—Seth Rolbein

—Updated by Carolyn Heller

☝ The **National Marine Life Center,** on the mainland, has a small exhibit area devoted to whales, dolphins, seals, and other marine life. In summer, there are weekly story hours for preschoolers, marine-life educational programs for older kids, and evening lectures about the ocean environment for adults. In 2000, the center hopes to break ground on an expanded facility for rehabilitating stranded marine animals that will include a marine animal hospital and nursery, rehabilitation pools, and additional exhibit space. ✉ *120 Main St., Buzzards Bay,* ☎ *508/ 759–8722.* ▱ *Free.* ☉ *Memorial Day–Labor Day, Mon.–Sat. 10–6, Sun. noon–6.*

A monument to the birth of commerce in the New World, the **Aptucxet Trading Post Museum** was erected on the foundation of the original post archaeologically excavated in the 1920s. Here, in 1627, Plimoth Plantation leaders established a way station between the Native American encampment at Great Herring Pond 3 mi to the northeast, Dutch colonists in New Amsterdam (New York) to the south, and English colonists on Cape Cod Bay. Before the canal was built, the Manomet River connected Herring Pond with Buzzards Bay (no, scavengers don't frequent it—it was misnamed for the migrating osprey that do), and a short portage connected the pond to Scusset River, which met Cape Cod Bay. The Native Americans traded furs; the Dutch traded linen cloth, metal tools, glass beads, sugar, and other staples; and the Pilgrims traded wool cloth, clay beads, sassafras, and tobacco (which they imported from Virginia). Wampum was the medium of exchange.

Inside the post are 17th-century cooking utensils hanging from the original brick hearth, beaver and otter skins, furniture, and other artifacts such as arrowheads, tools, and tomahawks. Also on the grounds are a gift shop in a Dutch-style windmill, a saltworks, herb and wildflower gardens, a picnic area overlooking the canal, and a small Victorian railroad station built for the sole use of President Grover Cleveland, who had a summer home in Bourne. To get here, take the first right from the Bourne Bridge rotary onto Trowbridge Road and follow the signs. Note that the site is also open on holiday Mondays in season. ✉ *24 Aptucxet Rd.,* ☎ *508/759–9487.* ▱ *$3.50.* ☉ *May–Columbus Day, Tues.–Sat. 10–5, Sun. 2–5; also open Mon. July–Aug. 10–5.*

☝ A break for energetic kids pent up in a car for too many miles, **Adventure Isle** has minibikes, a giant slide, a Ferris wheel, children's rides, an arcade, bumper boats, batting cages, a double gyroscope (for those with strong stomachs), and a miniature golf course. ✉ *Rte. 28, 2 mi south of Bourne Bridge,* ☎ *508/759–2636 or 800/535–2787.* ▱ *$1.75–$3.75 per ride or $10.50 per day for unlimited rides.* ☉ *Mid-Mar.–Nov., daily 10 AM–11 PM.*

Dining

$$ ✕ **Mitchell's Tavern.** Another roadside attraction, Mitchell's delivers the American goods without a lot of unnecessary frills: good steaks, straight-up seafood, thick chowder, and cold beers. The term "tavern" is overused in this neck of the woods, but here it makes sense, as there's a comfortable bar beside an unpretentious dining room. It won't make for a romantic dinner for two, but it's a fine place to give yourself ballast for a busy day. ✉ *570 MacArthur Blvd., Pocasset,* ☎ *508/563–1811. AE, DC, MC, V. Closed Tues.*

$$ ✕ **Stir Crazy.** One of just a few authentic Asian restaurants on the Cape— owner Bopha Samms hails from Cambodia—Stir Crazy fits the bill when you reach your inevitable limit of seafood and Yankee cooking. Overlook the anonymous location (beside self-storage lockers, in a building that also houses a real estate office), because the real spice is where it belongs: in the food. Dishes blur the ethnic line with lively

Cambodian-Thai-Vietnamese influences. Look for *nhem shross* (an appetizer of vegetables and shrimp) and beef *lock lack* (sirloin tips on a bed of watercress). ⊠ *626 MacArthur Blvd., Pocasset,* ☎ *508/564-6464. Reservations not accepted. MC, V. No smoking. Closed Mon. No lunch Sat.–Thurs.*

$ ✕ **My Tinman.** "The family diner with a heart" is one of the only real diners (architecturally speaking) left on the Cape. The outside is covered in silver aluminum; inside, the pink booths share space with *Wizard of Oz* photos and paraphernalia. As you'd expect, it's diner food all the way, and it's all good, especially the meat loaf. Most dishes are named after the film: Lionhearted sandwiches, Scarecrow Garden Salad, and so on. Breakfast is served all day; the diner is open from 5 AM to 2 PM. ⊠ *MacArthur Blvd., near the Massachusetts Military Reservation rotary, Pocasset,* ☎ *no phone. Reservations not accepted. No credit cards. No dinner.*

Nightlife and the Arts

The **Army Corps of Engineers** (☎ 508/759–4431), which maintains the Cape Cod Canal via a field office in Buzzards Bay, offers free daily programs in summer, including slide shows about the canal, sing-alongs, night walks, and storytelling around campfires at the Bourne Scenic Park and Scusset Beach State Park. Call for program details and locations.

In Bourne, **town band concerts** are held Thursday evenings in July and August starting at 7 in Buzzards Bay Park (⊠ Main St., ☎ 508/759–6000).

Outdoor Activities and Sports

BASEBALL

The **Bourne Braves** (☎ 508/888–5050) of the collegiate Cape Cod Baseball League play home games at Coady School (⊠ Trowbridge Rd., Bourne) from mid-June to mid-August.

BIKING

An easy, straight trail stretches on either side of the **Cape Cod Canal,** 6½ mi on the south side, 7 mi on the north, with views of the bridges and ship traffic on the canal. Directly across the street from the canal bike path on the mainland, **P & M Cycles** (⊠ 29 Main St., Buzzards Bay, ☎ 508/759–2830) rents a large selection of mountain and hybrid bikes at reasonable rates.

FISHING

The Cape Cod Canal is a good place to fish, from the service road on either side, for blues, flounder, herring, mackerel, and striped bass seasonally making their way through the passage (April–November). The Army Corps of Engineers has a **canal fishing hot line** (☎ 508/759–5991).

HIKING AND WALKING

The Army Corps of Engineers sponsors guided walks, bike trips, and hikes. Outside its **Herring Run Visitor Center,** on a bank of the canal with an excellent view, are picnic tables (close to noisy U.S. 6), access to the canal bike path, a herring run through which the fish travel on their spawning run in May, and short self-guided walking trails through woodland. The visitor center is on the mainland side of the canal on U.S. 6 in Bournedale, between the bridges. ⊠ *U.S. 6,* ☎ *508/759–4431; 508/759–5991 for tides, weather, and special events.*

On the Cape side of the canal, the Army Corps of Engineers manages the **Tidal Flats Recreation Area** (⊠ Shore Rd., ☎ 508/759–4431), a small but peaceful canal-side park near the Cape railroad bridge. It's a pleasant spot for picnicking or fishing, with a great view of the canal's ship traffic; there's access to the canal bike path, too. In the late afternoon, generally sometime between 4:30 and 5:30, you can watch the bridge lower to allow a train to cross the canal. After crossing the Bourne Bridge, follow Trowbridge Road to Shore Road to the recreation area.

ICE-SKATING AND ROLLER-SKATING

John Gallo Ice Arena (⊠ 231 Sandwich Rd., ☎ 508/759–8904) is the place to go for ice-skating September through June. Hours vary widely; call for details.

SCUBA DIVING

Rentals, instruction, group dives, and information are available through **Aquarius Diving Center** (⊠ 3239 Cranberry Hwy., Buzzards Bay, ☎ 508/759–3483), across the Bourne Bridge on the mainland.

Shopping

Tanger Outlet Center (⊠ U.S. 6 at the Buzzards Bay rotary, Bourne, ☎ 800/406–8435) sells women's, men's, and children's apparel from designers such as Izod, Nine West, Levi's, and Liz Claiborne.

En Route Before crossing the Bourne Bridge on your way to the Cape, you might stop in the towns of Wareham and Buzzards Bay, which have some unusual attractions and adventures for road-weary travelers.

The Massachusetts Maritime Academy (⊠ Taylor's Point, Buzzards Bay), founded in 1891, is the oldest such academy in the country. Future members of the Merchant Marine receive their training at its 55-acre campus in Buzzards Bay. The library has nautical paintings and scale models of ships from the 18th century to the present and is open to the public at no charge (hours are extensive but vary widely; ☎ 508/830–5000, ext. 1201). For a 20- to 30-minute tour of the academy weekdays at 10 and 2, call 48 hours in advance (ext. 1102).

☾ A wet and wild adventure for the kids awaits at the **Water Wizz Water Park,** with a 50-ft-high water slide complete with tunnels and dips, a river ride, three tube rides, two enclosed water mat slides, a children's slide, a pool, miniature golf, and food. The enclosed Black Wizard water slide descends 75 ft in darkness. ⊠ *U.S. 6 and Rte. 28, Wareham, 2 mi west of the Bourne Bridge,* ☎ *508/295–3255.* ⊡ *$22.* ☾ *Memorial Day–mid-June, weekends 11–4; mid-June–Labor Day, daily 10–6:30.*

West and North Falmouth

9 mi south of Bourne.

Several villages along Route 28 between Bourne and Falmouth proper might not offer a tremendous amount of interest in their own right, but they are worth a stop on the way to larger towns. Route 28 from the Bourne Bridge south to Falmouth is overly commercial in many areas, while Route 28A between Pocasset and West Falmouth is more scenic, with side roads leading to attractive beaches, particularly Old Silver Beach (☞ Outdoor Activities and Sports, *below*), and small harbors. The area is steeped in history. Native American names serve as reminders of the true first settlers here, and houses that date from the 18th century line the streets.

NEED A
BREAK?   **Peach Tree Circle Farm** (⊠ 881 Old Palmer Ave., West Falmouth, ☎ 508/548–4006) includes a bakery, a farm stand, and a cheery tearoom. Inexpensive lunches of soups, sandwiches, salads, and a few entrées like quiche and chicken potpie are served year-round amid the smells of baking bread and herbs hung to dry.

Lodging

$$$–$$$$ 🏠 **Inn at West Falmouth.** This luxurious, 1898 estate house inn is in a secluded area of an exclusive village. A mixture of contemporary and antique furnishings and polished hardwood floors sets an elegant but relaxed mood. Guest rooms have king- or queen-size beds (some with canopies), Italian marble bathrooms with whirlpool tubs, phones, hair dryers, and wall safes; some have fireplaces and private decks. Beyond the French doors, off the pale pink-and-green sunroom, a patio spilling over with lush potted plants and trees overlooks woods, gardens, and a tennis court and leads to the small pool and deck. ⊠ *Off Blacksmith Shop Rd., Box 1208, West Falmouth 02574,* ☎ *508/540–7696 or 800/ 397–7696,* 𝖥𝖠𝖷 *508/548–6974. 8 rooms. Pool, tennis court. No smoking. AE, MC, V. CP.*

$$$–$$$$ 🏠 **Sea Crest Resort.** Location and amenities are strong draws at this conference center and resort, whose eight buildings sprawl along one end of beautiful Old Silver Beach. Rooms are crisp and clean, done in dark blues and pastels. Many rooms have ocean views, and some have gas-log fireplaces. A number of lodging packages are available. ⊠ *350 Quaker Rd., North Falmouth 02556,* ☎ *508/540–9400 or 800/225– 3110,* 𝖥𝖠𝖷 *508/548–0556. 266 rooms, 8 suites. Restaurant, deli, piano bar, room service, indoor-outdoor pool, hot tub, sauna, putting green, 2 tennis courts, health club, shuffleboard, video games, children's programs (ages 3–12). AE, DC, MC, V.*

Nightlife and the Arts

Sea Crest Resort (⊠ 350 Quaker Rd., North Falmouth, ☎ 508/540– 9400; ☞ Dining and Lodging, *above*) has a summer and holiday-weekend schedule of nightly entertainment on the outdoor terrace, including dancing to country, Top 40, reggae, and jazz bands and a big-band DJ, as well as karaoke and comedy.

Outdoor Activities and Sports

BEACH

Old Silver Beach, off Quaker Road in North Falmouth, is a long, beautiful crescent of soft white sand, with Sea Crest Resort (☞ *above*) at one end. It is especially good for small children because a sandbar keeps it shallow at one end and creates tidal pools full of crabs and minnows. The beach has lifeguards, rest rooms, showers, and a snack bar. There's a $10 fee for parking in summer.

HORSEBACK RIDING

Haland Stables (⊠ 878 Rte. 28A, West Falmouth, ☎ 508/540–2552) offers lessons and trail rides, by reservation, Monday–Saturday.

TENNIS

Ballymeade Country Club (⊠ 125 Falmouth Woods Rd., off Rte. 151, North Falmouth, ☎ 508/457–7620) has six Har-Tru and four hard courts, a grass tennis court, lessons, clinics, ball machines, and a pro shop (☎ 508/457–7620) that accepts court-time reservations from mid-June through mid-October.

Falmouth

④ *2 mi south of West Falmouth, 15 mi south of the Bourne Bridge, 4 mi north of Woods Hole.*

The Cape's second-largest town, Falmouth was settled in 1660 by Congregationalists from Barnstable who had been ostracized by their church and deprived of voting privileges and other civil rights for being sympathizers with the Quakers (then the victims of severe repression). Much of Falmouth today is suburban, with a mix of old and new developments and a large year-round population. Many residents commute to towns on the Cape, to southeastern Massachusetts, and even to Boston. The **Village Green,** added to the National Register of Historic Places in 1996, was used as a militia training field in the 18th century and a grazing ground for horses in the early 19th. Today it is flanked by attractive old homes, some built by sea captains, and the 1856 **Congregational Church,** built on the timbers of its 1796 predecessor, with a bell made by Paul Revere. The bell's cheery inscription reads: "THE LIVING TO THE CHURCH I CALL, AND TO THE GRAVE I SUMMON ALL."

The **Falmouth Historical Society** maintains two museums that represent life in colonial Cape Cod. The 1790 **Julia Wood House** retains wonderful architectural details—a widow's walk, wide-board floors, leaded-glass windows, and a colonial kitchen with wide hearth. It is filled with antique embroideries, baby shoes and clothes, toys and dolls, portraits, furniture, and the trappings of an authentically equipped doctor's office, from the house's onetime owner. Out back, the Hallett Barn Museum displays antique farm implements, a 19th-century horse-drawn sleigh, and other interesting items. The smaller **Conant House** next door is a 1794 half-Cape (an asymmetrical, 1½-story building). Inside are military memorabilia, whaling items, scrimshaw, sailors' valentines, and a genealogical and historical research library. There's also a collection of books, portraits, and things relating to Katharine Lee Bates, the native daughter who wrote "America the Beautiful." Guides give tours of the museums, and a pretty formal garden with a gazebo and flagstone paths is adjacent. Free walking tours of the town are available Tuesday at 4 in July and August, as are historical trolley tours; call for prices and times. ⊠ *Village Green, off Palmer Ave.,* ☎ *508/548–4857.* ☜ *$3.* ☉ *Mid-June–mid-Sept., Tues. 9–2, Wed.–Sun. 2–5.*

The 1812 white Cape house at 16 Main Street marks the **birthplace of Katharine Lee Bates.** Now owned by the Falmouth Historical Society (☞ *above*), it is no longer open to the public, but a plaque out front commemorates Bates's birth, in 1859.

❺ The **Charles D. and Margaret K. Spohr Garden,** 3 planted acres on Oyster Pond, is a pretty, peaceful, privately owned place. The springtime explosion of more than 700,000 daffodils gives way in turn to the tulips, azaleas, magnolias, flowering crabapples, rhododendrons, lilies, and climbing hydrangeas that inspire garden goers in summer. A collection of old millstones, bronze church bells, and ships' anchors decorates the landscape. ⊠ *Fells Rd., off Oyster Pond Rd.* ☜ *Free.* ☉ *Daily sunrise– sunset.*

☾ A good place for kids on a rainy day, the **Leary Family Amusement Center** (⊠ 23 Town Hall Sq., off Rte. 28, ☎ 508/540–4877) has videogame rooms and candlepin bowling.

Dining and Lodging

$$$ ✕ **Regatta of Falmouth-by-the-Sea.** One of the Cape's nicest dining
★ rooms offers beautiful views of Nantucket Sound and Martha's Vineyard and a menu that evolves constantly, responding to culinary innovations while maintaining a traditional appeal. The dining room is modern and subdued, with soft colors, lamplight, and an intimate, romantic ambience. Continental and Asian cuisines have been mingling on the menu, resulting in dishes such as the sautéed shellfish sampler: scallops, mussels, lobster, and shrimp with a sensational curried lobster sauce over Asian greens. Three menus are served each night: lighter fare, regular fare, and a three-course early dinner menu. The Regatta of Cotuit (☞ Dining and Lodging *in* Cotuit, *below*) is a sibling. ⊠ 217

Clinton Ave., Falmouth Harbor, ☎ *508/548–5400. AE, MC, V. Closed Tues., and Oct.–Memorial Day. No lunch Sat.*

$$ ✕ **Quarterdeck Restaurant.** Part bar, part restaurant—but all Cape Cod—this spot is across the street from Falmouth's town hall, so the lunch talk tends to focus on local politics. The stained glass is not old and authentic, but the huge whaling harpoons certainly are. Low ceilings and rough-hewn beams seem a good match for the menu, which features hearty sandwiches like Reubens and grilled chorizo, and then specials at night. The swordfish kebab, skewered with mushrooms, onion, and green pepper and served over jasmine rice, is especially good. ✉ *164 Main St. (Rte. 28),* ☎ *508/548–9900. AE, D, DC, MC, V.*

$–$$ ✕ **Betsy's Diner.** An authentic-looking American treasure, Betsy's is a shiny, happy, busy place with a reassuring pink neon sign urging you to EAT HEAVY. The generous dining room, gleaming counter, and stools and booths by the big windows are all done in pretty pastel mauve and cream tones. Memorabilia and neon grace the walls. A classic diner menu with pancakes, waffles, and omelets is served all day, and dinner is meat loaf and mashed potatoes, knockwurst and sauerkraut, charbroiled pork chops—that kind of thing. ✉ *457 Main St. (Rte. 28),* ☎ *508/540–4446. Reservations not accepted. MC, V.*

$$–$$$ ✕🏨 **Coonamessett Inn.** Delightfully sunk in the past, this is one of the
★   best—and oldest (since 1953)—of many "quaint" inn-restaurants on the Cape. The main dining room is lovely, and the Cape Cod Room looks out over a pond and garden. The menu, not surprisingly, is also traditional, maybe too much so for adventuresome palates; the many seafood choices include charbroiled swordfish with grilled vegetable vinaigrette, steamed or baked and stuffed lobster, and baked scrod. Five buildings of one- or two-bedroom suites range around a broad, landscaped lawn that spills down to a scenic wooded pond; several suites directly overlook the pond. Rooms are casually decorated, with bleached wood or pine paneling and New England antiques or reproductions. There's also a one-bedroom cottage with a full kitchen. A large collection of Cape artist Ralph Cahoon's work is displayed throughout the inn. ✉ *311 Gifford St., at Jones Rd., 02540,* ☎ *508/548–2300,* FAX *508/540–9831. 28 suites, 1 cottage. Restaurant, bar, no-smoking rooms. AE, MC, V. CP.*

$$$ 🏨 **Holiday Inn.** This chain link is a dependable option for families—children under 18 stay and eat free with their parents. The tried-and-true comfort formula has been applied here: large rooms with contemporary pastel decor; suites with king-size beds; a large pool area surrounded by patio furniture and greenery. The restaurant is open for breakfast and dinner year-round. The hotel is across from a pond ½ mi outside Falmouth center. ✉ *291 Jones Rd., 02540,* ☎ *508/540–2000,* FAX *508/548–2712. 93 rooms, 5 suites. Restaurant, no-smoking rooms, room service, indoor pool, exercise room, video games. AE, D, DC, MC, V.*

$$–$$$ 🏨 **Inn on the Sound.** Although far from secluded, this inn, perched on a bluff overlooking Vineyard Sound and offering glimpses of the island itself, is blissfully quiet. The living room and 9 of the 10 guest rooms (all named for various Falmouth area landmarks) face the water. Guest rooms have queen-size beds and unfussy contemporary furnishings such as natural oak tables, unbleached cottons, and ceiling fans; four rooms have private decks. Common areas include the art-laden living room, with its oversize boulder fireplace, oversize windows, and modern white couches, a bistrolike breakfast room, and a large porch with even more stunning water views. ✉ *313 Grand Ave., Falmouth Heights 02540,* ☎ *508/457–9666 or 800/564–9668,* FAX *508/457–9631. 10 rooms. Beach. No smoking. AE, D, MC, V. BP.*

$$–$$$ ⌂ **Palmer House Inn.** This turn-of-the-century Queen Anne home is set on a tree-lined street in the historic heart of Falmouth, just a short stroll past the village green. The Victorian interior may seem slightly suffocating—dark hardwoods, heavy period furniture, endless lace, and ornate stained-glass windows. Each room has an antique, wicker, or four-poster bed and a ceiling fan. One good bet is the third-floor Tower Room, with a view across the treetops into Woods Hole and beyond. The large rooms in the 1910 carriage house are also airier, with more tailored appointments. The inn added four rooms, all with whirlpool baths, in 1999; three have king-size beds and all have traditional but less ornate decor. There's a private cottage, set off in the backyard, with a whirlpool tub. A candlelight breakfast is served and afternoon refreshments are available. ⊠ *81 Palmer Ave., 02540,* ☎ *508/548–1230 or 800/472–2632,* FAX *508/540–1878. 16 rooms, 1 cottage. Air-conditioning, bicycles. No smoking. AE, D, DC, MC, V. BP.*

$$–$$$ ⌂ **Wildflower Inn.** You'll find many instances of what innkeepers Phil
★ and Donna Stone call their "old made new again" decorating style: tables are constructed from early 1900s pedal sewing-machine bases, and the living room–breakfast area's sideboard was once a '20s Hotpoint electric stove. Each of the inn's five rooms (two with whirlpool tubs) is also innovatively decorated. The bed in the romantic Moonflower Room, tucked under the eaves, is draped in netting and has a skylight above for moon watching, while the bright and cheerful Geranium Room, with baskets of fresh geraniums, has a white iron bed topped with a geranium-print comforter. The Loft Cottage, once a stable, has a spiral staircase that winds up to the bedroom. Donna whips up delicious concoctions using the edible wildflowers she grows out back. (Her floral feasts have been featured on the PBS series *Country Inn Cooking.*) The wraparound porch serves as the summer's breakfast nook; one morning the five-course breakfast might include sunflower crepes, the next, calendula corn muffins. ⊠ *167 Palmer Ave., 02540,* ☎ FAX *508/548–9524 or 800/294–5459. 5 rooms, 1 cottage. Air-conditioning. No smoking. AE, MC, V. BP.*

$$ ⌂ **Admiralty Inn.** This large roadside motel outside Falmouth center has a wide range of rooms and suites, and its kid-friendly facilities make it a good bet for families. Standard rooms have two queen-size beds or one queen and one Murphy bed. King Jacuzzi rooms have king-size beds and whirlpool tubs in the bedroom. Town-house suites have cathedral ceilings with skylights, two baths (one with whirlpool), a loft with a king-size bed, a living room with a sofa bed and a queen-size or king-size bed. Children under 12 stay free. ⊠ *51 Teaticket Hwy. (Rte. 28), 02540,* ☎ *508/548–4240 or 800/341–5700,* FAX *508/457–0535. 68 rooms, 30 suites. Restaurant, bar, 1 indoor and 1 outdoor pool, hot tub. AE, D, DC, MC, V.*

$$ ⌂ **Capt. Tom Lawrence House.** Steps from downtown yet set back from the street enough to feel secluded, this pretty white house with a cupola and black shutters is surrounded by a lawn shaded by old maple trees. Built in 1861 for a whaling captain, the intimate B&B has romantic rooms with antique and painted furniture, French country wallpaper, soft colors, thick carpeting, cable TV, and refrigerators. The beds, all queen-size (several with canopies) or king-size, have firm mattresses, Laura Ashley or Ralph Lauren linens, and down comforters in winter. A family-friendly efficiency apartment is bright and spacious, with a fully equipped, eat-in kitchen and a private entrance. The large common room has a piano and a fireplace. The full breakfast is lavish and delicious. ⊠ *75 Locust St., 02540,* ☎ *508/540–1445 or 800/266–8139,* FAX *508/457–1790. 6 rooms, 1 efficiency. Air-conditioning. No smoking. MC, V. Closed Jan. BP.*

$$ ☒ **Mostly Hall.** Set in a landscaped park far back from the street and
★ separated from it by tall bushes, trees, and a wrought-iron fence, Car-
oline and Jim Lloyd's inn looks very much like a private estate. (The
house got its name when a young turn-of-the-century visitor exclaimed
to his mother, "Look! It's mostly hall!") The imposing 1849 house has
a wraparound porch and a dramatic widow's walk fitted as a guest
den with travel library and TV/VCR. The huge, comfortably elegant
living room has a marble fireplace and a piano. Accommodations are
in corner rooms, with shuttered casement windows, reading areas, an-
tique pieces, and reproduction queen-size canopy beds; most baths are
small. First-floor rooms have towering 13-ft ceilings. You can lounge
on an Adirondack chair in the lush gardens behind the house. ☒ 27
Main St. (Rte. 28), 02540, ☎ *508/548–3786 or 800/682–0565,* FAX *508/
457–1572. 6 rooms. Air-conditioning, bicycles, library. No smoking.
AE, D, MC, V. Closed Jan.–mid-Feb. BP.*

Nightlife and the Arts

THE ARTS

The **College Light Opera Company** (☒ Highfield Theatre, off Depot
Ave., ☎ 508/548–0668), founded in 1969, presents music and theater
majors from Oberlin and other colleges performing nine musicals or
operettas, each running one week during the summer. The company
includes more than 30 singers and an 18-piece orchestra. Be fore-
warned: when the shows are good, they are mildly enjoyable. When
they are bad—and it does happen—they are dreadful.

The **Cape Cod Theatre Project** (☎ 508/457–4242) was established in
1994 to help develop new American plays through a series of staged
readings. Each summer the project stages three or four readings, which
are followed by audience discussion with the playwright. Recent pro-
ductions have included *One Under* by Gloucester Stage Company di-
rector Israel Horovitz and works by Pulitzer Prize winners Lanford
Wilson and Paula Vogel. Performances are held in the Woods Hole Com-
munity Hall (☒ Water St., Woods Hole) or at Falmouth Academy (☒
7 Highfield Dr., off Depot Ave., Falmouth).

Falmouth's **town band concerts** are held on Thursday evenings start-
ing at 8 in summer (☒ Marina Park, Scranton Ave., ☎ 508/548–8500
or 800/526–8532).

NIGHTLIFE

Coonamessett Inn (☒ 311 Gifford St., ☎ 508/548–2300) has dancing to
soft piano, jazz trios, or other music in its lounge on weekends year-round.

Nimrod Inn (☒ 100 Dillingham Ave., ☎ 508/540–4132) offers jazz and
contemporary music at least six nights a week, including the Big Band
and jazz sounds of Stage Door Canteen, one of the Cape's best bands,
every Thursday evening from September through June.

The **Wharf** (☒ 286 Grand Ave. S, Falmouth Heights, ☎ 508/548–0777)
is the Upper Cape's hot beachfront club, with dancing in the nightclub
and on the outdoor deck to high-energy rock and Top 40 bands in sea-
son. Saturday-afternoon beach parties with entertainment and activi-
ties (volleyball tournaments, raft races, and the like) add to the fun.
Keep up your energy with selections from the deli or the upstairs
restaurant's full or light menu.

Outdoor Activities and Sports

BASEBALL

The **Falmouth Commodores** (☎ 781/862–1762) of the collegiate Cape
Cod Baseball League play home games at Guv Fuller Field (☒ 790 E.
Main St.) from mid-June to mid-August.

BIKING

The **Shining Sea Trail** is an easy 3½-mi route between Locust Street, Falmouth, and the Woods Hole ferry parking lot. It follows the coast, giving views of Vineyard Sound and dipping into oak and pine woods; a detour onto Church Street takes you to Nobska Light. A brochure is available at the trailheads. If you're going to Martha's Vineyard with your bike, you can park your car in one of Falmouth's Steamship Authority lots and ride the Shining Sea Trail to the ferry. (The free shuttle buses between the Falmouth lots and the Woods Hole ferry docks also have bike carriers; ☞ Martha's Vineyard A to Z *in* Chapter 3).

Corner Cycle (✉ 115 Palmer Ave., Falmouth, ☎ 508/540–4195) rents tandem and trail bikes by the hour, day, or week. It also does on-site repairs. **Holiday Cycles** (✉ 465 Grand Ave., Falmouth Heights, ☎ 508/540–3549) has surrey, tandem, and other unusual bikes.

FISHING

Freshwater ponds are good for perch, pickerel, trout, and more; the required license (along with rental gear) is available at tackle shops, such as **Eastman's Sport & Tackle** (✉ 150 Main St. [Rte. 28], Falmouth, ☎ 508/548–6900).

Patriot Boats (✉ 227 Clinton Ave., Falmouth Harbor, ☎ 508/548–2626; 800/734–0088 in MA) has deep-sea fishing from party or charter boats. Midweek you can often get a spot on the party boat without reservations, although advance bookings are recommended; reserve ahead for weekend trips.

ICE-SKATING

Fall through spring, ice-skating is available at the **Falmouth Ice Arena** (✉ 9 Skating La., off Palmer Ave., ☎ 508/548–9083). You'll need to bring your own skates, though; rentals are not available.

TENNIS AND RACQUETBALL

Falmouth Sports Center (✉ 33 Highfield Dr., ☎ 508/548–7433) is a huge facility with three all-weather tennis, six indoor tennis, and three racquetball-handball courts, as well as steam rooms and saunas, free weights, and physical and massage therapist services. Day and short-term rates are available.

Shopping

Bean & Cod (✉ 95 Palmer Ave., ☎ 508/548–8840 or 800/558–8840), a specialty food shop, carries cheeses, breads, and gourmet picnic fixings, along with pastas, coffees and teas, and unusual condiments. The store also packs and ships gift baskets.

Eight Cousins Children's Books (✉ 189 Main St. (Rte. 28), ☎ 508/548–5548) is the place to find reading material for toddlers through young adults. The well-stocked shop, which has nice sections on oceans and marine life, Native American peoples, and other Cape topics, also carries audiotapes and games.

Howlingbird (✉ 91 Palmer Ave., ☎ 508/540–3787) carries detailed, hand-silk-screened, marine-theme T-shirts and sweatshirts, plus hand-painted cards and silk-screened hats and handbags.

Maxwell & Co. (✉ 200 Main St. (Rte. 28), ☎ 508/540–8752) has traditional men's and women's clothing with flair from European and American designers, handmade French shoes and boots, and leather goods and accessories.

Woods Hole

6 *4 mi southwest of Falmouth, 19 mi south of the Bourne Bridge.*

The village of Woods Hole, which dangles at the Cape's southwestern tip, has a unique personality shaped by its substantial intellectual community. It is also the departure point for ferries to Martha's Vineyard, and draws crowds of visitors as a result in season.

Well known as a center for international marine research, Woods Hole is home to several major scientific institutions. The National Marine Fisheries Service was here first, established in 1871 to study fish management and conservation. In 1888 the Marine Biological Laboratory (MBL), a center for research and education in marine biology, moved in across the street. Then in 1930 the Woods Hole Oceanographic Institution (WHOI) arrived, and the U.S. Geological Survey's Branch of Marine Geology followed suit in the 1960s.

Most of the year, Woods Hole is a peaceful community of intellectuals quietly going about their work. In summer, however, the basically one-street village overflows with the thousands of scientists and graduate students who come from around the globe either to participate in summer studies at MBL, WHOI, or the National Academy of Sciences conference center or to work on independent research projects. A handful of waterside cafés and shops along Water Street compete for the most bicycles stacked up at the door.

What accounts for this incredible concentration of scientific minds is, in part, the variety and abundance of marine life in Woods Hole's unpolluted waters, and the natural deepwater port. In addition, there is the opportunity for easy interchange of ideas and information and the stimulation of daily lectures and discussions (many open to the public) by important scientists. The pooling of resources among the various institutions makes for economies that benefit each while allowing all access to highly sophisticated equipment.

A good example of the joining of scientific forces in Woods Hole is the **Marine Biological Laboratory–Woods Hole Oceanographic Institution Library** (✉ 7 Marine Biological Laboratory St., off Water St.), one of the best collections of biological, ecological, and oceanographic literature in the world. On top of its access to more than 200 computer databases and the Internet, the library subscribes to more than 5,000 scientific journals in 40 languages, with complete collections of most from their first issues. During World War II, the librarian arranged with a German subscription agency to have German periodicals sent to neutral Switzerland, to be stored until the end of the war. Thus the library's German collections are uninterrupted, where even many German institutions' are incomplete. All journals are always accessible, because they cannot be checked out and because the library is open 24 hours a day. The Rare Books Room contains photographs, monographs, and prints, as well as journal collections that date from 1665.

Unless you are a scientific researcher, the only way you'll get to see the library is by taking the **Marine Biological Laboratory tour** (☎ 508/289–7623 or 508/548–3705; call for reservations and meeting instructions at least a week in advance if possible). The 1½-hour tours are led by retired scientists (mid-June–August, weekdays at 1, 2, and 3 PM) and include an introductory slide show, as well as stops at the library, the marine resources center (where living sea creatures collected each day are kept), and one of the many working research labs.

The **Woods Hole Oceanographic Institution (WHOI)** is the largest independent, private oceanographic laboratory in the world. Several buildings in the village of Woods Hole house its shore-based facilities; others are on a 200-acre campus nearby. During World War II its research focused on underwater explosives, submarine detection, and the development of antifouling paint. Today its $87 million annual budget helps operate many specialized laboratories with state-of-the-art equipment. A graduate program is offered jointly with MIT, in addition to undergraduate and postdoctoral studies. WHOI's several research vessels roam the world's waters. Its staff led the successful U.S.–French search for the *Titanic* (found about 400 mi off Newfoundland) in 1985.

The institution itself (⊠ 86 Water St.) is not open to the public, but you can learn about it at the small **WHOI Exhibit Center,** with videos and exhibits on the institution and its various projects, including research vessels. ⊠ *15 School St.,* ☎ *508/289–2663.* ☒ *$2 suggested donation.* ☉ *Late May–early Sept., Mon.–Sat. 10–4:30, Sun. noon–4:30; Apr. and Nov.–Dec., Fri.–Sat. 10–4:30, Sun. noon–4:30; early–mid-May, mid-late Sept., and Oct., Tues.–Sat. 10–4:30, Sun. noon–4:30.*

The **National Marine Fisheries Service Aquarium** displays 16 tanks of regional fish and shellfish. There are magnifying glasses and a dissecting scope to examine marine life, and several hands-on pools with banded lobsters, crabs, snails, starfish, and other creatures. The top attraction is two harbor seals, which can be seen in the outdoor pool near the entrance in summer. The exhibits aren't sophisticated and the facility could be better maintained, but this popular place is definitely kid-friendly. ⊠ *Corner of Albatross and Water Sts.,* ☎ *508/495–2267, 508/495–2001 for recorded information.* ☒ *Free.* ☉ *Late June–mid-Sept., daily 10–4; mid-Sept.–late June, weekdays 10–4.*

A three-building complex, the **Woods Hole Historical Museum** (formerly known as the Bradley House Museum) displays paintings, a restored Woods Hole Spritsail boat, boat models, and a model of the town as it looked in the 1890s. In the archives of the historical collection you'll find old ships' logs, postcards, newspaper articles, maps, diaries and photographs, more than 200 tapes of oral history provided by local residents, and a 100-volume library on maritime history. Free guided walking tours of the village are available Tuesday at 4 in July and August from the museum, which is across from the Martha's Vineyard ferry parking lot. ⊠ *573 Woods Hole Rd.,* ☎ *508/548–7270.* ☒ *Donations accepted.* ☉ *Museum mid-June–late Sept., Tues.–Sat. 10–4. Archives year-round, Tues. and Thurs. 10–2.*

The 1888 **Episcopal Church of the Messiah,** a stone church with a conical steeple and a small medicinal herb garden in the shape of a Celtic cross, is a good place for some quiet time. The garden is enclosed by a holly hedge and has a bench for meditation. Inscriptions on either side of the carved gate read ENTER IN HOPE and DEPART IN PEACE. ⊠ *22 Church St.,* ☎ *508/548–2145.* ☒ *Free.* ☉ *Daily sunrise–sunset.*

Nobska Light (⊠ Church St.) is an impressive sight, as are the spectacular views from its base of the nearby Elizabeth Islands and of Martha's Vineyard, across Vineyard Sound. The 42-ft cast-iron tower, lined with brick, was built in 1876 with a stationary light. It shows red to indicate dangerous waters or white for safe passage. Since the light was automated in 1985, the adjacent keeper's quarters have been the headquarters of the Coast Guard group commander—a fitting passing of the torch from one safeguarder of ships to another. The lighthouse is not open to the public except during special tours.

Dining and Lodging

$$$ ✕ **The Dome.** An astonishing, somewhat ominous period piece, the Dome is a great half-sphere designed in 1953 by Buckminster Fuller himself. The canopied ceiling holds a large, flashy chandelier that truly defines the taste of the era. The dining room is a bit like a cruise-ship ballroom, and a big band plays for after-dinner dancing several nights a week in summer (☞ Nightlife and the Arts, *below*). The Dome menu is classic, with few surprises: scallops Provençale, baked shrimp with a sherried lobster stuffing, and four styles of prime rib. The wine list is fine, and a board lists nightly specials. The Dome has been revived after a period of dormancy but still looks a little past its prime. Then again, maybe the '60s never die. ⊠ *533 Woods Hole Rd.,* ☎ *508/548–0800. AE, D, MC, V. Closed mid-Oct.–Apr.*

$$ ✕ **Fish Monger's Café.** To say that this is the best restaurant in Woods
★ Hole sounds like faint praise in the scheme of Cape and island restaurants, but the menu is ambitious—particularly the inventive daily specials that take a new look at traditional seafood. The fried calamari appetizer is light and perfectly fried and served with a hot pepper sauce, and the hearty *bruschetta* (broiled bread slices) with ricotta, fresh herbs, basil leaves, and olives is a treat. Many grilled seafood dishes come with tropical fruit sauces or glazes; mango and cilantro sauce over grilled salmon is particularly delectable. The main dining room overlooks the water, and there is a bar attached to the restaurant. Breakfast and lunch are also served. ⊠ *25 Water St.,* ☎ *508/540–5376. Reservations not accepted. AE, MC, V. Closed Dec.–mid-Feb. and Tues. Nov.–Mar..*

$$ ⌸ **The Marlborough.** This gem is somewhat hard to find, but look for the white fence and colonial-style black-and-white sign. A classic Cape house built in 1942, it has five rooms in the main house, each with private bath and each named for its predominant color. Whether you choose the Green Room or the Yellow, Rose, Blue, or Pink, expect to find the same basic touches: wicker or brass beds, lace curtains, hooked rugs, fresh flowers, and floral print bedcoverings and pillows. The scent of lavender permeates not only the sheets but the rooms themselves. A small cottage is out back, next to the kidney-shape in-ground pool; it has redbrick floors, a queen-size bed, and a sitting room. ⊠ *320 Woods Hole Rd., 02543,* ☎ *508/548–6218 or 800/320–2322,* ℻ *508/457–7519. 5 rooms, 1 cottage. Pool, Ping-Pong. No smoking. AE, MC, V. BP.*

$$ ⌸ **Woods Hole Passage.** This century-old carriage house and barn have been tastefully converted into a romantic showcase. The large, rose-hued common room radiates comfort, with lace curtains, overstuffed furniture, and a yellow pine floor. There are five rooms, all with queen beds; one (the smallest) is in the main house, and the others are in the restored barn. In good weather, you can have breakfast on the flagstone patio. The inn is close to the Martha's Vineyard ferry stop, and owner Deb Pruitt sells (at cost) tickets to avoid lines at the dock. Early risers can request a "breakfast-in-a-bag" to take with them. ⊠ *186 Woods Hole Rd., 02540,* ☎ *508/548–9575 or 800/790–8976,* ℻ *508/540–4771. 5 rooms. Air-conditioning, croquet, horseshoes, bicycles. No smoking. AE, D, DC, MC, V. BP.*

Nightlife and the Arts

THE ARTS

The **Cape Cod Theatre Project** (☎ 508/457–4242; ☞ Falmouth, *above*) helps develop new American plays through a series of three or four staged readings each summer. Performances are held in the Woods Hole Community Hall (⊠ Water St., Woods Hole) or at Falmouth Academy (⊠ 7 Highfield Dr., off Depot Ave., Falmouth).

Woods Hole Folk Music Society (✉ Community Hall, Water St., ☎ 508/
540–0320) presents professional and local folk and blues in a no-
smoking, no-alcohol environment, with refreshments available during
intermission. There are concerts of nationally known performers the
first and third Sundays of the month from October to April, as well
as on the first Sunday of May.

Woods Hole Theater Company (✉ Community Hall, Water St., ☎ 508/
540–6525), the community's resident theater group since 1974, presents several productions each year, generally between late spring and
early fall.

NIGHTLIFE

The **Dome** (✉ 533 Woods Hole Rd., ☎ 508/548–0800) has dancing
to a jazz band in its lounge, under an authentic Bucky Fuller geodesic
dome, on Sunday in July and August; there is easy-listening piano on
Friday and Saturday in season, and a jazz brunch on Sunday. On
Thursday evenings in July and August, the Stage Door Canteen big band
moves from Falmouth's Nimrod Inn to the Dome.

East Falmouth and Waquoit

5 mi northeast of Woods Hole.

These bucolic villages (bucolic, at least, once you leave Route 28) just
east of Falmouth have several places of interest to nature lovers.

❼ Overseen by the Massachusetts Audubon Society, **Ashumet Holly and
Wildlife Sanctuary** is true to its name and its original plantsman, Wil-
fred Wheeler, with its 1,000-plus holly trees and shrubs, composed of
65 American, Asian, and European varieties. Like Heritage Plantation
in Sandwich, this 45-acre tract of woodland, shady groves, meadows,
and hiking trails was purchased and donated by Josiah K. Lilly III to
preserve local land. Grassy Pond is home to numerous turtles and frogs,
and in summer, 35 nesting pairs of barn swallows live in open rafters
of the barn—the sanctuary director can show them to you. Tours to
nearby Cuttyhunk Island (on a 50-ft sailing vessel) leave Falmouth Harbor every Sunday from mid-July to mid-October. In December the reserve holds a three-day holly sale. Self-guided-tour maps are available.
✉ 286 Ashumet Rd., East Falmouth, ☎ 508/563–6390. ⬚ $3. ☼ Trails
daily sunrise–sunset.

☙ **Waquoit Bay National Estuarine Research Reserve** encompasses 2,500
acres of estuary and barrier beach around the bay, making it a good
birding spot. **South Cape Beach** is part of the reserve; you can lie out
on the sand or join one of the interpretive walks. **Flat Pond Trail** runs
through a variety of habitats, including fresh- and saltwater marshes.
Washburn Island is accessible by boat (your own) or by Saturday-morn-
ing tours (call to reserve); it offers 330 acres of pine barrens and trails,
swimming, and 11 wilderness campsites (permit required; ☎ 877/
422–6762). At reserve **headquarters**, a 23-acre estate, a new exhibit
center that opened in 1999 includes displays about the bay's plants and
animals, the Cape Cod watershed, and local Wampanoag culture. An
interactive exhibit allows you to trace the path of a raindrop. In July
and August, the center schedules various daily nature programs for children and families. A Tuesday-evening series is held midsummer (bring
picnics) on environmental, historical, and artistic subjects; call for
program updates. ✉ Rte. 28, 3 mi west of Mashpee rotary, Waquoit,
☎ 508/457–0495.

Tony Andrews Farm and Produce Stand has pick-your-own strawberries (mid-June–early July); peas (June–July); lettuce, squash, cucumbers,

and peppers (mid-June–mid-Aug.); herbs (late-Jun–Aug.); and beans and tomatoes (August), as well as other produce on the stand. Hayrides are available in summer and fall. You can pick your own pumpkins in fall and choose your Christmas tree in December. ⊠ *398 Old Meeting House Rd., East Falmouth,* ☎ *508/548–5257.* ◷ *June–Dec.; call for hrs.*

Coonamessett Farm operates a farm store, where you can assemble your own gift baskets or purchase produce and specialty foods, as well as a small café serving soups, salads, baked goods, and beverages. You can tour the greenhouses and fields, learn about hydroponic growing systems, and examine a crayfish-culture research project. Members of the farm's "Pick Your Own" club ($10 per year membership) can pick strawberries, lettuces, herbs, rhubarb, and other fruits and vegetables. The farm also rents canoes for use on the adjacent Coonamessett Pond. ⊠ *277 Hatchville Rd., East Falmouth,* ☎ *508/563–2560.* ◷ *Call for seasonal hrs.*

Rows and rows of grapevines, 8,000 in all, line the fields of the **Cape Cod Winery.** Kristina and Antonio Lazzari established their winery in 1994. They now produce five wines, and in 1998, their Nobska Red won a Bronze Medal at the International Eastern Wine Competition. ⊠ *681 Sandwich Rd., East Falmouth,* ☎ *508/457–5592.* ◷ *July–Aug., tastings Thurs.–Sun. noon–5, tours weekends at 2; Memorial Day–June and Sept.–early Dec., tastings weekends noon–5.*

Dining

$ ✕ **McGann's of Falmouth Pub and Restaurant.** A discovery to everyone but the local crowd, McGann's calls itself "a touch of Ireland on Cape Cod." The McGann family should know, because they also have a pub in the town of Doolin, County Galway, Ireland. The place does have the slightly frayed grit of a true Irish country tavern, with its worn floorboards and dusty ceramic poteen jugs lined up on a high, gloomy shelf. McGann's offers typical bar food, with an Irish twist: Irish-style fish-and-chips, Gaelic chicken in an Irish whiskey and bacon sauce, garlic mussels over pasta, and a genuine "full Irish breakfast" with eggs, sausage, and blood pudding served all day long. Though Guinness reigns, the bar claims 200 beers on draft. There's music every night but Tuesday, and Monday night karaoke. The air-conditioning is like the Irish Arctic. ⊠ *734 Teaticket Hwy. (Rte. 28), East Falmouth,* ☎ *508/540–6656. Reservations not accepted. MC, V.*

Mashpee

❽   *7 mi east of East Falmouth, 10 mi south of Sandwich.*

Mashpee is one of two Massachusetts towns (the other is Aquinnah, formerly known as Gay Head, on Martha's Vineyard) that have municipally governed, as well as Native American–governed, areas. In 1660 the missionary Reverend Richard Bourne gave a 16-square-mi parcel of land to the Wampanoags (what irony—an outsider "giving" natives their own land). Known as the Mashpee Plantation and governed by two local sachems, it was the first Indian reservation in the United States. In 1870 Mashpee was founded as a town. In 1974 the Mashpee Wampanoag Tribal Council was formed to continue its government with a Chief, Supreme Sachem, Medicine Man, and Clan Mothers. More than 600 residents are descended from the original Wampanoags, and some continue to observe their ancient traditions.

Housed in a 1793 half-Cape, the **Wampanoag Indian Museum** is a small and somewhat disappointing museum on the history and culture of the tribe. Exhibits include baskets, weapons, hunting and fishing tools, clothing, arrowheads, and a small diorama depicting a scene from an early settlement. If you're curious, don't hesitate to ask questions of the Wampanoag staff. There is also a herring run on site, a small tidal stream that runs from the ocean into a pond. In spring, thick schools of herring swim to the calm safety of the pond to spawn. The tribe observed this cycle and would net great numbers of herring as the fish made their way back to the sea. At press time, the museum was renovating but expected to be fully operational by June 2000. ⊠ *416 Rte. 130, near Great Neck Rd. N,* ☎ *508/477–1536.* ⊡ *Donations accepted.* ☉ *Mon.–Sat. 10–2; call to confirm.*

The town landing gives a spectacular view of the interconnecting **Mashpee and Wakeby ponds** (⊠ Off Rte. 130), the Cape's largest freshwater expanse, popular for swimming, fishing, and boating.

The **Old Indian Meeting House** was originally built on Santuit Pond in 1684, and later moved to its present site on Route 28. The oldest standing church on Cape Cod, the Meeting House is still used by the Mashpee tribe for worship and meetings. In summer, memorials and religious events are held, some incorporating traditional Wampanoag practices. ⊠ *Meeting House Rd., off Rte. 28,* ☎ *508/477–0208.* ☉ *By appointment only.*

The **Old Indian Burial Ground,** near the meeting house on Meeting House Road, is an 18th-century cemetery with interesting headstones typical of the period, carved with scenes and symbols and inscribed with witty sayings.

☾ The spacious facility of the **Cape Cod Children's Museum** welcomes children of all ages with interactive play, science exhibits, a 30-ft pirate play ship, a portable planetarium, and other playtime activities for toddlers and parents most mornings. ⊠ *577 Great Neck Rd. S,* ☎ *508/ 539–8788.* ⊡ *$3.50.* ☉ *Mon.–Sat. 10–5, Sun. noon–5.*

A perfect place for bird-watching, fishing, or canoeing, the **Mashpee River Woodlands** comprises 391 acres of conservation land along the Mashpee River. More than 8 mi of trails meander through the marshlands and pine forests. Park on Quinaquisset Avenue, River Road, or Mashpee Neck Road (where there is a public landing for canoe access). Trail maps are available at the Mashpee Chamber of Commerce (☞ Visitor Information *in* Cape Cod A to Z, *below*).

Golfers, take note: The resort-residential community of **New Seabury** (☞ Lodging, *below*), a division of Mashpee, has one of the best golf courses on the Cape.

Dining and Lodging

$$$ ✕ **Contrast at The Commons.** New to Mashpee Commons and sister to a similarly named restaurant in Dennis, Contrast is a warm, sophisticated place in which to eat excellent food and study the unique and carefully executed decor. The "contrast" theme is highlighted by color-block walls, hand-painted tables, and modern sculpture that give a sense of sleek, but not cold, urban style. Besides the fine dinner menu there is innovative bistro fare and fancy sandwiches. Try the individual grilled pizzas served on a very thin, crisp Middle Eastern lavash crust; on the shrimp version you can actually see and taste good-size shrimp. Everything is available for take-out, too. ⊠ *Market St., Mashpee Commons,* ☎ *508/477–1299. Reservations essential. AE, MC, V.*

$$$ ✕ **Popponesset Inn.** You'll see a wedding or two at the Popponesset Inn every weekend in summer, and for good reason. The food may not be exceptional—traditional offerings include baked stuffed lobster,

grilled swordfish, and steak—but the atmosphere is. The site is picture-
perfect with old Cape Cod saltbox houses, lovely Nantucket Sound in
the background, and perfect evening light. The restaurant has a lounge,
Poppy's, and a number of small dining rooms, some with skylights and
others looking over the water through glass walls. Best of all, sit outside, either under the tent or at one of the umbrella tables. There's dancing to a band on weekends. The Popponesset is in the New Seabury
Resort (☞ *below*). ⊠ *Shore Dr.,* ☎ *508/477–1100 or 508/477–8258.
AE, DC, MC, V. Closed Nov.–Mar. and Mon.–Tues. Labor Day–Apr.
No lunch Labor Day–mid-June.*

$$ ✕ **The Flume.** The Cape and islands belonged to the Wampanoags for
★ centuries before the Pilgrims arrived, and the Flume, owned for more
than 25 years by Wampanoag elder (and author) Earl Mills, pairs
great food with reminders of that cultural tradition; Native American
artifacts decorate the dining room. The food concentrates on a few New
England staples, and the chowder is considered to be among the best
on the Cape. Traditional codfish cakes and beans, Yankee pot roast,
soft-shell crabs in season, and Indian pudding are done to perfection.
The Sunday roast turkey is a genuine treat, as are Aunt Jan's desserts.
If you have any questions about Mashpee's remarkable Wampanoag
history, Earl will happily provide the answers. ⊠ *Lake Ave., off Rte.
130,* ☎ *508/477–1456. MC, V. Closed Thanksgiving–Easter. No lunch
Oct. 12–Thanksgiving.*

$$$$ ✕⊞ **New Seabury Resort and Conference Center.** On a 2,000-acre point
★ surrounded by the waters of Nantucket Sound, this self-contained re-
sort community rents apartments in some of its 13 "villages." For ex-
ample, Maushop Village is a gray-shingled oceanfront complex of
buildings set among narrow lanes of crushed seashells, with rugosa roses
trailing over white picket fences and trellises; the interiors attractively
mix Cape-style and modern furnishings. Town-house units in Sea
Quarters have solariums with whirlpool baths and gas-log fireplaces.
All units have full kitchens and washer-dryers. Among the amenities
(many of them seasonal) are fine oceanfront dining, a lounge and
restaurant overlooking the fairways, a vast tennis facility, a 3-mi pri-
vate beach and an oceanfront pool, miles of jogging trails through the
woods, and Popponesset Marketplace (☞ Shopping, *below*). Golf and
other packages are available. ⊠ *Off Great Neck Rd. S, Box 549, New
Seabury 02649,* ☎ *508/477–9400 or 800/999–9033,* ℻ *508/477–
9790. 167 1- or 2-bedroom units. 2 restaurants, 2 pools, 2 18-hole golf
courses, miniature golf, 16 tennis courts, health club, jogging, beach,
windsurfing, boating, jet skiing, bicycles, pro shops. AE, DC, MC, V.*

Nightlife and the Arts

Bobby Byrne's Pub (⊠ Mashpee Commons, Rtes. 28 and 151, ☎ 508/
477–0600), now past the quarter-century mark, offers a comfortable
pub atmosphere, an outdoor café, a jukebox, and good light and full
menus.

The **Boch Center for the Performing Arts** (☎ 508/477–2580) presents
top-name performers year-round and is home to the Annual New En-
gland Jazz Festival, held in late August. Plans are under way to con-
struct a complex of buildings, including an amphitheater to accommodate
2,000 people, on an idyllic 10-acre tract of countryside in Mashpee.
Until the complex is completed, performances are held at Mashpee Com-
mons (☞ Shopping, *below*) or in the auditoriums of local high schools.

The 90-member **Cape Symphony Orchestra** (☎ 508/362–1111) comes
to Mashpee in July for its annual Sounds of Summer Pops Concert (it
also performs an August concert in Orleans). The performance takes
place at the Mashpee Commons (☞ Shopping, *below*).

Outdoor Activities and Sports

BEACH

South Cape Beach in Mashpee is a 2½-mi-long state and town beach on warm Nantucket and Vineyard sounds, accessible via Great Neck Road south from the Mashpee rotary. Wide, sandy, and pebbly in parts, with low dunes and marshland, it's a beach where you can walk to get a bit of privacy. Its only services are portable toilets. A hiking trail loops through marsh areas and ponds, linking it to the Waquoit Bay National Estuarine Research Reserve (☞ East Falmouth and Waquoit, *above*). A $2 parking fee is charged in summer.

GOLF

New Seabury Country Club (✉ Shore Dr., New Seabury, ☎ 508/477–9111, ext. 1540) has a superior 18-hole, par-72 championship layout on the water and an 18-hole, par-70 course. Both are open to the public September–May, depending on availability; reservations four days in advance are recommended, and proper attire is required.

HIKING AND WALKING

The **Lowell Holly Reservation** (✉ S. Sandwich Rd., off Rte. 130, ☎ 781/821–2977), administered by the Trustees of Reservations, has 4 mi of walking trails amid American beeches, hollies, white pines, and rhododendrons on a peninsula between Mashpee and Wakeby ponds. The reservation has picnic tables and a small swimming beach.

Shopping

Mashpee Commons (✉ Junction of Rtes. 28 and 151, ☎ 508/477–5400) has about 80 stores, including restaurants, art galleries, and a mix of local boutiques and national chains, in an attractive village square setting. There's also a multiscreen movie theater and free outdoor entertainment in summer.

Popponesset Marketplace (✉ Off Great Neck Rd. S, 2½ mi south of Rte. 28 from Mashpee rotary, New Seabury, ☎ 508/477–9111), open late spring to early fall, has 20 shops (boutique clothing, antiques), eating places (a raw bar, pizza, ribs, Ben & Jerry's), miniature golf, and weekend entertainment (bands, fashion or puppet shows, sing-alongs) by the sea.

THE MID CAPE

The designation Mid Cape is one that actually makes sense. It comprises the central section of the Cape and the major towns of Barnstable, the commercial hub of **Hyannis**, and **Hyannis Port**, a well-groomed enclave and site of the Kennedy compound. You'll find some of the most heavily populated and touristed areas along the Mid Cape here, in addition to a number of historic districts, and scenic back roads.

Barnstable is first in line, with its villages of **West Barnstable**, **Barnstable Village**, **Cotuit**, **Osterville**, **Centerville**, **Marstons Mills**, and **Hyannis**. The **Yarmouths** on both Routes 6A and 28 follow. Then come the **Dennis** townships on both the bay and sound sides.

Barnstable

🔾 *11 mi east of Sandwich, 4 mi north of Hyannis.*

With more than 43,000 year-round residents, Barnstable is the largest town on the Cape. It's also the second oldest—it was founded in 1639, two years after Sandwich, its lone predecessor. You'll get a feeling for its age in Barnstable Village, on and near Main Street (Route 6A), a

The Mid Cape

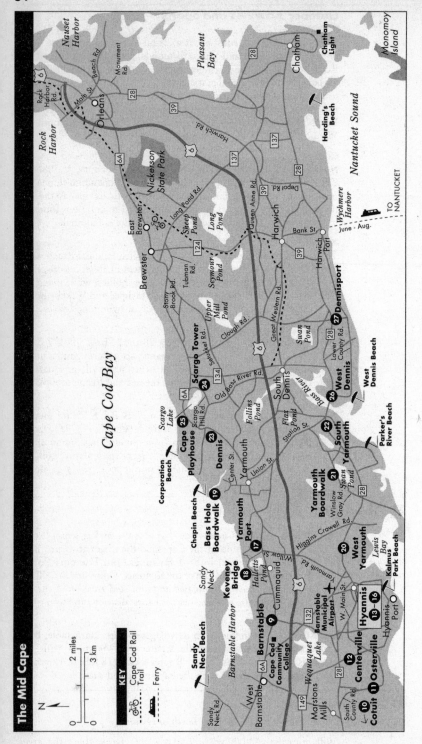

KEY

Cape Cod Rail
Trail
Ferry

N

0   2 miles
0   3 km

Cape Cod Bay

Nantucket Sound

Monomoy Island

Nauset Harbor

Pleasant Bay

Rock Harbor

Chatham

Chatham Light

Orleans

Brewster

East Brewster

Nickerson State Park

Harding's Beach

Harwich

Harwich Port

Wychmere Harbor

June - Aug.

TO NANTUCKET

Sheep Pond

Long Pond

Seymour Pond

Upper Mill Pond

Scargo Tower

Scargo Lake

Corporation Beach

Cape Playhouse

Dennis

Swan Pond

West Dennis

West Dennis Beach

Dennisport

South Dennis

Bass River

Yarmouth

Follins Pond

Flax Pond

Parker's River Beach

South Yarmouth

Yarmouth Boardwalk

Swan Pond

Chapin Beach

Bass Hole Boardwalk

Yarmouth Port

Keveney Bridge

Sandy Neck

Sandy Neck Beach

Barnstable

Barnstable Harbor

Cummaquid

Halletts Pond

West Yarmouth

Lewis Bay

Kalmus Park Beach

Hyannis

Hyannis Port

Barnstable Municipal Airport

Cape Cod Community College

Centerville

Osterville

Cotuit

West Barnstable

Wequaquet Lake

Marstons Mills

South County Rd.

Sandy Neck Rd.

lovely area of large old homes dominated by the Barnstable County Superior Courthouse. Behind the courthouse is a complex of government buildings best avoided. The Village Hall is home to the Barnstable Comedy Club, one of the oldest community theater groups in the country. The Cape Cod Conservatory of Music and Arts and Cape Cod Community College are also in the municipality. Barnstable is also known for beautiful Sandy Neck Beach.

The **Olde Colonial Courthouse,** built in 1772 as the colony's second courthouse, is the home of the historical society **Tales of Cape Cod** (✉ 3018 Main St. [Rte. 6A], ☎ 508/362–8927), which is restoring it to serve as a museum. A series of slide-illustrated lectures, given by guest speakers, is held Tuesday nights in July and August. From the courthouse, take a peek across the street at the old-fashioned English gardens at St. Mary's Episcopal Church.

Set in a 1644 building listed on the National Register of Historic Places, the **Sturgis Library** was established in 1863. Its holdings date from the 17th century and include hundreds of maps and land charts, the definitive collection of Cape Cod genealogical material ($5 daily fee for nonresidents), and an extensive maritime history collection. ✉ *3090 Main St. (Rte. 6A),* ☎ *508/362–6636.* ☽ *Mon. and Thurs. 10– 2; Tues. 1–9; Wed., Fri., and Sun. 1–5; Sat. 10–4.*

Barnstable's maritime past is on display at the **Trayser Museum Complex.** Listed on the National Register of Historic Places, the red-painted brick main building houses a small collection of maritime exhibits— telescopes, captains' shaving boxes, items brought back from voyages, ship models and paintings—as well as ivory, Sandwich glass, and arrowheads. The downstairs re-creates the way the building looked in 1856, when it served as a customs house; don't miss the ornate bronze Corinthian columns. A restored customs-keeper's office with an original safe and a view of the harbor are on the second floor. Also on the grounds are a jail, circa 1690, with two cells bearing former inmates' graffiti, and a carriage house with early tools, fishing implements, and a 19th-century horse-drawn hearse. ✉ *3353 Main St. (Rte. 6A),* ☎ *508/ 362–2092.* ✉ *$2 suggested donation.* ☽ *Mid-June–mid-Oct., Tues.– Sun. 1:30–4:30.*

If you are interested in Cape history, the **Nickerson Memorial Room** at **Cape Cod Community College** has the largest collection of information on Cape Cod, including books, records, ships' logs, oral-history tapes, photographs, films, and more. It also has materials on the islands of Martha's Vineyard and Nantucket. ✉ *2240 Iyanough Rd., off Rte. 132, West Barnstable,* ☎ *508/362–2131, ext. 4445.* ☽ *Mon., Wed., and Fri. 8:30–4; Tues. 8:30–3.*

Dining and Lodging

$$–$$$ ✕ **Barnstable Tavern & Grille.** This handsome old building right in the village center, across from the courthouse, holds both a serious restaurant and a more relaxed tavern. The tavern booths are a good compromise of atmosphere and informality. The rack of lamb and the tavern mixed grill are specialties, both hearty and straightforward. The tavern menu lists very big burgers and a turkey club sandwich that anyone would want to gobble. Sunday brunch from 11 to 3 features a 50-foot "cruise ship" from which the buffet is served, and that's something worth waking up for. ✉ *3176 Main St. (Rte. 6A),* ☎ *508/362–2355. AE, D, MC, V.*

$$–$$$ ✕ **Dolphin Restaurant.** Want to know who's running for what local office, or what the next controversy is likely to be at the planning commission? Eavesdrop at the Dolphin. For decades, this has been the place

where opinions clash and deals are cut. There is a colonial feel inside, dark and inviting; the food clings to what might be called historically appropriate preparation. This is a place to go basic, ordering the baked stuffed haddock or the prime rib. The bar is small but inviting, and your political secrets are safe with Joseph, one of Cape Cod's famous bartenders. ✉ *3250 Main St. (Rte. 6A),* ☎ *508/362–6610. AE, MC, V.*

\$\$–\$\$\$ ⊞ **Ashley Manor.** Set back from the Old King's Highway by high privet hedges and a wide lawn, this fine B&B is just a short walk from the village. The inn preserves its antique wide-board floors and has open-hearth fireplaces, one with a beehive oven, in the living room, the dining room, and the keeping room. The rooms are toasty, too—all but one have a working fireplace or woodstove, and the four suites have whirlpool tubs. Antique and country furnishings, Oriental rugs, and glimmers of brass and crystal create an elegant atmosphere. Breakfast is served on the backyard terrace, which looks onto fruit trees, a gazebo, and the tennis court, or in the formal dining room. ✉ *3660 Main St. (Rte. 6A), Box 856, 02630,* ☎ *508/362–8044 or 888/535–2246,* FAX *508/362–9927. 2 rooms, 4 suites. Air-conditioning, tennis court, bicycles. No smoking. D, MC, V. BP.*

\$\$–\$\$\$
★ ⊞ **Beechwood Inn.** Debbie and Ken Traugot's yellow and pale green 1853 Queen Anne is trimmed with gingerbread, wrapped by a wide porch with wicker furniture and a glider swing, and shaded by old beech trees. While the parlor is pure mahogany-and-red-velvet Victorian, guest rooms (all with queen or king beds) are decorated with antiques in lighter Victorian styles, including Eastlake. Three have fireplaces (two new fireplaces are in the works for 2000), and one has a water view. Bathrooms have pedestal sinks and antique lighting fixtures. Breakfast is served in the dining room, which has a pressed-tin ceiling, a fireplace, and lace-covered tables set with hurricane lamps and fresh flowers. Afternoon tea and homemade snacks are also available. ✉ *2839 Main St. (Rte. 6A), 02630,* ☎ *508/362–6618 or 800/609–6618,* FAX *508/362–0298. 6 rooms. Air-conditioning, refrigerators, bicycles. No smoking. AE, D, MC, V. BP.*

\$\$–\$\$\$ ⊞ **Cobb's Cove.** Proprietors Henri-Jean and Evelyn Chester have created a rustic hideaway for guests who want both quiet and comfort. Lush, wild gardens filled with bird feeders and fountains surround the house. The interior has huge wood beams, rough burlap walls, and heavy wooden doors studded (just as they did in the olden days) with nail heads. Guest rooms are large; each has a dressing area and a private bath with whirlpool tub and robes. The two top-floor rooms have glass walls, and from the sitting areas you can enjoy the spectacular view of Cape Cod Bay—on a good day, you can see all the way to Provincetown. Breakfast is served in the rustic dining room, dominated by a Count Rumford–designed fireplace. Historic Barnstable village, beaches, and even whale-watching boats in the marina are a short stroll away. ✉ *31 Powder Hill Rd., Box 208, 02630,* ☎ FAX *508/362–9356. 6 rooms. No smoking. AE, D, MC, V. BP.*

\$\$–\$\$\$
★ ⊞ **Heaven on High.** There's no more appropriately named B&B on the Cape. Deanna and Gib Katten's haven is indeed heaven, nestled high on a hill, on one of the Cape's oldest roads, overlooking dunes, Great Salt Marsh, and the Bay at Sandy Neck. The modern house's decor is a meld of California beach house and Cape Cod comfort—light, airy, and breezy. The Great Room is filled with overstuffed chairs and couches, a fireplace, TV, and natural oak floors. Sliding glass doors lead to the living room and also to the deck, which runs the full length of the house, offering panoramic views of sand and surf. Deanna is an avid collector of, well, you name it, and she has filled every nook with her treasures. Each room is named for the expansive collection that it houses; the Silhouettes and Mirrors Room, for instance, has—you

guessed it—silhouettes and mirrors of all types, as well as a queen-size bed, fireplace, and a large private deck. The breakfasts, served on fine china and Tiffany sterling, are almost angelic. ✉ *70 High St., Box 346, West Barnstable, 02668,* ☎ *508/362–4441 or 800/362–4044,* FAX *508/362–4465. 3 rooms. Air-conditioning, refrigerators, putting green. No smoking. D, MC, V. Closed Nov.–Dec. BP.*

$$ 🏨 **Acworth Inn.** Cheryl and Jack Ferrell, self-described "corporate drop-outs," have run Acworth since 1994. Jack will help prepare your sightseeing excursions, while Cheryl sees to fresh flowers and chocolates in your room. Their historic 1860 house, which has been added to throughout the years, has four large rooms, plus a spacious two-room suite. The rooms are decorated with soft pastels, lacy designer linens, and tasteful, hand-painted furniture. The suite, with modern furnishings, also has a fireplace, whirlpool tub, TV/VCR, and refrigerator. Cheryl is known for her breakfasts (one specialty is homemade granola, with strawberries that come from the strawberry patch out back), cinnamon rolls, and chocolate chip cookies. The inn is 1 mi east of Barnstable Village. ✉ *4352 Main St. (Rte. 6A), Box 256, Cummaquid 02637,* ☎ *508/362–3330 or 800/362–6363,* FAX *508/375–0304. 4 rooms, 1 suite. Bicycles. No smoking. AE, D, MC, V. BP.*

$$ 🏨 **Honeysuckle Hill.** Innkeepers Mary and Bill Kilburn ran an inn in Vermont before relocating to the Cape in 1998, and their experience and graciousness shine through in lots of little touches: a guest fridge stocked with sodas and water bottles, beach chairs with umbrellas (perfect for nearby Sandy Neck Beach), and an always-full cookie jar in the sunny dining room. The airy, country-style guest rooms in this expansive, gray-shingled 1810 Queen Anne–style cottage with white trim have lots of white wicker, feather beds, checked curtains, and pastel-painted floors. The spacious Wisteria Room, overlooking the lush yard and flower gardens, is a particularly comfortable retreat, with its own entrance under a wisteria arbor. The screened-in porch is a peaceful spot for early morning coffee. ✉ *591 Rte. 6A, West Barnstable 02668,* ☎ *508/362–8418 or 800/441–8418. 3 rooms, 1 suite. Air-conditioning. No smoking. AE, D, MC, V. BP.*

Nightlife and the Arts

The **Barnstable Comedy Club** (✉ Village Hall, Rte. 6A, ☎ 508/362–6333), the Cape's oldest amateur theater group (it celebrated its 75th anniversary in 1997), gives much-praised musical and dramatic performances throughout the year. Some folks who appeared here before they made it big are Geena Davis, Frances McDormand, and Kurt Vonnegut, a past president of the BCC.

Outdoor Activities and Sports

BEACH

Hovering above Barnstable Harbor and the 4,000-acre **Great Salt Marsh**, **Sandy Neck Beach** stretches some 6 mi across a peninsula that ends at **Sandy Neck Light**. The beach is one of the Cape's most beautiful—dunes, sand, and sea spread endlessly east, west, and north. The marsh used to be harvested for salt hay; now it is a haven for birds, which are out and about in greatest number morning and evening, at low tide, and during spring and fall migration. The lighthouse, standing just a few feet from eroding shoreline at the tip of the neck, has been out of commission since 1952. It was built in 1857 to replace an 1827 light, and it used to run on acetylene gas. It is now privately owned and no longer accessible from the beach. If you like to hike, ask at the ranger station for a trail brochure. The main beach at Sandy Neck has lifeguards, a snack bar, rest rooms, and showers. As you travel east along Route 6A from Sandwich, Sandy Neck Road is just *before* the Barnstable line, although the beach itself is in West Barnstable. ✉ *Sandy*

Neck Rd., West Barnstable. 🅿 *Parking $10 Memorial Day–Labor Day.*
🕐 *Daily 9–9, but staffed only until 5 PM.*

FISHING

The **Barnstable Harbor Charter Fleet** (✉ 186 Millway, ☎ 508/362–
3908) has fishing trips on 10 sportfishing vessels from spring through
fall. Reservations are recommended but not required.

WHALE-WATCHING

On **Hyannis Whale Watcher Cruises** out of Barnstable Harbor, a naturalist narrates and comments on whale sightings and the natural history of Cape Cod Bay. Trips last about four hours, there are concessions
on board, and in July and August you can cruise at sunset, too. Reservations are required; book a day or two in advance. ✉ *Millway Marina, off Phinney's La.,* ☎ *508/362–6088 or 800/287–0374.* 🅿 *$24.*
🕐 *Apr.–Oct.*

Shopping

Black's Handweaving Shop (✉ 597 Rte. 6A, West Barnstable, ☎ 508/
362–3955), in a barnlike shop with working looms, makes beautiful
handwoven goods in traditional and jacquard weaves. If you don't see
what you want on display, you can commission it.

The **Crystal Pineapple** (✉ 1540 Rte. 6A, West Barnstable, ☎ 508/362–
3128 or 800/462–4009) has cranberry glass and many collectibles
lines, including Dept. 56, Snowbabies, Swarovski crystal, and Disney
Classics.

Maps of Antiquity (✉ 1022 Rte. 6A, West Barnstable, ☎ 508/362–7169)
sells original and reproduction maps of Cape Cod, New England, and
other parts of the world. Some date back to the 1700s.

Whippletree (✉ 660 Rte. 6A, West Barnstable, ☎ 508/362–3320) is
a large barn, decorated for each season and filled with country gift items
and a year-round Christmas section. Offerings include German nutcrack-
ers, from Prussian soldiers to Casanovas.

Cotuit

❿ *9 mi southwest of Barnstable, 2½ mi southeast of Mashpee.*

Once called Cotuit Port, this small, picturesque town was formed
around seven Crocker family homesteads. The center of town is not
much more than a crossroads with a post office, old-time coffee shop,
local pizza parlor, and general store, which all seem unchanged since
the 1940s. Large waterfront estates line sections of Main Street and
Ocean View Drive, where small coves hide the uncrowded Loop Beach
and Ropes Beach. It's best to get to the beaches by bike, since traffic
is light and beach parking is for residents only.

The **Cahoon Museum of American Art** is in one of the old Crocker family buildings, a 1775 Georgian colonial farmhouse that was once a tavern and an overnight way station for travelers on the Hyannis–Sandwich
Stagecoach line. Its several rooms display selections from the permanent collection of American primitive paintings by Ralph and Martha
Cahoon along with other 19th- and early 20th-century art. Special exhibitions, classes, talks, and demonstrations are held throughout the
summer. ✉ *4676 Rte. 28,* ☎ *508/428–7581.* 🅿 *Donations accepted.*
🕐 *Mar.–Jan., Tues.–Sat. 10–4.*

The first motor-driven fire-fighting apparatus on Cape Cod, a 1916
Model T Chemical Fire Engine, is housed in the **Santuit–Cotuit Historical Society Museum,** behind the **Samuel Dottridge Homestead,** which

itself dates from the early 1800s. ⊠ *1148 Main St.,* ☎ *508/428–0461.* ☞ *Free.* ⊙ *Mid-June–mid-Oct., Thurs.–Sun. 2:30–5.*

Dining and Lodging

$$$$ ✕ **Regatta of Cotuit.** Like its sister restaurant in Falmouth (☞ *above*), the Cotuit Regatta serves three nightly menus in a softly elegant setting. The menu reaches for a wider global cuisine, and a younger audience, but it is still much more haute than hot. The classic yet original fare includes pâtés of rabbit, veal, and venison, and a signature seared loin of lamb with cabernet sauce, surrounded by chèvre, spinach, and pine nuts. The restored colonial stagecoach inn is plushly filled with wood, brass, and Oriental carpets, and the cozy taproom has its own bar menu. ⊠ *4613 Falmouth Rd. (Rte. 28),* ☎ *508/428–5715. AE, MC, V. No lunch.*

$–$$ ☉ **Josiah Sampson House.** Since there's no sign on this regal 1793 Federal-style house, you may mistake it for a private estate, but inside, the atmosphere is a comfortable mix of colonial and casual. The guest parlor is stocked with videos and games, while the spacious dining room has traditional colonial furnishings and an oversize fireplace. The guest rooms, some with fireplaces, are furnished with canopy beds (twins, doubles, or a queen), needlepoint rugs, and an attractive mix of antiques and what owner Michael Hughes calls "flea market finds." Hannah's Room, formerly the kitchen, has a queen-size four-poster, built-in window seats, and a massive working fireplace. It's also the roomiest; Hughes and his wife, Mal, who have little ones of their own, welcome families and can add a roll-away bed here for the kids. Upstairs, the double-bedded Sampson Room has an extra-large bathroom and a view of the backyard. Guests have tennis privileges at the Kings Grant Racquet Club next door. ⊠ *40 Old Kings Rd., off Main St., 02635,* ☎ *508/428–8383 or 877/574–6873,* ☏ *508/428–0116. 5 rooms. Outdoor hot tub, bicycles. AE, MC, V. CP.*

Outdoor Activities and Sports

The **Cotuit Kettlers** (☎ 508/428–3358) of the collegiate Cape Cod Baseball League play home games at Lowell Park (⊠ Lowell St., 2 mi south of Rte. 28) from mid-June to mid-August.

Shopping

The **Sow's Ear Antique Company** (⊠ 4698 Rte. 28, ☎ 508/428–4931), next to the Cahoon Museum, specializes in folk art—dolls, ship's models, wood carvings, antique quilts, and paintings—in a house that dates from the late 1600s.

Osterville

⑪ *3 mi east of Cotuit, 7 mi southwest of Barnstable.*

A wealthy Barnstable enclave southwest of the town center, Osterville is lined with elegant waterfront houses, some of which are large "cottages" built in the 19th century, when the area became popular with a monied set.

An 1824 sea captain's house is the setting for the **Osterville Historical Society Museum,** which displays antiques, dolls, and exhibits on Osterville's history. Two wooden boat museums, each showcasing various sailing vessels, as well as the Cammett House (dating from the early 18th century) are also on the property. ⊠ *155 West Bay Rd.,* ☎ *508/ 428–5861.* ☞ *$3.* ⊙ *Mid-June–Oct., Thurs.–Sun. 1:30–4:30.*

NEED A BREAK? | **Gone Chocolate** (⊠ 858 Main St., ☎ 508/420–0202) will tempt you with old-fashioned chocolate-pecan turtles, saltwater taffy, ice cream, and other confections.

Dining

$$ **Wimpy's.** In spite of its name and namesake, this is not a fast-food hamburger joint but a Cape standby with an extensive menu that favors Italian food and fried fish, from chicken picatta to the seafood platter. The restaurant occupies an expanded space that used to be the 1821 Charles Boult House, Wimpy's has built a large and loyal clientele that fills a big family dining room, a sunny atrium, and a dark, traditional tavern with cozy booths and a fine old bar. The frying batter and fish selections are on the bland side, so opt for the more inventive specials such as tortilla-crusted salmon topped in a caper sauce, or a simple prime rib (when available). You can get takeout here, too. This is just about the only choice in town, so make the most of it. ⊠ *752 Main St.,* ☎ *580/428–6300; 508/428–3474 for takeout. AE, DC, MC, V.*

Outdoor Activities and Sports

Holly Hill Farm (⊠ 240 Flint St., Marstons Mills, ☎ 508/428–2621) offers horseback-riding instruction and day camps but no trail rides.

Shopping

Oak & Ivory (⊠ 1112 Main St., ☎ 508/428–9425) specializes in Nantucket lightship baskets made on the premises, as well as gold miniature baskets and scrimshaw. It also sells china, gold jewelry, and gift items.

Centerville

⑫ *2½ mi northeast of Osterville, 4 mi southwest of Barnstable.*

Centerville was once a busy seafaring town, which is evident from the 50 or so shipbuilders' and sea captains' houses along its quiet, tree-shaded streets. Offering the pleasures of both sheltered ocean beaches on Nantucket Sound, such as **Craigville Beach** (☞ *below*), and freshwater swimming in Lake Wequaquet, it has been a popular vacation spot since the mid-19th century. Shoot Flying Hill Road, named by the Native Americans, is the highest point of land on the Cape, with panoramic views to Plymouth and Provincetown to the north and to Falmouth and Hyannis to the south.

Set in a 19th-century house, the **Centerville Historical Society Museum** exhibits furnished period rooms, Sandwich glass, miniature carvings of birds by Anthony Elmer Crowell, models of ships, marine artifacts, military uniforms and artifacts, antique tools, perfume bottles (dating from 1760 to 1920), 300 costumes (from 1650 to 1950), quilts, and a research library. Each summer there are special costume exhibits or other shows. ⊠ *513 Main St.,* ☎ *508/775–0331.* ⊡ *$3.* ☉ *Mid-June–mid-Oct., Wed.–Sat. noon–4:30.*

The **1856 Country Store** (⊠ 555 Main St., ☎ 508/775–1856) sells penny candy, except that these days the candy costs at least 25 pennies. The store also carries newspapers, coffee, crafts, jams, and all kinds of gadgets and toys. You can sip your coffee—and take a political stance—by choosing one of the wooden benches out front, marked DEMOCRAT and REPUBLICAN.

NEED A BREAK? Sample the homemade offerings at **Four Seas Ice Cream** (⊠ 360 S. Main St., ☎ 508/775–1394), a tradition with generations of summer visitors. It's open Memorial Day–Labor Day.

Lodging

$$–$$$ 🏨 **Tradewinds Inn.** Cape Cod conjures up images of sand and surf, and since 1963, the motel-style Tradewinds Inn has offered both—and a lot more. The 6-acre property, overlooking the Atlantic Ocean, Lake Elizabeth, and the pretty village of Craigville, has large, family-friendly ocean-view rooms, all with private balconies or patios. There are also three efficiencies with fully equipped kitchenettes, but skip the less attractive, non-water-view rooms in the detached buildings. The furnishings are simple but appealing: whitewashed furniture; floral quilts; and tasteful, if somewhat unspectacular, prints dotting the walls. A small, sandy private beach just for guests is down the path from the main lodge. The wicker-festooned, knotty-pine paneled lobby has a fireplace and a cocktail bar. ⊠ *780 Craigville Beach Rd., 02636,* ☎ *508/775–0365 or 877/444–7966,* 𝔽𝔸𝕏 *508/790–1404. 28 rooms, 4 suites, 3 efficiencies. Air-conditioning, lobby lounge, putting green, beach. AE, MC, V. Closed Nov.–Apr. CP.*

Outdoor Activities and Sports

Craigville Beach, on Craigville Beach Road, is a long, wide strand that is extremely popular with the collegiate crowd. (It's also known by its nickname, Muscle Beach.) The beach has lifeguards, showers, rest rooms, and food nearby. An $8 parking fee is charged in summer.

Hyannis

⑬–⑯   *3½ mi east of Centerville, 23 mi east of the Bourne Bridge.*

Hyannis was named for the Native American Sachem Iyanno, who sold the area for £20 and two pairs of pants. He would have sold it for far more had there been any indication that Hyannis would become known as the "home port of Cape Cod" or that the Kennedys would have pitched so many tents here. Hyannis is effectively the transportation center of the Cape; it's near the airport, and ferries depart here for Nantucket and (in season) Martha's Vineyard. The busy roads feeding into the town are lined with big-box stores you'll find anywhere.

A bustling year-round hub of activity, Hyannis has the Cape's largest concentration of businesses, shops, malls, hotels and motels, restaurants, and entertainment hot spots. Main Street is lined with used-book and gift shops, jewelers, clothing stores, summer-wear and T-shirt shops, and ice cream and candy stores, but the street can have a somewhat forlorn, down-at-the-heels feeling, as the malls outside downtown have taken their toll on business. There are, however plenty of fun and fancy eateries.

Perhaps best known for its association with the Kennedy clan, the Hyannis area was also a vacation spot for President Ulysses S. Grant in 1874 and later for President Grover Cleveland. Hyannis is making an effort to preserve its historical connection with the sea. By 1840 more than 200 shipmasters had established homes in the Hyannis-Hyannisport area. Aselton Park (at the intersection of South and Ocean streets) and the Village Green on Main Street are the sites of events celebrating this history, and Aselton Park marks the future starting point of the scenic Walkway to the Sea, which is planned to extend to the dock area.

Three parallel streets run through the heart of town. Busy, shop-filled Main Street is one-way from east to west; South Street runs from west to east; and North Street is open to two-way traffic. The airport rotary connects with the heavily trafficked routes 132 and 28, and with U.S. 6.

⑬   Located in Main Street's Old Town Hall, the surprisingly sparse **John F. Kennedy Hyannis Museum** explores JFK's Cape years (1934–63) through enlarged and annotated photographs, culled from the archives of the JFK Library near Boston, as well as a seven-minute video. The gift shop sells mugs, T-shirts, and presidential memorabilia. ⊠ *397 Main*

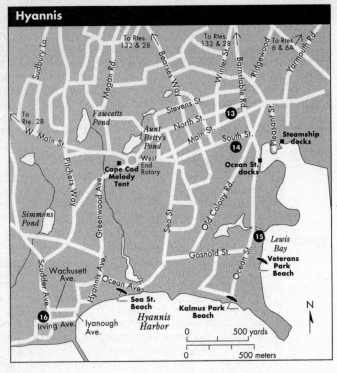

St., ☎ *508/790–3077.* 💌 *$3.* ☉ *Mid-Apr.–mid-Oct., Mon.–Sat., 10–4, Sun. 1–4; last admission at 3:30. Call for off-season hrs.*

⑭ The **St. Francis Xavier Church** (✉ 347 South St., ☎ 508/775–0818) is where Rose Kennedy and her family worshiped during their summers on the Cape; the pew that John F. Kennedy used regularly is marked by a plaque.

Beyond the bustling docks where waterfront restaurants draw crowds, and ferries, harbor tour boats, and deep-sea fishing vessels come and **⑮** go, the quiet esplanade by the **John F. Kennedy Memorial** ✉ Off Ocean St., south of Channel Point) overlooks boat-filled Lewis Bay. JFK loved to sail these waters, and in 1966 the people of Barnstable erected a plaque and fountain pool here in his memory. Adjacent to the memorial is **Veterans Park**, with a beach, a tree-shaded picnic and barbecue area, and a playground.

Hyannis Port was a mecca for Americans during the Kennedy presi-**⑯** dency, when the **Kennedy Compound** became the summer White House. The days of hordes of Secret Service men and swarms of tourists trampling down the bushes are gone, and the area is once again a community of quietly posh estates, though the Kennedy mystique is such that tourists still seek it out. The best way to get a glimpse of the compound is from the water on one of the many harbor tours or cruises.

Joseph P. and Rose Kennedy bought their house here—the largest one, closest to the water—in 1929, as a healthful place to summer with their soon-to-be-nine children. (Son Ted bought the house before his mother's death in 1995.) Sons Jack and Bobby bought neighboring houses in the 1950s. Jack's is the one at the corner of Scudder and Irving, with the 6-ft-high stockade fence on two sides. Bobby's is next to it, with the white fieldstone chimney. Ted bought a home on Squaw Island, a private island connected to the area by a causeway at the end of Scudder Avenue. It now belongs to his ex-wife, Joan. Eunice (Kennedy) and Sargent Shriver have a house near Squaw Island, on Atlantic Avenue.

The compound is relatively self-sufficient in terms of entertainment: Rose Kennedy's former abode (with 14 rooms and nine baths) has a movie theater, a private beach, a boat dock, a swimming pool, a tennis court, and a sports field that was the scene of the famous Kennedy touch-football matches. More recently, Maria Shriver, Caroline Kennedy, and other family members have had their wedding receptions here. In summer 1999, family members waited here for confirmation of John Kennedy Jr.'s death in a plane crash off Martha's Vineyard. He and his wife were flying her sister to the Vineyard before continuing on to a cousin's wedding in Hyannis; all three were killed.

☾ Perfect for a rainy day, **Ryan Family Amusement Center** is replete with video-game rooms and that old seaside favorite, Skee-ball. ⊠ *Cape Cod Mall, Rte. 132,* ☎ *508/775–5566.* ☉ *Daily; hrs vary.*

OFF THE BEATEN PATH

CAPE COD POTATO CHIPS – There's a standing invitation on the back of the bag: come for a free factory tour and get free samples of the crunchy, all-natural chips hand-cooked in kettles in small batches. ⊠ *Independence Park, Breeds Hill Rd., off Rte. 132,* ☎ *508/775–7253.* ☉ *July–Aug., weekdays 9–5, Sat. 10–4; Sept.–June, weekdays 9–5.*

Dining and Lodging

$$$ ✕ **Roadhouse Café.** For 20 years now, Dave and Melissa Colombo's ★ restaurant has been one the smartest spots for a night out in Hyannis. Candlelight flickers off the white linen tablecloths and dark wood wainscoting. The roasted red peppers and goat cheese appetizer is a savory combination, and shrimp and basil pesto over linguine is full of sun-dried tomatoes and whole roasted garlic cloves. All desserts are made on the premises, so do indulge in the rich tiramisu. In the more casual bistro and the mahogany bar, you can order from a separate menu, which offers thin-crust pizza as well as burgers, sandwiches, and other lighter fare. On Monday nights year-round in the bistro is the best straight-ahead jazz on Cape Cod, with regulars like pianist Dave McKenna and Lou Colombo (the trumpet-playing father of Dave). There's a piano bar every other night of the week between July 4 and Labor Day; it continues on Friday and Saturday in the off-season. ⊠ *488 South St.,* ☎ *508/775–2386. Reservations essential. AE, D, MC, V. No lunch.*

$$–$$$ ✕ **The Paddock.** For more than 30 years, the Paddock has been syn- ★ onymous with excellent, formal dining on the Cape—authentically Victorian with sumptuous upholstery in the main dining room and old-style wicker on the preferable, breezy summer porch. Its menu manages to be traditional yet deceptively innovative, combining fresh ingredients in novel ways. A salad of duck, apple, sharp Vermont cheddar, and walnuts on baby greens with cider-mustard vinaigrette is but one example. Steak au poivre, with the promise of five varieties of crushed peppercorns, is masterful; the superb Pacific Rim chicken is a grilled breast topped with oranges and mangoes, served on mixed greens and Asian noodles. Terrific brawny reds are on the award-winning wine list. An older crowd enjoys live music in the evenings at the bar, where Manhattans are still the drink of choice. ⊠ *W. Main St. rotary, next to Melody Tent,* ☎ *508/775–7677. AE, DC, MC, V. Closed mid-Nov.–Mar.*

$$–$$$ ✕ **Penguin Sea Grill.** The fact that a penguin is a bird that swims has symbolic import for this restaurant: owner-chef Bobby Gold experiments carefully, never losing sight of the fresh grilled seafood that he

prepares so well. Baked stuffed lobster (from 1 to 3 pounds) is outstanding, with crabmeat stuffing topped with fresh sea scallops. There are a number of excellent pasta dishes, again with seafood, such as pasta Fiore: shrimp, scallops, and lobster with mushrooms, scallions, sherry, and cream sauce on angel-hair pasta. All of the breads and desserts are homemade. The dining room is on two levels, with wood and brick and carvings of sea life galore. ⊠ *331 Main St.,* ☎ *508/775–2023. AE, DC, MC, V. No lunch weekends.*

$$–$$$ ✕ **RooBar.** A hit of Manhattan on Main Street, RooBar has a dark, sophisticated feel, aided by good music, low light, and a crowded, hip bar scene at night. It's all crowned by a flickering wood-fired oven in the back wall. From this oven come "hand-spun to order" pizzas like scallop and prosciutto with asparagus and goat cheese. The scene gleams at night, but the lunch menu is fresh and inventive and not to be overlooked. Try the Big-Ass Grilled Shrimp appetizer, three "enormous" grilled shrimp in a red curry and coconut sauce, and the fire-roasted half chicken entrée rubbed with toasted fennel and cumin seeds. The owner is a member of actor Christopher Reeve's family, and a portion of all profits goes to the Christopher Reeve Foundation for Spinal Cord Research. ⊠ *586 Main St.,* ☎ *508/778–6515. Reservations essential. AE, MC, V.*

$$ ✕ **Fazio's.** Now in the old Montilio's Bakery, Fazio's moved last year from the west to the east end of Main Street, after a brief hiatus in California, but continues to serve up appealing Italian fare. The new Fazio's looks like a trattoria, with wood floors, high ceilings, and a deli case full of fresh pasta, breads, and cheeses. There's also an espresso and cappuccino bar. The menu leans on simple, fresh ingredients and herbed pastas, such as thick, rough-cut black pepper tagliatelle with sausage and eggplant chunks in a garlicky tomato sauce. All ravioli, pastas, and breads are homemade. Take home some fresh cannoli for dessert. ⊠ *294 Main St.,* ☎ *508/775–9400. Reservations not accepted. AE, D, MC, V.*

$$ ✕ **Harry's.** Homesick for a little bit of the French Quarter on Cape
★ Cod? Harry's feels as though it's transplanted from New Orleans and serves accordingly—both Cajun and Creole—with great spices and sizable portions. The menu features a number of meal-size sandwiches and blackened local fish that's done to perfection, with a jambalaya that makes you wonder if there isn't a bayou nearby. It's also a prime spot for music: you can hear the blues on Friday and Saturday nights (Wednesday and Thursday as well, Memorial Day through Labor Day). There was a change in the ownership structure in 1999, but the same nice vibes and solid southern food are here. ⊠ *700 Main St.,* ☎ *508/778–4188. Reservations not accepted. AE, DC, MC, V.*

$$ ✕ **Starbuck's.** No, it's not another branch of the Seattle-based coffee company but something more like a T. G. I. Friday's with an edge. Walls and rafters are hung with doodads and hoo-has of every description, but un-themed: a tuba here, a couple of mannequins there, a miniature World War I fighter plane from out of nowhere. The menu matches the decor, with selections yanked from all over the planet: ostensibly Asian shrimp deep-fried in a coconut-tempura batter, Buck's beef burrito from the Tex-Mex column, and Italian standards like spaghetti and meatballs. There's also an assortment of burgers and Buckwiches. This might not be for everyone, but it's good if you're in the mood for something raucous. Reservations are essential on weekends. ⊠ *645 Rte. 132,* ☎ *508/778–6767. AE, D, DC, MC, V.*

$–$$ ✕ **Barbyann's.** Sooner or later, your kids are likely to reach their limit of seafood, even fish-and-chips. When it happens, pack everyone off to Barbyann's for an inexpensive family meal—steak and seafood, pizza and burgers, a couple of hardly authentic but kid-pleasing Mexican dishes, and loads of appetizers. Best of all are the Buffalo chicken wings, hot and spicy and filling. There's an outdoor patio with umbrella tables, and "night bird" specials are offered all evening Monday–Thursday for $8.95. ✉ *120 Airport Rd.,* ☎ *508/775–9795. Reservations not accepted. AE, D, DC, MC, V.*

$–$$ ✕ **Baxter's Fish N' Chips.** Fried seafood being the Cape staple that it is, you may want to plan ahead for a trip to pay homage to one of the best fry-o-lators around. Fried clams are delicious and generous, cooked up hot to order with french fries and homemade tartar sauce. Outside, a number of picnic tables allow you to lose no time in the sun with lobster, burgers, or something from the excellent raw bar. Indoors, Baxter's Boat House Club, slightly more upscale, serves the same menu, but with a number of very good specials as well; no one under 21 is allowed here, however. The restaurant is right on Hyannis Harbor, and it's always been a favorite of boaters and bathers alike. ✉ *Pleasant St.,* ☎ *508/775–4490. Reservations not accepted. AE, MC, V. Closed Columbus Day–Apr. and weekdays Labor Day–Columbus Day.*

$–$$ ✕ **Sam Diego's.** The bar is busy with people seeing and being seen, and the menu has satisfyingly authentic Mexican tortillas, burritos, and delicious *mole poblano* (chicken with a spicy, bittersweet cocoa sauce). The prop-shop decor may be a little cheesy—sombreros, Aztec birds, and the like—but the atmosphere is fun and friendly. Especially in the early evenings, this place is popular with families, thanks in part to the all-you-can-eat chili and taco bar—a good option when the kids need a little change of culinary pace. An interesting dessert, crusty deep-fried ice cream, is served in a giant goblet. Later on, the bar scene picks up steam; dinner is served until midnight. ✉ *950 Iyanough Rd. (Rte. 132),* ☎ *508/771–8816. AE, D, MC, V.*

$$$–$$$$ 🏨 **Sheraton Hyannis Resort.** For its beautifully landscaped setting, extensive services and pampering, and superior resort facilities, it's hard to beat the Sheraton. The lobby area is elegant, but the rooms, each with a private balcony, are admittedly a bit dull—standard contemporary hotel style. Views are best from rooms overlooking the golf greens or the courtyard garden. ✉ *West End rotary, 02601,* ☎ *508/775–7775,* FAX *508/778–6039. 224 rooms. Restaurant, pub, room service, air-conditioning, indoor-outdoor pool, beauty salon, 18-hole golf course, putting green, 2 tennis courts, health club, business services. AE, D, DC, MC, V.*

$$$ 🏨 **Simmons Homestead Inn.** This 1820 former sea captain's country estate is a delightful, inviting escape from the world, even though it's only two minutes from congested downtown Hyannis. Gregarious innkeeper Bill Putman doesn't hesitate to share his opinions, and he encourages guests to return around 6 each evening for a wine-and-social hour. If you can't stand smoke, though, beware: although the bedrooms are no-smoking, Putnam—a smoker himself—allows smoking in some public spaces. Each of the rooms in the main house or the detached barn is named for an animal. They have antique, wicker, or canopied four-poster beds topped with brightly colored quilts; some have fireplaces and private decks. The Bird Room, the largest and cheeriest, has an old-fashioned cast-iron tub and a private deck. You can borrow the 10-speed mountain bikes to explore the town, or simply enjoy the expansive backyard from the wraparound porch. Simmons Pond is a short jaunt away on the property's trail. Dogs are permitted, with advance notice, for $25. ✉ *288 Scudder Ave., Box 578, Hyannis Port 02647,* ☎ *508/778–4999 or 800/637–1649,* FAX *508/790–1342. 12 rooms, 1 suite. No-smoking rooms, hot tub, bicycles, billiards. AE, D, MC, V. BP.*

$$ 🏨 **Breakwaters.** If you were staying any closer to the water, you'd be
★ *in* the water—that's how close these charming, weathered gray-shingled
cottages are to Nantucket Sound. Privately owned condos that are rented
as cottages per day or week, the one-, two-, and three-bedroom units
offer all the comforts of home, including linens and towels. There's an
in-ground heated pool less than 200 ft from the lifeguarded town
beach. Each unit has one or two full baths; kitchens with microwave,
coffeemaker, refrigerator, toaster, and stove; TV and phone (local calls
are free); and a deck or patio with grill and picnic table. Most have
water views. An added plus is daily (except Sunday) maid service. The
laundromat at the end of the street (at North Street) will wash and fold
your dirty duds for a nominal fee. From June through August, you must
rent by the week. ⊠ *432 Sea St., Box 118, 02601, ☎ FAX 508/775–*
6831. 18 cottages. Refrigerators, pool, beach, baby-sitting. No credit
cards. No smoking. Closed mid-Oct.–Apr.

$$ 🏨 **Comfort Inn Hyannis.** All the rooms at this business- and family-
oriented cinder-block motel just off the highway have white-oak-ve-
neer furnishings, including one king-size or two double beds, a table
and chairs or a desk and chair, and a wardrobe. Some king rooms have
sofa beds. The quietest rooms are those on the top floor that face the
pond and woods; all have free HBO movies. Guests have free use of
the nearby Barnstable Athletic Club, and children under 18 stay free.
⊠ *1470 Iyanough Rd. (Rte. 132), 02601, ☎ 508/771–4804 or 800/*
228–5150, FAX 508/790–2336. 104 rooms. Indoor pool, sauna. AE, D,
DC, MC, V. CP.

$–$$ 🏨 **HoJo Express Inn.** This centrally located inn—squarely placed on
downtown Main Street—is in walking distance to all of Hyannis's major
sights. The no-surprises rooms have large double beds and typical
motel-chain furniture; most, unfortunately, have views of the drab
parking lot. A value-conscious package plan includes discount shopping coupons and a meal allowance at four nearby restaurants. ⊠ *447*
Main St., 02601, ☎ 508/775–3000, FAX 508/771–1457. 39 rooms, 1
suite. Restaurant, bar, indoor pool. AE, D, DC, MC, V. CP.

$–$$ 🏨 **Hyannis Inn Motel.** The second-oldest motel in Hyannis, this mod-
est, two-story motel has been family-owned and -run for the past 45
years. It also has a link to the Kennedys: during JFK's presidential cam-
paign, the main building served as press headquarters. The main building's immaculate rooms, nicely decorated in shades of dark blue and
rose, have double, queen-, or king-size beds, cable TV, and direct-dial
phones; some have whirlpool tubs. The newer deluxe rooms—built in
1981 in a separate wing out back—are larger, sunnier, and quieter (they
don't face Main Street) and offer queen- or king-size beds, sleeper sofas,
walk-in closets, and refrigerators. The restaurant serves breakfast only.
Children under 12 stay free. ⊠ *473 Main St., 02601, ☎ 508/775–0255*
or 800/922–8993, FAX 508/771–0456. 77 rooms. Restaurant, pub, air-
conditioning, indoor pool, sauna. AE, D, MC, V. Closed Dec.–Jan.

$–$$ 🏨 **Inn on Sea Street.** Charming and relaxed, this B&B is just a short
walk from the beach and downtown Hyannis. Guest rooms, in the 1849
main house or the mansard-roof Victorian across the street, have
canopy beds, antique furnishings, and claw-foot tubs. The across-the-
street rooms are generally larger; all have queen-size beds, one has a
private porch, and there's also a common living room and shared
kitchen. Innkeepers Sylvia and Fred LaSelva, who took over the inn in
1999, are gracious and welcoming hosts. Breakfasts are served on
china, silver, and crystal in the antiques-and-lace dining room of the
main house or in the glassed-in sunporch. Out back, a small, charming cottage all in white has its own kitchen. ⊠ *358 Sea St., 02601, ☎*
508/775–8030, FAX 508/771–0878. 9 rooms, 7 with bath; 1 cottage.

Air-conditioning. No smoking. AE, D, MC, V. Closed Nov.–late-Apr. BP.

$–$$ 🖼 **Sea Breeze Inn.** The Irish accent of owner-innkeeper Patricia Gib-
★ ney helps make this cedar-shingle B&B, two blocks from the beach,
even more welcoming. Each room has antique or canopied beds and
is simply decorated with well-chosen antiques. Larger families may want
to stay in one of the three detached cottages; the nicest is the Rose Garden, with three bedrooms (two on the second level), two baths, a TV
room, a fireplace, even a washer and dryer. If that's booked, try the
Honeymoon Cottage, which has a canopy bed and inviting double
Jacuzzi. (The cottage is fenced in for total privacy.) Patricia's breakfasts are worth getting up early for; you can eat in the dining room or
in the outdoor gazebo, surrounded by picture-perfect gardens. ⊠ *270
Ocean Ave., at Sea St., 02601,* ☎ *508/771–7213,* ℻ *508/862–0663.
14 rooms, 3 cottages. Air-conditioning, no-smoking rooms. AE, D, MC,
V. CP.*

$ 🖼 **Capt. Gosnold Village.** An easy walk to the beach and town, this
colony of motel rooms and cottages is ideal for families. Children can
ride their bikes around the quiet street, and the pool is fenced in and
watched by a lifeguard. In some rooms, walls are attractively paneled
with painted pine; floors are carpeted, and furnishings are colonial or
modern, simple, and pleasant. All cottages have decks and gas grills,
and receive maid service (except Sundays). The cottages are divided
into rooms, efficiencies, and 1- to 3-bedroom cottages. ⊠ *230 Gosnold St., 02601,* ☎ *508/775–9111. 18 cottages. Picnic area, pool, basketball. MC, V. Closed Nov.–mid-Apr.*

Nightlife and the Arts

The **Boston Pops Esplanade Orchestra** (☎ 508/362–0066) wows the
crowds with its annual Pops By the Sea concert, held in August at the
Hyannis Village Green. Each year, a guest conductor strikes up the band;
recent baton bouncers have included Olympia Dukakis, Joan Kennedy,
Mike Wallace, and Art Buchwald.

In 1950 the actress Gertrude Lawrence and her husband, producer-
manager Richard Aldrich, opened the **Cape Cod Melody Tent** (⊠ 21
W. Main St., at the West End rotary, ☎ 508/775–9100) to showcase
Broadway musicals and concerts. Today it is the Cape's top venue for
popular music concerts and comedy shows, and the performers who
play here, in the round, include Aretha Franklin, Willie Nelson, Tom
Jones, Ziggy Marley, KC and the Sunshine Band, Anne Murray, and
Tony Bennett. The Tent also hosts a Wednesday-morning children's theater series in July and August.

The 90-member **Cape Symphony Orchestra** (☎ 508/362–1111), under
former D'Oyly Carte Opera conductor Royston Nash, gives regular
classical and children's concerts, with guest artists, October through
May. Performances are held at the Barnstable Performing Arts Center
(⊠ 744 W. Main St., Hyannis).

In July and August, **town band concerts** (☎ 508/362–5230 or 800/449–
6647) are held on Wednesday evenings starting at 7:30 on the Village
Green on Main Street.

Bobby Byrne's Pub (⊠ Rte. 28 at Bearses Way, ☎ 508/775–1425) is
a branch of this local chain; it's comfortable and unpretentious.

Bud's Country Lounge (⊠ Bearses Way and Rte. 132, ☎ 508/771–2505)
has pool tables and provides live country music, dancing, and line-
dancing lessons year-round.

Club 477 (⊠ 477 Yarmouth Rd., ☎ 508/771–7511), in the old Hyannis train station, is the Upper and Mid Cape's only gay club. There's a piano bar on the lower level and a dance bar on the upper floor with music almost as hot as the crowd.

The **Prodigal Son** (⊠ 10 Ocean St., ☎ 508/771–1337) is home to some of the best up-and-coming bands and musicians in New England. The lineup includes acoustic, blues, jazz, rock, and even "spoken word" performers. Their high-octane java keeps the joint jumpin'. Call for schedule.

The **Roadhouse Café** (⊠ 488 South St., ☎ 508/775–2386; ☞ Dining, *above*) has great jazz year-round.

Starbuck's (⊠ 645 Iyanough Rd. (Rte. 132), ☎ 508/778–6767; ☞ Dining, *above*) presents live acoustic entertainment in its bar many nights year-round.

Outdoor Activities and Sports

BASEBALL

The **Hyannis Mets** (☎ 508/420–0962) of the collegiate Cape Cod Baseball League play home games at McKeon Field (⊠ High School Rd.) from mid-June to mid-August.

BEACHES

Kalmus Park Beach, at the south end of Ocean Street, is a fine, wide sandy beach with an area set aside for windsurfers and a sheltered area that's good for children. It has a snack bar, rest rooms, showers, and lifeguards. Parking fee is $8 in season.

Veterans Park, next to the John F. Kennedy Memorial on Ocean Street, has a small beach that is especially good for children; it's sheltered from waves and fairly shallow. There are picnic tables, barbecue facilities, showers, rest rooms, and a playground. Parking fee is $8 in season.

BIKING

Cascade Motor Lodge (⊠ 201 Main St., ☎ 508/775–9717), by the bus and train station, rents bikes.

BOATING

Eastern Mountain Sports (⊠ 1513 Iyanough Rd. (Rte. 132), ☎ 508/362–8690) rents kayaks and camping gear.

Sailing tours aboard the catboat **Eventide** (⊠ Ocean St. Dock, ☎ 508/775–0222) offer a variety of 1½-hour cruises through Hyannis Harbor and out into Nantucket Sound, including a nature tour and a sunset cruise.

Hy-Line (⊠ Ocean St. Dock, ☎ 508/778–2600) offers cruises on replicas of old-time Maine coastal steamers. The one-hour tours of Hyannis Harbor and Lewis Bay include a view of the Kennedy compound and other points of interest.

FISHING

Fishing trips are operated on a walk-on basis in spring and fall by **Hy-Line** (⊠ Ocean St. Dock, ☎ 508/790–0696). Reservations are mandatory during the summer season.

GOLF

Sheraton Hyannis Resort (⊠ West End rotary, ☎ 508/775–7775) has a beautifully landscaped, challenging 18-hole, par-3 course open to nonguests. You may bump into some famous faces: many performers from the Cape Cod Melody Tent tee off here while in town.

Barnstable Athletic Club (⊠ 55 Attucks La., Independence Park, off Rte. 132, ☎ 508/771–7734) has four racquetball-wallyball courts (wallyball is volleyball played on a racquetball court), a squash court, basketball, an aerobics room, whirlpools, sauna and steam rooms, and cardiovascular and free-weight equipment. Day care and day and short-term memberships are available.

Hyannis Athletic Club (⊠ Sheraton Hyannis Resort, West End rotary, ☎ 508/775–7775) has two outdoor tennis courts, a fitness club, and indoor and outdoor pools. Day and short-term memberships are available.

ICE-SKATING

The **Kennedy Memorial Skating Rink** (⊠ Bassett La., ☎ 508/790–6345) offers skating October through March; you can rent skates there.

MINIATURE GOLF

Cape Cod Storyland Golf is a 2-acre miniature golf course set up as a mini–Cape Cod, with each of the 18 holes a Cape town. The course winds around small ponds and waterfalls, a full-size working gristmill, and reproductions of historic Cape buildings. The picture possibilities are great. There's a $4.50 additional charge for the bumper boats. ⊠ *70 Center St., by the railroad depot,* ☎ *508/778–4339.* 🖅 *$6.* ☉ *Mid-Apr.–Oct., daily 8 AM–midnight.*

Shopping

Cape Cod Mall (⊠ Between Rtes. 132 and 28, ☎ 508/771–0200), already the Cape's largest, completed a major expansion in 1999. It now has 120 shops, including department stores from Macy's to Marshall's, and a 12-screen movie complex.

A mix of Disneyesque fantasy and Victorian excess, the Hyannis branch of the **Christmas Tree Shops** (⊠ 655 Iyanough Rd. [Rte. 132], ☎ 508/778–5521) is the largest on the Cape. Many people come just to gawk at the glass-enclosed clock out front, made in the '20s and imported from Cincinnati.

Colonial Candle of Cape Cod (⊠ 388 Main St., ☎ 508/771–2790 or 508/771–3916) has its touristy elements, but the candles are top-notch.

Hyannis Antique Co-op (⊠ 500 Main St., ☎ 508/778–0512) has a large selection of jewelry, glassware, porcelain, furniture, dolls, prints, and collectibles at good prices.

Nantucket Trading Company (⊠ 354 Main St., ☎ 508/790–3933) sells an incredible array of neat necessities for your home, including edibles, table linens, cooking gadgets, and kitchen accessories.

The handsome flagship **Puritan** (⊠ 408 Main St., ☎ 508/771–3277) store carries upscale clothing brands from the North Face to Eileen Fisher and Ralph Lauren and also sells outdoor gear. Service is great here; there are five other stores around the Cape.

If you're tired of wearing T-shirts and beach cover-ups, duck into **12 West** (⊠ 558 Main St., ☎ 508/771–7000) for casually upscale women's clothing and accessories.

Yarmouth Port

⑰ *4 mi northeast of Hyannis, 21 mi east of the Sagamore Bridge, 4 mi east of Barnstable.*

Once known as Mattacheese, or "the planting lands," Yarmouth was settled in 1639 by farmers from the Plymouth Bay Colony. Yarmouth Port wasn't incorporated as a separate village until 1829. By then the Cape had begun a thriving maritime industry, and men turned to the sea to make their fortunes. Many impressive sea captains' houses—some now B&Bs and museums—still line the streets, and Yarmouth Port has some real old-time stores in town.

★ For a peek into the past, make a stop at **Hallet's,** a country drugstore preserved as it was in 1889, when the current owner's grandfather, Thacher Hallet, opened it. Hallet served not only as druggist but as postmaster and justice of the peace as well. At the all-marble soda fountain with swivel stools, you can order the secret-recipe ice cream soda as well as an inexpensive lunch. Above Hallet's Store, the **Thacher Taylor Hallet Museum** displays photographs and memorabilia of Yarmouth Port and the Hallet family. ⊠ *139 Main St. (Rte. 6A),* ☎ *508/362–3362.* ⊠ *Donations accepted for museum.* ☉ *Apr.–mid-Nov.; call for hrs.*

The 1886 **Village Pump,** a black wrought-iron mechanism long used for drawing household water, is topped by a lantern and surrounded by ironwork with cutouts of birds and animals. In front is a stone trough that was used for watering horses. It's across from the Parnassus Book Service (⊠ 220 Main St.). The 1696 **Old Yarmouth Inn** (⊠ Main St., near Summer St.), near the village pump, is the Cape's oldest inn and a onetime stagecoach stop.

The **Botanical Trails of the Historical Society of Old Yarmouth,** right behind the post office (⊠ 231 Main St.), provide a good look at the area's flora in 50 acres of oak and pine woods and a pond, accented by blueberries, lady's slippers, Indian pipes, rhododendrons, hollies, and more. Stone markers and arrows point out the 2 mi of trails; you'll find trail maps in the gatehouse mailbox. Just beyond the historical society's trails, the little **Kelley Chapel** was built in 1873 by a father for a daughter grieving over the death of a child. The simple interior is dominated by an iron woodstove and a pump organ. ⊠ *Off Main St. (Rte. 6A).* ⊠ *$1 suggested donation.* ☉ *Gatehouse July–Aug., daily 1–4. Trails during daylight hrs year-round.*

The 1780 **Winslow Crocker House** is an elegantly symmetrical two-story Georgian with 12-over-12 small-pane windows and rich paneling in every room. After Crocker's death, his two sons built a wall dividing the house in half. The house was moved here from West Barnstable in 1936 by Mary Thacher, who donated it—along with her collection of 17th- to 19th-century furniture, pewter, hooked rugs, and ceramics—to the Society for the Preservation of New England Antiquities, which operates it as a museum. Tours are given every hour on the hour. ⊠ *250 Main St. (Rte. 6A),* ☎ *508/362–4385.* ⊠ *$4.* ☉ *June–mid–Oct., weekends 11–4.*

Built in 1840 onto an existing 1740 house for a sea captain in the China trade, then bought by another, who swapped it with a third captain, the **Captain Bangs Hallet House** is a white Greek Revival building with a hitching post out front and a weeping beech in back. The house and its contents typify a 19th-century sea captain's home, with pieces of pewter, china, nautical equipment, antique toys and clothing, and more on display. The kitchen has the original 1740 brick beehive oven and butter churns. ⊠ *11 Strawberry La., off Rte. 6A,* ☎ *508/362–3021.* ⊠ *$3.* ☉ *June–Oct., Sun. 1–3:30; tours at 1, 2, and 3.*

Purchased in 1640 and established as a prosperous farm in the late 1700s, the **Taylor-Bray Farm** (⊠ Bray Farm Rd., ☎ 508/385–6499) is still a working farm, listed on the National Register of Historic Places. The farm is open to the public by making an appointment with the tenants; it has picnic tables, walking trails, and a great view of the tidal marsh.

For a scenic loop with little traffic, turn north off Route 6A in town onto Church Street or Thacher Street, then left onto Thacher Shore Road. In fall this route is especially beautiful, with its impressive stands of blazing red burning bush. Wooded segments alternate with open views of marsh. Keep bearing right, and at the WATER STREET sign, the dirt road on the right will bring you to a wide-open view of marshland as it meets the bay. Don't drive in too far, or you may get stuck. As you **❶⑧** come out, a right turn will take you to **Keveney Bridge,** a one-lane wooden bridge over marshy Hallet's Mill Pond, and back to Route 6A.

★ ⑲ One of Yarmouth Port's most beautiful spots is Bass Hole, which stretches from Homer's Dock Road to the salt marsh. **Bass Hole Boardwalk** (✉ Trail entrance on Center St. near the Gray's Beach parking lot) extends over a marshy creek; amid the salt marshes, vegetated wetlands, and upland woods meander the 2½-mi **Callery-Darling nature trails.** Gray's Beach is a little crescent of sand with still water good for children. At the end of the boardwalk, benches provide a place to relax and look out over abundant marsh life and, across the creek, the beautiful, sandy shores of Dennis's Chapin Beach. At low tide you can walk out on the flats for almost a mile. It's a far cry from the days when an 18th-century harbor here was the site of a schooner shipyard.

Dining and Lodging

$$$ ✕ **Abbicci.** Unassuming to a fault from the outside, Abbicci tells an entirely different story on the inside, with stunning modern decor, explosions of color, and a handsome black slate bar. One of the first to bring northern Italian cooking to Cape Cod, chef-owner Marietta Hickey has remained true to the tradition and ahead of the crowd. She prepares rich and full-tasting yet heart-healthy fare, thanks to a light touch with olive oil and a watchful eye over the fat content of her dishes. One of the most pleasing is braised rabbit with fresh green beans and tiny onions over garlic mashed potatoes. In summer, fish and a dozen elegant pasta dishes take over. ✉ *43 Main St. (Rte. 6A),* ☎ *508/362–3501. AE, D, DC, MC, V.*

$$–$$$ ✕ **Aardvark Cafe.** This pretty place has gingerbread running down the roof and cream, mauve, and teal paint. The kitchen has steadily built a reputation for very fine, well-presented meals, and the dinners add a strong Vietnamese and Thai influence to the regular fish, steaks, and chicken. *Pho,* for example, is a Vietnamese dinner soup with shredded sirloin, rice noodles, scallions, and cilantro in a delicate, aromatic broth. Continental breakfast is served with gourmet coffees and a wide pastry selection. A pretty outdoor patio holds three tables, but the highway is too close, so go inside the cozy, converted old home. ✉ *134 Main St. (Rte. 6A),* ☎ *508/362–9866. Reservations essential. AE, D, MC, V. Closed Mon. No lunch Sun., no dinner Tues.*

$$–$$$ ✕ **Inaho.** Yuji Watanabe, the chef-owner of the Cape's best Japanese **★** restaurant, makes early morning journeys to Boston's fish markets to shop for the freshest local catch. His selection of sushi and sashimi is vast and artful, and vegetable and seafood tempura come out of the kitchen fluffy and light. If you're a teriyaki lover, you can't do any better than the chicken's beautiful blend of sweet and sour. One remarkable element of the restaurant is its artful lighting: small pinpoint lights on the food accentuate the presentation in a dramatic way. The serene and simple Japanese garden out back has a traditional goldfish pond. ⊠ *157 Main St. (Rte. 6A),* ☎ *508/362–5522. MC, V. Closed Mon. No lunch.*

$–$$ ✕ **Jack's Outback.** Tough to find, tough to forget, this eccentric little
★   serve-yourself-pretty-much-anything-you-want joint is right down the
driveway by Inaho (☞ *above*) and goes by the motto "Good food, lousy
service." The quintessential local hangout, it lives up to its motto in
every way. Solid breakfasts give way by midday to thick burgers,
freshly concocted sandwiches, pasta salads, homemade soups, and
then traditional home-cooked favorites like Yankee pot roast and fried
chicken. The owner, Jack Braginton Smith, is a local historian of note.
(As far as locals are concerned, if he doesn't insult you on the way in
and out, you've been insulted.) Jack's has no liquor license, and you
may not BYOB. ⊠ *161 Main St. (Rte. 6A),* ☎ *508/362–6690. Reservations not accepted. No credit cards. No dinner Sun.–Mon.*

$$–$$$ ▦ **Blueberry Manor.** Owners Jerry Rosen and Victoria Schuh, who
moved from a Brooklyn loft to this quiet, early 19th-century Greek Revival, have completely restored their new home to create a wonderfully sophisticated yet homey B&B. The living room pairs Victorian
furnishings and a marble fireplace with modern amenities, including
a TV/VCR, a stereo, and a stash of puzzles, games, and books. Upstairs, the guest rooms feel crisp and clean; although the furnishings
are traditional, there are no fussy lace treatments or curio shelves. The
Lavender Room has a queen-size four-poster bed with a handmade quilt,
an antique armoire, and a modern bath under the eaves with a skylight. Across the hall, the Rose Room has an exquisitely painted queen
bed and cheery pink walls. The fruit from the blueberry bushes in the
lush backyard and garden turns up at breakfast in homemade coffee
cakes and other baked goods. ⊠ *438 Main St. (Rte. 6A), 02675,* ☎
508/362–7620, ℻ *508/362–0053. 3 rooms. Air-conditioning. No
smoking. No credit cards. BP.*

$$–$$$ ▦ **The Inn at Cape Cod.** A stately white Greek Revival building with
imposing columns, the inn sits back from Route 6A in a parklike lawn
adjacent to the Botanical Trails (☞ *above*). The interior is eclectic. On
the first floor, the large Joshua Sears Room with a mahogany king four-poster bed, Oriental rug, and antique furnishings is a traditional Victorian chamber, while the Far East Room—iron-and-wicker bed,
Chinese curio chest, and wicker wing chairs—would feel at home in
Beijing's Forbidden City. Upstairs, the romantic Village Suite with its
Italian armoire and cherry writing desk opens to the front porch, and
the frilly Victorian Room has its own fireplace. Some smaller rooms,
particularly the basic pine Guest Room, are pint-size. Innkeepers Doug
and Mary Heywood, who serve a hearty buffet breakfast, bought the
inn in 1999 and have embarked on renovations, with two new rooms
in the works for 2000. ⊠ *4 Summer St., 02675,* ☎ *508/375–0590 or
800/850–7301,* ℻ *508/362–9520. 7 rooms, 1 suite. Air-conditioning.
No smoking. AE, MC, V. BP.*

$$–$$$ ▦ **Wedgewood Inn.** This handsome Greek Revival building, white with
★   black shutters and a fanlight, is on the National Register of Historic
Places and dates from 1812. The interior is sophisticated but welcoming,
with a mix of fine colonial antiques, upholstered wing chairs, sporting prints, and maritime paintings. In the guest rooms, antique quilts
top handcrafted cherry pencil-post beds. Two spacious suites in the main
building have canopy beds, fireplaces, and porches; one has a separate
sitting room. Three additional suites, built in the restored barn behind
the house, have king-size beds, TV, and large bathrooms. Innkeeper
Gerrie Graham cooks elegant breakfasts such as Belgian waffles with
whipped cream and strawberries, or egg dishes with hollandaise. Milt,
her husband, a former Boston Patriot (before the football team was
renamed the New England Patriots) and FBI agent, serves breakfast

and helps guests make plans for the day. ⊠ *83 Main St. (Rte. 6A), 02675,* ☎ *508/362–5157 or 508/362–9178,* ﬀ *508/362–5851. 4 rooms, 5 suites. Air-conditioning. No smoking. AE, DC, MC, V. BP.*

$$ 🏠 **Lane's End Cottage.** Indeed, owner-innkeeper Valerie Butler's house sits at the end of a dirt lane, moved here in 1860 by oxen to make room for the neighboring church. And what a magical setting it is: a white picket fence, an English cottage garden, an English antiques–filled common room–library with a fireplace. Each guest room has tasteful appointments and beds with firm mattresses, feather comforters, and white spreads. The sun-drenched first-floor Terrace Room has a fireplace and French doors that lead to a cobblestone patio overlooking a flower-rimmed garden. Pets are allowed (only in the off-season) with prior notice. ⊠ *268 Main St. (Rte. 6A), 02675,* ☎ *508/362–5298. 3 rooms. Library. No smoking. No credit cards. BP.*

$–$$ 🏠 **Village Inn.** Many of the guests who stay here will say it's just like staying at your grandmother's—provided, of course, your grandmother has the kind of clean, snug rooms found in Esther Hickey's 1795 sea captain's house. It's old-fashioned—some might say faded—but the rooms with their wide pine floorboards are lessons in history. The Provincetown Room, for instance, served as the house's schoolroom; the original (now unused) light fixtures are still in place. Room sizes and amenities fluctuate; avoid the Wellfleet Room, which has a half-size tub and is about as big as the oyster that bears its name. Families should note that the Brewster, Truro, and Hyannis rooms connect and that the first-floor Yarmouth Room is the most spacious, with its own library, bathroom with fireplace, and private entrance. The common rooms have as many books as some public libraries. ⊠ *92 Main St. (Rte. 6A), Box 1, 02675,* ☎ *508/362–3182. 10 rooms. No smoking. MC, V. BP.*

Nightlife and the Arts

Oliver's Restaurant (⊠ 6 Bray Farm Rd., off Rte. 6A, ☎ 508/362–6062) has live acoustic music in its tavern weekends year-round.

Shopping

Cummaquid Fine Arts (⊠ 4275 Rte. 6A, Cummaquid, ☎ 508/362–2593) has works by contemporary resident Cape Cod artists, beautifully displayed in an old home.

Parnassus Book Service (⊠ 220 Main St. [Rte. 6A], ☎ 508/362–6420), occupying a three-story 1840 former general store, has a huge selection of old and new books—Cape Cod, maritime, Americana, antiquarian, and others—and is a great place to browse. (The book stall on the shop's side is open 24 hours a day and works on the honor system; tally up your purchases and leave the money in the mail slot.) Parnassus also carries Robert Bateman's nature prints.

Peach Tree Designs (⊠ 173 Main St. [Rte. 6A], ☎ 508/362–8317) carries home furnishings and decorative accessories, some from local craftspeople, all beautifully made.

Pewter Crafters of Cape Cod (⊠ 933 Main St. [Rte. 6A], ☎ 508/362–3407) handcrafts traditional and contemporary pewter objects, from baby cups to tea services.

West Yarmouth

㉕ *4 mi south of Yarmouth Port, 3 mi east of Hyannis.*

There's no getting around it: the part of the Cape people love to hate is Route 28. Passing through the area, it's one motel, strip mall, nightclub, and miniature golf course after another. In 1989, as *Cape Cod*

Life magazine put it, "the town [began] to plant 350 trees in hopes that eventually the trees' leaves, like the fig leaf of Biblical lore, cover the shame of unkempt overdevelopment." Regardless of the glut of tacky tourist traps, there are some interesting sights in the little villages along the way. So take Route 28 if you want to intersperse amusements with your sightseeing, because you could amuse yourself to no end on this section of 28. A sensible option if you want to avoid it entirely: take speedy U.S. 6 to the exit nearest what you want to visit, and then cut south across the interior.

The village of West Yarmouth was settled in 1643 by Yelverton Crowe, who acquired his land from a Native American sachem who told him he could have as much land as he could walk on in an hour in exchange for an "ox-chain, a copper kettle . . . and a few trinkets." The first settlers were farmers; in the 1830s, when Central Wharf near Mill Creek was built, the town turned to more commercial ventures as headquarters for the growing packet service that ferried passengers from the Cape to Boston.

Listed on the National Register of Historic Places, the 1710 **Baxter Grist Mill,** by the shore of Mill Pond, is the only mill on Cape Cod that is powered by an inside water turbine; the others use either wind or paddle wheels. The mill was converted to the indoor metal turbine in 1860 because of the pond's low water level and the damage done to the wooden paddle wheel by winter freezes. The original metal turbine is displayed on the grounds, and a replica powers the restored mill. A videotape tells the mill's history. ✉ *Rte. 28,* ☎ *508/398–2231 ext. 292.* 🎟 *Free.* ☽ *Early June–Labor Day, weekends 1–5; also open Mon. or Fri. 1–5 on some holiday weekends.*

㉑ A unique and lovely walking trail, the **Yarmouth Boardwalk** (✉ Off Meadowbrook La.) stretches through swamp and marsh and leads to the edge of Swan Pond, a pretty pond ringed with woods. To get here, take Winslow Gray Road northeast from Route 28, turn right on Meadowbrook Lane, and take it to the end.

☾ An entertaining and educational stop for kids, **ZooQuarium** has sealion shows, a petting zoo with native wildlife, wandering peacocks, pony rides in summer, aquariums, and educational programs. The Children's Discovery Center presents changing exhibits such as "Bone Up on Bones" (all about skeletons), "Zoo Nutrition" (in which kids prepare meals), and the self-explanatory "Scoop on Poop." ✉ *674 Main St. (Rte. 28),* ☎ *508/775–8883.* 🎟 *$8.* ☽ *Mid-Feb.–June and Sept.–late Nov., daily 9:30–5; July–Aug., daily 9:30–6.*

NEED A BREAK?   **Jerry's Seafood and Dairy Freeze** (✉ 654 Main St. [Rte. 28], ☎ 508/775–9752) offers fried clams and onion rings, along with thick frappes, frozen yogurt, and soft ice cream, at good prices.

Lodging

$–$$ 🏨 **Inn at Lewis Bay.** This lovely 1920s Dutch Colonial overlooks Lewis Bay and is steps away from the beach. Enjoy, but be back by 4 PM, when innkeeper Liz Latshaw serves tea and home-baked cookies. Each room is furnished in country-antiques style, with Laura Ashley linens, fresh flowers, claw-foot tubs, and antique or canopy beds. The rooms also have a name and a theme, such as Secret Garden (ivy-print linens and wallpaper) and Sea Grass. Whalewatch, with its distinctive navys and maroons, is the one decidedly masculine room, and one of two with water views. Bountiful breakfasts are served in the candlelighted dining room, where the hand-stenciled strawberries on the ceiling match the wallpaper. ✉ *57 Maine Ave., 02673,* ☎ *508/771–3433 or 800/962–6679,* FAX *508/790–1186. 6 rooms. Beach. No smoking. AE, MC, V. BP.*

$ 🏨 **Americana Holiday Motel.** If you want the convenience of staying
★ on Route 28, this family-owned and -operated strip motel is a good
choice. All rooms have cable TV and a phone; those in the rear Pine
Grove section overlook serene sea pines and one of the motel's three
pools rather than traffic snarls. In the off-season, the rates simply
can't be beat. ✉ *99 Main St. (Rte. 28), 02673,* ☎ *508/775–5511 or*
800/445–4497, FAX *508/790–0597. 149 rooms, 4 suites. Coffee shop,*
air-conditioning, refrigerators, 1 indoor and 2 outdoor pools, hot tub,
sauna, putting green, shuffleboard, video games, playground. AE, D,
DC, MC, V. Closed Nov.–Mar. CP.

Nightlife and the Arts
Cape Cod Irish Village (✉ 512 Main St. [Rte. 28], ☎ 508/771–0100)
has dancing to two- or three-piece bands performing traditional and
popular Irish music year-round. The crowd is mostly couples and over-
35ers.

Clancy's (✉ 175 Main St. [Rte. 28], ☎ 508/775–3332) offers live entertainment, typically a mix of Irish, folk, and soft rock performed by
acoustic guitarist and vocalist Terry Brennan, on weekends year-round.

West Yarmouth's summertime **town band concerts** are held on Monday in July and August at 7 PM at Mattacheese Middle School (✉ Off
Higgins Crowell Rd., ☎ 508/778–1008).

Outdoor Activities and Sports
BIKE RENTAL
All Right Bike & Mower (✉ 627 Main St. [Rte. 28], ☎ 508/790–3191)
rents bikes and mopeds and does on-site repairs.

FISHING
Truman's (✉ 608 Main St. [Rte. 28], ☎ 508/771–3470) can supply
you with a required freshwater license and rental gear.

Shopping
The **Cranberry Bog Outlet Stores** (✉ Rte. 28, ☎ no phone) are on the
edge of a working cranberry bog. Bass, Van Heusen, and Izod are a
few of the shops here.

South Yarmouth

㉒ *3 mi east of West Yarmouth, 6 mi east of Hyannis.*

The Bass River divides the southern portions of the towns of Yarmouth
and Dennis. People also generally refer to the area of South Yarmouth
as Bass River. Here you'll find charter boats and boat rentals, as well
as a river cruise, plus seafood restaurants and markets. Like West
Yarmouth, the town has its stretch of blight and overdevelopment on
Route 28, but it also has some nice beaches that are good for families.

South Yarmouth was once called Quaker Village for the large numbers of Quakers who settled the area in the 1770s after a smallpox epidemic wiped out the local Native American population.

The 1809 **Quaker Meeting House** is still open for meetings. Two separate entrance doors and the partition down the center were meant to divide the sexes. The adjacent cemetery has simple markers with no
epitaphs, an expression of the Friends' belief that all are equal in God's
eyes. Behind the cemetery is a circa 1830 one-room Quaker schoolhouse.
✉ *58 N. Main St.,* ☎ *508/398–3773.* ☽ *Services Sun. at 10 AM.*

🕭 **Pirate's Cove** is the most elaborate of the Cape's many miniature golf setups, with a hill, a waterfall, a stream, and an 18-hole "Blackbeard's Challenge" course. ⊠ *728 Main St. (Rte. 28),* ☎ *508/394–6200.* ⊠ *$6.50.* 🕙 *July–Aug., daily 9 AM–11 PM; Apr.–June and Sept.–Oct., most days 10–8, but call.*

🕭 For rainy-day fun, the **Ryan Family Amusement Center** offers video-game rooms, Skee-ball, and bowling. ⊠ *1067 Main St. (Rte. 28),* ☎ *508/394–5644.* 🕙 *Daily; hrs vary.*

Lodging

$$$ 🏨 **Ocean Mist.** This three-story, upscale, motel-style resort sits on its own private sandy beach on Nantucket Sound. The rooms are designed to cover the bases: all have modern furnishings, cable TV, and either wet bars or fully stocked kitchenettes. The duplex loft suites are a step above, with cathedral ceilings, a sitting area with pull-out sofa, skylights, and one or two private balconies. ⊠ *97 S. Shore Dr., 02664,* ☎ *508/398–2633 or 800/248–6478,* FAX *508/760–3151. 32 rooms, 32 suites. Coffee shop, air-conditioning, indoor pool, hot tub, beach, coin laundry. AE, D, MC, V. Closed Dec. (except for the Christmas holidays)–mid-Feb.*

$$–$$$ 🏨 **Capt. Farris House.** Steps from the Bass River Bridge dividing South Yarmouth and West Dennis and a short spin away from congested Route 28 sits this imposing 1845 Greek Revival home, built by the sea captain for whom it's named. The rooms and suites—large and comfortable, despite their borderline excessiveness—have either antique or canopied queen- or king-size beds, extra pillows, plush comforters, fancy drapes, TVs, and tiled baths (all but one with a whirlpool tub). Some have fireplaces and sundecks, and the Honeymoon Suite has a private sundeck and a two-person whirlpool tub. Breakfast is served in the formal dining room or in the open, interior brick courtyard. Fresh baked goods and sherry are available for later-in-the-day nourishment. ⊠ *308 Old Main St., 02664,* ☎ *508/760–2818 or 800/350–9477,* FAX *508/398–1262. 6 rooms, 4 suites. Air-conditioning. No smoking. AE, MC, V. BP.*

$$ 🏨 **Belvedere B&B.** Elisha Baker, a local sea captain, built this quaint Federal home around 1820. The Hamilton Room is the most spacious, with some frilly touches: lace curtains, a lacy bedspread, green floral wallpaper, and old pink velvet chairs. Romantics may prefer the first-floor Boston Room, with green wicker chairs, a two-person whirlpool tub, and a queen-size bed topped with a rose quilt. The Virginia Anthony Room (with pink-and-white quilts on the twin four-poster beds) and the Florilla Room (with a queen bed, white wicker furnishings, and a pink wide-board floor) are both small but cozy and sunny; they share a bath across the hall. Breakfast, which may include sour cream cranberry bread or fresh eggs from the neighbors' chickens, is served in the formal dining room or on the screened-in porch. ⊠ *167 Old Main St., 02664,* ☎ *508/398–2533,* FAX *508/398–2523. 4 rooms, 2 with bath. No smoking. AE, D, MC, V. BP.*

$$ 🏨 **Seaside.** Right on a warm Nantucket Sound beach, this 5-acre village of Cape-style cottages (studios and one- or two-bedroom units) has a view of scalloped beaches in both directions. Seaside was built in the 1940s, and the decor varies from cottage to cottage, as each is individually owned. All have kitchens or kitchenettes, and many have wood-burning fireplaces. The oceanfront cottages, right off a strip of grass set with lounge and Adirondack chairs, have the best view and decor. Cottages in the adjacent pine grove are generally very pleasant, though the least expensive units, with knotty-pine walls and ceilings, have an outdated '50s look. Shoulder-season rates are very attractive. ⊠ *135*

S. Shore Dr., 02664, ☎ 508/398–2533, FAX 508/398–2523. 45 cottages. Kitchenettes, picnic area, beach. MC, V. Closed mid-Oct.–Apr.

Nightlife and the Arts

Betsy's Ballroom (✉ 528 Forest Rd., ☎ 508/362–9538) has Saturday-night ballroom dancing year-round to bands on the Cape's largest dance floor.

Outdoor Activities and Sports

BASEBALL

The **Yarmouth-Dennis Red Sox** (☎ 508/394–9466) of the collegiate Cape Cod Baseball League play home games at Red Wilson Field (✉ Station Ave.) from mid-June to mid-August.

BEACHES

Flax Pond (✉ N. Main St., between High Bank and Great Western Rds.) recreation area offers freshwater swimming, a lifeguard, and ducks, but no sand beach, just pine-needle-covered ground. There's a pine-shaded picnic area with grills, as well as tennis and basketball courts, and plenty of parking.

Parker's River Beach (✉ S. Shore Dr.), a flat stretch of sand on warm Nantucket Sound, is perfect for families. It has a lifeguard, a concession stand, a gazebo and picnic area, a playground, outdoor showers, and rest rooms. There's an $8 parking fee in season.

BIKE RENTAL

Outdoor Shop (✉ 50 Long Pond Dr., ☎ 508/394–3819) rents bikes and mopeds and does repairs.

GOLF

Blue Rock Golf Course (✉ Off Great Western Rd., ☎ 508/398–9295) is a highly regarded, easy-to-walk, 18-hole, par-3, 3,000-yard public course crossed by a pond. The pro shop rents clubs; reservations are mandatory in season.

HEALTH AND FITNESS CLUBS

Mid Cape Racquet Club (✉ 193 White's Path, ☎ 508/394–3511) has one racquetball, one squash, and nine indoor tennis courts; indoor basketball; a sauna, steam room, and whirlpools; massage services; and a free-weight and cardiovascular room—plus day care. It also offers spinning, kick boxing, and body pump classes. Daily rates are available.

Dennis

㉓ *4½ mi north of South Yarmouth, 4 mi east of Yarmouth Port, 5 mi north of Dennisport.*

The backstreets of Dennis still retain the colonial charm of seafaring days. The town was named for the Reverend Josiah Dennis and incorporated in 1793. There were 379 sea captains living in Dennis when fishing, salt making, and shipbuilding were the main industries, and the elegant houses that they constructed—now museums and B&Bs–still line the streets. In 1816 Dennis resident Henry Hall discovered that adding sand to his cranberry fields' soil improved the quality and quantity of the fruit. The decades soon after that saw cranberry farming and tourism become the Cape's main commercial enterprises. The town has a number of conservation areas and nature trails (take a look at the Dennis Chamber of Commerce guide), and numerous ponds for swimming.

West Dennis and Dennisport, off Route 28 on the south shore of the Cape, are covered separately below.

The **Josiah Dennis Manse,** a saltbox house with add-ons, was built in 1736 for Reverend Josiah Dennis. Inside, the rooms reflect life in Reverend Dennis's day. One room is set up as a child's room, with antique furniture and toys. The keeping room has a fireplace and cooking utensils, and the attic exhibits spinning and weaving equipment. Throughout you'll see china, pewter, and portraits of sea captains. The Maritime Wing has ship models, paintings, nautical artifacts, and more. On the grounds is a 1770 one-room schoolhouse, furnished with wood-and-wrought-iron desks and chairs. ⊠ *77 Nobscussett Rd., at Whig St.,* ☎ *508/385–2232.* ☒ *Donations accepted.* ☉ *July–Sept., Tues. 10–noon, Thurs. 2–4.*

㉔ On a clear day, from the top of **Scargo Tower** you'll have unbeatable panoramic views of Scargo Lake, the village's scattered houses below, Cape Cod Bay, and distant Provincetown. Winding stairs bring you to the top of the all-stone, 30-ft tower, which was rebuilt in 1890 after a fire destroyed the original wooden structure. (Don't forget to read the unsightly, but amusing, graffiti on the way up.) Expect crowds at sunrise and sunset. ⊠ *Scargo Hill Rd., off Rte. 6A or Old Bass River Rd.* ☒ *Free.* ☉ *Daily sunrise–sunset.*

NEED A BREAK? | If you're in the mood for something cold and sweet, sample the home-made ice cream and frozen yogurt at the **Ice Cream Smuggler** (⊠ 716 Main St. [Rte. 6A], near the Dennis Public Market, ☎ 508/385–5307).

★ ☺ ㉕ For Broadway-style dramas, comedies, and musicals, as well as children's plays, you can attend a production at the **Cape Playhouse,** the oldest professional summer theater in the country. In 1927 Raymond Moore, who had been working with a theatrical troupe in Provincetown, bought an 1838 former Unitarian Meeting House and converted it into a theater. The original pews still serve as seats. The opening performance was *The Guardsman,* starring Basil Rathbone; other stars who performed here in the early days, some in their professional stage debuts, include Bette Davis (who first worked here as an usher), Gregory Peck, Lana Turner, Ginger Rogers, Humphrey Bogart, Tallulah Bankhead, and Henry Fonda, who appeared with his then-unknown 20-year-old daughter, Jane. Cape resident Shirley Booth was such an admirer of the theater she donated her Oscar (for *Come Back Little Sheba*) and her Emmy (for *Hazel*) to the theater; both are on display in the lobby during the season. Behind-the-scene tours are also given in season; call for a schedule. The Playhouse offers children's theater on Friday mornings during July and August. Also on the 26-acre property, now known as the Cape Playhouse Center for the Arts, are a restaurant, the **Cape Museum of Fine Arts** (☞ *below*), and the **Cape Cinema,** whose exterior was designed in the style of the Congregational Church in Centerville. Inside, a 6,400-square-ft heavenly skies mural, designed by Massachusetts artist Rockwell Kent, who also designed the gold sunburst curtain, covers the ceiling. ⊠ *820 Main St. (Rte. 6A),* ☎ *508/385–3911 or 877/385–3911.* ☉ *Call for tour schedule.*

The **Cape Museum of Fine Arts** exhibits a permanent collection of more than 850 works by Cape-associated artists. Important pieces include a portrait of a fisherman's wife by Charles Hawthorne, the father of the Provincetown art colony; a 1924 portrait of a Portuguese fisherman's daughter by William Paxton, one of the first artists to summer in Provincetown; a collection of wood-block prints by Varujan Boghosian, a member of Provincetown's Long Point Gallery cooperative; an oil sketch by Karl Knaths, who painted in Provincetown from 1919 until his death in 1971; and works by abstract expressionist Hans Hoffman and many of his students. The museum also hosts film festivals, lectures, art classes, and trips. A major expansion was beginning in late 1999, with new gallery space scheduled to open in summer 2000; call to check hours and status before visiting. ✉ *60 Hope La. (on the grounds of the Cape Playhouse), off Rte. 6A,* ☎ *508/385–4477.* 📷 *$5.* ⊘ *Late May–Nov., Mon.–Sat. 10–5, Sun. 1–5; Dec.–mid-May, Tues.–Sat. 10–5, Sun. 1–5.*

Dining and Lodging

$$$ ✕ **Red Pheasant Inn.** This is one of the Cape's best cozy country inns, with a consistently good kitchen; the hearty American food is prepared with elaborate sauces and herb combinations. For instance, rack of lamb is served with an intense port and rosemary reduction, and exquisitely grilled veal chops come with a dense red wine and Portobello mushroom sauce. Deep-fried goat cheese ravioli is another winner. Try to reserve a table in the more intimate Garden Room. The expansive wine list is excellent. Men may want to wear a jacket. ✉ *905 Main St. (Rte. 6A),* ☎ *508/385–2133. D, MC, V. No lunch.*

$$ ✕ **Gina's by the Sea.** Some places are less than the sum of their parts;
★ Gina's is more. The funky old building is tucked into a sand dune, so that the aroma of fine northern Italian cooking blends with a fresh breeze off the bay. The dining room is tasteful, cozy, and especially wonderful in the fall when the fireplace is blazing. Blackboard specials could include angel-hair pastas or linguine with clams. If you don't want a long wait, come early or late. ✉ *134 Taunton Ave.,* ☎ *508/385–3213. Reservations not accepted. AE, MC, V. Closed Dec.–Mar. and Mon–Wed. Oct.–Nov. No lunch Apr.–June and Sept.–Nov.*

$$ ✕ **Scargo Café.** Because the Cape Playhouse is right across the street, this café is a favorite before- and after-show haunt. Excellent early-bird specials for the show crowd include scallops cooked in Harpoon beer (a Boston brew) and fettuccine Alfredo. The menu focuses on lighter fare for summer, but there's still plenty of richness, and a rather good wine cellar to complement it. Mussels Ferdinand features farm-raised mussels with a buttery Pernod sauce over pasta. An added plus: the kitchen stays open until midnight in summer. ✉ *799 Main St. (Rte. 6A),* ☎ *508/385–8200. AE, D, MC, V.*

$ ✕ **Cap'n Frosty's.** This locally much-acclaimed though very modest fried seafood and ice cream joint has a regular menu, a small specials board, and a counter where you order and take a number written on a french-fries box. The staff is young and hard working, pumping out fresh fried clams and fish-and-chips on paper plates. All frying is done in 100% canola oil, and rice pilaf is offered as a substitute for fries. There's seating inside and outside on a shady brick patio. ✉ *219 Main St. (Rte. 6A),* ☎ *508/385–8548. Reservations not accepted. No credit cards. Closed Oct.–Mar.*

$ ✕ **Red Cottage Restaurant.** Up Old Bass River Road just a half mile north of the town hall, the Red Cottage is indeed a red cottage that serves breakfast and lunch year-round. This friendly place has a long counter with swiveling stools, and the grill is in plain view. Breakfasts actually rate higher than lunches, but both are no-nonsense and just plain reliably good. The menu has something of an emphasis on "health," meaning egg-white omelets are available alongside the usuals, and "lite" cheese is used. ✉ *36 Old Bass River Rd.,* ☎ *508/394–2923. Reservations not accepted. No credit cards. No dinner.*

$$ 🏠 **Scargo Manor.** Location, location, location: that's what this 1895 sea captain's home has, a prime one right on Scargo Lake. Inside, there's plenty of room to spread out on the big screened porch with green wicker chairs, in the sitting room (with TV and fireplace), in the more formal living room, or in a red wicker chair in the cozy third-floor reading room (also with a TV). If you want a lake view, choose the all-blue Hydrangea Room with a pineapple-topped queen four-poster bed;

you can watch the stars through the skylight overhead. If you need lots of space, the Captain Howes Suite has a king canopy bed, plus a separate sitting room with a working fireplace that's bigger than the guest rooms at many B&Bs. Don't miss innkeeper Jane MacMillin's yummy cinnamon bread; it's enough to make you forget that the house's exterior, while a tasteful white, has been covered with nonwood siding. ⊠ *909 Main St. (Rte. 6A), 02638,* ☎ *508/385–5534 or 800/595–0034,* FAX *508/385–3992. 4 rooms, 2 suites. Breakfast room, beach. No smoking. AE, D, DC, MC, V. CP.*

$–$$ 🏠 **Four Chimneys Inn.** This three-story, four-chimney, 1881 Queen Anne Victorian gem, once home to the town doctor, is now a relaxing getaway. Rooms vary in size and decor, but all are tastefully furnished with cherry four-poster, wicker, or antique pine or oak beds; chenille comforters; and hand-stenciled trim. Three rooms have fireplaces, and all have views of either Scargo Lake (across the street) or of the surrounding woods and flowering gardens. You can enjoy breakfast in the high-ceilinged dining room; the screened-in summer porch, with its lovely garden views, is an even more soothing spot to start the day. Having afternoon tea under the wisteria-draped arbor is a wonderful way to wind down. ⊠ *946 Main St. (Rte. 6A), 02638,* ☎ *508/385–6317 or 800/874–5502,* FAX *508/385–6285. 7 rooms, 1 suite. No smoking. AE, MC, V. Closed Dec.–mid-Feb. CP.*

$–$$ 🏠 **Isaiah Hall B&B Inn.** Lilacs and pink roses trail along the white picket
★   fence outside this 1857 Greek Revival farmhouse on a residential road on the bay side of town. Inside, guest rooms are decorated with country antiques, floral-print wallpapers, TVs, and homey touches such as quilts and priscilla curtains. In the attached carriage house, rooms have three walls stenciled white and one knotty pine, and some have small balconies overlooking a wooded lawn with gardens, grape arbors, and berry bushes. The carriage-house suite has a king-size bed, a separate sitting area with a pull-out couch, and a refrigerator. Make-it-yourself popcorn, tea, coffee, and soft drinks are always available. ⊠ *152 Whig St., 02638,* ☎ *508/385–9928 or 800/736–0160,* FAX *508/385–5879. 9 rooms, 1 suite. Picnic area, air-conditioning, badminton, croquet. No smoking. AE, MC, V. Closed mid-Oct.–mid-Apr. CP.*

Nightlife and the Arts

The oldest professional summer theater in the country is the **Cape Playhouse** (⊠ 820 Main St. [Rte. 6A], ☎ 508/385–3911 or 877/385–3911), a former 1838 former Unitarian Meeting House, where top stars appear each summer (☞ *above*). The Playhouse also mounts children's shows on Friday mornings during July and August.

The **Nau-Sets** (⊠ Dennis Senior Center, Rte. 134, ☎ 508/255–5079 or 508/385–9841) hold weekly square dances on Tuesday.

The **Reel Art Cinema** at the Cape Museum of Fine Arts (⊠ 60 Hope La., ☎ 508/385–4477) shows avant-garde, classic, art, and independent films on weekends. Call for a schedule.

Outdoor Activities and Sports

BEACHES

Parking at all Dennis beaches is $10 a day in season for non-residents. **Chapin Beach** (⊠ Chapin Beach Rd.) is a lovely dune-backed bay beach with long tidal flats that at low tide allow walking far out. It has no lifeguards or services.

Corporation Beach (⊠ Corporation Rd.) has lifeguards, showers, rest rooms, and a food stand. At one time a packet landing owned by a corporation of townsfolk, the beautiful crescent of white sand backed by low dunes now serves a decidedly noncorporate use as a public beach.

For freshwater swimming, **Scargo Lake** (⊠ Access off Rte. 6A or Scargo Hill Rd.) has two beaches that offer rest rooms and a picnic area. The sandy-bottom lake is shallow along the shore, which is good for kids. It is surrounded by woods and stocked for fishing.

BIKING

The popular 25-mi-long **Cape Cod Rail Trail** offers a scenic ride through the area. Following the right-of-way of the old Penn Central Railroad, the paved path stretches from South Dennis to South Wellfleet, passing through woods, marshes, and Nickerson State Park. The terrain is easy to moderate (☞ Close-Up: Riding the Rail Trail, *below*).

Shopping

Robert C. Eldred Co. (⊠ 1483 Main St. [Rte. 6A], East Dennis, ☎ 508/385–3116) holds more than two dozen auctions per year, dealing in Americana, estate jewelry, top-quality antiques, marine, Asian, American, and European art, tools, and dolls. Its "general antiques and accessories" auctions put less expensive wares on the block.

Scargo Pottery (⊠ 30 Dr. Lord's Rd. S, off Rte. 6A, ☎ 508/385–3894) is set in a pine forest, where potter Harry Holl's unusual wares—such as his signature castle birdhouses—sit on tree stumps and hang from branches. Inside are the workshop and kiln, plus work by Holl's four daughters. With luck you'll catch a potter at the wheel; viewing is, in fact, encouraged.

West Dennis

㉖ *6 mi south of Dennis, 1 mi east of South Yarmouth.*

In another one of those tricks of Cape geography, the village of West Dennis is actually south of South Dennis on the east side of the Bass River. Dennisport is farther east, near the Harwich town line. If you're driving between West Dennis and Harwich, Lower County Road, with occasional glimpses of the sea between the cottages and beach-front hotels, is a more picturesque alternative to overdeveloped Route 28.

What is now the **Jericho House Museum,** a classic Cape with a bow roof and large central chimney, was built in 1801 for Captain Theophilus Baker. A subsequent owner named it, noticing that the walls seemed to be tumbling down. Antique furnishings in the fully restored house include 1850s portraits and exotic items brought home from overseas by sea captains. Antique cranberry-harvesting and woodworking equipment, a model saltworks, marine antiques, and 19th-century sleighs and wagons are in the barn museum. Also here is a 150-piece driftwood zoo: a local man collected wood on a beach, then added eyes and beaks to bring out animal shapes. ⊠ *Trotting Park Rd. at Old Main St.* ☎ *508/398–6736.* ⊠ *Donations accepted.* ☉ *July–Aug., Wed. and Fri. 2–4, and by appointment.*

The oldest working organ in the United States and a priceless chandelier made out of Sandwich glass can be found at the 1835 **South Parish Congregational Church** (⊠ 234 Old Main St., ☎ 508/394–5992). The cemetery beside the church has markers dating from 1795, many of which were raised for early sea captains and read "Lost at sea." One stone in the graveyard reads, even more simply, "The Chinese Woman."

Dining and Lodging

$$–$$$ ✕ **Christine's.** This family-run restaurant is sprawling, spacious, and a little generic, with a big bar in its own room, a private function room, and a separate show club with a glittering stage offering cabaret, comedy, impersonators, and bands from all over the country. The menu here is mostly typical American restaurant fare, with basic Italian

RIDING THE RAIL TRAIL

N THE LATE 1800S, visitors to Cape Cod could take the train from Boston all the way to Provincetown. But with the construction of the Sagamore and Bourne bridges in the mid-1930s, the age of the automobile truly arrived on the Cape. Today, although passenger trains no longer serve Cape Cod, the former train paths provide another, more leisurely way to explore the Cape—by bicycle. For many people, riding the trail through the fragrant woods is as quintessential a Cape experience as leaping into the cold Atlantic on a dune-backed beach.

The Cape's premier bike path, the Cape Cod Rail Trail was constructed in 1978 and extended in the mid-1990s and now offers a scenic ride from South Dennis to South Wellfleet. Following the paved right-of-way of the old Penn Central Railroad, it is 25 mi long, passing salt marshes, cranberry bogs, ponds, and Nickerson State Park, which has its own path.

Some serious bikers whiz along at top speed, but that's not the only way to travel. Along the way there are plenty of tempting places to veer off to spend an hour or two on the beach, to stop for lunch or ice cream, or just to smell the pine trees and imagine what the Cape looked like years ago. So relax: the terrain is easy to moderate and is generally quite flat, making it great for kids.

The trail starts at the parking lot off busy Route 134 south of U.S. 6, near Theophilus Smith Road in South Dennis, a far-from-scenic spot that will make you appreciate the trail even more. It ends at the post office in South Wellfleet. The Dennis Chamber of Commerce (☞ Visitor Information in Cape Cod A to Z below) will give you a free rail trail map, with distance markings to various points along the trail. It also notes the location of parking lots en route if you want to cover only a segment: in Harwich (across from Pleasant Lake Store on Pleasant Lake Avenue), in Brewster (at Nickerson State Park), and in Eastham (at the Salt Pond Visitor Center). Several bike shops near the trail in Den-

nis, Brewster, and Eastham can also provide information as well as convenient rentals.

If you want to ride the entire length and back in one day, you're in for a long ride. Experienced rail-trailers suggest doing the trail in segments, perhaps starting in the middle near Nickerson State Park and looping to one end and back. If you want to return to your starting point by public transportation, the easiest way is to start in Dennis, ride to Orleans, and catch the bike-rack-equipped H20 line bus back to Dennis; contact the Cape Cod Regional Transit Authority (☞ Getting Around in Cape Cod A to Z, below) for schedule and route information.

The Cape Cod Rail Trail is a popular spot for in-line skaters and pedestrians, as well as bicyclists. Remember that wheels yield to heels, so cyclists should give walkers the right of way. Pass slower traffic on the left, and call out a warning before you pass. Kids under 13 must wear helmets. As you ride through Orleans, a stretch of the trail is on busy town streets rather than on a dedicated bike thoroughfare, so use extra caution. And at one point in Harwich, you will cross a major highway. The trail can get crowded at times, especially in summer; if you prefer solitude (or cooler temperatures), set out earlier in the morning or later in the afternoon.

Busy bike trails share the same fate as roads: maintenance projects and expansion. A 19-mi section of the rail trail is scheduled for resurfacing in 2000. A new 3-mi spur leads from the rail trail through Harwich to the Chatham line; there is a cute little bike rotary on the main trail where the spur joins it. Eventually this spur will go into Chatham center. Also in the works are plans to extend the trail westward into Yarmouth. Contact the Cape Cod Commission (☎ 508/362–3828) for an update before setting out. For other resources for riders, see Web Sites in Smart Travel Tips A to Z.

–by Carolyn Heller

dishes and some seafood and steak. A nice touch is Lebanese specials such as a pine nut and almond crusted haddock with tahini sauce, and *kafta*, fresh ground lamb and beef blended with onions, mint, and Lebanese spices, grilled and served with almond rice and hummus. To help work off dinner, there's dancing year-round (☞ Nightlife and the Arts, *below*). Christine's has a "30-foot cruise ship–style buffet" every Sunday from 10 AM to 2 PM. ✉ *581 Main St. (Rte. 28),* ☎ *508/394–7333. AE, D, MC, V.*

$$$$ **⊞ Lighthouse Inn.** On a small private beach adjacent to West Dennis Beach, this traditional Cape resort has been in family hands since 1938. The main inn was built around a still-operational 1855 lighthouse and has five guest rooms. Scattered along a landscaped lawn are 23 individual, weathered, shingled Cape cottages (one-room to three-bedroom, no kitchens) and five multiroom buildings. Cottages have decks, knotty-pine and some painted walls, and generally nice, cabiny bedrooms. The oceanfront Guest House has a common room with a fireplace. In the main inn are a living room, a library, and a restaurant in three waterfront rooms that serves New England cuisine and seafood. In summer, supervised activities and dinners for children give parents some private time. ✉ *1 Lighthouse Rd., Box 128, 02670,* ☎ *508/398–2244,* FAX *508/398–5658. 40 rooms, 23 cottages. Restaurant, bar, room service, pool, miniature golf, tennis court, shuffleboard, beach, fishing, billiards, nightclub, recreation room, library, children's programs (ages 3–12), playground. MC, V. Closed mid-Oct.–mid-May. BP; MAP available.*

$ **⊞ Beach House Inn.** This is the kind of house you'd expect when Nantucket Sound is your backyard: shingles weathered gray from the salt air; white wicker and natural oak furniture that's practical yet comfortable; walls of glass that frame the beauty—and sometimes ferocity—of Mother Nature. Some rooms have brass or four-poster beds, and all have TVs, ceiling fans, and decks, some of which overlook the front yard. The best room is undoubtedly Room 2, with its second-story waterfront deck and a private staircase leading to the inn's beach. The common room has a TV and wide assortment of hit movies on video. You can use the barbecue grills or the fully equipped kitchen, which has a microwave, to cook meals. ✉ *61 Uncle Stephen's Rd., Box 494, 02670,* ☎ *508/398–4575, 617/489–4144 Columbus Day–Memorial Day,* FAX *508/298–8220. 7 rooms. Beach, playground. No smoking. No credit cards. CP.*

Nightlife and the Arts

Christine's (✉ 581 Main St. [Rte. 28], ☎ 508/394–7333; ☞ Dining, *above*) has entertainment nightly in season in its 300-seat show room. Concerts, sometimes with dancing, feature name bands from the 1950s to 1970s, Top 40 bands, or jazz. There are also stand-up comedy nights. Off-season, the schedule includes live entertainment and dancing to a DJ on weekends, as well as special events.

The **Sand Bar** (✉ Lighthouse Rd., ☎ 508/398–7586) presents the boogie-woogie piano playing of local legend Rock King, who's been tickling the ivories—and people's funny bones—here every summer for 40 years. The club is closed from mid-October to mid-May.

Sundancer's (✉ 116 Main St. [Rte. 28], ☎ 508/394–1600) has dancing to a DJ and live bands in season. It's closed December and January.

Outdoor Activities and Sports

BEACHES

The **West Dennis Beach** (✉ Lighthouse Rd., off Lower County Rd.) is one of the best on the south shore. A breakwater was started here in 1837 in an effort to protect the mouth of Bass River but was abandoned when a sandbar formed on the shore side. It is a long, wide, and popular sandy beach, stretching for 1½ mi, with marshland and the

Bass River across from it. A popular spot for windsurfers, the beach also has bathhouses, lifeguards, a playground, concessions, and parking for 1,000 cars. Non-residents pay a $10 parking fee per day in season.

ICE-SKATING

Fall through spring, plus summer Saturdays and some evenings (call for schedule), ice-skating is available at the **Tony Kent Arena** (⊠ 8 Gages Way, South Dennis, ☎ 508/760–2400). Keep your eyes peeled: this is where Nancy Kerrigan and Paul Wylie train. Rental skates are available.

JOGGING

Lifecourse (⊠ Bob Crowell Rd. and Old Bass River Rd., South Dennis) is a 1½-mi jogging trail through woods, with 20 exercise stations along the way. It is part of a recreation area that includes basketball and handball courts, ball fields, a playground, and a picnic area.

Dennisport

㉗ *1 mi east of West Dennis, 10 mi west of Chatham.*

The Mid Cape's last southern village is Dennisport, a prime summer resort area, with gray-shingled cottages, summer houses and condominiums, and lots of white picket fences covered with rambling roses. The Union Wharf Packing Company was here in the 1850s, and the shore was lined with sail makers and ship chandlers. The beach where sea clams were once packed in the sands is now packed with sunbathers.

☺ The **Cape Cod Discovery Museum** is a small but lively indoor play space for kids from preschool age through about 2nd grade. Legos, musical instruments, play dinosaurs, magnetic word games, and puzzles, plus visits from iguanas, snakes, or the resident parrot, will amuse the little ones. At press time the museum was expanding, adding a new ocean exhibit, a tropical reef display, and walking trails. ⊠ *444 Main St. (Rte. 28),* ☎ *508/398–1600.* ⊡ *$4.50.* ☉ *Mid-June–Labor Day, Mon.–Sat. 9:30–6, Sun. noon–6; Labor Day–mid-June, Mon.–Sat. 9:30–5:30.*

NEED A BREAK?
> Set in a rustic mid-19th-century barn decorated with such memorabilia as a working nickelodeon, the **Sundae School Ice Cream Parlor** (⊠ 387 Lower County Rd., ☎ 508/394–9122), open mid-April–mid-October, serves great homemade ice cream and frozen yogurt with lots of toppings, sugar-free ice cream, real whipped cream, and old-fashioned sarsaparilla and cream soda from an antique marble soda fountain.

Dining and Lodging

$$–$$$ ✕ **Clancy's.** A local landmark set on the bucolic Swan River, Clancy's is a popular spot with a parking lot that's often jammed by 5 PM. Calling itself a county (not country) tavern, this is an enormous operation with long family tables, round tables, bar tables, booths, a deck overlooking the river, two bars, and many, many, servers. On the seemingly endless menu you'll find several variations of nachos, salads, and chili if you're looking for light fare. Clancy's likes to put cute names on things, so there's Steak Lucifer (sirloin topped with lobster, asparagus, and béarnaise sauce) and a Sunday brunch menu with crab, steak, or eggs "benny." ⊠ *8 Upper County Rd.,* ☎ *508/394–6661. Reservations not accepted. AE, DC, MC, V.*

$$ ✕ **Swan River Restaurant and Fish Market.** From the right table, you can have a beautiful view of the Swan River marsh and Nantucket Sound beyond at this informal little spot, which turns out great fresh fish, both traditional and creative. Besides the usual fried and broiled choices,

try mako shark au poivre or scrod San Sebastian, simmered in garlic broth with littleneck clams. This restaurant is also a fish retailer and wholesaler, often a good indicator of high quality. ⊠ *5 Lower County Rd.,* ☎ *508/394–4466. AE, MC, V. Closed mid-Sept.–late May. No lunch late May–mid-June.*

$–$$ ✕ **Bob Briggs' Wee Packet.** Cute as can be, and maybe a little too cute, this tiny dinette is decorated in classic Cape kitsch with screaming-yellow tables, seascapes on the walls, and driftwood, seashells, and little bits of moss everywhere. The food is very good, very traditional, and very plain: plenty of local seafood (broiled swordfish and fish-and-chips are very reliable) as well as sandwiches and salads. Try bread pudding with lemon sauce for dessert. You can pick up homemade freshly baked goods of all kinds at the adjoining bakery and doughnut shop. Bob Briggs himself will greet you at the door, no doubt wearing his signature suspenders, just as he has been greeting customers for more than 30 years. ⊠ *79 Depot St.,* ☎ *508/398–2181. Reservations not accepted. MC, V. Closed Oct.–Apr.*

$ ✕ **Bob's Best Sandwiches.** Bob Theobald is a hands-on owner in the best sense; he makes his own bread, roasts his own turkey, opens every day at 7 AM, and doesn't close until around dinnertime. The result is one of the better breakfast and lunch spots around, as well as a busy catering business. The French toast for breakfast is a true treat, even better than the excellent omelets. For lunch, get a big roast beef sandwich and you're ready for anything. ⊠ *613 Main St. (Rte. 28),* ☎ *508/394–8450. Reservations not accepted. No credit cards. No dinner.*

$ ✕ **Kream 'N Kone.** This is how it's been since 1953: order up some fried clams, a shake or a soda, get a number, wait five minutes, and sit down to some of the best fast food anywhere. For some reason the onion rings in particular are a knockout. The fried food overflows a paper plate onto a plastic tray, but it's so good that what you thought you'd never be able to finish somehow vanishes. At times the prices are surprisingly high, but not for what you get. A sister restaurant of the same name, owned and operated by the same family, serves up the same great stuff down Route 28 a few miles into Chatham. ⊠ *Main St. (Rte. 28),* ☎ *508/394–0808. No credit cards. Closed Nov.–Apr.*

$$ ▦ **The Garlands.** There are innumerable strip motels and cottage colonies lining Old Wharf Road in Dennisport, but few places offer comfort and views to match this bi-level, motel-style complex. There are 20 units in all—18 are two-bedroom suites. Each unit has a fully equipped kitchen, cable TV, private sundeck or patio, and daily maid service. The oceanfront VIP suites, simply named A and B (two bedrooms) and C and D (one bedroom), are the best picks here—the nearly floor-to-ceiling windows offer unobstructed water views; at high tide, you're almost in the surf. ⊠ *117 Old Wharf Rd., Box 506, 02639,* ☎ *508/398–6987. 20 suites. Beach. No credit cards. Closed mid-Oct.–mid-Apr.*

Nightlife and the Arts

Clancy's (⊠ 8 Upper County Rd., ☎ 508/394–6661; ☞ Dining, *above*) has contemporary piano year-round.

Outdoor Activities and Sports

Cape Cod Waterways (⊠ 16 Main St. [Rte. 28], ☎ 508/398–0080) rents canoes, kayaks, and electric paddleboats for leisurely travel on the Swan River.

Shopping

Factory Shoe Mart (⊠ 271 Main St. [Rte. 28], ☎ 508/398–6000) has such brand names as Capezio, Dexter, Clark, Esprit, Nike, Reebok, L.A. Gear, and Rockport.

THE LOWER CAPE

The Lower Cape is the least developed part of the Cape, and the place that many people most treasure as a result. **Brewster** and **Harwich**, rich in history and Cape flavor, are west of **Chatham**, out at the elbow, a traditional town with good shopping and strolling. South of Chatham, the Monomoy National Wildlife Refuge is a twin-island bird sanctuary. Nickerson State Park in Brewster offers plenty of recreation and the Cape's prime camping in a forest setting. The beaches, woods, swamps, walking trails, historic sights, and visitor centers of the Cape Cod National Seashore are next on the east side, with the small and pretty fishing town of **Wellfleet** opposite on the bay side. As you continue north, the sweeping dunes of **Truro** and the Province Lands follow. Last but not least, **Provincetown** is a quiet fishing village in winter. In summer it dons a motley gown and draws crowds to its galleries, crafts shops, whale-watch boats, restaurants, nightlife, and crowds—yes, crowds of people watching crowds of people. These last three towns are often referred to as the Outer Cape; they are covered in their own section, below.

Brewster

28 *6 mi north of Chatham, 5 mi west of Orleans, 20 mi east of Sandwich.*

Brewster, on Cape Cod Bay, is a perfect place to learn about the natural history of the Cape. The Cape Cod Museum of Natural History is here, and the area is rich in conservation lands, state parks, forests, freshwater ponds, and brackish marshes. When the tide is low in Cape Cod Bay, you can stroll the beaches and explore tidal pools up to 2 mi from the shore on the Brewster flats. When it's high, the water is relatively warm and very calm for swimming.

Named for Plymouth leader William Brewster, the area was settled in 1659 but was not incorporated as a separate town until 1803. In the early 1800s, Brewster was the terminus of a packet cargo service from Boston and home to many seafaring families. In 1849 Thoreau wrote that "this town has more mates and masters of vessels than any other town in the country." A large number of mansions built for sea captains remain today, and quite a few have been turned into handsome B&Bs. In the 18th and 19th centuries, the bay side of Brewster was the site of a major salt-making industry. Of the 450 saltworks operating on the Cape in the 1830s, more than 60 were located here.

Windmills used to be prominent in Cape Cod towns; the Brewster area once had four. The 1795 **Higgins Farm Windmill** (Off Rte. 6A, just west of the Cape Cod Museum of Natural History; ☞ *below*)—an octagonal type mill shingled in weathered pine with a roof like an upturned boat—was moved here in 1974 and has been restored. The millstones are original. At night the mill is often spotlighted and makes quite a sight.

On the grounds of the Higgins Farm Windmill (☞ *above*) is a one-room house from 1795, the **Harris-Black House.** Once, amazingly enough, home to a family of 13, the restored 16-ft-square building is today partially furnished and dominated by a brick hearth and original woodwork. ✉ *Off Rte. 6A, just west of the Cape Cod Museum of Natural History (☞ below),* ☎ *508/896–9521.* ▣ *Free.* ۞ *July–Aug., Tues.–Fri. 1–4.*

29 A short drive outside of Brewster is the **Stony Brook Grist Mill,** a restored, operating, 19th-century fulling (i.e., shrinking and thickening cloth) mill that is now also a museum. The scene is wonderfully picturesque, with the old mill's waterwheel slowly turning in a small, tree-lined brook. Inside, exhibits include old mill equipment and looms; you can watch corn-

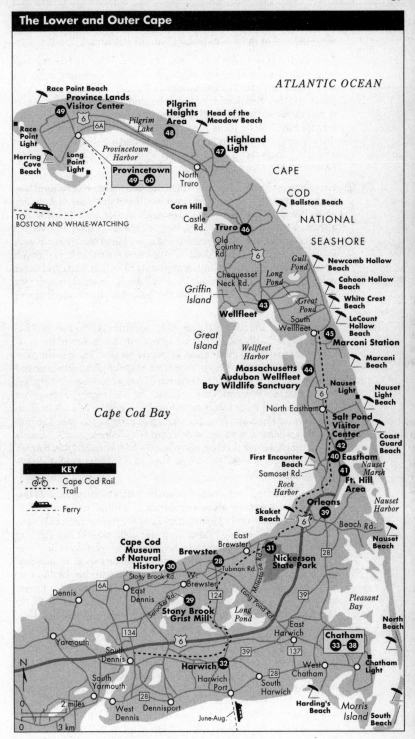

The Lower and Outer Cape

ATLANTIC OCEAN

Race Point Beach
Province Lands
Visitor Center

49

Race
Point
Light

Pilgrim Heights Area

48

Head of the
Meadow Beach

Highland Light

47

Pilgrim Lake

Herring Cove Beach

Long Point Light

Provincetown Harbor

Provincetown
49—60

North Truro

CAPE

COD

Ballston Beach

TO
BOSTON AND WHALE-WATCHING

Corn Hill

Castle Rd.

Truro
46

NATIONAL

Old Country Rd.

6

SEASHORE

Gull Pond

Newcomb Hollow Beach

Chequesset Neck Rd.

Long Pond

Cahoon Hollow Beach

Griffin Island

Great Pond

White Crest Beach

Wellfleet
43

South Wellfleet

LeCount Hollow Beach

Great Island

Wellfleet Harbor

Marconi Station
45

Marconi Beach

Massachusetts Audubon Wellfleet Bay Wildlife Sanctuary

44

6

Nauset Light

Nauset Light Beach

Cape Cod Bay

North Eastham

Salt Pond Visitor Center

42

Coast Guard Beach

First Encounter Beach

Eastham
40

Samoset Rd.

Rock Harbor

41

Ft. Hill Area

Nauset Marsh

KEY

Cape Cod Rail Trail

Ferry

Orleans

39

Nauset Harbor

Skaket Beach

6

Beach Rd.

Nauset Beach

East Brewster

31

Cape Cod Museum of Natural History
30

Brewster
28

Nickerson State Park

28

Stony Brook Rd.

Tubman Rd.

W Brewster

Dennis

6A

East Dennis

Schnuckel Rd.

29

124

Long Pond

Pleasant Bay

North Beach

Stony Brook Grist Mill

Long Pond Rd.

East Harwich

39

Chatham
33—38

Yarmouth

134

South Dennis

6

39

Chatham Light

N

South Yarmouth

Harwich
32

137

West Chatham

0   2 miles

28

Harwich Port

South Harwich

Harding's Beach

Morris Island

South Beach

0   3 km

West Dennis

Dennisport

28

June-Aug.

meal being stone-ground and get a lesson in weaving on a 100-year-old loom. Out back, across wooden bridges, a bench has a pleasant view of the pond and of the sluices leading into the mill area.

Early each spring, in April and early May, Stony Brook's **Herring Run** boils with alewives (herring) making their way to spawning waters; it is an amazing sight. The fish swim in from Cape Cod Bay up Paine's Creek to Stony Brook and the ponds beyond it. The rushing stream is across the street from the mill. The herring run consists of ladders that help the fish climb the rocky waters. Farther down the path to the stream, there is an ivy-covered stone wishing well and a wooden bridge with a bench. ⊠ *Setucket Rd., off Rte. 6A,* ☎ *no phone.* ☎ *Donations accepted.* ☉ *May–Aug., Thurs.–Sat. 2–5.*

🖐 ㉚ For nature enthusiasts, a visit to the **Cape Cod Museum of Natural History** is a must; it's just a short drive west from the heart of Brewster along Route 6A. The museum and grounds include guided field walks, a shop, a natural history library, lectures, classes, nature and marine exhibits such as a working beehive and a pond- and sea-life room with live specimens, and self-guided trails (one goes out to the bay) through 80 acres of forest, marshland, and ponds, all rich in birds and other wildlife. The exhibit hall upstairs has a wall display of aerial photographs documenting the process by which the famous Chatham sandbar was split in two.

Combining art and nature, the monthly exhibitions in the Personal Response to the Earth gallery display artists' interpretations of the environment; most of the multimedia works are for sale. The museum also offers guided canoe and kayak trips from May through September and several cruises that explore different Cape waterways: Nantucket Sound, Pleasant Bay, and Nauset Marsh. Onboard naturalists point out the wildlife and relay historical information unique to each habitat. Call for tour times and fees, and sign up as early as you can. The museum has wildlife movies and slide lectures on Wednesday at 7:30, early July through August, in the auditorium. ⊠ *869 Main St. (Rte. 6A),* ☎ *508/896–3867, 800/479–3867 in MA.* ☎ *$5.* ☉ *Mon.–Sat. 9:30–4:30, Sun. 11–4:30.*

🖐 Set on a re-created 19th-century common with a picnic area, the **New England Fire & History Museum** exhibits 35 antique vehicles, including the only surviving 1929 Mercedes-Benz fire engine, the late Boston Pops conductor Arthur Fiedler's private collection of fire-fighting memorabilia, 14 mannequins in historical uniforms depicting firefighters through the centuries, a Victorian apothecary shop, an animated diorama of the Chicago Fire of 1871 complete with smoke and fire, an historic working forge, and medicinal herb gardens. Guided tours are given. ⊠ *1439 Main St. (Rte. 6A),* ☎ *508/896–5711.* ☎ *$5.* ☉ *Mid-May–Labor Day, weekdays 10–4; Labor Day–Columbus Day, weekends noon–4.*

At the junction of Route 124, the **Brewster Store** (⊠ 1935 Main St. [Rte. 6A], ☎ 508/896–3744) is a local landmark. Built in 1852 as a church, it is a typical New England general store—God love 'em!—providing such essentials as the daily papers, penny candy, and benches out front for conversation. There's even a selection of Cape books to add to your collection. It's a good stop for quick grocery-type refreshments, as the bicycles piled up out front in summer attest. The Brewster Scoop out back serves ice cream mid-June through Labor Day. Upstairs, the old front of the store has been re-created, and memorabilia from antique toys to World War II bond posters are displayed. Downstairs is an antique nickelodeon that you can play.

Known as the Church of the Sea Captains, the handsome **First Parish Church** (✉ 1969 Main St. [Rte. 6A], ☎ 508/896–5577), with Gothic windows and a capped bell tower, is full of pews marked with the names of famous Brewster seamen. Out back is an old graveyard where militiamen, clergy, farmers, and sea captains rest side by side.

For a look at some nonnative species, visit the 20-acre **Bassett Wild Animal Farm,** home to domestic and exotic birds, a lion, a tiger, monkeys, llamas, and the animals at a petting zoo. Hayrides, pony rides, a snack bar, and a picnic area are available. ✉ *Tubman Rd. between Rtes. 124 and 137,* ☎ *508/896–3224.* ☑ *$6.75.* ☉ *Mid-May–mid-Sept., daily 10–5.*

The **Brewster Historical Society Museum,** in an 1830s house, is made up of a sea captains' room with paintings and artifacts, an 1890 barbershop, a child's room with antique toys and clothing, a room of women's period gowns and accessories, and other exhibits on local history and architecture. Out back, a ¼-mi nature trail over dunes leads to the bay. ✉ *3371 Main St. [Rte. 6A],* ☎ *508/896–7593.* ☑ *Free.* ☉ *June and Sept., weekends 1–4; July–Aug., Tues.–Sun. 1–4.*

For a lovely hike or run through the local wilds, the **Punkhorn Parklands,** studded with freshwater kettle-hole ponds, has 45 mi of scenic trails meandering through 800 acres of meadows, marshes, and pine forests. ✉ *End of Run Hill Rd., off Stony Brook Rd.*

Although today they are open to the public for recreation, the 1,961 acres encompassed by **Nickerson State Park** were once part of a vast estate belonging to Roland C. Nickerson, son of Samuel Nickerson, a Chatham native who became a multimillionaire and founder of the First National Bank of Chicago. At their long, private beach or their hunting lodge, Roland and his wife, Addie, lavishly entertained such visitors as President Grover Cleveland in English country-house style, with coachmen dressed in tails and top hats and a bugler announcing carriages entering the front gates.

The estate was like a village unto itself. Its gardens provided much of the household's food, supplemented by game from its woods and fish from its ponds. It also had its own electric plant and a nine-hole golf course by the water. The enormous mansion Samuel built for his son in 1886 burned to the ground 20 years later, and Roland died two weeks after the event. The even grander stone mansion built to replace it in 1908 is now part of the Ocean Edge resort (☞ Dining and Lodging, *below*). In 1934 Addie donated the land for the state park in memory of Roland and their son, who died during the 1918 flu epidemic.

The park itself consists of acres of oak, pitch pine, hemlock, and spruce forest dotted with seven freshwater kettle ponds that were formed by glacial action. Some ponds are stocked with trout for fishing. Other recreational opportunities include swimming in the ponds, canoeing, sailing, motorboating, biking along 8 mi of paved trails that have access to the Cape Cod Rail Trail, picnicking, and cross-country skiing in winter. Bird-watchers seek out the thrushes, wrens, warblers, woodpeckers, finches, larks, Canada geese, cormorants, great blue herons, hawks, owls, ospreys, and other species that frequent the park. Occasionally, red foxes and white-tailed deer are spotted in the woods. Tent and RV camping is extremely popular here (☞ Dining and Lodging, *below*), and visitor programs are offered in season. A map of the park is available on-site. ✉ *3488 Rte. 6A,* ☎ *508/896–3491.* ☑ *Free.* ☉ *Daily dawn–dusk.*

Dining and Lodging

$$$$ ✕ **Chillingsworth.** This has generally been regarded as the crown jewel
★ of Cape restaurants for many years, although as other dining here has
become more sophisticated, its extremely formal, somewhat stiff pre-
sentation seems a less essential experience. Even so, the excellent, terri-
bly pricey classic French menu and wine cellar continue to win award
after award. Every night, the seven-course table d'hôte menu rotates
through an assortment of appetizers, entrées, and "amusements." Recent favorites have been a super-rich risotto, roast lobster, and grilled
venison. At dinner, a more modest bistro menu is served in the Garden
Room, a sort of patio in the front of the restaurant. The whole experience is as close as you get on the Cape to formal extravagance. If you
want to linger, there are some guest rooms here, too. ✉ *2449 Main St.
(Rte. 6A),* ☎ *508/896–3640. AE, DC, MC, V. Closed Mon. mid-June–
Thanksgiving; closed some weekdays Memorial Day–mid-June and mid-
Oct.–Thanksgiving; closed entirely Thanksgiving–Memorial Day.*

$$$$ ✕ **High Brewster.** High Brewster is the real thing, a working country
★ inn that serves up some of the finest food on the Cape. The restored
colonial farmhouse has low ceilings and exposed beams overhead; it
overlooks a picture-perfect New England landscape. The five-course
prix-fixe menu ($35–$55) changes frequently as it explores classic interpretations of American regional cooking. Longtime favorites include
squash soup, grilled duck breast with black currant reduction, and apple
rum ice cream. Rack of lamb is always on the menu, and perfectly prepared. Summertime sees the arrival of swordfish and striped bass. A
six-course tasting dinner ($40–$42) is offered once a week in the summer (call ahead for the schedule). Accommodations at the inn are also
available. ✉ *964 Setucket Rd.,* ☎ *508/896–3636 or 800/203–2634.
Reservations essential. AE, MC, V. Closed 1st 2 wks in Jan.; call for
weekday hrs off-season. No lunch.*

$$–$$$ ✕ **Brewster Fish House.** Long overshadowed by its pricier neighbors,
the Fish House has carved a niche for itself. Old Cape standards are
starting to take a backseat to new ideas and an expanded menu. Management doesn't seem entirely convinced that a wholesale shift to an
upscale menu will carry the day, so classic scrod and boiled dinners
are still playing backup to evolving experimentation with duck, rack
of lamb, Cornish game hen, and tenderloin of beef in the classic style.
The wine list offers a half dozen whites and a half dozen reds that you
don't often see by the glass. ✉ *2208 Rte. 6A,* ☎ *508/896–7867. Reservations not accepted. MC, V.* ☽ *Call for off-season schedule.*

$$ ✕ **Laurino's Cape Cod Tavern.** With warm wood paneling, generous
booth-style seating, and red-and-white check tablecloths, there's some-
thing timeless about Laurino's in a basic American-Italian way. It's an
easy place to feed the whole family lunch and dinner but not a place
for Cape Cod fish, so steer instead to the burger or the specialty piz-
zas that come in two sizes. Try a "Buffalo Chicken Pizza" or the
"Kitchen Sink," with plenty of toppings. At the long, friendly bar you
can sit with a buddy over a beer and a big plate of "Macho Nachos."
Know that since Orleans has become a no-smoking restaurant town,
this place (right over the border) has become a smoky bar, indeed, though
the restaurant section is in the clean air. ✉ *3668 Main St. (Rte. 6A),*
☎ *508/896–6135. Reservations not accepted. AE, MC, V.*

$–$$ ✕ **New England Fish Factory.** Not exactly a factory, this establishment
offers a generous breakfast, lunch, a limited take-out menu until 6 PM,
early-bird specials, and a predictable New England dinner. The emphasis
is on fish and salad—and hey, if you eat here five times, you get a T-shirt.
The raw bar has ice-cold oysters, cherrystones, and littlenecks. For some
reason the menu proudly features lobsters from Maine. Is there something wrong with Cape Cod lobsters from the back shore? ✉ *2671*

Main St. (Rte. 6A), ☎ *508/896–1067. Reservations not accepted. AE, D, MC, V.*

$$$$ 🏨 **Ocean Edge.** This huge, self-contained resort is almost like a town. Sports facilities are superior, and activities such as concerts, tournaments, and clambakes are scheduled throughout the summer. Accommodations range from oversize hotel rooms in the conference center, with sitting areas and direct access to the health club and tennis courts, to luxurious one- to three-bedroom condominiums in the woods. Two- to three-bedroom beachfront villas offer immediate access to the resort's private beach. All are decorated with pastel fabrics and fresh wood furnishings in modern style. Condominiums have washer-dryers and some fireplaces, and many units have ocean views. The resort is so spread out that you may need a car to get from your condo to the pool. MAP plans are subject to availability. ✉ *2907 Main St. (Rte. 6A), 02631,* ☎ *508/ 896–9000 or 800/343–6074,* ☏ *508/896–9123. 197 condominium units, 90 hotel rooms. 4 restaurants, pub, room service, 2 indoor and 4 outdoor pools, ponds, saunas, driving range, golf privileges, putting greens, 11 tennis courts, basketball, exercise room, beach, bicycles, children's programs (ages 4–17), concierge. AE, D, DC, MC, V.*

$$–$$$$ 🏨 **Captain Freeman Inn.** A splendid 1866 Victorian built for a packet-
★ schooner-fleet owner continues to show off its original opulence with a marble fireplace, herringbone-inlay flooring, ornate Italian plaster ceiling medallions, tall windows, and 12-ft ceilings. Guest rooms have hardwood floors, antiques and Victorian reproductions, and beds with eyelet spreads and fishnet or lace canopies. The eight "luxury rooms" are truly indulgent, with queen-size canopy beds, sofas, fireplaces, TV with VCR, minirefrigerators, and French doors leading to small enclosed porches with private whirlpool spas. Winter weekend cooking schools share the innkeeper's skills, as do diners (on request for an extra charge) in the off-season. ✉ *15 Breakwater Rd., 02631,* ☎ *508/896– 7481 or 800/843–4664,* ☏ *508/896–5618. 12 rooms. Pool, badminton, croquet, bicycles. No smoking. AE, MC, V. BP.*

$$–$$$ 🏨 **Brewster Farmhouse.** This restored 1846 farmhouse on historic Route 6A has several comforting touches, from the goose-down pillows in the guest rooms to the turndown service with bedside sherry and chocolates. One room has a fireplace, another a king-size canopy bed and sliders out to a private deck. In 1999, an ambitious expansion in the form of another structure added three luxury-size rooms with antiques and reproduction pieces, including a white wrought-iron canopy bed. These new rooms all have fireplaces and whirlpool baths. In good weather, a breakfast prepared by the inn's owners, Carol and Gary Concors, is served on a patio looking onto the 2-acre backyard with apple trees and gardens on its edges and a heated pool and whirlpool in its center. ✉ *716 Main St. (Rte. 6A), 02631,* ☎ *508/896–3910 or 800/892–3910,* ☏ *508/896–4232. 8 rooms, 1 suite. Pool, bicycles. No smoking. AE, D, DC, MC, V. BP.*

$$–$$$ 🏨 **Isaiah Clark House.** A former sea captain's residence just west of the town proper, this inn provides modern amenities without sacrificing its 18th-century heritage and character. The original inhabitants are not forgotten here, from the scrawled signature of 13-year-old son Jeremiah in a closet and framed historic documents and photographs to the namesake of each of the rooms (all Clark family women). Having been lovingly preserved and updated, the inn retains all its old touches of wide-plank flooring and low, sloping ceilings and is further enhanced by a varied selection of antiques. Most rooms have queen four-poster or canopy beds, braided rugs, and fireplaces. The extensive gardens yield some of the fruit used in the homemade pies, muffins, and breads. ✉ *1187 Main St. (Rte. 6A), 02631,* ☎ *508/896–2223 or 800/822–4001. 7 rooms. AE, D, DC, MC, V. BP.*

$$–$$$ ⊞ **The Ruddy Turnstone.** Built in the early 1800s, this beautifully pre-
served Cape homestead is set on 3 acres that gently slope to a marsh
at the edge of the property. Pine-board floors with braided rugs in the
main house, the original barn-board walls of the Carriage House,
quilts, and antiques take you back in time, while modern amenities pam-
per you. Rooms have queen-size beds and large baths, most with
shower-tub combos. An upstairs common sitting room offers an incredible vista of the marsh and the bay beyond; another common
room has a fireplace and small library. One spectacular upstairs room
has fine bay views through generous windows (no need to lift your head
from the pillow). A delicious country breakfast is served at little tables
on the porch or in the dining room. ⊠ *463 Main St. (Rte. 6A), 02631,*
☎ *508/385–9871 or 800/654–1995,* FAX *508/385–5696. 5 rooms. Air-
conditioning. No smoking. MC, V. BP.*

$–$$$ ⊞ **Old Sea Pines Inn.** Fronted by a white-columned portico and
★   wraparound veranda overlooking a broad lawn, the Old Sea Pines evokes
the atmosphere of a summer estate from an earlier time. A sweeping
staircase leads to guest rooms decorated with reproduction wallpaper,
antiques, and framed old photographs. Many rooms are very large; some
have fireplaces, including the inn's best room, which also has a sitting
area in an enclosed sunporch. Rooms in a newer building are sparsely
but well decorated, with bright white modern baths, and have cast-
iron queen-size beds. The shared-bath rooms are *very* small but sweetly
done, and a steal in summer. There's Sunday dinner and a musical revue
in season. ⊠ *2553 Main St. (Rte. 6A), Box 1070, 02631,* ☎ *508/896–
6114,* FAX *508/896–7387. 23 rooms, 18 with bath; 5 suites. Restaurant.
No smoking. AE, D, DC, MC, V. Closed Jan.–Mar. BP.*

$$ ⊞ **Greylin House.** Set slightly back off Route 6A and surrounded with
prettily manicured gardens is this 1837 B&B, where good things ac-
tually do come in smaller packages. The four guest rooms are individually
decorated with reproduction antiques, canopy beds, and painted, wide
pine flooring. The baths (one bath is a quick hop across the hall) are
on the small side but comfortable and well equipped; you'll probably
be spending more time on the outdoor brick patio overlooking the gardens and greenhouse. ⊠ *2511 Main St. (Rte. 6A), 02631,* ☎ *508/896–
0004 or 800/233–6662. 4 rooms. AE, D, DC, MC, V. BP.*

$ ⚠ **Nickerson State Park.** The Cape's largest and most popular camp-
ing site is on almost 2,000 acres teeming with wildlife, white pine, hemlock, and spruce forest. The area is jammed with opportunities for trout
fishing, walking, or biking along 8 mi of paved trails; canoeing; sailing; motorboating; and bird-watching. Basic sites cost $6; 23 pre-
mium sites, situated on the edges of ponds, are $7. RVs must be
self-contained. Facilities include showers, bathrooms, picnic tables, barbecue areas, and a store. Maps and schedules of park programs are
available at the park entrance. ⊠ *3488 Main St. (Rte. 6A), 02631,* ☎
508/896–3491, 877/422–6762 for reservations, FAX *508/896–3103.
418 sites. No credit cards.*

Nightlife and the Arts

The **Cape Cod Repertory Theatre Co.** (⊠ 3379 Main St. [Rte. 6A], ☎
508/896–1888) performs several impressive productions, from original works to classics, in its new indoor Arts and Crafts–style theater
way back in the woods. Mesmerizing entertainment for children, in
the form of lively outdoor (and often interactive) theater, is provided
here, too. Performances of fairy tales, music, and folktales are given
on Tuesday and Friday mornings at 10 AM in July and August. The
theater is just west of Nickerson State Park.

Sunday evenings by the bay are filled with the sounds of the **town band
concerts,** held in the gazebo on the grounds of Drummer Boy Park (⊠

Rte. 6A). The park is about ½ mi west of the Cape Cod Museum of Natural History, on the western side of Brewster.

The **Woodshed** (✉ 1993 Main St. [Rte. 6A], ☎ 508/896–7771), the rustic bar at the Brewster Inn, is a good place to soak up local color and listen to pop duos or bands that perform nightly. It's open May through October.

Outdoor Activities and Sports

BASEBALL

The **Brewster Whitecaps** (☎ 508/896–9284 in summer; 781/784–7409 in winter) of the collegiate Cape Cod Baseball League play home games at Cape Cod Regional Tech High School (✉ Rte. 124, Harwich) from mid-June to mid-August.

BEACHES

Flax Pond in Nickerson State Park (3488 Main St. [Rte. 6A], ☎ 508/896–3491), surrounded by pines, offers picnic areas, a bathhouse, and water-sports rentals.

Breakwater Landing, Linnell Landing, Paine's Creek, Point of Rocks, and **Robin's Hill** bay beaches all have access to the flats that at low tide make for very interesting tidal-pool exploration. Eponymous roads to each beach branch off Route 6A; there's limited parking. Some beaches have a daily $8 parking fee; ask at the town hall ☎ (508/896–3701) about various seasonal parking passes, which may require a proof-of-stay form.

BIKING

The **Cape Cod Rail Trail** (☞ Dennis, *above*) cuts through Brewster with many access points: Long Pond Road, Underpass Road, and Mill-stone Road, to name a few.

Open during summer only but located right alongside the Cape Cod Rail Trail is the tiny **Idle Times Bike Shop** (✉ Rte. 6A, just west of Nickerson State Park, ☎ 508/896–9242), with bikes both big and small for rent. You can't beat the proximity to the trail and the easy parking.

The **Rail Trail Bike Shop** (✉ 302 Underpass Rd., ☎ 508/896–8200) rents bikes, including children's bikes, and in-line skates. There's free parking and a picnic area, with easy access to the Rail Trail.

BOATING

Jack's Boat Rentals (✉ Flax Pond, Nickerson State Park, Rte. 6A, ☎ 508/896–8556) rents canoes, kayaks, Seacycles, Sunfish, pedal boats, and sailboards; guide-led kayak tours are also offered.

FISHING

Many of Brewster's freshwater ponds offer good fishing for perch, pick-erel, and more; five ponds are well stocked with trout. Especially good for fishing is Cliff Pond in Nickerson State Park. You'll need a **fishing license,** available from the town hall (✉ 3918 Main St. [Rte. 6A], ☎ 508/896–3701).

When fishing guidance is in order, you can sign up with **Brewster Flats Fishing & Outfitters** (✉ 2655 Main St. [Rte. 6A], ☎ 508/896–2460) for custom sport-fishing trips that include bait, tackle, and all-weather gear.

GOLF

The par-72, 18-hole **Captain's Golf Course** (✉ 1000 Freeman's Way, ☎ 508/896–5100) is an excellent public course.

Ocean Edge Golf Course (✉ Villages Dr., off Rte. 6A, ☎ 508/896–5911), an 18-hole, par-72 course winding around five ponds, features

Scottish-style pot bunkers and challenging terrain. Three-day residential and commuter golf schools are offered in spring and early summer.

Moby Dick Farm (⊠ 179 Great Fields Rd., ☎ 508/896–3544) offers instruction and trail rides to riders of all levels.

Woodsong Farm (⊠ 121 Lund Farm Way, ☎ 508/896–5555) has instruction and day programs but no trail rides; it also has a horsemanship program for children 5–18.

The **Ocean Edge** resort (⊠ 2907 Main St. [Rte. 6A], ☎ 508/896–9000) has five clay and six Plexipave courts. It offers lessons and round-robins and hosts a tennis school, with weekend packages and video analysis.

Run by the town and open to the public at no charge are four **public tennis courts,** located just behind the fire and police stations on Route 6A. Two basketball courts are also for public use.

Shopping

B. D. Hutchinson (⊠ 1274 Long Pond Rd., ☎ 508/896–6395), a watch and clock maker, sells antique and collectible watches, clocks, and music boxes.

Brewster Book Store (⊠ 2648 Main St. [Rte. 6A], ☎ 508/896–6543) prides itself on being a special Cape bookstore. It's filled to the rafters with all manner of books by local and international authors and has an extensive children's section. A full schedule of author signings and kids' story times continues year-round.

Kemp Pottery (⊠ 258 Main St. [Rte. 6A], ☎ 508/385–5782) has functional and decorative stoneware and porcelain, fountains, garden sculpture, pottery sinks, and stained glass.

Kingsland Manor (⊠ 440 Main St. [Rte. 6A], ☎ 508/385–9741) has ivy covering the facade, fountains in the courtyard, and everything "from tin to Tiffany"—including English hunting horns, full-size antique street lamps, garden and house furniture, weather vanes, jewelry, and chandeliers.

Kings Way Books and Antiques (⊠ 774 Main St. [Rte. 6A], ☎ 508/896–3639) sells out-of-print and rare books, including a large medieval section, plus small antiques, china, glass, silver, coins, and linens.

Punkhorn Bookshop (⊠ 672 Main St. [Rte. 6A], ☎ 508/896–2114), an antiquarian and out-of-print bookseller, specializes in natural history, the Cape and region, fine arts, and biography, and sells antique prints and maps.

Open from April through October, the **Satucket Farm Stand** (⊠ 76 Harwich Rd. [Rte. 124], just off Rte. 6A, ☎ 508/896–5540) is reminiscent of the well-stocked and freshly fragrant side-of-the-road farm stands that make us all nostalgic. Most of the produce is grown on the premises, and you can fill your basket with the finest of the harvest, from home-baked scones and breads to fruit pies, produce, herbs, and flowers.

The **Spectrum** (⊠ 369 Main St. [Rte. 6A], ☎ 508/385–3322) has a great selection of imaginative American arts and crafts, including pottery, stained glass, art glass, and more.

Sydenstricker Galleries (⊠ 490 Main St. [Rte. 6A], ☎ 508/385–3272) stocks glassware handcrafted by a unique process, which you can watch in progress.

Harwich

32 *3 mi east of Dennisport, 6 mi south of Brewster.*

Originally known as Setucket, Harwich separated from Brewster in 1694 and was renamed after the famous seaport in England. Like other townships on the Cape, Harwich is actually a cluster of seven small villages, including Harwich Port. Three naturally sheltered harbors on Nantucket Sound make the town, like its English namesake, a popular spot for boaters. Wychmere Harbor is particularly beautiful.

The Cape's famous cranberry industry took off in Harwich in 1844, and Alvin Cahoon was its principal grower at the time. Each September Harwich holds a great **Cranberry Festival** to celebrate the importance of this indigenous berry; the festival is usually scheduled during the second week after Labor Day. There are cranberry bogs throughout Harwich.

Once a private school offering the first courses in navigation, the pillared 1844 Greek Revival building of the **Brooks Academy Museum** now houses the museum of the **Harwich Historical Society.** In addition to a large photo-history collection and exhibits on artist Charles Cahoon (grandson of cranberry grower Alvin), the socio-technological history of the cranberry culture, and shoe making, the museum displays antique clothing and textiles, china and glass, fans, toys, and much more. There is also an extensive genealogical collection for researchers. On the grounds is a powder house that was used to store gunpowder during the Revolutionary War, as well as a restored 1872 outhouse that could spur your appreciation for indoor plumbing. ✉ *80 Parallel St.,* ☎ *508/432–8089.* ✉ *Donations accepted.* ☉ *June–mid-Oct., Wed.–Sat. 1–4.*

✋ **Brooks Park** on Main Street (Rte. 28) is a good place to stretch your legs, with a playground, picnic tables, a ball field, tennis courts, and a bandstand where summer concerts are held.

✋ **Grand Slam Entertainment** has softball and baseball batting cages and pitching machines, including one with fastballs up to 80 mph, a Wiffle-ball machine for younger kids, a bumper-boat pool, and a video-arcade room. ✉ *322 Main St. [Rte. 28], Harwich Port,* ☎ *508/430–1155.* ✉ *$1.50 for 10 pitches, $5 for 40 pitches, or $10 for 100 pitches; $5 per bumper-pool ride.* ☉ *Apr.–May and Sept.–mid-Oct., Mon.–Sat. 11–7, Sun. 11–9; June–Aug., daily 9 AM–11 PM.*

For kids who have spent too much time in the car watching you drive, ✋ a spin behind the wheel of one of 20 top-of-the-line go-carts at **Bud's Go-Karts** may be just the thing. ✉ *9 Sisson Rd., off Rte. 28, Harwich Port,* ☎ *508/432–4964.* ✉ *$5 for 6 mins.* ☉ *June–Labor Day, Mon.–Sat. 9 AM–11 PM, Sun. 1–11.*

✋ The **Trampoline Center** has 12 trampolines—a perfect activity to release some of that boundless, bouncing energy. They are set up at ground level over pits for safety. ✉ *296 Main St. [Rte. 28], West Harwich,* ☎ *508/432–8717.* ✉ *$4 for 10 mins.* ☉ *Apr.–mid-June, weekends (hrs vary widely, call ahead); mid-June–Labor Day, daily 9 AM–11 PM.*

Dining and Lodging

$$ ✗ **Brax Landing.** In this local stalwart perched alongside busy Saquatucket Harbor, you'll get a menu tip-off as you pass by tanks full of steamers and lobsters in the corridor leading to the dining room. The restaurant sprawls around a big bar that serves drinks like the "Moxie" (pink lemonade and vodka, "calm seas guaranteed"). The swordfish and the Chatham scrod are favorites, both served simply and well. There's a notable children's menu, and Sunday brunch, served from 10 to 2, is an institution. ⊠ *Rte. 28 at Saquatucket Harbor, Harwich Port,* ☎ *508/432–5515. Reservations not accepted. AE, DC, MC, V.*

$$ ✕ **400 East.** This big, dark restaurant buzzing with conversation is in a nondescript shopping plaza. The menu includes teriyaki tuna and chicken, prime rib, and baked scrod but lists excellent pizza offerings as well, with toppings like wild mushrooms, blue cheese, and Cajun chicken and corn. Eating at the busy, U-shape bar can be a great alternative to waiting for a table, provided you don't mind a television set in the picture. The 400 has a "cousin" restaurant (also called the 400) on Main Street that is not as much fun. ⊠ *1421 Rte. 39,* ☎ *508/432–1800. AE, D, MC, V.*

$$$–$$$$ ⊞ **Winstead Inn and Beach Resort.** Two equally inviting properties, one in the heart of historic Harwich, the other on a private Nantucket Sound beach, combine to make an enticing getaway. Since they're under the same management, the facilities of both are open to all guests; an old "woodie" shuttles between the two. The inn is a grand colonial building, with fireplaces and a baby grand piano in the common room. The antiques-filled guest rooms are in two separate wings; many have balconies or decks that overlook the pool and garden. The beach resort is reminiscent of an earlier era, with a turret and a wraparound porch. Its elegant guest rooms are also dotted with antiques, and some baths have whirlpool tubs. From umbrella tables on the deck you can watch the sweep of coast and surrounding grasslands while enjoying a generous Continental breakfast. Off-season, there's a fire burning in the common room. ⊠ *328 Bank St., 02645, and* ⊠ *4 Braddock La., Harwich Port 02646,* ☎ *508/432–4444 or 800/870–4405. 44 rooms. Restaurant, pool. MC, V. Closed Mar. CP.*

$$–$$$$ ⊞ **Dunscroft by the Sea.** With romance as its main motto, this gambrel-roof, cedar-shingle inn provides such lush amenities as antique sleigh, laced canopy, and four-poster beds, two-person whirlpool tubs, and terry robes for its guests. Rooms are generously sized and individually and colorfully decorated, with floral curtains and reproduction pieces; some have working fireplaces. The calming waters of Nantucket Sound are just a few paces away. ⊠ *24 Pilgrim Rd., Harwich Port 02646,* ☎ *508/432–0810 or 800/432–4345. 8 rooms, 1 cottage. Beach. AE, D, MC, V. BP.*

$$$ ⊞ **Augustus Snow House.** This grand old Victorian is the epitome of
★ elegance. Common areas include the oak-paneled front room, with tall windows and a fireplace, and a wicker-filled screened porch. The stately dining room is the setting for the three-course breakfast, with dishes such as baked pears in raspberry and cream sauce. Guest rooms are individually decorated with Victorian-print wallpapers, luxurious carpets, and fine antiques and reproduction furnishings. All have quilts, TVs, fireplaces, and antique brass bathroom and lighting fixtures; three also have whirlpool tubs. Downstairs, a lovely gardenlike tearoom is open to the public on Thursday, Friday, and Saturday for afternoon tea. ⊠ *528 Main St. (Rte. 28), Harwich Port 02646,* ☎ *508/430–0528 or 800/320–0528,* Ⅲ *508/432–6638 ext. 15. 5 rooms. Air-conditioning. AE, D, MC, V. BP.*

$$ ⊞ **Sea Heather Inn.** Resting majestically amid sculptured lawns with views of Nantucket Sound, this is one of the grand dames of the area. The main house, a stately and rambling Cape-style building built in the 1840s, is in the perpetual process of renewing itself; the owners are adding painted wainscoting and wide plank flooring. Rooms in the main house are filled with antiques and reproductions, and several offer water views. A larger, hotel-style complex on the property provides rooms with more modern furnishings in a decidedly hotel-style area, complete with game room for those in need of entertainment. The inn is a short walk

from several beaches. ✉ *28 Sea St., Harwich Port 02646,* ☎ *508/432–1275 or 800/789–7809. 22 rooms. Air-conditioning. AE, D, MC, V. BP.*

$–$$ 🖬 **Seadar Inn.** While it won't win any awards for elegant decor, the
★ friendly Seadar brings comfort and cleanliness with a great draw—location. The only obstacle between you and the beach on Nantucket Sound is the small parking lot and possibly the ice cream truck. The homey, motel-style rooms are unfussy and practical in a colonial style, with knotty-pine walls, frilly curtains, and the kind of furniture you might see in your grandmother's house; some have water views. Outdoor grills are available. ✉ *Braddock La. at Bank St. Beach, Harwich Port 02646,* ☎ *508/432–0264 or 800/888–5250. 23 rooms. AE, D, MC, V. Closed mid-Oct.–May. BP.*

$ 🖬 **Handkerchief Shoals Motel.** This single-story property about 2 mi from Harwich Port and 3 mi from downtown Chatham is set back from the highway on a deep skirt of lawn. The large rooms are sparkling clean, with sitting and desk areas, tiled baths, cable TV, and a refrigerator and microwave. All in all, it's a very good value for the area. ✉ *888 Rte. 28, at Deep Hole Rd., Box 306, South Harwich 02661,* ☎ *508/432–2200. 26 rooms. Pool, Ping-Pong. D, MC, V. Closed mid-Oct.–mid-Apr.*

Nightlife and the Arts

THE ARTS

The **First Congregational Church** (✉ Main St., corner of Rtes. 39 and 124, Harwich, ☎ 508/432–1053) closes its day of worship with Sunday evening Candlelight Concerts at 7:30 from July through September.

Harwich Junior Theatre (✉ 105 Division St., West Harwich, ☎ 508/432–2002) gives theater classes for children year-round and presents four family-oriented summer productions.

Town band concerts in Harwich take place in summer on Tuesday at 7:30 in Brooks Park (☎ 508/432–1600).

NIGHTLIFE

Country Inn (✉ 86 Sisson Rd. [Rte. 39], West Harwich Port, ☎ 508/432–2769) complements its dinner menu with dancing every Friday and Saturday evening. You can dance between courses to music of the 1940s with a piano player on Friday nights and a pianist and bass player on Saturday evenings from 7.

Irish Pub (✉ 126 Main St. [Rte. 28], West Harwich, ☎ 508/432–8808) has dancing to bands—playing Irish, American, and dance music—as well as sing-alongs, pool, darts, sports TV, and pub food in the bar.

Jake Rooney's Pub (✉ 119 Brooks Rd., off Rte. 28, Harwich Port, ☎ 508/430–1100) has a comfortable pub atmosphere, keno, and live entertainment five nights a week.

Outdoor Activities and Sports

BASEBALL

The **Harwich Mariners** (☎ 508/432–0662) of the collegiate Cape Cod Baseball League play home games at Whitehouse Field (✉ Harwich High School, Oak St.) from mid-June to mid-August.

BEACHES

Harwich has 22 beaches, more than any other Cape town. Most of the ocean beaches are on Nantucket Sound, where the water is a bit calmer and warmer. Freshwater pond beaches are also abundant.

BOATING

Whether you're in the mood to sail under the moonlight, hire a private charter or learn to navigate yourself, **Cape Sail** (✉ 337 Saquatucket

Harbor, off Rte. 28, Harwich Port, ☎ 508/896–2730) can accommodate any whim.

Cape Water Sports (✉ 337 Main St. [Rte. 28], Harwich Port, ☎ 508/432–7079) rents Sunfish, Hobie Cats, Lasers, powerboats, surfbikes, day sailers, and canoes and gives instructions.

The year 2000 marks the 10th annual **Sails Around Cape Cod** regatta (☎ 508/430–1165). The late-August race circumnavigates the Cape, a distance of 140 nautical mi, beginning at the east end of the Cape Cod Canal and ending at the west end.

FISHING

Fishing trips are operated on a walk-on basis from spring through fall on the **Golden Eagle** (✉ Wychmere Harbor, Harwich Port, ☎ 508/432–5611).

The **Yankee** (✉ Saquatucket Harbor, Harwich Port, ☎ 508/432–2520) invites passengers aboard its 65-ft party boat in search of fluke, scup, sea bass, and tautog. Two trips depart daily Monday through Saturday, and there's one on Sunday. Reservations are recommended.

GOLF

Cranberry Valley Golf Course (✉ 183 Oak St., ☎ 508/430–7560) has a championship layout of 18 well-groomed holes surrounded by cranberry bogs.

Harwich Port Golf Club (✉ South and Forest Sts., Harwich Port, ☎ 508/432–0250) has a nine-hole course that's great for beginners.

SCUBA DIVING

Water temperatures vary from 50°F to 70°F in Nantucket Sound and from 40°F to 65°F on the ocean side and in Cape Cod Bay. Check with a dive shop about local conditions and sites, as well as about dive boats. Wrecks in area waters include a steamship and schooners. Rentals, instruction, group dives, and information are available through **Cape Cod Divers** (✉ 815 Main St. [Rte. 28], Harwich Port, ☎ 508/432–9035 or 800/348–4641).

SWIMMING

Cape Cod Divers (☞ Scuba Diving, *above*) has a heated indoor pool and swimming lessons year-round.

Shopping

Cape Cod Braided Rug Co. (✉ 537 Main St. [Rte. 28], Harwich Port, ☎ 508/432–3133) specializes in braided rugs made on the premises in a variety of colors, styles, and sizes.

Merlyn Auctions (✉ 204 Main St., North Harwich, ☎ 508/432–5863) are held every Saturday night, with moderate to inexpensive prices for antique and used furniture.

Wychmere Book & Coffee (✉ 587 Main St. [Rte. 28], Harwich Port, ☎ 508/432–7868) is a place to savor the comforts of browsing, reading, and sipping good coffee. Special events with authors and a children's summer reading hour further enhance the scene.

Chatham

33–**38**   *5 mi east of Harwich, 8 mi south of Orleans.*

In 1656 William Nickerson traded a boat for the 17 square mi of land that make up Chatham. In 1712 the area separated from Eastham and was incorporated as a town; the surnames of the Pilgrims who first settled here still dominate the census list. Although Chatham was originally a

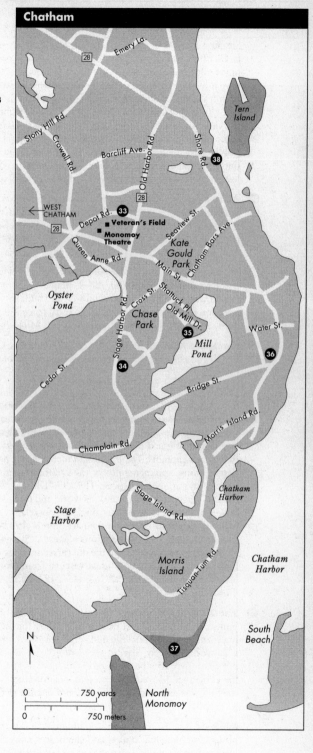

Chatham

Emery La.

28

Stony Hill Rd.

Crowell Rd.

Barcliff Ave.

Old Harbor Rd.

Shore Rd.

Tern
Island

38

28

← WEST
  CHATHAM

Depot Rd.

33

■ Veteran's Field

■ Monomoy
  Theatre

Seaview St.

Kate
Gould
Park

Chatham Bars Ave.

28

Queen Anne Rd.

Main St.

Oyster
Pond

Stage Harbor Rd.

Cross St.

Shattuck Pl.

Chase
Park

Old Mill Dr.

35

Mill
Pond

Water St.

34

36

Cedar St.

Bridge St.

Morris Island Rd.

Champlain Rd.

Stage Island Rd.

Chatham
Harbor

Stage
Harbor

Morris
Island

Tisquan-Tum Rd.

Chatham
Harbor

N

South
Beach

37

0   750 yards

0   750 meters

North
Monomoy

farming community, the sea finally lured townspeople to turn to fishing for their livelihood, an industry that has held strong to this day.

Situated at the bent elbow of the Cape, with water nearly surrounding it, Chatham has all the charm of a quietly posh seaside resort, with relatively little commercialism. And it is charming: gray-shingled houses with tidy awnings and cheerful flower gardens, an attractive Main Street with crafts and antiques stores alongside homey coffee shops, and a five-and-ten. It's a traditional town, where elegant summer cottages share the view with stately houses of purebred Yankee architecture, including some of the finest bow-roof houses in the country. There is none of Provincetown's flash, yet it's not overly quaint—just well-to-do without being ostentatious, casual and fun but refined, and never tacky (unless you feel that a few large new "trophy houses" qualify as tacky).

③③ Authentic all the way, the **Railroad Museum** is set in a restored 1887 depot. Exhibits include a walk-through 1910 New York Central caboose, old photographs, equipment, thousands of train models, and a diorama of the 1915 Chatham rail yards. ⊠ *153 Depot Rd.,* ☏ *no phone.* ◨ *Donations accepted.* ⊙ *Mid-June–mid-Sept., Tues.–Sat. 10–4.*

☾ A unique playground, the **Play-a-round,** a multilevel wooden playground of turrets, twisting tubular slides, jungle gyms, and more, was designed with the input of local children and built by volunteers. There's a section for people with disabilities and a fenced-in area for small children. ⊠ *Depot Rd., across from Railroad Museum.*

On **Queen Anne Road** around Oyster Pond, half-Cape houses, open fields, and rolling pastures reveal the area's colonial and agricultural history.

③④ Built by sea captain Joseph C. Atwood in 1752 and occupied by his descendants until it was sold to the Chatham Historical Society in 1926, the **Atwood House Museum** has a gambrel roof, variable-width floor planks, fireplaces, an old kitchen with a wide hearth and a beehive oven, and some antique dolls and toys. The New Gallery displays portraits of local sea captains. The Joseph C. Lincoln Room has the manuscripts, first editions, and mementos of the Chatham writer, and in the basement is an antique tool room. The 1974 Durand Wing houses collections of seashells from around the world and threaded Sandwich glass, as well as Parian ware figures, unglazed porcelain vases, figurines, and busts. In a remodeled freight shed are murals (1932–45) by Alice Stallknecht Wight portraying religious scenes in Chatham settings. On the grounds are an herb garden, the old turret and lens from the Chatham Light, and a simple camp house rescued from eroding North Beach. ⊠ *347 Stage Harbor Rd.,* ☏ *508/945–2493.* ◨ *$3.* ⊙ *Mid-June–Sept., Tues.–Fri. 1–4.*

③⑤ The **Old Grist Mill,** one of a number of windmills still on the Cape, was built in 1797 by Colonel Benjamin Godfrey for the purpose of grinding corn. How practical the mill actually was is a matter of debate: for it to work properly, a wind speed of at least 20 mph was necessary, but winds over 25 mph required the miller to reef the sails, or quit grinding altogether. Moved to its present location from Miller Hill in 1956, the mill was extensively renovated and opened to the public in 1957. ⊠ *Old Mill Dr.* ⊙ *July–Aug., weekdays 10–3.*

Mill Pond is a lovely place to stop for a picnic. There's fishing from the bridge, and often the "bullrakers" can be seen at work, plying the pond's muddy bottom with 20-ft rakes in search of shellfish.

Stage Harbor, sheltered by Morris Island, is where Samuel de Champlain anchored in 1606. The street on its north side is, not surprisingly, called Champlain Road. A skirmish here between Europeans and Native Americans marked the first bloodshed in New England between native people and the new arrivals.

★ ③⑥ The famous view from **Chatham Light** (⊠ Main St., near Bridge St., ☎ 508/945–5199)—of the harbor, the offshore sandbars, and the ocean beyond—justifies the crowds that gather to share it. The lighthouse is especially dramatic on a foggy night, as the beacon's light pierces the mist. Coin-operated telescopes allow a close look at the famous "Chatham Break," the result of a fierce 1987 nor'easter that blasted a channel through a barrier beach just off the coast; it is now known as North and South beaches. The Cape Cod Museum of Natural History in Brewster (☞ *above*) has a display of photos documenting the process of erosion leading up to and following the break. The U.S. Coast Guard Auxiliary, which supervises the lighthouse, offers tours on the first and third Wednesdays, April–September. The lighthouse is also open by appointment, and on three special occasions during the year: Seafest, an annual tribute to the maritime industry held in mid-October; mid-May's Cape Cod Maritime Week; and June's Cape Heritage Week.

★ **Monomoy National Wildlife Refuge** is a 2,500-acre preserve including the Monomoy Islands, a fragile, 9-mi-long barrier-beach area south of Chatham. Monomoy's North and South islands were created when a storm divided the former Monomoy Island in 1978. Monomoy was itself separated from the mainland in a 1958 storm. A paradise for birdwatchers, the island is an important stop along the North Atlantic Flyway for migratory waterfowl and shore birds—peak migration times are May and late July. It also provides nesting and resting grounds for 285 species, including gulls—great black-backed, herring, and laughing—and several tern species. White-tail deer also live on the islands, and harbor and gray seals frequent the shores in winter. The only structure on the islands is the **South Monomoy Lighthouse.** Built in 1849, the shiny red-orange structure, along with the keeper's house, was refurbished in 1988.

Monomoy is a quiet, peaceful place of sand and beach grass, of tidal flats, dunes, marshes, freshwater ponds, thickets of bayberry and beach plum, and a few pines. Because the refuge harbors several endangered species, visitors' activities are limited. Certain areas are fenced off to protect nesting areas of terns and the threatened piping plover. The Massachusetts Audubon Society in South Wellfleet, the Cape Cod Museum of Natural History in Brewster, and other groups conduct tours of the islands, many with a focus on bird-watching. The *Rip Ryder* (☎ 508/945–5450) will take you over from Chatham in season for some lone bird-watching. Rates vary greatly: if you catch a ride out with the seal-watching cruise, it's $14 per person; if you charter a private ride, rates are $45 per person round-trip or $10 per person for three or more passengers.

③⑦ The **Monomoy National Wildlife Refuge headquarters,** on the misleadingly named Morris Island (it is connected to the mainland), has a visitor center and bookstore (⊠ Off Morris Island Rd., ☎ 508/945–0594), open daily 8–5, with gaps, where you can pick up pamphlets on Monomoy and the birds, wildlife, and flora and fauna found there. A ¾-mi interpretive walking trail, closed at high tide, around Morris Island gives a good view of the refuge and the surrounding waters.

③⑧ The **Fish Pier** (⊠ Shore Rd. and Barcliff Ave.) bustles with activity when Chatham's fishing fleet returns, sometime between noon and 2 PM daily, depending on the tide. The unloading of the boats is a big local event, drawing crowds who watch it all from an observation deck. From their fishing grounds 3 to 100 mi offshore, fishermen bring in haddock, cod, flounder, lobster, halibut, and pollack, which is packed in ice and shipped to New York and Boston or sold at the fish market here. You might also see sand sharks being unloaded. They typically go fresh and frozen to French and German markets. Also here is *The Provider*, a monument to the town's fishing industry, showing a hand pulling a fish-filled net from the sea.

The **Chatham Winery** (✉ 1291 Rte. 28, ☎ 508/945–0300) is open year-round for tours and tastings of the fruit and flower wines produced here.

Known for their artful contemporary treatment of blown glass, Jim Holmes and Deborah Doane of the **Chatham Glass Company** (☞ Shopping, *below*) create everything from candle holders to unique vases in a vast spectrum of color. You can watch the fascinating process of glassblowing here. ✉ *758 Main St.,* ☎ *508/945–5547.* ☉ *Memorial Day–Labor Day, Mon.–Sat. 10–5; Labor Day–Memorial Day, daily 10–5.*

Dining and Lodging

$$$ ✕ **Christian's.** The influences at this landmark town establishment stem from two continents. Downstairs, the dining room mixes Old Cape and country French decor: Pilgrim blue with lace. Lunch and dinner are also both French and New England: boneless roast duck with raspberry sauce, and flaky sautéed sole with lobster and lemon-butter sauce. The mahogany-paneled bar and deck upstairs serve a lighter menu that remains strong on seafood but adds some Mexican influences, like tacos and quesadillas, that are well suited to the summer. In some ways, this is one of those situations where less is more; as nice as the formal downstairs remains, the upstairs is more of a happening scene. ✉ *443 Main St.,* ☎ *508/945–3362. AE, D, DC, MC, V. Closed weekdays Jan.–Mar.*

$$–$$$ ✕ **Vining's Bistro.** Chatham's restaurants have tended to the conser-
★ vative end of the culinary spectrum, but this bistro is convincing everyone that it deserves mention not only for its exceptionally inventive menu but for its determination not to rest on its laurels. The wood grill is the center of attention here, where the chef employs zesty rubs and spices from all over the globe. The wonderful, exotic Bangkok fisherman's stew has almost too much seafood crammed in; spit-roasted Jamaican chicken competes with a Portobello mushroom sandwich as the restaurant's signature dish. Go for the "Mahogany Fire Noodles," an awe-inspiring shrimp and chicken dish. The restaurant is upstairs at the Gallery building, and many of the windows look out on the art below. ✉ *595 Main St.,* ☎ *508/945–5033. Reservations not accepted. AE, D, MC, V. Closed mid-Jan.–Apr.*

$$ ✕ **Chatham Squire.** What had been a bar and not much more has now
★ evolved into an excellent dining experience. This is the kind of place where if you order anything local, you can't go wrong. The fish is as fresh and good as you get on Cape Cod, and the kitchen continues to innovate while not forgetting its Cape roots. The calamari is always tender, the oysters a lovely mouthful. The Squire is not as inexpensive as it was (or as its exterior implies), but it is much finer. Expect a long wait in season, in which case a visit to the bar side is not the worst fate. ✉ *487 Main St.,* ☎ *508/945–0945. Reservations not accepted. AE, D, MC, V.*

$$ ✕ **The Sou'wester.** You're more likely to see someone in a yellow slicker and rubber boots than a sports jacket and loafers in this small spot, the most unpretentious bar-restaurant in Chatham, if not the Lower Cape. The decor could hardly even be called that: eight booths, low light, and what look like fake Oriental rugs for wall hangings. The handwritten menu is heavy on steak tips, sirloin, and pork chops, with fish

In case you want to see the world.

At American Express, we're here to make your journey a smooth one. So we have over 1,700 travel service locations in over 130 countries ready to help. What else would you expect from the world's largest travel agency?

do more

Travel

Call 1 800 AXP-3429 or visit
www.americanexpress.com/travel

In case you want to be welcomed there.

We're here to see that you're always welcomed at establishments everywhere. That's why millions of people carry the American Express® Card – for peace of mind, confidence, and security, around the world or just around the corner.

do more · AMERICAN EXPRESS Cards

In case you're running low.

We're here to help with more than 190,000 Express Cash locations around the world. In order to enroll, just call American Express at 1 800 CASH-NOW before you start your vacation.

do more **AMERICAN EXPRESS**

Express Cash

And in case you'd rather be safe than sorry.

We're here with American Express® Travelers Cheques. They're the safe way to carry money on your vacation, because if they're ever lost or stolen you can get a refund, practically anywhere or anytime. To find the nearest place to buy Travelers Cheques, call 1 800 495-1153. Another way we help you do more.

do more

Travelers Cheques

cakes and beans for the fishermen patrons who haven't had their fill of fish for the day. A long-neck Bud seems the appropriate accompaniment. On weekends there's good, loud, get-down live music in the bar, known as the Lincoln Lodge. ⊠ *1563 Main St.,* ☎ *508/945–4424. AE, MC, V.*

$$$$ ✕🏨 **Chatham Bars Inn.** This 1914 landmark inn is an oceanfront resort in the old, extravagant style. High above the beach on a windswept bluff, the inn claims a stunning view of the ocean through floor-to-ceiling windows. The formal dining-room menu leans on current American hits like rich, seared foie gras and steamed swordfish with clams. Grand Sunday dinner buffets include a raw bar with caviar and half lobsters. The Tavern is open for more casual lunch and dinner, and the Beach House Bar opens in season for breakfast and lunch down by the water. The inn consists of a main building flanked with wings— on the ground floor the grand lobby gives way to the formal restaurant on one side and a porch-fronted lounge on the other—and 26 one-to eight-bedroom cottages on 22 landscaped acres overlooking the ocean. Under seemingly perpetual renovation, the once bland rooms are now filled with hand-painted furnishings by local artists and colorful fabrics depicting sunny seaside scenes. Although the ocean views from some rooms may be spectacular, when push comes to shove, the value for the money is not exceptional. ⊠ *Shore Rd., 02633,* ☎ *508/945–0096 or 800/527–4884,* 𝔽𝔸𝕏 *508/945–5491. 205 rooms. 3 restaurants, bar, lobby lounge, pool, putting green, 4 tennis courts, exercise room, volleyball, beach, baby-sitting, children's programs. AE, DC, MC, V.*

$$$$ 🏨 **Wequassett Inn Resort & Golf Club.** This exquisite traditional resort
★ offers first-rate accommodations in 20 Cape-style cottages and an attractive hotel complex. Partly surrounded by the mild waters of Pleasant Bay and shaded by oaks and pines on its 22 acres, the Wequassett provides luxury in an informal setting. Along with attentive service and evening entertainment, you'll find plenty of sunning and sporting opportunities, including the brand-new, very exclusive Cape Cod National Golf Club (guests have golf privileges). Thoughtfully decorated with fresh pine furniture, floral bedcoverings or handmade quilts and such homey touches as overflowing window boxes and duck decoys, rooms are spacious and welcoming. ⊠ *173 Orleans Rd. (Rte. 28), Pleasant Bay, 02633,* ☎ *508/432–5400 or 800/225–7125,* 𝔽𝔸𝕏 *508/432–5032. 102 rooms, 2 suites. Restaurant, grill, piano bar, room service, pool, 4 tennis courts, exercise room, windsurfing, boating. AE, D, DC, MC, V. Closed Nov.–Apr. FAP.*

$$$–$$$$ 🏨 **Chatham Wayside Inn.** Once a stop on a turn-of-the-century stagecoach route, the inn may still be an oasis for weary travelers, but its decor does not hark back to those earlier times. Everything is crisp and colorful here, from the floral comforters and wallpapers to freshly painted walls and bright wall-to-wall carpeting. Some rooms include private balconies, fireplaces, and whirlpool tubs. You'll find modern, tasteful comfort here, with the added benefit of a location smack in the center of town: you may not have to leave your room to hear the sounds of the weekly town band concerts. ⊠ *512 Main St., 02633,* ☎ *508/ 945–5550 or 800/391–5734,* 𝔽𝔸𝕏 *508/945–3407. 56 rooms. Restaurant, pool. AE, D, MC, V. BP.*

$$$–$$$$ 🏨 **Cranberry Inn.** Within close range of the heart of town, the inn has the added benefit of a protected marsh area in its backyard—a fine spot from which to spy great blue herons and the occasional deer or fox. Billed as the oldest continuously operating lodging establishment in Chatham, the inn reinforces the tradition with decor that reflects a country-inspired theme, such as antique and reproduction furniture and an array of handmade quilts. Rooms have telephones and televisions; some offer fireplaces or private balconies. ⊠ *359 Main St., 02633,* ☎

508/945–9232 or 800/332–4667, FAX 508/945–3769. 18 rooms. Restaurant. AE, D, MC, V. BP.

$$$–$$$$ ★ **Queen Anne Inn.** Built in 1840 as a wedding present for the daughter of a famous clipper-ship captain, the building first opened as an inn in 1874, at which time a north wing was added; a south wing was added much later, in the 1950s. The quite-grand resulting structure has large guest rooms furnished in a casual yet elegant style. Some have working fireplaces, private balconies, and hot tubs. Lingering and lounging are encouraged—around the large heated outdoor pool, at the tables on the veranda, in front of the fireplace in the cozy sitting room, and in the plush parlor. The tastefully designed restaurant, which serves a delicious breakfast, is also open to the public for dinner. ⊠ *70 Queen Anne Rd., 02633,* ☎ *508/945–0394 or 800/545–4667,* FAX *508/945–4884. 31 rooms. Restaurant, bar, air-conditioning, pool, 3 tennis courts. AE, D, MC, V.*

$$–$$$$ ★ **Captain's House Inn.** Finely preserved architectural details, superb interiors, and an overall feeling of warmth and quiet comfort are just part of what makes Jan and Dave McMaster's inn one of the Cape's finest. Each room in the four inn buildings has its own personality. Some are quite large, and most have fireplaces; some are lacy and feminine, others refined and elegant. Authentic details of another era abound, from a Victorian tile ceiling to wide-board floors and elaborate moldings and wainscoting. The gorgeous Hiram Harding Room in the bow-roofed Captain's Cottage has 200-year-old hand-hewn ceiling beams, a wall of raised walnut paneling, and a large, central, working fireplace. The luxury suites in the former stables are particularly spacious and have every amenity imaginable, including whirlpool baths, fireplaces, TV/VCR, minirefrigerators, and private patios or balconies. ⊠ *371 Old Harbor Rd., 02633,* ☎ *508/945–0127,* FAX *508/945–0866. 16 rooms, 3 suites. Croquet, bicycles. No smoking. AE, D, MC, V. BP.*

$$–$$$ ★ **Moses Nickerson House.** Each room in this 1839 house has an individual look: one with dark woods, leathers, Ralph Lauren fabrics, and English hunting antiques; another with a high canopy bed and a hand-hooked rug. Still others are bedecked with handmade quilts, floral wallcoverings, and canopy or four-poster beds. Some rooms have gas-log fireplaces. The constants are the queen beds, televisions, telephones, and complete modem and computer hookups. Breakfast is served in a pretty glassed-in sunroom with views of the garden and fishpond. ⊠ *364 Old Harbor Rd., 02633,* ☎ *508/945–5859 or 800/628–6972,* FAX *508/945–7087. 7 rooms. Air-conditioning, in-room data ports. No smoking. AE, D, MC, V. BP.*

$$ **Hawthorne Motel.** Known not just for its immediate proximity to the water, this popular motel overlooking Pleasant Bay, the Atlantic, and Chatham Harbor is also cherished for its reasonable prices. Nearly all the rooms, whether they are the spotless no-nonsense, simply decorated motel rooms or the fully equipped efficiency units, have the advantage of stunning water views. The center of town is just a short walk away. ⊠ *196 Shore Rd., 02633,* ☎ *508/945–0372. 16 rooms, 10 efficiencies. AE, D, MC, V. Closed mid-Oct.–mid-May.*

Nightlife and the Arts

THE ARTS

Chatham Drama Guild (⊠ 134 Crowell Rd., ☎ 508/945–0510) stages several productions in the summer season, including musicals, comedies, and dramas.

The **Creative Arts Center** (⊠ 154 Crowell Rd., ☎ 508/945–3583) is a thriving year-round arts center with classes, changing gallery exhibitions, demonstrations, lectures, and other activities.

In July and August, the **Guild of Chatham Painters** presents an outdoor art gallery on Thursdays and Fridays from 9:30 to 5 on the lawn of the Main Street School (✉ Main St.).

The **Monomoy Theatre** (✉ 776 Main St., ☎ 508/945–1589) presents summer productions—thrillers, musicals, classics, modern drama—by the Ohio University Players.

Chatham's summer **town band concerts** (✉ Kate Gould Park, Main St., ☎ 508/945–5199) begin at 8 on Friday and draw up to 6,000 people. As many as 500 fox-trot on the roped-off dance floor, and there are special dances for children and sing-alongs for all.

NIGHTLIFE
Chatham Squire (✉ 487 Main St., ☎ 508/945–0945), with four separate bars including a raw bar, is a rollicking year-round local hangout, drawing a young crowd to the bar side and a mixed crowd of locals to the restaurant (☞ Dining and Lodging, *above*).

Wequassett Inn Resort & Golf Club (✉ 173 Orleans Rd. [Rte. 28]), Pleasant Bay, ☎ 508/432–5400; ☞ Dining and Lodging, *above*) has a jazz duo or piano music nightly in its lounge in July and August (jacket requested).

Outdoor Activities and Sports

BASEBALL
The **Cape Cod Baseball League,** begun in 1885, is an invitational league of college players that counts Carlton Fisk, Ron Darling, and the late Thurman Munson as alumni. Considered the country's best summer league, it is scouted by all the major-league teams. Players have included Mo Vaughn and Nomar Garciaparra. Ten teams play a 44-game season from mid-June to mid-August; games held at all 10 fields are free (☞ Close-Up: The Cape Cod Baseball League, *below*). The **Chatham A's** games (✉ Veteran's Field, Main and Depot Sts. by the rotary, ☎ 508/996–5004 for schedule) are great entertainment.

Baseball clinics (✉ Veteran's Field, Main and Depot Sts. by the rotary, ☎ 508/432–6909) for children 6–8, 9–12, and 13–17 are offered in one-week sessions by the Chatham A's in summer. The other nine town teams in the Cape league also conduct clinics (☎ 508/996–5004 for information).

BEACHES
If you're looking for a crowd-free sandy beach, boats at Chatham Harbor—such as the **Rip Ryder** (☎ 508/945–5450)—will ferry you across to North Beach ($10–$12 per person), which is a sand spit adjoining Orleans's Nauset Beach to South Beach ($10), or to Monomoy ($45, or $10 per person for three or more passengers).

Outermost Harbor Marine (✉ Morris Island Rd., ☎ 508/945–2030) runs shuttles to South Beach; rides cost $10 round-trip for adults. The cost includes parking.

Harding's Beach (✉ Harding's Beach Rd., off Barn Hill Rd.), west of Chatham center, is open to the public and charges daily parking fees to nonresidents in season. Lifeguards are stationed in summer.

BIKING
Bert & Carol's Lawnmower & Bicycle Shop (✉ 347 Orleans Rd. [Rte. 28], North Chatham, ☎ 508/945–0137) rents a variety of bikes.

Bikes & Blades (✉ 195 Crowell Rd., ☎ 508/945–7600) rents all manner of bikes as well as in-line skates.

THE CAPE COD BASEBALL LEAGUE

AT THE BASEBALL HALL OF FAME in Cooperstown, New York, you'll find a poster announcing a showdown between arch rivals Sandwich and Barnstable. The date? July 4, 1885. In the hundred-plus years since that day, the Cape's ball-playing tradition has continued unabated, and if you're a sports fan, a visit to a Cape Cod Baseball League summer game is a must. Seeing a game on the Cape is to come into contact with baseball's roots. You'll remember why you love the sport, and you'll have a newfound sense of why it became the national pastime.

As they have since the 1950s, top-ranked college baseball players from around the country descend on the Cape when school lets out, in time to begin the season in mid-June. This is no sandlot, catch-as-catch-can scene. Each player joins one of the league's 10 teams, which are based in Bourne, Wareham, Falmouth, Cotuit, Hyannis, Dennis-Yarmouth, Harwich, Brewster, Chatham, and Orleans. The teams are the Bourne Braves, Wareham Gatemen, Falmouth Commodores, Cotuit Kettleers, Hyannis Mets, Dennis-Yarmouth Red Sox, Harwich Mariners, Brewster Whitecaps, Chatham Athletics (A's), and the Orleans Cardinals.

Players lodge with local families and work day jobs cutting lawns, painting houses, or giving baseball clinics in town parks. In the evenings, though, their lives are given over to baseball, as they don uniforms and head for the field.

To judge by the past, Cape League veterans are tomorrow's major-league stars. By latest count, one of every eight active major league ballplayers spent a summer in the Cape League on the way up. The Boston Red Sox's recent starting infield—Mo Vaughn, John Valentin, Tim Naehring, and Nomar Garciaparra—all played in the Cape League in different years, for different teams. Add names like Frank Thomas, Jeff Bagwell, Albert Belle (before he lost his manners), Will Clark, and Walt Weiss, and you begin to get a sense of the quality on display.

As good as the baseball is—and you'll often see bunches of major-league scouts at a game—another great reason to come out to the ballpark is . . . the ballpark. Chatham's Veterans Field is the Cape's 3Com Park at Candlestick Point, because, much like the San Francisco version, fog tends to engulf the games. Orleans's Eldredge Park is a local favorite—immaculate, cozy, and comfortable. Some parks have bleachers, while in others it's up to you to bring your own chair or blanket and stretch out behind a dugout or baseline. Kids are free to roam and can even try for foul balls, which they are, however, asked to return because, after all, balls don't grow on trees. When hunger hits, the ice cream truck and hot-dog stand are never far away.

Games start at either 5 or 7 PM, depending on whether the field has lights (there are occasionally afternoon games). Each team plays 44 games in a season, so finding one is rarely a problem. And best of all, they're always free. The Cape's baseball scene is so American, the ambience so relaxed and refreshing, that it's tempting to invoke the old Field of Dreams analogy. But the league needs no Hollywood comparison. This is the real thing. It was built a long time ago, and they are still coming.

—Seth Rolbein

Monomoy Sail & Cycle (✉ 275 Orleans Rd., North Chatham, ☎ 508/945–0811) rents sailboards and Sunfish.

GOLF

Chatham Seaside Links (✉ Seaview St., ☎ 508/945–4774), a nine-hole course, is good for beginners.

SURFING

The Lower and Outer Cape beaches, including North Beach in Chatham, are the best spots for surfing, which is tops when there's a storm offshore. Chatham does not have any surf shops, but you'll find them in nearby Orleans (☞ Outdoor Activities and Sports *in* Orleans, *below*).

TENNIS

Chatham Bars Inn (✉ Shore Rd., ☎ 508/945–0096, ext. 1155) offers three waterfront all-weather tennis courts, lessons, and a pro shop.

The town maintains two public tennis parks, one on Depot Road next to the Railroad Museum at No. 153 and the other at the middle school on Crowell Road.

Shopping

Main Street is a busy shopping area with upscale and conservative merchandise. Here you'll find galleries, crafts, clothing stores, bookstores, and a few good antiques shops.

Cape Cod Cooperage (✉ 1150 Queen Anne Rd., at Rte. 137, ☎ 508/432–0788), set in an old barn, sells woodenware made in a century-old tradition by an on-site cooper (barrel maker), as well as hand-decorated furniture, crafts supplies, and more. Daily classes are also scheduled in everything from stenciling to basket making, decorative painting to birdhouse building.

Chatham Glass Company (✉ 758 Main St., ☎ 508/945–5547) is a glass-works where you can watch glass being blown and buy it, too—objects including marbles, Christmas ornaments, jewelry, and art glass.

Chatham Jam and Jelly Shop (✉ 10 Vineyard Ave., at Rte. 28, West Chatham, ☎ 508/945–3052) sells preserves such as cranberry with strawberries and Maine wild blueberry, nutty conserves, and ice cream toppings, all made on-site in small batches.

Clambake Celebrations (✉ 1223C Main St., ☎ 508/945–7771 or 800/423–4038) prepares full clambakes, including lobsters, clams, mussels, corn, potatoes, onions, and sausage, for you to take away; it'll even loan a charcoal grill. The company also delivers or air-ships year-round. The food is layered in seaweed in a pot and ready to steam.

Fancy's Farm of Chatham (✉ 1291 Main [Rte. 28]), West Chatham, ☎ 508/945–1949) sells local and exotic produce, fresh-baked breads, pies, and pastries, dried flowers, baskets, frozen prepared gourmet foods, spices, and potpourri. A delicatessen provides take-out meats and sandwiches.

Marion's Pie Shop (✉ 2022 Main St. [Rte. 28], West Chatham, ☎ 508/432–9439) sells homemade and home-style fruit breads, pastries, prepared foods such as lasagna, Boston baked beans, chowder base, and, of course, pies, both savory and sweet.

The **Spyglass** (✉ 618 Main St., ☎ 508/945–9686) carries telescopes, barometers, writing boxes, maps, and other nautical antiques.

Yankee Ingenuity (✉ 525 Main St., ☎ 508/945–1288) stocks a varied selection of unique jewelry and lamps and a wide assortment of unusual, beautiful trinkets at some reasonable (especially for Chatham) prices.

Yellow Umbrella Books (⊠ 501 Main St., ☎ 508/945–0144) has an excellent selection of new books, many about Cape Cod, as well as used books.

En Route   North of Chatham, Route 28 winds through wooded upland toward **Pleasant Bay,** from which a number of country roads will take you to a nice view of Nauset spit and the islands in the bay.

Orleans

 8 mi north of Chatham, 4 mi southwest of Eastham, 35 mi east of the Sagamore Bridge.

Named for Louis-Philippe de Bourbon, duc d'Orléans, who reputedly visited the area during his exile from France in the 1790s, Orleans was incorporated as a town in 1797. Historically, it has the distinction of being the only spot in the continental United States to have received enemy fire during either world war. In July 1918 a German submarine fired on commercial barges off the coast. Four were sunk, and one shell is reported to have fallen on American soil.

Today Orleans is a mix of quiet seaside village and a bustling center with a pleasant downtown and some major strip malls. The commercial hub of the Lower Cape, Orleans is one of the more steadily populated areas, year-round, of this section of the Cape. It has a long heritage in fishing and seafaring, and many beautifully preserved homes remain from the colonial era. As you head north, this is the first Cape town to touch both Cape Cod Bay and the Atlantic Ocean. Nauset Beach, on the Atlantic, is enormously popular.

A walk along Rock Harbor Road, a pleasant winding street lined with gray-shingled Cape houses, white picket fences, and neat gardens, leads to the bay-side **Rock Harbor,** a former packet landing and the site of a War of 1812 skirmish in which the Orleans militia kept a British warship from docking. In the 19th century Orleans had an active saltworks, and a flourishing packet service between Rock Harbor and Boston developed. Today the former packet landing is the base of charter-fishing and party boats in season, as well as of a small commercial fishing fleet whose catch hits the counters at the fish market and small restaurant here. Sunsets over the harbor are spectacular.

The 1890 **French Cable Station Museum** was the stateside landing point for the 3,000-mi-long transatlantic cable that originated in Brittany. Another cable laid between Orleans and New York City completed the France–New York link, and many important messages were communicated through the station. In World War I it was an essential connection between army headquarters in Washington and the American Expeditionary Force in France, and the station was under guard by the marines. By 1959 telephone service had rendered the station obsolete, and it closed. The equipment is still in place. ⊠ *41 S. Orleans Rd.,* ☎ *508/240–1735.* ⊠ *Donations accepted.* ☉ *June–Labor Day, Mon.–Sat. 1–4.*

The **Jonathan Young Windmill,** a pretty, if somewhat incongruous, sight on the busy highway, is a landmark from the days of salt making in Orleans, when it would pump saltwater into shallow vaults for evaporation. A program explaining the history and operation of the mill demonstrates the old millstone and grinding process. ⊠ *Rte. 6A and Town Cove.* ☉ *July–Aug., daily 11–4; June and Sept., weekends 11–4.*

⟲ The **Academy of Performing Arts** (✉ 5 Giddiah Hill Rd., ☎ 508/255–5510) offers two-week sessions of theater, music, and dance classes to children 8 to 12 years old, with a show at the end of each session. It also schedules year-round classes for ages 4 to adult in dance, music, and drama. The academy's theater is at 120 Main St.

Dining and Lodging

$$–$$$ ✕ **Kadee's Lobster & Clam Bar.** A summer landmark that harks back to an era when drive-ins were the norm and not the exception, Kadee's serves good clams and fish-and-chips that you can grab on the way to the beach from the take-out window. Or sit down in the smoke-free indoor dining room for steamers and mussels, pasta and seafood stews, or the famous Portuguese kale soup. Even the service staff seems plucked from a few decades ago—clean-cut college kids working their way through the summer. There's a gift shop as well, and a miniature golf course out back. The only serious problem here is that, for what is served, the prices seem to have gone through the roof. ✉ *212 Main St.,* ☎ *508/255–6184. Reservations not accepted. MC, V. Closed day after Labor Day–week before Memorial Day and weekdays in early June.*

$$–$$$ ✕ **Nauset Beach Club.** What once was the unsung local hero has now ★ become widely known for its fine dining. You might feel as if you're eating in someone's former living room (you are), but the sophisticated food, rooted in contemporary Italian cuisine, is beyond that of even the finest home cooks. *Zuppa di pesce* (seafood stew) features shrimp, scallops, calamari, and lobster in a sauce Provençale served on pasta. The *penne puttanesca* (penne pasta with olives, garlic, peppers, and anchovies) delivers a whole medley of tastes. Unfortunately, the bar is too small and uncomfortable for the long waits (reservations are accepted only for parties of six or more), so stop in early or late for what will prove to be a superb meal. ✉ *222 Main St., East Orleans,* ☎ *508/ 255–8547. Reservations not accepted. AE, D, DC, MC, V. No lunch. No dinner Sun. and Mon. mid-Oct.–Memorial Day.*

$$–$$$ ✕ **Rosina's Cafe.** Originally a classic mom-and-pop Italian restaurant off Main Street, Rosina's has expanded into a full-blown, full-service place. Some feel that the food, which was some of the best homestyle Italian cooking on Cape Cod, has not survived the move all that well, but with a little care in your choice you can still find that fresh, natural style. The pasta primavera makes the grade, as does Angela's stuffed halibut (often on special), a good chunk of fish stuffed with scallops, cheeses, pine nuts, bread crumbs, and garlic. The puttanesca remains a signature, rewarding dish. The wine list mimics the food, veering into the conventional. ✉ *15 Cove Rd.,* ☎ *508/240–5513. AE, D, MC, V.*

$$ ✕ **The Jailhouse.** The symbol next to the entrance of this rambling restaurant, added on to what was an old stone lockup, is a big set of golden jailer's keys. The theme continues, with a light touch, throughout the decor and menu. On the long, varied menu are headings like "A Light Sentence" for salads and appetizers and "The Lineup" for the sandwich list. Foods for sharing include a whole wheel of baked Brie with homemade Boursin cheese, crackers and fruit, and deep-fried fresh vegetables with ranch dip. Entrées lean toward basic seafood, steak, veal, and chicken dishes. The restaurant has a flower-hung atrium, a long oak bar, and the new Courthouse addition for group events. ✉ *28 West Rd.,* ☎ *508/255–5245. Reservations not accepted. D, MC, V.*

$$ ✕ **Lobster Claw.** If you're over 6 ft tall, keep an eye out for the fishing nets hanging from the ceiling inside this goofy little seafood spot. Tables are lacquered turquoise, portions are huge, and the lobster roll is one of the best. You can get all the Cape basics here: fish and seafood poached, broiled, baked, or fried, and an assortment of steaks for variety. The kids' choices include some good seafood picks as well as the usual chicken tenders. ⊠ *Rte. 6A,* ☎ *508/255–1800. Reservations not accepted. AE, D, DC, MC, V.*

$$ ✕ **Mahoney's Atlantic Bar and Grill.** A recent arrival, Mahoney's has overcome some bad vibes at an excellent location and now seems ready to make a good go of it. The chef, indeed a Mahoney who cooked for years at one of Provincetown's busiest restaurants, really knows his stuff. The lunch and dinner menu are extending appetizers to new heights, emphasizing grilled vegetables and polenta, drunken littlenecks steamed in ale, and a New Orleans classic, oyster po'boys (why this hasn't come to Cape Cod sooner is a mystery). The bar is long and comfortable, although the California wine list is a little over-priced and the beer selection should improve. ⊠ *28 Main St.,* ☎ *508/255–5505. AE, D, DC, MC, V.*

$–$$ ✕ **Land Ho!** Orleans's flagship local scene is definitely fun and bois-terous even if the typical tavern fare on the blackboard menu doesn't always live up to the atmosphere. Hanging from the rafters are dozens of homemade wooden signs; anybody who's anybody in town has one made up. The burgers and the sea-clam pie are both excellent—much better than the fish-and-chips. The conversation is generally tastier (and saltier) than the chowder. At one table near the back, a group of local thinkers often chews over the world's problems. It's a good place for a rainy-day lunch. The place has expanded not only into the store next door but also down to Costa Rica, where owner John Murphy has set up another Land Ho! ⊠ *Rte. 6A and Cove Rd.,* ☎ *508/255–5165. Reser-vations not accepted. AE, MC, V.*

$–$$ ✕ **Sir Cricket's Fish and Chips.** If you have a sudden craving for a beau-tifully turned-out fish sandwich, you can pull off the highway into this tiny local favorite, a hole-in-the-wall attached to the Nauset Lobster Pool. Built mainly for takeout, this clean, no-frills fried-food joint does have three or four tiny tables and a soda machine. Try the fresh oyster roll or go for a full fisherman's platter. Be sure to check out the chair seats as you gobble those fries. Each is an exquisitely rendered mini-mural of Orleans history or a personality painted by legendary local artist Dan Joy. ⊠ *Rte. 6A, near Stop & Shop,* ☎ *508/255–4453. Reservations not accepted. No credit cards.*

$–$$ ✕ **The Yardarm.** Orleans's version of a roadhouse, the Yardarm feels smoky even though smoking is not allowed anymore. The tube over the bar is likely to be tuned to a sports game, and the only pool table in town is always busy (though not in use when dinner is being served). The hearty, well-cooked food is a great value, especially the baked sole, barbecued ribs or chicken, and the pot roast; thanks to the big por-tions, you can expect to take some of your dinner home. It's also a great place to stop in for a burger-and-beer lunch. If you're lucky, Lenny will be holding court behind the bar, and Patience will take your order into the kitchen. ⊠ *48 Rte. 28,* ☎ *508/255–4840. Reservations not accepted. AE, DC, MC, V.*

$$ ✕🏨 **Barley Neck Inn.** The hotel-like lodge, adjacent to the restaurant building, has both standard and luxury rooms, all very spacious, that are outfitted in pretty florals and colored wicker or wood furnishings. Modern conveniences such as televisions and small refrigerators are standard. It took a little time, but the inn's restaurant, in a restored 1850s sea captain's house, has shucked off its staidness and become a popular new destination. The fairly formal main dining area and a buzzing, relaxed bar called Joe's have equally satisfying menus (the bar is cheaper); the chef updates classic Cape fish dishes with a French in-fluence. The kitchen hums with innovation, particularly in its new array of salsas and sauces. Off-season, there is often live jazz on Sunday af-ternoons and a good fire burning in the huge stone fireplace. ⊠ *5 Beach*

Rd., East Orleans 02643, ☎ 508/255–8484; 508/255–0212 for restaurant, ☒ 508/255–3626. 18 rooms. 2 restaurants, refrigerators, pool. AE, MC, V.

$$ ☒ **Kadee's Gray Elephant.** A mile from Nauset Beach, next to shops,
★ a grocery store, a farm stand, a post office, and Kadee's Lobster & Clam Bar (☞ *above*), this 200-year-old house offers small vacation studio and one-bedroom apartments. They're a cheerful riot of color, from wicker painted lavender or green to bright pink bows and flowers painted on furniture to beds layered in quilts and comforters mixing plaids and florals. Kitchens are fully equipped with microwaves, attractive glassware, irons and boards—and even lobster crackers. ☒ *216 Main St., Box 86, East Orleans 02643, ☎ 508/255–7608, ☒ 508/240–2976. 6–8 apartments. Restaurant, miniature golf, gift shop. MC, V.*

$–$$ ☒ **Nauset House Inn.** You could easily spend a day trying out all the places to relax here. There's a parlor with comfortable chairs and a large fireplace, an orchard set with picnic tables, and a lush conservatory with a weeping cherry tree in its center. Rooms in both the main building and the adjacent Carriage House have stenciled walls, quilts, and unusual antique pieces, as well as hand-painted furniture, stained glass, and prints done by one of the owners. The beach is only ½ mi distant (they'll set you up with beach chairs and towels), and the attractions of town are close, but not too close. ☒ *143 Beach Rd., Box 774, East Orleans 02643, ☎ 508/255–2195. 14 rooms. Breakfast room. D, MC, V. BP.*

$–$$ ☒ **Skaket Beach Motel.** This convenient-to-everything motel prides it-
★ self on its commitment to absolute cleanliness. Rooms are traditional motel style but are sparkling and well sized, available in standard, deluxe, or poolside variety. Outdoors are a number of distractions from horseshoes to the heated pool; you can even use one of the outdoor grills. The location on the busy roadside is less appealing, though the motel is convenient to local amenities from shops to beaches and still retains a semblance of privacy. ☒ *203 Rte. 6A, 02643, ☎ 508/255–1020 or 800/835–0298, ☒ 508/255–6487. 46 rooms. Pool, croquet, horseshoes. MC, V. Closed late Nov.–Mar. CP.*

Nightlife and the Arts

The **Academy Playhouse** (☒ 120 Main St., ☎ 508/255–1963), one of the oldest community theaters on the Cape, presents 12 or 13 productions year-round, including original works.

The **Cape & Islands Chamber Music Festival** (☒ Box 2721, 02653, ☎ 508/255–9509) presents three weeks of top-caliber performances, including a jazz night, at various locations in August.

The 90-member **Cape Symphony Orchestra** (☎ 508/362–1111) sails into Orleans in late August for one of two Sounds of Summer Pops concerts (the other is in Mashpee in July). The performance takes place at the Eldridge Field Park (☒ Rte. 28 and Eldredge Pkwy.). Call for a year-round schedule of events.

Free ocean-side concerts are held in the gazebo at **Nauset Beach** each Monday evening from 7 to 9 in July and August. The resident fried-clam shack stays open until 10.

Outdoor Activities and Sports

BASEBALL

The **Orleans Cardinals** (☎ 508/240–2867) of the collegiate Cape Cod Baseball League play home games at Eldredge Park (☒ Rte. 28) from mid-June to mid-August.

BEACHES

The town-owned **Nauset Beach** (⊠ Beach Rd.)—not to be confused with Nauset Light Beach up a ways at the national seashore—is a wide, 10-mi-long sweep of sandy ocean beach with low dunes and large waves good for bodysurfing or board surfing. The beach has lifeguards, rest rooms, showers, and a food concession (something the national seashore beaches lack). It's open to off-road vehicles with a special permit. Daily parking fees of $8 are charged, or you can buy a one-week pass for $25, a two-week pass for $45, or a season pass for $65. Entrance is free with a resident sticker. For more information, call the parks department (☎ 508/240–3775).

Freshwater seekers can access **Pilgrim Lake** (⊠ Pilgrim Lake Rd., off Monument Rd. and Rte. 28) with the same parking and sticker fees as Nauset Beach (☞ *above*).

Skaket Beach (⊠ Skaket Beach Rd.) on Cape Cod Bay is a sandy stretch with calm warm water good for children. There are rest rooms, lifeguards, and a snack bar. Daily parking fees are the same as at Nauset Beach (☞ *above*). For more information, call the parks department (☎ 508/240–3775).

BOATING

Arey's Pond Boat Yard (⊠ 43 Arey's La., off Rte. 28, South Orleans, ☎ 508/255–0994) has a sailing school with individual and group lessons.

FISHING

Many of Orleans's freshwater ponds offer good fishing for perch, pickerel, trout, and more. The required fishing license, along with rental gear, is available at the **Goose Hummock Shop** (⊠ 15 Rte. 6A, ☎ 508/255–0455).

Bait, equipment rentals, and tide charts can be found at **MacSquids** (⊠ 85 Lowell Square, ☎ 508/240–0778).

The **Osprey** (☎ 508/255–1266) leaves Rock Harbor for both half- and full-day sport-fishing trips. All tackle, bait, and cleaning services are provided.

Rock Harbor Charter Boat Fleet (⊠ Rock Harbor, ☎ 508/255–9757; 800/287–1771 in MA) goes for bass and blues in the bay from spring through fall. Walk-ons and charters are both available.

ICE-SKATING

Ice-skating, lessons, hockey, clinics, and camps are available at the **Charles Moore Arena** (⊠ O'Connor Way, ☎ 508/255–5902). Kids 9–14 ice-skate to DJ-spun rock and flashing lights at Rock Night, which takes place Friday from 8 to 10 PM.

SPORTS EQUIPMENT RENTALS

Nauset Sports (⊠ Jeremiah Sq. Rte. 6A at the rotary, ☎ 508/255–4742) rents surf, body, skim, and wake boards, kayaks, wet suits, in-line skates, and tennis racquets.

For bike rentals just across the way from the Cape Cod Rail Trail, head to **Orleans Cycle** (⊠ 26 Main St., ☎ 508/255–9115).

SURFING

The Lower and Outer Cape beaches, including Nauset Beach in Orleans, are the best spots for surfing, especially when there's a storm offshore. For a surf report—water temperature, weather, surf, tanning factor—call 508/240–2229.

Pump House Surf Co. (⊠ 9 Rte. 6A, ☎ 508/240–2226) rents wet suits and sells other surf gear.

Shopping

Baseball Shop (✉ 26 Main St., ☎ 508/240–1063) sells licensed products relating to baseball and other sports—new and collectible cards (and non-sports cards) as well as hats, clothing, and videos.

Bird Watcher's General Store (✉ 36 Rte. 6A, ☎ 508/255–6974 or 800/562–1512) sells nearly everything avian but the birds themselves: feeders, paintings, houses, books, binoculars, calls, bird-theme apparel—ad infinitum.

Compass Rose Bookshop (✉ 43 Main St., ☎ 508/255–1545) is just what an independent bookstore should be: friendly, comfortable, and full of books on all kinds of subjects, including works by local authors and those of regional interest. You'll also find a generous collection of unique greeting cards and specialty items. Changing art exhibits showcase the talents of local artists, and Internet access is available on a sign-up, fee basis.

Fancy's Farm Stand (✉ 199 Main St., East Orleans, ☎ 508/255–1949) sells local produce, fresh sandwiches and roll-ups, salads (salad bar or prepared varieties), homemade soup, ice cream, fresh-baked breads, and other supplies for a great picnic. A wide assortment of flowers, both dried and fresh, are sold, adding great color to the beautiful, beamed, old-style barn.

Hannah (✉ 47 Main St., ☎ 508/255–8234) has women's casual dresses, scarves, and hats with flair, by such labels as Hannah, No Saint, and Angel Heart.

Heaven Scent You (✉ 13 Cove Rd., ☎ 508/240–2508) offers massage, spa services, and beauty treatments—everything you need for some relaxation and rejuvenation.

Kemp Pottery (✉ 9 Rte. 6A, ☎ 508/255–5853) has functional and decorative stoneware and porcelain, fountains, garden sculpture, sinks, and stained glass.

The **Orleans Farmers' Market** (✉ Cape Cod Five Operations Center, 19 West Rd.), held Saturday mornings throughout the summer, features local delicacies such as fresh shellfish, produce, flowers, and homemade goodies. It opens at 8, and early birds get the best selection—things tend to disappear quickly.

ART AND CRAFTS GALLERIES

The **Addison Holmes Gallery** (✉ 43 Rte. 28, ☎ 508/255–6200), in four rooms of a brick-red Cape house, represents more than two dozen regional artists and sells a broad range of contemporary works, many of which are inspired by life on Cape Cod. The sculpture garden in the side yard is a perfect complement to the tasteful gallery. Receptions, where you can often meet the week's featured artist, are held from 5 to 7 Saturday nights.

Left Bank Gallery (✉ 8 Cove Rd., ☎ 508/247–9172) carries an eclectic mix of handcrafted jewelry, fine art by both local and national artists, hand-painted furniture, pottery, and handmade clothing.

In July and August, **Nauset Painters** presents outdoor juried art shows every Tuesday (✉ Depot Sq. at Old Colony Way) from 10 to 5 and Sunday (✉ Sandwich Cooperative Bank, 51 Main St.) from 10 to 5.

The **Orleans Art Association** holds outdoor art shows from 10 to 5 each Thursday and Friday in July and August on the grounds of the American Legion Hall (✉ 137 Main St.).

Tree's Place (✉ Rte. 6A, at Rte. 28, ☎ 508/255–1330), one of the Cape's best and most original shops, has a collection of handcrafted kaleidoscopes, as well as art glass, hand-painted porcelain and pottery, hand-blown stemware, jewelry, and imported ceramic tiles as well as fine art. Tree's displays the work of New England artists including Robert Vickery, Don Stone, and Elizabeth Mumford (whose popular folk art is bordered in mottoes and poetic phrases). Champagne openings are held on Saturday nights in summer.

Eastham

40 *3 mi north of Orleans, 6 mi south of Wellfleet.*

Eastham holds the Salt Pond Visitor Center, one of the Cape Cod National Seashore's main centers, and beautiful natural areas such as Ft. Hill. Unlike the other towns, it has no official town center or Main Street; busy U.S. 6 bisects Eastham, and the town is spread out on both Cape Cod Bay and the Atlantic. This is where the Cape's spectacular stretches of dune-backed beach begin.

It was here in 1620 that Myles Standish and company landed on First Encounter Beach and met the Nauset tribe. The meeting was peaceful, but the Pilgrims moved on to Plymouth anyway. Nearly a quarter century later, they returned to settle the area, which they originally called by its Native American name, Nawsett. Eastham was incorporated as a town on June 7, 1651.

Like many of the towns on the Cape, Eastham started as a farming community and later turned to the sea and to salt making for its livelihood; at one time there were more than 50 saltworks in town. A more atypical industry here was asparagus growing; from the late 1800s through the 1920s, Eastham was known as the "Asparagus Capital." The runner-up crop, Eastham turnips, are still the pride of many a harvest table.

41 The road to the Cape Cod National Seashore's **Ft. Hill Area** (✉ Ft. Hill Rd., off U.S. 6) winds past the **Captain Edward Penniman House** (☞ *below*), ending at a parking area with a lovely view of old farmland traced with stone fences that rolls gently down to **Nauset Marsh** (☞ *below*) and a red-maple swamp. Appreciated by bird-watchers and nature photographers, the 1-mi **Red Maple Swamp Trail** begins outside the Penniman House and winds through the area, branching into two separate paths, one of which eventually turns into a boardwalk that meanders through wetlands. The other path leads directly to Skiff Hill, an overlook with benches and informative plaques that quote Samuel de Champlain's account of the area when he moored off Nauset Marsh in 1605. Also on Skiff Hill is Indian Rock, a large boulder that was moved to the hill from the marsh below. Once used by the local Native American tribe as a sharpening stone, the rock is cut with deep grooves and smoothed in circles where ax heads were whetted.

The French Second Empire–style **Captain Edward Penniman House** was built in 1868 for a whaling captain. The impressive exterior is notable for its mansard roof; its cupola, which once commanded a dramatic view of bay and sea; and the whale-jawbone entrance gate. Though still in the process of renovation, the interior is open for guided tours or for browsing through changing exhibits. Call ahead to find out when tours are available. ✉ *Ft. Hill Rd., Ft. Hill Area,* ☎ *508/255–3421.* 🎫 *Free.* ☉ *Weekdays 1–4.*

The park at Samoset Road has as its centerpiece the **Eastham Windmill,** the oldest windmill on Cape Cod. A smock mill built in Plymouth in the early 1680s, it was moved to this site in 1793 and is the only

Cape windmill still on the site where it was used commercially. The mill was restored by local shipwreck historian William Quinn and friends. ✉ *U.S. 6 at Samoset Rd.* ⌗ *Free.* ☉ *Late June–Labor Day, Mon.–Sat. 10–5, Sun. 1–5.*

Frozen in time, the 1741 **Swift-Daley House** was once the home of Gustavus Swift, founder of the Swift meatpacking company. Inside the full Cape with bow roof you'll find beautiful pumpkin-pine woodwork and wide-board floors; a ship's-cabin staircase, which, like the bow roof, was built by ships' carpenters; and fireplaces in every downstairs room. The colonial-era furnishings include an old cannonball rope bed, tools, a melodeon, and a ceremonial quilt decorated with beads and coins. Among the antique clothing is a stunning 1850 wedding dress. Out back is a tool museum. ✉ *U.S. 6, next to the Eastham Post Office,* ☎ *no phone.* ⌗ *Free.* ☉ *July–Aug., weekdays 1–4; Sept., Sat. 1–4.*

A great spot for watching sunsets over the bay, **First Encounter Beach** (✉ End of Samoset Rd., off U.S. 6) is rich in history. Near the parking lot, a bronze marker commemorates the first encounter between local Native Americans and passengers from the *Mayflower,* led by Captain Myles Standish, who explored the entire area for five weeks in November and December 1620 before moving on to Plymouth. The remains of a navy target ship retired after 25 years of battering now rest on a sandbar about 1 mi out.

★ The Cape's most expansive national treasure, the **Cape Cod National Seashore** was established in 1961 under the administration of President John F. Kennedy, for whom Cape Cod was home and haven. The 27,000-acre seashore, extending from Chatham to Provincetown, encompasses and protects 30 mi of superb ocean beaches, great rolling dunes, swamps, marshes, and wetlands, pitch pine and scrub oak forest, all kinds of wildlife, and a number of historic structures. Self-guided nature trails, as well as biking and horse trails, lace through these landscapes. Hiking trails lead to a red-maple swamp, **Nauset Marsh,** and **Salt Pond,** in which breeding shellfish are suspended from floating "nurseries"—their offspring will later be used to seed the flats. Also in the seashore, the Buttonbush Trail is a nature path for people with vision impairments. A hike or bike ride to Coast Guard Beach leads to a turnout looking out over marsh and sea. A section of the cliff here was washed away in 1990, revealing remains of a prehistoric dwelling.

㊷ **Salt Pond Visitor Center** is the first visitor center of the Cape Cod National Seashore; the other, the **Province Lands Visitor Center,** is in Provincetown (☞ Provincetown, *below*). The Salt Pond center, overlooking pretty Salt Pond, offers guided walks, tours, boat trips, demonstrations, and lectures from mid-April through Thanksgiving, as well as evening beach walks, campfire talks, and other programs in summer.

The center includes a museum with several displays: on whaling and the old saltworks, early Cape Cod artifacts including scrimshaw, the journal that Mrs. Penniman kept while on a whaling voyage with her husband, and some of the Pennimans' possessions, such as their tea service and the captain's top hat. A good bookstore and an air-conditioned auditorium showing films on geology, sea rescues, whaling, Henry David Thoreau, and Marconi are also here. Something's up most summer evenings at the outdoor amphitheater, from slide-show talks to military-band concerts. ✉ *Doane Rd., off U.S. 6,* ☎ *508/255-3421.* ⌗ *Free.* ☉ *Mar.–June and Sept.–Dec., daily 9–4:30; July–Aug., daily 9–5; Jan.–Feb., weekends 9–4:30.*

Roads and bicycle trails lead to **Coast Guard and Nauset Light beaches** (✉ Off Ocean View Dr.), which begin an unbroken 30-mi stretch of barrier beach extending to Provincetown—the "Cape Cod Beach" of Thoreau's 1865 classic, *Cape Cod.* You can still walk its length, as Thoreau did, though the Atlantic continues to claim more of the Cape's eastern shore every year. The site of the famous beach cottage of Henry Beston's 1928 book, *The Outermost House,* is to the south, near the end of Nauset spit. Designated as a literary landmark in 1964, the cottage was, alas, completely destroyed in the Great Blizzard of February 1978.

Moved 350 ft back from its perch at cliff's edge in 1996, the much-photographed red-and-white **Nauset Light** (⊠ Ocean View Dr. and Cable Rd.) still tops the bluff where the Three Sisters Lighthouses once stood; the Sisters themselves can be seen in a little landlocked park surrounded by trees, reached by paved walkways off Nauset Light Beach's parking lot. How the lighthouses got there is a long story. In 1838 three brick lighthouses were built 150 ft apart on the bluffs in Eastham, overlooking a particularly dangerous area of shoals (shifting underwater sandbars). In 1892, after the eroding cliff dropped the towers into the ocean, they were replaced with three wooden towers. In 1918 two were moved away, as was the third in 1923. Eventually the National Park Service acquired the Three Sisters and brought them together here, where they would be safe, rather than returning them to the eroding coast. The Fresnel lens from the last working lighthouse is on display at the **Salt Pond Visitor Center** (☞ *above*). Lectures on, and guided walks to, the lighthouses are conducted throughout the season. In 1999 tours of Nauset Light were given on Sunday between 4:30 and 7:30 PM in July and August, on Sunday from 1 to 4 PM after Labor Day, and by appointment; the plan was to repeat this schedule in 2000, but call in advance (☎ 508/240–2612) to confirm.

Dining and Lodging

$–$$ ✕ **Fairway Restaurant and Pizzeria.** The newly renovated, family-run Fairway is not as cozy as it used to be but still serves up Italian comfort food in a casual, friendly setting. Attached to the Hole in One Donut shop (very popular among locals), the Fairway puts a jar of crayons on every paper-covered table and sells its own brand of root beer. Entrées come with salad and homemade rolls. Try the orange tequila shrimp and scallops with a little Cajun heat, eggplant Parmesan, or a well-stuffed calzone. You can order from the extensive breakfast menu from 6:30 to 11:30. ⊠ *4295 U.S. 6,* ☎ *508/255–3893. Reservations not accepted. AE, D, DC, MC, V.*

$ ✕ **Lori's Family Restaurant.** Omelets, pancakes, French toast, waffles—admit it, they're a part of being on vacation. Fresh mushrooms and sprouts to accompany the eggs are typical of the perfect, extra touches that make every plate special. Lori's serves only breakfast (it's open daily from 6 AM to 1 PM). ⊠ *Main St. Mercantile, U.S. 6, North Eastham,* ☎ *508/255–4803. Reservations not accepted. MC, V.*

$$$$ 🔛 **Four Points Sheraton.** At the entrance to the national seashore, this Sheraton offers standard modern-decor rooms with two double beds or one king-size bed, and tiled baths. Rooms have views of the tropical indoor pool, complete with lush plants, pirate-theme bar, and resident live parrot, the parking lot, or the woods. Outside rooms are a little bigger and brighter and have minirefrigerators. Children under 17 stay free. ⊠ *3800 U.S. 6, 02642,* ☎ *508/255–5000 or 800/533–3986,* FAX *508/ 240–1870. 107 rooms, 2 suites. Restaurant, lobby lounge, no-smoking rooms, room service, 1 indoor and 1 outdoor pool, saunas, 2 tennis courts, exercise room, video games. AE, D, DC, MC, V. BP.*

$$$–$$$$ 🔛 **Whalewalk Inn.** Named for the widow's walk atop the building, this 1830 whaling master's home is situated on 3 acres of rolling lawns, gardens, and meadows. Lots of windows give the place an open, airy feeling, while wide-board pine floors, fireplaces, and 19th-century country antiques provide historical appeal. Guest rooms are spacious, with four-poster twin, double, or queen-size beds; floral fabrics; and antique or reproduction furniture. Besides the rooms in the main inn, there are suites with fully equipped kitchens in the converted barn and guest house. A secluded saltbox cottage has a fireplace, kitchen, and private patio. Deluxe rooms in the carriage house have fireplaces, whirlpool tubs, and air-conditioning. Breakfast is served each morning in the cheerful sunroom or on the garden patio. ⊠ *220 Bridge Rd., 02642,* ☎ *508/255–0617. 11 rooms, 5 suites. Bicycles. No smoking. MC, V. BP.*

$$$　🏨 **Over Look Inn.** If it weren't for the vivid yellow paint job on this three-story inn, it would be lost among the trees, even though it's right along U.S. 6. Both the Cape Cod Rail Trail and the Salt Pond Visitor Center are just across the road from this 19th-century oasis. Victorian touches abound, from the graceful high ceilings to the intricate interior wood molding. Each room has antiques, brass beds, and soft down comforters; some have genuine claw-foot tubs, which are great to slide into after a day at the beach. The innkeeper's Scottish hospitality promises some unusual and traditional breakfast fare each morning. ⊠ *3085 U.S. 6, 02642,* ☎ *508/255–1886,* FAX *508/240–0345. 14 rooms. AE, D, MC, V. BP.*

$$–$$$　🏨 **Penny House Inn.** Tucked behind a wave of privet hedge, this rambling gray-shingle inn offers mostly spacious rooms, furnished with a combination of antiques, collectibles, and wicker. Captain's Quarters, the grandest room, has a sitting area with a wood-burning fireplace, a king-size brass bed, miniature library, and a lovely view of the garden. Common areas include the Great Room, with a fireplace and lots of windows, a combination sunroom-library, and a garden patio set with umbrella tables. A full homemade breakfast starts the day, and afternoon tea is available. ⊠ *4885 County Rd., U.S. 6, 02642,* ☎ *508/ 255–6632 or 800/554–1751,* FAX *508/255–4893. 11 rooms. Air-conditioning, library. No smoking. AE, D, MC, V. BP.*

$–$$　🏨 **Cove Bluffs Motel.** Nestled among the trees and very near the waters of Town Cove and several nature trails is this old-fashioned haven for families. The entire complex is reminiscent of a cottage colony, with several structures dotted beneath the pines, divided among standard motel rooms and several fully equipped, one- to two-bedroom housekeeping units. Decor is simple, consisting of painted knotty-pine interiors and plain but practical bed coverings. Outdoors holds plenty for busy kids—basketball courts, shuffleboard, swing sets, a playhouse, and sandbox—as well as a selection of swinging hammocks in the shade. You're welcome to use the outdoor grills, too. ⊠ *U.S. 6 and Shore Rd., 02642,* ☎ *508/240–1616. 5 rooms, 8 housekeeping units. No-smoking rooms, pool, basketball, shuffleboard, coin laundry. MC, V. Closed Nov.– Mar.*

$　🏨 **Hostelling International–Mid Cape.** On 3 wooded acres near the Cape Cod Rail Trail and a 15-minute walk to the bay, this hostel has eight cabins that sleep six to eight each; two of them can be used as family cabins. It has a common area and a kitchen, and a number of programs are available for guests. ⊠ *75 Goody Hallet Dr., 02642,* ☎ *508/255–2785. 8 cabins. Volleyball, Ping-Pong. MC, V. Closed mid-Sept.–Mid-May.*

$　⛺ **Atlantic Oaks Campground.** This campground is conveniently located less than a mile north of the Salt Pond Visitor Center. Primarily an RV camp, it offers limited tenting as well. The setting is a pine and oak forest, and you're minutes from Cape Cod National Seashore. There are bikes for rent and direct access to the Cape Cod Rail Trail. Movies for kids are shown at night. RV hookups, including cable TV, cost $35 for two people; tent sites are $26 for two people. Showers are free. ⊠ *3700*

U.S. 6, 02642, ☎ *508/255–1437 or 800/332–2267. 100 RV sites, 30 tent sites. Bicycles, playground, coin laundry. D, MC, V. Closed Nov.–Apr.*

Nightlife and the Arts

The **Cape Cod National Seashore** (☎ 508/255–3421 for information) offers summer evening programs, such as slide shows, sunset beach walks, concerts by local groups or military bands, and campfire sing-alongs.

The **Eastham Painters Guild** holds outdoor art shows every Thursday, Friday, and holiday weekend from 9 to 5, July through October, at the Schoolhouse Museum (⊠ Next to the Salt Pond Visitor Center, off U.S. 6).

First Encounter Coffee House (⊠ Chapel in the Pines, Samoset Rd., ☎ 508/255–5438) presents a mixture of professional and local folk and blues in a no-smoking, no-alcohol environment, with refreshments available during intermission. National acts are booked for the second and fourth Saturday. It's closed May and December.

Outdoor Activities and Sports

BEACHES

On the bay side of the Outer Cape, **First Encounter Beach** (⊠ End of Samoset Rd., off U.S. 6) is open to the public and charges daily parking fees of $5 (weekly and season passes are also available; call the Town Hall at ☎ 508/240–5972) to nonresidents in season. Parking fees or passes also apply to several other bay beaches and ponds, both saltwater and freshwater.

Coast Guard Beach (⊠ Off Ocean View Dr.), part of the national seashore, is a long beach backed by low grass and heathland. A handsome former Coast Guard station is also here, though it is not open to the public. The beach has no parking lot of its own, so park at the Salt Pond Visitor Center (☞ *above*) or the lot up Doane Road from the center and take the free shuttle to the beach. There are showers, and lifeguards are posted between June and August. A daily charge of $7 for cars or a season pass (by far the best bargain) for $20 grants admission to all seven national seashore beaches.

Nauset Light Beach (⊠ Off Ocean View Dr.), adjacent to Coast Guard Beach, continues the national-seashore landscape of long, sandy beach backed by tall dunes, grass, and heathland, with the lighthouse for a little extra Cape atmosphere. It has showers and lifeguards in summer, but as with other national seashore beaches, there is no food concession. For fees, *see* Coast Guard Beach, *above*.

BIKING

The **Idle Times Bike Shop** (⊠ U.S. 6 and Brackett Rd., ☎ 508/255–8281) provides bikes of all sizes and kinds and is located right near the Cape Cod Rail Trail.

The **Little Capistrano Bike Shop** (⊠ Salt Pond Rd. across from the Salt Pond Visitor Center, ☎ 508/255–6515) rents a variety of different bikes and trailers and is conveniently located between the Cape Cod Rail Trail and the National Seashore Bike Trail.

Nauset Trail is maintained by the Cape Cod National Seashore and stretches 1⅗ mi from Salt Pond Visitor Center through groves of apple and locust trees to Coast Guard Beach.

HEALTH AND FITNESS CLUBS

The **Norseman Athletic Club** (⊠ 4730 U.S. 6, North Eastham, ☎ 508/255–6370 or 508/255–6371) has four racquetball, two squash, and six indoor tennis courts; one NBA indoor basketball court; an Olympic-size, indoor heated pool; swimming lessons; aerobics and children's self-defense classes; plus Nautilus, free weights, and cardiovascular machines.

You can relax in the whirlpool, steam room, or sauna; there's also a pro shop and a restaurant. There are daily and weekly guest membership passes.

THE OUTER CAPE

A part of and often synonymous with the Lower Cape, the Outer Cape forms the wrist and fist of Cape Cod. There's a sense of abandon here, both in the hedonistic frenzy of Provincetown in summer and on the windswept landscape of sand dunes and salt marsh. The scenery becomes flatter and the vegetation more sparse, and the sea feels closer as the land narrows. Much of the area is undeveloped, protected by the Cape Cod National Seashore. Long dune-backed beaches seem to stretch on forever, and trails wind through wind-stunted forests of scrub pine, beech, and oak. **Wellfleet** is a quiet town, with art galleries and upscale shops along Main Street, and an active harbor. With its expanse of high dunes, estuaries, salt marshes, pine forests, rivers, and winding back roads, **Truro** is the least developed and least populated of the Outer Cape towns. The promise of solitude draws artists and writers, who come here to escape the summer crowds of neighboring towns. **Provincetown** has two faces—a quiet little fishing village in winter and a magnet for throngs of pleasure-seekers in summer, who come to enjoy the vast sandy beaches, streets lined with historical houses, the unique nightlife, shops that sell everything from antiques to zoot suits, and the galleries, readings, and art classes that are a part of Provincetown's rich history as an art colony.

Wellfleet and South Wellfleet

6 mi north of Eastham, 13 mi southeast of Provincetown.

43 Still famous for its world-renowned and succulent namesake oysters and, with Truro, a colonial whaling and cod-fishing port, **Wellfleet** is also a center for artists and writers. Less than 2 mi wide, it is one of the more tastefully developed Cape resort towns, with a number of fine restaurants, historic houses, art galleries, and a good old main street in the village proper. South Wellfleet borders North Eastham and is home to a wonderful Audubon sanctuary and a drive-in theater that doubles on weekends as a flea market.

★ **44** A trip to the Cape isn't complete without a visit to the informative **Massachusetts Audubon Wellfleet Bay Wildlife Sanctuary,** a 1,000-acre haven for more than 250 species of birds attracted by the varied habitats found here. The jewel of the Massachusetts Audubon Society, the sanctuary is a superb place for walking, birding, and looking west over the salt marsh and bay at wondrous sunsets.

The Audubon Society hosts a great variety of naturalist-led wildlife tours around different parts of the Cape, including the Monomoy Islands (☞ Chatham, *above*), year-round. There are bay cruises, bird and insect walks, hikes, snorkeling, winter seal cruises, and birding, canoe, and kayak trips. The sanctuary also has camps for children in July and August and weeklong field schools for adults. Phone reservations are required ahead of time, as some programs are very popular. ⊠ *Off U.S. 6, Box 236, South Wellfleet 02663,* ☎ *508/349–2615.* ⚏ *$3.* ⊙ *Daily 8 AM–dusk.*

45 **Marconi Station** on the Atlantic side of the Cape's forearm is the site of the first transatlantic wireless station erected on the U.S. mainland. From here, Italian radio and wireless-telegraphy pioneer Guglielmo Marconi sent the first American wireless message to Europe—"most cordial greetings and good wishes" from President Theodore Roosevelt to Edward VII of England—on January 18, 1903. The station broadcasted news for 15 years. An outdoor shelter contains a model of the original station, of which only fragments remain as a result of cliff erosion; parts of the tower bases are sometimes visible on the beach below, where they fell. The Cape Cod National Seashore's administrative headquarters is here, and though it is not an official visitor center, it can provide information at times when the centers are closed. Inside there is a mock-up of the spark-gap transmitter used by Marconi. Off the parking lot a 1¼-mi trail and boardwalk lead through the **Atlantic White Cedar Swamp**; it's one of the most beautiful trails on the seashore. Free maps and guides are available at the trailhead. **Marconi Beach,** south of the station on Marconi Beach Road, is another of the National Seashore's ocean beaches (☞ Beaches, *below*). ⊠ *Marconi Site Rd., South Wellfleet,* ☎ *508/349–3785.* ☞ *Free.* ☉ *Daily 8–4:30.*

For a **scenic loop** through a classic Cape landscape near Wellfleet's Atlantic beaches—with scrub and pines on the left, heathland meeting cliffs and ocean below on the right—take LeCount Hollow Road just north of the Marconi Station turnoff. All of the beaches on this strip rest at the bottom of a tall, grass-covered dune, which lend dramatic character to this outermost shore. The first of the four, **LeCount Hollow,** is restricted to residents or temporary residents in season, as is the last, **Newcomb Hollow,** with a scalloped shoreline of golden sand. In between, **White Crest** and **Cahoon Hollow** are town-managed public beaches. On breezy days, hang gliders fly from the cliffs. Cahoon has a hot restaurant and dancing spot, the Beachcomber (☞ Nightlife and the Arts, *below*). Backtrack to Cahoon Hollow Road and turn west for the southernmost entrance to the town of Wellfleet proper, across U.S. 6.

Wellfleet's **First Congregational Church** (⊠ 200 Main St., ☎ 508/349–6877), a handsome 1850 Greek Revival building, is said to have the only town clock in the world to strike on ship's bells. The church's interior is lovely, with pale blue walls, a brass chandelier hanging from an enormous gilt ceiling rosette, subtly colored stained-glass windows, and pews curved to form an amphitheater facing the altar and the 1873, 738-pipe Hook and Hastings tracker-action organ. To the right is a Tiffany-style window depicting a clipper ship, with a dedication to the memory of a sea captain. Concerts are given in July and August on Sunday at 8 PM.

For a glimpse into Wellfleet's past, the **Wellfleet Historical Society Museum** exhibits furniture, paintings, shipwreck salvage, needlework, navigation equipment, early photographs, Native American artifacts, clothing, and more. The society's Samuel Rider House is no longer open to the public. In July and August, short guided walks around the center of town are given Tuesday and Friday mornings at 10:15 for $3. ⊠ *266 Main St.,* ☎ *508/349–9157.* ☞ *$1.* ☉ *Late June–mid-Sept., Tues.–Sat. 1–4.*

The comfortable **Wellfleet Public Library** (⊠ 55 W. Main St., ☎ 508/349–0310) is a great place to spend a rainy afternoon. The library is a reflection of the literary life of Wellfleet, as are the two wonderful bookstores in town (☞ Shopping, *below*). Among the writers who have spent time here are Mary McCarthy, Edmund Wilson, Annie Dillard, and Marge Piercy.

Main Street is a good place to start if you're in the mood for shopping (☞ Shopping, *below*). **Commercial Street** has all the flavor of the fishing town that Wellfleet remains. Galleries and shops occupy small weathered-shingle houses, some of which look like fishing shacks. A good stroll around town would take in Commercial and Main streets, ending perhaps at **Uncle Tim's Bridge** (⊠ Off E. Commercial St.). The short walk across this arcing landmark—with its beautiful, much-photographed view over marshland and a tidal creek—leads to a small wooded island.

Follow Commercial Street to the **Wellfleet Pier,** busy with fishing boats, sailboats, yachts, charters, and party boats. At the twice-daily low tides you can fish on the tidal flats for oysters, clams, and quahogs (☎ 508/349–9818 for a permit).

Chequesset Neck Road makes for a pretty 2½-mi drive from the harbor to the bay past Sunset Hill—a great place to catch one. At the end, on the left, is a parking lot and wooded picnic area, from which nature trails lead off to **Great Island** (✉ Off Chequesset Neck Rd.), perfect for the beachcomber and solitude seeker. The "island" is actually a peninsula connected by a sand spit that was built by tidal action. Over 7 mi of trails wind along the inner marshes and the water; these are the most difficult on the seashore, since they're mostly in soft sand. In the 17th century there were lookout towers here for shore whaling, as well as a tavern. Animals were pastured, and oystering and cranberry harvesting were undertaken. By 1800 the hardwood forest that had covered the island had been cut down for use in ship- and home-building. The pitch pines and other growth you see here (and all over the Cape) today were introduced in the 1830s to keep the soil from washing into the sea. Cape Cod National Seashore offers occasional guided hikes on Great Island and, from February through April, seal walks. To the right of the Great Island lot, a road leads to **Griffin Island,** with its own walking trail.

Dining and Lodging

$$$ ✕ **Aesop's Tables.** A worthy choice for a special dinner, Aesop's spe-
★ cializes in seafood entrées and appetizers that often take the local Wellfleet oyster to new heights. Inside this 1805 captain's house are five dining rooms; aim for a table on the porch overlooking the center of town. The signature dish is an exotic bouillabaisse, with mounds of fresh-off-the-boat seafood in a hot saffron broth; the homemade sourdough bread is the perfect accompaniment. The marinated duck breast is another favorite. When it's time for dessert, you're likely to see lots of diners tempting fate with "Death by Chocolate," a heavy mousse cake. Some nights in summer, there's live jazz in the tavern, where the mood and the menu are more casual; the chairs are so comfortable, you may have trouble getting up. ✉ *316 Main St., Wellfleet,* ☎ *508/349–6450. AE, DC, MC, V. Closed Columbus Day–Mother's Day. No lunch.*

$$–$$$ ✕ **Painter's.** Named for chef-owner Kate Painter (not for all the local artists), this fresh restaurant has survived the start-up years but still seems to be in flux from season to season. A redesign has now closed the upstairs to the public. Harder to understand is a downstairs that has eliminated a lovely old bar for a new one that is just as cramped but not as atmospheric. The kitchen also seems to be a little lost. One moment the food seems fresh and excellent, the next uncertain and unsophisticated. The 10 to 15 seafood dishes run from traditional Portuguese fare like clam *cataplana* (hearty clam stew with a spicy red wine sauce) to a new American version of pan-seared tuna, encrusted with sesame and mustard seeds. All the desserts are homemade as well; the flourless chocolate Armagnac fig cake begs to be devoured. Be careful ordering wine; even a simple house chardonnay is seriously overpriced. ✉ *50 Main St., Wellfleet,* ☎ *508/349–3003. AE, MC, V. Closed Dec.–Apr.*

$$ ✕ **Captain Higgins.** Fish is the specialty (of course) at this popular spot at the turn of the road around Wellfleet's town pier. Besides being close to the fishing fleet and town beach, Captain Higgins has a broad outdoor deck overlooking a beautiful green and gold marsh. You can watch the slender reeds sway in the breeze as you sip an icy Seabreeze and finish a plate of fresh Wellfleet oysters or a marinated calamari appetizer. This is a good place to get a big boiled lobster dinner or fresh bluefish with a sweet mustard glaze. A more surprising option is a delicious 100% ostrich burger, similar to beef but lower in fat and calories. Reservations are accepted if you call before 6. ⊠ *Town Pier, Wellfleet,* ☎ *508/349–6027. MC, V. Closed Nov.–Apr.*

$$ ✕ **Finely JP's.** This unassuming little roadside spot right on U.S. 6 gives
★   no hint that chef John Pontius consistently turns out wonderful food full of the best Italian influences and ingredients. The dining room is small and noisy, but the fish and pasta dishes (which emphasize good olive oil and plenty of lemon) silence all. Appetizers are especially good, among them a warm spinach and scallop salad or blackened beef with charred pepper relish. The Wellfleet paella draws raves and a steady handful of locals, but the chef is not afraid to cook a Delmonico steak either. A warning to anyone prone to the odd moment of dyslexia: be sure not to confuse this place with PJ's (☞ *below*). ⊠ *U.S. 6, South Wellfleet,* ☎ *508/349–7500. Reservations not accepted. D, MC, V. Closed Mon.–Wed. Thanksgiving–Memorial Day; Mon.–Tues. Memorial Day–mid-June and Oct.–Thanksgiving; Tues. Labor Day–Oct.*

$$ ✕ **Serena's.** The name is Italian for "mermaid," and images of the sirens crop up everywhere. A family place that caters to kids, Serena's offers an assortment of "blackboard specials" every night. The Italian menu is short on the contemporary northern cuisine you'll find at many other places; red sauces still prevail here. Try the seafood *fra diavolo,* a bouillabaisse-like stew that can be ordered hot and extremely hot. The bar side of the restaurant is reserved for smokers. ⊠ *U.S. 6, South Wellfleet,* ☎ *508/349–9370. Reservations not accepted. AE, D, DC, MC, V. No lunch.*

$–$$ ✕ **Bayside Lobster Hutt.** There is no hut, though there are plenty of lobsters, as well as fishing nets draped on the side of the building. Diners share meals with strangers at long tables and, often as not, wind up neighbors on the beach the next day. The food is nothing fancy, but the emphasis is always on freshness and quality; try the sea-clam pie (in fact a clam potpie). You're encouraged to bring your own beer or wine. ⊠ *91 Commercial St., Wellfleet,* ☎ *508/349–6333. Reservations not accepted. No credit cards. BYOB. Closed mid-Sept.–Memorial Day.*

$–$$ ✕ **PJ's Family Restaurant.** There's always a good-size but fast-moving line in front of this entrenched Wellfleet tradition, waiting for a heap of steamers or a creamy soft-serve cone. The inside is clean, airy, and unpretentious, with slanting knotty-pine paneling, swirling overhead fans, the ubiquitous starfish-studded fishnet—and a view of the vast parking lot. The open kitchen gleams and the staff hustles. At PJ's you place your order and take a number. Food is served in utilitarian style: Styrofoam soup bowls, paper plates, plastic forks. The lobster and corn chowder doesn't have much lobster in it, so stick to the traditional clam chowder. Fried calamari and clam or oyster plates are generous and fresh. Try the dense, spicy stuffed clams and a pile of crispy homemade onion rings, but stay far, far away from the veggie burger. ⊠ *U.S. 6, at the first turn into town,* ☎ *508/349–2126. Reservations not accepted. No credit cards. Closed mid-Oct.–mid-Apr.*

$ ✕ **Moby Dick's.** A meal at this good-natured, rough-hewn fish shack named for you-know-who is an absolute Cape Cod tradition for some people. Many, many clams have given their lives to make the sparkling white driveway. Moby Dick's has a giant blackboard menu (order up front and food is brought to you); a big, breezy, screened-in "porch" to eat in; and red-check tablecloths. The owners claim to serve the freshest seafood and to buy, whenever possible, from local fishermen, and what they serve supports the claim. The frying oil is filtered twice daily—

essential for light and crisp clams, fish, and scallops. Go for a "Nantucket Bucket": one pound of Monomoy steamers, one pound of native mussels, and corn on the cob served in a bucket. Don't miss the unique Outer Cape Onion, a whole onion cut in such a way that when it's dipped in batter and deep-fried, it opens like a flower. ⊠ *U.S. 6, on the Truro side of town center,* ☎ *508/349–9795,* FAX *. Reservations not accepted. No credit cards. Closed Oct.–Apr.*

$ ✕ **Lighthouse Restaurant.** There are no fireworks, but there's still a line out the door on summer mornings for a classic bacon-and-egg breakfast—this place is authentic all the way down the line. A plate of steamers and a beer for lunch? Chowder, burger, and another beer for dinner? You got it. ⊠ *Main St.,* ☎ *508/349–3681. Reservations not accepted. D, MC, V.*

$$–$$$ ⊞ **Surf Side Colony Cottages.** There's very little in the way of accom-
★ modations on the Atlantic shore of the Outer Cape, so these one- to three-bedroom cottages are an especially good find. Scattered on either side of Ocean View Drive, they range from units in a piney grove to well-equipped ocean-side cottages; the two closest to the water have the best views. The cottages are a one-minute walk from Maguire's Landing town beach (Le Count Hollow), a beautiful, wide strand of sand, dunes, and surf. Though the exteriors are retro Florida, with pastel shingles and flat roofs, cottage interiors are tastefully decorated in Cape style, including knotty-pine paneling. All units have phones, wood-burning fireplaces, screened porches, kitchens, (mostly) tiled baths, rattan furniture, carpeting, and grills. Some have roof decks with an ocean view and outdoor showers. Ocean-side cottages have dishwashers. ⊠ *Ocean View Dr., Box 937, South Wellfleet 02663,* ☎ *508/349–3959,* FAX *508/349–3959. 18 cottages. Picnic area, coin laundry. 1- to 2-wk minimum in summer. MC, V. Closed Nov.–Mar.*

$$–$$$ ⊞ **Wellfleet Motel & Lodge.** A mile from Marconi Beach, opposite the Audubon sanctuary, is this well-maintained and tasteful highway-side complex, which sits on 12 wooded acres. In the single-story motel, the rooms, which are renovated each winter, are decorated in rich green and burgundy, with standard oak furniture. Rooms in the two-story lodge are bright and spacious, with king- or queen-size beds, TV with HBO, and balconies or patios. The property offers direct access to the Cape Cod Rail Trail. ⊠ *146 U.S. 6, Box 606, South Wellfleet 02663,* ☎ *508/349–3535 or 800/852–2900,* FAX *508/349–1192. 57 rooms, 8 suites. Bar, coffee shop, air-conditioning, 2 pools, hot tub, basketball, meeting room. AE, DC, MC, V. Lodge and facilities closed Dec.–Mar.*

$–$$ ⊞ **Even'tide.** Long a summer favorite, this motel is set back off the main road, surrounded by trees and sitting close to the Cape Cod Rail Trail. A central attraction is the 60-ft indoor pool (although Wellfleet's beaches are not far), but guests return year after year for the hospitality and the motel's reputation for cleanliness. Rooms are furnished in simple motel style and include some with queen or double beds, two-room family suites, and efficiencies with kitchens. Speckled about the property are cottages, available for week-or-more stays. ⊠ *650 U.S. 6, South Wellfleet 02663,* ☎ *508/349–3410,* FAX *508/349–7804. 31 units, 10 cottages. Air-conditioning, refrigerators, indoor pool, playground. 1- to 2-wk minimum for cottages in summer. MC, V. Closed Nov.–Apr.*

$–$$ ⊞ **Holden Inn.** If you're watching your budget and can deal with modest basics, try this old-timey place just out of the town center. Rooms have hardwood floors and are simply decorated with grandma's-house wallpapers, ruffled sheers or country-style curtains, and antiques like brass-and-white iron or spindle beds or a marble-top table. Private baths with old porcelain sinks are available in adjacent 1840 and 1890 buildings. A suite has a queen bed and two twins for a small family. The lodge has shared baths, an outdoor shower, and a large, screened-in porch with a lovely view of the bay and Great Island far below. The main house has a common room and a screened front porch with rockers and a bay view through trees. There are picnic tables and gardens in the backyard. ⊠ *140 Commercial St., Box 816, Wellfleet 02667,* ☎ *508/349–3450. 25 rooms, 10 with bath. No credit cards. Closed mid-Oct.–mid-Apr.*

$ ⌂ **Inn at Duck Creek.** Set on 5 wooded acres by a duck pond, creek, and salt marsh, this old inn consists of the circa-1815 main building and two other old houses. Rooms in the main inn (except rustic third-floor rooms) and in Saltworks have a simple charm. Typical furnishings include claw-foot tubs, country antiques, lace curtains, chenille spreads, and rag rugs on hardwood floors. The two-room Carriage House is cabiny, with rough barn-board and plaster walls. There's fine dining at Sweet Seasons or pub dining with entertainment at the Tavern Room (☞ Nightlife and the Arts, *below*). ⊠ *70 Main St., Box 364, Wellfleet 02667,* ☎ *508/349–9333,* FAX *508/349–0234. 25 rooms, 17 with bath. 2 restaurants. 2-night minimum weekends July–Aug. AE, MC, V. Closed mid-Oct.–mid-Apr. CP.*

Nightlife and the Arts

THE ARTS

Jim Wolf, Master Storyteller (☎ 508/349–0103 for information) beguiles folks of all ages with his dramatic tellings of both past and present Cape Cod lore and legend. July and August show times are Wednesday through Friday at 7:30 PM at the Wellfleet United Methodist Church (⊠ Main St.).

During July and August, the First Congregational Church (⊠ 200 Main St., Wellfleet, ☎ 508/349–6877) trades the serenity of worship for **Sunday evening concerts.** The music begins at 8 PM and has included opera, blues, jazz, and chamber music.

The drive-in movie is alive and well on Cape Cod at the **Wellfleet Drive-In Theater** (⊠ 51 U.S. 6, Eastham-Wellfleet line, ☎ 508/349–7176 or 508/255–9619); films start at dusk nightly in season, and there's a miniature golf course.

On Saturday evenings in July and August during the **Wellfleet Gallery Crawl,** Wellfleet's art galleries are open for cocktail receptions to celebrate show openings. You can walk from gallery to gallery meeting the featured artists and checking out their works.

The well-regarded **Wellfleet Harbor Actors Theater** (⊠ Kendrick St., past E. Commercial St., Wellfleet, ☎ 508/349–6835) presents world premieres of American plays, satires, farces, and black comedies in its mid-May–mid-October season. This is the place for provocative, experimental theater.

NIGHTLIFE

Beachcomber (⊠ Ocean View Dr., Cahoon Hollow Beach, off U.S. 6, Wellfleet, ☎ 508/349–6055) is big with the college crowd. It's right on the beach, with national touring acts most nights, weekend happy hours with live reggae, and dancing nightly in summer. Indoors or at tables by the beachfront bar, you can order from a menu of fun appetizers, salads, burgers, seafood, barbecue, and frozen drinks. There's also a raw bar.

A number of organizations sponsor outdoor activities at night, including the **Massachusetts Audubon Wellfleet Bay Wildlife Sanctuary**'s (☞ *above*) night hikes and lecture series.

The **Tavern Room** (⊠ 70 Main St., Wellfleet, ☎ 508/349–7369), set in an 1800s building with a beamed ceiling, a fireplace, and a bar covered in nautical charts, has live entertainment from jazz to pop to country to Latin ensembles. Munchies are served alongside the menu of traditional and Latin/Caribbean-inspired dishes.

Kick up your heels and grab a twirling partner for a long-standing Wellfleet tradition, the **Wednesday Night Square Dance.** Down at the town pier in July and August, the music and live calling by master caller Toots begins at 7 PM and lasts as long as you can.

Outdoor Activities and Sports

BEACHES

Public Beaches. The spectacular dune-drop Atlantic beaches **White Crest** and **Cahoon Hollow** charge daily parking fees of $10 to nonresidents in season only. Cahoon Hollow has lifeguards, rest rooms, and a restaurant and music club on the sand (☞ Nightlife and the Arts, *above*). **Marconi Beach,** part of Cape Cod National Seashore, charges $7 for daily parking or $20 for a season pass that provides access to all seven national seashore beaches. **Mayo Beach** just west of Wellfleet Harbor is free. You can also park free at the small lot by **Great Island** on the bay.

Restricted Beaches. Resident or temporary resident parking stickers are required for access to Wellfleet beaches in season only, from the last week of June through Labor Day. (Some hotels and rental agencies give these to their guests or to people renting houses.) To get a weekly ($25) or season ($75) pass, visit the Beach Sticker Booth on the town pier with your car registration in hand and a proof-of-stay form, available from rental agencies and hotels. For the rest of the year, anyone can visit the beaches for free. Note that people arriving on foot or by bicycle can visit the beaches at any time; the sticker is for parking only. **LeCount Hollow** and **Newcomb Hollow** are the restricted ocean beaches; **Indian Neck** harbor beach and the **Duck Hollow** bay beach past Great Island are also restricted. For more information call the Wellfleet Chamber of Commerce (☎ 508/349–2510).

The **Wellfleet Ponds,** nestled in the woods between U.S. 6 and the ocean, were formed by glaciers and are fed by underground springs. Mild temperatures and clear, clean water make swimming pleasant for the whole family, a refreshing change from the bracing, salty surf of the Atlantic. They are also perfect for canoeing, sailing, or kayaking (boats are available from Jack's Boat Rentals; ☞ *below*). These fragile ecosystems have called for restricted use, and a Wellfleet beach sticker (☞ *above*) is required in season. The sticker is for cars, however, so anyone can walk over or ride a bike to the ponds and dive in. Motorized boats are not allowed.

BIKING

The Cape Cod Rail Trail ends at the South Wellfleet post office. Other scenic routes for bicyclists include the winding, tree-lined Old County Road, just outside Wellfleet center at the end of West Main Street. Ambitious riders can bike all the way to Truro on this often bumpy road, but do watch for vehicular traffic around the tight curves. Ocean View Drive, on the ocean side, provides for many miles of cycling in wooded areas. If you get too hot, there are several ponds along the route to sink into.

Black Duck Sports Shop (✉ U.S. 6 at LeCount Hollow Rd., South Wellfleet, ☎ 508/349–9801; 508/349–2335 off-season) rents a variety of bikes.

Wellfleet Cycles Ltd. (✉ 54 E. Commercial St., Wellfleet, ☎ 508/349–9322) rents bicycles in a convenient, in-town location. Sailing lessons are also available.

BOATING

Fun Seekers (☎ 508/349–1429) offers windsurfing instruction and guided mountain-bike and kayak tours by appointment. Children's programs are available; the company closes in the off-season.

Jack's Boat Rentals (✉ Gull Pond, Wellfleet, ☎ 508/349–7553; ✉ U.S. 6, Wellfleet, ☎ 508/349–9808 for long-term rentals) provides canoes, kayaks, sailboards, Sunfish, pedal boats, surfboards, boogie boards, and sailboards. Guided tours are also available.

Wellfleet Marine Corp. (✉ Town Pier,, ☎ 508/349–2233) rents motorboats in various sizes and sailboats by the hour or daily.

FISHING

Fishing trips are operated on a walk-on basis from spring through fall on the *Navigator* (✉ Town Pier, Wellfleet, ☎ 508/349–6003). Rods, reels, and bait are included.

You can climb aboard the charter boat *Jac's Mate* (✉ Town Pier, Wellfleet, ☎ 508/255–2978) for fishing expeditions in search of bass and blues.

GOLF AND TENNIS

Wellfleet maintains several tennis courts down at **Baker's Field** near the Town Pier. Court time is $10 for singles per hour and $12 for doubles per hour and may be reserved by calling the Recreation Department (☎ 508/349–0330).

Chequessett Yacht Country Club (✉ Chequessett Neck Rd., Wellfleet, ☎ 508/349–3704) is a semiprivate club (public use on space-available basis) with a nine-hole golf course and five hard-surface tennis courts by the bay. Lessons are available.

Oliver's (✉ U.S. 6, Wellfleet, ☎ 508/349–3330) has one Truflex and seven clay courts, offers lessons, and arranges matches.

SURFING

The Atlantic-coast **Marconi and White Crest beaches** are the best spots for surfing. Surfboard rentals can be arranged at Jack's Boat Rentals (☞ *above*).

Shopping

Blue Heron Gallery (✉ 20 Bank St., Wellfleet, ☎ 508/349–6724) is one of the Cape's best galleries, with contemporary works—including Cape scenes, jewelry, sculpture, and pottery—by regional and nationally recognized artists, among them Steve Allrich and Del Filardi.

Eccentricity (✉ 361 Main St., Wellfleet, ☎ 508/349–7554) keeps the corner of Main and Briar offbeat. One of the most interesting stores on the Cape, it sells gorgeous kimonos, ethnic-inspired cotton clothing, carved African wooden sculpture, barbershop paintings, odd Mexican items, and trinkets.

Herridge Books (✉ 11 E. Main St. between U.S. 6 and town center, Wellfleet, ☎ 508/349–1323) is a perfect store for a town that has hosted so many writers. Its dignified literary fiction, art and architecture, literary biography and letters, mystery, Americana, sports, and other sections are full of used books in very nice condition. Herridge also catries new books on the Cape and its history.

Karol Richardson (✉ 11 W. Main St., Wellfleet, ☎ 508/349–6378) fashions women's wear in luxurious fabrics and sells interesting shoes, hats, and jewelry. The store may look and sound a little New York for Wellfleet, but the clothing is original.

Kendall Art Gallery (⊠ 40 E. Main St., Wellfleet, ☎ 508/349–2482) carries contemporary art, including Harry Marinsky's bronzes in the sculpture garden, John French's brightly colored ceramic renderings of real and whimsical building facades, and watercolors by Walter Dorrell.

Off Center (⊠ Off Main St., Wellfleet, diagonally across from Eccentricity, ☎ 508/349–3634), another of the Eccentricity (☞ *above*) owners' enterprises, sells mainstream yet stylish women's clothing.

The giant **Wellfleet Flea Market** (⊠ 51 U.S. 6, Eastham-Wellfleet line, ☎ 508/349–2520) sets up shop in the parking lot of the Wellfleet Drive-In Theater mid-April–June and September–October, weekends and Monday holidays 8–4; July and August, Monday holidays, Wednesdays, Thursdays, and weekends 8–4. There's a snack bar and playground. You'll find antiques, sweat socks, old advertising posters, books, Beanie Babies, sweaters from Guatemala, trinkets, plants, and plenty more.

En Route If you're in the mood for a quiet, lovely ride winding through what the Cape might have looked like before Europeans arrived, follow **Old County Road** from Wellfleet to Truro on the bay side. It's bumpy and beautiful—let's hope it stays that way—with a stream or two to pass. So cycle on it, or drive slowly, or just stop and walk to take in the nature around you.

Truro

46 *2 mi north of Wellfleet, 7 mi southeast of Provincetown.*

Settled in 1697, Truro has had several names. It was originally called Pamet after the local Indians, but in 1705 the name was changed to Dangerfield in response to all of the sailing mishaps off its shores. "Truroe" was the final choice, and Truro became the namesake of a Cornish town that homesick settlers thought it to resemble. The town relied on the sea for its income—whaling, shipbuilding, and cod fishing were the main industries.

Today a town of high dunes, estuaries, and rivers fringed by grasses, rolling moors, and houses sheltered in tiny valleys, Truro is a popular retreat of artists, writers, politicos, and numerous vacationing psychoanalysts. Edward Hopper summered here from 1930 to 1967, finding the Cape light ideal for his austere brand of realism.

One of the largest towns in terms of area—almost 43 square mi—it is the smallest in population, with about 1,400 year-round residents. If you thought neighboring Wellfleet's downtown was small, wait until you see—or don't see—Truro's. It's a post office, a town hall, a shop or two. You'll know it by the sign that says DOWNTOWN TRURO at a little plaza entrance. There's also a library, a firehouse, and a police station, but that's about all. Truro is the Cape's narrowest town, and from a high perch you can see the Atlantic Ocean on one side and Cape Cod Bay on the other.

NEED A BREAK? **Jams** (⊠ 14 Truro Center Rd., off U.S. 6 in Truro Center, ☎ 508/349–1616) has the answer for whoever is looking for a great picnic lunch, sandwiches, fresh produce, a bottle of wine or Evian, or a sweet treat. You won't be able to stay for lunch unless you're content getting your knees knocked on the bench outside, but with the best part of the Cape just outside the door, who would want to?

☾ For a few hours of exploring, take the kids to **Pamet Harbor** (⊠ Depot Rd.). At low tide you can walk out on the flats and discover the creatures of the salt marsh. A nearby plaque identifies the plants and animals and tells of the ecological importance of the area.

On **Corn Hill** (✉ Off Corn Hill Rd.), near the beach area of the same name, a tablet commemorates the finding of a buried cache of corn by Standish and the *Mayflower* crew. They took it to Plymouth and used it as seed, returning later to pay the Indians for the corn they'd taken.

The **Truro Center for the Arts at Castle Hill,** housed in a converted 19th-century barn, offers summer arts-and-crafts workshops for children, as well as courses and single classes in art, crafts, photography, and writing for adults. Teachers have included notable New York– and Provincetown-based artists. ✉ *10 Meeting House Rd., Box 756, 02666,* ☎ *508/349–7511,* FAX *508/349–7513.*

Built at the turn of the century as a summer hotel, the **Truro Historical Museum** is a great little gem, a repository of 17th-century firearms, mementos of shipwrecks, early fishing and whaling gear, ship models, a pirate's chest, scrimshaw, and more. One room exhibits wood carvings, paintings, blown glass, and ship models by Courtney Allen, artist and founder of Truro's historical society. The museum also hosts some ambitious local art and artifact shows each year. ✉ *6 Lighthouse Rd., off S. Highland Rd., North Truro,* ☎ *508/487–3397.* ✇ *$3.* ☉ *Memorial Day–Sept., daily 10–4:30.*

❹⓻ Truly a breathtaking sight, **Highland Light,** also called Cape Cod Light, is the Cape's oldest lighthouse. It was the last to have become automated, in 1986. The first light on this site, powered by 24 whale-oil lamps, began warning ships of Truro's treacherous sandbars in 1798— the dreaded Peaked Hills Bars alone, to the north, have claimed hundreds of ships. The current light, a white-painted 66-ft tower built in 1857, is powered by two 1,000-watt bulbs that are reflected by a huge Fresnel lens. Its beacon is visible for 20 mi.

One of four active lighthouses on the Outer Cape, Highland Light has the distinction of being listed in the National Register of Historic Places. Thoreau used it as a stopover in his travels across the Cape's back side, as the Atlantic side of the Outer Cape is called. Erosion threatened to cut this lighthouse from the 117-ft cliff on which it stood and drop it into the sea. Thanks to a concerted effort by local citizens and lighthouse lovers, the necessary funds were raised and the lighthouse was moved back 450 ft to safety in 1996; it is still surrounded by the Highland Links golf course, however. Twenty-five minute tours of the lighthouse are given daily in the summer. For those with children, all must be 51" tall to climb the tower. ✉ *Off S. Highland Rd.,* ☎ *508/487–1121.* ✇ *$3.* ☉ *Mid-June–Sept., daily 10–sunset.*

The gardens of **A Touch of Heaven** are a beautiful place and, unlike most other gardens, are meant to be picked. The lawns are set with benches and birdbaths. The flowers are so abundant you don't feel guilty gathering a bunch to take home. ✉ *Pond Village Heights, North Truro,* ☎ *no phone.* ✇ *Free.* ☉ *Daily, dawn–dusk.*

❹⓼ At the **Pilgrim Heights Area** of the Cape Cod National Seashore (✉ Off U.S. 6), a short trail leads to the spring where a Pilgrim exploring party stopped to refill their casks, tasting their first New England water. Walking through this still-wild area of oak, pitch pine, bayberry, blueberry, beach plum, and azalea gives you a taste of what it was like for these voyagers in search of a new home. "Being thus passed the vast ocean . . ." William Bradford wrote in *Of Plimoth Plantation,* "they had no friends to welcome them, no inns to entertain them or refresh their weather-beaten bodies; no houses, or much less towns to repair to, to seek for succour."

From an overlook you can see the bluffs of High Head, where glaciers pushed a mass of earth before melting and receding. Another path leads to a swamp, and a bike trail leads to Head of the Meadow Beach (☞ Outdoor Activities and Sports, *below*), often a less crowded alternative to others in the area.

Dining and Lodging

$$–$$$ ✕ **Adrian's.** Adrian Cyr's restaurant crowns a high bluff overlooking Pilgrim Lake and all of Provincetown; his cooking also hits the heights. Cayenne-crusted grilled salmon with maple-mustard sauce is one of the well-prepared dishes. Tuscan salad is a constant hit, with tomatoes, olives, fresh basil, plenty of garlic, and balsamic vinegar. Pizzas, too, are standouts, especially one made with cornmeal dough and topped with shrimp and artichokes. The outdoor deck, always a fun spot, bursts at the very popular breakfasts and brunches, served every day in season. ⊠ *Outer Reach Hotel, 535 U.S. 6, North Truro,* ☎ *508/ 487–4360. Reservations not accepted. AE, MC, V. Closed mid-Oct.– Memorial Day.*

$$–$$$ ✕ **Blacksmith Shop.** Here's the spot in Truro where the locals like to linger at the bar, gossiping about what's going on at town hall while choosing from an eclectic menu with everything from seafood to Mexican items. The restaurant looks like it might have been a place to bring your horse for a shoeing, but these days it's a nice out-of-the-way spot for company. There are excellent steaks as well as an emphasis on greens and gently cooked vegetables that would keep a Californian happy. A short bar menu has moved south of the border, listing wraps and bean dishes that could use a little more salsa heat. Local shellfishermen like Keith Rose deliver excellent quahogs and oysters and then hang out to find out what's the latest on the building inspector. ⊠ *Off Rte. 6A in Truro Center,* ☎ *508/349–6554. AE, D, MC, V. Closed weekdays Nov.–May.*

$$–$$$ ✕ **Montano's.** This place looms on the side of U.S. 6, a friendly, cavernous, Italian-style restaurant with vaulted ceilings and hanging plants. Old harpoons, fish barrels, and lobster-pot "chandeliers" add the requisite nautical touch, and the ever-smooth Tony Bennett croons in the background. Built to handle a tour bus crowd, Montano's serves comfortable, predictable, Italian-American fare with a leaning toward seafood and a solid selection of steaks. You can't go wrong with classics like linguine and mussels in a red or white sauce, or a simple thick, center-cut filet mignon with roasted garlic butter. The 14-inch pizzas are made on fresh dough, and you can taste the difference. Montano's is one of the endangered species that still offer an unlimited salad bar. This is a good place to take a big family. ⊠ *481 U.S. 6,* ☎ *508/487– 2026. AE, MC, V. No lunch.*

$$–$$$ ✕ **Terra Luna.** An insider's favorite for a special breakfast, Terra Luna has become a wonderful choice for dinner as well. The dining room may lean toward cramped instead of intimate, but the food is stylish and well presented, with surprising sauces for both fish and meat dishes. The striped bass is grilled but not over-grilled, and spicy stuffed lamb chops are an excellent alternative to the usual fish. Here is a kitchen that never took "nouveau" too seriously, so the servings remained ample. ⊠ *104 Shore Rd. (Rte. 6A), North Truro,* ☎ *508/487–1019. AE, MC, V. Closed late Oct.–May.*

$–$$ 🏠 **East Harbour.** This meticulously maintained complex outside Provincetown offers simple accommodations ranged around a manicured lawn and separated from the bay beach by low grasses. The two-bedroom cottages have paneled walls, colonial-style furnishings, and full kitchens. Motel rooms have large picture windows, minirefrigerators and coffeemakers, light paneling, and '60s motel-style furnishings. A newer apartment is all white and bright, with skylights, Shaker-reproduction furnishings, a modern kitchen, and second-floor views of the harbor from a private deck. All units have individual heat, microwaves, and cable TV. ⊠ *618 Shore Rd. (Rte. 6A), Box 183, North Truro 02652,* ☎ *508/487–0505,* FAX *508/487–6693. 7 cottages, 9 rooms, 1 apartment. Picnic area, beach, coin laundry. In season, 1-wk minimum for cottages, 2-night minimum for rooms. AE, D, MC, V. Closed Nov.–Mar.*

$–$$ ⊞ **Moorlands Inn.** A proud Victorian beauty, this inn shines both inside and out. Artful touches include the creative works—both visual and musical—of innkeepers Bill and Skipper Evaul, artists and musicians, that fill the walls and rooms with lovely images and sounds. Antiques adorn the bright, uncluttered rooms in the main house, and fresh blues and whites are balanced with natural wood accents. The spacious penthouse provides a full kitchen, two bedrooms, plenty of living space, and a deck. Carriage House guests have their own private outdoor whirlpool, and other guests can gather in the communal hot tub out back. Truro is naturally quiet, and this is a beautiful place from which to enjoy the solitude. ⊠ *11 Hughes Rd., North Truro 02652,* ☎ *508/487–0663. 5 rooms, 1 apartment, 3 cottages. Croquet, outdoor hot tub. MC, V. BP.*

$–$$ ⊞ **Truro Vineyards of Cape Cod Inn.** Set on 5 acres of working vineyard, this 1836 former farmstead has been transformed into an elegant inn. The decor reflects the wine motif: antique casks and presses stand in the corners, and deep greens and burgundies predominate. Guest rooms have four-poster king- and queen-size beds and modern tiled baths. The luxury room includes a king bed and an extra large bath with a two-person whirlpool bath. Homegrown berries often garnish dishes at breakfast, which is served in the sunroom or, in nice weather, outside on the patio. A large common sundeck has sweeping views of the vineyard. ⊠ *11 Shore Rd. (Rte. 6A), North Truro 02652,* ☎ *508/487–6200,* FAX *508/487–4248. 5 rooms, 4 with bath. No smoking. MC, V. BP.*

$ ⊞ **Hostelling International–Truro.** In a former Coast Guard station right on the dunes, this handsome, well-placed hostel has kitchen facilities, a common area, and naturalist-led programs. It's also right by the ½-mi Cranberry Bog Trail, which takes you by a refurbished cranberry bog and an old bog house. ⊠ *N. Pamet Rd., Box 402, Truro 02666,* ☎ *508/349–3889. 42 beds. MC, V. Closed Labor Day–mid-June.*

Outdoor Activities and Sports

BEACHES

A number of Truro's **town beaches,** including Coast Guard Beach and Ballston Beach on the Atlantic, are reserved for residents and renters in season, although anyone can walk or bicycle in. Ask at Town Hall (☎ 508/349–3635) about a seasonal sticker.

Head of the Meadow Beach (⊠ Head of the Meadow Rd., off U.S. 6) in North Truro, part of Cape Cod National Seashore, is often less crowded than others in the area. It has only temporary rest-room facilities available in summer and no showers since the bathhouse burned down. The daily parking fee is $7 in season, or the beach can be accessed with the purchase of a season pass ($20) good for all national seashore locations.

BIKING

The **Head of the Meadow Trail** is 2 mi of easy cycling between dunes and salt marshes from High Head Road, off Route 6A in North Truro, to the Head of the Meadow Beach parking lot. Bird-watchers also love the area.

Bayside Bikes (✉ 102 Rte. 6A, North Truro, ☎ 508/487–5735) rents bicycles by the hour, day, or week, with easy access to the Head of the Meadow Trail.

The **Highland Golf Links** (✉ Lighthouse Rd., North Truro, ☎ 508/487–9201), a nine-hole, par-36 course on a cliff overlooking the Atlantic and Highland Light, is unique for its resemblance to Scottish links, instead of the well-manicured and less-challenging courses that are more typical.

Longnook Beach (✉ End of Longnook Rd., off U.S. 6 is a good surfing spot.

Shopping

Atlantic Spice Co. (✉ U.S. 6 at Rte. 6A, North Truro, ☎ 508/487–6100) stocks a fragrant array of spices, teas, and potpourris, as well as herbs, dried flowers, locally made soaps, sauces, and kitchenware items

Whitman House Gift Shop (✉ County Rd., just off U.S. 6, N. Truro, ☎ 508/487–3204) sells Amish quilts and other country items.

Provincetown

49–60 *7 mi northwest of Truro, 27 mi north of Orleans, 62 mi from the Sagamore Bridge.*

The Cape's smallest town in area and the second-smallest in year-round population, Provincetown comprises 8 square mi packed with history. The curled fist at the very tip of the Cape, Provincetown has shores that curve protectively around a natural harbor, the perfect spot for visitors from any epoch to anchor. Historical records show that Thorvald, brother of Viking Leif Erikson, came ashore here in AD 1004 to repair the keel of his boat and consequently named the area "Kjalarness," or Cape of the Keel. Bartholomew Gosnold came to Provincetown in 1602 and named the area Cape Cod after the abundant codfish he found in the local waters.

The Pilgrims remain Provincetown's most famous visitors. On Monday, November 21, 1620, the *Mayflower* dropped anchor in Provincetown Harbor after a difficult 63-day voyage from England; while in the harbor they signed the Mayflower Compact, the first document to declare a democratic form of government in America. One of the first things the ever-practical Pilgrims did was to come ashore to wash their clothes, thus starting the ages-old New England tradition of Monday wash day. They stayed in the area for five weeks before moving on to Plymouth. Plaques and parks commemorate the landing throughout town.

During the American Revolution, Provincetown Harbor was controlled by the British, who used it as a port from which to sail to Boston and launch attacks on colonial and French vessels. In November 1778 the 64-gun British frigate *Somerset* ran aground and was wrecked off Provincetown's Race Point. Every 60 years or so the shifting sands uncover her remains.

Incorporated as a town in 1727, Provincetown was for many decades a bustling seaport, with fishing and whaling as its major industries. Fishing is still an important source of income for many Provincetown locals, while the town ranks fourth in the world as a whale-watching, rather than hunting, mecca.

Provincetown

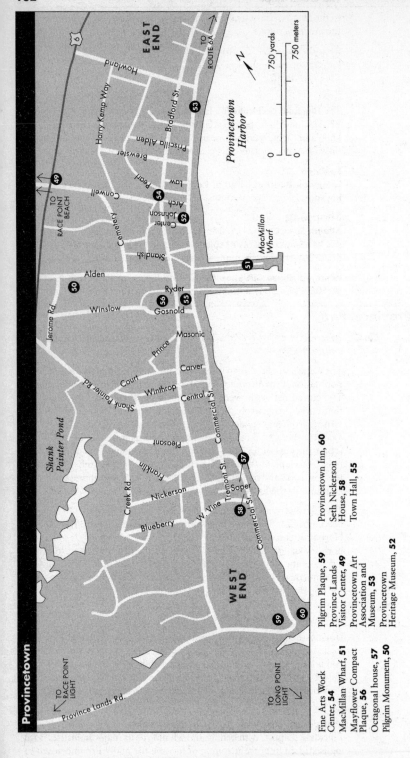

Fine Arts Work Center, **54**
MacMillan Wharf, **51**
Mayflower Compact Plaque, **56**
Octagonal house, **57**
Pilgrim Monument, **50**

Pilgrim Plaque, **59**
Province Lands Visitor Center, **49**
Provincetown Art Association and Museum, **53**
Provincetown Heritage Museum, **52**

Provincetown Inn, **60**
Seth Nickerson House, **58**
Town Hall, **55**

Artists began coming here in 1899 for the unique Cape Cod light—in fact, Provincetown is the nation's oldest continuous art colony. Poets, writers, and actors have also been part of the art scene. Eugene O'Neill's first plays were written and produced here, and the Fine Arts Work Center continues to have in its ranks some of the most important writers of our time.

During the early 1900s, Provincetown became known as Greenwich Village North. Artists from New York and Europe discovered the town's unspoiled beauty, special light, lively community, and colorful Portuguese flavor. By 1916, with five art schools flourishing here, painters' easels were nearly as common as shells on the beach. This bohemian community, along with the availability of inexpensive summer lodgings, attracted young rebels and writers as well, including John Reed (*Ten Days That Shook the World*) and Mary Heaton Vorse (*Footnote to Folly*), who in 1915 began the Cape's first significant theater group, the Provincetown Players. The young, then-unknown Eugene O'Neill joined them in 1916, when his *Bound East for Cardiff* premiered in a tiny wharf-side fish house in the East End that was minimally fitted out as a theater. After 1916 the Players moved on to New York. Their theater, at present-day 571 Commercial Street, is long since gone, but a model of it and of the old Lewis Wharf on which it stood is on display at the Pilgrim Monument museum.

Provincetown is a place of creativity, sometimes startling originality, and great diversity. In the busy downtown, Portuguese-American fishermen mix with painters, poets, writers, whale-watching families, cruise-ship passengers on brief stopovers, and many lesbian and gay residents and visitors, for whom P-town, as it's almost universally known, is one of the most popular East Coast seashore spots. In summer Commercial Street is packed with sightseers and shoppers hunting for treasures in the overwhelming number of galleries and crafts shops. At night, raucous music and people spill out of bars, drag shows, and sing-along lounges galore. It's a fun, crazy place, with the extra dimension of the fishing fleet unloading their catch at MacMillan Wharf, in the center of the action.

Near the Provincetown border, **massive dunes** actually meet the road in places, turning U.S. 6 into a sand-swept highway. Scattered among the dunes are primitive cottages, called dune shacks, built from flotsam and other found materials, that have provided atmospheric as well as cheap lodgings to a number of famous artists and writers over the years—among them poet Harry Kemp, Eugene O'Neill, e. e. cummings, Jack Kerouac, and Norman Mailer. The few surviving shacks are privately leased from the Cape Cod National Seashore, whose proposal to demolish the shacks was halted by their inclusion on the National Register of Historic Places in 1988. The dunes are fragile and should not be walked on, but there are paths leading through them to the ocean. You can see some of the shacks by van on Art's Dune Tours (☞ Guided Tours *in* Cape Cod A to Z, *below*).

The **Province Lands** begin at High Head in Truro and stretch to the tip of Provincetown. The area is scattered with ponds, cranberry bogs, and scrub; unfortunately this terrain provides optimal conditions for the deer tick, so use extra caution. Bike and walking trails lace through forests of stunted pines, beech, and oak and across desertlike expanses of rolling dunes. Protected against development, the Province Lands are the "wilds" of the Cape.

A beautiful spot to stop for lunch before biking to the beach, the **Beech Forest picnic area** (⊠ Race Point Rd.) in the national seashore borders a small pond covered with water lilies. The adjacent bike trails lead to Herring Cove and Race Point beaches, both part of the seashore.

49 Inside the **Province Lands Visitor Center** in the Cape Cod National Seashore you'll find literature and nature-related gifts, frequent short films—on local geology, the U.S. Life Saving Service, and more—and exhibits on the life of the dunes and the shore. You can also pick up information on guided walks, birding trips, lectures, bonfires, and other current programs throughout the seashore, as well as on the Province Lands' own beaches, Race Point and Herring Cove, and the walking, biking, and horse trails. Don't miss the wonderful 360-degree view of the dunes and the surrounding ocean from the observation deck. ⊠ *Race Point Rd.,* ☎ *508/487–1256.* ⊙ *Apr.–Nov., daily 9–5.*

Not far from the present Coast Guard station is the **Old Harbor Station,** a U.S. Life Saving Service building towed here by barge from Chatham in 1977 to rescue it from an eroding beach. It is reached by a boardwalk across the sand, and plaques along the way tell about the lifesaving service and the whales seen offshore. Inside are displays of such equipment as Lyle guns, which shot rescue lines out to ships in distress when seas were too violent to launch a surfboat, and breeches buoys, in which passengers were hauled across those lines to safety. At 6:30 on Thursday nights in summer there are reenactments of the old-fashioned lifesaving procedure. ⊠ *Race Point Beach, end of Race Point Rd.,* ☎ *no phone.* 🎫 *Donations accepted; Thurs. night $3.* ⊙ *July–Aug., daily 10–4.*

Provincetown's main downtown thoroughfare, **Commercial Street,** is 3 mi from end to end. In season, driving from one end of the main street to the other could take forever, so walking is definitely the way to go; you'll see signs for parking lots as you head into town. A casual stroll will allow you to see the many different architectural styles (Greek Revival, Victorian, Second Empire, and Gothic, to name a few) used to build impressive houses for wealthy sea captains and merchants. Be on the lookout for blue plaques fastened to housefronts explaining their historical significance—practically the entire town has been designated part of the Provincetown Historic District. The Historical Society puts out a series of walking-tour pamphlets, available for about $1 each at many shops in town, with maps and information on the history of many buildings and the more or less famous folk who have occupied them. You may also want to pick up a free Provincetown gallery guide.

The center of town is where the crowds and most of the touristy shops are. The quiet East End is mostly residential, with some top galleries, and the similarly quiet West End has a number of small inns with neat lawns and elaborate gardens. Narrated trolley sightseeing tours make the downtown circuit throughout the day, or the romantically inclined can hire a **horse-drawn carriage** (☎ 508/487–4246) from the stand in front of the Town Hall (⊠ 260 Commercial St.).

50 The first thing you'll see in Provincetown is the **Pilgrim Monument,** stretching into the sky. This somewhat grandiose edifice, which seems oddly out of proportion to the rest of this low-rise town, commemorates the first landing of the Pilgrims in the New World and their signing of the Mayflower Compact, America's first rules of self-governance, before they set off from Provincetown Harbor to explore the mainland. Climb the 252-ft-high tower (116 steps and 60 ramps) for a panoramic view—dunes on one side, harbor on the other, and the entire bay side of Cape Cod beyond. On an exceptionally clear day, you can see the Boston skyline. At the base is a museum of Lower Cape and Provincetown history, with exhibits on whaling, shipwrecks, and scrimshaw, a diorama of the *Mayflower,* and another of a glass factory. The site is also the summer home of the Provincetown Repertory Theater (☞ Nightlife and the Arts, *below*), which stages several fine productions throughout the season in a small theater here.

The tower was erected of granite shipped from Maine, according to a design modeled on a tower in Siena, Italy. President Theodore Roosevelt laid the cornerstone in 1907, and President Taft attended the 1910 dedication. On Thanksgiving Eve, in a ceremony that includes a museum tour and open house, 5,000 white and gold lights that drape the tower are illuminated—a display that can be seen as far away as the Cape Cod Canal. They are lit nightly into the New Year. ✉ *High Pole Hill Rd.,* ☎ *508/487–1310.* 🎟 *$5.* ⏲ *Apr.–June and Sept.– Nov., daily 9–5; July–Aug., daily 9–7; last admission 45 mins before closing.*

51 **MacMillan Wharf** (✉ Off Commercial St.), with its large municipal parking facility, is a sensible place to start a tour of town. It is one of the remaining 5 of 54 wharves that once jutted into the bay. The wharf is the base for P-town whale-watch boats, fishing charters, and party boats. The **Chamber of Commerce** is also here, with all kinds of information and events schedules. Kiosks at the wharf have rest-room and parking-lot locations, bus schedules, and other information for visitors.

In 1997 renovations were completed on the former **Provincetown Marina building** on MacMillan Wharf, and it opened as the **Expedition Whydah Sea Lab and Learning Center,** the new home for artifacts and treasure recovered from the *Whydah,* a pirate ship that sank off the coast of Wellfleet more than 265 years ago, and the only pirate shipwreck ever authenticated in the world. The new museum is both entertaining and educational, with a display featuring the conservation and restoration processes at work on actual artifacts, and a history component that gives the untold story of 18th-century pirating life. Eventually the museum hopes to collect all of the recovered pieces, some of which are presently on loan to other museums across the country. ✉ *16 MacMillan Wharf,* ☎ *508/487–8899 or 800/949–3241.* 🎟 *$5.* ⏲ *Memorial Day–Labor Day, daily 10–7; Apr.–Memorial Day and Labor Day–Oct. 15, daily 10–5; Oct. 16–Dec., weekends 10–5.*

52 Housed in an 1860 Methodist church listed on the Register of Historical Places, the **Provincetown Heritage Museum** displays scenes of domestic life and workplaces from centuries past. Exhibits include antique fire-fighting equipment, fishing artifacts, and artwork donated by Provincetown-related artists. There are also antique prints and watercolors of schooners, wax figures, and a half-scale model, 66 ft long, built by a master shipbuilder, of the fishing schooner *Rose Dorothea,* which won the Lipton Cup in 1907. The museum was closed for renovations for much of the 1999 season but should be open in 2000. ✉ *356 Commercial St.,* ☎ *508/487–7098.* 🎟 *$3.* ⏲ *Memorial Day–mid-Oct., daily 10–5:30.*

NEED A BREAK?

The **Provincetown Portuguese Bakery** (✉ 299 Commercial St., ☎ 508/487–1803) makes fresh Portuguese breads and pastries and serves breakfast and lunch all day from March to October. Novices should ask the counter person which pastries to try. It's open until 11 PM in summer.

53 Founded in 1914 to collect and show the works of Provincetown-associated artists, the **Provincetown Art Association and Museum** (PAAM) houses a 1,650-piece permanent collection, displayed in changing exhibits that combine up-and-comers with established 20th-century artists. Some of the work hung in the four bright galleries is for sale. The museum store has books by or about local artists, authors, and

topics, as well as posters, crafts, cards, and gift items. PAAM-sponsored year-round courses (one day and longer) offer the opportunity to study under such talents as Sal Del Deo, Carol Whorf Westcott, and Tony Vevers. ⊠ *460 Commercial St.,* ☎ *508/487–1750.* 🖾 *$3.* ☉ *Nov.–Apr., weekends noon–4 and by appointment; Memorial Day–Labor Day, daily noon–5 and 8–10; May and Sept.–Oct., Fri.–Sun. noon–5.*

To see or hear the work of up-and-coming artists, visit the gallery or
❺❹ attend a reading at the **Fine Arts Work Center** (FAWC). A nonprofit organization founded in 1968, the FAWC sponsors 10 writers and 10 artists from October through May each year with a place to live and work, and access to artists and teachers. A new Summer Program has open-enrollment workshops in both writing and the visual arts. The buildings in the complex around the center, which it owns, were formerly part of Day's Lumber Yard Studios, built above a lumberyard by a patron of the arts to provide poor artists with cheap accommodations. Robert Motherwell, Hans Hoffmann, and Helen Frankenthaler have been among the studios' roster of residents over the years. ⊠ *24 Pearl St.,* ☎ *508/487–9960.* ☉ *Weekdays 9–5.*

The former studios of two noted artists, Edwin W. Dickinson, at 46 Pearl Street, and Charles W. Hawthorne, at 48 Pearl Street, give an idea of the proliferation of now-famous artists that worked in the area. Hawthorne's **Cape Cod School of Art,** established here in 1899 (now managed by Lois Griffel, a former student of Henry Hensche, one of Hawthorne's disciples), put the town on its path to becoming a major art colony. The school runs weeklong workshops in summer; call ahead to get the catalog. The year 1999 marked the school's centennial, and the town celebrated being home to the nation's oldest continuous art colony. ⊠ *22 Brewster St.,* ☎ *508/487–0101.* ☉ *Late May—late Sept.; call for hrs.*

❺❺ The **Town Hall** was used by the Provincetown Art Association as its first exhibit space and still exhibits paintings donated to the town over the years, including Provincetown scenes by Charles Hawthorne and WPA-era murals by Ross Moffett. ⊠ *260 Commercial St.,* ☎ *508/487–7000.* ☉ *Weekdays 8–5.*

❺❻ In a little park behind the town hall is the **Mayflower Compact Plaque** (⊠ Bradford St.) carved in bas-relief by sculptor Cyrus Dalin, depicting the historic signing.

NEED A BREAK?   The **Provincetown Fudge Factory** (⊠ 210 Commercial St., ☎ 508/487–2850), across from the post office, makes silky peanut-butter cups, chocolates, saltwater taffy, yard-long licorice whips, custom-flavor frozen yogurt, and the creamiest fudge on the Cape—a must stop for those with a discriminating sweet tooth—and will ship goodies to you, too.

❺❼ An **octagonal house** (⊠ 74 Commercial St., between Soper and Nickerson Sts.) built in 1850 is an interesting piece of Provincetown architecture in the West End. The house is not open to the public.

The oldest building in town, dating from 1746, is the small Cape-style
❺❽ **Seth Nickerson House** (⊠ 72 Commercial St., at Soper St.), still a private home. It was built by a ship's carpenter, with massive pegged, hand-hewn oak beams and wide-board floors. Renovated in 1998, the house does not offer the glimpse into centuries past that it once did, but it's still impressive.

❺❾ The bronze **Pilgrim Plaque** (⊠ West end of Commercial St.), set into a boulder at the center of a little park, commemorates the first footfall of the Pilgrims onto Cape soil—Provincetown's humble equivalent of the Plymouth Rock.

60 In the **Provincetown Inn** (✉ 1 Commercial St., ☎ 508/487–9500) you can see a series of 19 murals, painted in the 1930s from old postcards, depicting life in the 19th-century town. The inn still operates as a hotel; the murals are in the lobby and hallways.

Dining and Lodging

$$$$ ✕ **Chester.** Understated and golden-hued, Chester is the newest, most expensive addition to Provincetown's upscale dining scene. Named for a 10-year-old pet terrier, the single-room restaurant in a Greek Revival sea captain's house has a small, elegant contemporary menu that changes regularly. The owners' philosophy that fresh quality food need not be masked with extraneous ingredients has created a reputation for memorable, beautifully presented food. The menu lists locally procured meats and seafood, and the chef collects tomatoes, herbs, and lettuces from a garden behind the restaurant. Try seasonal choices such as asparagus and fiddlehead risotto, and lamb with cranberry jus, potatoes, and vegetables. The carefully crafted wine list has 100 selections, all the better to help you create unusual food and wine pairings, as the owners suggest. ✉ *404 Commercial St., ☎ 508/487–8200. Reservations essential. AE, MC, V. Closed part of Dec.–Mar; call for Dec. dates.*

$$$ ✕ **Café Edwige.** Nancy Meads now owns the restaurant she has run
★ for years, which is good news for one and all. Delicious contemporary American food, relaxed and friendly service, and an eclectic, homey upstairs setting—Café Edwige delivers all this night after night. Begin with a Maine crab cake, warm goat cheese on crostini, or a refreshing field-green-and-wild-lettuce salad, and then consider lobster and Wellfleet scallops over pasta with a wild mushroom, Asiago, and tomato broth, or planked local codfish with roasted corn and shiitakes. Don't pass on the wonderful desserts such as the Cape Cod cranberry crumble served with vanilla ice cream. The tasty breakfast here is a town institution. ✉ *333 Commercial St., ☎ 508/487–2008. AE, MC, V. Closed Nov.–May.*

$$$ ✕ **Front Street.** Front Street is so good, so consistent, and so roman-
★ tic that many locals consistently rate it as a contender for the title of best restaurant in P-town. Chef-owners Donna Aliperti and Kathleen Cotter link classic Italian cooking to offerings from other Mediterranean regions such as Greece and southern France and even North Africa. Duck smoked in Chinese black tea is dense and luscious, served with a different lusty sauce every day; a current favorite is fresh tropical fruit with mixed peppercorns. An aromatic smoked salmon chowder comes and goes from the menu (there ought to be a town meeting to put it on permanently). Littleneck clams and calamari with butternut squash in a roast garlic broth is essentially a simple dish, but its unique flavors show off these traditional ingredients in a new light. The wine list is also a winner. Make sure to call well ahead for a reservation even during the shoulder seasons, when the menu turns purely Italian. ✉ *230 Commercial St., ☎ 508/487–9715. Reservations essential. AE, D, MC, V. Closed Jan.–mid-May.*

$$$ ✕ **Martin House.** Provincetown can be such a zoo that it is a genuine
★ relief to find this island of calm and creative contemporary fare right on crazy Commercial Street. The house's 1850s woodwork lends an historic feeling, and the walls are graced with Provincetown paintings. The menu has become less innovative in recent years, but there are some wonderful and soothing offerings. Some of the more interesting dishes include Oysters Claudia, which matches native Wellfleets-on-the-half-shell with an Asian dipping sauce, wasabi, and pickled ginger, and pan-

roasted lamb rib eye with an exotic mint chutney and quinoa–wild rice tabbouleh. ✉ *157 Commercial St.,* ☎ *508/487–1327. AE, D, DC, MC, V. Closed Wed. and Thurs. Jan.–Mar.*

$$$ ✕ **The Mews.** This town favorite is still going strong, with a menu that
★ focuses on seafood with a cross-cultural flair. Some popular entrées are rich and spicy scallops, shrimp-and-crab mousse in a wonton on grilled filet mignon, and a decadent French lentil ragout with chipotle aioli sauce. Downstairs, the main dining room opens onto magnificent harbor views. A piano bar upstairs serves lunch (weekdays in summer) and dinner from a light café menu. The view of the bay from the bar is near perfect, and the gentle lighting makes this a romantic spot for a drink. Brunch is also served every day in season. ✉ *429 Commercial St.,* ☎ *508/487–1500. Reservations not accepted. AE, D, DC, MC, V. Closed Jan. No lunch weekdays off-season or Sat. between Columbus Day and Memorial Day.*

$$$ ✕ **Provincetown Ferry Restaurant.** Chef Joseph Martello serves up trendy food with an international touch right in the heart of the happening West End. The Ferry has been freshly redesigned in blues, grays, reds, and blond tones. The small, airy back room is decked out with four screens constantly playing adult contemporary music videos, and a bar in front, still lushly dark, has new urban-industrial overtones. The seared-tuna ferryboats appetizer is rare tuna and fried wontons with a tamari-ginger-soy "splash." Some main-course choices are a vegetarian risotto du jour with fresh seasonal vegetables and (a rare find these days) bone-in prime rib served au jus or Philly style, smothered in onions, peppers, and cheese. One caveat: the house salad at $6 is too expensive. On the fine breakfast and brunch menu are items such as Mom's deep-dish French toast. ✉ *177 Commercial St.,* ☎ *508/487–0120. AE, MC, V. Closed Nov.–mid-Apr.*

$$–$$$ ✕ **Dancing Lobster Café Trattoria.** Chef and owner Pepe Berg put in
★ some time at Harry's Bar in Venice and brought back to P-town rich Italian flavors and stylish whimsy. Berg has moved for the third time in four years, this time back to the restaurant where his father held court for years, (known then as Pepe's Wharf). This feels like a homecoming, and while the food is becoming more upscale, it remains among the best prepared in Provincetown. The presentations are innovative and sophisticated, outstanding in every way. Appetizers are pure classics—carpaccio is a favorite—and the *zuppa di pesce* (Italian seafood stew) with couscous is complex and filling. The chef can sometimes be a bit too generous with the olive oil, but think of it as more of a good thing. The lobster may not dance, but the customers will— sometimes joined by Robert the bartender, a great local favorite. ✉ *371 Commercial St.,* ☎ *508/487–0900. AE, D, MC, V. Closed mid-Nov.–mid-May.*

$$–$$$ ✕ **Lobster Pot.** Provincetown's Lobster Pot is fit to do battle with all the Lobster Pots anywhere (and everywhere) on the Cape. As you enter you'll pass through one of the hardest-working kitchens on the Cape, which turns out classic New England cooking: lobsters galore, generous and filling seafood platters, and some of the best chowder around. The upstairs deck overlooks the harbor, and every time you turn around it seems to expand. It now ranks as the best lunch location in town. There's also a take-out lobster market and bakery on the premises. The bad news is that you'll have to wait in line; the good news is that the line is in the center of town, great for people-watching. ✉ *321 Commercial St.,* ☎ *508/487–0842. Reservations not accepted. AE, D, DC, MC, V. Closed Jan.*

$$–$$$ ✕ **Lorraine's.** In its new, much bigger location in the East End of town, Lorraine's has an ambience that is more robust than intimate, but the Mexican-inspired menu is as finely prepared as ever. After four successful years, Lorraine still keeps her hand in the kitchen—and welcomes her mother to cook alongside her on her trips from California. Specials are always worth a listen. An appetizer of three large shrimp stuffed with cheese and fresh jalapeños packs a punch, and the *mujeres* clams (steamed littlenecks in a cilantro citrus broth) are addictive. Also wonderful is a dish called simply *carnitas,* slow-cooked pork tenderloin with fresh guacamole, salsa, sour cream, and lots of frilly greens. The vessel-shape bar draws a loyal, lively clientele. ⊠ *463 Commercial St.,* ☎ *508/487–6074. Reservations essential. MC, V. Closed Jan.–Mar. No lunch.*

$$–$$$ ✕ **The Moors.** Buoys and nets hang everywhere—an authentic testament to the fine Portuguese seafood the Moors has been serving for almost 40 years. If this place looks like it was just tossed up by an errant wave, that's because in a way it was. After a fire destroyed it years ago, locals scoured the outer beaches for driftwood, which was used to rebuild the establishment. Mylan Costa passed the torch to new owners in 1998; patrons are happy to report that they haven't noticed that much of a difference. Specialties include a delicious soup made from *chouriço* (pork sausage) and *linguiça* (garlic-flavored sausage), sea-clam pie, and marinated swordfish steaks. Prix-fixe Portuguese dinners with a choice of three entrées are offered ($16–$20). There's entertainment in the lounge (☞ Nightlife and the Arts, *below*). ⊠ *5 Bradford St. W,* ☎ *508/487–0840. AE, D, DC, MC, V. Closed Nov.–Mar.*

$$–$$$ ✕ **Napi's.** No visit to Provincetown is complete without dinner at
★ Napi's, an excellent Mediterranean-style restaurant. The food and the interior share a penchant for unusual, striking juxtapositions—a classical sculpture in front of an abstract canvas, for instance. On the gustatory front, look for sharp combinations such as shrimp flambé in ouzo and Metaxa, served with a tomato, garlic, and onion sauce. The menu is strong on vegetarian items with an international flair—rice heaped with spicy vegetables is one example. If you arrive early and see a man at the bar drinking a glass of muscadet in summer and a martini in winter, hunched over the *New York Times* crossword puzzle, introduce yourself: it's Napi himself, with his wife, Helen, soon to appear from the kitchen. ⊠ *7 Freeman St.,* ☎ *508/487–1145. Reservations essential. AE, D, DC, MC, V. No lunch June–mid-Sept.*

$$–$$$ ✕ **Sal's Place.** Sal has sold the trattoria that bears his name, so he's no longer cooking commercially (though he is still painting). Even so, this little waterfront place still serves up massive portions of southern Italian specialties. Calamari and linguine, *vongole* (tiny clams) over pasta, and delicious vegetarian spinach lasagna are all longtime favorites. Determined carnivores will want to tackle the steak *pizzaiola*: a massive 25-ounce rib steak served with marinara sauce. Opinions on the decor depend on one's commitment to the authenticity of wine bottles in wicker, but the back dining room overlooks the harbor—the best decor there is. ⊠ *99 Commercial St.,* ☎ *508/487–1279. MC, V. Closed Nov.–Apr. and Mon.–Thurs. Oct. 2–mid-June. No lunch.*

$$ ✕ **Bubala's by the Bay.** Personality bubbles up at this funky joint, which
★ once was a staid standby. When owner John Yingling took over in 1993, he and his crew pumped up the funk as well as the quality—the building is painted bright yellow and adorned on top with campy carved birds. The result is an inviting, mellow-delic seaside '60s feel. The kitchen rarely stops, serving breakfast, lunch, and dinner; it's strong on seafood bought directly off local boats and cut in back just hours before it's served. The Cuban cod would surprise any Cuban because it has little to do with that cuisine (except the beans), but it's wonderfully fresh and tasty. The same thing can be said of the Jamaican fish stew. The wine list is priced practically at retail, and the U-shape bar picks up into the evening. Outdoor seating along Commercial Street is a social

focal point, while quieter indoor seating reaches right down to the bay. ⊠ *183 Commercial St.,* ☎ *508/487–0773. AE, D, MC, V. Closed Halloween–April Fool's Day.*

$–$$ ✕ **Pucci's Harborside.** Here's a friendly, casual standby if you're looking for an easy lunch or dinner way out in the quieter East End. Perched out over the harbor on high tides, Pucci's is a relatively small place with a great water view and airy feel. It blew down several years ago during Hurricane Bob and has been sturdily rebuilt. The house specialties are a big plateful of fiery chicken wings or a wonderful, big stuffed artichoke, gleaming with garlic butter. This is a good place for a solid mushroom and blue cheese burger, a Gorgonzola salad with mixed greens and roasted red peppers, a messy nachos Fiesta, and a decent shrimp scampi. The bartender serves up big, frosty Bloody Marys for steamy summer afternoons. ⊠ *539 Commercial St.,* ☎ *508/487–1964. AE, MC, V. Closed mid-Oct.–late Apr.*

$ ✕ **Mojo's.** This is Provincetown's fast-food institution, where any-
★ body who knows anything about food and happens to be in a hurry goes to grab a bite. The tiniest of kitchens turns out one of the most varied and eclectic menus in town, everything from fresh-cut French fries to fried clams with the bellies, steak subs, tacos, tofu burgers (and the regular kind), tacos, hummus, roll-up sandwiches, salads, and the best fried fish. How they crank it out, so fast and so good, is anybody's guess. It's hard to believe Mojo's has been around for 27 years, but it's even harder to believe it hasn't always been a part of Provincetown. There's some seating in the back at colorfully painted picnic tables. ⊠ *5 Ryder St. Ext.,* ☎ *508/487–3140. Reservations not accepted. No credit cards. Closed mid-Oct.–early May, depending on weather and crowds.*

$ ✕ **Spiritus.** The local bars close at 1 AM, at which point this pizza joint–coffee stand becomes the town's epicenter. The crowd gets so big and flamboyant that Commercial Street virtually shuts down for an hour. It's the ultimate place to see and be seen, pizza slice in hand and witty banter at the ready. In the morning, the same counter serves up restorative coffee and croissants. ⊠ *190 Commercial St.,* ☎ *508/487–2808. No credit cards. Closed Nov.–Apr.*

$$–$$$ ✕🏠 **The Commons.** Built as an inn in the 1860s, this combination guest house and bistro had long suffered a reputation for tackiness until Carl Draper and Chuck Rigg took the helm in 1994. The rooms are now comfortable and tasteful, with wide-board floors, antique furnishings, Oriental carpets, and marble-tiled baths. Most rooms have a view of the bay; some have private balconies. All have TVs and fans or air-conditioning. The bistro has an innovative, ever-changing Continental menu, with dishes like seared halibut with lobster risotto. You can relax in the garden or at the deck bar that overlooks the bay. ⊠ *386 Commercial St. 02657,* ☎ *508/487–7800 or 800/487–0784,* 𝔽𝔸𝕏 *508/ 487–0358. 14 rooms. Restaurant, bar. AE, MC, V. Restaurant closed Jan.–mid-Feb.; guest house closed Jan.–Easter. CP.*

$$$$ 🏠 **Brass Key.** Conveniently close to restaurants, shops, galleries, and
★ nightlife, this complex of buildings is fast becoming Provincetown's most luxurious resort. The main house, originally an 1828 sea captain's home, is beautifully restored, and there are several other carefully groomed buildings and cottages. Rooms include antique furniture with a decidedly Victorian flavor, floral wallcoverings, and ultramodern amenities; all have Bose stereos, minirefrigerators, and TV/VCRs (there's a videocassette library). Deluxe rooms also have gas fireplaces and whirlpool baths or French doors opening out to wrought-iron balconies. A widow's-walk sundeck has a panoramic view of Cape Cod Bay. Complimentary cocktails are served in the courtyard; in winter, wine is served before a roaring fire in the common room. The Brass Key has long been favored by a largely gay clientele, but the owners and staff make every-

one feel welcome and pampered. ⊠ *67 Bradford St., 02657, ☎ 508/487–9005 or 800/842–9858, FAX 508/487–9020. 36 rooms. Air-conditioning, in-room safes, in-room VCRs, pool. No smoking. AE, D, MC, V. CP.*

$$–$$$$ 🏠 **Beaconlight Guesthouse.** It may be Provincetown outside, but within the walls of this inn is the elegance of the English countryside. The casual nature of the place fits in just fine with the designer wallpapers, freshly painted walls, antiques, and luxurious touches such as six pillows per bed and televisions and VCRs. Outside, three different decks offer varied, stunning views of the entire town and the harbor, and an outdoor hot tub invites soaks under the night skies. The guest house is between busy Commercial and Bradford Streets, so it's close to everything but still a bit quieter than places on the main thoroughfares. ⊠ *12 Winthrop St., 02657, ☎ 508/487–9603 or 800/696–9603. 7 rooms, 3 suites. In-room modem lines, outdoor hot tub. AE, D, DC, MC, V. CP.*

$$$ 🏠 **Best Western Chateau Motor Inn.** This may be part of a chain, but the personal attention of owners Charlotte and Bill Gordon, whose family has run the place for decades, shows in the landscaped grounds and in the well-maintained modern rooms with wall-to-wall carpeting and tiled baths. Atop a hill with expansive views from picture windows of marsh, dunes, and sea, the motel is a longish walk to the center of town. Children under 18 stay free. ⊠ *105 Bradford St. Ext., Box 558, 02657, ☎ 508/487–1286 or 800/528–1234, FAX 508/487–3557. 54 rooms. Pool. AE, D, DC, MC, V. CP. Closed Nov.–Apr.*

$$–$$$ 🏠 **Bayshore.** Formerly known as the Hargood House, this apartment
★ complex on the water, ½ mi from the town center, is a great option for longer stays. Many of the individually decorated units have decks and large water-view windows; all have full kitchens, modern baths, and phones. Number 8 is like a light, bright beach house on the water, with three glass walls, cathedral ceilings, private deck, dining table, and chairs. Number 20 has a fireplace and a home-style kitchen. Rental is mostly by the week in season; there's a two-night minimum off-season. Pets are welcome. ⊠ *493 Commercial St., 02657-2413, ☎ FAX 508/487–9133. 25 apartments. Beach. AE, MC, V.*

$$–$$$ 🏠 **Fairbanks Inn.** This comfortable, nicely decorated inn on the next street over from Commercial Street includes the 1776 main house and auxiliary buildings. Guest rooms have four-poster or canopy beds, Oriental rugs on wide-board floors, and antique furnishings, and some have fireplaces or kitchens. Many original touches remain here, from the 18th-century wallpaper to artifacts from the inn's first residents. The baths are on the small side, but they help preserve the colonial integrity of the home. The wicker-filled sunporch and the garden are good places for afternoon cocktails. ⊠ *90 Bradford St., 02657, ☎ 508/487–0386 or 800/324–7265, FAX 508/487–3540. 13 rooms, 1 efficiency. Parking (free). AE, MC, V. CP.*

$–$$$ 🏠 **The Captain and His Ship.** Built in 1887 for a sea captain, this stately, mansard-roof Victorian is only a short walk from the center of town, and across the street from the Provincetown bay. Jim Baer, who has owned the house since 1980, fills his immaculate, spacious rooms with period antiques and Oriental carpets. Room 3, done in subtle earth tones, has a king-size bed, a gas fireplace, and private access to the garden. Most rooms have water views; all have color TVs, VCRs, minirefrigerators, and hair dryers. Seven rooms have private baths, while two have hallway baths. Some have private decks. A Continental breakfast is included in July and August. There's a fee for the limited parking. ⊠ *164 Commercial St., 02657, ☎ 508/487–1850 or 800/400–2278. 9 rooms, 7 with bath. Air-conditioning. No smoking. MC, V. Closed Nov.–Apr.*

$–$$$ ⊡ **The Masthead.** Hidden away in the quiet west end of Commercial Street, the Masthead is a charming cluster of shingled houses that overlook a lush lawn, a 450-ft-long boardwalk, and a private beach. Spacious rooms, efficiencies, apartments, and fully outfitted cottages offer a wide range of lodging options. The cottages, for instance, which sleep four to seven, are an ideal choice for families or larger groups and for longer stays (children under 12 stay free). The deepwater and in-shore moorings right on the property make this a great choice if you're boating into town. This is classic Provincetown—friendly, unpretentious, and homey. ✉ *31–41 Commercial St., Box 577, 02657,* ☎ *508/ 487–0523 or 800/395–5095,* 𝔽𝔸𝕏 *508/487–9251. 7 apartments, 3 cottages, 2 efficiencies, 9 rooms. Beach, dock. AE, D, DC, MC, V.*

$ ⊡ **The Meadows.** At the far west end of Bradford Street, between the town center and the beach, these motel-like rooms may not have the convenience of an in-town location, but they do offer a good value, especially for families. Rooms are bright, clean, and comfortable, furnished in standard motel style. All have TVs with HBO and minirefrigerators. Bicycle rentals and tennis courts are nearby. ✉ *122 Bradford St. Ext., 02657,* ☎ *508/487–0880 or 888/675–0880,* 𝔽𝔸𝕏 *508/487–4691. 20 rooms. MC, V.*

Nightlife and the Arts

THE ARTS

The **Beach Plum Music Festival,** held in August at the Provincetown Town Hall (✉ 260 Commercial St., ☎ 508/349–6874), is a series of popular folk and jazz concerts by performers such as Wynton Marsalis, Arlo Guthrie, Queen Ida, and Holly Near.

The **Provincetown Playhouse Mews Series** (✉ Town Hall, 260 Commercial St., ☎ 508/487–0955) presents classical chamber, folk, ethnic, and jazz concerts in summer.

The **Provincetown Repertory Theatre** (☎ 508/487–0600) stages a summer lineup of classic and modern drama, presenting Equity actors and local talent. The theater makes its home in the museum building of the Pilgrim Monument.

The **Provincetown Theatre Company** (☎ 508/487–8673) presents classics, modern drama, and new works by local authors year-round, as well as staged readings and playwriting workshops.

NIGHTLIFE

Atlantic House (✉ 6 Masonic Pl., ☎ 508/487–3821), the grandfather of the gay night scene and the only gay bar open year-round, is frequented mostly by men. It has several lounge areas and an outdoor patio.

Boatslip Beach Club (✉ 161 Commercial St., ☎ 508/487–1669) holds a mixed gay and lesbian tea dance daily from 3:30 to 6:30 on the outdoor pool deck. The club has indoor and outdoor dance floors. There is ballroom dancing here, as well as two-stepping Thursday through Sunday nights.

The **Cape Cod National Seashore** offers summer evening programs, such as slide shows, sunset beach walks, concerts (local groups, military bands), and sing-alongs, at its Province Lands Visitor Center (✉ Race Point Rd., ☎ 508/487–1256), and sunset campfire talks on the beaches in Provincetown.

Club Euro (✉ 258 Commercial St., ☎ 508/487–2505) has weekend concerts by big names in world music, including African music, Jamaican reggae, Chicago blues, and Cajun zydeco. The venue itself is fantastic: the 1843 Congregational church, later a movie theater, is an eerie ocean dreamscape with oceanic sea-green walls with a half-submerged, three-dimensional mermaid; spouting fish; and a black ceiling high above. Pool tables and a late-night menu are available.

The **Crown & Anchor Complex** (⊠ 247 Commercial St., ☎ 508/487–1430) in the heart of town was ravaged by fire in 1998. The restoration of the building's original facade and its many different venues kept contractors working through most of the 1999 summer season. By summer 2000 the complex should be as it was, with several bars, a cabaret with drag shows, and a game room.

Governor Bradford Restaurant (⊠ 312 Commercial St., ☎ 508/487–9618) is perhaps better known as a sometimes-rowdy pool and dance hall. In the afternoon you can play chess or backgammon at the tables by the window. After 8 PM the place revs up with live music (on weekends) or a DJ spinning everything from hip-hop to disco. The pool tables are downstairs.

The **Moors** (⊠ 5 Bradford St. Ext., ☎ 508/487–0840; ☞ Dining, *above*) has presented Lenny Grandchamp in its lounge for nearly 20 years. He plays the piano, sings, tells jokes, and leads sing-alongs up to six nights a week in season.

Napi's (⊠ 7 Freeman St., ☎ 508/487–1145; ☞ Dining, *above*) offers easy-listening piano in its upstairs lounge on weekends, nightly in season.

Pied Piper (⊠ 193A Commercial St., ☎ 508/487–1527) draws hordes of gay men to its post–tea dance gathering at 6:30 every evening in July and August and weekends in the shoulder seasons. Later in the evening, though, the crowd is mostly, though not exclusively, women. The club has a deck overlooking the harbor, a small dance floor with a good sound system, and two bars.

Outdoor Activities and Sports

BEACHES

Race Point Beach (⊠ Race Point Rd.), one of the Cape Cod National Seashore beaches in Provincetown, has a wide swath of sand stretching far off into the distance around the point and Coast Guard station. Behind the beach is pure duneland, and bike trails lead off the parking lot. Because of its position, on a point facing north, the beach gets sun all day long, whereas the east-coast beaches get fullest sun early in the day. Parking is available, and lifeguards are stationed in season; the beach has showers and rest rooms. From mid-June through Labor Day, parking costs $7 per day, or $20 for a yearly pass good at all national seashore beaches.

Herring Cove Beach, a national seashore beach, is calmer (and a little warmer) than Race Point Beach, though it's not as pretty since the parking lot isn't hidden behind dunes. But the parking lot to the right of the bathhouse is a great place to watch the sunset, and there's a hot-dog stand. Lifeguards are on duty in season, and there are showers and rest rooms. For fees, *see* Race Point Beach, *above*.

For a day of fairly private beachcombing and great views, you can walk across the stone jetty at low tide to **Long Point,** a sand spit south of town with two lighthouses and two Civil War bunkers, named Fort Useless and Fort Ridiculous because they were hardly needed. It's a 2-mi walk across soft sand—beware of poison ivy and deer ticks if you detour from the path—or hire a boat at Flyer's (☎ 508/487–0898) to drop you off and pick you up.

BIKING

The **Province Lands Trail** is a 5¼-mi loop off the Beech Forest parking lot on Race Point Road, with spurs to Herring Cove and Race Point beaches and to Bennett Pond. The paths wind up and down hills amid dunes, marshes, woods, and ponds, affording spectacular views. More than 8 mi of bike trails lace through the dunes, cranberry bogs, and scrub pine of the national seashore, with many access points, including Herring Cove and Race Point.

The **Beech Forest** trail (⊠ Off Race Point Rd.) in the national seashore offers an especially nice ride through a shady forest to Bennett Pond.

Arnold's (⊠ 329 Commercial St., ☎ 508/487–0844) rents all types of bikes, children's included.

Nelson's Riding Stables and Bike Rentals (⊠ 43 Race Point Rd., ☎ 508/487–8849), across from the Beech Forest bike trail, rents a variety of bikes, including trailers, and has a deli with picnic-ready food; parking is free.

Ptown Bikes (⊠ 42 Bradford St., ☎ 508/487–8735) has Trek and Mongoose mountain bikes at good rates; the shop also provide free locks and maps.

BOATING

Flyer's Boat Rental (⊠ 131A Commercial St., ☎ 508/487–0898) has kayaks, surfbikes, Sunfish, Hobies, Force 5s, Lightnings, powerboats, and rowboats. Flyer's will also shuttle you to Long Point (☞ Beaches, *above*).

FISHING

You can go for fluke, bluefish, and striped bass on a walk-on basis from spring through fall with **Cap'n Bill & Cee Jay** (⊠ MacMillan Wharf, ☎ 508/487–4330 or 800/675–6723).

HORSEBACK RIDING

The **Province Lands Horse Trails** lead to the beaches through or past dunes, cranberry bogs, forests, and ponds.

Bayberry Hollow Farm (⊠ 27 W. Vine St. Ext., ☎ 508/487–6584) has pony rides year-round. It's fun for kids.

Nelson's Riding Stable (⊠ 43 Race Point Rd., ☎ 508/487–1112) offers trail rides by reservation.

KAYAKING

Kayaking has become increasingly popular on the Cape, and **Off the Coast Kayak Company** (⊠ 3 Freeman St., ☎ 508/487–2692 or 877/785–2925) has single and double kayaks for rent. It also schedules several-hour or half-day guided trips around Provincetown, Truro, and Wellfleet.

TENNIS

Bissell's Tennis Courts (⊠ 21 Bradford St. Ext., ☎ 508/487–9512) has five clay courts and offers lessons. It's open from Memorial Day to September.

Provincetown Tennis Club (⊠ 286 Bradford St. Ext., ☎ 508/487–9574) has several outdoor clay courts open to nonmembers; you can also take lessons with the resident tennis pro.

WHALE-WATCHING

One of the joys of Cape Cod is spotting whales while they're swimming in and around the feeding grounds at Stellwagen Bank, about 6 mi off the tip of Provincetown. On a sunny day, the boat ride out into open ocean is part of the pleasure, but the thrill, of course, is in seeing these great creatures. You might spot minke whales, humpbacks (who put on the best show when they breach), finbacks, or perhaps the most endangered great whale species, the right whale. Dolphins are a welcome sight as well, as they play in the boats' bow waves. Many people also come aboard for birding, especially during spring and fall migration. You can see a great variety of birds at sea—gannets, shearwaters, storm petrels, among many others.

Several boats take whale-watchers out to sea—and bring them back—with morning, afternoon, or sunset trips lasting three to four hours. All boats have food service, but remember to take sunscreen and a sweater or jacket—the breeze makes it chilly. Some boats stock seasickness pills, but if you're susceptible, come prepared.

The municipal parking area by the harbor in Provincetown fills up by noon in summer. Consider taking a morning boat to avoid crowds and the hottest sun. And although it may be cold in April, it is one of the better months for spotting whales, who at that time have just migrated north after mating and are very hungry. Good food is, after all, what brings the whales to this part of the Atlantic.

Dolphin Fleet tours are accompanied by scientists from the Center for Coastal Studies in Provincetown who provide commentary while collecting data on the whale population they've been monitoring for years. They know many of the whales by name and tell you about their habits and histories. Reservations are required. ⊠ *Ticket office in Chamber of Commerce building at MacMillan Wharf,* ☎ *508/349–1900 or 800/826–9300.* ⊡ *$18 (seasonal variations).* ☉ *Tours Apr.–Oct.*

The **Portuguese Princess** sails with a naturalist on board to narrate. The snack bar offers Portuguese specialties. ⊠ *Tickets available at 70 Shank Painter Rd. ticket office or at Whale Watchers General Store, 309 Commercial St.,* ☎ *508/487–2651 or 800/442–3188.* ⊡ *$15–$19.* ☉ *Tours May–Oct.*

The **Ranger V,** the fastest whale-watch boat, also has a naturalist on board. ⊠ *Ticket office on Bradford and Standish Sts.,* ☎ *508/487–3322 or 800/992–9333.* ⊡ *$18.* ☉ *Tours May–mid-Oct.*

Shopping

ART GALLERIES

Albert Merola Gallery (⊠ 424 Commercial St., ☎ 508/487–4424) has 20th-century and contemporary master prints and Picasso ceramics and features artists from in and around Provincetown, Boston, and New York, including James Balla and Richard Baker.

Berta Walker Gallery (⊠ 208 Bradford St., ☎ 508/487–6411) deals in Provincetown-affiliated artists, including Selina Trieff, Nancy Whorf, and many of the artists who migrated here from the now-defunct Long Point Gallery.

The **DNA Gallery** (⊠ 288 Bradford St., ☎ 508/487–7700) represents a wide variety of artists working in various media, including many former fellows from the Fine Arts Work Center. The gallery also hosts readings, films, and concerts.

New on the art scene, the **Schoolhouse Center** (⊠ 494 Commercial St., ☎ 508/487–4800) has already established itself as a vital addition to the town. Housing both the Driskel Gallery and the Silas Kenyon Gallery, it has changing exhibitions of antiques as well as the works of local and national artists and photographers. A full range of performing and visual arts classes is available year-round, and the center has a Summer Reading Series on Thursday evenings at 8. A true community organization, the center is open Thursday through Monday.

The **William Scott Gallery** (✉ 439 Commercial St., ☎ 508/487–4040) primarily shows contemporary works such as John Dowd's reflective, realistic Cape scapes.

SPECIALTY STORES

Giardelli Antonelli (✉ 417 Commercial St., ☎ 508/487–3016) specializes in handmade, quality clothing by local designers. Hand-knit sweaters are especially popular.

Impulse (✉ 188 Commercial St., ☎ 508/487–1154) has contemporary American crafts, including jewelry and an extraordinary kaleidoscope collection. The Autograph Gallery features framed photographs, letters, and documents signed by celebrities.

Kidstuff (✉ 381 Commercial St., ☎ 508/487–0714) carries unusual, colorful children's wear.

Marine Specialties, Inc. (✉ 235 Commercial St., ☎ 508/487–1730) is akin to a vast basement full of treasures, knickknacks, and clothing; it even has that same pleasantly musty smell. Here you can purchase some very reasonably priced casual and military-style clothing, as well as sea shells, marine supplies, stained-glass lamps, candles, rubber sharks (you get the idea), and prints of old advertisements.

Moda Fina (✉ 349 Commercial St., ☎ 508/487–6632) offers an eclectic selection of women's fashions, shoes, and jewelry. Style is the word here, from flowing linen or silk night wear to the funky and casual. Unique Mexican crafts are also for sale.

Remembrances of Things Past (✉ 376 Commercial St., ☎ 508/487–9443) deals with articles from the 1920s to the 1960s, including Bakelite and other jewelry, telephones, neon items, ephemera, and autographed celebrity photographs.

Silk & Feathers (✉ 377 Commercial St., ☎ 508/487–2057) carries an assortment of fine lingerie, women's clothing, and jewelry.

Tim's Used Books (✉ 242 Commercial St., ☎ 508/487–0005) has volumes of volumes, rooms of used-but-in-good-shape books, including some rare and out-of-print texts. It's a great place to browse for that perfect book to read on vacation.

West End Antiques (✉ 146 Commercial St., ☎ 508/487–6723) specializes in variety: $4 postcards, a $3,000 model ship, handmade dolls, and better-quality glassware—Steuben, Orrefors, and Hawkes.

CAPE COD A TO Z

Arriving and Departing

By Bus

Bonanza Bus Lines (☎ 508/548–7588 or 800/556–3815) offers direct service to Bourne, Falmouth, and the Woods Hole steamship terminal from Boston, Providence, Fall River, and New Bedford, as well as connecting service from New York and Connecticut. Another route travels between Boston, Wareham, and Buzzards Bay.

Plymouth & Brockton Street Railway (☎ 508/746–0378) provides bus service to Provincetown from Boston and Logan Airport, with stops en route. The "Logan Direct" airport express service bypasses downtown Boston and makes stops in Plymouth, Sagamore, Barnstable, and Hyannis.

By Ferry

Ferries shuttle between Boston, Plymouth, and Provincetown in season. Between the Cape and Islands, year-round boats run between Woods Hole, Hyannis, and Martha's Vineyard, and between Hyannis and Nantucket. There is also seasonal Cape–Islands service from these ports, from Falmouth to Martha's Vineyard, and from Harwich Port (east of Hyannis) to Nantucket. *See* Martha's Vineyard A to Z in Chapter 3 and Nantucket A to Z in Chapter 4 for details on Cape–Island ferry service.

TO AND FROM BOSTON

Bay State Cruise Company makes the three-hour trip between Commonwealth Pier in Boston and MacMillan Wharf in Provincetown daily from mid-June to Labor Day, and weekends only through Columbus Day. The company also runs a two-hour express boat from Boston to Provincetown's Fisherman's Wharf daily from June to Columbus Day. ☎ *617/748–1428 in Boston; 508/487–9284 in Provincetown.* ☒ *3-hr boat $18 one-way, $5 bicycles; same-day round-trip $30, $10 bicycles. 2-hr express boat $39 one-way, $5 bicycles; same-day round-trip $75, $10 bicycles.*

TO AND FROM PLYMOUTH

Capt. John Boats' passenger ferry makes the 1½- to 2-hour trip between Plymouth's State Pier and Provincetown from Memorial Day to mid-June, weekends; mid-June to Labor Day, daily. Schedules allow for day excursions. One-way fares are only available in May, June, and September. ☎ *508/747–2400; 800/242–2469 in MA.* ☒ *$25 round-trip, $14 one-way, bicycles $2.*

HARWICH PORT–NANTUCKET

The **Freedom Cruise Line** runs express ferries to Nantucket, allowing you to take a day trip from Harwich Port between May 15 and October 15 (☞ Nantucket A to Z *in* Chapter 4). Parking is free for the first 24 hours, then $10 per day. ☒ *Saquatucket Harbor, Harwich Port,* ☎ *508/432–8999.* ☒ *$35 round-trip, $10 bicycles; $20 one-way.*

By Car

From Boston (60 mi), take Route I–93 South to Route 3 South, across the Sagamore Bridge, which becomes U.S. 6, the Cape's main artery, which leads to Hyannis and Provincetown. From western Massachusetts, northern Connecticut, and northeastern New York State, take I–84 East to the Massachusetts Turnpike (I–90 East) and take I–495 to the Bourne Bridge. From Washington, D.C., Philadelphia, New Jersey, New York City, and all other points south and west, take I–95 North toward Providence, where you'll pick up I–195 East (toward Fall River/New Bedford) to Route 25 East to the Bourne Bridge. From the Bourne Bridge, you can take Route 28 south to Falmouth and Woods Hole (about 15 mi), or go around the rotary, following the signs to U.S. 6; this will take you to the Lower Cape and central towns more quickly.

Driving times can vary widely depending on traffic. In good driving conditions, you can reach the Sagamore Bridge from Boston in about 1¼ or 1½ hours, the Bourne Bridge from New York City in about 4½ or 5 hours.

On summer weekends, when more than 100,000 cars a day cross each bridge, make every effort to avoid arriving in the late afternoon, especially on holidays. U.S. 6 and Routes 6A and 28 are heavily congested eastbound Friday evenings, westbound Sunday afternoons, and in both directions on summer Saturdays.

By Plane

The Cape's two main airports are just a few minutes from the town centers. **Barnstable Municipal Airport** (✉ 480 Barnstable Rd., Rte. 28 rotary, Hyannis, ☎ 508/775–2020) is the region's main air gateway.

Provincetown Municipal Airport (✉ Race Point Rd., ☎ 508/487–0241) has year-round Boston service through Cape Air.

CARRIERS

Airline service is extremely unpredictable because of the seasonal nature of Cape travel—carriers come and go, while others juggle their routes. The Barnstable Municipal Airport will always know which carriers fly in, should you encounter difficulty in making reservations.

Cape Air/Nantucket Airlines (☎ 508/771–6944 or 800/352–0714) flies direct from Boston to Hyannis and Provincetown year-round and from New Bedford to Martha's Vineyard and Nantucket. Cape Air has joint fares with Continental, Delta, Midwest Express, and US Airways and ticketing-and-baggage agreements with eight major U.S. airlines and KLM.

Colgan Air/Continental Connection (☎ 800/272–5488) flies from Newark or New York to Hyannis and Nantucket year-round.

US Airways Express (☎ 800/428–4322) flies nonstop from Boston and New York to Hyannis year-round. Connect in Boston with the airline's other routes.

For charters, contact **Cape Air** (☞ *above*). **Westchester Air** (☎ 800/ 759–2929) offers charter service from White Plains, New York to Hyannis, Martha's Vineyard, and Nantucket.

By Train

Citing dwindling ridership, **Amtrak** (☎ 800/872–7245) stopped offering train service to the Cape in 1998. Amtrak's continuing fiscal woes make it improbable service will be restored, but it's possible it could start up again if there is enough interest; call for updates.

Getting Around

By Bicycle

The Cape will satisfy both the avid and the occasional cyclist. There are many flat back roads, as well as a number of well-developed and scenic bike trails. The 25-mi **Cape Cod Rail Trail** (☞ Dennis, *above*) follows the paved right-of-way of the old Penn Central Railroad line between South Dennis and South Wellfleet, with many access points.

By Bus

The **Cape Cod Regional Transit Authority** (☎ 508/385–8326; 800/ 352–7155 in MA; www.allcapecod.com/ccrta) operates several bus services that link Cape towns. All buses are wheelchair-accessible and equipped with bike racks. The SeaLine operates along Route 28 Monday–Saturday between Hyannis and Woods Hole. (Average fare is $3.50 one-way from Hyannis to Woods Hole.) Its many stops include Mashpee Commons, Falmouth, and the Woods Hole Steamship Authority docks. The SeaLine connects in Hyannis with the Plymouth & Brockton line, as well as the Villager, another bus line that runs along Route 132 between Hyannis and Barnstable Harbor. The driver will stop when signaled along the route.

The b-bus is composed of a fleet of minivans that will transport passengers door-to-door between any towns on the Cape. Service runs seven days a week, year-round, though reservations must be made in advance. The cost is $2 per ride, plus 10¢ per mile.

The H2O Line offers daily, regularly scheduled service year-round between Hyannis and Orleans along Route 28. The Hyannis–Orleans fare is $3.50; shorter trips are less. Buses connect in Hyannis with the SeaLine, the Villager, and Plymouth & Brockton lines.

Plymouth & Brockton Street Railway (☎ 508/746–0378) has service between Boston and Provincetown, with stops at many towns in between.

Bonanza (☎ 508/548–7588 or 800/556–3815) runs between Bourne, Falmouth, and Woods Hole. All service is year-round.

By Car

Traffic on Cape Cod in summer can be maddening, especially on Route 28, which traces the populous south shore. U.S. 6 is the main artery, a limited-access (mostly divided) highway running the entire length of the Cape. On the north shore, the Old King's Highway, Route 6A, parallels U.S. 6 and is a scenic country road passing through occasional towns. When you're in no hurry, use back roads—they're less frustrating and much more rewarding.

Massachusetts permits a right turn on a red light (after a stop) unless a sign says otherwise. Also, when you approach one of the Cape's numerous rotaries (traffic circles), note that the vehicles already in the rotary have the right of way and that those vehicles entering the rotary must yield. Be careful: some drivers can forget this principle.

By Limousine

The following companies provide 24-hour Cape-wide limo service: **Aristocrat Limousine** (☎ 508/420–5466 or 800/992–6163); **Black Tie Limousine** (☎ 508/775–1780); **Cape Escape Tours & East Coast Limousine Co.** (☎ 508/430–0666; 800/540–0808 in MA). **John's Taxi & Limousine** (☎ 508/394–3209) picks up in Dennis and Harwich only but will take passengers all over the Cape.

By Taxi

There are taxi stands at the Hyannis airport, the bus station, and at the Cape Cod Mall. In Hyannis, call **Hyannis Taxi** (☎ 508/775–0400 or 800/773–0600) and **Checker Taxi** (☎ 508/771–8294). Elsewhere on the Cape, call **All Village Taxi** (✉ Falmouth, ☎ 508/540–7200), **Always Available Transport** (✉ Orleans, ☎ 508/255–7557 or 800/339–9732), **Eldredge Taxi** (✉ Chatham, ☎ 508/945–0068), or **Cape Cab** (✉ Provincetown, ☎ 508/487–2222).

By Trolley

The **Cape Cod Regional Transit Authority** (☎ 508/385–8326; 800/352–7155 in MA) runs seasonal trolleys in Falmouth, Mashpee, Hyannis, Yarmouth, and Dennis. Fares and times vary; call for more information. In Sandwich, the **Glasstown Trolley** (☎ 508/428–9973) runs from the train station at Jarves Street to Heritage Plantation.

Contacts and Resources

Art and Antiques

Cape Cod Antiques & Arts (✉ Box 39, 02653–0039, ☎ 508/247–3200), a monthly supplement of the *Register* and the *Cape Codder* available at local newsstands, is chock-full of information on galleries, upcoming shows, Cape artists, antiques shops, auctions, and so forth.

B&B Reservation Agencies

In summer, lodgings should be booked as far in advance as possible—several months for the most popular cottages and B&Bs. Assistance with last-minute reservations is available at the Cape Cod Chamber of Commerce information booths. Off-season rates are much reduced, and service may be more personalized.

Bed and Breakfast Cape Cod (⊠ Box 1312, Orleans 02653, ☎ 508/255–3824 or 800/541–6226, FAX 508/240–0599, www.bedandbreakfastcapecod.com) lists about 150 B&Bs and small inns on the Cape and islands.

DestINNations (⊠ 572 Rte. 28, Suite 3, West Yarmouth 02673, ☎ 508/790–0566 or 800/333–4667, FAX 508/790–0565, www.destinnations.com) handles a limited number of upscale inns, resorts, and B&Bs on the Cape and islands but will arrange any and all details of a visit.

Provincetown Reservations System (⊠ 293 Commercial St., Provincetown 02657, ☎ 508/487–2400 or 800/648–0364, FAX 508/487–6517) makes reservations year-round for accommodations, shows, transportation, and more.

Camping

The Cape has many private campgrounds, as well as camping at state parks and forests. Call the Cape Cod Chamber of Commerce (☞ Visitor Information, *below*) for its listing.

Eastern Mountain Sports (⊠ 1513 Rte. 132, Hyannis, ☎ 508/362–8690) rents tents and sleeping bags.

Nickerson State Park (⊠ 3488 Rte. 6A, Brewster, ☎ 508/896–3491; 877/422–6762 for reservations) is huge (almost 2,000 acres) and hugely popular. It has plenty of facilities and guest programs.

Sandy Terraces (⊠ Box 98, Marstons Mills 02648, ☎ 508/428–9209), a surprise in this very traditional area, is a seasonal family nudist campground.

Although private campgrounds serve the area, the only camping permitted on the Cape Cod National Seashore itself is in nonrental, self-contained RVs at Provincetown's **Race Point Beach** (⊠ Provincetown, ☎ 508/487–2100).

Car Rentals

Rental cars are available at Barnstable Municipal Airport in Hyannis from: **Avis** (☎ 508/775–2888 or 800/831–2847), **Budget** (☎ 508/771–2744 or 800/527–0700), **Hertz** (☎ 508/775–5825 or 800/654–3131), and **National** (☎ 508/771–4353 or 800/227–7368). Budget offers seasonal rentals out of **Provincetown Municipal Airport** (☎ 508/487–4557).

Children's Activities

Each town has a recreation program open to visitors. The morning activities, including sports, trips, and crafts, provide a good opportunity for your kids to meet others.

The **Cape Cod YMCA** (⊠ Box 188, Rte. 132, West Barnstable 02668, ☎ 508/362–6500) offers one-week "fun clubs" (sports, crafts, nature) during school vacation weeks, kids' evenings, summer day camps, swimming classes, and more.

Hyannis Public Library (⊠ 401 Main St., Hyannis, ☎ 508/775–2280) has a children's multicultural center, created in collaboration with the Barnstable Public Schools, with books, tapes, and videos (some in foreign languages), programs, a play area with puzzles and games, and a children's reading club in summer.

Libraries usually offer regular children's story hours or other programs—check them out on a rainy day. Hours are listed in the newspapers each week. The wonderful **Wellfleet Public Library** (⊠ 55 W. Main St., ☏ 508/349–0310), in a town visited by numerous children's book authors, has a story hour.

The Cape has a variety of day and residential summer camps. For more information, write to the **Cape Cod Association of Children's Camps** (⊠ Box 38, Brewster 02631).

Cape Cod Baseball Camp (⊠ Box S, Buzzards Bay 02532, ☏ 508/432–6909) offers day camp sessions of a week or more for children 8–14.

The **Cape Cod Community College** (⊠ Rte. 132, West Barnstable 02668, ☏ 508/362–2131 or ext. 4365) offers summer sports programs.

Cape Cod Museum of Natural History (⊠ 869 Main St. [Rte. 6A], Brewster, ☏ 508/896–3867) has a full program of children's and family activities in summer, including one-day workshops and one- and two-week day camps of art and nature classes for preschoolers through grade 9.

Cape Cod Sea Camps (⊠ Box 1880, Brewster 02631, ☏ 508/896–3451) teach sailing and water sports to children ages 7 to 17.

Children's concerts, plays, and programs are offered by the **Cape Cod Melody Tent** (☏ 508/775–9100), the **Cape Cod Symphony Orchestra** (☏ 508/362–1111), the **Cape Rep Theater** (☏ 508/896–1888), and the **Cape Playhouse** (☏ 508/385–3911).

Massachusetts Audubon Wellfleet Bay Sanctuary (⊠ U.S. 6, Box 236, South Wellfleet 02663, ☏ 508/349–2615) has daily and weekly nature programs and camps for children.

Emergencies
Ambulance, fire, police (☏ 911).

For rescues at sea, call the **Coast Guard** (☏ 508/548–5151 in Woods Hole; ☏ 508/888–0335 in Sandwich and Cape Cod Canal; ☏ 508/945–0164 in Chatham; ☏ 508/487–0070 in Provincetown). Boaters should use channel 16 on their radios.

Massachusetts Poison Control Center (☏ 800/682–9211).

DENTISTS
Dental Associates of Cape Cod (⊠ 262 Barnstable Rd., Hyannis, ☏ 508/778–1200) accepts emergency walk-ins.

HOSPITALS
Cape Cod Hospital (⊠ 27 Park St., Hyannis, ☏ 508/771–1800) has a 24-hour emergency room.

Falmouth Hospital (⊠ 100 Ter Heun Dr., Falmouth, ☏ 508/548–5300) also has a 24-hour emergency room.

LATE-NIGHT PHARMACIES
Most of the Cape's **CVS** stores are open seven days a week. Two are open 24 hours a day, with the pharmacies open until midnight during the summer: in Falmouth (⊠ 64 Davis Straits, ☏ 508/540–4307) and Dennis (⊠ Patriot Square Mall, Rte. 134, ☏ 508/398–0724). They usually accept out-of-town prescription refills with the prescribing doctor's phone verification. Most pharmacies post emergency numbers on their doors.

Falmouth Walk-in Medical Center (⊠ 309 Main St., Rte. 28, Teaticket, ☎ 508/540–6790).

Mashpee Family Medicine (⊠ 800 Falmouth Rd., Mashpee, ☎ 508/477–4282).

Long Pond Medical Center(⊠ 525 Long Pond Dr., Harwich, ☎ 508/432–4100).

Mid Cape Medical Center (⊠ 489 Bearses Way, at Rte. 28, Unit A-4, Hyannis, ☎ 508/771–4092).

Outer Cape Health Services (⊠ 81 Old Colony Way, Orleans, ☎ 508/255–9700; ⊠ 3130 U.S. 6, Wellfleet, ☎ 508/349–3131; ⊠ 49 Harry Kemp Way, Provincetown, ☎ 508/487–9395).

Guided Tours

CRUISES

The gaff-rigged schooner ***Bay Lady II*** makes two-hour sails, including a sunset cruise, across Provincetown Harbor into Cape Cod Bay. Private charters are also available. ⊠ *MacMillan Wharf, Provincetown,* ☎ *508/487–9308.* 🖼 *$10–$15.*

Cape Cod Canal Cruises (two or three hours, narrated) leave from Onset, just northwest of the Bourne Bridge. A Sunday jazz cruise, sunset cocktail cruises, and Friday and Saturday dance cruises are available. Kids 12 and under cruise free on Family Discount Cruises, Monday through Saturday at 4. ⊠ *Onset Bay Town Pier,* ☎ *508/295–3883.* 🖼 *$10–$13.*

Cape Cod Duck Mobile takes you on a land-and-sea tour of downtown Hyannis and the harbor in a restored U.S. military amphibious vehicle. These 45-minute narrated tours depart on the hour, roll through downtown, then splash into Lewis Bay to cruise past the Kennedy compound and other sights. Tickets go on sale daily at 9:30 AM and, in summer, often sell out by noon. Call for details about where to purchase tickets. ⊠ *447 Main St., Hyannis,* ☎ *508/362–1117.* 🖼 *$12.*

Hy-Line runs one-hour narrated tours of Hyannis Harbor, including a view of the Kennedy compound. Sunset and evening cocktail cruises are available. ⊠ *Ocean St. dock, Pier 1,* ☎ *508/778–2600.* 🖼 *$10–$14.*

Patriot Boats offers two-hour day and sunset cruises between Falmouth and the Elizabeth Islands on the 68-ft schooner *Liberté*. Another nightly sunset cruise passes six lighthouses in the Falmouth area. Also available is an afternoon excursion to Cuttyhunk Island, with a guided walk around the island; this trip runs weekdays in summer from 1 to 5. Rates vary; call for details. ⊠ *227 Clinton Ave., Falmouth,* ☎ *508/548–2626; 800/734–0088 in MA.*

Starfish River Cruise offers 1½-hour water safari tours of the Bass River, past windmills, marshlands, and old captains' houses, on a 32-ft aluminum boat with an awning. ⊠ *Rte. 28, West Dennis, just east of the Bass River Bridge,* ☎ *508/362–5555.* 🖼 *$12.*

FLIGHTSEEING

Sightseeing by air is offered by **Cape Air** (Provincetown Municipal Airport, ⊠ Race Point Rd., ☎ 800/352–0714), **Cape Cod Flying Service** (⊠ Cape Cod Airport, 1000 Race La., Marstons Mills, ☎ 508/428–8732), **Cape Flight LTD** (Barnstable Municipal Airport, ⊠ 480 Barnstable Rd., Rte. 28 rotary, Hyannis, ☎ 508/775–8171), and **Chatham Municipal Airport** (⊠ George Ryder Rd., West Chatham, ☎ 508/945–

9000). **Cape Cod Soaring Adventures** (☎ 508/420–4201 or 800/660–4563) offers glider flights and lessons out of Marstons Mills.

TRAIN TOURS

In 1999, the **Cape Cod Central Railroad** began offering two-hour, 42-mi scenic rail tours from Hyannis to the Cape Cod Canal and back. Plans for a dinner train were also in the works at press time. ⊠ *Hyannis Train Depot, 252 Main St., Hyannis,* ☎ *508/771–3800 or 888/797–7245.* ☞ *2-hr tours $11.75.* ☉ *Memorial Day–Oct., Tues.–Sun.; Mar.–May, Christmas, New Year's, call for schedule.*

TROLLEY TOURS

The **Provincetown Trolley** leaves from the town hall, with pickups at other locations, on the hour from 10 to 7 and on the half hour from 10:30 to 4:30. Points of interest on the 40-minute narrated tours include the downtown area and the Cape Cod National Seashore. Riders can get on and off at four locations. ☎ *508/487–9483.* ☞ *$9.* ☉ *May–Oct.*

VAN TOURS

Art's Dune Tours, around for years, are hour-long narrated van tours through the national seashore and the dunes around Provincetown. ⊠ *Standish and Commercial Sts., Provincetown,* ☎ *508/487–1950; 800/894–1951 in MA.* ☞ *$12 daytime, $15 sunset.* ☉ *Tours mid-Apr.–late Oct.; call for schedule*

House Rentals

Many real-estate agencies can assist with house or apartment rentals; be sure to check local chambers' guidebooks and area telephone book yellow pages. Most agencies deal with only a segment of the Cape, and properties are often rented a year in advance, so plan ahead. Often, rental opportunities are greater in the smaller, quieter towns, such as Yarmouth, Chatham, Wellfleet, and Truro.

Mid Cape rentals are handled by **Century 21, Sam Ingram Real Estate** (⊠ 938 Rte. 6A, Yarmouth 02675, ☎ 508/362–8844 or 800/697–3340, FAX 508/362–7889).

Commonwealth Associates (⊠ 551 Main St., Harwich Port 02646, ☎ 508/432–2618, FAX 508/432–1771) can assist in finding vacation rentals in the Harwiches, including waterfront properties.

Compass Vacation Rentals (⊠ Main St. Mercantile Unit 19, U.S. 6, Eastham 02642, ☎ 508/240–7600 or 800/724–1307, FAX 508/240–6943, www.compassrealestate.com) is one of many realtors with a listing of available apartments and houses on the Lower Cape.

Donahue Real Estate (⊠ 850 Main St., Falmouth 02540, ☎ 508/548–5412, FAX 508/548–5148) lists both apartments and houses in Falmouth and vicinity.

Great Vacations Inc. (⊠ 2660 Rte. 6A, Brewster 02631, ☎ 508/896–2090) specializes in locating vacation rentals in Brewster, Dennis, and Orleans.

Peter McDowell Associates (⊠ 585 Main St. [Rte. 6A], Dennis 02638, ☎ 508/385–9114 or 888/385–9114 and ⊠ 11 Main St. [Rte. 28], Dennisport 02639, ☎ 508/394–5400 or 800/870–5401, www.capecodproperties.com) offers a wide selection of properties for rent by the week, month, or season; the company also rents larger homes for family reunions and other gatherings. Most places are in Dennis.

Real Estate Associates (⊠ Rtes. 151 and 28A, Box 738, North Falmouth 02556, ☎ 508/563–7173, FAX 508/563–6943, www.realestateassc.com)

HOME, SWEET RENTAL HOME

ONE OF THE JOYS OF A CAPE Cod vacation can be renting a furnished house—one with plenty of space to accommodate extended families or groups of friends, a backyard or deck where you can kick back with a cool drink, a kitchen where you can boil up some lobsters. If a house rental is in your plans, you must act early. Cape realtors report that it's not unusual to get bookings a year in advance, and by January the summer pickings in many prime beachfront areas may already be getting slim.

Most Cape Cod house rentals run weekly, from Saturday to Saturday. You can move in on Saturday afternoon, and you must be out the following Saturday morning. There may be some flexibility outside the peak summer season of July 4 through Labor Day, but otherwise you'll have to cross the bridges with the rest of the week-to-week renters. Two-week minimums for some choicer properties are not uncommon. Note that summer rental prices can vary even from week to week, depending on the most popular times; mid-to-late June and early September prices may be a bit lower.

If you're planning a summer rental, here are some tips on making your arrangements:

Decide where you'd like to be. Most Cape realtors deal with a particular town or area (☞ Contacts and Resources in *Cape Cod A to Z, below*), so narrow your search before you start asking about houses. Do you want to be on Cape Cod Bay or Nantucket Sound, or close to the beaches of Cape Cod National Seashore? Will you stay put, or do you want a central location that lets you explore the Cape easily? The towns on the Cape have different personalities, and that will be part of your decision making.

Know what you will need. How many bedrooms (with how many beds) and how many bathrooms? Is there a washer and dryer? What about a yard or a deck? How close to the beach? Is a water view important? Or a quiet street where the kids can play? Do you want to be close to a supermarket and other stores, or are you willing to drive a bit?

Ask what's included. Most Cape rentals do not include linens, so you'll need to bring your own sheets and towels. Most do provide a cleaning service before you arrive and after you leave, but ask whether you're responsible for taking trash to the dump or for handling other clean-up tasks. Inquire about using the phone; some owners restrict their tenants to local calls, while others ask for a deposit to cover your phone bill. If you want anything special—a crib, bicycles, a barbecue grill, air-conditioning—be sure to ask.

Request a photo. If you can't visit properties in person, ask the realtor or owner to send you pictures of the house. What is described as cozy may turn out to be cramped, and old-fashioned may sometimes be run-down; photos will help avoid misunderstandings.

Use the Internet. Some realtors now post photos of properties on their Web sites, and a growing number of property owners are handling their own rentals via the Net.

Before you head for the Cape, ask your realtor or the local chamber of commerce about beach stickers. Many towns with resident-only beaches or ponds will sell weekly beach permits to nonresidents if you present a copy of your lease at town hall or the town recreation department.

Then pack up the family, pick up some lobsters, and relax in that lawn chair. At least for the week, you're home.

—Carolyn Heller

lists properties ranging from beach cottages to waterfront estates, although the focus is on more expensive houses. It covers Falmouth, Bourne, Mashpee, and Sandwich on the Upper Cape.

Roslyn Garfield Associates (✉ 115 Bradford St., Provincetown 02657, ☎ 508/487–1308) lists rentals for Wellfleet, Truro, and Provincetown.

Waterfront Rentals (✉ 20 Pilgrim Rd., W. Yarmouth 02673, ☎ 508/778–1818, FAX 508/771–3563, www.waterfrontrentalsinc.com) covers Bourne to Truro, listing everything from one-bedroom condos to a seven-bedroom, seven-bath beachfront estate.

Libraries

Several area libraries have special collections. The **Centerville Library** (✉ 585 Main St., ☎ 508/790–6220) has a 42-volume noncirculating set of transcripts of the Nuremberg Trials. **Cotuit Library** (✉ 871 Main St., ☎ 508/428–8141) holds a noncirculating set of luxurious leather-bound classics. **Hyannis Public Library** (✉ 401 Main St., ☎ 508/775–2280) has a case full of books on JFK. **Barnstable's Sturgis Library** (✉ 3090 Rte. 6A, ☎ 508/362–6636) has extensive Cape genealogical and maritime materials. Other Cape libraries, though without special collections, are no less worthwhile. The **Brewster Ladies' Library** (✉ 1822 Main St. [Rte. 6A], ☎ 508/896–3913) occupies a restored Victorian building and a 1997 addition. The **Wellfleet Public Library** (✉ W. Main St., ☎ 508/349–0310) is a particularly nice one.

Outdoor Activities and Sports

BASEBALL

The **Cape Cod Baseball League** (☎ 508/996–5004), considered the country's best summer league, is scouted by all the major-league teams. Ten teams play a 44-game season from mid-June to mid-August; games held at all 10 fields are free (☞ Close-Up: The Cape Cod Baseball League *in* Chatham, *above*).

BEACHES

The beaches on Cape Cod range from the gentler waters of those on Cape Cod Bay to the cold, pounding surf of the Atlantic beaches. For information on specific beaches, *see* the Outdoor Activities and Sports section in individual towns.

BIKING

The Dennis Chamber of Commerce's guidebook includes bike tours and maps, and the Wellfleet chamber's pamphlet "Bicycling in Wellfleet" includes an annotated map. Check with local chambers for free maps, guidebooks and pamphlets.

The Cape's best bike path is the **Cape Cod Rail Trail** (☞ Close-Up: Riding the Rail Trail, in West Dennis, *above*), which links several towns and is undeniably scenic, if flat. There are a few parking lots along the route if you'd prefer to ride a segment of the trail instead of pedaling all 25 mi.

The Travel Center at the American Youth Hostels' Boston office (✉ 1105 Commonwealth Ave., Boston 02215, ☎ 617/779–0900) sells a "Cape Ann & North Shore/Cape Cod & Islands" bike map that includes information on the **Claire Saltonstall Bikeway** between Boston and Provincetown (135 mi) or Woods Hole (85 mi), using mostly bike paths and little-traveled roadways. Brochures about the bikeway may also be available from the Cape Cod Chamber of Commerce.

CANOEING AND KAYAKING

Cape Cod Coastal Canoe & Kayak (✉ 36 Spectacle Pond Dr., East Falmouth 02536, ☎ 508/564–4051; 888/226–6393 in MA) runs daily paddling tours of the Cape's tidal rivers, salt marshes, and coastal ponds April–October. The company provides all equipment (including canoes and solo or tandem kayaks) and a naturalist guide for tours that average 3–3½ hours. Call for a schedule of trips, which depart from sites across the Cape. Tours are $30 per paddler; children are free in a canoe with two adults. Trips are rated by difficulty, but you should be realistic about what you or your family can manage.

Off the Coast Kayak Company (☞ Outdoor Activities and Sports *in* Provincetown, *above*) rents kayaks and has guided paddles on the Outer Cape.

FISHING

Charter boats and party boats (per-head fees, rather than the charters' group rates) fish in season for bluefish, tuna, marlin, and mako and blue sharks. Throughout the year there's bottom fishing for flounder, tautog, scup, fluke, cod, and pollack.

The Cape Cod Chamber's *Sportsman's Guide* gives fishing regulations, surf-fishing access locations, a map of boat-launching facilities, and more. The state Division of Fisheries and Wildlife has a book with dozens of maps of Cape ponds. Remember, you'll need a license for freshwater fishing, available for a nominal fee at bait and tackle shops.

Molly Benjamin's fishing column in the Friday *Cape Cod Times* tells the latest in fishing on the Cape—what's being caught and where.

GOLF

The Cape Cod Chamber of Commerce has a "Golf Map of Cape Cod," locating dozens of courses on the Cape and islands. Summer greens fees range from $25 to $50.

RUNNING

Many road races are held in season. To run in the world-class **Falmouth Road Race** (✉ Box 732, Falmouth, 02541, ☎ 508/540–7000) in August, send a stamped, self-addressed envelope to request an entry form; the race typically closes to entrants in early spring. The **Cape Codder Triathlon** (✉ Box 307, West Barnstable 02668) takes place at Craigville Beach in Centerville in early summer.

Visitor Information

The **Cape Cod Chamber of Commerce** (✉ Junction of U.S. 6 and 132, Hyannis, ☎ 508/862–0700 or 888/332–2732) is open year-round, Monday–Saturday 9–5 and Sunday 10–4. There's also a year-round visitor information center (☎ 508/759–3814) on Route 25 on the way to the Bourne Bridge; it's open daily 9–5. From Memorial Day to Columbus Day, there are extended hours: Sunday–Thursday 8–6 and Friday–Saturday 8–7.

LOCAL CHAMBERS OF COMMERCE

Local chambers of commerce, many open only in season, put out literature on their area.

Brewster (✉ 2198 Main St. [Rte. 6A], Box 1241, 02631, ☎ 508/896–3500), in the Brewster town offices building. The office includes a visitor center and the offices of the Brewster Chamber of Commerce and Board of Trade United.

Cape Cod Canal Region, for Sandwich and Bourne and Wareham (✉ 70 Main St., Buzzards Bay 02532, ☎ 508/759–6000); information centers at the Sagamore rotary, at the train depot in Buzzards Bay, and on Rte. 130 in Sandwich).

Chatham (✉ Box 793, 02633, ☎ 508/945–5199 or 800/715–5567; visitor center: ✉ 2377 Main St., South Chatham; information booth at ✉ 533 Main St., Chatham).

Dennis (✉ Junction of Rtes. 28 and 134, West Dennis; ✉ Box 275, South Dennis 02660, ☎ 508/398–3568 or 800/243–9920).

Eastham (✉ U.S. 6 at Fort Hill Rd., Box 1329, 02642, ☎ 508/240–7211).

Falmouth (✉ Academy La., Box 582, 02541, ☎ 508/548–8500 or 800/526–8532).

Harwich (✉ Rte. 28, Box 34, Harwich Port 02646, ☎ 508/432–1600 or 800/441–3199).

Hyannis (✉ 1481 Rte. 132, 02601, ☎ 508/362–5230 or 800/449–6647).

Mashpee (✉ Rte. 151, Box 1245, 02649, ☎ 508/477–0792).

Orleans (✉ Box 153, 02653, ☎ 508/255–1386; information booth: ✉ Eldredge Pkwy., off Rte. 6A, ☎ 508/240–2484).

Provincetown (✉ MacMillan Wharf, Box 1017, 02657, ☎ 508/487–3424).

Provincetown Business Guild (✉ 115 Bradford St., Box 421, 02657, ☎ 508/487–2313) specializes in gay tourism.

Truro (✉ U.S. 6 at Head of the Meadow Rd., Box 26, North Truro 02652, ☎ 508/487–1288).

Wellfleet (✉ Box 571, 02667, ☎ 508/349–2510; information center off U.S. 6 in South Wellfleet).

Yarmouth Area (✉ 657 Rte. 28, West Yarmouth, 02673; ✉ Box 479, South Yarmouth, 02664, ☎ 508/778–1008 or 800/732–1008; information center on U.S. 6 heading east between Exits 6 and 7, ☎ 508/362–9796).

OTHER INFORMATION

You can call the **Army Corps of Engineers 24-hour recreation hot line** (☎ 508/759–5991) for canal-area events, tide, and fishing information.

Arts and entertainment events are listed in the *Cape Cod Times*'s "CapeWeek" section on Friday and in its daily editions. Extensive art happenings and unusual feature stories can be found in *A-Plus,* available free in galleries and as several newspaper supplements. Also check out listings in the *Barnstable Patriot* and the Tuesday and Friday editions of the *Cape Codder.* In Provincetown, look for the *Advocate,* the *Banner,* and *Provincetown Magazine,* all weeklies.

The **Cape Cod Jazz Society** operates a 24-hour hot line (☎ 508/394–5277) on jazz events throughout the Cape.

A recorded **tide, marine, and weather forecast hot line** is sponsored by local radio station WQRC (☎ 508/771–5522).

3 MARTHA'S VINEYARD

On today's star-studded Vineyard, the summertime bustle and crush of Vineyard Haven, Oak Bluffs, and Edgartown continue to belie the quieter feeling off-season visitors have come to love. In season, you can step back into rural time Up-Island at the wonderful West Tisbury Farmers' Market or in a conservation area's pine woods or rolling meadows. At all times a superb beach—that perennial favorite of island vacationing—beckons nearby.

Updated by
Karl Luntta

Dining
updated by
Seth Rolbein
and Ellen
LeBow

BARTHOLOMEW GOSNOLD charted Martha's Vineyard for the British Crown in 1602 and is credited with naming it, supposedly after his infant daughter or mother-in-law (or both) and the wild grapes he found growing in profusion. Later, Massachusetts Bay Colony businessman Thomas Mayhew was given a grant to the island, along with Nantucket and the Elizabeth Islands, from King Charles of England. Mayhew's son, Thomas Jr., founded the first European settlement here in 1642 at Edgartown, finding the resident Wampanoags good neighbors. Among other survival skills, they taught the settlers to kill whales on shore. When moved out to sea, this practice would bring the island great prosperity, for a time. Historians estimate a Wampanoag population of 3,000 upon Mayhew's arrival. Today there are approximately 300. The tribe is now working hard to reclaim and perpetuate its cultural identity, and it has managed to take back ancestral lands in the town of Aquinnah, formerly called Gay Head.

Europeans settled as a community of farmers and fishermen, and both occupations continue to flourish. In the early 1800s, the basis of the island's economy made a decided shift to whaling. Never as influential as Nantucket or New Bedford, Martha's Vineyard nonetheless held its own, and many of its whaling masters returned home wealthy men. Especially during the industry's golden age, between 1830 and 1845, captains built impressive homes with their profits. These, along with many graceful houses from earlier centuries, still line the streets of Vineyard Haven and Edgartown, both former whaling towns. The industry went into decline after the Civil War, but by then revenue from tourism had picked up, and those dollars just keep flooding in.

The story of the Vineyard's development as a resort begins in 1835, when the first Methodist Camp Meeting—a two-week gathering of far-flung parishes for group worship and a healthy dose of fun—was held in the Oak Bluffs area, barely populated at the time. From the original meeting's 9 tents, the number grew to 250 by 1857. Little by little, returning campers built permanent platforms arranged around the central preachers' tent. Then the odd cottage popped up in place of a tent. By 1880, Wesleyan Grove, named for Methodism's founder, John Wesley, was a community of about 500 tiny cottages built in a hybrid of European Gothic Revival styles. Lacy filigree insets of jigsaw-cut detail work began to appear on cottage facades, and the ornamented look came to be known as Carpenter Gothic.

Meanwhile, burgeoning numbers of cottagers coming to the island each summer helped convince speculators of its desirability as a resort destination, and in 1867 they laid out a separate secular community alongside the Camp Ground. Steamers from New Bedford, Boston, New York, and elsewhere brought in fashionable folk for bathing and taking in the sea air, for picking berries or playing croquet. Grand hotels sprang up around Oak Bluffs Harbor. A railroad followed, connecting the town with the beach at Katama. The Victorian seaside resort was called Cottage City before its name changed to Oak Bluffs.

More than 300 of the Camp Ground cottages remain. And just as Edgartown and Vineyard Haven reflect their origins as whaling ports, so Oak Bluffs—with its porch-wrapped beach houses and a village green where families still gather to hear the town band play in the gazebo —evokes the days of Victorian summer ease, of flowing white dresses and parasols held languidly against the sun.

Martha's Vineyard

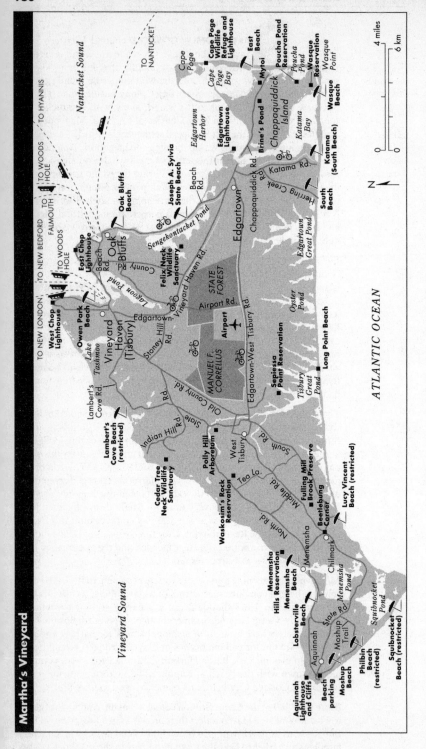

Far less developed than Cape Cod—thanks to a few conservation organizations—yet more cosmopolitan than neighboring Nantucket, Martha's Vineyard is an island with a double life. From Memorial Day through Labor Day the quieter, some might say real, Vineyard quickens into a vibrant, star-studded place. Edgartown floods with people who come to wander narrow streets flanked with elegant boutiques, stately whaling captains' homes, and charming inns. The busy main port, Vineyard Haven, welcomes day-trippers fresh off ferries and private yachts to browse in its own array of shops. Oak Bluffs, where pizza and ice cream emporiums reign supreme, attracts diverse crowds with its boardwalk-town air and nightspots that cater to high-spirited, carefree youth.

Summer regulars include a host of celebrities, among them William Styron, Art Buchwald, Walter Cronkite, Beverly Sills, Patricia Neal, Spike Lee, and Sharon Stone. President Clinton and his wife, Hillary, have been frequent visitors during his terms in office. Concerts, theater, dance performances, and lecture series draw top talent to the island, while a county agricultural fair, weekly farmers' markets, and miles of walking trails provide earthier pleasures.

Most people know the Vineyard's summer persona, but in many ways its other self has even more appeal, for the off-season island is a place of peace and simple beauty. Drivers traversing country lanes through the agricultural center of the island find time to linger over pastoral and ocean vistas, without being pushed along by a throng of other cars, bicycles, and mopeds. In nature reserves, the voices of summer are gone, leaving only the sounds of birdsong and the crackle of leaves underfoot. Private beaches open to the public, and the water sparkles under crisp, blue skies.

Locals are at their convivial best off-season. After the craziness of their short moneymaking months, they reestablish contact with friends and take up pastimes temporarily crowded out by work. The result for visitors—besides the extra dose of friendliness—is that cultural, educational, and recreational events continue year-round.

Pleasures and Pastimes

Dining

Upscale, downscale, flamboyant, and funky: the Vineyard offers an amazing variety of culinary choices, with less of the wash of pretense that increasingly characterizes dining in neighboring Nantucket (though it does come close to Nantucket's high prices). Edgartown and Oak Bluffs compete as the best restaurant scenes; Edgartown tends to the haute while Oak Bluffs goes for the hot. Vineyard Haven has its adherents as well, and Down-Island holds its own in wonderful little outposts that feel like the restaurant equivalent of a secluded, lovely beach.

It seems impossible in these times, but much of the Vineyard is dry. That means no liquor stores and no restaurant liquor service in the towns of Vineyard Haven, West Tisbury, Chilmark, Aquinnah (Gay Head), and Menemsha. The economies of Oak Bluffs and Edgartown benefit from the business their "wet" status brings in. Virtually all restaurants in the dry towns allow you to bring your own beer or wine, though almost all of them now charge a "set-up" or "corkage" fee of anywhere from $1 to $5. Many travelers keep a cooler handy and stop at a small package store like Our Market in Oak Bluffs as they begin their tour to Vineyard Haven and beyond.

If all this sounds quaint, rest assured that, in terms of food, the Vineyard is no backwater. Celebrities and high-powered executives may come here to relax in their cutoffs and sneakers, but *no one* takes a vacation without packing an appetite. You don't have to leave the island to sample the cuisines of France, Italy, New Orleans, or New York. And if you want to eat New England seafood, you'll find plenty of that, too. Keep in mind that the fish served in restaurants is much more likely to have come from a New Bedford trawler than a local day boat, but what reaches the plate still ranks among the best and freshest in the country. In recognition of that, sushi has made a major appearance; what's surprising is not that it's here but that it took so long to arrive. Then again, if the mood strikes you, you can hit a seafood market like Larsen's in Menemsha and cook up—or not cook up—some fish yourself.

For price-category information, *see* Dining *in* Smart Travel Trips A to Z.

Lodging

The variety of lodging on Martha's Vineyard ranges from historic whaling captains' mansions filled with antiques to sprawling ocean-front hotels to cozy cottages in the woods. When choosing your accommodations, keep in mind that each town has a different "personality": Oak Bluffs tends to cater to a younger, active, nightlife-oriented crowd, while Edgartown is more subdued. Chilmark has beautiful beaches and miles of conservation lands but not much of a downtown shopping area. Bear in mind that many of the island's B&Bs, set in vintage homes filled with art and antiques, have age restrictions—call ahead if you're traveling with a family. And remember that in July and August, the height of the summer season, minimum stays of as many as three nights may be required. If you're planning to visit for a week or more, you might consider renting a house. Advance reservations for summer stays should be made as far in advance as possible; early spring is not too early. Rates in season are very high but may go down by as much as 50% in the off-season.

For price-category information, *see* Lodging *in* Smart Travel Tips A to Z.

Outdoor Activities and Sports

BEACHES

On the Vineyard's south shore, the Atlantic Ocean side, surf crashes in refreshingly chilly waves—a great place for bodysurfing. The more protected beaches on the Nantucket and Vineyard sounds tend to have slightly warmer and calmer waters, perfect for swimmers and for families. A few freshwater beaches at inland ponds offer a change of pace from the salty sea.

Note that public beaches are split between free beaches such as the Joseph A. Sylvia State Beach, for which no parking fees are required, and several open to the public for which parking fees are collected, such as Moshup Beach in Aquinnah. Private beaches are reserved for permanent and summer residents, who must obtain parking or resident stickers from the appropriate town hall.

BIKING

Martha's Vineyard is a great place for cycling. Up-Island roads cross some hilly terrain, and during summer and fall roads island-wide can get very crowded. Still, cycling beats driving as a pleasant and often more practical way to tour the island. Cyclists have access to well-maintained, flat paved paths along the coast road from Oak Bluffs to Edgartown—very scenic—and inland from Vineyard Haven to Edgartown and South Beach. These connect with sometimes potholed paths that weave through the Manuel F. Correllus State Forest. Middle Road in Chilmark is a lovely, winding country road with less traffic than the main roads.

CONSERVATION AREAS

There are a great many conservation areas on the Vineyard in which you can indulge in biophilia (love of nature). Many are of the do-it-yourself variety, with beautiful walking trails meandering through diverse habitats—dunes and salt marshes among them—while others offer bird walks or special kids' programs.

FISHING

Huge trawlers unload abundant daily catches at the docks in Vineyard Haven and Menemsha, attesting to the richness of the waters surrounding the island. But some of the most zealous fishing is done by amateurs—the striped bass and bluefish derby in the fall is very serious business. One of the most popular spots for sport anglers is Wasque Point on Chappaquiddick. Two others are South Beach and the jetty at the mouth of the Menemsha Basin. Striped bass and bluefish are island stars. Several outfits offer deep-sea fishing trips if surf fishing is not your thing.

HIKING AND WALKING

The nature preserves and conservation areas are laced with well-marked, scenic trails through varied terrains and ecological habitats, and the island's miles of uninterrupted beaches are perfect for stretching your legs.

WATER SPORTS

Martha's Vineyard is an ideal place for windsurfing. Neophytes can practice on the protected waters of the many bays and inlets, while the ocean-side surf provides plenty of action for experts. Swimming, sailing, sea-kayaking, and canoeing are also favorite pastimes, with both ocean and freshwater locales from which to choose.

Shopping

A specialty of the island is wampum—beads made from black, white, or purple shells and fashioned into jewelry sold at the cliffs and elsewhere. Antique and new scrimshaw jewelry, and jewelry incorporating Vineyard and island-specific designs such as lighthouses or bunches of grapes, is also popular. Many island shops carry the ultraexpensive Nantucket lightship baskets, tightly woven creations of wood and rattan that were originally made by sailors but are now valued collectibles made by artisans. A good number of Vineyard shops close for the winter, though quite a few in Vineyard Haven and some stores in other locations remain open—call ahead before making a special trip.

The three main towns have the largest concentrations of shops. In Vineyard Haven, shops line Main Street. Edgartown's are clustered together within a few blocks of the dock, on Main, Summer, and Water streets. Casual clothing and gift shops crowd along Circuit Avenue in Oak Bluffs. At Aquinnah Cliffs, you'll find touristy Native American crafts and souvenirs in season.

The West Tisbury Farmers' Market, the largest farmers' market in Massachusetts, offers a different, more modest shopping experience. Elsewhere, some of the antiques stores hidden along back roads brim with the interesting and the unusual.

Exploring Martha's Vineyard

The island is roughly triangular, with maximum distances of about 20 mi east to west and 10 mi north to south. The west end of the Vineyard, known as Up-Island—from the nautical expression of going "up" in degrees of longitude as you sail west—is more rural and wild than the eastern Down-Island end, comprising Vineyard Haven, Oak Bluffs, and Edgartown. Conservation land claims almost a quarter of the island, with preservationist organizations acquiring more all the time. The Land Bank, funded by a tax on real-estate transactions, is a leading group, set up to preserve as much of the island in its natural state as is possible and practical.

Numbers in the text correspond to numbers in the margin and on the Vineyard Haven, Oak Bluffs, Edgartown, and Up-Island maps.

Great Itineraries

The itineraries below cover all the towns on the island, but you don't have to. You might want to spend a short time in Vineyard Haven before getting rural Up-Island or heading for a beach. Or you might prefer to go straight to Edgartown to stroll past the antique white houses, pop into a museum or two, and shop. If you just want to have fun, Oak Bluffs, with its harbor scene and nearby beaches, will be the place to go. In essence, pick and choose what you like best from what follows. The Vineyard is small enough, too, that you can pick one town as your base and explore other areas easily.

IF YOU HAVE 2 DAYS

Start your trip in **Vineyard Haven.** Historic houses line **William Street,** and you'll find shops and eateries along Main Street. Take a quick jaunt out to **West Chop** ⑥ for a great view over Vineyard Sound from the lighthouse; then head back through town toward **Oak Bluffs** via Beach Road. Spend some time wandering the streets of the **Oak Bluffs Camp Ground** ⑩, where tightly packed pastel-painted Victorian cottages vie with one another for the fanciest gingerbread trim. Then head into the center of Oak Bluffs for a ride on the Flying Horses, the oldest continuously operating carousel in the country.

Instead of going to Oak Bluffs from Vineyard Haven, you could head straight to **Edgartown.** Take the On-Time ferry to **Chappaquiddick Island** ㉕ to visit the **Mytoi** preserve or have a picnic at Brine's Pond. If conservation areas are your thing, the **Cape Poge Wildlife Refuge** on the island is a must. You'll need a few hours on Chappaquiddick to make the visit worthwhile. If you spend the afternoon in Edgartown, take your pick of shops and interesting museums. After dinner, attend a performance at the Old Whaling Church. Spend the night in Edgartown or back in Oak Bluffs.

On the second day, head all the way out to **Aquinnah** ㉟ (formerly Gay Head), one of the most spectacular spots on the island. Go to the lookout at the cliffs for the view, or take the boardwalk to the beach and walk back to see the cliffs and Aquinnah Light from below. In the afternoon, **West Tisbury** ㉖ has great nature preserves and a public beach on the south shore. The Field Gallery in the town center has whimsical statues set about the lawn.

You could also spend the afternoon in the fishing village of **Menemsha** ㉞. As the day comes to an end, pick up some seafood and bring it to Menemsha Beach for a sunset picnic. Spend the night Up-Island.

IF YOU HAVE 4 DAYS

Follow the two-day itinerary at a slower pace. If conservation areas appeal, **Felix Neck Wildlife Sanctuary** northwest of Edgartown is a great spot. Chappaquiddick conservation areas are also wonderful. Start your tour in **Vineyard Haven,** but spend two nights in **Edgartown,** with jaunts into Oak Bluffs to sample the nightlife. If schedules permit, catch a show at the Vineyard Playhouse or at the amphitheater at Tashmoo Overlook, or enjoy a performance at the Wintertide Coffeehouse.

Spend two days Up-Island as well, where the beaches are some of the best on the Vineyard. Visit one of the **West Tisbury** ㉖ farms, some of which have pony rides for kids or fruit picking, or the **Winery at Chicama Vineyards** ㉘. The **Mayhew Chapel and Indian Burial Ground** are interesting and offer an almost eerie look into the past. Because you'll have more time, don't miss the **Aquinnah Cliffs** ㊳ via **Moshup Beach,** and spend some time sunning and swimming at this breathtaking spot. (A note to the modest: the beach attracts nude sunbathers; though it's illegal, the officials usually look the other way.) Spend two nights Up-Island. If you choose West Tisbury, be sure to take time on its gorgeous beach.

IF YOU HAVE 6 DAYS

With nearly a week on your hands, follow the suggestions mentioned in the four-day tour, allowing plenty of time in each place. Give yourself whole days on the beach and take a fishing trip from one of the harbors. Bike the trails from town to town or through the state forest. You'll have plenty of time for shopping.

Up-Island, bird-watchers can enjoy leisurely walks around **Sepiessa Point Reservation** or **Wompesket Preserve**'s wet meadow—the conservation areas here have much to offer. The **Menemsha Hills Reservation, Cedar Tree Neck Wildlife Sanctuary,** and **Waskosim's Rock Reservation** are also quite good. Get out of the car and walk around the rural towns of West Tisbury and Chilmark. Since you'll be on the island for Wednesday and/or Saturday, you won't want to miss the **West Tisbury Farmers' Market.** If you are a John Belushi fan, stop by the **Chilmark Cemetery** to see the booze bottles and cigarette collections left beside the rock bearing his name. (It is a memorial stone only; Belushi's real grave is unmarked to deter overzealous fans.) Travel the backroads to find some interesting, out-of-the-way antiques shops. And be sure to catch sunset from this side of the island—from the cliffs or from a Menemsha beach or its harbor.

When to Tour Martha's Vineyard

Summer is the most popular season on the Vineyard, the time when everyone is here and everything is open and happening. With weather perfect for all kinds of activities, the island hosts special events from the Martha's Vineyard Agricultural Fair to the Edgartown Regatta. Another busy season, fall brings cool weather, harvest celebrations, and fishing derbies. Tivoli Day, an end of summer/start of fall celebration, includes a street fair. The island does tend to curl up in winter, when many shops and restaurants close. However, for the weeks surrounding the Hanukkah–Christmas–New Year's holidays, the Vineyard puts bells on for all kinds of special events and celebrations, most notably in Edgartown and Vineyard Haven. Spring sees the island awaken from its slumber in a burst of garden and house tours as islanders warm up for the busy season.

DOWN-ISLAND

The three towns that compose Down-Island Martha's Vineyard—Vineyard Haven, Oak Bluffs, and Edgartown—are the most popular and the most populated. Here you'll find the ferry docks, the shops, and a concentration of things to do and see, including the centuries-old houses and churches that document the island's history. A stroll through any one of these towns allows you to look into the past while enjoying the pleasures of the present.

Vineyard Haven (Tisbury)

3½ mi west of Oak Bluffs, 8 mi northwest of Edgartown by the inland route.

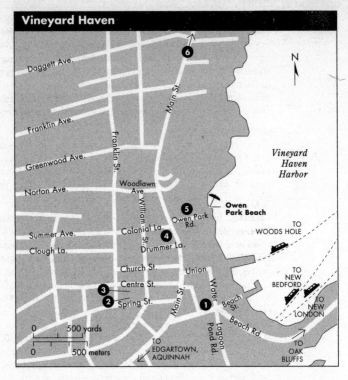

Most people call this town Vineyard Haven for the name of the port where the ferry pulls in, but its official name is in fact Tisbury. Not as high-toned as Edgartown nor as honky-tonk as Oak Bluffs, Vineyard Haven blends the past and the present with a touch of the bohemian. Settled in the mid-1600s when the island's first governor-to-be purchased rights to the land from local Wampanoags, it is the busiest year-round community on Martha's Vineyard. Visitors arriving here step off the ferry right into the bustle of the harbor, a block from the shops that line Main Street.

① If you need to stock up on maps or information on the island, **Martha's Vineyard Chamber of Commerce** is a good place to get your bearings. The office is around the corner from the steamship terminal (where you'll find a small information booth, open daily 8–8 in season) on Beach Road. ⊠ *24 Beach Rd.,* ☎ *508/693–0085.* ☉ *Weekdays 9–5.*

NEED A BREAK?	The **Black Dog Bakery**'s (⊠ 11 Water St., ☎ 508/693–4786) delicious breads, pastries, and quick-lunch items are simply not to be missed—it's a popular stop for good reason (☞ Dining and Lodging, *below*).

② The stately, neoclassic 1844 **Association Hall** (⊠ 51 Spring St., ☎ 508/696–4200) houses the town hall and the **Katharine Cornell Memorial Theatre**, created in part with funds that Cornell (1898–1974)—one of America's foremost stage actresses in the 1920s, '30s, and '40s, and a longtime summer resident—donated in her will. The walls of the theater on the second floor are painted with murals depicting such island scenes as whaling expeditions and a Native American gathering, while the ceiling resembles a blue sky with seagulls overhead. Island artist Stan Murphy painted the murals on the occasion of the town's tercentenary in 1971. In addition to theatrical performances, the theater holds concerts and dances.

Finally, a travel companion that doesn't snore on the plane or eat all your peanuts.

MCI WORLDCOM WorldPhone®

123 456 7891 2345
J.D. SMITH

When traveling, your MCI WorldCom Card is the best way to keep in touch. Our operators speak your language, so they'll be able to connect you back home—no matter where your travels take you. Plus, your MCI WorldCom Card is easy to use, and even earns you frequent flyer miles every time you use it. When you add in our great rates, you get something even more valuable: peace-of-mind. So go ahead. Travel the world. MCI WorldCom just brought it a whole lot closer.

You can even sign up today at www.mci.com/worldphone or ask your operator to make a collect call to 1-410-314-2938.

EASY TO CALL WORLDWIDE

1 Just dial the WorldPhone access number of the country you're calling from.
2 Dial or give the operator your MCI WorldCom Card number.
3 Dial or give the number you're calling.

Australia ♦	
To call using OPTUS	1-800-551-111
To call using TELSTRA	1-800-881-100
Bahamas/Bermuda	1-800-888-8000
British Virgin Islands	1-800-888-8000
Costa Rica ♦	0-800-012-2222
Denmark	8001-0022
Norway ♦	800-19912
India	000-127
For collect access	000-126
United States/Canada	1-800-888-8000

For your complete WorldPhone calling guide, dial the WorldPhone access number for the country you're in and ask the operator for Customer Service. In the U.S. call 1-800-431-5402.

♦ Public phones may require deposit of coin or phone card for dial tone.

EARN FREQUENT FLYER MILES

AmericanAirlines®
A'Advantage®

Continental Airlines
OnePass

▲ Delta Air Lines
SkyMiles®

♦ MILEAGE PLUS.
United Airlines

US AIRWAYS
DIVIDEND MILES

MCI WorldCom, its logo and the names of the products referred to herein are proprietary marks of MCI WorldCom, Inc. All airline names and logos are proprietary marks of the respective airlines. All airline program rules and conditions apply.

MCI WORLDCOM

Distinctive guides packed with up-to-date expert advice and smart choices for every type of traveler.

Fodor's. For the world of ways you travel.

❸ The **Centre Street Cemetery** (✉ Centre St., between William and Franklin Sts.), where tall pine trees shade grave markers dating as far back as 1817, stands as a reminder of the town's past. Some stones are simple gray slate slabs, while others are carved with such motifs as the death's-head—a skull, common on tombstones of the era. A more recent grave is that of the actress Katharine Cornell, who died in 1974 and whose largesse helped build the theater (housed in the Association Hall; ☞ *above*) named for her.

A stroll down **William Street,** a quiet stretch of white picket fences and Greek Revival houses, many of them built for prosperous sea captains, lets you imagine the town as it was in the 19th century. Now a part of a National Historic District, the street was spared when the Great Fire of 1883 claimed much of the old whaling and fishing town.

108 William Street, set back on a wide lawn behind a wrought-iron fence, is an imposing monument to a later source of the town's prosperity: tourism. The elegantly detailed three-story house was built in 1873 by Benjamin C. Cromwell—captain not of a whaling ship but rather of a steamer that brought New Bedford folk to the island. It is not open to the public.

❹ Built in 1829, the **Old Schoolhouse Building** was the first town school and today houses the Vineyard Seaman's Society and Bethel Maritime Collection. You can view items brought back from voyages during whaling days, including Inuit and Polynesian tools, as well as antique musical instruments, clothing, and the school records of 19th-century schoolchildren. Out front, the **Liberty Pole** was erected by the Daughters of the American Revolution in honor of three patriotic girls who blew up the town's liberty pole in 1776 to prevent it from being taken for use on a British warship. The museum has experienced staffing problems recently, so call for current opening times. ✉ *110 Main St.,* ☎ *508/693–9317.* ☞ *$2.* ✆ *Mid-June–mid-Sept., Tues.–Fri. and Sun. noon–4.*

❺ For a little relaxation, try the tree-shaded benches in **Owen Park** (✉ Off Owen Park Rd.), a lovely spot for a picnic and for summer concerts held at the bandstand. At the end of the lawn is a public beach with a swing set and a close-up view of the boats sailing in and out of the harbor. In the 19th century this harbor was one of the busiest ports in the world, welcoming thousands of vessels each year. Lighthouses still stand at the headlands—West Chop in Vineyard Haven and East Chop in Oak Bluffs—to help bring ships safely into port. Both areas were largely settled in the late-19th to early 20th centuries, when the very rich from Boston and Newport built expansive bluff-top "summer cottages." These shingle-style houses, characterized by broad gable ends, dormers, and, of course, natural shingle siding that weathers to gray, were meant to eschew pretense, though they were sometimes gussied up with a turret or two.

❻ Beautiful and green, **West Chop** retains its exclusive air and claims some of the island's most distinguished residents. An approximately 2-mi walk, drive, or bike ride along Vineyard Haven's Main Street—which becomes increasingly residential on the way—will take you there.

One of two lighthouses that mark the opening to the harbor, the 52-ft white-and-black **West Chop Lighthouse** (✉ W. Chop Rd. [Main St.]), was built in 1838 of brick to replace an 1817 wood building. It has been moved back twice from the edge of the eroding bluff. (It is not open to the public.) Just beyond the lighthouse, on the point, is a scenic overlook with a landscaped area and benches.

West Chop Woods is an 85-acre conservation area with marked walking trails through pitch pine and oak. The area is just south and west of the West Chop lighthouse, with entrances and parking spots on Main Street and Franklin Street.

Martha's Vineyard Shellfish Group grows seed clams, scallops, and oysters to stock lagoons and beds throughout the county. From spring through fall, tours of the solar shellfish hatchery on Lagoon Pond in Vineyard Haven can be arranged with advance notice. ⊠ *Weaver La.,* ☎ *508/693–0391.* 🎟 *Free.* ☉ *Call for appointment.*

Dining and Lodging

$$$–$$$$ ✕ **Le Grenier.** Up narrow stairs, a life-size rendering of a stereotypical goateed French chef greets you at the door. Le Grenier is like that chef: probably startling and fresh 20 years ago but unchanged since then, and so reading the menu is almost like peering into a time warp. Although a truly French restaurant in a dry town is certainly a stretch, what is served here is authentic and expert and always aims for the Continental and classic. For frogs' legs, sweetbreads, tournedos, and calves' brains served as they were a decade or more ago, Le Grenier is the clear choice. ⊠ *Upper Main St.,* ☎ *508/693–4906. AE, MC, V. BYOB. No lunch.*

$$$ ✕ **Black Dog Tavern.** The black dog on the tavern's signature label had his hat backward for a while; now it's on straight again. A Jungian specialist on the collective unconscious could find plenty to analyze in the power of the black dog/Martha's Vineyard connection—at this point, a cultural leash is in order. The waterfront tavern itself hasn't changed, but locals have generally adopted Yogi Berra's line: it's so crowded, no one goes there anymore. Regardless, prices seem to go up every year. The menu has all the usual suspects, such as codfish and pasta, and the truth is that the food (if that still matters) is just fine breakfast, lunch, or dinner. Even the bakery out front has gotten so popular that a bakery-café has opened down State Road (it's about a 15-minute walk). ⊠ *Beach St. Ext.,* ☎ *508/693–9223. Reservations not accepted. AE, D, MC, V. BYOB. No smoking.*

$$$ ✕ **Stripers.** Lush mint grows alongside the winding walkway at this creative, mostly seafood restaurant, tucked behind the Vineyard Haven Marina. A series of airy rooms includes two upstairs verandas (furnished, alas, in white patio plastic) that overlook the yachts below, and blue fish-print tablecloths and fresh blue and white walls give the place a lighthearted feel. Chef Daniel Sweimler follows the modern American trend of contrasting "global village" ingredients in surprising combinations. A salad of roasted beets, endive, and pear comes with a ricotta and tomato-*chipotle* (hot chili pepper) confit. There's a seaweed-crusted tuna entrée and pan-seared scallops with pineapple-mango salsa, fried plantain, coconut ginger rice, and braised greens. The $5 cork fee is outlandish; save your money for a root beer float with homemade butter cookies for dessert. ⊠ *52 Beach Rd.,* ☎ *508/693–8383. MC, V. BYOB. Closed mid-Oct.–mid-May.*

$$ ✕ **Cafe Moxie.** They've hit the right combination here: great food and a stylish ambience. Fancy pizzas and salads make up most of the lunch choices, but at night the menu typically includes something intriguing from each of the major staples: salmon, scallops, steak, chicken, and shrimp. Moxie has the moxie to invite some of the most interesting young chefs from Boston for one-night stands, and a little tradition of partnering is in the making. Last year Laura Brennan from the former Mercury Bar and Steve Rosen from Salts both showed up, with memorable results. The restaurant is across the street from the movie theater; if you're trying to make the previews, let your server know. ⊠ *Main St. at Centre St.,* ☎ *508/693–1484. D, MC, V. Closed Mon.*

$$$$ 🏨 **Thorncroft Inn.** Set on 3½ wooded acres about 1 mi from the ferry,
★ this inn's main building, a 1918 Craftsman bungalow, combines fine
Colonial and richly carved Renaissance Revival antiques with tasteful
reproductions to create a somewhat formal environment. Ten of the
rooms have working fireplaces. Deluxe rooms are outfitted with minirefrigerators, and some have canopy beds; three rooms have two-
person whirlpool baths and two have private hot-tub spas. Set apart
from the main house and reached via a breezeway, the private, ultra-
deluxe room has a king-size bed and a whirlpool tub and is wheelchair
accessible. Owners Karl and Lynn Buder deliver a newspaper to your
room each morning and serve full breakfasts in two seatings, as well
as afternoon tea. No smoking is permitted. ⊠ *460 Main St., Box
1022, 02568,* ☎ *508/693–3333 or 800/332–1236,* FAX *508/693–5419.
14 rooms. Library. AE, D, DC, MC, V. BP.*

$$$–$$$$ 🏨 **Martha's Place.** Since it opened in 1997, Martin Hicks and Richard
★ Alcott's B&B has set a standard on the island. This 1840s Greek Re-
vival house, built by a descendant of the island's founder, now bubbles
with hospitality. The interior's carefully selected antiques and luscious
fabrics reveal the presence of a design pro (Martin); he never spills over
into frou-frou. Then there are the generous details: thick terry-cloth
robes, beautifully presented Continental breakfasts, and tennis rack-
ets and bicycles provided gratis to guests. The property overlooks the
harbor (some rooms have water views); it's a few blocks from the ferry
landing, just west of the village center. ⊠ *114 Main St., Box 1182, 02568,*
☎ FAX *508/693–0253. 6 rooms. Breakfast room, bicycles. AE, MC, V. CP.*

$$–$$$$ 🏨 **Captain Dexter House.** An 1843 sea captain's house at the edge of
the shopping district is the setting for this intimate B&B. Small guest
rooms are appointed with period-style wallpapers, velvet wing chairs,
and 18th-century antiques and reproductions, including several four-
poster canopy beds with lace or fishnet canopies and hand-sewn quilts.
The Captain Harding Room is larger, with the original wood floor as
well as a fireplace, bay windows, canopy bed, desk, and bright bath
with claw-foot tub. There is a common refrigerator, and in season afternoon lemonade and cookies and evening sherry are served. ⊠ *92
Main St., Box 2457, 02568,* ☎ *508/693–6564,* FAX *508/693–8448. 7
rooms, 1 suite. No pets. No smoking. AE, MC, V. CP.*

$$$ 🏨 **Hanover House.** Set on a half acre of landscaped lawn within walk-
ing distance of the ferry, this inn offers comfortable rooms decorated
with a combination of antiques and reproduction furniture. Each room
has its individual flair, some with floral wallpaper and quilts, others
sponge-painted and filled with whimsical, creative furnishings such as
an antique sewing machine that serves as a TV stand. Three suites in
the separate carriage house are roomy, with private decks or patios;
two have kitchenettes. The owners include touches such as Heming-
way paperbacks on night tables. Homemade breads and muffins and
a special house cereal are served each morning on a sunporch bright-
ened with fresh flowers from the gardens. ⊠ *28 Edgartown Rd., Box
2107, 02568,* ☎ *508/693–1066 or 800/339–1066,* FAX *508/696–6099.
12 rooms, 3 suites. No pets, no smoking, no children under 8 in Aug.
AE, D, MC, V. Closed Dec.–Mar. CP.*

$$$ 🏨 **Tisbury Inn.** At the center of the shopping district, this three-story
hotel—dating to 1794—offers tiled bathrooms with tub showers, firm
beds, and amenities that include a well-equipped health club, cable TV,
air-conditioning, and ceiling fans. Pastel colors, floral fabrics, and simple decor lend the rooms an islandy feel; on the downside, rooms are
small and those facing the main street tend to be noisy. Number 32's
windows on two walls let in plenty of sunshine and allow a smidgen
of a view of the harbor. Look for special packages in summer. ⊠ *9 Main*

St., Box 428, 02568, ☎ 508/693–2200 or 800/332–4112, FAX 508/693–4095. 28 rooms, 4 suites. Restaurant, indoor pool, health club. No pets, no smoking. AE, D, DC, MC, V. CP.

$
★ ⚠ **Martha's Vineyard Family Campground.** Wooded sites, a ball field, camp store, bicycle rentals, and electrical and water hookups are among the facilities at this 20-acre campsite. A step up from tents are eight rustic one- or two-bedroom cabins with electricity, refrigerators, and gas grills. Book for a week and receive discounts. No dogs or motorcycles are allowed. ⊠ *569 Edgartown–Vineyard Haven Rd., Box 1557, 02568, ☎ 508/693–3772, FAX 508/693–5767. 180 sites, 8 cabins. Picnic area, bicycles, recreation room, playground, coin laundry. D, MC, V. Closed mid-Oct.–mid-May.*

Nightlife and the Arts

Island Theatre Workshop (☎ 508/693–5290), the island's oldest year-round company, performs at various venues.

The **Vineyard Playhouse** (⊠ 24 Church St., ☎ 508/693–6450 or 508/696–6300) has a year-round schedule of community theater and professional productions. Mid-June through early September, a mostly Equity troupe performs drama, classics, and comedies on the air-conditioned main stage, as well as summer Shakespeare and other productions at the natural amphitheater at Tashmoo Overlook on State Road in Vineyard Haven—bring insect repellent and a pillow. Children's programs and a summer camp are also offered, as well as local art exhibitions throughout the year. One performance of each summer main-stage show is interpreted in American sign language.

Sunday night **Vineyard Haven Town Band concerts** (☎ 508/693–0085) take place on alternate weeks in summer at 8 PM at Owen Park in Vineyard Haven and at the gazebo in Ocean Park on Beach Road in Oak Bluffs.

Wintertide Coffeehouse (⊠ Five Corners, at Beach St., Beach St. Extension, Beach Rd., Lagoon Pond Rd., and Water St., ☎ 508/693–8830) presents live folk, blues, jazz, and other music showcasing local and national talent, and open-mike nights, in a homey alcohol- and smoke-free environment. Light meals, desserts, and freshly ground coffees and cappuccino are served at candlelighted tables year-round.

Outdoor Activities and Sports

BEACHES

Lake Tashmoo Town Beach (⊠ End of Herring Creek Rd.) invites swimming in the warm, relatively shallow, brackish lake or in the cooler, gentle Vineyard Sound. There is a lifeguarded area and some parking.

Owen Park Beach, a small, sandy harbor beach off Main Street, is a convenient spot with a children's play area, lifeguards, and a harbor view.

BIKING

Martha's Bike Rentals (⊠ 4 Lagoon Pond Rd. at Five Corners, ☎ 508/693–6593) rents bicycles, helmets, and baby seats. It also handles repairs and will deliver and pick up your bike free anywhere on the island.

Martha's Vineyard Strictly Bikes (⊠ 24 Union St., ☎ 508/693–0782) rents a variety of bicycles. It also does repairs.

BOATING

Wind's Up! (⊠ 199 Beach Rd., ☎ 508/693–4252 or 508/693–4340; ☞ Shopping, *below*) rents day sailers, catamarans, surfboards, sea kayaks, canoes, and Sunfish, as well as Windsurfers and boogie boards, and offers lessons.

GOLF

The semiprivate **Mink Meadows Golf Club** (⊠ Golf Club Rd. at Franklin St., ☎ 508/693–0600), on West Chop, has nine holes and ocean views. Reservations must be made 48 hours in advance.

HEALTH AND FITNESS CLUBS

The **Health Club at the Tisbury Inn** (⊠ 9 Main St., ☎ 508/693–7400) has Lifecycle, Nautilus, Universal, and StairMaster machines, bikes, free-weight rooms, tanning facilities, aerobics classes, and personal trainers. The club also has a large heated pool, a hot tub, and a sauna. Short-term memberships, from one day to a month, are available.

MINIATURE GOLF

Island Cove Mini Golf (⊠ State Rd., ☎ 508/693–2611) offers an 18-hole course with bridges, a cave, rocklike obstacles, sand traps, and a stream that powers a water mill. Next door is Mad Martha's, where the winners can be treated to ice cream.

TENNIS

Tennis is very popular on the island, and at all times reservations are strongly recommended. The public clay courts on Church Street are open in season only and charge a small fee (reserve a court with the attendant a day in advance).

On rainy days you can head down to the **Vineyard Tennis Center** (⊠ 22 Airport Rd., ☎ 508/696–8000) at the entrance to the airport. For a fee you can play at the indoor courts until 10 at night.

Shopping

All Things Oriental (⊠ 123 Beach Rd., ☎ 508/693–8375) has jewelry, porcelains, paintings, furniture, and more, with an Asian theme.

Black Dog General Store (⊠ Between the Black Dog Tavern and the Bakery on Water St., ☎ 508/696–8182) sells T-shirts, sweatshirts, beach towels, and many other gift items, all emblazoned with the telltale Black Dog.

Bramhall & Dunn (⊠ 19 Main St., ☎ 508/693–6437) carries 19th-century English country pine furniture, as well as fine crafts, linens, and housewares, and hand-knit sweaters and original women's accessories and shoes.

Brickman's (⊠ 8 Main St., ☎ 508/693–0047) sells beach and sports gear, such as camping, fishing, and snorkeling equipment and boogie boards. It also carries sportswear, surf-style clothing, and major-label footwear for the family.

Bunch of Grapes Bookstore (⊠ 68 Main St., ☎ 508/693–2291) carries a wide selection of new books, including many island-related titles, and sponsors book signings—watch the papers for announcements.

C. B. Stark Jewelers (⊠ 126 Main St., ☎ 508/693–2284) creates one-of-a-kind pieces for both women and men, including island charms. It also carries other fine jewelry and watches.

Cronig's Market (⊠ 109 State Rd., ☎ 508/693–4457) supports local farmers and specialty-item producers—and carries whatever edibles you might need.

Island Children—Althea and Emily Designs (⊠ 94 Main St., ☎ 508/693–6130) has children's and women's clothing in 100% cotton, hand block–printed with unique African- and Caribbean-inspired and classic designs.

Lorraine Parish (⊠ 18 S. Main St., ☎ 508/693–9044) sells sophisticated, upscale women's dresses (some with a summery island feel), suits,
and blouses in natural fibers, all designed by Lorraine Parish, the designer of Carly Simon's wedding dress.

Murray's of the Vineyard (⊠ 72 Main St., ☎ 508/693–2640), sister
shop of Nantucket's Murray's Toggery, carries designer men's and
women's fashions, shoes, and accessories, from such names as Ralph
Lauren and Liz Claiborne. You can also buy the signature all-cotton
Nantucket Red pants, which fade to pink with washing.

Paper Tiger (⊠ 29 Main St., ☎ 508/693–8970) offers a wide array of
handmade paper, cards, and gift items, plus wind chimes, pottery,
writing utensils, and works by local artists.

Pyewacket's (⊠ 135 Beach Rd., ☎ 508/696–7766) carries an interesting conglomeration of antiques, island crafts, handmade soaps and
candles, and jewelry.

Rainy Day (⊠ 86 Main St., ☎ 508/693–1830) is the ultimate home
store, with high-quality cookware and home furnishings, including reasonably priced kilim rugs.

Sioux Eagle Designs (⊠ 29 Main St., ☎ 508/693–6537) sells unusual
handmade jewelry from around the world.

Wind's Up! (⊠ 199 Beach Rd., ☎ 508/693–4340; ☞ Outdoor Activities and Sports, *above*) sells swimwear, windsurfing and sailing equipment, boogie boards, and other outdoor gear.

Oak Bluffs

*3½ mi east of Vineyard Haven, 6 mi northwest of Edgartown, 22 mi
northeast of Aquinnah.*

Purchased from the Indians in the 1660s, Oak Bluffs was a farming
community that did not come into its own until the 1830s, when
Methodists began holding summer revivalist meetings in a stand of oaks
known as Wesleyan Grove, named for Methodism's founder, John
Wesley. As the camp meetings caught on, attendees built small cottages
in place of tents. Then the general population took notice and the area
became a popular summer vacation spot. Hotels, a dance hall, a roller-
skating rink, and other shops and amusements were built to accommodate the flocks of summer visitors.

Today Circuit Avenue is the bustling center of action in Oak Bluffs,
the address of most of the town's shops, bars, and restaurants. Oak
Bluffs Harbor, once the setting for a number of grand hotels—the
1879 Wesley Hotel on Lake Avenue is the last of them—is still crammed
with gingerbread-trimmed guest houses and food and souvenir joints.
With its whimsical cottages, long beachfront, and funky shops, the small
town is more honky-tonk than tony, more fun than refined.

East Chop is one of two points of land that jut out into the Nantucket-
Vineyard sound, creating the sheltered harbor at Vineyard Haven and
some fine views. From Oak Bluffs, take East Chop Drive, or you can
loop out to the point on your way from Vineyard Haven by taking Highland Drive off Beach Road after crossing the drawbridge.

❼ The **East Chop Lighthouse** was built of cast iron in 1876 to replace an
1828 tower—used as part of a semaphore system of visual signaling
between the island and Boston—that burned down. The 40-ft structure stands high atop a bluff with spectacular views of Nantucket

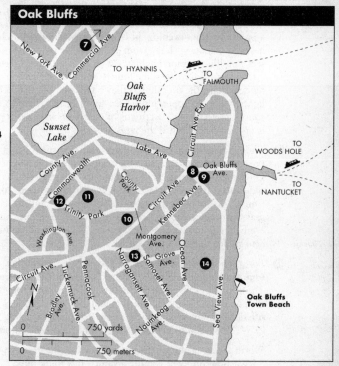

Oak Bluffs

Sound. ✉ *E. Chop Dr.,* ☎ *508/627–4441.* ✉ *$2.* ☉ *Late June–late
Sept., hr before sunset–hr after sunset.*

❽ The **information booth** will help you get your bearings and point the
way to the not-to-be-missed spots in Oak Bluffs, with some good tips
for gingerbread-trim lovers. ✉ *Corner of Lake and Oak Bluffs Aves.,*
☎ *508/693–4266.* ☉ *Mid-May–mid-Oct., daily 9–5.*

☝ ❾ A National Historic Landmark, the **Flying Horses Carousel** is the nation's oldest continuously operating carousel. The carousel was handcrafted in 1876 (the horses have real horse hair and glass eyes) and
offers children a taste of entertainment from a Nintendo-free time. While
waiting in line, you can munch on popcorn or cotton candy or slurp a
slush. The waiting area has a number of arcade games. ✉ *Oak Bluffs
Ave.,* ☎ *508/693–9481.* ✉ *Rides $1; $8 for a book of 10.* ☉ *Memorial
Day–Labor Day, daily 10–10; Easter–Memorial Day, weekends 10–5;
Labor Day–Columbus Day, weekdays 11–4:30, weekends 10–5.*

NEED A
BREAK?

The **Coop de Ville** (✉ Dockside Marketplace, Oak Bluffs Harbor, ☎
508/693–3420) often teems with people eager to sample the delecta-
bles from the raw bar and the simple fried seafood. Eat out on the patio
deck overlooking the water—the oysters are fantastic. It's open May
through Columbus Day.

Some like it sweet, and with all its homemade ice cream, the long-
standing local joint **Mad Martha's** (✉ 117 Circuit Ave., ☎ 508/693–
9151) is just the place for a sweet tooth. There's a great jukebox, too.
It's open from May through August and stays open until midnight in July
and August.

★ ❿ Don't miss a look at **Oak Bluffs Camp Ground** (✉ Off Circuit Ave.),
a 34-acre warren of streets tightly packed with more than 300 Car-

penter Gothic Victorian cottages with wedding-cake trim, gaily painted in pastels. As you wander through this fairy-tale setting, imagine it on a balmy summer evening, lit by the warm glow of hundreds of Japanese paper lanterns hung from every cottage porch. This describes the scene on Illumination Night at the end of the Camp Meeting season—attended these days by some fourth- and fifth-generation cottagers. Attendees mark the occasion as they have for more than a century, with lights, song, and open houses for families and friends. Note that because of overwhelming crowds of onlookers in seasons past, the date is not announced until the week before.

⑪ The **Tabernacle,** an impressive open-air structure of iron and wood at the center of Trinity Park, is the original site of the Methodist services. On Wednesdays at 8 PM in season, visitors are invited to join in on an old-time community sing-along. If you know tunes like "The Erie Canal" or just want to listen in, drop by the Tabernacle and take a seat. Also, music books are available for a donation. Sunday services are held in summer at 9:30 AM. The 1878 **Trinity Methodist Church** also stands in the park.

⑫ For a glimpse at life in Cottage City during its heyday, visit the **Cottage Museum,** in an 1868 Creamsicle-hue cottage near the Tabernacle. The two-story museum exhibits cottage furnishings from the early days, including photographs, hooked rugs, quilts, and old Bibles. The gift shop offers Victorian and nautical items. ⊠ *1 Trinity Park,* ☎ *508/693–7784.* 🖃 *$1 donation requested.* ☉ *Mid-June–Sept., Mon.–Sat. 10–4.*

Worth at least a glance, the house known as the **Wooden Valentine** (⊠ 25 Washington Ave.) is quite a sight—just think pink.

⑬ An octagonal, nonsectarian house of worship, **Union Chapel** (⊠ Corner of Kennebec and Samoset Aves., ☎ 508/693–1093) was constructed in 1870 for the Cottage City resort folk who lived outside the Camp Ground's 7-ft-high fence. In summer, concerts are held here, as are 10 AM Sunday services.

⑭ A long stretch of green facing the sea, **Ocean Park** (⊠ Sea View Ave.) fronts a crescent of large shingle-style cottages with numerous turrets, breezy porches, and pastel facades. Band concerts take place at the gazebo here on summer nights, and in August the park hosts hordes of island families and visitors for a grand fireworks display over the ocean.

Dining and Lodging

$$$–$$$$ ✕ **Lola's.** "Where Oak Bluffs meets Edgartown," jokes Lola Domitrovich, and in a way that's true. On the beach road between the towns, Lola's actually is closer to Oak Bluffs in every respect. Boisterous, open 364 days a year (closed only on Christmas), with a huge kitchen, this is the spot for a Mardi Gras crowd. The menu started as pure Louisiana, with standards like jambalaya, but is now getting into things like ribs. The bar is big and welcoming, the wall mural full of familiar local faces. Year-round residents very much appreciate the live music into the dead of winter. ⊠ *Beach Rd., just over 1 mi from Oak Bluffs,* ☎ *508/693–5007. D, MC, V.*

$$$–$$$$ ✕ **Sweet Life Café.** This island favorite, with its warm tones and low
   ★   lighting, will make you feel like you've entered someone's home, but the cooking is more sophisticated than home-style. For proof of this, try the lobster *barigoule* (stuffed in artichokes) or the crispy sweetbread salad with Portobello mushrooms. Main courses have become a bit earthier in the past year, including grilled prime sirloin with a marrow crust. The desserts remain superb. There's outdoor dining by candlelight in a shrub-enclosed garden. ⊠ *Upper Circuit Ave., at the far end of*

town, ☎ *508/696–0200. Reservations essential. AE, D, MC, V. Closed Jan.–Mar.*

$$–$$$ ✕ **Offshore Ale Company.** Buckle down to study the microbrews in this handsome, dark room with big copper vats behind the stand-up bar. The Downtown Nut Brown can be a little too bitter, but the Oak Bluff-berry tastes just fine. Take your own peanuts in a jar by the door and drop the shells on the floor, or eat from a shellfish- and burger-type menu. While some ads talk of oysters in here, actually, there aren't any. ⊠ *30 Kennebec Ave.,* ☎ *508/693–2626. Reservations not accepted. AE, MC, V.*

$$–$$$ ✕ **Smoke 'n Bones.** Opened in 1997, this is the island's only rib joint, with a smoker out back and a cord of hickory, apple, oak, and mesquite wood stacked up around the lot. The place has a cookie-cutter, prefab feeling, with all the appropriate touches like neon flames around the kitchen and marble bones for doorknobs. But it's fun, with details kids can really enjoy, like a hole in each tabletop for a bucket to hold dis-carded ribs. The allusions to pot smoking don't seem to bother anybody, the beer is cold and the mugs are big (although there is no bar), and, as in any good rib spot, there is a thriving take-out business. As the menu says, Bone appetit. ⊠ *Siloam Rd., about 7 blocks from Oak Bluffs,* ☎ *508/696–7427 (RIBS). Reservations not accepted. No credit cards.*

$$ ✕ **Jimmy Sea's.** This place is unabashedly proud of the deep, irresistible fragrance of sautéed garlic rolling out its doors, beckoning to passersby. The only reason to pass by would be the extent of the waiting crowd (reservations are accepted only for eight or more). For eight years, with the sound of Sinatra crooning in the background, Jimmy Sea's has brought to the table generous portions of classic Italian dishes from *von-gole* (whole littleneck clams) marinara to linguine *puttanesca* (spicy tomato sauce with capers, olives, and anchovies). A brightly colored porch and painted ceilings add to the obvious charm of the place. ⊠ *32 Ken-nebec Ave.,* ☎ *508/696–8550. Reservations not accepted. MC, V.*

$$ ✕ **Zapotec Cafe.** Southwest meets Gingerbread at one of the island's sweetest, most cheerful, and unpretentious restaurants. The crowded quarters, dressed in warm Caribbean and fruit colors and strung with chili-pepper Christmas lights, add to its character. On the menu are fine original versions of classic Mexican-American fare. *Tacos de pescado* lays barbecued swordfish over a creamy yogurt sauce in soft flour tortillas. Do not pass up the outstanding mussels Oaxaca, a big bowlful steamed with wine, chipotle peppers, lime, cilantro, and cream. ⊠ *Kennebec Ave.,* ☎ *508/693–6800. Reservations not accepted. AE, MC, V. Closed mid-fall–mid-spring; call for exact months.*

$–$$ ✕ **Chow Baby—Gourmet to Go.** The new kid on the block is a small place with a big counter and an appealing menu. Although focused mostly on takeout and catering, it has a crooked little brick patio with a few tables out front, and indoors there are a few more. Besides daily deli specials like Israeli couscous with black olives, feta, artichokes, and peppers, you can find pasta-less vegetable lasagna or a rosemary roasted pork sandwich with cranberry-mustard mayonnaise. Lunch or dinner gourmet picnic boxes have to be ordered by noon the previous day, party platters and hors d'oeuvres 24 hours in advance. Bring in your own daily catch and they'll even prepare it for you. ⊠ *18 Ken-nebec Ave.,* ☎ *508/696–8494. Reservations not accepted. MC, V. Closed Oct.–May.*

$–$$ ✕ **Linda Jean's.** This is a classic local hangout. Want to eat breakfast at
★ 6 AM? No problem. Want to eat breakfast at 11:30 AM? No problem. Tired of the gourmet world and want something close to good diner food, with comfortable booths, friendly waitresses, and few frills? No prob-lem. The only problem? You may have to wait. ⊠ *34 Circuit Ave.,* ☎ *508/693–4093. Reservations not accepted. No credit cards.*

$–$$ ✕ **Seasons Eatery and Pub.** The somewhat frenetic, young scene here includes quite acceptable food. Dodge the Irish theme night and karaoke and order a B. B. King burger (with blue cheese—get it?), giant nachos, hand-cut fried calamari, or one of the many pasta dishes. Surprisingly, the food arrives with a sophisticated touch to the presentation. Seating is built around the bar, and at last count 11 televisions were up and running around the place. Why does any establishment truly need 11 televisions, especially when you can look at all the beautiful, hand-painted murals of Oak Bluffs instead? ⊠ *19 Circuit Ave.,* ☎ *508/693-7129. AE, D, DC, MC, V.*

$ ✕ **Amity Cafe.** With breakfast always available, the Amity is a good spot for getting the day's most important meal whenever you like. There's a *Jaws* motif, with a "Benchley Breakfast Burrito" and a big shark cruising the wall mural. If you make it through the breakfast "shark attack"— three eggs, choice of bacon, sausage, or ham, pancakes, French toast, home fries, and coffee for $7.95—you may find yourself dead in the water. You can also grab an "Amity stroller" (corn tortilla wrap) for an on-the-hoof lunch. ⊠ *1 Park Ave.,* ☎ *508/696-9922. No credit cards.*

$$$ ▥ **Oak House.** The wraparound veranda of this pastel-painted 1872
★   Victorian looks across a busy street to the beach. Several rooms have private terraces; if you're bothered by noise, ask for a room at the back. Inside, the reason for the inn's name becomes clear: everywhere you look you will see richly patinated oak in ceilings, wall paneling, wainscoting, and furnishings. All this well-preserved wood creates an appropriate setting for the choice antique furniture and nautical-theme accessories. An elegant afternoon tea with cakes and cookies is served in a glassed-in sunporch. With its white wicker, plants, floral-print pillows, and original stained-glass window accents, it's a lovely place to while away the end of the day. ⊠ *75 Sea View Ave., Box 299, 02557,* ☎ *508/693-4187 or 800/245-5979,* ℻ *508/696-7385. 8 rooms, 2 suites. No pets, no smoking, no children under 10. AE, D, MC, V. Closed mid-Oct.–mid-May. CP.*

$$–$$$ ▥ **Admiral Benbow Inn.** Located on a busy road between Vineyard Haven and Oak Bluffs Harbor, and recently spruced up with new paint and a new porch, the Benbow is endearing in its funkiness. The small B&B was built for a minister at the turn of the century, and it is decked out with elaborate woodwork, a comfortable hodgepodge of antique furnishings, and a Victorian parlor with a stunning tile-and-carved-wood fireplace. Guests have access to an ice machine and refrigerator in the kitchen. Next door to the rather drab yard is a gas station, but the price is right, and the location a few blocks from the harbor is convenient. Manager Joyce Dodge serves a Continental-plus breakfast that includes seasonal fruit, yogurt, and homemade cereal. ⊠ *81 New York Ave., Box 2488, 02557,* ☎ *508/693-6825,* ℻ *508/ 693-1131. 6 rooms. No smoking. AE, D, MC, V. CP.*

$$–$$$ ▥ **Dockside Inn.** Just yards from the Oak Bluffs ferry and in the thick of the town's bustle, the modern Dockside is a good bet for folks who want to be close to the action. The pink lobby and rich florals of the rooms might be a bit vivid for some, but the overall ambience is warm. Kids are welcome, and they'll have plenty to do in town and at nearby beaches. Rooms that open onto building-length balconies have air-conditioning, cable TV, and reproduction antique furniture; some have full kitchens or kitchenettes. A small cottage at the back of the main building, the inn's quiet spot, houses two suites (one with hot tub, both with private decks) and a roof-top widow's walk. There's no restaurant here, but several are within walking distance. ⊠ *9 Circuit Ave. Ext., Box 1206, 02557,* ☎ *508/693-2966 or 800/245-5979,* ℻ *508/696-7293. 17 rooms, 5 suites. AE, D, MC, V. Closed late Oct.–Mar. CP.*

$$-$$$ 🏨 **Pequot Hotel.** All the bustle of downtown Oak Bluffs is a pleasant five-minute walk past Carpenter Gothic houses from this casual cedar-shingle inn. The furniture won't win any prizes, but the old wing has a bit more atmosphere and no televisions. In the main section of the building, the first floor has a wide porch with rocking chairs—perfect for getting in some reading and for enjoying coffee or tea with the cookies that are set out in the afternoon—and a small breakfast room where you help yourself to bagels, muffins, and cereal in the morning. The hotel is one block from the beaches that line the Oak Bluffs–Edgartown road. Weekend rates are higher than weekday rates. ⊠ *19 Pequot Ave., 02557,* ☎ *508/693–5087 or 800/947–8704. 29 rooms, 1 3-bedroom apartment. Breakfast room. AE, MC, V. Closed mid-Oct.–Apr. CP.*

$$-$$$ 🏨 **Sea Spray Inn.** In late 1997, Carol Dennis purchased this porch-wrapped Victorian B&B and spiffed it up with new king-size, four-poster feather beds and other personal touches. Room 3's iron-and-brass bed is positioned for viewing the sunrise through five windows draped in lacy curtains, and the cedar-lined bath includes an extra-large shower. A garden-side room has a bed with gauze canopy and a private enclosed porch. The inn is set on a quiet drive circling an open park that borders an ocean beach; public tennis and the beach are within walking distance. ⊠ *2 Naumkeag Ave., Box 2355, 02557,* ☎ *508/693–9388,* FAX *508/696–7765. 6 rooms, 1 suite. No smoking, no children under 12. MC, V. Closed Dec.–Apr. CP.*

$$ 🏨 **Martha's Vineyard Surfside Motel.** These two buildings stand right in the thick of things, so it tends to get noisy in summer. Rooms are spacious and bright (corner rooms more so), and many have been recently upgraded with new carpets, wallpaper, and tile floors; each comes with typical motel furnishings and a table and chairs. Deluxe rooms have water views. Four suites have whirlpool baths, while two are wheelchair-accessible. Midweek rates are reduced by $10–$20. ⊠ *Oak Bluffs Ave., Box 2507, 02557,* ☎ *508/693–2500 or 800/537–3007,* FAX *508/693–7343. 34 rooms, 4 suites. Hot tub. AE, D, MC, V.*

$ 🏨 **Attleboro House.** This guest house, part of the Methodist Association campgrounds, is across the street from bustling Oak Bluffs Harbor. The big 1874 gingerbread Victorian has wraparound verandas on two floors and small, simple rooms with powder-blue walls, lacy white curtains, and a few antiques. Some rooms have sinks. Singles have three-quarter beds, and every room is provided linen exchange but no chambermaid service during a stay. The five shared baths are rustic and old but clean. ⊠ *42 Lake Ave., Box 1564, 02557,* ☎ *508/693–4346. 9 rooms without bath. MC, V. Closed Oct.–mid-May. CP.*

Nightlife and the Arts

Atlantic Connection (⊠ 124 Circuit Ave., ☎ 508/693–7129) offers fancy light and sound systems (including a strobe-lighted dance floor topped by a glitter ball) to highlight live reggae, R&B, funk, and blues.

The **Lampost** (⊠ 111 Circuit Ave., ☎ 508/696–9352), a nightclub and sports bar, is popular with younger crowds.

The **Rare Duck** (⊠ 111 Circuit Ave., ☎ 508/696–9352), next to the Lampost (☞ *above*), is a dark cocktail lounge that occasionally has live music.

The **Ritz Café** (⊠ 109 Circuit Ave., ☎ 508/693–9851), a popular bar with a pool table (off-season) and a jukebox, presents an eclectic mix of live music Monday through Saturday in summer and on weekends in the off-season.

The **Tabernacle** (☞ *above*) is the scene of a popular, old-timey Wednesday-evening community sing-along at 8, as well as other family-oriented entertainment. For a schedule, contact the Camp Meeting Association (⊠ Box 1176, Oak Bluffs 02557, ☎ 508/693–0525).

Sunday-night summer **town band concerts** (☎ 508/693–0085) alternate weeks between the gazebo in Ocean Park on Beach Road in Oak Bluffs and Owen Park in Vineyard Haven.

Outdoor Activities and Sports

BEACHES

Joseph A. Sylvia State Beach, between Oak Bluffs and Edgartown off Beach Road, is a 6-mi-long sandy beach with a view of Cape Cod across Nantucket Sound. The calm, warm water and food vendors make it popular with families. There's parking along the roadside, and the beach is accessible by bike path or shuttle bus.

Oak Bluffs Town Beach, between the steamship dock and the state beach off Sea View Avenue, is a crowded, narrow stretch of calm water on Nantucket Sound, with snack joints, lifeguards, parking, and rest rooms at the steamship office.

BIKING

Anderson's (⊠ Circuit Ave. Ext., ☎ 508/693–9346), on the harbor, rents several different styles of bicycle. **DeBettencourt's** (⊠ Circuit Ave. Ext., ☎ 508/693–0011) rents bikes, mopeds, scooters, and Jeeps. **Harbor Rentals** (⊠ Circuit Ave. Ext., ☎ 508/693–1300) rents several different types of bicycle, as well as mopeds. **Ride-On Mopeds and Bikes** (⊠ Circuit Ave. Ext., ☎ 508/693–2076 or 508/693–4498) rents bicycles and mopeds. **Sun 'n' Fun** (⊠ Lake Ave., ☎ 508/693–5457) rents bikes, cars, and Jeeps.

BOATING

Vineyard Boat Rentals (⊠ Dockside Marketplace, Oak Bluffs Harbor, ☎ 508/693–8476) rents Boston Whalers, Bayliners, and Jet-Skis.

FISHING

Dick's Bait and Tackle (⊠ New York Ave., ☎ 508/693–7669) rents gear, sells accessories and bait, and keeps a current copy of the fishing regulations.

The party boat *Skipper* (⊠ Oak Bluffs Harbor, ☎ 508/693–1238) leaves for deep-sea fishing trips out of Oak Bluffs Harbor in July and August. Reservations are mandatory.

GOLF

Farm Neck Golf Club (⊠ County Rd., ☎ 508/693–3057), a semiprivate club on marsh-rimmed Sengekontacket Pond, has 18 holes in a championship layout and a driving range. Reservations are required 48 hours in advance.

Windfarm Golf Driving Range (⊠ 203 Edgartown–Vineyard Haven Rd., ☎ 508/693–4842) is open daily for duffers in need of a few practice swings. Tees are covered for rainy-day play, and lessons are available.

ICE-SKATING

Martha's Vineyard Arena (⊠ Edgartown–Vineyard Haven Rd., ☎ 508/693–5329) is open mid-July–March.

SCUBA DIVING

Vineyard waters hold a number of sunken ships, among them several schooners and freighters off East Chop and Aquinnah. Visibility is decent, though the water clarity isn't in the same league as that of the Caribbean. Guided dives are the norm.

Vineyard Scuba (⊠ S. Circuit Ave., ☎ 508/693–0288) has diving information and equipment rentals. Certification classes are given; they can also arrange for dive guides.

TENNIS

Tennis is very popular on the island, and at all times reservations are strongly recommended. Hard-surface courts in **Niantic Park** (☎ 508/693–6535) cost a small fee and are open year-round.

Farm Neck Golf Club (⊠ County Rd., ☎ 508/693–9728) is a semiprivate club with four clay tennis courts, lessons, and a pro shop. It's open mid-April through mid-November; reservations are required.

Island Inn Tennis Club (⊠ Beach Rd., ☎ 508/693–6574) has three Har-Tru courts and a pro shop; it's open May–Columbus Day.

Shopping
Book Den East (⊠ New York Ave., ☎ 508/693–3946) is an amazing place to browse and buy, with 20,000 out-of-print, antiquarian, and paperback books housed in an old barn.

Laughing Bear (⊠ 138 Circuit Ave., ☎ 508/693–9342) carries fun children's and women's wear made of Balinese or Indian batiks and other unusual materials, plus jewelry and accessories from around the world.

The **Secret Garden** (⊠ 41 Circuit Ave., ☎ 508/693–4759), set in a yellow gingerbread cottage, sells lace, baby gifts, wicker furniture, and prints.

Tisbury Marketplace (⊠ 31 Beach Rd. between Oak Bluffs and Vineyard Haven) is a collection of crafts and gift shops, a toy store, a music store, a sporting-goods shop, and a pizza parlor.

Edgartown

6 mi southeast of Oak Bluffs, 9 mi southeast of Vineyard Haven via Beach Rd., 8½ mi east of West Tisbury.

Edgartown has long been the Vineyard's toniest town. Ever since Thomas Mayhew, Jr., landed here in 1642 as the Vineyard's first governor, the town has served as the county seat. Plenty of settlers inhabited the area, making it the island's first Colonial settlement, but the town was not officially named until 1652. First called Great Harbour, the town was renamed for political reasons some 30 years later, after the three-year-old son of the Duke of York.

Once a well-to-do whaling town, Edgartown has managed to preserve the elegance of that wealthy era. Lining the streets are 18th- and 19th-century sea captains' houses, many painted white, set among well-manicured gardens and lawns. The uniformity—of both the quality of houses originally built and their current condition—sets Edgartown apart from the two other major Vineyard towns as a sort of museum piece. There are plenty of shops here, as well as other sights and activities to occupy the crowds who walk the streets to see and be seen. A stroll is definitely the best way to absorb it all.

To orient yourself historically before making your way around town, you might want to stop off at a complex of buildings and lawn exhibits ★ ⑮ that constitutes the **Vineyard Museum and Oral History Center.** The opening hours and admission listed below apply to all the buildings and exhibits—including the Thomas Cooke House, the Francis Foster Museum, the Capt. Francis Pease House, and the Carriage Shed—unless otherwise noted. The museum, administered by the Martha's Vineyard Historical Society, sells an excellent Edgartown walking-tour

180

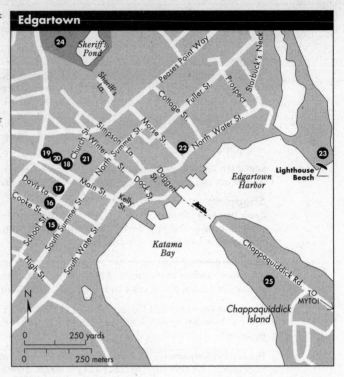

Edgartown

booklet full of anecdotes and the history of the people who have lived in the old houses over the past three centuries. You can purchase it at the entrance gatehouse in summer or at the library in winter. ⊠ *Corner of Cooke and School Sts.,* ☎ *508/627–4441.* ▨ *$6.* ☉ *Mid-June–mid-Oct., Tues.–Sat. 10–5; mid-Oct.–mid-June, Wed.–Fri. 1–4, Sat. 10–4.*

The one Vineyard Museum property open mid-June–mid-October only is the **Thomas Cooke House** (⊠ School St., ☎ 508/627–4441), set in the 1765 home of a customs collector. The house itself is part of the display, evoking the past with its low doorways, wide-board floors, original raised-panel woodwork with fluted pilasters, and hearths in the summer and winter kitchens. Docents conduct tours of the 12 rooms, whose exhibits reveal the island's history with furniture, tools, costumes, portraits, toys, crafts, and various household objects. One room is set up as a 19th-century parlor, illustrating the opulence of the golden age of whaling with such period pieces as a pianoforte. Upstairs are ship models, whaling paraphernalia, old customs documents, and a room tracing the evolution of the Camp Meeting through photographs and objects.

The **Francis Foster Museum** (⊠ School St., ☎ 508/627–4441) houses a small collection of whaling implements, scrimshaw, navigational instruments, and many old photographs. One interesting exhibit is a collection of 19th-century miniature photographs of 110 Edgartown whaling masters, grouped by family. The **Gale Huntington Reference Library** is also in the building, with genealogical records, rare island books, and ships' logs from the whaling days, as well as some publications for sale.

The **Capt. Francis Pease House** (⊠ School St., ☎ 508/627–4441), an 1850s Greek Revival, houses a permanent exhibit of Native American, prehistoric, pre-Columbian, and later artifacts, including arrowheads and pottery, plus changing exhibits from the collection. The Children's Gallery presents changing exhibits created by children, and the museum shop sells books, maps, jewelry, and island crafts.

The **Carriage Shed** (⊠ School St., ☎ 508/627–4441) displays a number of vessels and vehicles, among them a whaleboat, a snazzy 1855 fire engine with stars inlaid in wood, and an 1830 hearse, considerably less ornate than the fire engine. The shed also houses some peculiar gravestones that mark the eternal resting places of an eccentric poet's strangely beloved chickens. In the yard outside are a replica of a 19th-century **brick tryworks,** used to process whale oil from blubber aboard ship, and the 1,008-prism **Fresnel lens** installed in the Aquinnah Lighthouse (☞ Aquinnah, *below*) in 1854 and removed when the light was automated in 1952. Each evening the lens lamp is lighted briefly after sundown. The **tool shed** contains harvesting tools used both on land and at sea in the early 19th century.

⑯ **60 Davis Lane** (not open to the public) is a particularly handsome, white clapboard Greek Revival with black shutters and a fan ornament, surrounded by gardens. It was built in 1825 as a private school.

⑰ A monumental, white Greek Revival fronted with four solid Doric columns, **20 School Street** was built as a Baptist church in 1839. It is now a private residence.

⑱ The **Old Whaling Church** (⊠ 89 Main St., ☎ 508/627–8619 for tour), which opened in 1843 as a Methodist church and is now a performing-arts center (☞ Nightlife and the Arts, *below*), is a massive building with a six-column portico, unusual triple-sash windows, and a 92-ft clock tower that can be seen for miles. The simple, graceful interior is brightened by light from 27-ft-tall windows and still contains the original box pews and lectern. Aside from attending performances, you can get inside only if you join one of the historical walking tours offered by Liz Villard (☞ Contacts and Resources *in* Martha's Vineyard A to Z, *below*).

⑲ A truly elegant sight is the graceful **Dr. Daniel Fisher House** (⊠ 99 Main St.), with a wraparound roof walk, a small front portico with fluted Corinthian columns, and an architecturally economical, elegant side portico with thin fluted columns. It was built in 1840 for one of the island's richest men, who was a doctor, the first president of the Martha's Vineyard National Bank, and the owner of a whale-oil refinery, a spermaceti (whale-oil) candle factory, and a gristmill, among other pursuits. It is interesting to note that the good doctor came to a portion of his fortune through marriage—as a wedding gift, his generous but presumably eccentric father-in-law presented him with the bride's weight in silver. The house is now used for functions and office space, and you can gain access only on Liz Villard's historical walking tours (☞ Contacts and Resources *in* Martha's Vineyard A to Z, *below*).

⑳ The island's oldest dwelling is the 1672 **Vincent House.** It was moved to its present location behind the Dr. Daniel Fisher House (☞ *above*) in 1977, restored, and furnished with pieces that date from the 17th to the 19th century. A tour of this weathered, shingle farmhouse takes you along a time line that starts with the sparse furnishings of the 1600s and ends in a Federal-style parlor of the 1800s. ⊠ Main St., ☎ 508/627–4440. ☞ $3. ⊙ Late May–Oct., Mon.–Sat. 10:30–3.

㉑ A good place to stop for directions or suggestions is the **Edgartown Visitors Center** (⊠ Church St., ☎ no phone), which offers information, rest rooms, and snacks in season.

NEED A
BREAK?

If you need a pick-me-up, pop into **Espresso Love** (⊠ 3 S. Water St., ☎ 508/627–9211) for a cappuccino and a homemade raspberry scone or blueberry muffin. If you prefer something cold, the staff makes fruit smoothies with fruit and apple juice. Light lunch fare is also served: bagel sandwiches, soups, and delicious pastries and cookies—all homemade, of course. (The First Family has been known to make breakfast stops here.)

The architecturally pristine, much-photographed upper part of North Water Street is lined with many fine captains' houses. There's always an interesting detail on this stretch that you never noticed before—like a widow's walk with a mannequin poised, spyglass in hand, watching for her seafaring husband to return. The 1832 house where this piece

㉒ of whimsy can be seen stands at **86 North Water Street,** which the Society for the Preservation of New England Antiquities maintains as a rental property.

㉓ The **Edgartown Lighthouse,** surrounded by a public beach, offers a great view (but seaweedy bathing). The original light guarding the harbor was built in 1828 and set on a little island made of granite blocks. The island was later connected to the mainland by a bridge. By the time the 1938 hurricane made a new light necessary, sand had filled in the gap between the island and the mainland. The current white, cast-iron tower was floated by barge from Ipswich, Massachusetts, in 1938. This area, called Starbuck's Neck, is a good place to wander about and take in views of the ocean, harbor, a little bay, and moorland. ⊠ Off N. Water St. 🎫 $2. ⊙ Late June–late Sept., hr before sunset–hr after sunset.

㉔ A pleasant walking trail circles an old ice pond at the center of **Sheriff's Meadow Sanctuary,** (⊠ Planting Field Way, ☎ 508/693–5207), 17 acres of marsh, woodland, and meadow. One of the area's many wildlife preserves, Sheriff's Meadow contains a variety of habitats.

★ ☙ The Vineyard's conservation areas are a good way to get acquainted with local flora and fauna. The 350-acre **Felix Neck Wildlife Sanctuary,** a Massachusetts Audubon Society preserve 3 mi out of Edgartown toward Oak Bluffs and Vineyard Haven, has 6 mi of hiking trails traversing marshland, fields, oak woods, seashore, and waterfowl and reptile ponds. Nesting ospreys and barn owls also call the sanctuary home. A full schedule of events unfolds throughout the year, including sunset hikes along the beach, explorations of the salt marsh, stargazing, snake or bird walks, snorkeling, canoeing, and more, all led by trained naturalists. An exhibit center has trail maps, aquariums, snake cages, and a gift shop. A bit of summer fun and learning experience combined, the sanctuary's **Fern & Feather Day Camp** is a great way for children to learn about wildlife, plants, and the stars. It offers one- or two-week summer sessions that include overnight camping expeditions. Early registration is advised and begins in February. ⊠ Off Edgartown–Vineyard Haven Rd., ☎ 508/627–4850. 🎫 $3. ⊙ Center mid-June–mid-Sept., daily 8–4; mid-Sept.–mid-June, Tues.–Sun. 9–4. Trails sunrise–7 PM.

Dining and Lodging

$$$$ ✕ **L'étoile.** Perhaps the Vineyard's finest traditional restaurant, L'étoile
★ carries on a long history of excellent dining. Both the food and the setting in the stunning Charlotte Inn (☞ below) are unforgettable. The glass-enclosed dining room reminds you why hunter green, dark wood, and glass became so popular—and imitated. Preparations are at once classic and creative. Not to be missed are a terrine of grilled vegetable appetizer, roasted ivory king salmon with a wonderful horseradish and

scallion crust, and Black Angus sirloin with zinfandel and oyster sauce. The outstanding wine list has selections from California and Europe that are solid, if a little pricey. An outdoor patio is ideal for brunch ($24 prix fixe). During the shoulder seasons (May–mid-June, September) the restaurant's weekday schedule varies. ⊠ *27 S. Summer St.,* ☎ *508/627–5187. Reservations essential. AE, MC, V. Closed Jan.–mid-Feb. and weekdays Oct.–Dec. and late Feb.–Apr. No lunch.*

$$$$ ✕ **Savoir Fare.** With guests from Walter Cronkite to William Styron
★ to President Clinton, Savoir Fare has carved out a reputation as the Vineyard's celebrity favorite. At first glance there's no obvious reason: the big black-and-white diamonds painted on the wood floor are nice but not so special, the buff walls and gauzy white linen can be found everywhere, and even the view of the small garden and patio is island typical. What is it, then? The food! "Summer on a Plate" presents roasted striped bass with ripe peach and tomato jelly, grilled Vidalia onion and basil salad, and handmade potato chips. You can be sure the fish and meat are top quality, but "Salad Like the Chefs Eat" (hot potato salad and cold iceberg lettuce with "salad bar vegetables") is a cute concept that shouldn't cost $9.50. ⊠ *14 Church St., in courtyard opposite Main St.'s town hall,* ☎ *508/627–9864. Reservations essential. AE, MC, V. Closed Nov.–Apr. No lunch.*

$$$–$$$$ ✕ **Alchemy Bistro and Bar.** According to the menu, the dictionary meaning of *alchemy* is "a magic power having as its asserted aim the discovery of a panacea and the preparation of the elixir of longevity"— high goals for yet another French-style bistro. This high-class version has elegant gray wainscoting, classic paper-covered white tablecloths, old wooden floors, and an opening cut into the ceiling to reveal the second-floor tables. The only things missing are the patina of age, experience, cigarette smoke—and French working folk's prices. The same people own Savoir Fare, so you can expect quality and imagination. One example is a cumin-crusted halibut with roasted yucca and watercress. The alcohol list, long and complete, includes cognacs, grappas, and beers. ⊠ *71 Main St.,* ☎ *508/627–9999. AE, MC, V.*

$$$ ✕ **The Navigator.** This is Edgartown's version of big: a big room with a big view of big boats, with a big menu, a big patio, a big blue awning, and a big bar. None of this comes, of course, without paying big prices for basic seafood. It's not a bad place to get a big boiled lobster. Probably the best time to visit is for a big Bloody Mary late in the afternoon. ⊠ *2 Main St.,* ☎ *508/627–4320. AE, D, DC, MC, V. Closed mid-Oct.–Apr.*

$$ ✕ **Seafood Shanty.** The best lure here is the beautiful, panoramic harbor view. On the lunch menu, look for the blackened bluefish special. The seafood chili has various shellfish simmering in a spicy stock; it's more of a stew than chili, and the better for it. Come dinnertime there probably are better options than eating at this restaurant. If you're here in the evening between June and Labor Day, head upstairs to the pub for a light menu and entertainment—perhaps some live music. ⊠ *31 Dock St.,* ☎ *508/627–8622. Reservations not accepted. AE, MC, V. Closed mid-Sept.–mid-May.*

$–$$ ✕ **Lattanzi's Pizzeria.** Albert and Cathy Lattanzi's big brick oven gets fired up by 2:30 PM, and the pizza that slides out come evening is delicious—baby clams with plum tomatoes, oregano, spinach, roasted garlic, and Asiago cheese is just one example. A Tuscan landscape mural with Bacchus presiding over his harvest circles the walls; you'll be able to salute him year-round. ⊠ *Old Post Office Sq.,* ☎ *508/627–9084. AE, D, DC, MC, V. No lunch.*

$–$$ ✕ **Newes from America.** Sometimes a nearly subterranean, darkened scene feels right on a hot summer afternoon, in which case the Newes is the perfect spot for an informal lunch or dinner. Inside, there's plenty of wood and greenery, and many things "olde." The food is mostly Americana (burgers and fries), though some dishes like "Roquefort stilettos" (French bread, Roquefort cheese, and bacon) have made their way onto the menu. There's a massively inclusive list of microbrew beers, and the staff is well equipped to make recommendations. Once again named the best local bar-pub by the readers of the *Vineyard Gazette,* the Newes returns the vote of confidence by staying open from 11 AM until midnight every single day of the year except Christmas. ⊠ *23 Kelly St.,* ☎ *508/627–4397. Reservations not accepted. AE, D, MC, V.*

$ ✕ **Edgartown Deli.** A no-frills place with a down-home, happy feeling, this deli has walls and a glass counter plastered with specials written on multicolored paper. Brightly lighted booths fill one side of the room, while customers line up at the counter for orders to go. Breakfast specials served from 8 until 10:45 include egg, cheese, and *linguiça* (garlicky Portuguese sausage) "deli Macs," and two eggs on a roll. At lunch, look for sandwiches with corned beef and swiss, roast beef, turkey, pastrami, or steak and cheese. ⊠ *52 Main St.,* ☎ *508/627–4789. Reservations not accepted. No credit cards. Closed Nov.–Apr. No dinner.*

$$$$ ✕🏨 **Charlotte Inn.** From the moment you walk up to the dark-wood Scottish barrister's desk at check-in you'll be surrounded by the trappings
★ and customs of a bygone era. Guests' names are handwritten into the register by the dignified and attentive staff. Beautiful antique furnishings, *objets,* and paintings fill the property—the book you pick up in your room might be an 18th-century edition of Voltaire, and your bed could be a hand-carved four-poster. All rooms have hair dryers, phones, robes, and (except for one room) TVs. This elegant atmosphere extends to the outstanding restaurant L'étoile (☞ *above*). ⊠ *27 S. Summer St., 02539,* ☎ *508/627–4751,* FAX *508/627–4652. 23 rooms and 2 suites in 5 buildings. Restaurant. No children under 14. AE, MC, V. CP.*

$$$$ 🏨 **Harbor View Hotel.** The centerpiece of this historic hotel is a gray-shingle 1891 Victorian building with wraparound veranda and a
★ gazebo. Accommodations are also in a complex of buildings in the rear that take up a great chunk of a residential neighborhood a few minutes from downtown. Town houses have cathedral ceilings, decks, kitchens, and large living areas with sofa beds. Rooms in other buildings, however, very much resemble upscale motel rooms, so ask for main-building or town-house rooms for more colorful lodgings. A beach, good for walking, stretches ¾ mi from the hotel's dock, and the sheltered bay is a great place for kids to swim. The hotel also has a cigar bar. Packages and theme weekends, as well as rooms with kitchenettes, are available. ⊠ *131 N. Water St., Box 7, 02539,* ☎ *508/627–7000 or 800/225–6005,* FAX *508/627–8417. 102 rooms, 22 suites. Restaurant, room service, pool, 2 tennis courts, dock, laundry service, concierge. AE, DC, MC, V.*

$$$$ 🏨 **Kelley House.** At the center of town, this sister property of the Harbor View (☞ *above*) combines services and amenities with a country-inn feel. The 1742 white clapboard main house and the adjacent Garden House are surrounded by pink roses; inside, the decor is an odd mix of country French and Shaker. Large suites in the Chappaquiddick House and the two spacious town houses with full kitchens in the Wheel House have porches (most with harbor views) and living rooms. All guest rooms have cable TVs, phones, and air-conditioning. The 1742 pub, with original hand-hewn timbers and ballast-brick walls, serves light fare and microbrewed beers on tap. ⊠ *23 Kelly St., Box 37, 02539,* ☎ *508/627–7900 or 800/225–6005,* FAX *508/627–8142. 42 rooms, 9 suites, 2 town-house units. Pub, pool, 2 tennis courts, babysitting, laundry service. AE, DC, MC, V. Closed Nov.–Apr. CP.*

$$$$ ⊞ **Mattakesett.** The Mattakesett resort recently purchased the inn next door and redubbed it the Winnetu. Now the resort complex consists of individually owned three- and four-bedroom homes and studios or one- to three-bedroom condominiums, all within walking distance of South Beach. Both sets of accommodations share facilities, including a restaurant. All Mattakesett units are spacious, sleep eight, and have phones, full kitchens with dishwashers, washer-dryers, fireplaces, and decks (some with bay and ocean views). The children's programs and facilities have been expanded, and the pool and barbecue grills add to the family atmosphere. Bookings at Mattakessett are taken on a per-week basis only and at Winnetu for a minimum of three nights. To book, call the off-island reservations number weekdays. ⊠ *Katama Rd., 02539,* ☎ *508/627–8920,* 𝔽𝔸𝕏 *508/627–7015; reservations c/o* ⊠ *Stanmar Corp., 130 Boston Post Rd., Sudbury, MA 01776,* ☎ *978/443–1733,* 𝔽𝔸𝕏 *978/443–0479. 92 units at Mattakesett, 23 units at Winnetu. Restaurant, 2 pools, 8 tennis courts, aerobics, children's programs (ages 3–teens). No credit cards. Closed Columbus Day– Memorial Day.*

$$$$ ⊞ **Shiverick Inn.** Innkeepers Denny and Marty Turmelle add warmth
★ and a sense of humor to the elegance of this inn, set in a striking 1840 house with mansard roof and cupola. Rooms are airy and bright, with high ceilings, lots of windows, American and English antiques, and rich fabrics and wallpapers. Beds are mostly queen-size with canopies or carved four-posters. Several rooms have fireplaces or woodstoves. Breakfast is served in a lovely summerhouse-style room with a wood-burning fireplace. There's a library with cable TV and a stereo, and a flagstone garden patio. The inn is about a five-minute walk from the heart of downtown. ⊠ *5 Peases Point Way, at Pent La., Box 640, 02539,* ☎ *508/627–3797 or 800/723–4292,* 𝔽𝔸𝕏 *508/627–8441. 10 rooms. No smoking, no children under 12. AE, D, MC, V. CP.*

$$$$ ⊞ **Tuscany Inn.** Inspired by the eponymous region, the Tuscany Inn manages to combine European sophistication and New England style, rather like an Italian villa with Victorian leanings. Rooms are decorated with fine fabrics and treasures that the owners have collected. The inn has king, queen, or twin accommodations; some baths have whirlpool tubs and harbor views. Guests can mingle in front of the fire in the parlor, read a book out on the wicker-furnished veranda, or sip cappuccino and munch on homemade biscotti on the patio in the side yard, surrounded by lovely gardens and twinkling white lights. Breakfast, which may include frittatas, fresh-baked bread, and fresh fruit, is a highlight, and dining in the intimate La Cucina restaurant will make you feel as if you're in Italy. ⊠ *22 N. Water St., Box 2428, 02539,* ☎ *508/627–5999,* 𝔽𝔸𝕏 *508/627–6605. 8 rooms. AE, DC, MC, V. Closed Jan.–Mar. BP.*

$$$–$$$$ ⊞ **Harborside Inn.** Right on the harbor, with boat docks at the end of a nicely landscaped lawn, the large inn offers a central town location, harbor-view decks, and plenty of amenities. Seven two- and three-story buildings sprawl around formal rose beds, brick walkways, a brick patio, and a pool. Rooms have Colonial-style furnishings, brass beds and lamps, and textured wallpapers. ⊠ *3 S. Water St., Box 67, 02539,* ☎ *508/ 627–4321 or 800/627–4009,* 𝔽𝔸𝕏 *508/627–7566. 89 rooms, 3 suites. Pool, hot tub, sauna. AE, MC, V.*

$$$–$$$$ ⊞ **Victorian Inn.** White with the classic black shutters of the town's historic homes, and fronted by ornate columns, this appropriately named inn a block from the downtown harbor area was built as the home of 19th-century whaling captain Lafayette Rowley. Today the inn's three floors are done in dark woods and bold floral wallpapers, with rugs over wood floors. Several rooms hold handmade reproduction four-poster beds, while others have quiet vestibules and balconies;

the French doors of Number 11 open for wide views of the harbor and Chappaquiddick Island. Breakfast, served in season in the brick-patio garden, consists of four courses including creative muffins and breads, and a glass of cream sherry greets all arrivals. ⊠ *24 S. Water St., 02539,* ☎ *508/627–4784. 14 rooms. No children under 8. MC, V. BP.*

$$$ ✸ **Colonial Inn.** The inn, part of a busy downtown complex of shops, ★ is perfect if you like having modern conveniences and being at the center of the action. It was built in 1911 but doesn't have the same antique quality as the sea captains' houses. Rooms are decorated in soft floral peaches and pastel blues, with white pine furniture, wall-to-wall carpeting, and brass beds and lamps. Each has a good-size bath, and suites come with a sofa bed; the cable TV system has recently been upgraded. One common fourth-floor deck has a superb view of the harbor, as do some rooms. Holiday theme weekends, celebrating Halloween and Thanksgiving, are family-friendly. ⊠ *38 N. Water St., Box 68, 02539,* ☎ *508/ 627–4711 or 800/627–4701,* FAX *508/627–5904. 39 rooms, 2 suites, 2 efficiencies. Restaurant. AE, MC, V. Closed Dec.–Apr. CP.*

$$$ ✸ **Daggett House.** The flower-bordered lawn that separates the main ★ house from the harbor makes a great retreat after a day of exploring town, a minute away. All four inn buildings—the main 1660 Colonial house, the Captain Warren house across the street, the Henry Lyman Thomas house around the corner, and a three-room cottage between the main house and the water—are decorated with fine wallpapers, antiques, and reproductions (including some canopy beds). Much of the buildings' historical ambience has been preserved, including a secret stairway that's now a private entrance to an upstairs guest room. The Widow's Walk Suite has a full kitchen and a private roof walk with a superb water view and a hot tub. Six other rooms have kitchenettes, and another has a hot tub; some have TVs. Breakfast and dinner are served in the 1750 tavern. ⊠ *59 N. Water St., Box 1333, 02539,* ☎ *508/627–4600 or 800/946–3400,* FAX *508/627–4611. 27 rooms, 4 suites. No smoking. AE, D, MC, V.*

$$$ ✸ **Edgartown Commons.** This condominium complex of seven buildings, which includes an old house and motel units around a busy pool, is just a couple of blocks from town. Studios and one- or two-bedroom units all have full kitchens, and some are very spacious. Each has been decorated by its individual owner, so the decor varies—some have an older look, while some are new and bright (none have phones). Definitely family-oriented, the place buzzes with lots of kids, and units away from the pool are quieter. ⊠ *20 Peases Point Way, Box 1293, 02539,* ☎ *508/627–4671,* FAX *508/627–4271. 35 units. Picnic area, pool, playground, coin laundry. AE, D, MC, V. Closed Nov.–Apr.*

Nightlife and the Arts

Throughout the year, lectures, classic films, concerts, plays, and other events are held at the **Old Whaling Church** (⊠ 89 Main St., ☎ 508/ 627–4442); watch the papers, or check the kiosk out front.

Outdoor Activities and Sports

BEACHES

Some lovely beaches are on nearby Chappaquiddick Island (☞ *below*).

Bend-in-the-Road Beach (⊠ Beach Rd.), Edgartown's town beach, is a protected area marked by floats adjacent to Joseph A. Sylvia State Beach. Backed by low, grassy dunes and wild roses, Bend-in-the-Road has calm, shallow waters; some parking; and lifeguards. It is on the shuttle-bus and bike routes.

South Beach (⊠ Katama Rd.), also called Katama Beach, is the island's largest and most popular. A 3-mi ribbon of sand on the Atlantic, it sustains strong surf and occasional riptides, so check with the lifeguards before swimming. There is limited parking.

BIKING

Several bike paths lace through the Edgartown area, including a path to Oak Bluffs that has a spectacular view of Sengekontacket Pond on one side and Nantucket Sound on the other.

R. W. Cutler Bike (⊠ 1 Main St., ☎ 508/627–4052) rents and repairs all types of bicycles. **Triangle** (⊠ Upper Main St., ☎ 508/627–7099) has bicycles available for rent. **Wheelhappy** (⊠ 8 S. Water St., ☎ 508/627–5928) rents bicycles and will deliver them to you.

FISHING

The annual **Martha's Vineyard Striped Bass & Bluefish Derby** (⊠ Box 2101, Edgartown 02539, ☎ 508/693–0728), from mid-September to mid-October, offers daily, weekly, and derby prizes for striped bass, bluefish, bonito, and false albacore catches, from boat or shore. The derby is a real Vineyard tradition, cause for loyal devotion among locals who drop everything to cast their lines at all hours of day and night in search of that prizewinning whopper.

One of the most popular spots for surf casting is **Wasque Point** on Chappaquiddick Island (☞ Chappaquiddick Island, *below*).

Big Eye Charters (☎ 508/627–3649) offers fishing charters that leave from Edgartown Harbor.

Coop's Bait and Tackle (⊠ 147 W. Tisbury Rd., ☎ 508/627–3909) sells accessories and bait, rents fishing gear, and keeps a current listing of fishing regulations.

Larry's Tackle Shop (⊠ 141 Main St., ☎ 508/627–5088) rents gear and sells accessories and bait and has a copy of the fishing regulations.

Slapshot II (☎ 508/627–8087) is available for fishing charters from Edgartown Harbor.

RECREATION AREAS

Edgartown Recreation Area (⊠ Robinson Rd., ☎ 508/627–7574) has five tennis courts, a basketball court, a softball field, a roller hockey court, a picnic area, and playground equipment. Activities (published in local papers) include tennis round-robins, softball and basketball games, arts and crafts, and rainy-day events. Also see the "Island Recreation" section of the *Vineyard Gazette*'s calendar for open Frisbee, rugby, and other games.

TENNIS

Since tennis is so popular on the island, reservations are usually necessary for the hard-surface courts at the **Edgartown Recreation Area** (☞ *above*). There's a small fee, and the courts are open year-round.

Shopping

Bickerton & Ripley Books (⊠ Main St., ☎ 508/627–8463) carries a wide selection of current and island-related titles.

Brickman's (⊠ 33 Main St., ☎ 508/627–4700) sells beach and sports gear, such as camping, fishing, and snorkeling equipment, and boogie boards. It also carries sportswear, surf-style clothing, and major-label footwear for the family.

The **Colonial Inn Shops** (⊠ 38 N. Water St., ☎ 508/627–4711) sell art, crafts, pottery, and sports gear.

Edgartown Scrimshaw Gallery (⊠ 17 N. Water St., ☎ 508/627–9439) showcases a large collection of scrimshaw, including some antique pieces, as well as Nantucket lightship baskets and 14-karat lightship-basket jewelry.

The **Fligors** (⊠ 27 N. Water St., ☎ 508/627–4722) is the closest thing to a department store on the island, with varied offerings, including preppy clothing and a Christmas shop.

The **Gallery Shop** (⊠ 20 S. Summer St., ☎ 508/627–8508) has 19th- and 20th-century oils and watercolors, including English sporting prints, marine art, and works by major local artists, plus small English antiques.

Nevin Square (⊠ Winter St., ☎ no phone), a minimall, has shops that sell leather, clothing, art, antiques, and crafts.

Optional Art (⊠ 35 Winter St., ☎ 508/627–5373) carries fine jewelry mostly in 18-karat gold, handcrafted by 30 award-winning American artisans.

Vivian Wolfe Antiques (⊠ 42 Main St., ☎ 508/627–5822) offers antique and estate jewelry, as well as antique silver tea services and the like.

Willoughby's (⊠ 12 N. Water St., ☎ 508/627–3369) displays mostly island landscapes and scenes by Vineyard and Cape artists, including limited-edition prints and drawings.

Chappaquiddick Island

㉕ *6 mi southeast of Oak Bluffs, across the bay from Edgartown.*

A sparsely populated area with a great number of nature preserves, Chappaquiddick Island makes for a pleasant day trip or bike ride on a sunny day. If you are interested in covering a lot of it, cycling is the best way to go. The island is actually connected to the Vineyard by a long sand spit from South Beach in Katama—a spectacular 2¾-mi walk if you have the energy. If not, the On Time ferry (☞ Getting Around *in* Martha's Vineyard A to Z, *below*) makes the short trip from Edgartown across from 7 AM to midnight in season. The ferry departs every five minutes or so but posts no schedule, thereby earning its name—technically, it cannot be late.

The Land Bank's 41-acre **Brine's Pond** (⊠ Off Chappaquiddick Rd.) is a popular, scenic picnicking spot. Mown grasses surround a serpentine pond with an island in its center and a woodland backdrop behind—a truly lovely setting.

★   The Trustees of Reservations' 14-acre **Mytoi** preserve is a quiet, Japanese-inspired garden with a creek-fed pool, spanned by a bridge and rimmed with Japanese maples, azaleas, and irises. The garden was created in 1958 by a private citizen. Rest-room facilities are available. ⊠ *Dyke Rd., ⅛ mi from intersection with Chappaquiddick Rd.,* ☎ *508/693–7662.* 🎫 *Free.* ☉ *Daily sunrise–sunset.*

At the end of Dyke Road is **Dyke's Bridge,** infamous as the scene of the 1969 accident in which a young woman died in a car driven by Ted Kennedy. The rickety bridge has been replaced, after having been dismantled in 1991, but for ecological reasons, vehicle access over it is limited. The **Cape Poge Wildlife Refuge** (☞ *below*), which includes the spectacular **East Beach** and the **Cape Poge Light,** is across the bridge.

The **Poucha Pond Reservation,** near the southeast corner of the island, encompasses 99 acres of varied environments. Its trails wander among shady pitch pine and oak forests and around a marshy pond on one-time farmland. One trail end has a great view of the pond, the Dyke

Bridge, and the East Beach dunes in the distance. Bring binoculars for the birds—terns, various herons, gulls, plovers—and repellent for the mosquitoes. ⊠ *4 mi from Chappaquiddick ferry landing,* ☎ *508/627–7141.* ▨ *Free.* ☉ *Daily sunrise–sunset.*

A conglomeration of habitats where you can swim, walk, fish, or just sit and enjoy the surroundings, the **Cape Poge Wildlife Refuge** (⊠ East end of Dyke Rd., 3 mi from the Chappaquiddick ferry landing), on the easternmost shore of Chappaquiddick Island, is more than 6 square mi of wilderness. Its dunes, woods, cedar thickets, moors, salt marshes, ponds, tidal flats, and barrier beach serve as an important migration stopover and nesting area for numerous sea and shore birds. The best way to get to the refuge is as part of a naturalist-led **Jeep drive** (☎ 508/627–3599). You can also get there from Wasque Reservation (☞ *below*) on the south shore of the island. You'll need a four-wheel-drive vehicle to do that, and to get to much of the acreage. The Trustees of Reservations requires an annual permit ($70–$110) for a four-wheel drive, available on-site or through Coop's Bait and Tackle (☞ Outdoor Activities and Sports *in* Edgartown, *above*).

★ The 200-acre **Wasque Reservation** (pronounced "*wayce*-kwee"), mostly a vast beach, connects Chappaquiddick "Island" with the mainland of the Vineyard in Katama, closing off the south end of Katama Bay. You can fish, sunbathe, take the trail by Swan Pond, walk to the island's southeasternmost tip at Wasque Point, or dip into the surf—with caution, as there are strong currents. **Wasque Beach** is accessed by a flat boardwalk with benches overlooking the west end of Swan Pond. It's a pretty walk skirting the pond, with ocean views on one side and poles for osprey nests on the other. Atop a bluff is a pine-shaded picnic grove with a spectacular, practically 180-degree panorama. Below, Swan Pond teems with bird life, including the requisite swans, in the surrounding marsh and beach grasses. Beyond that lie beach, sky, and boat-dotted sea. From the grove, a long boardwalk leads down amid the grasses to **Wasque Point,** a prime surf-casting spot for bluefish and stripers. Rest rooms and drinking water are available. *Located at east end of Wasque Rd., 5 mi from Chappaquiddick ferry landing,* ☎ *508/627–7260.* ▨ *Cars $3, plus $3 per adult, Memorial Day–mid-Sept.; free rest of yr.* ☉ *Property 24 hrs. Gatehouse Memorial Day–Columbus Day, daily 9–5.*

Outdoor Activities and Sports
East Beach, one of the area's best beaches, is accessible by car from Chappaquiddick Road to Dyke Road, or by boat or Jeep from the Wasque Reservation (☞ *above*). It has heavy surf, good bird-watching, and relative isolation in a lovely setting. There is a $3 fee to enter the beach.

Wasque Beach, at the Wasque Reservation (☞ *above)*, is an uncrowded ½-mi sandy beach with sometimes strong surf and currents, a parking lot, and rest rooms.

UP-ISLAND

Much of what makes the Vineyard special is found in its rural reaches, in the agricultural heart of the island and the largely undeveloped lands south and west of the Vineyard Haven to Edgartown line. Country roads meander through woods and tranquil farmland, and dirt side roads lead past crystalline ponds, abandoned cranberry bogs, and conservation lands. In Chilmark, West Tisbury, and Aquinnah, nature lovers, writers, artists, and others have established close, ongoing summer communities. In winter, the isolation and bitter winds generally send even year-round Vineyarders from their Up-Island homes to places in the cozier Down-Island towns.

West Tisbury

26 *6½ mi southwest of Vineyard Haven, 12 mi northeast of Aquinnah.*

Founded in the 1670s by settlers from Edgartown, among them the son of Myles Standish and the son-in-law of the *Mayflower* Aldens, West Tisbury was known for its first 200 Westernized years simply as Tisbury. Among the settlement's advantages over Down-Island outposts, most important was a strong-flowing stream that ran into a pond, creating a perfect mill site—a rare thing on the Vineyard. A gristmill was built and a community developed. Farming, especially sheep farming, became Tisbury's mainstay.

West Tisbury has retained its rural appeal and maintains its agricultural tradition at several active horse and produce farms. The town center looks very much the small New England village, complete with a white, steepled church. Half the 5,146-acre Manuel F. Correllus State Forest lies within the town limits.

The weekly **West Tisbury Farmers' Market**—Massachusetts' largest— is held Wednesdays and Saturdays in summer at the 1859 **Old Agricultural Hall** (⊠ South Rd., ☎ 508/693–9549), near the town hall. The colorful stands overflow with fresh produce, most of it organic—a refreshing return to life before fluorescent-lighted, impersonal supermarkets (☞ Shopping, *below*).

Built in 1996, the **New Ag Hall** (⊠ 35 Panhandle Rd., ☎ 508/693–9549), about a mile from the Old Agricultural Hall (☞ *above*), is the setting for various shows, lectures, dances, and potluck dinners. A yearly county fair—including a woodsman contest, dog show, games, baked goods and jams for sale, and, of course, livestock- and produce-judging— is held here in late August (☞ Festivals and Seasonal Events *in* Chapter 1).

A rich and expansive collection of flora and serene walking trails are the attractions of the **Polly Hill Arboretum.** A horticulturist and part-time Vineyard resident, Polly Hill, now in her 90s, has over the years tended some 2,000 species of plants and developed nearly 100 species herself on her old sheep farm in West Tisbury. On site are azaleas, tree peonies, dogwoods, hollies, lilacs, magnolias, and more. Hill raised them from seeds without the use of a greenhouse, and her patience is the inspiration of the arboretum. Now run as a non-profit center, the arboretum also offers guided tours, a lecture series, and a visitor center and gift shop. ⊠ 809 State Rd., ☎ 508/693–9426. ☜ $5. ☉ Thurs.–Tues. 7–7; visitor center Memorial Day–early Oct.

An unusual sight awaits at the **Field Gallery** (⊠ State Rd., ☎ 508/693–5595), where Tom Maley's ponderous white sculptures, such as a Colonial horse and rider or a whimsical piper, are displayed on a wide lawn. Inside there are changing summer exhibitions of island artists' work, which is for sale.

Music Street, named for the numerous parlor pianos bought with the whaling money of successful sea captains, is lined with the oldest houses in West Tisbury.

NEED A BREAK?   Step back in time with a visit to **Alley's General Store** (⊠ State Rd., ☎ 508/693–0088), the heart of town since 1858. Alley's sells a truly general variety of goods: everything from hammers and housewares and dill pickles to all those great things you find only in a country store. The

Martha's Vineyard Preservation Trust purchased the building in 1993 and beautified it, preserving its rural character. Behind the parking lot, Back Alley's (☎ 508/693–7367) serves tasty sandwiches and pastries to go year-round.

The **Mill Pond** (✉ Edgartown–West Tisbury Rd.) is a lovely spot graced with swans—at the right time of year you might see a cygnet with the swan couple. The small building nearest the pond has been a grammar school, an icehouse, and most recently a police station, until a larger station house opened. The mill stands across the road. Originally a gristmill, it opened in 1847 to manufacture island wool for pea coats, which whalers wore. The Martha's Vineyard Garden Club uses the building now. The pond is just around the corner from the town center on the way toward Edgartown.

㉗ Its limbs twisting into the sky and along the ground, the **Old Oak Tree** stands near the intersection of State and North roads. This massive, much-loved member of the *quercus* family is thought to be about 150 years old, and it's a perennial subject for nature photographers.

The **Martha's Vineyard Glassworks** (✉ 529 State Rd., N. Tisbury, ☎ 508/693–6026) offers a chance to watch glass being blown—a fascinating process—by glassmakers who have pieces displayed in Boston's Museum of Fine Arts. Their work is also for sale.

West Tisbury has a wealth of conservation areas, each of them unique. A paradise for bird-watchers, **Sepiessa Point Reservation,** a Land Bank–Nature Conservancy property, consists of 164 acres on splendid Tisbury Great Pond, with expansive pond and ocean views, walking trails around coves and saltwater marshes, bird-watching, horse trails, swimming, and a boat launch. On the pond beach, watch out for razor-sharp oyster shells. Beaches across the pond along the ocean are privately owned. ✉ *New La., which becomes Tiah's Cove Rd., off W. Tisbury Rd.,* ☎ *508/627–7141.* 🎫 *Free.* ☉ *Daily sunrise–sunset.*

Long Point, a 633-acre Trustees of Reservations preserve with an open area of grassland and heath, provides a lovely walk with the promise of a refreshing swim at its end. The area is bounded on the east by freshwater Homer's Pond, on the west by saltwater West Tisbury Great Pond, and on the south by fantastic, mile-long South Beach on the Atlantic Ocean. Tisbury Great Pond and Long Cove Pond, a sandy freshwater swimming pond, are ideal spots for bird-watchers. Drinking water and a rest-room facility are available. Arrive early on summer days if you're coming by car, since the lot fills quickly. The Trustees of Reservations(☎ 508/693–7392) organizes informative and fun two-hour canoe trips through the reserve. Call ahead to reserve a spot on one of the two trips per day (Friday–Tuesday). ✉ *Mid-June–mid-Sept., turn left onto the unmarked dirt road (Waldron's Bottom Rd., look for mailboxes) ⁷⁄₁₀ mi west of airport on Edgartown–West Tisbury Rd.; at end, follow signs to Long Point parking lot. Mid-Sept.-mid-June, follow unpaved Deep Bottom Rd. (1 mi west of airport) 2 mi to lot.* ☎ *508/693–3678.* 🎫 *Mid-June–mid-Sept., $7 per vehicle, $3 per adult; free rest of yr.* ☉ *Daily 9–6.*

★ **㉘** A rather unique island undertaking, the **Winery at Chicama Vineyards** is the fruit of the Mathiesen family's labors. From 3 acres of trees and rocks, George—a broadcaster from San Francisco—his wife, Cathy, and their six children have built a fine vineyard. They started in 1971 with 18,000 vinifera vines, and today the winery produces nearly 100,000 bottles a year from chardonnay, cabernet, and other European grapes. Chenin Blanc, merlot, and a cranberry dessert wine are among their 10 or more tasty varieties. A shop selling their wine, along with herbed

Up-Island

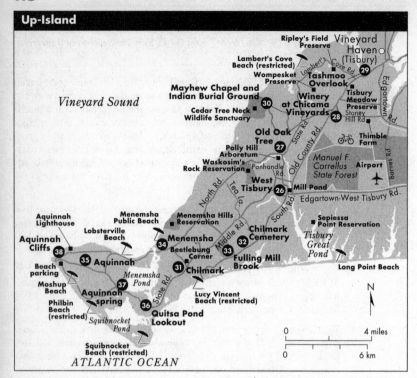

vinegars, mustards, jellies, and other foods prepared on the premises, is open year-round. A Christmas shop with glassware, gift baskets, wreaths, and wine-related items is open mid-November through New Year's Eve. ⊠ *Stoney Hill Rd.,* ☎ *508/693–0309.* 🎫 *Free tours and tastings.* ☉ *Memorial Day–Columbus Day, Mon.–Sat. 11–5, Sun. 1– 5; call for off-season hrs and tastings.*

In season you can pick your own strawberries and raspberries at **Thimble Farm,** where you can also buy pre-boxed fruit if you're not feeling quite so agrarian. The farm also sells cut flowers, melons, pumpkins, hydroponic tomatoes, and other produce. ⊠ *Stoney Hill Rd.,* ☎ *508/693–6396.* ☉ *June–early Oct., Tues.–Sun. 10–5.*

㉙ Just outside the center of Vineyard Haven, on the way to West Tisbury, the **Tashmoo Overlook** (⊠ State Rd. and Spring St.) surveys a public meadow leading down to Lake Tashmoo and Vineyard Sound beyond. Across the lane from the meadow is the amphitheater where summer Vineyard Playhouse productions are held.

NEED A BREAK?	In a little dale on the way out of Vineyard Haven you'll find the **Scottish Bakehouse** (⊠ State Rd., ☎ 508/693–1873), which has long fed islanders with breads, desserts, and pastries of all kinds. You can also pick up Scotch meat pies, jams and jellies, pickles, and chutneys here, and the shortbread is to die for.

One of the rare meadows open for hiking on the island, the 83-acre **Tisbury Meadow Preserve** (⊠ Trailhead on east side of State Rd., ½ mi south of Tashmoo Overlook) isn't being farmed but is mowed to keep it from reverting to woodland. An old farmstead sits on the property, and the back acres are wooded except for an 18th-century cart path. You can walk Tisbury Meadow in less than an hour or combine it with two other areas, the Wompesket and Ripley's Fields preserves across State Road, for a longer hike.

Ripley's Field Preserve (⊠ John Hoft Rd., off north end of Lambert's Cove Rd., ⅔ mi from State Rd.) gives an idea of what the island must have looked like 200 years ago. The 56-acre preserve spreads over undulating, glacier-formed meadows and woodland. A windmill and wildflowers are pleasant attractions. The preserve connects via old cart paths to Tisbury Meadow and Wompesket preserves in North Tisbury. A parking area and bike rack are on the left.

Bordering part of Merry Farm, **Wompesket Preserve** (⊠ Red Coat Hill Rd.) includes an interesting wet meadow and ponds that are good for birding. The walk to the 18-acre area overlooks the farm and the Atlantic in the distance. To get here, follow marked dirt roads from Ripley's Field or Tisbury Meadow Preserve.

30 Deep in the woods off a dirt road, the **Mayhew Chapel and Indian Burial Ground** (⊠ Off Indian Hill Rd., off State Rd.) are suffused with history. The tiny chapel, built in 1829 to replace an earlier one, and a memorial plaque are dedicated to the pastor Thomas Mayhew, Jr., leader of the original colonists who landed at Edgartown in 1642. Mayhew was a relatively enlightened man, noted for his fair dealings with the local Wampanoags. Within a few years, he had converted a number of them to Christianity. Called Praying Indians, they established a community here called Christiantown.

An overgrown wildflower garden grows near the chapel. Beyond the boulder with the plaque are rough-hewn stones marking Native American grave mounds—the dead are not named, for fear of calling down evil spirits. Behind the chapel is the beginning of a loop trail through the woods, which leads to a lookout tower. You'll find a map at the first trail fork.

Cedar Tree Neck Wildlife Sanctuary, 300 hilly acres of unspoiled West Tisbury woods managed by the Sheriff's Meadow Foundation, consists of varied environments, including a sphagnum bog and a pond. The sanctuary has interesting flora, including bayberry and swamp azalea bushes, tupelo, sassafras, and pygmy beech trees. Wooded trails lead to a stony but secluded North Shore beach (swimming, picnicking, and fishing prohibited), and from the summit of a headland there are views of Aquinnah and the Elizabeth Islands. To get here, follow Indian Hill Road off State Road for 2 mi, and then turn right 1 mi on an occasionally steep, rocky dirt road to the parking lot. ⊠ Indian Hill Rd., ☎ 508/693–5207. ☒ Free. ☉ Daily sunrise–sunset.

★ At the center of the island, the **Manuel F. Correllus State Forest** is a 2,000-acre pine and scrub-oak forest crisscrossed with hiking trails and circled by a paved but rough bike trail (mopeds are prohibited). There's a 2-mi nature trail, a 2-mi par course, and horse trails. The West Tisbury side of the state forest joins with an equally large Edgartown parcel to virtually surround the airport. ⊠ Headquarters on Barnes Rd. by the airport, ☎ 508/693–2540. ☒ Free. ☉ Daily sunrise–sunset.

A memorial to Thomas Mayhew, Jr., called **Place on the Wayside,** stands along the Edgartown–West Tisbury Road, just east of the airport entrance on the south side of the road. A plaque identifies the spot where Mayhew had his "last worship and interview with them [the Wampanoags] before embarking for England" in 1657, never to return: the ship was lost at sea. Wampanoags passing this spot would leave a stone in Mayhew's memory, and the stones were later cemented together to form the memorial.

Dining and Lodging

$$$$ ✕ **Red Cat.** It's hard to resist a restaurant with a name like Red Cat,
★ especially if it also seems to be situated in what feels like the middle
of nowhere. The first thing you see is a lawn littered with red, yellow,
and blue sculpted figures, some about to fall into a compromising po-
sition. Inside is one square room and a screened-in side porch, with
tawny walls and ivory painted beams with swirling ceiling fans. The
creative menu favors scallops, salmon, bass, lamb, and beef, and each
preparation changes daily. A yellowfin tuna sushi tower with Maine
crab salad, grilled pineapple salsa, and wasabi aioli appetizer is as eclectic as you get. It all seems to work, because reservations are "a must."
⊠ *688 State Rd., near North Rd.,* ☎ *508/693–9599. Reservations essential. MC, V. BYOB. No smoking. Closed Mon. No lunch. Call for
off-season hrs.*

$$–$$$ ✕⊞ **Lambert's Cove Country Inn.** A narrow road winds through pine
★ woods to this secluded inn, set on a lawn surrounded by gardens and
old stone walls. Rooms in the 1790 farmhouse have light floral wallpapers and a sweet country feel. Rooms in outbuildings have screened
porches or decks. Among the common areas is a library with fireplace.
At the restaurant ($$$–$$$$), the soft candlelight and excellent Con-
tinental cooking make it another destination for a special dinner,
whether you stay the night or not. The chef's delicate, refined creations
rely on local produce and seafood. Especially good are the crisp-baked
soft-shell crab appetizer, red and yellow Belgian endive salad, and
grilled Muscovy duck breast on caramelized onions. Reservations are
essential at the restaurant, and it's BYOB. ⊠ *Off Lambert's Cove Rd.,
W. Tisbury;* ⊠ *R.R. 1, Box 422, Vineyard Haven 02568,* ☎ *508/693–
2298,* ℻ *508/693–7890. 15 rooms. Restaurant, tennis court, library.
AE, MC, V. BP.*

$ ⊞ **Hostelling International–Martha's Vineyard.** The only budget, roof-
over-your-head alternative in season, this hostel is one of the country's
best. The large, common kitchen is outfitted with multiple refrigera-
tors and stoves (barbecue grills are available, too), the common room
has a fireplace and plenty of books, and you'll catch wind of local events
on the bulletin board. Morning chores are required in summer. The
hostel offers summer programs on island history, as well as nature tours.
It is near a bike path and is 2 mi from the airport and about 3 mi from
the nearest beach. The Island Shuttle makes a stop out front. ⊠ *Edgar-
town–West Tisbury Rd., Box 158, 02575,* ☎ *508/693–2665 or 800/
909–4776. 78 dorm-style beds. Volleyball, coin laundry. MC, V. 11 PM
curfew June–Aug. Closed daytime 10–5 and completely Nov.–Apr.*

Nightlife and the Arts

Granary Gallery (⊠ Red Barn Emporium, Old County Rd., ☎ 508/
693–0455 or 800/472–6279) showcases sculptures and mostly repre-
sentational paintings by island and international artists, including the
photographs of the late Alfred Eisenstaedt. Biweekly shows spotlight-
ing a local artist are preceded by Sunday-evening receptions.

Hermine Merel Smith Fine Art (⊠ 548 Edgartown Rd., ☎ 508/693–
7719) specializes in paintings and drawings by contemporary Ameri-
can realists and impressionists.

Hot Tin Roof (⊠ Martha's Vineyard Airport, Edgartown–West Tisbury
Rd., ☎ 508/693–1137), opened by Carly Simon in 1976 and later closed,
was reopened by the singer in 1996 and is now the island's hottest club.
Simon sometimes shows up to perform (unannounced), but it's usu-
ally other big names—Jimmy Cliff and Jerry Lee Lewis, for instance—
crowding the stage. Look for comedy nights in season.

Outdoor Activities and Sports

BEACHES

Lambert's Cove Beach (⊠ Lambert's Cove Rd.), one of the island's prettiest, has fine sand and very clear water. The Vineyard Sound–side beach has calm waters good for children and views of the Elizabeth Islands. In season it is restricted to residents and those staying in West Tisbury.

Long Point (☞ *above*), a Trustees of Reservations preserve, has a beautiful beach on the Atlantic, as well as freshwater and saltwater ponds for swimming, including the brackish Tisbury Great Pond. There are rest rooms.

Uncle Seth's Pond is a warm freshwater pond on Lambert's Cove Road, with a small lifeguarded beach right off the road. Car parking is very limited.

HORSEBACK RIDING

Arrowhead Farm (⊠ Indian Hill Rd., ☎ 508/693–8831) offers riding lessons for adults and children year-round, as well as children's summer horsemanship programs. The farm has an indoor ring and leases horses but does not offer trail rides.

Manuel F. Correllus State Forest (⊠ Access off Barnes Rd., Old County Rd., and Edgartown–West Tisbury Rd.) is laced with horse trails open to the public, but it has no stables.

You can arrange for a horse at **Scrubby Neck Farm** (⊠ Edgartown–West Tisbury Rd., across from airport entrance, ☎ 508/693–3770) and ride in Manuel F. Correllus State Forest.

Misty Meadows Horse Farm (⊠ Old County Rd., ☎ 508/693–1870) organizes trail rides. Be sure to call ahead to reserve.

TENNIS

Stop by to reserve hard-surface courts at the grammar school on Old County Road in West Tisbury. There is a small fee for using the courts, which are open year-round.

Shopping

Alley's General Store (⊠ State Rd., ☎ 508/693–0088), in business since 1858, deals in everything from fresh fruit and preserves to shoelaces, suntan lotions, and vintage (though horrendously pricey) tablecloths and cookie jars. There's even a post office.

Chilmark Pottery (⊠ Fieldview La., off State Rd., ☎ 508/693–6476) is a workshop and gallery selling hand-formed stoneware, porcelain, and Raku-ware by island potters.

Cronig's (⊠ 469 State Rd., ☎ 508/693–2234) supports local farmers and specialty food producers and carries most food items that you'll need.

The **Field Gallery** (☞ *above*) is a good source for works by local artists.

Martha's Vineyard Glassworks (☞ *above*) displays glass creations made locally.

West Tisbury Farmers' Market—with booths selling fresh flowers, plants, fruits and vegetables, honey, and homemade baked goods and jams—is held at the Agricultural Hall (⊠ South Rd., ☎ 508/693–9549) mid-June to mid-October, Wednesday and Saturday from 9 to noon.

Chilmark

31 *5½ mi southwest of West Tisbury, 12 mi southwest of Vineyard Haven*

A rural, unspoiled village with scenic ocean-view roads, rustic woodlands, and no crowds, Chilmark draws chic summer visitors and, hard on their heels, stratospheric real-estate prices. Lucy Vincent Beach (residents only in summer) here is perhaps the island's most beautiful. Laced with ribbons of rough roads and winding stone fences that once separated fields and pastures, Chilmark reminds visitors what the Vineyard was like in an earlier time, before developers took over.

Waskosim's Rock Reservation, bought by the Land Bank in 1990 from a developer who had planned to build 40 houses on it, comprises diverse habitats—rolling green hills, wetlands, oak and beetlebung (black gum) woods, and 1,500 ft of frontage on Mill Brook—as well as the ruins of an 18th-century homestead. Waskosim's Rock itself was deposited by the retreating glacier 10,000 years ago and is said to resemble the head of a breaching whale. It is one of the highest points on the Vineyard, situated on a ridge above the valley, from which there is a panoramic view of more than 1,000 acres of protected land. At the trailhead off North Road, a map outlines a 3-mi hike throughout the 166 acres. ⊠ *Parking areas on North Rd.,* ☎ *508/627–7141.* ⌨ *Free.* ☉ *Daily sunrise–sunset.*

32 **Chilmark Cemetery** (⊠ South Rd.) offers an interesting look into the island's past. Longtime summer resident and writer Lillian Hellman, one of many who continued the Vineyard's tradition of liberal politics, is buried here, as is John Belushi, in an unmarked grave. A boulder, deeply engraved with the comedian's name and sitting near the entrance, is a decoy placed to deter overzealous fans from finding the actual burial site. Visitors often leave odd tokens of remembrance.

Beetlebung Corner (⊠ Middle, State, South, and Menemsha Cross Rds.), a crossroads named for the stand of beetlebung trees that grows here, marks Chilmark's town center. Here are the town's public buildings, including the firehouse and the post office, as well as the **Chilmark Community Center** (☎ 508/645–9484), where events such as town meetings, auctions, children's activities, and chamber music concerts take place. In summer, a general store, a clothing boutique, a restaurant and breakfast café, a gallery, and a bank turn the little crossroads into a mini-metropolis.

NEED A BREAK?
The **Chilmark Store** (⊠ 7 State Rd., ☎ 508/645–3655) has the basics that you'd expect as well as Primo's Pizza, a solid take-out lunch spot. If you've bicycled into town, the wooden rockers on the porch may be just the place to take a break—or find a picnic spot of your own nearby to enjoy a fish burger or a slice of the pizza of the day. It's open from May to mid-October.

33 Jointly owned by the Land Bank and the town, **Fulling Mill Brook** (⊠ Middle or South Rd.) is a 50-acre conservation area. Its easy walking trail slopes gently down toward the lowlands along the brook, where there are boulders to sit and sun on, and to the property's edge at South Road, where there's a bike rack.

Dining and Lodging

$$$–$$$$ ✕ **Feast of Chilmark.** Civilized, calm, and calming, the Feast is a wel-
★   come break from the busyness of the Vineyard's bigger-town joints. Photographer Peter Simon's work adds much to the ambience in the bright and airy dining room, where the clientele is generally laid-back. Lots of seafood interpretations, light appetizers, and fresh salads play

up summer tastes and flavors. For starters, try oven-seared scallops with spinach and casino butter. A fine main course is a grilled swordfish steak with cilantro lime butter. The whole menu takes advantage of local produce, and the mixed green salad is simple and perfect. One unfortunate annoyance is the $3 corkage fee—per bottle—when you bring your own wine. ⊠ *Beetlebung Corner,* ☎ *508/645–3553. AE, MC, V. BYOB. No lunch.*

$$$–$$$$ ✕⌸ **Inn at Blueberry Hill.** Exclusive and secluded, this cedar-shingle
★ retreat and its 56 acres of former farmland put you in the heart of the rural Vineyard. The restaurant is relaxed and elegant, and the fresh, health-conscious food is thoughtfully prepared. A cold breakfast is included in the room rate, and a box lunch (about $15) is available for a picnic on the beach (the restaurant is open to the public for dinner by reservation only). Guest rooms are sparsely but tastefully decorated with Shaker-inspired, island-made furniture, and beds are fitted with handmade mattresses with all-cotton sheets and duvets. Most rooms have glass doors that open onto terraces or private decks set with Adirondack chairs. There is a large parlor-library with a fireplace and a casual den and fitness center. Be aware that less expensive rooms may be small, and consider whether you'd prefer staying upstairs in the main building or in one of the three detached cottages. ⊠ *74 North Rd., R.R. 1, Box 309, Chilmark 02535,* ☎ *508/645–3322 or 800/356–3322,* ℻ *508/645–3799. 25 rooms, 1- to 3-room suites available. Dining room, lap pool, massage, tennis court, exercise room, meeting room, airport shuttle. AE, MC, V. BP. Closed Nov.–Apr.*

Nightlife and the Arts

Chilmark Community Center (⊠ Beetlebung Corner, Chilmark, ☎ 508/ 645–9484) holds square dances and other events for different age groups throughout the summer; watch for announcements in the papers.

Chilmark Writing Workshop (☎ 508/645–9085), a series of weeklong summer seminars, is lead by Nancy Slonim Aronie, a former visiting writer at Trinity College and NPR commentator. It's best to reserve a spot in the spring.

Martha's Vineyard Chamber Music Society (☎ 508/696–8055), formerly called the Chilmark Chamber Players, performs 10 summer concerts and 3 in winter at various venues.

The **Yard** (⊠ Off Middle Rd., Chilmark, ☎ 508/645–9662)—a colony of dancers and choreographers formed in 1973—gives several performances throughout the summer at its 100-seat Barn Theater in a wooded setting. Artists are selected each year from auditions held in New York. Dance classes are available to visitors.

Outdoor Activities and Sports

BEACHES

Lucy Vincent Beach (⊠ Off South Rd.), on the south shore, is perhaps the island's most beautiful. The wide strand of fine sand is backed by high clay bluffs and fronted by the Atlantic surf. Keep walking to the left for the unofficial nude beach. In season, Lucy Vincent is restricted to town residents and visitors with passes. Off-season a stroll here is the perfect getaway. Parking is available.

A narrow beach that is part smooth rocks and pebbles, part fine sand, **Squibnocket Beach** (⊠ Off South Rd.), on the south shore, offers an appealing boulder-strewn coastline and gentle waves. During the season, this beach is restricted to residents and visitors with passes.

Shopping

A shop at **Allen Farm** (⊠ South Rd., ☎ 508/645–9064) sells handwoven blankets and knitted items made from the farm's wool. The farm—seen from the road across pastureland protected by the Land Bank—is vast and impressive.

Chilmark Chocolates (⊠ State Rd., ☎ 508/645–3013) sells superior chocolates and the world's finest butter crunch, which you can sometimes watch being made in the back room. Don't forget to pick up a catalog—mail orders are available except during warm months.

Menemsha

★ ㉞   *1½ mi northwest of Chilmark, 3½ mi east of Aquinnah.*

A fishing village unspoiled by the "progress" of the past few decades, Menemsha is a jumble of weathered fishing shacks, fishing and pleasure boats, drying nets and lobster pots, and parents and kids pole-fishing from the jetty. Though the picturesque scene is not lost on myriad photographers and artists, this is very much a working village. The catch of the day, taken off boats returning to port, is sold at markets along Dutcher's Dock. Romantics bring picnic suppers to the public **Menemsha Beach** to catch perfect sunsets over the water. If you feel you've seen this town before, you probably have: it was used for location shots in the film *Jaws.*

Very different from most other island conservation areas, **Menemsha Hills Reservation,** a 210-acre Trustees of Reservations property, includes a mile of rocky shoreline and high sand bluffs along Vineyard Sound. Its hilly walking trails through scrub oak and heathland have interpretive signs at viewing points, and the 309-ft Prospect Hill, the island's highest, affords excellent views of the Elizabeth Islands and beyond. Call ahead about naturalist-led tours. ⊠ *Off North Rd., 1 mi east of Menemsha Cross Rd.,* ☎ *508/693–7662.* ⊡ *Free.* ☉ *Daily sunrise–sunset.*

Dining and Lodging

$$$ ✕ **Homeport.** When does an institution become institutionalized? For Homeport's many fans, it hasn't happened yet. Still, unless you get broiled chicken (and why come to Menemsha for chicken?), the prices are as high as at the fanciest French joint. You pay for the location—away from the bustle of the town, with outdoor seating overlooking the harbor. The Homeport has expanded over the years, pretty much obliterating the handsome lines of the original building, and symbolically that says much. What should be a great island treat, from raw bar to lobster, takeout or sit down, winds up feeling vaguely like someone's taking advantage of you. ⊠ *At the end of North Rd.,* ☎ *508/645–2679. Reservations essential. MC, V. BYOB. Closed mid-Oct.–mid-Apr. No lunch.*

$ ✕ **The Bite.** Fried everything—clams, fish-and-chips, you name it—is on the menu at this simple, roadside shack, where two outdoor picnic tables are the only seating options. Small, medium, and large are the three options: all of them are perfect if you're craving that classic seaside fried lunch. But don't come on a rainy day, unless you want to get wet. The Bite closes at 3 PM weekdays, 7 PM weekends. ⊠ *Basin Rd.,* ☎ *no phone. No credit cards. Closed Oct.–late-Mar.*

$ ✕ **Larsen's.** Dutcher's Dock would not be the same without this au-
★   thentic, funky port-side stopover. Basically a retail fish store, with reasonable prices for the island and superb quality, Larsen's also will open some oysters for you, rustle up fish cakes, and stuff quahogs. You can grab some fish stock or a handful of herring roe and even bait squid for the bluefish you want to catch. The best deal is a plate of in-

credible, fresh littlenecks or cherrystones for $7 a dozen. Oysters at a buck apiece are not a bad alternative. Another temptation is the seafood chowder, which packs in tastes of scallops, shrimp, swordfish, mussels, tuna, lobster, flounder, and cod. The food tastes especially good with a bottle of your own wine, as you sit at one of the two outdoor picnic tables or on a blue bench, back against the wall, with upturned fish crates for tables. If it's lobster without fanfare that you want, do it here, but be sure to call ahead. Larsen's closes at 6 PM weekdays, 7 PM weekends. ⊠ *Dutcher's Dock,* ☎ *508/645–2680. MC, V. BYOB. Closed mid-Oct.–mid-May.*

$$$$ ✕🏨 **Beach Plum Inn.** Innkeeper Craig Arnold took over this faltering property in 1998 and in short order added new room carpets, linens, and artwork. The main draws of the 10-acre retreat are its woodland setting, panoramic views of the ocean and Menemsha Harbor, and restaurant with spectacular sunset views over the harbor. Chef James McDonough serves up the fresh catch of the day, sea bass, and lobster in season. (Reservations are essential, and it's BYOB.) Cottages are decorated in casual beach style, and rooms—some with private decks offering great views—have modern furnishings and small baths; all have TVs and twice-daily maid service. The hotel provides residence passes to nearby Lucy Vincent Beach. ⊠ *50 Beach Plum La., 02552,* ☎ *508/ 645–9454,* 🖷 *508/645–2801. 5 inn rooms, 4 cottages. Restaurant, tennis court, croquet. No pets, no smoking. AE, D, MC, V. Closed mid-Oct.–mid-May. BP.*

$$–$$$ 🏨 **Menemsha Inn and Cottages.** For 40 years the late *Life* photogra-
★ pher Alfred Eisenstaedt returned to his cottage on the hill for the panoramic view of Vineyard Sound and Cuttyhunk beyond the trees below. All with screened porches, fireplaces, and full kitchens, the cottages are nicely spaced on 10 acres and vary in privacy and view. You can also stay in the 1989 inn building or in the pleasant Carriage House, both of which have plush blue or sea green carpeting and Appalachian light pine reproduction furniture. All rooms and suites have private decks, most with sunset views. Suites include sitting areas, desks, minirefrigerators, and big tiled baths. The Continental breakfast is available at the inn and Carriage House only. ⊠ *North Rd., Box 38, 02552,* ☎ *508/645–2521. 9 rooms, 6 suites, 12 cottages. No pets. No credit cards. Closed Nov.–Apr. CP.*

Outdoor Activities and Sports

BEACHES
Menemsha Public Beach, adjacent to Dutcher's Dock, is a pebbly beach with gentle surf on Vineyard Sound and, with views to the west, a great place to catch the sunset. Fishing boats and anglers on the jetty add atmosphere. On site are rest rooms and lifeguards. Snack stands and restaurants are a short walk from the parking lot.

FISHING
North Shore Charters (⊠ Menemsha Harbor, ☎ 508/645–2993) has boats for charter.

Shopping
Pandora's Box (⊠ Basin Rd., ☎ 508/645–9696) sells unique women's clothing and accessories.

Aquinnah

㉟ *4 mi west of Menemsha, 12 mi southwest of West Tisbury, 20 mi west of Edgartown.*

Aquinnah, formerly called Gay Head, is an official Native American township. In 1987, after more than a decade of struggle in the courts, the Wampanoag tribe won guardianship of 420 acres of land, which are being held in trust by the federal government in perpetuity and constitute the Aquinnah Native American Reservation. In 1997, the town voted to change the town's name from Gay Head back to its original Native American name, Aquinnah (pronounced "a-*kwih*-nah"), Wampanoag for "land under the hill." The vote was then passed by the Massachusetts legislature, with the name officially changing on August 1, 1998. While the name has changed, it will take some time for the state and Martha's Vineyard authorities to convert road signs, maps, and other documents to the new name—so you can expect minor confusion. Some private businesses that use the name Gay Head might elect to retain it, so keep in mind that Gay Head and Aquinnah refer to the same place.

The "center" of Aquinnah consists of a combination fire and police station, the town hall, a Tribal Council office, and a public library, formerly the little red schoolhouse. Because the town's year-round population hovers around 650, Aquinnah children attend schools in other towns. Also in Aquinnah is the 380-acre estate of the late Jacqueline Onassis.

36 **Quitsa Pond Lookout** (✉ State Rd.) has a good view of the adjoining Menemsha and Nashaquitsa ponds, the woods, and the ocean beyond.

37 **Aquinnah spring** (✉ State Rd.), from a roadside iron pipe, gushes water cold enough to slake a cyclist's thirst on the hottest day. Feel free to fill a canteen. Locals come from all over the island to fill jugs. The spring is just over the town line.

★ **38** The spectacular, dramatically striated walls of red clay at **Aquinnah Cliffs** (✉ State Rd), a National Historic Landmark and part of the Wampanoag reservation land, are the island's major tourist attraction, as evidenced by the tour bus–filled parking lot. Native American crafts and food shops line the short approach to the overlook, from which you can see the Elizabeth Islands to the northeast across Vineyard Sound and Noman's Land Island, part wildlife preserve, part military bombing-practice site, 3 mi off the Vineyard's southern coast.

If you've reached a state of quiet, vacationland bliss, keep in mind that this *is* a heavily touristed spot, and it might turn out to be a shock to your peace of mind. When you come, consider going to Aquinnah Lighthouse (☞ *below*) first, then down and around to the beach and cliffs. If you're famished when you arrive, you can eat at L'Osteria at the Aquinnah (☞ Dining and Lodging, *below*), at the top of the loop by the lighthouse.

There is no immediate access to the beach from the light—nothing like an easy staircase down the cliffs to the sand below. To reach the cliffs, park in the Moshup Beach (☞ Beaches *in* Outdoor Activities and Sports, *below*) lot by the lighthouse loop, walk five-plus minutes south on the boardwalk, then continue another 20 or more minutes on the sand to get back around to the lighthouse. The cliffs themselves are pretty marvelous, and you should plan ahead if you want to see them. It takes a while to get to Aquinnah from elsewhere on the island, and in summer the parking lot and beach fill up, so start early to get a jump on the throngs.

Aquinnah Lighthouse, adjacent to the Aquinnah Cliffs overlook, is the largest of the Vineyard's five, precariously stationed atop the rapidly eroding cliffs. In 1799 a wooden lighthouse was built here—the island's first—to warn ships of Devil's Bridge, an area of shoals ¼ mi offshore. The current incarnation, built in 1856 of red brick, carries on with its alternating pattern of red and white flashes. Despite the light, the Vineyard's worst wreck occurred here in January 1884, when the *City of Columbus* sank, taking with it into the icy waters more than 100 passengers and crew. The original Fresnel lens was removed when the lighthouse was automated in 1952, and it is preserved at the Vineyard Museum in Edgartown (☞ *above*). The lighthouse is open to the public for sunsets Fridays, Saturdays, and Sundays in summer, weather permitting; private tours can also be arranged. ⊠ *Lighthouse Rd.*, ☎ *508/645–2211.* 🖾 *$2.*

A scenic route worth the trip is West Basin Road, which takes you along the Vineyard Sound shore of Menemsha Light and through the **Cranberry Lands,** an area of cranberry bogs gone wild that is a popular nesting site for birds. No humans can nest here, but you can drive by and look. At the end of the road, with marshland on the right and low dunes, grasses and the long blue arc of the bight on the left, you get a terrific view of the quiet fishing village of Menemsha, across the water. **Lobsterville Road Beach** here is public, but public parking is limited to three spots, so get here early if you want one of them.

Dining and Lodging

\$\$–\$\$\$ ✕ **L'Osteria at the Aquinnah.** At the far end of a little row of shops owned and operated by members of the Wampanoag tribe, L'Osteria at the Aquinnah offers straightforward, generic seaside servings, better for lunch than for dinner. Most imaginative is a bluefish burger, served just like a hamburger. If the feel is generic, the view is not. The deck is world class, high on the Aquinnah bluffs. The ocean rolls to the horizon, while clay and sand along the shore make for Caribbean colors far below. The owners have one serious request: please don't feed the seagulls. ⊠ *State Rd.*, ☎ *508/645–9654. AE, MC, V. Closed mid-Oct.–mid-Apr.*

\$\$\$\$ ✕🏠 **Outermost Inn.** Hugh and Jeanne Taylor's B&B by the Aquinnah
★ Cliffs, their former home, takes full advantage of the location: standing alone on acres of moorland, the house is wrapped in windows revealing views of sea and sky in three directions. A wide porch extends along another side of the house, providing great views of the Aquinnah Lighthouse. At the restaurant, crab cakes are a great appetizer (the menu calls them "The Best"), and the baked stuffed seafood platter is also easy to recommend. The restaurant seats twice for dinner, at 6 and 8 PM, four to six nights a week from spring through fall. Dinners are all prix fixe at $65 (reservations are essential, and it's BYOB). The decor of the inn is clean and contemporary, with white walls and polished light-wood floors. Each room has a phone, and one has a whirlpool tub. The beach is a 10-minute walk away. Hugh has sailed area waters since childhood and captains his 50-ft catamaran on excursions to Cuttyhunk Island. ⊠ *Lighthouse Rd., R.R. 1, Box 171, 02535,* ☎ *508/645–3511,* 🖷 *508/645–3514. 7 rooms. Restaurant. No pets, no children under 12. AE, D, MC, V. Closed mid-Oct.–May. BP.*

\$\$–\$\$\$ 🏠 **Duck Inn.** Elise LeBovit's Duck Inn, originally an 18th-century home built by Native American seafarer George Belain, sits on a bucolic 5-acre bluff overlooking the ocean, with the Aquinnah Lighthouse standing sentinel to the north. The only sounds at night are crickets and the ocean surf some 10 minutes away by foot. The eclectic decor blends peach stucco walls, Native American rugs and wall hangings, and ducks. The duck sign on State Road that directs you to the inn's winding dirt track is just one clue that Elise is big on waterfowl. Three upstairs rooms come with balconies, a suite in the stone-wall lower level (cool in summer, warm in winter) offers views of the rolling fields, and a small attached cabin (closed in winter) with separate bath is the least expensive room. The first floor's common room, with a working 1928

Glenwood stove, piano, and fireplace, is the heart of the inn. Massage and facial therapies are available, and breakfast fare includes waffles with strawberries, chocolate crepes, and omelets. Kids and pets are welcome. ⊠ *State Rd., Box 160, 02535,* ☎ *508/645–9018,* FAX *508/645–2790. 4 rooms, 1 suite. Outdoor hot tub. MC, V. BP.*

Outdoor Activities and Sports

BEACHES

Moshup Beach is, according to the Land Bank, "probably the most glamorous" of its holdings, because the beach provides access to the awesome Aquinnah Cliffs. The best views of the cliffs and up to the lighthouse are from a 25-plus-minute walk via boardwalk and beach. There is a drop-off area close to the beach, but you still must park in the lot and walk to the sand. The island shuttle bus stops here, too, and there are bike racks on the beach. Come early in the day to ensure both a quieter experience and an available parking spot. Keep in mind that climbing the cliffs is against the law—they're eroding much too quickly on their own. It's also illegal to take any of the clay with you. ⊠ *Parking lot at intersection of State Rd. and Moshup Trail* ⊠ *Parking fee Memorial Day–Labor Day $15.*

Lobsterville Beach encompasses 2 mi of beautiful sand and dune beach directly off Lobsterville Road on the Vineyard Sound. It is a seagull nesting area and a favorite fishing spot. Though the water tends to be cold, the beach is protected and suitable for children. There is limited public parking.

MARTHA'S VINEYARD A TO Z

Arriving and Departing

By Bus

Bonanza Bus Lines (☎ 508/548–7588 or 800/556–3815) travels to the Woods Hole ferry port on Cape Cod from Rhode Island, Connecticut, and New York year-round.

By Ferry

Car-and-passenger ferries travel to Vineyard Haven from Woods Hole on Cape Cod year-round. In season, passenger ferries from Falmouth and Hyannis on Cape Cod, and from New Bedford, serve Vineyard Haven and Oak Bluffs. All provide parking lots where you can leave your car overnight ($6–$10 per night).

FROM WOODS HOLE

The **Steamship Authority** runs the only car ferries, which make the 45-minute trip to Vineyard Haven year-round and to Oak Bluffs from late May through September.

If you plan to take a car to the island (or to Nantucket) in summer or weekends in the fall, you *must* have a reservation. (Passenger reservations are never necessary.) You should book your car reservation as far ahead as possible; in season, call weekdays from 5 AM to 9:55 PM for faster service. Standby car reservations to the island are only available on Tuesdays, Wednesdays, and Thursdays; there are no standby car reservations to Nantucket. Those with confirmed car reservations must be at the terminal 30 minutes (45 minutes in season) before sailing time. ☎ *508/477–8600 for information and car reservations; 508/693–9130 on the Vineyard; 508/540–1394 TTY for information and car reservations; 508/548–3788 for day-of-sailing information.* ⊠ *Passengers one-way year-round $5, bicycles $3. Cars one-way in sea-*

*son (mid-May–mid-Oct.) $47 per car (not including passengers). Call
for off-season rates.*

A number of **parking lots** in Falmouth hold the overflow of cars when
the Woods Hole lot is filled, and free shuttle buses take passengers to
the ferry, about 15 minutes away. Signs along Route 28 heading south
from the Bourne Bridge direct you to open parking lots, as does AM
radio station 1610, which can be picked up within 5 mi of Falmouth.

A free **Martha's Vineyard Chamber of Commerce reservations phone**
at the ticket office in Woods Hole connects you with many lodgings
and car- and moped-rental firms on the island.

FROM HYANNIS

Hy-Line makes the 1¾-hour run to Oak Bluffs May–October. From June
to mid-September, the "Around the Sound" cruise makes a one-day
round-trip from Hyannis with stops at Nantucket and Martha's Vineyard ($36). The parking lot fills up in summer, so call to reserve a space
in high season. ⊠ *Ocean St. dock,* ☎ *508/778–2600 or 888/778–1132;
508/778–2602 for reservations; 508/693–0112 in Oak Bluffs.* 🖭 *One-
way $12, bicycles $5.*

FROM FALMOUTH

The **Island Queen** makes the 35-minute trip to Oak Bluffs from late
May through Columbus Day. ⊠ *Falmouth Harbor,* ☎ *508/548–4800.*
🖭 *Round-trip $10, bicycles $6; one-way $6, bicycles $3.*

Patriot Boats (☎ 508/548–2626) allows passengers ($6 one-way) on
its Falmouth Harbor–Oak Bluffs mail runs (mornings only, daily in-
season, more frequently during off-season) and operates a year-round
24-hour water taxi. You can also charter a boat—for about $300.

FROM NEW BEDFORD

The **Schamonchi** travels between Billy Woods Wharf and Vineyard Haven
from mid-May to mid-October. The 600-passenger ferry makes the 1½-
hour trip at least once a day, several times in high season, allowing you
to avoid Cape traffic. Note that round-trip fares apply only for same-
day travel; overnight stays require the purchase of two one-way tickets. ☎ *508/997–1688 in New Bedford; Martha's Vineyard ticket office:*
⊠ *Beach Rd., Vineyard Haven,* ☎ *508/693–2088.* 🖭 *Round-trip
$17, bicycles $5; one-way $9.50, bicycles $2.50.*

FROM NEW LONDON

Fox Navigation carries passengers between State Pier in New London,
Connecticut, and Vineyard Haven from the end of May to mid-October.
The 257-passenger high-speed ferry makes the two-hour trip Friday
through Sunday only, at least twice per day. There is no deck on the
enclosed ferry; passengers sit in either Clipper Class or the more expensive Admiral Class, which has wider seats, water views, and expanded
food service. ☎ *800/724–5369;* ⊠ *Pier 44, Beach Rd., Vineyard
Haven.* 🖭 *Round-trip Admiral Class $89, Clipper Class $59.*

FROM NANTUCKET

Hy-Line makes 2¼-hour runs to and from Oak Bluffs from early June
to mid-September—the only interisland passenger service. (To get a car
from Nantucket to the Vineyard, you must return to the mainland and
drive from Hyannis to Woods Hole.) ☎ *508/778–2600 in Hyannis;
508/693–0112 in Oak Bluffs; 508/228–3949 on Nantucket.* 🖭 *One-
way $11, bicycles $5.*

By Plane

Martha's Vineyard Airport (⊠ Edgartown–West Tisbury Rd., ☎ 508/
693–7022) is in West Tisbury, about 5 mi west of Edgartown.

Air New England (☎ 508/693–8899) offers an island-based charter service year-round. **Cape Air/Nantucket Airlines** (☎ 508/771–6944 or 800/352–0714) connects the Vineyard year-round with Boston (including an hourly summer shuttle), Hyannis, Nantucket, and New Bedford. It offers joint fares and ticketing and baggage agreements with several major carriers. **Continental Express** (☎ 800/525–0280) has seasonal nonstop flights to the Vineyard from Newark. **Direct Flight** (☎ 508/693–6688) is a year-round charter service based on the Vineyard. **Ocean Wings** (☎ 508/693–4646 or 800/253–5039) flies to and from New England cities and New York. **US Airways Express** (☎ 800/428–4322) has year-round service to the Vineyard, as well as Hyannis and Nantucket, out of Boston and New York City's LaGuardia Airport, and seasonal service from Washington, D.C. **Westchester Air** (☎ 800/759–2929) flies charters out of White Plains, New York.

By Private Boat

Town harbor facilities are available at **Vineyard Haven** (☎ 508/696–4249), **Oak Bluffs** (☎ 508/693–4355), **Edgartown** (☎ 508/627–4746), and **Menemsha** (☎ 508/645–2846). Private marine companies include **Vineyard Haven Marina** (☎ 508/693–0720), **Dockside Marina** (☎ 508/693–3392) in Oak Bluffs, and **Edgartown Marine** (☎ 508/627–4388).

Getting Around

By Car

In season, the Vineyard is overrun with cars, and many innkeepers will advise you to leave your car at home, saying you won't need it. This is true if you are coming over for just a few days and plan to spend most of your time in the three main towns—Oak Bluffs, Vineyard Haven, and Edgartown—which are connected in summer by a shuttle bus. Otherwise, you'll probably want a car. Driving on the island is fairly simple. There are few main roads, and they are all well marked. Local bookstores sell a number of excellent maps of the island. You can book rentals through the Woods Hole ferry terminal free phone.

By Ferry

The three-car **On Time** ferry—so named because it has no printed schedules and therefore can never be late—makes the five-minute run to Chappaquiddick Island Memorial Day–mid-October, about every five minutes daily 7 AM–midnight, less frequently off-season. ⊠ *Dock St., Edgartown,* ☎ *508/627–9427.* 🚢 *Round-trip individual $1, car and driver $5, bicycle and rider $3, moped or motorcycle and rider $4.*

By Four-Wheel-Drive

Four-wheel-drive vehicles are allowed from Katama Beach to Wasque Reservation with $50 annual permits ($75 for vehicles not registered on the island) sold on the beach in summer or anytime at the **Dukes County Courthouse** (⊠ Treasurer's Office, Main St., Edgartown 02539, ☎ 508/627–4250). Wasque Reservation has a separate mandatory permit (also available at the courthouse) and requires that vehicles carry certain equipment, such as a shovel, tow chains, and rope; call the rangers before setting out for the dunes. Be aware that due to the protected status of the piping plover, which uses the shore for nesting, some sections are occasionally closed off to vehicular traffic.

Jeeps are a good idea for exploring areas approachable only by dirt roads, but the going can be difficult in over-sand travel, and even Jeeps can get stuck. Stay on existing tracks whenever possible, since wet sand by the water line can suck you in. Most rental companies don't allow their Jeeps to be driven over sand for insurance reasons. Renting a four-wheel-drive vehicle costs $45–$140 per day (seasonal prices fluctuate widely).

By Limousine

Holmes Hole Car Rentals & Limo Service (✉ 36 Water St., Five Corners, Vineyard Haven, ☎ 508/693–8838) provides limo service on-island and occasionally travels off-island.

Muzik's Limousine Service (✉ 10 Kennebec Ave., Oak Bluffs, ☎ 508/693–2212) provides limousine service on- and off-island.

By Shuttle Bus

From late June to early September, shuttles operate daily from 6 AM to 12:45 AM between Vineyard Haven (pickup on Union Street in front of the steamship wharf), Oak Bluffs (by the Civil War statue), and Edgartown (on Church Street opposite the Old Whaling Church). Shuttle tickets cost $1.75–$2.25 one-way and up to $3.25 for round-trip excursions among the three towns. An all-day, unlimited pass is $5, and weekly ($15) and monthly ($50) passes are also available. For the current **bus schedule,** call the shuttle hot line (☎ 508/693–1589 or 508/693–0058) or flip through a Steamship Authority schedule.

Buses from the Down-Island towns to Aquinnah—stopping at the airport, West Tisbury, Chilmark, and on demand wherever it's safe to do so—run every couple of hours between 9 AM and 5 PM in July and August. At other times, call to confirm. Cost is $1–$5 one-way.

By Taxi

Taxis meet all scheduled ferries and flights, and there are taxi stands by the Flying Horses Carousel in Oak Bluffs, at the foot of Main Street in Edgartown, and by the Steamship office in Vineyard Haven. Fares range from $4 within a town to $35–$40 one-way from Vineyard Haven to Aquinnah. Rates double after midnight.

Companies serving the island include **All Island Taxi** (☎ 508/693–3705 or 800/693–8294), **Marlene's** (☎ 508/693–0037 or 800/281–8294), and **Martha's Vineyard Taxi** (☎ 508/693–8660).

By Minibus in Edgartown

The **Martha's Vineyard Transit Authority** has three shuttle-bus routes, two in Edgartown and one in Vineyard Haven. One-way fares are $1.50 or less; senior citizens and children 12 and under are free. For information on weekly, monthly, or seasonal passes, call ☎ 508/627–9663 or 508/627–7448.

DOWNTOWN

From mid-May to mid-September, white-and-purple shuttle buses make a continuous circuit downtown, beginning at free parking lots on the outskirts—at the Triangle off Upper Main Street, at the Edgartown School on Robinson Road (take a right off the West Tisbury Road before Upper Main), and on Mayhew Lane. It's well worth taking it to avoid parking headaches in town, and it's cheap (50¢ each way) and convenient. The shuttle buses run every 15 minutes from 7:30 AM to 11:30 PM daily (mid-May–June, 7:30–7) and can be flagged along the route. Service is also available between Vineyard Haven (free parking lot near Cronig's Market) and the steamship terminal. Minibuses run every 15 minutes from the first ferry in the morning to the last ferry at night. Cost is 50¢ each way and seasonal passes are available; senior citizens and kids under 12 ride free.

SOUTH BEACH

Shuttle-bus service to South Beach via Herring Creek and Katama roads is available mid-June–mid-September for $1.50 one-way (10-trip pass, $10). Pickup is at the corner of Main and Church streets. In good weather there are frequent pickups daily between 10 and 6:30, every half hour in inclement weather, or you can flag a shuttle bus whenever you see one. In July and August, evening service to and from South Beach runs to 9:45 PM.

Contacts and Resources

B&B Reservation Agencies

You can reserve a room at many island establishments via the toll-free phone inside the waiting room at the Woods Hole ferry terminal. The Chamber of Commerce maintains a listing of availability in the peak tourist season, from mid-June to mid-September. During these months, rates are, alas, astronomical, and reservations are essential. **Martha's Vineyard and Nantucket Reservations** (⊠ Box 1322, Lagoon Pond Rd., Vineyard Haven 02568, ☎ 508/693–7200; 800/649–5671 in MA) books cottages, apartments, inns, hotels, and B&Bs. **DestINNations** (☎ 508/428–5600 or 800/333–4667) handles a limited number of Vineyard hotels and B&Bs, but the staff will arrange any and all details of a visit.

Car Rentals

Budget (☎ 508/693–1911), **Hertz** (☎ 508/693–2402), and **All Island** (☎ 508/693–6868) arrange rentals from their airport desks.

Adventure Rentals (⊠ Beach Rd., Vineyard Haven, ☎ 508/693–1959) rents cars (through Thrifty), as well as mopeds, Jeeps, and buggies, and offers half-day rates. Cost is $40–$65 per day for a basic car. **Atlantic Rent-A-Car** (⊠ 15 Beach Rd., Vineyard Haven, ☎ 508/693–0480) rents cars, Jeeps, vans, and convertibles. **Vineyard Classic and Specialty Cars** (☎ 508/693–5551) rents classic Corvettes, a '57 Chevy, and other cars, as well as Harley Davidson motorcycles, mopeds, and mountain bikes.

Emergencies

Dial **911** for the hospital, physicians, ambulance services, police, fire departments, or Coast Guard.

Martha's Vineyard Hospital (⊠ Linton La., Oak Bluffs, ☎ 508/693–0410).

Vineyard Medical Services (⊠ State Rd., Vineyard Haven, ☎ 508/693–6399) provides walk-in care; call for days and hours.

Guided Tours

CRUISES

The 50-ft sailing catamaran **Arabella** (☎ 508/645–3511) makes day and sunset sails out of Menemsha to Cuttyhunk and the Elizabeth Islands with Captain Hugh Taylor, co-owner of the Outermost Inn.

The teakwood sailing yacht **Ayuthia** (☎ 508/693–7245) offers half-day, full-day, and overnight sails to Nantucket or the Elizabeth Islands out of Coastwise Wharf in Vineyard Haven.

Mad Max (☎ 508/627–7500), a 60-ft high-tech catamaran, offers day sails and charters out of Edgartown.

The **Shenandoah** (☎ 508/693–1699), a square topsail schooner, offers six-day cruises including meals; passengers are ferried to ports, which may include Nantucket, Cuttyhunk, New Bedford, Newport, Block Island, or others. One or two weeks each summer, day sails with lunch are offered (call for schedule). Cruises depart from Coastwise Wharf in Vineyard Haven. "Kids Cruises" (throughout the summer) are for 10- to 18-year-olds only.

FLIGHTSEEING

Warbird Flight (⊠ Martha's Vineyard Airport, Edgartown–West Tisbury Rd., West Tisbury, ☎ 508/806–9030) will take you on one- or two-hour island tours, including buzzes over Nantucket and Woods Hole on Cape Cod, in a vintage 1948 L-17 warplane.

ORIENTATION

Buses meet all ferries for two-hour narrated tours of the island from spring through fall, with a stop at the Aquinnah Cliffs. They are crowded and claustrophobic, so see the island another way if at all possible.

WALKING

Liz Villard (☎ 508/627–8619) leads walking tours of Edgartown's "history, architecture, ghosts, and gossip" that include visits to the historic Dr. Daniel Fisher House, the Vincent House, and the Old Whaling Church. Tours are given April–December; call for times. Liz and her guides also lead similar tours of Oak Bluffs and Vineyard Haven. Walks last a little over an hour.

House Rentals

Martha's Vineyard Vacation Rentals (⊠ 107 Beach Rd., Box 1207, Vineyard Haven 02568, ☎ 508/693–7711 or 800/556–4225) and **Sandcastle Vacation Home Rentals** (⊠ 256 Vineyard Haven Rd., Box 2488, Edgartown 02539, ☎ 508/627–5665) can help you find rentals for long-term visits.

Late-Night Pharmacy

Leslie's Drug Store (⊠ 65 Main St., Vineyard Haven, ☎ 508/693–1010) is open daily year-round and has a pharmacist on 24-hour call for emergencies.

Vineyard Activities

BIKING

The **Martha's Vineyard Chamber of Commerce** (☞ Visitor Information, *below*) has a pamphlet called *Biking in Martha's Vineyard,* with regulations and trails. The Martha's Vineyard Land Bank's public conservation lands map, also available at the chamber, is useful, too. All town maps carried by the chamber have marked bike paths.

For information on unofficial group rides, call **Cycleworks** (⊠ 351 State Rd., Vineyard Haven, ☎ 508/693–6966).

CHILDREN'S ACTIVITIES

The following towns offer recreational programs for children: **Edgartown** (☎ 508/627–6145), **Oak Bluffs** (☎ 508/693–2303), **Vineyard Haven** (☎ 508/696–4200), and **West Tisbury** (☎ 508/696–0147).

Storytelling hours for children are offered by all the island's libraries. Call towns about days and times: **Chilmark** (⊠ State Rd., ☎ 508/645–3360), **Edgartown** (⊠ N. Water St., ☎ 508/627–4221), **Oak Bluffs** (⊠ Circuit Ave., ☎ 508/693–9433), **Vineyard Haven** (⊠ Upper Main St., ☎ 508/696–4212), and **West Tisbury** (⊠ State Rd., ☎ 508/693–3366).

CLAMBAKES AND PICNICS

Don't feel like cooking on vacation? Box or picnic lunches are available at **Vineyard Gourmet** (⊠ Main St., Vineyard Haven, ☎ 508/693–5181). **Bill Smith** (☎ 508/627–8809 or 800/828–6936) prepares clambakes to go. **New England Clambake Co.** (☎ 508/627–7462) will cater clambakes for parties of 10 or more.

CONSERVATION AREAS

A free map to the islands' conservation lands is available from the **Martha's Vineyard Land Bank** (⊠ 167 Main St., Edgartown 02539, ☎

508/627–7141) or from some town halls and libraries. It is one of the best general maps covering the Vineyard, and it includes detailed directions, parking information, and usages permitted in conservation areas.

Conservation-area bird walks, children's programs, and a schedule of events are listed in newspapers year-round and in the *Best Read Guide,* available free in shops and hotels.

NIGHTLIFE AND THE ARTS

Both **island newspapers,** the *Martha's Vineyard Times* and the *Vineyard Gazette,* as well as the *Cape Cod Times,* publish weekly calendars of events. Also scan the *Best Read Guide,* free at many shops and hotels.

The 24-hour movie hot line (☎ 508/627–6689) has schedules for the **Capawock** (✉ Main St., Vineyard Haven), **Island Theater** (✉ Circuit Ave., Oak Bluffs), and the **Strand** (✉ Oak Bluffs Ave. Ext., Oak Bluffs). **Entertainment Cinemas** (✉ Main St., Edgartown, ☎ 508/627–8008) has two screens showing first-release films. Films are also shown at other locations from time to time, so check local papers.

RESTRICTED BEACHES

Inns occasionally lend guests parking stickers for town beaches that are otherwise limited to residents. These restricted beaches are often much less crowded than public beaches, and some, such as Lucy Vincent and Lambert's Cove, are the most beautiful. These beaches are restricted only seasonally, roughly mid-June to Labor Day. At other times they are accessible to the public.

SHELLFISHING

Each town issues shellfish licenses for the waters under its jurisdiction. For a permit, contact the town hall of the town in which you wish to fish; you can also obtain information on good spots and a listing of areas closed because of seeding projects or contamination: **Aquinnah** (☎ 508/645–2300), **Chilmark** (☎ 508/645–2100), **Edgartown** (☎ 508/627–6100), **Oak Bluffs** (☎ 508/693–5511), **Vineyard Haven** (☎ 508/696–4200), and **West Tisbury** (☎ 508/696–0148).

Visitor Information

Martha's Vineyard Chamber of Commerce is two blocks from the Vineyard Haven ferry. The chamber information booth by the Vineyard Haven steamship terminal is open Memorial Day–last weekend in June, Friday–Sunday 8–8; July–Labor Day, daily 8–8; and Labor Day–Columbus Day, Friday–Sunday 8:30–5:30. There are also town information kiosks on Circuit Avenue in Oak Bluffs and on Church Street in Edgartown. ✉ *Beach Rd., Box 1698, Vineyard Haven 02568,* ☎ *508/693–0085.* ☺ *Weekdays 9–5.*

4 NANTUCKET

Herman Melville may never have set foot on Nantucket, but he was right about its exuberance—in summer, the place brims over with activity. To the eye, Nantucket Town's museum-quality houses and the outlying beaches and rolling moors make the island an aesthetic world unto itself. So hop a ferry to the Gray Lady of the Sea to measure your gait on its historic streets, stand knee-deep in surf casting for stripers, pick up some old whaling lore, or set yourself up on the sand as the sun arcs its way across the sky.

Updated by
Laura V. Scheel

Dining
updated by
Seth Rolbein
and Ellen
LeBow

AT THE HEIGHT OF ITS PROSPERITY in the early to mid-19th century, the little island of Nantucket was the foremost whaling port in the world. Its harbor bustled with the coming and going of whaling ships and coastal merchant vessels putting in for trade or outfitting. Along the wharves a profusion of sail lofts, ropewalks, ship's chandleries, cooperages, and other shops stood cheek by jowl. Barrels of whale oil were off-loaded from ships onto wagons, then wheeled along cobblestone streets to refineries and candle factories. On strong sea breezes the smoke and smells of booming industry were carried through the town as inhabitants eagerly took care of business. It's no wonder that Herman Melville's Ishmael, of the novel *Moby-Dick,* felt the way he did about the place:

My mind was made up to sail in no other than a Nantucket craft, because there was a fine, boisterous something about everything connected with that famous old island, which amazingly pleased me.

But the island's boom years didn't last long. Kerosene came to replace whale oil, sought-after sperm whales were overhunted and became scarce, and a sandbar at the mouth of the harbor silted up. Before the prosperity ended, however, enough hard-won profits went into building the grand houses that remind us of the glory days. And wharves once again teem with shops of merchants who tend to the needs of incoming ships—ferry boats, mostly, bringing visitors who crave T-shirts and chic handbags rather than ropes and barrels.

Thanks in no small part to the island's isolation, 30 mi out in the open Atlantic—its original Native American name, Nanticut, means faraway land—and to an economy that experienced frequent depressions, Nantucket has managed to retain much of its 17th- to 19th-century character. The town itself hardly seems to have changed since whaling days—streets are still lined with hundreds of beautifully preserved houses and lit by old-fashioned lamps. This remarkable preservation also owes much to the foresight and diligence of people working to ensure that Nantucket's uniqueness can be enjoyed by generations to come. In 1955 legislation was initiated to designate the island an official National Historic District. Now any outwardly visible alterations to a structure, even the installation of air conditioners or a change in the color of paint, must conform to a rigid building code.

The code's success shows in the fine harmony of the buildings, most covered in weathered gray shingles, sometimes with a clapboard facade painted white or gray. Local wood being in short supply, clapboard facades were a sign of wealth. In town, which is more strictly regulated than the outskirts, virtually nothing jars. You'll find no neon, stoplights, billboards, or fast-food franchises. In spring and summer, when the many tidy gardens are in bloom and cascades of roses cover the gray shingles, it all seems perfect.

The desire to protect Nantucket from change extends to the land as well. When the 1960s tourism boom began, it was clear that something had to be done to preserve the breezy, wide-openness of the island—its miles of clean, white-sand beaches and heath-covered moors—that is as beautiful as the historic town. A third of the 14-by-3-mi island's 30,000 acres are now protected from development, thanks to the ongoing efforts of several public and private organizations and the generosity of Nantucketers, who have donated thousands of acres to the cause. The Nantucket Conservation Foundation (NCF), established in 1963, has acquired through purchase or gift more than 8,200 acres, including working cranberry bogs and great tracts of moorland.

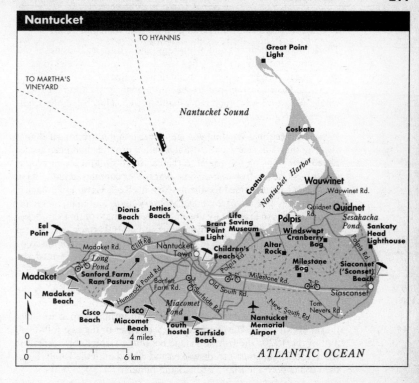

A land bank funded by a 2% tax on real-estate transactions was instituted in 1984 and has since acquired more than 1,000 acres. Most of these are open to the public and marked with roadside signs.

While builders today are enjoying a more than fruitful run of business—the smell of fresh lumber and the sounds of construction of expensive homes are as commonplace as the overhead gulls—the expansion is bound to be short-lived and contained. Nantucket's residents remain dedicated to preserving a vital sense of open space and natural habitat.

The first Europeans came to the island to escape repressive religious authorities on the mainland. Having themselves fled to the New World to escape persecution in England, the Puritans of the Massachusetts Bay Colony proceeded to persecute Quakers and those who were friendly with them. In 1659 Thomas Macy, who had obtained Nantucket through royal grant and a deal with the resident Wampanoag tribe, sold most of the island to nine shareholders for £30 and two beaverskin hats. These shareholders then sold half shares to people whose skills the new settlement would need. The names of these families—Macy, Coffin, Starbuck, Coleman, Swain, Gardner, Folger, and others—appear at every turn in Nantucket, where many descendants continue to reside three centuries later.

The first year, Thomas Macy and his family, along with Edward Starbuck and the 12-year-old Isaac Coleman, spent fall and winter at Madaket, getting by with the assistance of local Wampanoags. The following year, 1660, Tristram Coffin and others arrived, establishing a community—later named Sherburne—at Capaum Harbor on the north shore. When storms closed the harbor early in the 18th century, the center of activity was moved to the present Nantucket Town. Relations with the Wampanoags seem to have been cordial, and many of the tribe became expert whalers. Numbering about 3,000 when the settlers arrived, the native population was greatly reduced in 1763 by a plague. The last full-blooded Wampanoag on the island died in 1855.

The settlers tried their hand at farming, though their crops never did well in the sandy soil. In 1690 they sent for a Yarmouth whaler to teach them to catch right whales from small boats just offshore. In 1712 a boat was blown farther out to sea and managed to capture a sperm whale, whose oil was much more highly prized. Thus began the whaling era on Nantucket.

In the 18th century, whaling voyages never lasted much longer than a year. By the 19th century the usual whaling grounds had been so depleted that ships had to travel to the Pacific to find their quarry and could be gone for five years. Some Nantucket captains actually have South Sea islands named for them—Swain's Reef, Gardner Pinnacles, and so forth. The life of a whaler was very hard, and many never returned home. An account by Owen Chase, first mate of the Nantucket whaling ship *Essex,* of "the mysterious and mortal attack" of a sperm whale, which in 1820 ended in the loss of the ship and most of the crew, fascinated a young sailor named Herman Melville and formed the basis of his 1851 novel, *Moby-Dick*.

The fortunes of Nantucket's whaling industry rose and fell with the tides of three wars and ceased altogether in the 1860s. By the next decade tourism was being pursued, and hotels began springing up at Surfside, on the south shore. Developments at Siasconset to the east followed, and in the 1920s the fishing village became a fashionable resort for theater folk. The tourist trade waxed and waned until the 1960s. Since then it has been the island's bread and butter.

Like the original settlers, most people who visit Nantucket today come to escape—from cities, from stress, and in some ways from the mayhem of the new millennium. Nantucket has a bit of nightlife, including two raucous year-round dance clubs, but that's not what the island is about. It's about small gray-shingled cottages covered with pink roses in summer, about daffodil-lined roads in spring. It's about moors swept with brisk salt breezes and scented with bayberry, wild roses, and cranberries. Perhaps most of all, it's about rediscovering a quiet place within yourself and within the world, getting back in touch with the elemental and taking it home with you when you go.

Pleasures and Pastimes

Dining

"You're looking for a great, cheap place to eat?" mused a Nantucket cabdriver. "Try Cape Cod."

There is sad truth to the joke. Nantucket has adopted Manhattan prices, a solid 20% higher than comparable fare on the Cape. This remains true even as Cape prices creep higher; Nantucket seems to have no problem keeping pace. For years, this was justified by saying that transportation costs to the remote island are high. But ferry charges for freight are not so exorbitant that a simple salad in virtually every restaurant must cost $8, and besides, no one thinks twice about making the argument while simultaneously trumpeting their use of local fish and produce. Finally, there's the fact that Martha's Vineyard somehow manages to use the ferries and keep prices within sight.

One visitor from the mainland, browsing through the restaurants in town, put it simply as he and his wife were trying to decide where to eat that night. "Do you think," he wondered, "that we'll find a place where a piece of salmon costs less than $35?"

In the end, there's simply no getting around it: Nantucket is expensive and basically takes the attitude that if you can't handle it, don't bother to come.

But come dinnertime, it's best to grin, bear it, hand over the plastic, and don't let cynicism spoil the meal. Because the other truth is that this competitive little island has some great chefs, sophisticated and well schooled. Their venues are usually small, carefully appointed, and full of personality. Their wine lists are by and large superb—so much so that establishments that don't have some sort of award from a national wine magazine seem a little behind the times. And a few cheaper, more family-style holdouts can help hold the monthly service charges down.

There are two schools of thought for handling Nantucket on a fixed budget. One advocates going for the $12 breakfasts and $25 lunches and then eating very lightly for dinner. The other basically suggests fasting though the day and then thoroughly enjoying a beautiful supper at night. Who knows, perhaps this approach might be given a name one day: the Nantucket Diet.

Most restaurants open and close seasonally on Nantucket, although most also stay open or reopen for the Christmas Stroll weekend in early December. Come off-season, generally from late October through Memorial Day, and you'll find only a handful of the less expensive places still serving. Dining rooms associated with inns are the best bet year-round. Some restaurants outside of town offer taxi vouchers, the ultimate in responsible designated driving.

For price-category information, *see* Dining *in* Smart Travel Trips A to Z.

Lodging

Nantucket has only 1,200 beds available at any given time, and in summer, as many as 40,000 people per day descend on the place. With such a captive audience swamping them year in and year out, it seems that some lodging places get lazy, as well as increasingly expensive. At the same time, others are wonderful and have attentive innkeepers and staff. Apart from cottages and a few inns and hotels scattered across the island, Nantucket's lodging places are in the busy town. Those in the center are convenient, but houses are close together, right on the street. In season there may be street noise until midnight. Inns a 5- or 10-minute walk from the center are quieter.

If appliances like coffeemakers, mini-refrigerators, or televisions are important to your stay, ask about them when you reserve a room; you should also ask about minimum stays that may be required in season. Many inns have fragile antiques and do not welcome children, so ask when you book. You can also consider larger inns, which may be better equipped for families. If you're visiting during summer, be sure to make reservations well in advance. For summer weekends, early spring would not be too early. House or condominium rentals are an option for stays of a week or longer; again, make your plans well ahead.

For price-category information, *see* Lodging *in* Smart Travel Tips A to Z.

Outdoor Activities and Sports

BEACHES

The shores of Nantucket are lined with beaches, most of which are open to the public. From mid-June into October the water is usually warm, especially on the Nantucket Sound side. The south and east shores, fronting the Atlantic, have strong surf and undertow, while those on the north and west sides are calmer and warmer; this variety allows for all types of activities, from wading with kids to surfing. Some beaches are accessible by bike path, others by shuttle bus, and others by foot or four-wheel-drive. Most have facilities and lifeguards, and public beaches do not charge parking or entrance fees.

BIKING

One of the best ways to tour Nantucket is by bicycle. Miles of paved bike paths wind through all types of terrain from one end of the island to the other; it is possible to bike around the entire island in a day. Several paths lead from town out to beaches and have drinking fountains and benches placed in strategic spots along the way. The paths are also perfect for runners and rollerbladers.

BIRD-WATCHING

Nantucket is among the 100 best birding spots in the country—more than 354 species flock to the island's moors, meadows, and marshes in the course of a year. Birds that are rare in other parts of New England thrive here due to the lack of predators and the abundance of wide-open, undeveloped space. Northern harriers, short-eared owls, and Savannah sparrows nest in the grasslands; oystercatchers, gulls, plovers, and tiny least terns nest on sands and in beach grasses; snowy egrets, great blue herons, and ospreys stalk the marshlands; and ring-necked pheasants, mockingbirds, and Carolina wrens inhabit the tangled bogs and thickets. Take a pair of binoculars and wander through the conservation areas or along the bike trails or beaches and you're sure to catch sight of interesting bird life, not just in migratory season but year-round.

CONSERVATION AREAS

The island of Nantucket has a fascinating array of landscapes—wild, open tracts of bog land and moors; groves of scrub oak and pitch pine; and wide, sandy beaches that stretch seemingly forever. A diverse assortment of plant and animal species, many of which are endangered or threatened, thrive here as nowhere else. The windswept heathlands that compose much of Nantucket's acreage are becoming globally rare and are protected on the island by various conservation organizations that use carefully controlled fires to burn away encroaching shrubs and trees. Flowering plants are especially prolific after these burns and include such rare species as bush rockrose, pink lady's slipper, and the Eastern silvery aster.

Other local species of flora and fauna to keep watch for are the white flowers of the Nantucket shadbush, brilliant red cardinal flowers, bird's-foot violets, false heather, pink Virginia roses, wild morning glories, and big, beautiful red-orange wood lilies; in the fall, look for asters, goldenrod, and the tall purple spikes and thistlelike flowers of the endangered New England blazing star. Although cranberries are the most abundant berry, there are also blueberries, raspberries, blackberries, and huckleberries. Beach plums, beach peas, and the fragrant non-native rosa rugosa grow well near the sea in the sandiest soil. In the meadows and groves are mice, moles, meadow voles, white-tailed deer, and cottontail rabbits—and a distinct lack of predatory mammals such as raccoons, skunks, and opossums due to Nantucket's distance from the mainland. On the beach and in the sea, mollusks such as oysters, mussels, steamers, quahogs, and blue crabs are plentiful and can be harvested as long as you have the proper shellfishing permit.

Please remember that these conservation areas are set aside to preserve and protect Nantucket's fragile ecosystems—tread carefully.

FISHING

Surf fishing is very popular on Nantucket, especially in the late spring when bluefish are running. Blues and bass are the main island catches— bluefishing is best at Great Point—but there are plentiful numbers of other flavorful fish as well. Freshwater fishing is also an option at many area ponds.

WATER SPORTS

Surfing and sailing are both popular on Nantucket; surfing is especially good on the south and east shores, where the wild Atlantic crashes. Canoeing and kayaking on the inland ponds and in Nantucket Harbor are other wonderful ways to cruise the waters.

Shopping

From the early 1800s on, Nantucket has had an active shopping scene. Sea captains brought merchandise back from their sailing excursions to ports all over the world to trade and sell. When the whaling boom encouraged the men to take to the seas, the women of Nantucket ran the shops, earning the name "Petticoat Row" for a concentrated stretch of women-run shops on Centre Street.

Nantucket Town's commercial district—bounded approximately by the waterfront and Main, Broad, and Centre streets and continuing along South Beach Street—contains virtually all of the island's shops. Old South Wharf, built in 1770, is filled with crafts, clothing, and antiques stores, a ship's chandlery, and art galleries in small, connected "shanties." Straight Wharf, where the Hy-Line ferry docks, is lined with T-shirt and other tourist-oriented shops, a gallery, a museum, and restaurants. (Phones and rest rooms are at the end of the wharf.) The majority of Nantucket's shops are seasonal, opening sometime after April and closing between Labor Day and November, though an active core stay open longer.

The island specialty is the Nantucket lightship basket, woven of oak or cane, with woven covers adorned with scrimshaw or rosewood. First made in the 19th century by crew members passing time between chores on the lightships that stood off Sankaty Head (☞ Close-Up: Nantucket's Lightship Baskets: Ship-Bored Enterprise, *below*), the baskets are now used as purses by those who can afford them—prices range from $300 for new baskets to well over $3,000 for vintage ones. Miniature versions of the baskets are made by plaiting fine threads of gold or silver wire. Some have working hinges and latches, and some are decorated with plain or painted scrimshaw or small gems. Prices start at around $300 for gold versions. Another signature island product is a pair of all-cotton pants called Nantucket Reds, which fade to pink with washing. They're sold at Murray's Toggery Shop. There is something for nearly everyone here—apart from a few too many sweatshirts—from unique decorative items to handwoven clothing, antiques, and island-made jams and jellies.

Exploring Nantucket

The 14-by-3-mi island of Nantucket has one town, called Nantucket. The village of Siasconset, known as 'Sconset, is in the southeast corner, with a fair number of services and essential stores. North of 'Sconset, Wauwinet is an old residential enclave with a landmark inn. It is the gateway to the sprawling beach and reserves of Coatue, Coskata, and Great Point. The village of Madaket on the west end has a beach and harbor, great sunsets, a seasonal restaurant, and bluefishing off the point. Madaket also has a number of residential areas with no commercial or tourist facilities. Although major roads will take you to most of these areas, exploring must often be done on dirt roads. Bike paths lead east from the town of Nantucket to 'Sconset, south to Surfside Beach, and west to Madaket.

NANTUCKET LIGHTSHIP BASKETS: SHIP-BORED ENTERPRISE

IN THE CASE OF THE NANTUCKET LIGHT-**SHIP** baskets, boredom was the mother of invention. First created in the 1820s by Nantucket sailors, these woven rattan baskets with wooden bottoms were quite different from the typical "Indian basket" used at the time. The form mimicked the construction of wooden barrels and casks made in great quantities on Nantucket for the whaling industry. It was not until 1856, when basket molds were brought aboard the *South Shoal Lightship*, that they were dubbed "lightship baskets."

Anchored 24 mi off Nantucket, the lightship was a sort of floating lighthouse, outfitted with two bright beacon-lights and a bell. Men spent nine-month stretches aboard ship, their sole responsibility to warn passing vessels of the treacherous shoals around Sankaty Head. In bad weather the crew was on high alert, searching the fog-enshrouded waters for ships headed for trouble; otherwise, there was not much to do. The weaving of lightship baskets was well suited to such a constrained lifestyle. It was a time-consuming activity and the necessary materials were easily obtained during on-shore leave.

The basket's construction borrowed heavily from coopering. It was based on a round wooden circle (or sometimes oval) turned on a lathe from local hardwood and scored with a deep groove along the outer edge. A mold of the basket form was then screwed to the bottom of the circle, and staves—thin strips cut from oak or hickory—were soaked until pliable, wedged into the scored slot, shaped to the mold, and tied in place with cord. When dry, the staves served as the ribs of the basket, and the mold was removed. A long, thin strip of rattan woven in and out of the staves completed the body of the basket. The lip was then fitted with hoops of oak that served as the rim (another technique borrowed from coopering); often these rims were wrapped with rattan.

Lids were made of separate rounds of woven rattan, often incorporating wooden pieces with carved designs, or scrimshaw ornaments depicting the ever-popular sperm whale or other marine-related scenes. Some were made as nesting sets.

Sailors generally gave these baskets as gifts to their families for household use as shopping baskets, sewing baskets, and the like. By the turn of the century, they were being produced on shore as well. In 1905 the namesake lightship was taken out of service, but by then the baskets had attracted tourists' attention.

In 1948, at the request of his wife, who wanted to use her lightship basket as a handbag, José Formoso Reyes altered the design of the basket by attaching the cover with a strip of leather. In addition, the top of the basket was adorned with an ebony whale ornament. Today a decorated top can add several hundred dollars to a basket's price.

The Nantucket Lightship Basket Makers Merchants Association now has about 90 members, who are eager to educate buyers about the authenticity of their baskets. Baskets made by these members come with a certificate with the maker's name and location on it. Fake baskets made in Japan or Hong Kong may have a loose weave; cane, rather than oak, handles; square, instead of rounded, edges on top and bottom; and stamped, rather than carved, scrimshaw for decoration.

The baskets' popularity has never ebbed; today jewelers even make miniature versions in gold and silver. Prices for the traditionally made basket range from $300 for a plain 8-inch open basket to $3,000 and up for a vintage basket—which brings new meaning to the old phrase "putting all your eggs in one basket."

—Dorothy Antczak

Numbers in the text correspond to numbers in the margin and on the Nantucket Town map.

Great Itineraries

The island is small enough to get around it all reasonably in four days, three if you really dash about. In two days you can explore Nantucket Town and one other area. Whatever time you have, try not to rush too much; relax and absorb the spirit of the place.

IF YOU HAVE 2 DAYS

Spend the first day of your trip in ☷ **Nantucket Town** absorbing the island's history. Visit the **Peter Foulger Museum and Edouard A. Stackpole Library and Research Center** ⑤ and the **Whaling Museum** ④; to see them properly will take up much of the morning. Then stop off at one of the town's cafés for lunch, or take lunch to **Lily Pond Park** for a picnic. Afterward, stroll along the streets and take note of the magnificent captains' homes built during the prosperous whaling era. Climb the tower at the **First Congregational Church** ⑧ for a panoramic view of moors, ponds, beaches, Sankaty Head Lighthouse, Great Point, and Muskeget and Tuckernuck islands. Visit the **Macy-Christian House** ㉓ to get an idea of how Nantucketers lived in past centuries. Wander among the cobblestone streets of the town center, or if you are eager for some swimming and sunning, Children's Beach is close by, and Surfside Beach is only a 3-mi bike ride away.

Start day two with a visit to the **Hinchman House** ⑮, a natural history museum with examples of local flora and fauna. Then pack a lunch and head off (the best way to tour the island is by bicycle) to explore the walking trails at the **Sanford Farm, Ram Pasture, and the Woods.** Continue on to spend the afternoon at beautiful **Eel Point** beach, walking, relaxing, and enjoying the views. Surf fishing is good here, and the area is great for birding as well.

You could otherwise head for **Siasconset,** with a stop at the Milestone Bog to get a good view of the famous Nantucket bogs. If you are here in the fall you'll want to spend extra time observing the cranberry harvest. From 'Sconset, take the short trip to see Sankaty Head Lighthouse. As the day fades, walk around 'Sconset's little village. Be sure to stroll along Evelyn, Lily, and Pochick streets, which remain much as they were in the 1890s. Treat yourself to dinner at one of the village restaurants, and if possible, spend the night in a cottage by the beach.

IF YOU HAVE 4 DAYS

Spend the first day and night of your trip in ☷ **Nantucket Town,** following suggestions for the two-day itinerary above.

Cycle out toward **Madaket** the next day and take the 6½-mi (round-trip) trail that leads to the shore via Hummock Pond—a superb route for bird-watchers. Surfers and swimmers will want to hang out at the beach here. Go on along a south-shore road to Madaket Beach to catch the sunset; then head back to Nantucket Town for dinner.

In the morning on day three, walk out to **Brant Point Light** and take in the view of the harbor; then continue to **Jetties Beach** and rent a kayak or sailboat, or take a swim. Walk the Black Heritage Trail and discover the heritage of African-Americans living on Nantucket in the 19th century. Go back through town and take Polpis Road to the interesting, unique **Nantucket Life Saving Museum.** Go inland a bit to explore the trails that wind through the moor around **Altar Rock,** which has wonderful views. Cut across the moor to Sesachacha Pond and take the path that leads around the pond to the Audubon wildlife area, another great birding spot. Stop by the **Milestone Bog** to get a look at what was once the largest contiguous natural cranberry bog (until it was subdivided after 1959). During harvest season, you'll want to stay for a while and watch the cranberry-collecting process. Then head for Siasconset for dinner.

Golfers might want to spend the next morning at the Siasconset Golf Club; others might enjoy tennis at the Siasconset Casino. 'Sconset Beach is a fine place to swim or surf, or simply relax in the sun. From 'Sconset, head to the gateway of **Coatue–Coskata–Great Point,** an unpopulated sand spit comprising three cooperatively managed wildlife refuges. Take a Jeep tour, or if you're feeling energetic, walk around Coskata Pond. If you feel like getting on the water, reserve a spot on the beautiful sloop *Endeavor* to sail out to Coatue. The Trustees of Reservations sponsors a naturalist-led Great Point natural history tour, which is another option. Spend the afternoon exploring the area or walking on the beach. Coatue is open for shellfishing, surf casting, and birdwatching, and though swimming is discouraged, the beach is a beautiful place to sit and read or picnic. You may want to plan ahead for dinner at the Wauwinet Inn.

When to Tour Nantucket

Summer is Nantucket's most popular season, when everything is open and positively bustling. The Nantucket Harborfest in June celebrates Nantucket's ties to the sea with all sorts of festivities. From house tours to sand-castle competitions, there's always something going on.

Autumn is harvesttime, and on Nantucket that means one thing—cranberries. The harvesting process is fascinating to watch, and the landscape is particularly lovely at this time of year.

Winter is quiet, with many shops and restaurants closed, but it's a perfect time to visit if you enjoy roaming the streets and beaches in solitude. Around the holidays, the town comes to life and the throngs return for the Christmas Stroll, an old-time celebration including carolers, theatrical performances, art exhibitions, crafts fairs, and a tour of historical homes.

Spring is heralded by a profusion of blooms, most notably daffodils—they are everywhere. The four-day Daffodil Festival culminates in a procession of narcissi-adorned antique cars that head to Siasconset for tailgate picnics.

NANTUCKET TOWN

Steeped in history, Nantucket Town has one of the country's finest historic districts. Beautiful 18th- and 19th-century architecture abounds, and museums have carefully preserved Nantucket's important whaling history. Located on a magnificent harbor, the town remains the center of island activity, as it has since the early 1700s. A small commercial area of a few square blocks leads up from the waterfront. Beyond it, quiet residential roads fan out to points around the island; Siasconset lies 7 mi to the east, Surfside 3 mi to the south, and Madaket 6 mi west of town.

A stroll through town is the best way to absorb the history of Nantucket. Most of the Greek Revival houses you will see were built to replace buildings lost in the Great Fire of 1846. As you wander you may notice a small round plaque by some doorways. Issued by the Nantucket Historical Association, the plaques certify that the house dates from the 17th century (silver), 1700–1775 (red bronze), 1776–1812 (brass), 1813–1846 (green), or 1847–1900 (black). Unfortunately, the signs all seem to turn coppery green or black with age.

Nantucket Town

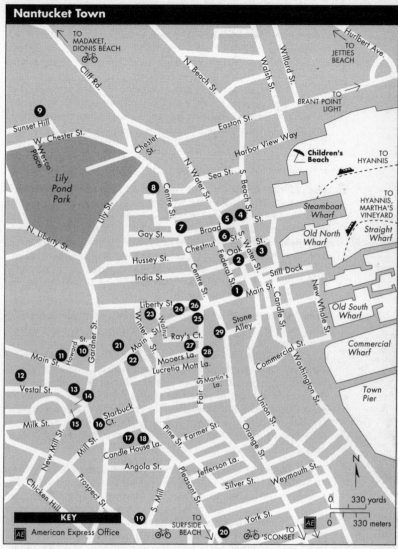

TO MADAKET, DIONIS BEACH

Cliff Rd

N. Beach St.

Walsh St.

Willard St.

Hurlbert Ave.

TO JETTIES BEACH

TO BRANT POINT LIGHT

9 Sunset Hill

W. Chester St.

W. Westco Place

Chester St.

Easton St.

Harbor View Way

Children's Beach

TO HYANNIS

Lily Pond Park

Lily St.

N. Liberty St.

Centre St.

N. Water St.

Sea St.

S. Beach St.

St.

Steamboat Wharf

Old North Wharf

TO HYANNIS

TO HYANNIS, MARTHA'S VINEYARD

Straight Wharf

8 First Congregational Church

Gay St.

7

Broad

Chestnut

5 **4**

6

Oak

S. Water St.

3

Hussey St.

India St.

Centre St.

Federal St.

2

1

Main St.

Still Dock

Candle St.

New Whale St.

Old South Wharf

Liberty St.

23 **24** **26**

25

29

Stone Alley

Ray's Ct.

27

Winter St.

Walnut

Main St.

21

22

Mooers La.

28

Lucretia Mott La.

Commercial St.

Washington St.

Commercial Wharf

Howard St.

Gardner St.

Main St.

11 **10**

12

Vestal St.

13 **14**

Fair St.

Martin's La.

Union St.

Orange St.

Town Pier

Milk St.

15 **16**

Starbuck Ct.

Mill St.

17 **18**

Candle House La.

Pine St.

Farmer St.

Angola St.

New Mill St.

Prospect St.

S. Mill St.

Pleasant St.

Jefferson La.

Silver St.

Weymouth St.

N

Chicken Hill

KEY

19 Old Mill

TO SURFSIDE BEACH

20

York St.

TO 'SCONSET

AE

0 330 yards

0 330 meters

AE American Express Office

African School and Church, **20**

Atheneum, **2**

Coffin houses, **24**

Dreamland Theatre, **3**

1800 House, **17**

Fire Hose Cart House, **10**

First Congregational Church, **8**

Greater Light, **11**

Hadwen House, **22**

Hinchman House, **15**

Jared Coffin House, **7**

John Wendell Barrett House, **25**

Macy-Christian House, **23**

Maria Mitchell Science Library, **14**

Mitchell House, **13**

Moors' End, **18**

Nantucket Information Bureau, **6**

Old Gaol, **12**

Old Mill, **19**

Oldest House, **9**

Pacific Club, **1**

Pacific National Bank, **26**

Peter Foulger Museum and Edouard A. Stackpole Library and Research Center, **5**

Quaker Meeting House, **27**

St. Paul's Episcopal Church, **28**

Starbuck refinery and candle works, **16**

"Three Bricks," **21**

Unitarian Universalist Church, **29**

Whaling Museum, **4**

NOTE: Fourteen historic properties (2 museums, 8 historic buildings, 4 historic sites) along Nantucket Town's streets are operated as museums by the **Nantucket Historical Association.** At any one of them you can purchase an NHA Visitor Pass ($10), which entitles you to free entry at all 14, or you can pay single admission at each (prices vary). You can also buy a pass at the association's gift shop (⊠ 11 Broad St.), open April–December. Most sites are open daily from Memorial Day to Columbus Day, except the one or two closed each year for maintenance. The **Whaling Museum** (☞ *below*) has longer hours; it closes after the Christmas Stroll and reopens weekends after April 1. ⊠ *2 Whaler's La.,* ☎ *508/228–1894.* ☉ *NHA hrs vary from year to year. The general schedule is as follows: Memorial Day–Labor Day, daily 10–5; Labor Day–Columbus Day, daily 11–3.*

❶ The redbrick **Pacific Club** (⊠ Main and Federal Sts.) building still houses the elite club of Pacific whaling masters for which it is named. Since the last whaling ship was seen here in 1870, the club now admits whalers' descendants, who gather for the odd cribbage game or a swapping of tales. The building began in 1772 as the counting house of William Rotch, owner of the *Dartmouth* and *Beaver,* two of the three ships that hosted a famous tea party in Boston. According to the NHA, the plaque outside the Pacific Club identifying the third ship, the *Eleanor,* as Rotch's is incorrect.

The most photographed view of **Main Street** is from the Pacific Club (☞ *above*) at the bottom end. The cobblestone square has a harmonious symmetry. The Pacific Club anchors the foot of it, and the Pacific National Bank (☞ *below*), another redbrick building, squares off the head. The only broad thoroughfare in town, Main Street was widened after the Great Fire of 1846 leveled all its buildings except those made of brick, to safeguard against flames hopping across the street in the event of another fire. The cobblestones were brought to the island as ballast in returning ships and laid to prevent the wheels of carts heavily laden with whale oil from sinking into the dirt on their passage from the waterfront to the factories.

At the center of Lower Main is an old horse trough, today overflowing with flowers. From here the street gently rises. At the bank it narrows to its pre-fire width and leaves the commercial district for an area of mansions that escaped the blaze. The simple shop buildings that replaced those lost are a pleasing hodgepodge of sizes, colors, and styles. Elm trees—thousands of which were planted in the 1850s by Henry and Charles Coffin—once formed a canopy over Main Street, but Dutch elm disease took most of them. In 1991 Hurricane Bob took two dozen more.

You might want to stop at the **Chamber of Commerce** to get your bearings. You'll find maps and island information available on weekdays. ⊠ *Upstairs at 48 Main St.,* ☎ *508/228–1700.*

NEED A BREAK?	You can breakfast or lunch inexpensively at several soup-and-sandwich places, including **David's Soda Fountain** (Congdon's Pharmacy, 47 Main St., ☎ 508/228–4549).
	Nantucket Pharmacy (⊠ 45 Main St., ☎ 508/228–0180) has a lunch counter that offers a quick, inexpensive lunch of simple fare, mostly sandwiches. The local favorite is tuna salad—try one!

The great white Greek Revival building with the odd windowless façade and fluted Ionic columns is the **Atheneum,** Nantucket's town library. Completed in 1847 to replace a structure lost to the fire, this is
❷

one of the oldest libraries in continuous service in the United States. The famous astronomer Maria Mitchell (☞ Mitchell House, *below*) was its first librarian. Opening ceremonies included a dedication by Ralph Waldo Emerson, who—along with Daniel Webster, Henry David Thoreau, Frederick Douglass, Lucretia Mott, and John James Audubon— later delivered lectures in the library's second-floor Great Hall. In the 19th century the hall was the center of island culture, hosting public meetings, suffrage rallies, and county fairs.

Closed for more than a year for renovations, the Atheneum reopened in 1996; the inside is beautifully restored and the space used in a way that is far more functional. Check out the periodicals section on the second floor to get all the local news. A morning story hour is held weekly; call ahead for the schedule. The adjoining Atheneum Park is a wonderful spot in which to read. ✉ *1 Lower India St.,* ☎ *508/228– 1110.* ☉ *Memorial Day–Labor Day, Mon., Wed., and Fri.–Sat. 9:30– 5, Tues. and Thurs. 9:30–8; Labor Day–Memorial Day, Tues. and Thurs. 9:30–8, Wed. and Fri.–Sat. 9:30–5.*

❸ Currently a summer cinema, the handsome wooden **Dreamland The- atre** (✉ 17 S. Water St., ☎ 508/228–5356) was built as a Quaker meet- ing house in 1829 and then became a straw factory and, later, an entertainment hall. It was moved to Brant Point as part of the grand Nantucket Hotel in the late 19th century and then was floated across the harbor by barge about 1905 and installed in its present location— a good illustration of early Nantucketers' penchant for the multiple use of dwellings as well as the relocation of houses. Trees (and there- fore lumber) were so scarce that Herman Melville joked in *Moby-Dick* that "pieces of wood in Nantucket are carried about like bits of the true cross in Rome."

★ ☾ ❹ A wonderful way to learn about the whaling era is a visit to the **Whal- ing Museum,** set in an 1846 factory built for refining spermaceti and making candles. This museum immerses you in Nantucket's whaling past with exhibits that include a fully rigged whaleboat; harpoons and other implements; portraits of sea captains; a large scrimshaw collec- tion; a full-size tryworks once used to process whale oil aboard ship; the skeleton of a 43-ft finback whale; replicas of cooper, blacksmith, and other ship-fitting shops; and the original 16-ft-high glass prism from the Sankaty Head Lighthouse. The knowledgeable and enthusiastic staff gives a 20- to 30-minute introductory talk peppered with tales of a whaler's life at sea (call for tour times). Spermaceti candles, inciden- tally, gave off a clean, steady light and only a slight fragrance, which is why they became such popular replacements for smelly tallow can- dles; due to the depletion of the sperm whale, authentic spermaceti can- dles are no longer made. Don't miss the museum's gift shop next door. ✉ *13 Broad St.,* ☎ *508/228–1894.* ▦ *$5 or NHA pass. Dec.–Mar., Sat lecture and guided tour at 1:30; Apr. and Columbus Day–Nov., weekends 11–3; May, daily 11–3; Memorial Day–Columbus Day, daily 10–5.*

❺ The **Peter Foulger Museum and Edouard A. Stackpole Library and Re- search Center** offer a peek into Nantucket's genealogical past. The mu- seum displays changing exhibits from the permanent collection, including portraits, textiles, porcelains, silver, and furniture. The research cen- ter's extensive collection of manuscripts, photographs, ships' logs and charts, and genealogical records is open only to those doing research. ✉ *15 Broad St.,* ☎ *508/228–1655.* ▦ *$4 or NHA pass. Research per- mit $10 (2 days).* ☉ *Memorial Day–mid-June and Columbus Day– Thanksgiving, weekends 11-3; mid-June–Labor Day, daily 10–5; Labor Day–Columbus Day, daily 11–3.*

NEED A
BREAK?
The **Juice Bar** (✉ 12 Broad St., ☎ 508/228–5799) serves homemade
ice cream with lots of toppings, waffle cones, and baked goods. There
are also fresh-squeezed juices, frozen yogurt, and specialty coffees.
Long lines signal good things coming to those who wait. It's open from
April to mid-October.

6 The **Nantucket Information Bureau** has public phones, rest rooms,
and a bulletin board posting events. The staff (though it may be just
one person manning the desk) gives candid recommendations and can
assist with reservations. This is the best place to turn to if you're
tempted to extend your stay and need accommodations. ✉ *25 Federal
St.,* ☎ *508/228–0925.* ۞ *July–Labor Day, daily; Labor Day–June, weekdays. Call for hrs.*

7 The handsome **Jared Coffin House** (✉ 29 Broad St., ☎ 508/228–2400
or 800/248–2405; ☞ Dining and Lodging, *below*) has operated as an
inn since the mid-19th century. Coffin was a wealthy merchant, and
he built this brick house with Ionic portico, parapet, hip roof, and
cupola—the only three-story structure on the island at the time—for
his wife, who wanted to live closer to town. They moved here in 1845
from their home on Pleasant Street, but (so the story goes) nothing would
please Mrs. Coffin, and within two years they left the island altogether
for Boston.

★ **8** The **First Congregational Church**, also known as the Old North Church,
is Nantucket's largest and most elegant. Its tower—whose steeple is
capped with a weather vane depicting a whale catch—rises 120 ft, providing the best view of Nantucket to be had. On a clear day the reward for climbing the 92 steps (many landings break the climb) is a
panorama encompassing Great Point, Sankaty Head Lighthouse,
Muskeget and Tuckernuck islands, moors, ponds, beaches, and the winding streets and rooftops of town. Peek in at the church's interior, with
its old box pews, a turn-of-the-century organ, and a trompe l'oeil ceiling done by an Italian painter in 1850 and since restored. (Organ aficionados may want to have a look at the 1831 Appleton organ—one
of only four extant—at the United Methodist Church next to the Pacific National Bank on Main Street.) The Old North Vestry in the rear,
the oldest house of worship on the island, was built in 1725 about a
mile north of its present site. The main church was built in 1834. ✉
62 Centre St., ☎ *508/228–0950.* ▣ *Tour $2.* ۞ *Mid-June–mid-Oct.,
Mon.–Sat. 10–4; call for times of scheduled tower tours. Services Sun.
at 8 AM and 10 AM.*

Twenty-six-foot tall, white-painted **Brant Point Light** (✉ End of Easton St., across a footbridge) sits on Brant Point, which has views of
the harbor and town. The beach here is not large, but it's a great place
to watch boats coming and going. The point was the site of the second-
oldest lighthouse in the country (1746), though the present, much-
photographed light was built in 1902. The existing lighthouse is the
10th to occupy this historic spot; its reassuring light is visible from 10
mi offshore.

History and architecture buffs should be sure to get a look at the hill-
9 top **Oldest House**, also called the Jethro Coffin House, built in 1686
as a wedding gift for Jethro and Mary Gardner Coffin. The most striking feature of the saltbox—the oldest house on the island—is the massive central brick chimney with brick horseshoe adornment. Other
highlights are the enormous hearths and diamond-pane lead-glass windows. Cutaway panels show 17th-century construction techniques. The
interior's sparse furnishings include an antique loom. ✉ *Sunset Hill
(a 10- to 15-min walk out Centre St. from Main St.),* ☎ *508/228–1894.*

🎫 *$3 or NHA pass.* ☉ *Memorial Day–Columbus Day, daily 10–5; call for spring hrs.*

Lily Pond Park (✉ N. Liberty St.), a 5-acre Land Bank conservation area on the edge of the town center, is a prime bird-watching spot. Its lawn and wetlands—there is a trail, but it's muddy—foster abundant wildlife, including birds, ducks, and deer. You can pick blackberries, raspberries, and grapes in season wherever you find them.

➓ Built in 1886 as one of several neighborhood fire stations—Nantucketers had learned their lesson after the 1846 conflagration—the **Fire Hose Cart House** displays a small collection of fire-fighting equipment used a century ago, including dousing buckets and a hand-pumped fire cart. ✉ *8 Gardner St.,* ☎ *508/228–1894.* 🎫 *Free.* ☉ *Memorial Day–Columbus Day, daily 10–5.*

➑ A whimsical blend of necessity and creativity, **Greater Light** (✉ *8 Howard St.*) is an example of the summer homes of the artists who flocked to Nantucket in its early resort days. In the 1930s two unusual Quaker sisters from Philadelphia—actress Hanna and artist Gertrude Monaghan—converted a barn into what looks like the lavish set for an old movie. The exotic decor includes Italian furniture, Native American artifacts and textiles, a wrought-iron balcony, bas-reliefs, and a coat of arms. The sisters also remodeled the private house next door, called Lesser Light, for their parents. (This is still a private home, so it's closed to the public.) Greater Light, closed for the past few years, may be open in 2000, depending on fund-raising success, but get the latest scoop at the Chamber of Commerce (☎ 508/228–1700).

➓ It's tough to escape the law when you live on an island. Those who did not obey the rules and regulations ended up in the **Old Gaol,** an 1805 jailhouse in use until 1933. Shingles mask the building's construction of massive square timbers, plainly visible inside. Walls, ceilings, and floors are bolted with iron. The furnishings consist of rough plank bunks and open privies, but you needn't feel too much sympathy for the prisoners: most of them were allowed out at night to sleep in their own beds. ✉ *15R Vestal St.* 🎫 *Free.* ☉ *Memorial Day–Labor Day, daily 10–5, Labor Day–Columbus Day, daily 11–3.*

The **Maria Mitchell Association** (☎ 508/228–9198), established in 1902 by Vassar students and astronomer Maria Mitchell's family, administers the Mitchell House, the Maria Mitchell Science Library, the Hinchman House, the Maria Mitchell Aquarium, and the Loines Observatory (☞ *below* for information on these sites). A combination admission ticket to all sites is $7.

Women played a strong role in Nantucket's history. During the whaling days men would be gone for up to five years at a time—and it was up to the women to keep the town going. They became leaders in every arena, from religion to business. Mary Coffin Starbuck helped establish Quakerism on the island and was a celebrated preacher. Lucretia Coffin Mott was a powerful advocate of the antislavery and women's-rights movements. During the post–Civil War depression, Centre Street near Main Street became known as "Petticoat Row," a reflection of the large number of women shopkeepers.

➌ Astronomy aficionados will appreciate the **Mitchell House,** birthplace of astronomer and Vassar professor Maria (pronounced "mah-*rye*-ah") Mitchell, who in 1847, at age 29, discovered a comet while surveying the sky from the top of the Pacific National Bank (☞ *below*). Her family had moved to quarters over the bank, where her father—also an astronomer—worked as a cashier. One of 10 children of Quaker parents, Mitchell was the first woman astronomy professor in the United States, and the first woman to discover a comet. The restored 1790 house contains family possessions and Maria Mitchell memorabilia, including the telescope with which she spotted the comet. The kitchen, of authentic wide-board construction, retains the antique utensils, iron pump, and sink of the time. Tours of the house and the roof walk are included in the admission price. The adjacent observatory is used by researchers and is not open to the public. ⊠ *1 Vestal St.,* ☎ *508/228–2896.* ☜ *$3 or association pass.* ☉ *Mid-June–Aug., Tues.–Sat. 10–4.*

⑭ The **Maria Mitchell Science Library** contains an extensive collection of science books and periodicals, including field-identification guides and gardening books, as well as books on Nantucket history. ⊠ *2 Vestal St.,* ☎ *508/228–9219.* ☜ *Free.* ☉ *Mid-June–mid-Sept., Tues.–Sat. 10–4; mid-Sept.–mid-June, Wed.–Fri. 2–5, Sat. 9–noon.*

⑮ If you're interested in the natural history of Nantucket, the **Hinchman House** displays specimens of local birds, shells, insects, and plants; exhibits habitats; and offers bird and wildflower walks and children's nature classes. The building also houses the Maria Mitchell Association's gift shop. ⊠ *7 Milk St.,* ☎ *508/228–0898.* ☜ *$3 or association pass.* ☉ *Mid-June–Sept., Tues.–Sat. 10–4.*

Loines Observatory offers "open nights" on Monday year-round, and more frequently in high season, so that you can get in a little stargazing. ⊠ *Milk St. Ext.,* ☎ *508/228–9198 or 508/228–9273.* ☜ *$5 or association pass.* ☉ *Memorial Day–Columbus Day, Mon., Wed., and Fri. 9 PM–10:30 PM; Columbus Day–Memorial Day, Mon. 9 PM–10:30 PM.*

Nantucket is packed with places that speak of its history. Off New Dollar Lane by Milk Street, and down a long driveway, the remains of the **⑯** **Starbuck refinery and candle works** are now used as apartments and garages.

⑰ To see how the other half lived, stop by the **1800 House** (⊠ *10 Mill St.*), a typical Nantucket home—one not enriched by whaling money—of that time. Once the residence of the high sheriff, the house has locally made furniture and other household goods, a six-flue chimney with beehive oven, and a summer kitchen. The house is scheduled for repairs in late 1999 and may be closed in 2000; check its status with the NHA (☎ *508/228–1894*).

⑱ Built between 1829 and 1834, the handsome Federal brick house known as **Moors' End** (⊠ *19 Pleasant St.*) is where merchant Jared Coffin lived before moving to what is now the Jared Coffin House (☞ *above*)—the proximity to the fumes from the Starbuck refinery was one of Mrs. Coffin's complaints. It is a private home, so you won't be able to see Stanley Rowland's vast murals of the whaling era on the walls or the scrawled notes about shipwreck sightings in the cupola in person; instead, keep an eye out for pictures in any number of coffee-table books about Nantucket. Behind high brick walls is the largest walled garden on Nantucket; like the house, it is not open to the public.

⑲ Several windmills sat on Nantucket hills in the 1700s, but only the **Old Mill,** a 1746 Dutch-style octagonal windmill built with lumber from shipwrecks, remains. The Douglas-fir pivot pole used to turn the cap and sails into the wind is a replacement of the original pole, a ship's foremast. The mill's wooden gears work on wind power, and when the wind is strong enough, corn is ground into meal that is sold here. ⊠ *50 Prospect St., at S. Mill St.,* ☎ *508/228–1894.* ☜ *$2 or NHA pass.* ☉ *Memorial Day–Labor Day, daily 10–5; Labor Day–Columbus Day, daily 11–3.*

As far back as the early 1700s, there was a small African-American population on Nantucket; the earliest blacks were slaves of the island's earliest settlers. When slavery was abolished on the island in 1773, Nantucket became a destination for free blacks and escaping slaves. Today nine sights associated with the island's African-American heritage are on the self-guided Black Heritage Trail tour (☞ Guided Tours *in* Nantucket A to Z, *below*). Of these, the **African School and Church** is the only extant public building constructed and occupied by the island's African-American populace in the 19th century. Built in the 1820s, the meeting house also served first as a schoolhouse and then, after 1848 when the schools were integrated, as a church, up until 1911. A complete restoration, both inside and out, has returned the site to its authentic 1880s appearance. Newly completed spaces for lectures, concerts, and readings help portray the experiences of African-Americans and Cape Verdeans on Nantucket. ☒ *York and Pleasant Sts.,* ☎ *508/228–4058 or 617/739–1200.* ☜ *Call; not set at press time.* ☉ *Call for seasonal hrs.*

★ ㉑ Many of the mansions of the golden age of whaling were built on Upper Main Street. The well-known **"Three Bricks"** (☒ 93–97 Upper Main St.), identical redbrick mansions with columned, Greek Revival porches at their front entrances, were built between 1836 and 1838 by whaling merchant Joseph Starbuck for his three sons. One house still belongs to a Starbuck descendant. The Three Bricks are similar in design to the Jared Coffin House (☞ *above*) but have only two stories. They are not open to the public.

While you're touring Main Street, the magnificent white, porticoed Greek Revival mansions you'll see—referred to as the Two Greeks—were built in 1845 and 1846 by wealthy factory owner William Hadwen, a Newport native who made his money in whale oil and candles. No. 94, built as a wedding gift for his adopted niece, was modeled on the Athenian Tower of the Winds, with Corinthian capitals on the entry columns, a domed-stair hall with statuary niches, and an oculus. The Hadwens' ㉒ own domicile, at No. 96, is now a museum, the **Hadwen House,** which reflects how the wealthy of the period lived. The house has been restored to its mid-19th-century origins, with classic Victorian gas chandeliers and furnishings, as well as reproduction wallpapers and window treatments. A guided tour points out such architectural details as the grand circular staircase, fine plasterwork, and carved Italian-marble fireplace mantels. A second-floor gallery houses an exhibition that changes each year; the 1999 show was about lightship baskets. Behind the house are period gardens. ☒ *96 Main St.,* ☎ *508/228–1894.* ☜ *$3 or NHA pass.* ☉ *Memorial Day–Labor Day, daily 10–5; Labor Day– Columbus Day, daily 11–3.*

㉓ The **Macy-Christian House,** a two-story lean-to, built circa 1740 for Nathaniel Macy, has a great open hearth flanked by brick beehive ovens and old paneling. Part of the house reflects the late-19th-century Colonial Revival style of the 1934 renovation by the Christian family. The formal parlor and upstairs bedroom are in authentic Colonial style. ☒ *12 Liberty St.,* ☎ *508/228–1894.* ☜ *$2 or NHA pass.* ☉ *Memorial Day– Labor Day, daily 10–5; Labor Day–Columbus Day, daily 11–3.*

㉔ Built for brothers, and facing each other, are the two attractive brick **Coffin houses** (☒ 75 and 78 Main St.): the **Henry Coffin House** and the **Charles G. Coffin House.** Wealthy shipping agents and whale-oil merchants, the Coffins used the same mason for these 1830s houses and the later Three Bricks (☞ *above*). These are privately owned and not open to the public.

㉕ One of Nantucket's grand Main Street homes, the **John Wendell Barrett House** (✉ 72 Main St.) was built in 1820 in early Greek Revival style. Legend has it that Lydia Mitchell Barrett stood on the steps and refused to budge when, during the Great Fire, men tried to evacuate her so they could blow up the house to stop the spread of the fire. Luckily, a shift in the wind settled the showdown.

㉖ The 1818 **Pacific National Bank** (✉ 61 Main St.), like the Pacific Club (☞ *above*) it faces, is a monument to the far-flung voyages of the Nantucket whaling ships it financed. Inside, above old-style teller cages, are murals of street and port scenes from the whaling days. But this is no relic—the bank is still in use today.

Murray's Toggery, near the top of the hill in town, marks the site of R. H. Macy's first retail store (☞ Shopping, *below*). ✉ 62 Main St.

㉗ Built around 1838 as a Friends school, the **Quaker Meeting House** is now a Quaker place of worship in summer. A small room of quiet simplicity, with white-and-gray walls, 12-over-12 windows with antique glass, and unadorned wood benches, it is in keeping with the tenets of these peaceful people, who believe that the divine spirit is within each person and that no one requires an intermediary to worship God. An unattractive 1904 concrete building attached to the meeting house holds the **Fair Street Museum,** which presents rotating exhibits such as the NHA's collection of antique lightship baskets and portraits of historical Nantucket figures. ✉ *1 Fair St.,* ☎ *508/228–0316.* 🎫 *$3 or NHA pass.* ☉ *Services Sun. at 10 AM.*

㉘ On a hot day, peek into the 1901 **St. Paul's Episcopal Church,** a massive granite structure adorned at the front and back by beautiful Tiffany windows. The interior is cool and white, with dark exposed beams, and offers a quiet sanctuary from the crowds and the heat. ✉ *20 Fair St.,* ☎ *508/228–0916.* ☉ *Church office open Mon.–Sat., 9–1; services Sun. at 8 AM and 10 AM.*

㉙ The 1809 **Unitarian Universalist Church,** also known as South Church, has a gold-domed spire that soars above town, just as the First Congregational Church's slender white steeple does. Also like First Congregational (☞ *above*), South Church has trompe-l'oeil ceiling painting, this one simulating an intricately detailed dome; it was executed in 1840 by a European painter. Here, however, illusion is taken to greater lengths: the curved chancel and paneled walls you see are also creations in paint. The 1831 mahogany-cased Goodrich organ in the loft is played at services and concerts (☞ Music *in* Nightlife and the Arts, *below*). In the octagonal belfry of the tower, which houses the town clock, there is a bell cast in Portugal that has been ringing out the noon hour since it was hung in 1815. ✉ *11 Orange St., at Stone Alley,* ☎ *508/228–2730.* ☉ *Service Sun. at 10:45 AM.*

�! **Maria Mitchell Aquarium** fills its salt- and freshwater tanks with local marine life, including flukes, skates, and lobsters. Kids can pick up crabs and starfish from the hands-on tank; family marine ecology trips are given four times weekly in season. ✉ *28 Washington St., near Commercial Wharf,* ☎ *508/228–5387.* 🎫 *$1 or association pass.* ☉ *Mid-June–Aug., Tues.–Sat. 10–4.*

As you look beyond the island horizons, a bit of whimsy is found on the wall of the last building on the left on **Washington Street,** at Main Street—notice the sign listing distances from Nantucket to various points of the globe. It's 14,650 mi to Tahiti.

Dining and Lodging

$$$$ ✕ **Company of the Cauldron.** There's only one menu each night, and often only a single seating as well, so pick your night with care—luckily, just about anything coming out of this kitchen is excellent. The special could include chilled white gazpacho with sliced lobster meat and fresh basil and chocolate ganache cake with raspberries. The interior has a dark, Northern European tavern feel, with ivy tumbling over the windows, and tables lined up in rows that are more comradely than intimate. ⊠ *7 India St.,* ☎ *508/228–4016. Reservations essential. MC, V. No smoking. No lunch.*

$$$$ ✕ **The Pearl.** Walking into this new place, which is as superslick and upscale as Nantucket gets, is like entering a rather chilly stratosphere. All is minimalist, sumptuous design, in pale colors such as cream and ice blue. The bar is translucent white onyx, lit from within, and an enormous fish tank with tinted blue water divides the dining areas from the entrance. Tables in the left side of the room are too crowded together "bistro style" for such a fancy place; stay to the more intimate right side instead. This is a restaurant in which to feel elegant, enjoy fine wine, and eat such dishes as salmon tartare with cucumber noodles and roasted beet oil. The only problem is, it all feels as if they might check your credentials at the door. ⊠ *12 Federal St.,* ☎ *508/228–9701. Reservations essential. AE, MC, V.*

$$$$ ✕ **Straight Wharf.** Kate and Steve Cavagnaro, originally from Hartford, Connecticut, run this old place nestled on bustling Straight Wharf with a simple, interesting menu and superior wine list. The room is pretty, with a peaked wood ceiling, but the covered deck overlooking the water is the choice place to sit in summer. The high-end main menu presents the usual choices—fresh salmon, tuna, rack of lamb—along with original touches such as seared Nantucket sea scallops and foie gras "BLT," and striped bass tapenade with a tomato, artichoke, and pepper *panzanella* (an Italian bread salad). The restaurant also has a summer grill menu with more basic fare and prices (though a food minimum of $29 applies) and a beautiful dessert list. ⊠ *6 Harbor Sq., Straight Wharf,* ☎ *508/228–4499. Reservations essential. AE, MC, V. No lunch. Closed Labor Day–Memorial Day.*

$$$–$$$$ ✕ **American Seasons.** The culinary context here is geographic: chef and
★ owner Michael Getter gathers specialties from the four corners of the continental United States. You can roam the menu's territories, choosing Nantucket lobster for an appetizer and then a loin of pork for the main course. In the "Wild West" there's an excellent green peppercorn–crusted aged sirloin of beef, while "Down South" jumbo shrimp are covered by crispy cornmeal. New England offerings favor monkfish and tuna, a surprise to traditionalists. Pastoral murals add a rustic charm, although eating on the patio is a fine alternative. As is fitting, expect only American wines, which definitely hold their own. ⊠ *80 Centre St.,* ☎ *508/228–7111. AE, MC, V. No smoking. Closed mid-Dec.–early Apr. No lunch.*

$$$–$$$$ ✕ **The Boarding House.** Sneak through a happening street-level bar into this handsome, mural-lined basement dining room. Executive chef Seth Carter Raynor is expanding his horizons at the Pearl (☞ *above*), but he retains a good hand with fresh fish; the grilled, rare yellowfin tuna is exceptional. Outdoor tables let you do a bit of people-watching, and the bistro menu can make the evening easier on the wallet. Another plus: this excellent restaurant stays open year-round. ⊠ *12 Federal St.,* ☎ *508/228–9622. AE, MC, V. No dinner Mon., Tues.*

$$$–$$$$ ✕ **DeMarco.** *Cape Cod Life* has given this restaurant an award as "Best Ethnic Restaurant" on the island; it perhaps says more about Nantucket than DeMarco that basic, good, northern Italian food is considered ethnic here. The antipasto menu includes *vitello tonnato* (tender

poached veal with a creamy tuna-caper-anchovy sauce). The selection of pasta dishes is strong; try "badly cut" fresh pasta in a sauce of wild mushrooms, prosciutto, and fresh sage with a dollop of mascarpone. Another strength here is the excellent wine list. The dining room is a bit generic, especially upstairs. Dining downstairs near the curving bar is definitely a better bet. ⊠ *9 India St.,* ☎ *508/228–1836. AE, MC, V. Closed Jan.–Apr. No lunch.*

$$$–$$$$ ✕ **Le Languedoc.** This busy little place has a café downstairs, a somewhat more formal dining room upstairs, and a garden terrace where a tapas menu is offered from 6 to 10 PM. The cuisine blends Continental and American styles; for instance, the pan-roasted lobster comes with a champagne grapefruit butter. The back room is particularly handsome, with dark red walls over dove-gray paneling and white tablecloths. Reservations in the more formal area are for one of the two seatings per night, at 7 or 8:45 PM. The same kitchen serves the café, in a more relaxed and less expensive way. ⊠ *24 Broad St.,* ☎ *508/ 228–2552. AE, MC, V. BYOB. Closed Jan.–mid-Apr. and Sun. off-season. No lunch July–Aug.*

$$$–$$$$ ✕ **21 Federal.** Proprietor Chick Walsh and chef Russell Jaehnig have
★ created sophisticated, gentrified island dining. This is a place to see and be seen, as well as to enjoy some of the island's best new and traditional American cuisine. An informal dining room extends into the dark-paneled bar. Beyond are two other rooms, with traditional gray wainscoting, black-suede banquettes, and damask-covered tables; a curving staircase leads to a similar second floor, although the first floor has better ambience and more people exposure. Entrées have luxurious touches, such as sautéed halibut with saffron risotto, morels, and osetra caviar. ⊠ *21 Federal St.,* ☎ *508/228–2121. AE, MC, V. Closed Jan.–Mar.; may close Mon. in Apr., May, Oct., and Nov.*

$$$ ✕ **Cioppino's.** The name, from the robust fish stew, is said to come from poor San Franciscans who used to go from fishing boat to fishing boat asking the Italian captains to throw a fish or two into the communal pot. "Chip in-o, chip in-o," they called, adding the "o" to mimic the sound of Italian. Whatever its origin, the stew is the house specialty, but the menu also lists plenty of meat and new seafood specials every night. (Many items change every two weeks.) Owner Tracy Root worked for years at Chanticleer (☞ Siasconset, Polpis, and Wauwinet, *below*) before opening his own place nine years ago and remains a passionate, engaged restaurateur, proud of his interesting wine selection (look for the Californians). Locals pack the small, eight-stool bar up front. ⊠ *20 Broad St.,* ☎ *508/228–4622. D, DC, MC, V. Closed Oct.–Apr.*

$$–$$$ ✕ **Atlantic Cafe.** With its booths in the back and serious beer-drink-
★ ing up front, the Atlantic has been the island's belly-up-to-the-bar place since 1978. Two big, salty codfish cakes with plenty of slaw and fries will make the beer taste even better, and you can still actually order food like nachos and potato skins without endangering your reputation. "Mary and the Boys" is a Bloody Mary with six shrimp, and it's a good deal. The painting over the big bar reveals a few old, bearded Nantucket salts in a card game; any rainy afternoon, you'll find some young salts in the corner mimicking the scene. ⊠ *15 S. Water St.,* ☎ *508/228–0570. AE, DC, MC, V.*

$$–$$$ ✕ **Center Street Bistro.** What was the Off-Center Café has been renamed; owners Ruth and Tim Pitts have gone upscale a bit but not changed all that much. As in most American "bistros," the menu experiments with ingredients and ethnicities. You can find a smoked salmon and potato "taco" with capers and cream cheese, or try sautéed shrimp with red curry, coconut rice noodles, and mango cilantro relish. Serving only beer and wine, the Pitts offer 15 wines by the glass and a private label beer. The walk here through a little minimall is kind of strange, but you do have a nice sense of being tucked away in back. There's seating for only 20, and the tables are jammed together. Outdoor seating is basically on the sidewalk, making for great people-watching. You can get breakfast here, too. ⊠ *29 Centre St.,* ☎ *508/228–8470. No credit cards. No lunch.*

\$\$–\$\$\$ ✕ **Nantucket Tapas.** The first thing you see when you step into this small, converted cottage—a "culinary concept" from Nantucket's Sushi by Yoshi (☞ *below*)—is a big glass counter beckoning with rich desserts that can round off a meal of tasty appetizer-size dishes. One side of the room is lined with family-style tables set on big old barrels, the other with more intimate, white-cloth tables set for dinner only. The 33 items on the main tapas menu are eclectic with an Asian bend, and expensive. The idea is to pick and choose, maybe share a taste of this and a taste of that. Try the seared tuna carpaccio with greens and crème fraîche, and grilled Peking duck with an Asian sauce. The place fills up fast, especially during the day, so expect a wait or take advantage of the take-out option. *15 S. Beach St.,* ☎ *508/228–2033. AE, MC, V.*

\$\$ ✕ **Cap'n Tobey's Chowder House.** A don't-rock-the-boat fish house, Cap'n Tobey's is nothing if not comfortable. It's in a nice location though it lacks a great water view; the menu and decor run to the dependably familiar. Some dishes, like seafood au gratin and baked stuffed jumbo shrimp, have an anachronistic feel to them here in chic Nantucket, but that might suit you down to the ground. ⊠ *Straight Wharf,* ☎ *508/228–0836. AE, D, DC, MC, V. Closed mid-Oct.–May.*

\$–\$\$ ✕ **Vincent's.** Pizza under a warmer, calzones, plenty of pasta, free delivery—these are hardly island staples, but Vincent's does them all and has since 1954. Don't get into anything fancy—in this case, "fancy" means fettuccine Alfredo—just order some pizzas, pitas, and focaccia and fill up. Whether you eat in or out, enjoy it, because this place is an endangered species on Nantucket. It's open for breakfast, too. ⊠ *21 S. Water St.,* ☎ *508/228–0189. MC, V.*

\$ ✕ **Espresso Cafe.** This appealing spot for breakfast, lunch, pastries, express takeout, special coffees, and killer iced espresso drinks resembles a turn-of-the-century ice cream parlor, with its white and pink entrance and hanging petunias. Inside, a huge room has an ornate, pressed-tin ceiling and black-and-white tiled floor. A long counter showcasing desserts and breakfast items from the bakery (described by one sweet tooth as a "dream counter") is rumored to have the best scones in town. The menu is extensive. The café's motto is "No waiting!! No kidding!!" ⊠ *40 Main St.,* ☎ *508/228–6930. Reservations not accepted. D, MC, V. No dinner.*

\$ ✕ **Rose and Crown.** A place for college kids to raise harmless hell at night is also a fun place to eat lunch on a rainy afternoon. The Rose and Crown is cavernous and worn, the walls and ceiling hung with old restaurant signs and hula hoops. Lively young servers bring mounds of nachos, French fries with the skins on, big grilled hot dogs, pesto and goat cheese pizzas, and excellent Bloody Marys flecked with horseradish. The stage up front is perpetually set for the live music at night, and there's got to be a dartboard somewhere. ⊠ *23 S. Water St.,* ☎ *508/228–2595. Reservations not accepted. AE, MC, V. Closed Nov.–mid-Apr.*

\$ ✕ **Schooner's.** This could be your first stop off the Nantucket ferry. Schooner's is true to its nautical motif: old wooden floors, beams strung with ships' flags, and a sidewalk café enclosed with navy blue canvas. Among the rooms to choose from is an airy blue and white one upstairs that overlooks the wharf. The absolutely straightforward menu features chicken tenders and tenderloin tips, Caesar salad and fajitas. A spinach artichoke dip comes with many-color tortilla chips.

Live acoustic music plays nightly. ⊠ *31 Easy St.,* ☎ *508/228–5824. Reservations not accepted. AE, MC, V. Closed mid-Oct.–Mar.*

$ ✕ **Something Natural.** Of all of the few really good take-out places on the island—for sandwiches, desserts, loaves of bread—this one deserves special mention, if only for the picnic area that comes in so handy for an occasional quick, inexpensive lunch. ⊠ *50 Cliff Rd.,* ☎ *508/228–0504. No credit cards.*

$$$$ ✕🖬 **Harbor House.** Giant mergers seem to be the way of the times,
★ and with them come many changes; Harbor House is now part of Nantucket Island Resorts. This family-oriented complex provides scads of amenities like its more upscale sibling, the White Elephant (☞ *below*), at a lower price. The restaurant, now called the Food Fare at the Hearth, is a traditional island favorite with a lovely outdoor patio. Ideal for families with hungry children in tow, the restaurant has five separate stations—an extensive salad bar, a pasta section, a meat-carving table, a children's section, and a dessert table—that can be grazed upon for one price. The 1886 main inn and several "town houses" are set on a flower-filled quadrangle very near the town center. Standard rooms are done in English-country style, with bright floral fabrics and queen-size beds. Some have French doors that open onto decks. The generally larger town-house rooms, in buildings grouped around the pool, have a more traditional look, with upscale pine and pastels. Some have cathedral ceilings, sofa beds, and decks. All rooms have phones and TVs. The Garden Cottage has its own garden and a private-house feel, but its rooms are smaller. ⊠ *S. Beach St., Box 1139, 02554,* ☎ *508/228–1500, 800/475–2637 for reservations,* ℻ *508/228–7639. 109 rooms. Restaurant, lounge, concierge, children's programs (ages 5–13), business services. AE, D, DC, MC, V. CP.*

$$$$ ✕🖬 **White Elephant.** Long a hallmark of service and style on the island, the White Elephant offers, above all, a choice location—right on Nantucket Harbor, separated only by a wide lawn. The main hotel, wrapped by a deck with a fine view of the bobbing boats, has a formal restaurant with a waterside outdoor café. The Brant Point menu indulges in rich combinations, focusing on ocean-fresh seafood. The recent merger with the Harbor House (☞ *above*) means that extensive changes are afoot. At press time, massive renovation and redecoration were slated to begin in fall 1999; June 2000 was the projected date for the reopening. The new face of this old standby was yet to be determined. ⊠ *Easton St., Box 1139, 02554,* ☎ *508/228–2500, 800/ 475–2637 for reservations,* ℻ *508/325–1195. 54 rooms. Restaurant, lounge, room service, putting green, dock, concierge, meeting rooms. AE, D, DC, MC, V. Seasonal months of operation not determined at press time.*

$$$–$$$$ ✕🖬 **Jared Coffin House.** This collection of four buildings has been hosting guests for more than a century (☞ Exploring, *above*). Jared's restaurant ($$$)—famous, formal, and safe—is an elegant dining room. Dinner is predictable, never veering far from perfectly grilled swordfish and herb-encrusted tenderloin. Service is impressive, and the wine list is expansive. (Dinner is not served January–April.) Downstairs, the Tap Room ($$), open year-round, is dark and cozy, with lots of exposed wood and nautical art. The fare includes prime rib, fried clams, and pasta—things you'll never find upstairs at Jared's. You can lunch on the outdoor patio, weather permitting. The main inn building, an 1845 three-story brick mansion topped by a cupola, has an historic tone. The public and guest rooms are furnished with period antiques (the other buildings, with reproductions), Oriental carpets, and lace curtains. The Harrison Gray House, an 1842 Greek Revival mansion across the street, offers larger guest rooms with large baths and queen-size canopy beds. Two newer buildings are close by on

Center Street, but they don't have the historical appeal of the main inn and the Harrison Gray House. All rooms have phones and cable TV. Small, inexpensive single rooms are available. ⊠ *29 Broad St., Box 1580, 02554,* ☎ *508/228–2400 or 800/248–2405,* ℻ *508/228–8549. 60 rooms. Restaurant, bar, café, concierge. AE, D, DC, MC, V. BP.*

$$$$ **Cliffside Beach Club.** Once you've gotten here, you may not be in-
★ clined to leave—enjoying the beach may be occupation enough. Although the cedar-shingle exterior, landscaped with climbing roses and hy-drangeas, and the pavilion on the private sandy beach 1 mi from town reflect the club's 1920s origins, the interiors are done in contemporary summer style, with white walls, white or natural wood furniture, cathedral ceilings, and local art. Some have kitchenettes, fireplaces, wet bars, or private decks. Two large "town-house suites" have full kitchens and decks overlooking dunes, moors, and Nantucket Sound. Front rooms are reserved for adults only; children are welcome in the apartments. ⊠ *46 Jefferson Ave., Box 449, 02554,* ☎ *508/228–0618,* ℻ *508/325–4735. 26 rooms, 3 suites, 2 apartments, 1 cottage. Restaurant, piano bar, exercise room, beach, playground. AE. Closed mid-Oct.–May. CP.*

$$$$ **Wharf Cottages.** These weathered shingle cottages sit on a wharf in Nantucket Harbor, with yachts moored just steps away—in fact, with reservations, you could arrive by boat and tie up at the marina. Each unit has a little garden and sitting area, a fully equipped kitchen, and attractive modern decor with a nautical flavor: white walls, navy blue rugs, light-wood floors and furniture. Studios have a sofa bed for sleeping. Other cottages have one to three bedrooms. All spaces have water views, though they're not always equal—some cottages have extra-large windows. There's a three-night minimum in high season. All of the amenities available at the Harbor House (☞ *above*) extend here, including the children's programs. ⊠ *New Whale St., Box 1139, 02554,* ☎ *508/228–4620, 800/475–2637 for reservations,* ℻ *508/228–7639. 25 cottages. Kitchenettes, dock. AE, D, DC, MC, V. Closed mid-Oct.–late Apr.*

$$$–$$$$ **Beachside at Nantucket.** Those who prefer rooms-around-a-pool mo-tels with all the creature comforts will find a very nice one here, though it's a bit of a walk from the town center. Each unit in the one- and two-story buildings is furnished in wicker and florals and has a queen-size or two double beds, a tiled bath, and a small refrigerator and coffeemaker. Some rooms have French doors opening onto pool-view decks. Pub-lic tennis courts are adjacent. ⊠ *30 N. Beach St., 02554,* ☎ *508/228–2241 or 800/322–4433,* ℻ *508/228–8901. 90 rooms, 3 2-bedroom suites. Pool, meeting rooms. AE, D, DC, MC, V. CP. Closed mid-Oct.–mid-Apr.*

$$$–$$$$ **Centerboard Guest House.** The look and polish of this no-smoking
★ inn help differentiate it from any other Nantucket property. White walls, some with murals of moors and sky in soft pastels; blond-wood floors; and natural woodwork create a cool, dreamy atmosphere. There is yet more white in the lacy linens and puffy comforters on the feather beds. Touches of color are added by stained-glass lamps, antique quilts, and fresh flowers. The first-floor suite (right off the entry hall) is stunning, with 11-ft ceilings, a Victorian living room with fireplace and bar, in-laid parquet floors, and a green-marble bath with whirlpool bath. This island of calm isn't isolated, however; it's just a few blocks from the center of town. ⊠ *8 Chester St., Box 456, 02554,* ☎ *508/228–9696. 6 rooms, 1 suite. AE, MC, V. CP.*

$$$–$$$$ **Lyon Street Inn.** Ann Marie and Barry Foster have combined an en-
★ thusiasm for history and an eye for detail to create a truly unique guest house. Their mostly new, air-conditioned house has been rebuilt with historical touches such as variable-width plank floors, salvaged Colo-nial mantels on the fireplaces, and hefty ceiling beams of antiqued red

oak. The white walls and blond woodwork provide a clean stage for antique Oriental rugs in deep, rich colors; choice antiques, such as Room No. 1's French tester bed draped in white mosquito netting; and English floral fabrics, down comforters, and big pillows. Bathrooms are white and bright. Several have separate showers and antique tubs, and all have antique porcelain pedestal sinks and brass fixtures. The inn is just a five-minute walk from the center of town. ⌧ *10 Lyon St., 02554,* ☎ *508/228–5040. 7 rooms. MC, V. Closed mid-Dec.–mid-Apr. CP.*

$$$–$$$$ 🖼 **Manor House.** The screened and open porches of this no-smoking hotel in the heart of the historic district are perfect for a casual bit of people-watching. Rooms in the 1846 house are spacious, with reproduction rice-carved beds (king or queen). Seven rooms have king canopy beds and working fireplaces. All have TV, air-conditioning, and phones. A small cottage next door done in wicker and chintz has two bedrooms and a fully equipped kitchen. Packages are available. ⌧ *31 Centre St., Box 1436, 02554–1436,* ☎ *508/228–0600 or 800/673–4559,* 📠 *508/325–4046. 15 rooms, 1 cottage. D, MC, V. CP.*

$$$–$$$$ 🖼 **Westmoor Inn.** Built in 1917 as a Vanderbilt summer house, this yel-
★   low Federal-style mansion with widow's walk and portico is a mile from town and a short walk to a quiet ocean beach, just off the Madaket bike path. There are plenty of places to settle down to read, including a wide lawn set with Adirondack chairs and a garden patio secluded behind 11-ft hedges. A wicker-filled sunroom has a common TV. Guest rooms are beautifully decorated in French-country style, most with soft florals and stenciled walls. One extra-large first-floor room has a giant bath with whirlpool tub and French doors opening onto the lawn. Some third-floor rooms are built into the eaves, which gives them odd angles and low ceilings—be sure to watch your head. During breakfast you can look out through the dining room's glass walls and ceiling. The inn is no smoking. ⌧ *Cliff Rd., 02554,* ☎ *508/228–0877 or 888/236–7310,* 📠 *508/228–5763. 14 rooms. Bicycles. AE, MC, V. Closed early Dec.–mid-Apr. CP.*

$$–$$$$ 🖼 **Century House.** This 1833 late-Federal-style sea captain's home became a rooming house in the 1870s and has operated as a guest house ever since. Rooms are furnished with a mix of antiques and reproductions, but all the beds are beautiful old pieces—sleigh beds, spool beds, and canopy four-posters. A lavish buffet breakfast is served in the pine-paneled country kitchen; if you're feeling languid, you can relax in a rocking chair on the wraparound veranda. The innkeepers also manage two cottages, one in 'Sconset across from the beach, another on Nantucket harbor. ⌧ *10 Cliff Rd., 02554,* ☎ *508/228–0530, 561/655–3127 off-season. 14 rooms. MC, V. CP.*

$$–$$$$ 🖼 **Chestnut House.** At this perfectly unpretentious, centrally located guest house, innkeepers Jeannette and Jerry Carl's hand-hooked rugs and paintings, along with their son's Tiffany-style lamps, are everywhere. Suites have a sitting room with sofa. The guest parlor reflects the Arts and Crafts style, and some rooms have William Morris–theme wallpapers. A spacious, cheery cottage sleeps four (queen-size bed and sofa bed) and has a full kitchen and bath and a small deck. Rates include a voucher for breakfast at a couple of local restaurants. No smoking is permitted. ⌧ *3 Chestnut St., 02554,* ☎ *508/228–0049,* 📠 *508/228–9521. 1 room, 4 suites, 1 cottage. AE, MC, V. BP.*

$$–$$$$ 🖼 **Martin House Inn.** Debbie Wasil's friendly and very nicely refurbished
★   B&B in an 1804 house offers a great variety of mostly spacious rooms (two suites and singles among them) with four-poster beds or canopies, pretty linens, and fresh flowers; several have queen-size beds, couches, and/or writing tables. Four rooms have fireplaces, including No. 21 on the second floor, which also has a queen-size canopy bed and a private porch overlooking the backyard. Third-floor shared-bath rooms

are sunny and bright, with a quirky under-eaves feel. The large living room with a fireplace and the wide porch invite lingering. ⊠ *61 Centre St., Box 743, 02554, ☎ 508/228–0678, FAX 508/325–4798. 11 rooms, 7 with bath; 2 suites. Piano. AE, MC, V. CP.*

$$–$$$$ 🏠 **Roberts House and Meeting House Inns.** These attractive, historic buildings are in the thick of Nantucket's shops and restaurants. Many of the guest rooms have high ceilings and a mix of antique and re-production furniture. All have queen-size or larger beds, TV, phones, and air-conditioning; some have Jacuzzis and small refrigerators. The bathrooms, though, are not all they could be. ⊠ *11 India St., at Centre St., Box 1436, 02554-1436, ☎ 508/228–9009 or 800/872–6817, FAX 508/325–4046. 24 rooms. D, MC, V. CP.*

$$$ 🏠 **Seven Sea Street.** You can get a lovely view of the harbor from this inn's widow's walk. There's a dash of Scandinavia inside, with plenty of tongue-in-groove light pine and red oak walls, some stenciled white walls, exposed-beam ceilings, and highly polished wide-board floors. Most rooms have braided rugs, queen-size beds with fishnet canopies and quilts, modern baths, and a desk area. All have TV/VCR, phones, air-conditioning, and mini-refrigerators. The deluxe Honeymoon Suite, good for longer stays, has a cathedral post-and-beam ceiling, a full kitchen, a gas fireplace, and a view of the harbor. The inn is no smoking. ⊠ *7 Sea St., 02554, ☎ 508/228–3577, FAX 508/228–3578. 11 rooms, 2 suites. Hot tub, steam room, library. AE, D, MC, V. CP.*

$$–$$$ 🏠 **Cliff Lodge.** Owners Debby and John Bennett have preserved much
★ of the old-house feeling of this 18th-century lodge. Moldings, wainscoting, and wide-board floors hark back a century or so; the large rooms have pastel hooked rugs on spatter-painted floors, country curtains and furnishings, and down comforters. Also in keeping with the house's age, some baths are quite small. The very pleasant apartment has a living room with a fireplace, a private deck and entrance, and a large eat-in kitchen. In addition to enjoying the attractive common rooms, you can lounge on the sunporch or garden patio, or head up to the roof walk for a great view of the harbor. Smoking is not permitted. ⊠ *9 Cliff Rd., 02554, ☎ 508/228–9480, FAX 508/228–6308. 11 rooms, 1 apartment. MC, V. CP.*

$$–$$$ 🏠 **18 Gardner Street.** The rooms in this 1835 house are comfortable without being completely casual, with wide-board floors, mostly queen-size beds (some canopy or four-poster) with eyelet sheets and hand-made quilts, and a handful of antiques. All have TV and air-conditioning; 10 have working fireplaces. The inn is no smoking. ⊠ *18 Gardner St., 02554, ☎ 508/228–1155 or 800/435–1450. 17 rooms, 15 with bath; 2 suites. Refrigerators, bicycles. AE, MC, V. CP.*

$$–$$$ 🏠 **Hawthorn House.** Innkeeper Mitch Carl and his wife, Diane, have filled their 1850 house with art, hooked rugs, and stained glass. The smallish rooms are decorated with antiques and homey, personal touches, like Mitch's stained-glass lamps and Diane's handmade quilts. A dark but conveniently located cottage sleeps two and has air-conditioning. Breakfast vouchers are included for a couple of local restaurants. ⊠ *2 Chestnut St., 02554, ☎ FAX 508/228–1468. 9 rooms, 7 with bath; 1 cottage. MC, V. BP.*

$$–$$$ 🏠 **Pineapple Inn.** The beauty of this 1838 Greek Revival whaling captain's home shines after a generous renovation, complete with a score of luxurious details. The pineapple was a symbol of hospitality in colonial times, and such old traditions are alive and thriving here. Named after local whaling captains, the rooms have king or queen four-poster canopy beds with goosedown quilts, antiques, and spacious baths finished in white marble, as well as telephones and voice mail. Morning diners are greeted with fresh-squeezed juices, espresso, and scrumptious homemade pastries. The inn is three blocks from the ferry land-

ing on a small one-way street, and the owners will happily make suggestions for your stay. ✉ *10 Hussey St., 02554,* ☎ *508/228–9992,* FAX *508/325–6051. 12 rooms. In-room data ports. AE, MC, V. Closed mid-Dec.–late Apr. CP.*

$$–$$$ ⌂ **76 Main Street.** Built in 1883 by a sea captain, this no-smoking B&B just beyond the bustle of the shops carefully blends antiques and reproductions, Oriental rugs, handmade quilts, and lots of fine woods. The cherry-wood Victorian entrance hall is dominated by a long, elaborately carved staircase. Room No. 3, originally the dining room, also has wonderful woodwork, a carved-wood armoire, and twin four-posters. Spacious No. 1, once the front parlor, has three large windows, massive redwood pocket doors, and a bed with eyelet spread and canopy. The motel-like rooms in the 1955 annex out back, set around a flagstone patio and gardens, have low ceilings but are quite spacious and are perfect for families. Owner Shirley Peters usually officiates over breakfast, which she serves in the bright kitchen; her homemade scones are wonderful. ✉ *76 Main St., 02554,* ☎ *508/228–2533. 18 rooms. Refrigerator. AE, D, MC, V. Closed Jan.–Mar. CP.*

$–$$ ⌂ **Nesbitt Inn.** This family-run guest house in the center of town offers comfortable, shared-bath rooms sweetly done in Victorian style, with lace curtains, some marble-top and brass antiques, and a sink in each room. There's a pair of inexpensive single rooms, as well as a pair of rooms with two twin beds apiece. Some beds are not as firm as they should be, and the location next door to a popular bar-restaurant means it gets traffic noise (ask for a room on the quieter side), but the Nesbitt is a very good buy in this town. The backyard is perfect for children. ✉ *21 Broad St., Box 1019, 02554,* ☎ *508/228–0156,* FAX *508/228–2446. 12 rooms without bath. No-smoking rooms, refrigerator. No pets. MC, V. Closed Jan.–Mar. CP.*

$ ⌂ **Hostelling International–Nantucket.** One of the most picturesque hostels in the country, this 49-bed facility occupies a former lifesaving station. It's in Surfside Beach, a 3-mi ride from town on the bike path. The hostel has common areas, a piano, a kitchen, and grills for cookouts, as well as a variety of educational, cultural, and recreational programs. Reservations, essential in July and August, are always strongly recommended. ✉ *31 Western Ave., 02554,* ☎ *508/228–0433 (Nov.–Mar.: ✉ Box 3158, W. Tisbury 02575,* ☎ *508/693–2665). Picnic area, volleyball. MC, V. Closed mid-Oct.–mid-Apr.*

Nightlife and the Arts

BARS AND CLUBS

The **Box** (a.k.a. Chicken Box; ✉ 16 Dave St., off Lower Orange St., ☎ 508/228–9717) is open daily year-round and has live music every night in season, weekends off-season. Lineups range from reggae to rock, with both local and visiting bands—one local favorite is E Cliff and the Swing Dogs.

Brotherhood of Thieves (✉ 23 Broad St., ☎ no phone) has live folk music year-round. The well-stocked bar offers an interesting selection of beers and ales, plus dozens of cordials and liqueurs. A major fire closed this place in mid-1999, but it should reopen for summer 2000.

The **Muse** (✉ 44 Surfside Rd., ☎ 508/228–6873) is where all ages dance to rock, reggae (especially popular on the island), and other music, live or recorded. It also has a take-out pizza shop (☎ 508/228–1471).

Rose and Crown (✉ 23 S. Water St., ☎ 508/228–2595; ☞ Dining and Lodging, *above*) is a friendly, noisy seasonal restaurant with a big bar, a small dance floor, live bands, DJs, and karaoke nights.

The **Tap Room** (⊠ Jared Coffin House, 29 Broad St., ☎ 508/228–2400; ☞ Dining and Lodging, *above*) has various lineups, from jazz trios to acoustic guitar. While the performers are local, the crowd is not.

FILM AND PHOTOGRAPHY

There are two first-run movie houses in Nantucket Town: **Dreamland Theatre** (⊠ 17 S. Water St., ☎ 508/228–5356) and **Gaslight Theatre** (⊠ 1 N. Union St., ☎ 508/228–4435).

Nantucket Filmworks presents a different slide show on Nantucket every year, created by one of the island's best photographers, Cary Hazlegrove. Shows are given at the Methodist church (⊠ 2 Centre St., at Main St., ☎ 508/228–3783) Monday–Saturday at 6:30 PM from mid-June to mid-September.

The **Nantucket Film Festival** (⊠ Box 688, Prince St. Station, New York, NY 10012, ☎ 508/325–6274 or 212/642–6339) runs annually for six days in mid-June, with film screenings, staged readings, panel discussions, and hobnobbing with screenwriters, actors, and directors. Weeklong passes should be purchased early.

MUSIC

Band concerts (☎ 508/228–7213) are held at 6 PM Thursdays and Sundays, July 4–Labor Day, at Children's Beach (⊠ S. Beach St.). Bring blankets, chairs, and bug repellent, and set yourself up in front of the bandstand; the music ranges from classical to rock-and-roll oldies.

Nantucket Arts Council (⊠ Coffin School, 4 Winter St., ☎ 508/228–2190) sponsors a music series (jazz, country, classical) September–June.

Nantucket Chamber Music Center (⊠ Coffin School, 4 Winter St., ☎ 508/228–3352) offers year-round choral and instrumental concerts as well as instruction.

Nantucket Musical Arts Society (⊠ Box 897, Nantucket 02554, ☎ 508/228–1287) holds Tuesday-evening concerts in July and August with internationally acclaimed musicians at the First Congregational Church (⊠ 62 Centre St.) and free, informal "Meet the Artists" gatherings elsewhere the previous evening.

Noonday concerts on an 1831 Goodrich organ are performed Thursdays at noon in July and August at the Unitarian Universalist Church (⊠ 11 Orange St., ☎ 508/228–5466).

THEATER

Actors Theatre of Nantucket (⊠ Methodist Church, 2 Centre St., at Main St., ☎ 508/228–6325) presents several Broadway-style plays Memorial Day–Columbus Day, plus children's post-beach matinees in July and August, comedy nights, late-night productions, and readings.

Theatre Workshop of Nantucket (⊠ Bennett Hall, 62 Centre St., ☎ 508/228–4305), a community theater since 1956, offers plays, musicals, and staged readings year-round.

Outdoor Activities and Sports

Murray Camp of Nantucket (⊠ Box 3437, 02584, ☎ 508/325–4600, FAX 508/325–4646) offers weekly summer day camps for children 5–14. Activities include French language instruction, tennis, sailing and other water sports, arts and crafts, drama and music, and environmental-awareness classes.

BEACHES

A calm area by the harbor, **Children's Beach** (⊠ S. Beach St.) is an easy walk from town, and it is perfect for small children. The beach has a grassy park with benches, a playground, lifeguards, food service, picnic tables, showers, and rest rooms. Tie-dyeing lessons are offered Fridays at noon mid-July–August.

Dionis Beach (✉ Eel Point Rd.) is, at its entrance, a narrow strip of sand that turns into a wider, more private strand with high dunes—it is the only Nantucket beach with dunes—and fewer children. The beach has a rocky bottom; calm, rolling waters; lifeguards; and rest rooms. Take the Madaket bike path to Eel Point Road and look for a white rock pointing to the beach, about 3 mi west of town.

Jetties (✉ Hulbert Ave.), a short bike or shuttle-bus ride from town, is the most popular beach for families because of its calm surf, lifeguards, bathhouse, rest rooms, and snack bar. It's a lively scene, especially with ferries passing, water-sports rentals (Windsurfer, sailboat, kayak), a playground and volleyball nets on the beach, and tennis courts adjacent. Swim lessons for children 6 and up are offered 9:30–noon, July 4–Labor Day. The concessions and rest rooms are wheelchair-accessible, and there is a boardwalk to the beach.

BIKING

The easy 2½-mi **Surfside Bike Path,** which begins on Surfside Road (from Main Street take Pleasant Street; then turn right onto Atlantic Avenue), leads to Surfside, the island's premier ocean beach (☞ Outdoor Activities and Sports *in* The South Shore, *below.* Benches and drinking fountains are placed at strategic locations along the path.

Nantucket Bike Shop (✉ Steamboat Wharf and ✉ Straight Wharf, ☎ 508/228–1999 for both), open April–October, rents bicycles and mopeds and provides an excellent touring map. Daily rentals typically cost $18–$30 for a bicycle and $45–$65 for a moped, though half-, full-, and multiple-day rates are available.

Nantucket Cycling Club (☎ 508/228–6066 or 508/228–1164) holds open races in summer.

Young's Bicycle Shop (✉ Steamboat Wharf, ☎ 508/228–1151) rents several different types of bicycle, plus cars and Jeep Wranglers. The shop provides an excellent touring map. Daily rentals typically cost $16–$35 for a bicycle, though multiple-day rates are available.

BIRD-WATCHING

Birding Adventures (☎ 508/228–2703) offers tours led by a naturalist who can wax eloquent on everything from raptors to oystercatchers. The **Maria Mitchell Association** (✉ 2 Vestal St., ☎ 508/228–9198) organizes wildflower and bird walks from June to Labor Day.

BOATING

Nantucket Boat Rentals (✉ Slip 1, Straight Wharf, ☎ 508/325–1001) rents powerboats. Security deposits are required for all boat rentals, and boats 17 ft or over require previous boating experience.

Nantucket Harbor Sail (✉ Swain's Wharf, ☎ 508/228–0424) rents sailboats. Security deposits are required for all boat rentals, and boats larger than 17 ft require previous boating experience.

Nantucket Island Community Sailing (✉ Jetties Beach, ☎ 508/228–5358 or 508/228–6600) rents Sunfish, Windsurfers, and kayaks; it also runs two-week sailing sessions at Polpis Harbor and offers classes for adults.

FISHING

Barry Thurston's Fishing Tackle (✉ Harbor Sq., ☎ 508/228–9595) will give you fishing tips and rents all the gear you'll need.

Beach Excursions Ltd. (☎ 508/228–3728) provides guided surf-casting trips and rents gear.

Bill Fisher Tackle (⊠ 14 New La., ☎ 508/228–2261) rents equipment and can point you in the direction of the best fishing spots.

Herbert T. (⊠ Slip 14, ☎ 508/228–6655) and other boats are available for seasonal charter from Straight Wharf.

Whitney Mitchell (☎ 508/228–2331) leads guided surf-casting trips with tackle by four-wheel-drive.

GOLF

Miacomet Golf Club ⊠ 12 W. Miacomet Ave., off Somerset La., ☎ 508/325–0333), a public course owned by the Land Bank and abutting Miacomet Pond and coastal heathland, has nine holes on very flat terrain.

HEALTH AND FITNESS CLUB

Club N. E. W. (⊠ 10 Young's Way, ☎ 508/228–4750) has StairMasters, Lifecycles, treadmills, rowers, Airdyne bikes, New Generation Nautilus, and free weights; aerobics, dance, and yoga classes; and a nutritionist, personal trainers, and baby-sitting. You can get a short-term pass that covers the machines, fitness classes, or both.

MINIATURE GOLF

Nobadeer Minigolf, an 18-hole miniature golf course set in gardens, is reached by a path connecting with the 'Sconset bike path. There's also a restaurant and a free shuttle from downtown. ⊠ *Nobadeer Farm and Sun Island Rds., off Milestone Rd. on the way to 'Sconset, ☎ 508/228–8977.* ⊟ *$6.* ⊙ *Daily 9 AM–11 PM in-season; hrs vary widely off-season.*

ROLLERBLADING

Nantucket Sports Locker (⊠ 14 Cambridge St., ☎ 508/228–5669) rents skates and protective gear.

SCUBA DIVING

The scuba diving around Nantucket is somewhat limited. Visibility is often only 5 ft, and there are no spectacular wrecks to visit. Most diving is done off the jetties. The **Sunken Ship** (⊠ Broad and S. Water Sts., ☎ 508/228–9226) offers complete dive-shop services, including lessons, guided dives, equipment rentals, and charters; it also rents water skis, boogie boards, tennis rackets, and fishing poles.

SWIMMING

The Olympic-size, indoor **Nantucket Community Pool** (⊠ Nantucket High School, Atlantic Ave., ☎ 508/228–7262) is open daily year-round for lap swimming and lessons.

TENNIS

There are six asphalt **town courts** (☎ 508/325–5334) at Jetties Beach. Sign up at the Park and Recreation Commission building for one hour of court time (usually the limit) or for lessons or tennis clinics. There is a charge for court maintenance: $5 per hour for singles, $20 per hour for doubles.

Brant Point Racquet Club (⊠ 48 N. Beach St., ☎ 508/228–3700), a short walk from town, has nine fast-dry clay courts and a pro shop and offers lessons, rentals, playing programs, and round-robins.

WHALE-WATCHING

Nantucket Whale Watch (⊠ Hy-Line dock, Straight Wharf, ☎ 508/283–0313 or 800/322–0013) offers naturalist-led full-day excursions every Tuesday mid-July–August. The cost is $75, and reservations are essential.

Shopping

ANTIQUES AND AUCTIONS

Forager House Collection (✉ 20 Centre St., ☎ 508/228–5977) specializes in folk art and Americana, including whirligigs, wood engravings, vintage postcards, Nantucket lightship baskets, and antique maps, charts, and prints.

Janis Aldridge (✉ 50 Main St., ☎ 508/228–6673) has beautifully framed antique engravings, including architectural and botanical prints, and home furnishings.

Nina Hellman Antiques (✉ 48 Centre St., ☎ 508/228–4677) carries scrimshaw, ship models, nautical instruments, and other marine antiques, plus folk art and Nantucket memorabilia.

Paul La Paglia (✉ 38 Centre St., ☎ 508/228–8760) has moderately priced antique prints, including Nantucket and whaling scenes, botanicals, and game fish.

Rafael Osona (✉ American Legion Hall, 21 Washington St., ☎ 508/228–3942; for a schedule, write to ✉ Box 2607, 02584) holds auctions of fine antiques from Memorial Day to early December. Items date from the 18th to the 20th century and include everything from furniture and art to Nantucket baskets and memorabilia.

Tonkin of Nantucket (✉ 33 Main St., ☎ 508/228–9697) has two floors of fine English antiques—including furniture, china, art, silver, marine and scientific instruments, and Staffordshire miniatures—as well as new sailors' valentines and lightship baskets.

ART GALLERIES

Robert Wilson Galleries (✉ 34 Main St., ☎ 508/228–6246 or 508/228–2096) carries outstanding contemporary American marine, impressionist, and other art.

Sailors' Valentine Gallery (✉ Macy's Warehouse, Lower Main St., ☎ 508/228–2011) has contemporary fine and folk art (including international "outsider art"), South American furnishings, sculpture, and exquisite sailors' valentines.

William Welch Gallery (✉ 14 Easy St., ☎ 508/228–0687) exhibits Welch's signature watercolors, pastels, and oils of Nantucket scenes, as well as the Nantucket oil paintings by Jack Brown.

BOOKS

Mitchell's Book Corner (✉ 54 Main St., ☎ 508/228–1080) has an excellent room full of books on Nantucket and whaling and stocks many ocean-related children's books, plus the usual bookstore fare. Authors appear weekly in summer.

Nantucket Bookworks (✉ 25 Broad St., ☎ 508/228–4000) carries an extensive assortment of hardcover and paperback books, with an emphasis on literary works and Nantucket-specific titles, as well as a children's-book room and unusual gift and stationery items.

CLOTHING

Cordillera Imports (✉ 18 Broad St., ☎ 508/228–6140) sells jewelry, affordable clothing in natural fibers for both men and women (though women get the lion's share), and crafts from Latin America, Asia, and elsewhere.

M. Hedgepath (✉ 42 Main St., ☎ 508/228–4500) carries women's and children's apparel with lots of lovely floral patterns, linens, giftware, jewelry, and candles.

Michelle's Romantic Clothing (⊠ 7 Centre St., ☎ 508/228–4409) offers lacy vintage dresses, antique jewelry, flower-bedecked hats, and shoes to match.

Murray's Toggery Shop (⊠ 62 Main St., ☎ 508/228–0437) sells traditional footwear and clothing—including the famous pants, Nantucket Reds—for men, women, and children. All the New England standards are here: chinos, turtlenecks, polos, and some of the small prints favored by the golf crowd.

Murray's Warehouse (⊠ 7 New St., ☎ 508/228–3584) has discounts of up to 50% on items sold in Murray's Toggery Shop (☞ *above*).

Nantucket Looms (⊠ 16 Main St., ☎ 508/228–1908) allows customers to watch weavers hand-fashioning sweaters, scarves, throws, and other items at two large wooden looms. The shop is open year-round and also carries distinctive furnishings for home and garden.

The **Peanut Gallery** (⊠ 8 India St., ☎ 508/228–2010) has a discriminating collection of children's clothing, including Cary, Flapdoodles, and island-made items.

Vis-à-Vis (⊠ 34 Main St., ☎ 508/228–5527) has unique, funky, and classic women's and children's clothing, accessories, and decorative objects, including hooked rugs, quilts, and collectibles.

CRAFTS

Claire Murray (⊠ 11 S. Water St., ☎ 508/228–1913 or 800/252–4733) carries the designer's Nantucket-theme and other hand-hooked rugs and rug kits, quilts, and knitting and needlework kits.

Erica Wilson Needle Works (⊠ 25 Main St., ☎ 508/228–9881) sells the famed designer's kits, as well as decorative items for the home, clothing, hats and accessories, and handmade jewelry by Heidi Weddendorf.

Four Winds Craft Guild (⊠ 6 Ray's Ct., ☎ 508/228–9623) carries a large selection of antique and new scrimshaw and lightship baskets, as well as ship models, duck decoys, and a kit for making your own lightship basket.

Golden Basket (⊠ 44 Main St., ☎ 508/228–4344) sells miniature gold and silver lightship baskets, pieces with starfish and shell motifs, and other fine jewelry.

Golden Nugget (⊠ Straight Wharf, ☎ 508/228–1019), with the same owner as the Golden Basket (☞ *above*), stocks similar merchandise.

Nantucket lightship basket makers include **Michael Kane** (⊠ 18½ Sparks Ave., ☎ 508/228–1548) and **Bill and Judy Sayle** (⊠ 112 Washington St. Ext., ☎ 508/228–9876).

Rosa Rugosa (⊠ 10 Straight Wharf, ☎ 508/228–5597) has items for the home, including furniture painted with roses, and antiques.

Scrimshander Gallery (⊠ 19 Old South Wharf, ☎ 508/228–1004) deals in new and antique scrimshaw.

The Spectrum (⊠ 26 Main St., ☎ 508/228–4606) sells distinctive art glass, wood boxes, jewelry, kaleidoscopes, and more.

FARM STANDS

Monday through Saturday in season, colorful farm stands are set up on Main Street to sell local produce and flowers.

At **Bartlett's Ocean View Farm & Greenhouses** (⊠ Bartlett Farm Rd. off Hummock Pond Rd., ☎ 508/228–9403), a 100-acre farm run by eighth-generation Bartletts, a farm stand is open in season. In June you can pick your own strawberries.

GIFT SHOPS

Museum Shop (⊠ 1 Broad St., next to the Whaling Museum, ☎ 508/228–5785) has island-related books, antique whaling tools, reproduction furniture, and toys, including reproduction 18th- and 19th-century whirligigs.

Seven Seas Gifts (⊠ 46 Centre St., ☎ 508/228–0958) stocks all kinds of inexpensive gift and souvenir items, including shells, baskets, toys, and Nantucket jigsaw puzzles. The building itself is unique, with addition after addition tacked on as the contents of the store required more space. Check out the pressed-tin ceilings and the fireplaces tucked in among the merchandise.

SIASCONSET, THE SOUTH SHORE, AND MADAKET

Beyond the hustle and bustle of Nantucket Town, the island has a more serene side. Several bike paths meander through the low shrubs and soft-colored heather of the moors and bogs, where all you'll hear is the song of birds. At the northern tip of the island, the vast, windswept beaches of the Coatue–Coskata–Great Point reserve stretch for miles—and offer limitless sun, sea, and solitude. A sleepy little town with rose-covered cottages lining narrow streets, Siasconset also has unparalleled bluffs overlooking the wild Atlantic. To the west, the dune-backed beaches of Madaket and Eel Point are the ideal place from which to watch the sun slide into the sea in a burst of brilliant color. The many conservation areas on these parts of the island showcase a variety of landscapes, from open heathlands to pine woods and sandy beaches. Even in the height of season, you'll be amazed to discover just what peaceful solitude awaits.

Siasconset, Polpis, and Wauwinet

7 mi east of Nantucket Town, 9 mi northeast of Surfside.

Originally a community of cod and halibut fishermen and shore whalers
★ from the 17th century, **Siasconset** was already becoming a summer resort during whaling days, when people from Nantucket Town would come here to get away from the smell of burning whale oil in the refineries. In 1884 the narrow-gauge railway—built three years earlier to take spiffily clad folk from the New Bedford steamers to the beach at Surfside—came to 'Sconset (as it's known locally), bringing ever more off-islanders. These included writers and artists from Boston in the 1890s, followed soon by Broadway actors on holiday during the theaters' summer hiatus. Attracted by the village's beauty, remoteness, sandy ocean beach, and cheap lodgings—converted one-room fishing shacks, and cottages built to look like them—they spread the word, and before long 'Sconset became a thriving actors' colony.

Today a charming village of pretty streets with tiny rose-covered cottages and driveways of crushed white shells, 'Sconset is almost entirely a summer community. The local postmaster claims that about 150 families live here through the winter, but you'd never know it. At the central square are the post office, a liquor store, a bookstore, a market, and two restaurants.

Siasconset makes a lovely day trip from Nantucket Town. Off-season there's not a lot to do in the village, but it still has its attractions, such as taking a stroll through some of the narrow streets. Plenty of beautiful beaches and conservation areas are close by, as well.

NEED A
BREAK? The **Nantucket Bake Shop** (✉ 79 Orange St., ☎ 508/228–2797) is a great place to stop on your way out of Nantucket Town to fill a knapsack with Portuguese bread and pastries. It's closed January–March.

★ The **Milestone Bog** (✉ Off Milestone Rd., west of Siasconset), more than 200 acres of working cranberry bogs surrounded by conservation land, is always a beautiful sight to behold, especially during the fall harvest. Cultivated since 1857, the bog was the world's largest contiguous natural cranberry bog until it was subdivided after 1959. The land was donated to the Nantucket Conservation Foundation (NCF) in 1968. The bogs are leased to a grower, who harvests and sells the crops.

The harvest begins in late September and continues for six weeks, during which time harvesters work daily from sunup to sundown in flooded bogs. The sight of floating bright red berries and the moors' rich autumn colors is not to be missed. At other times the color of the bog may be green, rust-red, or, in June and early July, the pale pink of cranberry blossoms. Any time of year, the bog and the moors have a remarkable, quiet beauty that's well worth seeing.

In 'Sconset, a stroll down three of the side streets—**Evelyn, Lily,** and **Pochick,** south of Main Street—will give you an idea of what Siasconset was like a century ago. The streets remain much as they were in the 1890s, when a development of tiny rental cottages in the fishing-shack style was built here. The summer blossoms of roses climbing all over many of the cottages are fantastic carpets of color.

An interesting reminder of the past is the **'Sconset Pump** (✉ Off Broadway St.), a nicely preserved well marked with a plaque proclaiming it "dug in 1776."

Despite its name, the 1899 **Siasconset Casino** (✉ New St., ☎ 508/257–6661) is in fact a tennis club (☞ Outdoor Activities and Sports, *below*) and bowling alley that was never used for gambling. During the actors'-colony heyday, it became a venue for theater productions. Some theater can still be seen here, but the casino is mostly a summer tennis club and cinema. Opposite the casino is the much-photographed entryway of the Chanticleer restaurant (☞ Dining and Lodging, *below*): a trellis arch topped by a sculpted hedge frames a rose garden with a flower-bedecked carousel horse at its center.

The **'Sconset Union Chapel** (✉ Chapel St., ☎ 508/257–6616), the village's only church, holds Roman Catholic mass at 8:45 AM and Protestant services at 10:30 on summer Sundays.

The red-and-white-striped **Sankaty Head Lighthouse** (✉ Off Polpis Rd.), overlooking the sea on one side and the Scottish-looking greens of the private Sankaty Head Golf Club on the other, is one of the Cape and islands' many endangered lighthouses. Standing on a 90-ft-high bluff that has lost as much as 200 ft of shoreline in the past 75 years, the 1849 lighthouse could be lost, as Great Point Light was in 1984, to further erosion. A fragile piece of land, Nantucket loses more of its shoreline every year, especially at Sankaty Head and on the south shore, where no shoals break the ocean waves as they do on the north shore. Some of that sand is simply moved along shore to the other end of the island, but that's no great consolation to Sankaty Head and 'Sconset dwellers. The lighthouse is not open to the public.

Alongside **Polpis Road,** which heads north out of 'Sconset on its loop back toward Nantucket Town, hundreds of thousands of daffodils bloom in spring. A million Dutch bulbs donated by an island resident were planted along Nantucket's main roads in 1974, and more have been planted every year since.

A good spot for bird-watching, **Sesachacha Pond** (pronounced "seh-*sah*-kah-cha" or, more often here, just "*sah*-kah-cha"), off Polpis Road, is circled by a walking path that leads to an Audubon wildlife area. The pond is separated from the ocean by a narrow strand on its east side. From the pond, there's a good view of Sankaty Head Lighthouse (☞ *above*) high above.

Throughout the year, the 205-acre **Windswept Cranberry Bog** (⊠ Off Polpis Rd., northwest of 'Sconset), part working bog, part conservation land, is a beautiful tapestry of greens, reds, and golds—and a popular hangout for many different bird species. The bog is especially vibrant in mid-October, when you can watch the cranberry harvest. A map, as well as the 30-page "Handbook for Visitors to the Windswept Cranberry Bog," is available for $4 ($5 by mail) from the NCF (☞ Guided Tours *in* Nantucket A to Z, *below*).

Wauwinet is a hamlet of beach houses on the northeastern end of Nantucket. European settlers found the neck of sand above it to be the easiest way to get to the ocean for fishing. Instead of rowing around Great Point, fishermen would go to the head of the harbor and haul their dories over the narrow strip of sand and beach grass separating Nantucket Harbor from the ocean. Hence the name for that strip: the haulover. Various storms have washed it out, allowing fishermen to sail clean through the area, but the moving sands have continued to fill it back in.

In the 1870s the first Wauwinet House started luring townspeople to its 75¢ shore dinners. Local historian Jane Lamb, resident of "Chaos Corner" on Polpis Road, relates the story of July 4, 1877, revelers who, while sailing back to town after dancing until 11 PM, were grounded on shoals, rolling back and forth until the tide rose with the sun. Happily, Wauwinet dinner cruises didn't die with that night, and you can still sail out to Wauwinet for dinner at the current inn.

Coatue–Coskata–Great Point, an unpopulated spit of sand comprising three cooperatively managed wildlife refuges, is a great place to spend a day exploring, relaxing, or pursuing a favorite activity, like bird-watching or fishing. **Coatue,** the strip of sand enclosing Nantucket Harbor, is open for many kinds of recreation—shellfishing for bay scallops, soft-shell clams, quahogs, and mussels (license required); surf casting for bluefish and striped bass (spring through fall); picnicking; or just enjoying the crowdless expanse. **Coskata**'s beaches, dunes, salt marshes, and stands of oak and cedar attract marsh hawks, egrets, oyster-catchers, terns, herring gulls, plovers, and many other birds, particularly during spring and fall migration. A successful program has brought ospreys here to nest on posts set up in a field by Coskata Pond. Don't come without field glasses.

Because of dangerous currents and riptides and the lack of lifeguards, swimming is strongly discouraged in the refuges, especially within 200 yards of the 70-ft stone tower of **Great Point Light.** Those currents, at the same time, are fascinating to watch at the Great Point tide rip. Seals and fishermen alike benefit from the unique feeding ground that it creates. The lighthouse is a 1986 re-creation of the light destroyed by a storm in 1984. The new light was built to withstand 20-ft waves and winds of up to 240 mph, and it was fitted with eight solar panels to power it.

The area may be entered only on foot or by four-wheel-drive vehicle, for which a permit ($85 for a year; $20 a day for a rental vehicle; ☎ 508/228–2884 for information) is required. Issued only for a vehicle that is properly registered and equipped—confirm this with the rental agent if you plan to enter the area—the permits are available at the **gatehouse at Wauwinet** (✉ End of Wauwinet Rd., ☎ 508/228–0006) June–September or off-season from a ranger patrolling the property. If you enter on foot, be aware that Great Point is a 5-mi walk from the entrance on soft, deep sand. Jeepless people often hitchhike here. Another alternative is a Jeep tour (☞ Nature Tours *in* Nantucket A to Z, *below*).

★ An unmarked dirt track off Polpis Road between Wauwinet and Nantucket Town leads to **Altar Rock,** from which the view is spectacular. The rock sits on a high spot in the midst of open moor and bog land—technically called lowland heath—which is very rare in the United States. The entire area, of which the Milestone Bog is a part, is laced with paths leading in every direction. Don't forget to keep track of the trails you travel in order to find your way back.

Housed in an interesting re-creation of an 1874 Life Saving Service station, the **Nantucket Life Saving Museum** displays items including original rescue equipment and boats, artifacts recovered from the wreck *Andrea Doria,* and photos and accounts of daring rescues. There are several rare pieces; the museum acquired a surfboat, one of four still extant, and a horse-drawn carriage from the Henry Ford Museum, and a beach cart (the only known original), all in mint condition. ✉ *Fulling Hill Rd., off Polpis Rd., 2½ mi east of Nantucket Town,* ☎ *508/228– 1885.* 🖾 *$3.* ☉ *Mid-June–Columbus Day, Tues.–Sun. 9:30–4.*

Dining and Lodging

$$$$ ✕ **Chanticleer.** Chanticleer deserves its due. For more than 20 years, Anne and Jean-Charles Berruet have been serving superb French food in a lovingly maintained, formal country setting, complete with gorgeous clematis cascading down the weathered shingles. The wine cellar is among the best in the country, reputed to hold more than 40,000 bottles. All that said, some have come to feel that the food and the ambience have both become heavy and overbearing. Others say that the wine is carrying the food, rather than vice versa. Yet for many a Nantucket trip would not be complete without getting dressed up, making the trip here, and easily spending hundreds of dollars on a sumptuous meal. Dining here is a commitment to a classic form of elegance—think of if as entering the set of an elaborate play. For the full effect, try to stay on center stage—the main dining room in front. ✉ *9 New St., Siasconset,* ☎ *508/257–6231. Reservations required. Jacket required. AE, MC, V. Closed Mon. and mid-Oct.–early May.*

$$–$$$ ✕ **'Sconset Café.** This place has a great location in the heart of town ★ and is BYOB to boot (a liquor store is next door). If you stop in and no tables are available, as is often the case, they will give you a beeper, send you down to the beach or over to the Summer House (☞ *below*) for a drink, and beep you when your table is ready. You can relax, wear jeans, and enjoy what is becoming both a better and a more expensive menu, with local fish and a few other items such as duck. Lunchtime menu items are reasonable, including lots of sandwiches and salads. ✉ *Post Office Sq., Siasconset,* ☎ *508/257–4008. No credit cards. BYOB. Closed Oct.–mid-May.*

$ ✗ **Claudette's.** For a great picnic in 'Sconset, stop here and pick up something for a nearby beach. ✉ *Post Office Sq., Siasconset,* ☎ *508/257–6622. No credit cards.*

$$$$ ✗⊞ **Summer House.** Here, across from 'Sconset Beach and clustered around a flower-filled lawn, are the rose-covered cottages associated with Nantucket summers. For the main restaurant (reservations essential), compliments and complaints abound—divided between those who love the place for its 'Sconset bluff ocean views and live piano music and those who are put off by the pompous, over-fussy service. Daily seafood specials are often the highlights on the menu. The Ocean Restaurant serves lunch only. The pre–World War II whitewashed beach-cottage look lends the dining room a sort of *Great Gatsby* vibe. Each one- or two-bedroom guest cottage is furnished in romantic, English country style: trompe-l'oeil-bordered white walls, white eyelet spreads, and stripped English-pine antique furnishings. Some cottages have fireplaces or kitchens, and most have marble baths with whirlpool tubs. Adirondack chairs dot the lawn; you won't need a book with this view to absorb. ✉ *Ocean Ave., Box 880, Siasconset 02564,* ☎ *508/257–4577,* ⅏ℵ *508/257–4590. 8 cottages. 2 restaurants, bar, piano bar, pool. AE, MC, V. Closed Nov.–late Apr. CP.*

$$$$ ✗⊞ **Wauwinet.** Some people would say that this historic 19th-century
★   hotel is the only place to stay on Nantucket, and its friendliness, exquisite location, impeccable furnishings, and first-rate restaurant make it easy to see why. Topper's restaurant is tasteful and elegant (dinner reservations are essential). Lobster-crab cakes with corn, jalapeño olives, and mustard sauce is a deserving favorite appetizer, as is the warm Nantucket oysters with caviar. Pan-seared sea scallops with lobster risotto and the roasted rack of *cervena* venison (a lean, farm-raised New Zealand deer) with creamy polenta and forest mushroom glaze are superb entrées. Around the inn itself, a sweeping lawn with white chaise lounges leads to a pebbly private harbor beach, where you can play with a life-size wooden chess set. Guest rooms and cottages are individually decorated in country-beach style, with pine antiques; some have water views. Activities here abound, including sailing in Nantucket catboats. There are also boat shuttles to Coatue beach across the harbor, and, perhaps best of all, the innkeeper runs a Land Rover tour of the Great Point reserve—all of which are included in the room rate. Jitney service to and from Nantucket Town, 8 mi away, plus Steamship pickup, makes it convenient if you don't have a car. In season, you can cruise to the inn in the gorgeous *Wauwinet Lady* skiff. ✉ *120 Wauwinet Rd., Box 2580, Nantucket 02584,* ☎ *508/228–0145 or 800/426–8718,* ⅏ℵ *508/228–7135. 25 rooms, 5 cottages. Restaurant, bar, room service, 2 tennis courts, croquet, beach, boating, mountain bikes, library, concierge, business services. AE, DC, MC, V. Closed Nov.–Apr. BP.*

$$–$$$$ ⊞ **Wade Cottages.** On a bluff overlooking the ocean, this complex of guest rooms, apartments, and cottages in 'Sconset couldn't be better located for beach lovers. The buildings, in the same family since the 1920s, are arranged around a central lawn with a great ocean view. Most inn rooms and cottages have sea views, and all have phones. Furnishings are generally in somewhat worn beach style, with some antique pieces. Note the minimum-stay requirements: three nights for rooms, one week for apartments, 2 weeks for cottages. ✉ *Shell St., Box 211, Siasconset 02564,* ☎ *508/257–6308, 212/989–6423 off-season,* ⅏ℵ *508/257–4602. 8 rooms, 4 with bath; 6 apartments; 3 cottages. Refrigerator, badminton, Ping-Pong, beach, coin laundry. AE, MC, V. Closed mid-Oct.–late May. CP.*

Nightlife and the Arts

Nantucket Island School of Design and the Arts (✉ 23 Wauwinet Rd., Wauwinet, ☎ 508/228–9248; for schedule, ✉ Box 958, Nantucket 02554) offers a year-round program of multicultural, environmental, nature, and arts-and-crafts classes, lectures, and slide shows for adults and children.

The **Siasconset Casino** (✉ New St., Siasconset, ☎ 508/257–6661) shows first-run films in season.

Outdoor Activities and Sports

BEACHES

Siasconset Beach (✉ End of Milestone Rd.), also known as 'Sconset Beach and Codfish Park, has a golden-sand beach with moderate to heavy surf, a lifeguard, showers, rest rooms, and a playground. Restaurants are a short walk away.

BIKING

The 8-mi **Polpis Bike Path,** a long trail with gentle hills, begins at the intersection of Milestone and Polpis Roads and winds alongside Polpis Road almost all the way into Siasconset. It goes right by the Life Saving Museum (☞ *above*), and has great views of the moors, the cranberry bogs, and Sesachacha Pond.

The 6½-mi **'Sconset Bike Path** starts at the rotary east of Nantucket Town and parallels Milestone Road, ending in 'Sconset. It is paved and mostly level, with some gentle hills and benches and drinking fountains at strategic locations along the way.

GOLF

Sankaty Head Golf Club (✉ Polpis Rd., Siasconset, ☎ 508/257–6391), a private 18-hole course, is open to the public from mid-June to late September. This challenging Scottish-style links course cuts through the moors and has spectacular views of the lighthouse and ocean from practically every hole.

Siasconset Golf Club (✉ Milestone Rd., ☎ 508/257–6596), begun in 1894, is an easy-walking nine-hole public course surrounded by conservation land.

NATURE TOURS

The Trustees of Reservations sponsors naturalist-led **Great Point Natural History Tours** (☎ 508/228–6799) from June to October.

SWIMMING

The **Summer House** (☞ Dining and Lodging, *above*) in 'Sconset offers its pool, on the bluff above the ocean beach, to diners at its poolside café in season.

TENNIS

Siasconset Casino (✉ New St., Siasconset, ☎ 508/257–6661) is a private club with seven clay courts and one poor hard court. Infrequently the club has openings at 1 or 2 PM. Call ahead to check.

The South Shore

3–4 mi from Nantucket Town.

The immediate presence of the Atlantic Ocean dominates the south shore. Its beaches—Cisco, Surfside, and Madaket—are known for challenging surf, steep dunes, and a more isolated, natural essence.

Miacomet Pond (✉ Off Miacomet Rd.) is a freshwater pond surrounded by grass and heath, separated from the ocean by a narrow strip of sandy Land Bank beach. The pond—in whose reedy fringes swans and snapping turtles are sometimes seen, along with the resident ducks—is a peaceful setting for a picnic or quiet time. A right turn off Surfside Road onto Miacomet Road (which begins paved and turns to dirt) will take you there.

Cisco is a beautiful area not far from Nantucket Town, with a stretch of beach that suffers the battering of wild, wind-tossed seas. Several oceanfront houses at Cisco have been lost or moved since 1990 because of massive bluff erosion due to fierce winter storms. To get to the area from Nantucket Town, take Main Street west to Milk Street and continue at its end on Hummock Pond Road to its end.

Five varieties of vinifera grapes grow at the **Nantucket Vineyard** and winery 2½ mi south of Nantucket Town. Tastings of red, white, and rosé wines are available year-round, as are bottles for purchase. ⊠ *3 Bartlett Farm Rd., off Hummock Pond Rd., Cisco,* ☎ *508/228–9235.* ☜ *Free.* ☉ *Mon.–Sat. 11–6, Sun. noon–5 (call first in winter).*

A 5- to 10-minute bike ride from Nantucket Town on the way to Madaket, the **Sanford Farm, Ram Pasture, and the Woods** offer a wonderful combination of habitats to explore. The area comprises more than 900 contiguous acres of wetlands, grasslands, forest, and former farmland off Madaket Road. Interpretive markers border the 6½-mi (round-trip) walking trail that leads to the shore via Hummock Pond and offers great ocean and heath views. It begins off the Madaket Road parking area near the intersection of Cliff Road, as do a 1½-mi loop and a 3-mi round-trip to a barn on high ground with views of the south shore. Stop at Something Natural (☞ Dining and Lodging *in* Nantucket Town, *above*) on Cliff Road on your way out of town to pick up a picnic. Maps are available through the NCF (☞ Guided Tours *in* Nantucket A to Z, *below*), which owns 767 acres, or the **Land Bank** (⊠ 22 Broad St., Nantucket 02554, ☎ 508/228–7240), which owns 165.

Outdoor Activities and Sports

Cisco (⊠ Hummock Pond Rd.) is a long, sandy beach with heavy surf, lifeguards, and rest rooms. It's not easy to get to from Nantucket Town, though. There are no bike trails to it, so you may need to walk or take a taxi. Also, the cliffs are severely eroded, so getting down onto the beach is difficult. Still, the waves make it a popular spot for body and board surfers.

Surfside (⊠ Surfside Rd.) is the island's premier surf beach, with lifeguards, rest rooms, a snack bar, and a wide strand of sand. It pulls in college students as well as families and is great for kite flying and surf casting. The best way to get here from Nantucket Town is by bike along the Surfside Bike Path (☞ Outdoor Activities and Sports *in* Nantucket Town, *above*).

Madaket

6 mi west of Nantucket Town, 15 mi west of Siasconset.

This rural, residential village at the westernmost point of Nantucket doesn't have much to offer by way of a town, but beautiful beaches and conservation areas well worth exploring are close by, including some of the most scenic places to observe the island's wildlife. A bike ride out from Nantucket Town over gentle hills takes 30 to 45 minutes.

A ¾-mi **Land Bank walking trail** begins at a set of picnic tables on the north side of Madaket Road, ½ mi west of the Eel Point Road intersection. It wanders upland to an overview of a swamp, through a hawthorn grove and blueberry patches, and across meadows. This short jaunt is a perfect introduction to Nantucket's many different habitats.

Long Pond (⊠ Off Madaket Rd., to dirt road across from Hither Creek sign) is a 64-acre Land Bank property that's especially good for birding. A 1-mi walking path along the pond, past meadows and a natural cranberry bog, makes for a pleasant, relaxing stroll.

★ An unspoiled conservation area perfect for a leisurely walk, particularly appealing to bird-watchers, **Eel Point** (⊠ Eel Point Rd., off Cliff Rd.) is a spit of sand with harbor on one side and shoal-protected ocean on the other. Covered here and there with goldenrod, wild grapes, roses, bayberries, and other coastal plants, the area is a nesting place for gulls and also attracts great numbers of other birds, including herons and egrets, which perch on small islands formed by a sandbar that extends out 100 yards or more. The water is shallow, and the surf fishing is good. Nature guides on Eel Point are available from the **Maria Mitchell Association** (⊠ 2 Vestal St., Nantucket 02554, ☎ 508/228–5387), $10 for nonmembers, or the NCF (☞ Guided Tours *in* Nantucket A to Z, *below*).

Outdoor Activities and Sports

BEACHES

Six miles from Nantucket Town and accessible only by foot, **Eel Point** (⊠ Eel Point Rd., off Cliff Rd.) near Madaket has one of the island's most beautiful and interesting beaches for those who don't necessarily need to swim—a sandbar extends out 100 yards, keeping the water shallow, clear, and calm. There are no services, just lots of birds, wild berries and bushes, and solitude.

Known for great sunsets and surf, **Madaket Beach** is reached by shuttle bus from Nantucket Town or the Madaket bike path (5½ mi) and has lifeguards and rest rooms.

BIKING

The **Madaket Bike Path,** reached via Cliff Road in Nantucket Town, is a hilly but beautiful 5½-mi paved route to the western tip of the island. There are picnic tables by Long Pond and benches and drinking fountains along the way.

NANTUCKET A TO Z

Arriving and Departing

By Ferry

Year-round service is available only from Hyannis on Cape Cod. Hy-Line has two boats, one of which runs between Nantucket and the Vineyard in summer only. The only way to get a car to Nantucket is on the Steamship Authority. To get a car from the Vineyard to Nantucket, you would have to return to Woods Hole, drive to Hyannis, and ferry it out from there.

FROM HYANNIS

The **Steamship Authority** runs car-and-passenger ferries to the island from Hyannis year-round. The trip takes 2¼ hours. A new, faster passenger ferry takes just an hour. For policies and restrictions, *see* Martha's Vineyard A to Z *in* Chapter 3. ⊠ South St. dock, ☎ 508/477–8600; 508/228–3274 on Nantucket for reservations; 508/228–0262 for information; 508/540–1394 TTD. ☒ One-way $11, bicycles $5. Cars one-way mid-May–mid-Oct. $110; mid-Oct.–mid-May $80. High-speed passenger ferry one-way $20, bicycles $5.

Hy-Line's high-end, high-speed boat, the *Grey Lady II,* ferries passengers from Hyannis and back year-round. The trip takes just under an hour. That speed has its downside in rough seas—lots of bucking and rolling that some find nauseating. Seating ranges from benches on the upper deck to airlinelike seats in side rows of the cabin to café-style tables and chairs in the cabin front. There is a snack bar on board. ⊠ *Ocean St. dock,* ☎ *508/778–0404 or 800/492–8082.* 🚲 *One-way $29, bicycles $5.*

Hy-Line's slower **ferry** makes the 1¾- to 2-hour trip from Hyannis early May–October 28. The M.V. *Great Point* offers a first-class section ($21 one-way) with a private lounge, rest rooms, upholstered seats, carpeting, complimentary Continental breakfast or afternoon cheese and crackers, a bar, and a snack bar. ⊠ *Ocean St. dock,* ☎ *508/778–2602 for reservations; 508/778–2600 for information; 508/228–3949 on Nantucket.* 🚲 *One-way $11, bicycles $5.*

FROM HARWICH PORT

Freedom Cruise Line runs passenger ferry service from May 15 to October 15 from this town west of Chatham on Cape Cod. The trip takes 90 minutes and offers an alternative to the crowds in Hyannis during the busy summer months. ⊠ *Saquatucket Harbor, off Rte. 28;* ☎ *508/432–8999 for reservations.* 🚲 *One-way $18, bicycles $5.*

FROM MARTHA'S VINEYARD

Hy-Line makes 2¼-hour runs to and from Nantucket from early June to mid-September—the only interisland passenger service. ☎ *508/778–2600 in Hyannis; 508/228–3949 on Nantucket; 508/693–0112 in Oak Bluffs.* 🚲 *One-way $11, bicycles $5.*

By Plane

Nantucket Memorial Airport (☎ 508/325–5300) is about 3½ mi southeast of town via Old South Road. A taxi from the airport to town costs $7.

Business Express/Delta Connection flies from Boston year-round and from New York (LaGuardia) in season. **Cape Air/Nantucket Air** flies from Hyannis on Cape Cod year-round and offers charters. **Colgan Air** (☎ 508/325–5100 or 800/272–5488) flies from Newark and Hyannis year-round. **Continental Connection** (☎ 800/523–3273) has nonstops from LaGuardia in New York year-round. **Island Airlines** (☎ 508/228–7575; 800/698–1109 in MA; 800/248–7779) flies from Hyannis year-round and offers charters. **New Island Connections** (☎ 508/228–4600 or 800/295–5842) flies year-round from Hyannis, and offers charters and air freight service. **Ocean Wings** (☎ 508/325–5548, 508/228–3350, or 800/253–5039) offers year-round charters from its Nantucket base. **Westchester Air** (☎ 914/761–3000 or 800/759–2929) flies charters out of White Plains, New York.

Getting Around

One of the attractions of a Nantucket vacation is escape from the fast lane. You might find yourself walking a lot more than usual and taking advantage of the island's miles of scenic bike paths. Even so, in high season the main streets are clogged with traffic (and parking spaces are filled), and residents beg you to leave your car at home. If your visit will be short and spent mostly in town and on the beaches, taxis and beach shuttles can supplement foot power adequately.

Some of the island's most beautiful and least-touristed beaches are accessible only by foot or four-wheel-drive vehicles. Yearlong permits are available for $20 for private vehicles, $100 for rental vehicles, at the **police department** (☎ 508/228–1212) on South Water Street. Coatue–Coskata–Great Point is open to Jeeps but requires a separate NCF permit.

By Bicycle and Moped

The main bike trails around the island are paved, but mountain bikes are best if you plan to explore the dirt roads. To drive a moped you must have a driver's license and a helmet. You may not use the vehicle within the town historic district between 10 PM and 7 AM, and you may never drive it on the bike paths. Moped accidents happen often on the narrow or dirt roads—watch out for loose gravel. There are several places to rent bicycles and mopeds in Nantucket Town (☞ Outdoor Activities and Sports, *in* Nantucket Town, *above*). Look for bike stands along Main Street, as there aren't many in the side streets; also, keep in mind that the cobblestones on Main Street make for rough riding. Be sure to keep an eye out for one-way signs, as you can be fined for going the wrong way.

The island's bicycle paths are very clearly marked. Both the Chamber of Commerce and the visitor information bureau (☞ Visitor Information, *below*) in Nantucket Town have maps and free guides. Bike rental shops have maps, too.

By Bus

From mid-June to Labor Day, **Barrett's Tours** (✉ 20 Federal St., ☎ 508/228–0174 or 800/773–0174), across from the Nantucket Information Bureau, runs beach shuttles to 'Sconset and Madaket ($5 round-trip, $3 one-way), Surfside ($3 round-trip, $2 one-way), and Jetties ($1 one-way) several times daily. Children pay half fare to 'Sconset and Surfside.

By Car

Having a car on the island is invariably expensive, whether you bring one over on the ferry or rent one once you arrive (☞ Car Rentals *in* Contacts and Resources, *below*). Yet you might find the experience of not having a car to bother with quite pleasant. With the seasonal island shuttle, a car may even be unnecessary if you're staying in a hotel. If you're staying in a house and need to shop for groceries, a car could be of use, but you should ask yourself whether it's worth the price of admission. Nantucket is small, so you won't be using much gas, but parking in town and dealing with traffic getting in and out is just ghastly in season.

By Island Shuttle

The **Nantucket Regional Transit Authority** (☎ 508/228–7025; 508/325–0788 TTY) runs shuttle buses around the island between June 1 and September 30. There are five routes with different timing on each; most service begins at 7 AM and ends at 11 PM. Call for schedules. Fares are 50¢ in Nantucket Town, $1 to 'Sconset and Madaket, $10 for a three-day pass, $15 for a seven-day pass, and $30 for a one-month pass. Seasonal passes are also available.

By Taxi

Taxis usually wait outside the airport or at the foot of Main Street by the ferry. Rates are flat fees, based on one person with two bags before 1 AM: $5 within town (1½-mi radius), $7 to the airport, $11 to 'Sconset, $13 to Wauwinet.

A-1 Taxi (☎ 508/228–3330 or 508/228–4084). **Aardvark Cab** (☎ 508/228–2223). **All Point Taxi** (☎ 508/228–5779). **B. G.'s Taxi** (☎ 508/228–4146). A seven-passenger van is available upon request. **Peterson's Taxi** (☎ 508/228–9227).

Contacts and Resources

Baby-sitting Service

Nantucket Babysitters' Service (☎ 508/228–4970) offers year-round professional baby-sitting and home-helper services.

B&B Reservation Agencies

DestINNations (☎ 800/333–4667) handles a limited number of Nantucket hotels and B&Bs but will arrange any and all details of a visit.

Heaven Can Wait Accommodations (✉ Box 622, Siasconset 02564, ☎ 508/257–4000) books inns and B&Bs and also plans island honeymoons.

Martha's Vineyard and Nantucket Reservations (✉ Box 1322, 73 Lagoon Pond Rd., Vineyard Haven, Martha's Vineyard 02568, ☎ 508/693–7200, 800/649–5671 in MA) books inns, hotels, B&Bs, and cottages.

Nantucket Information Bureau (✉ 25 Federal St., ☎ 508/228–0925) maintains a list of room availability in season and at holidays for last-minute bookings. At night, check the lighted board outside for available rooms.

Car Rentals

If you decide to rent a car, reserve one well in advance in season. **Budget** (☎ 508/228–5666 or 888/228–5666) rents cars, vans, and Ford Explorers. **Hertz** (☎ 508/228–9421 or 800/654–3131) has cars and Ford Explorers available.

The local company **Nantucket Windmill** (☎ 508/228–1227 or 800/228–1227) rents cars, vans, Ford Explorers, and Jeeps at low rates and with free mileage.

Thrifty (☎ 508/325–4626) rents cars, Jeeps, and Ford Explorers with free mileage and pick-up service.

Emergencies

Dial **911** to reach the police or fire department.

The **Nantucket Cottage Hospital** (✉ 57 Prospect St., ☎ 508/228–1200) has a 24-hour emergency room.

Guided Tours

CRUISES

Boats of all kinds leave from Straight Wharf on harbor sails throughout the summer; many are available for charter as well.

Anna W. II (✉ Slip 12, ☎ 508/228–1444) is a renovated lobster boat with shoreline, sunset, and moonlight cruises, as well as lobstering demonstrations and winter seal cruises.

The ***Endeavor*** (✉ Slip 15, ☎ 508/228–5585), a beautiful 31-ft Friendship sloop, offers harbor tours, sunset cruises, and sails to Coatue, where you are rowed ashore to spend a morning beachcombing.

The 40-ft sailing yacht ***Sparrow*** (✉ Slip 18, ☎ 508/228–6029), with a teak, brass, and stained-glass interior, offers 1½-hour sails for six guests, plus charters.

The ***"Around the Sound"*** cruise, a one-day round-trip from Hyannis with stops at Nantucket and Martha's Vineyard and six hours at sea, is available June–mid-September. ✉ *Hy-Line, Ocean St. Dock, Hyannis,* ☎ *508/778–2600 or 508/778–2602, 508/228–3949 on Nantucket.* 🖃 *$33, bicycles $15.*

GENERAL TOURS

Barrett's Tours (✉ 20 Federal St., ☎ 508/228–0174 or 800/773–0174) gives 75- to 90-minute narrated bus tours of the island from spring through fall; the Barrett family has lived on Nantucket for generations. Buses meet the ferries; reservations aren't necessary.

Carried Away (☎ 508/228–0218) offers narrated carriage rides through the town historic district in season.

Gail's Tours (☎ 508/257–6557) are lively 1½-hour van tours narrated by sixth-generation Nantucketer Gail Johnson, who knows all the inside stories.

"Historic Nantucket Walking Tours," a free, self-guided tour pamphlet published by the Nantucket Historical Association, is available at the Nantucket Information Bureau (☞ Visitor Information *below*).

Nantucket Island Tours (Straight Wharf, ☎ 508/228–0334) gives 75- to 90-minute narrated bus tours of the island from spring through fall; buses meet the ferries.

HISTORICAL TOURS

The self-guided **Black Heritage Trail** tour (✉ Box 1802, Nantucket 02544, ☎ 508/228–4058) covers nine sites in and around Nantucket Town that have associations with Nantucket's African-American population, including the African Meeting House, the Whaling Museum, and the Atheneum. The trail guide is free from the Friends of the African Meeting House on Nantucket.

NATURE TOURS

Great Point Natural History Tours (☎ 508/228–6799), led by naturalists, are sponsored by the Trustees of Reservations. Groups drive in for the three-hour tour, with stops to see points of interest and certain bird species and to stretch.

For a map of the **Nantucket Conservation Foundation**'s properties, visit or write NCF headquarters. The map costs $3, or $4 by mail. ✉ *118 Cliff Rd., Box 13, Nantucket 02554,* ☎ *508/228–2884.* ⊙ *Weekdays 8–5.*

Harbor Facilities

Harbor facilities are available in town year-round at the **Town Pier** (☎ 508/228–7260).

The **Boat Basin** (☎ 508/325–1350 or 800/626–2628) offers harbor facilities year-round, with shower and laundry facilities, electric power, cable TV, phone hookups, a fuel dock, and summer concierge service.

Madaket Marine (☎ 508/228–9086 or 800/564–9086) has moorings May–October and fuel and slips year-round for boats up to 29 ft in Hither Creek.

House Rentals

A number of realtors (complete lists are provided by the Chamber of Commerce and the Nantucket Information Bureau; ☞ Visitor Information, *below*) offer rentals ranging from in-town apartments in antique houses to new waterfront houses.

Congdon & Coleman (✉ 57 Main St., Nantucket 02554, ☎ 508/325–5000, ℻ 508/325–5025) has properties island-wide.

Country Village Rentals & Real Estate (✉ 4 Cherry St., Nantucket 02554, ☎ 508/228–8840 or 800/599–7368) has more than 250 homes for rent on the island.

'Sconset Real Estate (✉ Box 122, Siasconset 02564, ☎ 508/257–6335, 508/228–1815 in winter) lists properties in and around 'Sconset.

Island Activities

FISHING

Fishing licenses are needed only for freshwater fishing and shellfishing. **Freshwater licenses** can be obtained at local fishing outfitters or through the Marine, Harbormaster, and Shellfish Department (✉ 34 Washington St., ☎ 508/228–7260).

The **shellfish warden** (⊠ 34 Washington St., ☎ 508/228–7260) issues digging permits for littleneck and cherrystone clams, quahogs, and mussels. Family shellfishing permits are $15.

For listings of events, see the free seasonal weekly *Nantucket Map & Legend,* the ferry companion paper *Yesterday's Island,* and the island newspaper the *Inquirer and Mirror.*

Pharmacies

Congdon's (⊠ 47 Main St., ☎ 508/228–0020) is open nightly until 10 from mid-June to mid-September.

Island Pharmacy (⊠ Stop & Shop Plaza, Sparks Ave., ☎ 508/228–6400) is open daily until 8 or 9 during the summer.

Nantucket Pharmacy (⊠ 45 Main St., ☎ 508/228–0180) stays open until 10 nightly from Memorial Day to Labor Day.

Visitor Information

The **Chamber of Commerce** (⊠ 48 Main St., Nantucket 02554, ☎ 508/228–1700) is open weekdays 9–5 year-round.

The **Nantucket Visitors Service and Information Bureau** (⊠ 25 Federal St., ☎ 508/228–0925) is open daily July–Labor Day, weekdays Labor Day–June. Hours vary. Also look for information kiosks at Steamboat and Straight wharves.

5 PORTRAITS OF THE CAPE AND ISLANDS

The Cape's Six Seasons

A Brief History of the Cape

Cape and Islands Books

THE CAPE'S SIX SEASONS

SO MUCH HAS BEEN MADE of the difference between "the season" and "the off-season" that you might think there is a magic switch that flicks Cape Cod on and off. The truth is something more complicated. Far from having only two seasons, much less the traditional four, the Cape and islands really have six identifiable seasons, each distinct and dramatic.

From early April until Memorial Day, it's spring—a season that can be beautiful, bursting with wildflowers and green grass. Locals shake out the kinks and get ready. In the old days, you could smell tar and pitch as fishermen prepared their nets for another season at sea. Now, you're likelier to smell fresh paint as B&B owners put on a fresh coat. Provincetown's exotic little gardens, nurturing unusual plants brought home from seaports around the world, are in their glory. And it's a great time to enjoy bird walks, nature hikes, and country drives, along with lower prices and a lack of crowds.

"The season" is generally thought to start on Memorial Day, but, in fact, the holiday is a quick and busy harbinger, nothing more. After the long weekend, a lull sets in that lasts until the end of June, when schools finally let out. The weather is still iffy—balmy one minute, freezing the next—but everything is open, and not too many summer people have arrived yet. It's the calm before the rush—more anticipation than real hustle.

Then, all at once, comes the high tide of visitors—from late June through early September, with surges on July 4 and Labor Day. Inns, restaurants, beaches, and roads can be packed; everything is open and bustling, and the weather can be warm and beautiful. It's not a time for people who don't enjoy being in a crowd at least occasionally, although it's always possible to walk a bit farther on the beach and escape everyone.

For some people, Labor Day to Columbus Day is the most intriguing time on the Cape and islands. School's back in session, so families are gone. Yet summer often sticks around. And the ocean, not nearly as fickle as the air, holds on to its warmth. Many people who are not tied to summer vacations have discovered this "shoulder" season.

Columbus Day to New Year's becomes a time of slow retraction. Under crisp blue skies in the clear autumn light, the lower Cape and islands' cover of heather, gorse, cranberry, bayberry, box berry, and beach plum resembles, in Thoreau's words, "the richest rug imaginable spread over an uneven surface." Oaks and swamp maples burnish into beautiful, subtle tones, and fields of marsh grass that were green just a few weeks ago become tawny, like a miniature African savanna. Thanksgiving is a particularly evocative moment, when the Cape's Pilgrim history comes to the fore.

And then—winter. The mainland gets much more snow than the Cape, but nonetheless, it's a stark, tough time. The landscape has a desolate, moorish quality, which makes the inns and restaurants that do remain open all the more inviting. Many museums and shops close, although a year-round economy has emerged, especially around Hyannis, Falmouth, and Orleans. The Cape's community-theater network continues throughout the year, and many golf courses remain open, except when it snows (some open their courses to cross-country skiers). Intimate B&Bs and inns make romantic retreats after a day of ice fishing or pond skating.

Still, the farther toward the fringes you get, the quieter life becomes. If you believe that less can be more, this is the time to discover what others never could have found during the hectic high-season months.

Many towns on the Cape and islands celebrate Christmas in an old-fashioned way, with wandering carolers and bands, theatrical performances, crafts sales, and holiday house tours. Nantucket's Christmas Stroll is the best-known event. The Cape's holiday season extends from Thanksgiving to New Year's, with celebratory activities including First Night celebrations in many towns.

—by Seth Rolbein

A BRIEF HISTORY OF THE CAPE

THE FORTUNES of Cape Cod have always been linked to the sea. For centuries, fishermen in search of a livelihood, explorers in search of new worlds, and pilgrims of one sort or another in search of a new life—down to the beach-bound tourists of today—all have turned to the waters around this narrow peninsula arcing into the Atlantic to fulfill their needs and ambitions.

Although some maintain that the Viking Thorvald from Iceland broke his keel on the shoals here in 1004, European exploration of Cape Cod most likely dates from 1602, when Bartholomew Gosnold sailed from Falmouth, England, to investigate the American coast for trade opportunities. He first anchored off what is now Provincetown and named the cape for the great quantities of cod his crew managed to catch. He then moved on to Cuttyhunk in the Elizabeth Islands (which he named for the queen); on leaving after a few weeks, he noted that the crew were "much fatter and in better health than when we went out of England." Samuel de Champlain, explorer and geographer for the king of France, visited in 1605 and 1606; his encounter with the resident Wampanoag tribe in the Chatham area resulted in deaths on both sides.

None of these visits, however, led to settlement; that began only with the chance landing of the Pilgrims, some of whom were Separatists rebelling from enforced membership in the Church of England, others merchants looking for economic opportunity. On September 16, 1620, the *Mayflower*, with 101 passengers, set out from Plymouth, England, for an area of land granted them by the Virginia Company (Jamestown had been settled in 1607). After more than two months at sea in the crowded boat they saw land; it was far north of their intended destination, but after the stormy passage and in light of the approach of winter, they put in at Provincetown Harbor on November 21. Before going ashore they drew up the Mayflower Compact, America's first document establishing self-governance, because they were in an area under no official jurisdiction and dissension had already begun to surface.

Setting off in a small boat, a party led by Captain Myles Standish made a number of expeditions over several weeks, seeking a suitable site for a settlement in the wilderness of woods and scrub. Finally they chose Plymouth, and there they established the colony, governed by William Bradford, that is today re-created at Plimoth Plantation.

Over the next 20 years, settlers spread north and south from Plymouth. The first parts of Cape Cod to be settled were the bay-side sections of Sandwich, Barnstable, and Yarmouth (all incorporated in 1639), along an old Indian trail that is now Route 6A. (Martha's Vineyard was first settled in 1642, and Nantucket in 1659.) Most of the newcomers hunted, farmed, and fished; salt hay from the marshes was used to feed cattle and roof houses.

The first homes built by the English settlers on Cape Cod were wigwams built of twigs, bark, hides, cornstalks, and grasses, which they copied from those of the local Wampanoag people who had lived here for thousands of years before the Europeans arrived. Eventually, the settlers stripped the land of its forests to make farmland, graze sheep, and build more European-style homes, though with a New World look all their own. The steep-roofed saltbox and the Cape Cod cottage—still the most popular style of house on the Cape, and copied all over the country—were designed to accommodate growing families.

A newly married couple might begin by building a one- or two-room half-Cape, a rather lopsided 1½-story building with a door on one side of the facade and two windows on the other; a single chimney rose up on the wall behind the door. As the family grew, an addition might be built on the other side of the door large enough for a single window, turning the half-Cape into a three-quarter-Cape; a two-window addition would make it a symmetrical full Cape. Additions built onto the sides and back were called warts. An interesting feature of some Cape houses is the graceful bow roof, slightly curved like the bottom of a boat (not surprising, since ships' carpenters did much of the house building as well). More noticeable, often in the older houses, is a profusion of small, irregularly shaped and located windows in the gable ends; Thoreau wrote of one such house that it looked as if each of the various occupants "had punched a hole where his necessities required it." Many ancient houses have been turned into historical museums. In some, docents take you on a tour of the times as you pass from the keeping room—the heart of the house, where meals were cooked at a great hearth before which the family gathered for warmth—to the nearby borning room, in whose warmth babies were born and the sick were tended, to the "showy" front parlors where company was entertained. Summer and winter kitchens, backyard pumps, beehive ovens, elaborate raised-wall paneling, wide-board pine flooring, wainscoting, a doll made of corn husks, a spinning wheel, a stereopticon, a hand-stitched sampler or glove—each of these historic remnants gives a glimpse into the daily life of another age.

The Wampanoags taught the settlers what they knew of the land and how to live off it. Early on they showed them how to strip and process blubber from whales that became stranded on the beaches. To coax more whales onto the beach, men would sometimes surround them in small boats and make a commotion in the water with their oars until the whales swam to their doom in the only direction left open to them. By the mid-18th century, as the supply of near-shore whales thinned out, the hunt for the far-flung sperm whale began, growing into a major New England industry and making many a sea captain's fortune. Wellfleet, Truro, and Provincetown were the only ports on the Cape that could support deepwater distance whaling (and these were overtaken by Nantucket and New Bedford), but ports along the bay conducted active trade with packet ships carrying goods and passengers to and from Boston. Cape seamen were in great demand for ships sailing from Boston, New York, and other deep-water ports. In the mid-19th century, the Cape saw its most prosperous days, thanks largely to the whaling industry.

The decline in whaling hit the economies of Martha's Vineyard and Nantucket first and hardest, and both islands began cultivating tourism in the 19th century. Martha's Vineyard had played host to annual Methodist Camp Meetings since 1835, and Siasconset, on Nantucket, became a summer haven for New York theater folk when train service reached that remote end of the island in 1884. Whereas previously people traveled from Boston to and along the Cape only by stagecoach or packet boat, in 1848 the first train service from Boston began, reaching to Sandwich; by 1873 it had been extended little by little to Provincetown. In the 1890s President Grover Cleveland made his Bourne residence (now gone) the Cape's first "summer White House" (to be followed in the 1960s by John F. Kennedy). Grand seaside resorts grew up for summering families, and Cape Cod began to court visitors actively.

ARTISTS WERE DRAWN to Provincetown starting in the early part of the 20th century. In 1899, Charles W. Hawthorne opened the Cape Cod School of Art and taught the Impressionist *en plein air* style (outdoors) on the beach. It was the first of several art schools established over the next few years that promoted Provincetown as an art colony. Writers (including John Reed and the young Eugene O'Neill) started the Provincetown Players, which would be the germ of Cape community theater and professional summer-stock companies. The Barnstable Comedy Club, founded in 1922 and still going strong, is the most notable of the area's many amateur groups; novelist Kurt Vonnegut acted in its productions in the 1950s and 1960s and had some of his early plays produced by the group. Professional summer stock began with the still-healthy Cape Playhouse in Dennis in 1927, and its early years featured the likes of Bette Davis (who was first an usher there), Henry Fonda, Ruth Gordon, Humphrey Bogart, and Gertrude Lawrence. In 1928, the University Players Guild (today called Falmouth Playhouse) opened in Falmouth, attracting the likes of James Cagney, Orson Welles, Josh Logan, Tallulah Bankhead, and Jimmy Stewart (who, while on summer vacation from Princeton, had his first bit part during Falmouth's first season).

The idea of a Cape Cod canal, linking the bay to the sound, was studied as early as the 17th century, but not until 1914 did the privately built canal merge the waters of the two bays. It was not, however, a thunderous success; too narrow and winding, the canal allowed only one-way traffic and created dangerous currents. The federal government bought it in 1928 and had the U.S. Army Corps of Engineers rebuild it. In the 1930s three bridges—two traffic and one railroad—went up, and the rest is the latter-day history of tourism on Cape Cod.

The building of the Mid Cape Highway (U.S. 6) in the 1950s marked the great boom in the Cape's growth, and the presidency of John F. Kennedy, who summered in Hyannis Port, certainly added to the area's allure. In 1961, President Kennedy signed the legislation that established Cape Cod National Seashore. Today the Cape's sum-

mer population is more than 500,000, 2½ times the year-round population.

Though tourism, construction, and light industry are the mainstays of the Cape's economy these days, the earliest inhabitants' occupations have not disappeared. There are still more than 100 farms on the Cape, and the fishing industry—including lobstering, scalloping, and oyster aquaculture, as well as the fruits of fishing fleets such as those in Provincetown and Chatham—brings in $2 million a month.

Visitors are still drawn here by the sea: scientists come to delve into the mysteries of the deep, artists come for the light, and everyone comes for the charm of the beach towns, the beauty of the white sand, the soft breezes, and the roaring surf.

CAPE AND ISLANDS BOOKS

The Cape and islands have inspired a vast number of books, from hard-to-find, locally published autobiographical reminiscences to handsomely illustrated coffee-table books from national publishers. You can explore some of these before your trip at your local library, bookstore, or on-line bookseller, but try to make time to visit some of the many excellent bookstores on the Cape and islands. You may well make some special discovery that will illuminate your stay. For information about local newspapers and magazines, *see* Media in Smart Travel Tips A to Z.

General

CAPE COD

The classic works on Cape Cod are Henry David Thoreau's readable and often entertaining *Cape Cod,* an account of his walking tours in the mid-1800s, and Henry Beston's 1928 *The Outermost House,* which chronicles the seasons during a solitary year in a cabin at ocean's edge. Both reveal the character of Cape Codders and are rich in tales and local lore, as well as observations of nature and its processes. *Cape Cod: Henry David Thoreau's Complete Text with the Journey Recreated in Pictures,* by William F. Robinson, is a handsome New York Graphics Society edition (currently out of print), illustrated with prints from the period and current photographs. *Cape Cod Pilot,* by Josef Berger (alias Jeremiah Digges), is a WPA guidebook from 1937 that is filled with "whacking good yarns" about everything from religion to fishing, as well as a lot of still-useful information. *A Place Apart: A Cape Cod Reader* (1993), edited by Robert Finch, includes writings about the Cape from dozens of writers, from Melville to Adam Gopnik.

NANTUCKET

Nantucket Style, by Leslie Linsley and Jon Aron, is a look at 25 houses, from 18th-century mansions to rustic seaside cottages, with 300 illustrations. Recently reprinted is Henry Chandler Forman's architectural classic *Early Nantucket and Its Whale Houses.*

History

CAPE COD

Cape Cod, Its People & Their History, by Henry C. Kittredge (first published in 1930), is the standard history of the area, told with anecdotes and style as well as scholarship. Now out of print, *Sand in Their Shoes,* compiled by Edith and Frank Shay, is a compendium of writings on Cape Cod life throughout history. *Of Plimoth Plantation* is Governor William Bradford's 17th-century description of the Pilgrims' voyage to and early years in the New World. *Art in Narrow Streets,* by Ross Moffett, *Figures in a Landscape,* by Josephine Del Deo, *Provincetown as a Stage,* by Leona Rust Egan, and *Time and the Town: A Provincetown Chronicle,* by Provincetown Playhouse founder Mary Heaton Vorse, paint the social landscape of Provincetown in the first half of this century, concentrating on the lives and contributions of the many writers, artists, and actors that flocked to the town. An illustrated history for children, *The Story of Cape Cod,* by Kevin Shortsleeve (available through *Cape Cod Life,* ☎ 800/645–4482), is written in rhyming verse and sure to entertain. *In the Footsteps of Thoreau: 25 Historic and Nature Walks on Cape Cod,* by Adam Gamble, is a useful guide for naturalists and Thoreau admirers.

MARTHA'S VINEYARD

The many books written by Henry Beetle Hough, the Pulitzer Prize–winning editor of the *Vineyard Gazette* for 60 years, include his 1970 *Martha's Vineyard* and his 1936 *Martha's Vineyard, Summer Resort.*

NANTUCKET

Alexander Starbuck's 1924 *History of Nantucket,* now out of print, is the most comprehensive work on early Nantucket. *Nantucket: The Life of an Island,* by Edwin P. Hoyt, is a lively and fascinating popular history.

Fiction

Herman Melville's *Moby-Dick,* set on a 19th-century Nantucket whaling ship, captures the spirit of the whaling era. *Cape Cod,* by William Martin, is an historical novel and mystery following two families from the *Mayflower* voyage to the present, with lots of Cape history and flavor along the way. Norman Mailer's *Tough Guys Don't Dance* is a murder mystery set in Provincetown and Truro, and several other novels use Provincetown as a setting, including *Resuscitation of a Hanged Man,* by Denis Johnson, and Anne LeClaire's *Grace Point. Murder on Martha's Vineyard,* by David Osborn, and Alice Hoffman's lovely *Illumination Night* are set on the island. *Dark Nantucket Noon,* by Jane Langton, is a mystery full of island atmosphere. *Nantucket Daybreak* is set in off-season Nantucket and portrays the life of scallopers in a story of love and betrayal. Francine Mathews's *Death in Rough Water* stars detective Merry Folger and involves a fisherman accidentally killed during a gale. *Nightbirds on Nantucket,* by Joan Aiken, is a mystery for younger readers, set on the Nantucket moors. Other mystery writers who set their books on the Cape and islands are Margot Arnold, Rick Boyer, Philip A. Craig, Virginia Rich, Marie Lee, and Phoebe Atwood Taylor. *Cape Cod Stories,* edited by John Miller, is a collection of Cape-related short fiction by such luminaries as Edgar Allen Poe, John Cheever, and Sylvia Plath. *Cape Discovery,* edited by Bruce Smith and Catherine Gammon, an anthology of poetry and fiction by former fellows of the Fine Arts Work Center in Provincetown, includes the work of noted contemporary American writers such as Louise Glück, Michael Cunningham, Dean Albarelli, and Maria Flook. Many of the poems in *Passing Through,* Pulitzer Prize-winning poet Stanley Kunitz's latest collection, evoke the natural beauty of the Cape, and several refer to his garden on Commercial Street in Provincetown.

Memoir

In *Heaven's Coast,* Mark Doty, a Provincetown writer, recounts the death of his lover, Wally Roberts, from complications caused by AIDS. In a similar vein, David Gessner's *A Wild, Rank Place: One Year on Cape Cod* combines insights about the Cape with reminiscence about battling cancer and confronting his father's death. Gladys Taber chronicles her life on the Cape at Still Cove in *My Own Cape Cod.*

Natural History

Robert Finch, editor of *A Place Apart*(☞ *above*), has also written three lyrical books about natural history: *Outlands: Journeys to the Outer Edges of Cape Cod, Common Ground: A Naturalist's Cape Cod,* and *The Primal Place,* a meditation about life on the Cape, especially its natural rhythms and history. Finch is also the author of the attractively illustrated *Cape Cod: Its Natural and Cultural History,* a National Park Service handbook about the national seashore and the Cape. *In the Company of Light* traces John Hay's journey from Maine to Cape Cod, recounting his observations of light and luminescence—in nature and as revelation. Hay is a wonderful nature writer; other titles by him include *The Run,* about the life cycle of alewives, and *Great Beach. A Guide to Nature on Cape Cod and the Islands,* edited by Greg O'Brien, has sections by a variety of experts on the area's flora and fauna.

Photography

A Summer's Day (winner of the 1985 Ansel Adams Award for Best Photography Book) and *Cape Light* present color landscapes, still lifes, and portraits by Provincetown-associated photographer Joel Meyerowitz. *Martha's Vineyard* and *Eisenstaedt: Martha's Vineyard* are explorations of the island by *Life* magazine photographer Alfred Eisenstaedt, who summered on the island until his death in 1995. Robert Gambee's handsome *Nantucket* contains more than 525 color photographs along with detailed captions about island sights.

INDEX

NOTES

p. 44 Mostly Hall
recomended by book +
Cape cod life

p 79 Scargo Manor

NOTES

NOTES

NOTES

NOTES

NOTES

NOTES

NOTES

Looking for a different kind of vacation?

Fodor's makes it easy with a full line of specialty guidebooks to suit a variety of interests—from adventure to romance to language help.

L@@king

© FOR A

great place to go?

We know just the place. In fact, it attracts more than 125,000 visitors a day, making it one of the world's most popular travel destinations. It's previewtravel.com, the Web's comprehensive resource for travelers. It gives you access to over 500 airlines, 25,000 hotels, rental cars, cruises, vacation packages and support from travel experts 24 hours a day. Plus great information from Fodor's travel guides and travelers just like you. All of which makes previewtravel.com quite a find.

Preview Travel has everything you need to plan & book your next trip.

air, car & hotel reservations

vacation packages & cruises

destination planning & travel tips

24-hour customer service

previewtravel.com

preview travel℠

aol keyword: previewtravel

www.previewtravel.com